Selected Works of Peter A. Boodberg

Selected Works of Peter A. Boodberg

Compiled by Alvin P. Cohen

University of California Press
Berkeley • *Los Angeles* • *London*

University of California Press
Berkeley and Los Angeles, California

University of California Press, Ltd.
London, England

Copyright © 1979 by
The Regents of the University of California

ISBN 0-520-03314-0
Library of Congress Catalog Card Number: 76-24580
Printed in the United States of America

1 2 3 4 5 6 7 8 9

Contents

Preface

This book is dedicated to the memory of a great teacher, a scholar of outstanding creative imagination, and a warm and generous human being. The late Professor Peter A. Boodberg was extraordinary in his ability to inspire his students and colleagues both with his scholarly knowledge and with his personal qualities. He was such a complex man that I will not even attempt to discuss his life. Whatever can be said about him in mere words has been well, said in Professor Schafer's necrology. The rest will linger on in the memories of those of us fortunate enough to have known him.

The materials reprinted here comprise Professor Boodberg's most important writings. They also include selections from his rare personally published serials, an unpublished lecture, and articles from journals and *Festschriften* that are not readily available in many college libraries. I hope this volume will make his work familiar to a larger portion of the scholarly community.

The preparation for this book began with the compilation of Professor Boodberg's bibliography. This turned out to be a more difficult task than I had anticipated because most of his personally published writings of the 1930s are extremely rare. In my search for these rare publications it became necessary to solicit help from his colleagues and former students all over the world. The responses to my inquiries were both encouraging and fruitful, and enabled me to compile a bibliography with only a few missing items.

I am especially indebted to Charles E. Hamilton, of the East Asiatic Library of the University of California at Berkeley, for the great amount of help he so generously gave me. I am also grateful to Edward H. Schafer and William G. Boltz for providing me with extensive information and copies of many of the rare publications. My thanks are also due to those kind people who sent me copies of the rare publications and important information: Woodbridge Bingham, Albert E. Dien, Hans H. Frankel, L. Carrington Goodrich, Li Fang-kuei, Mrs. Anna Maenchen, Karl H. Menges, Mrs. Kate Olschki, Nicholas Poppe, Richard C. Rudolph, Hugh M. Stimson, Alex Wayman, Eugene Wu. My gratitude extends to Felicia G. Bock for her invaluable help and encouragement in bringing this volume to fruition, to Phyllis Schafer for preparing the typescript, to James E. Bosson for writing the Arabic and Mongol scripts, and to Edward H. Schafer for writing the Chinese characters. In addition, there were others, too numerous to name, who provided much help, encouragement, and information—to all of them I am truly grateful.

The publication of this volume was financed partly by the publisher and partly by the generous contributions of Elizabeth Huff and another donor who wishes to remain anonymous. Were it not for their generosity in these times of high costs and limited funds, this book would not have come into existence.

Finally I wish to thank the following journals and publishers for permission to reprint Professor Boodberg's articles (numbers refer to the items in the Bibliography):

Necrology and Bibliography, with the permission of the *Journal of the American Oriental Society.*

No. 27, with the permission of *Oriens.*

Nos. 16, 17, 18, 19, 21, 25, 28, with the permission of the *Harvard Journal of Asiatic Studies.*

Nos. 23 and 32, from *Philosophy East and West,* with the permission of The University Press of Hawaii.

No. 31, with the permission of the *Tsing Hua Journal of Chinese Studies.*

No. 29, reprinted from *Approaches to the Oriental Classics: Asian Literature and Thought in General Education,* edited by W. T. de Bary, New York: Columbia University Press, 1959, by permission of the publisher.

No. 20, with the permission of E. J. Brill, publisher of *T'oung Pao.*

No. 22, copyright © 1951 by The Regents of the University of California; reprinted by permission of the University of California Press.

A.P.C.
March 1977

Peter A. Boodberg,
1903-1972

by Edward H. Schafer

Journal of the American Oriental Society, 94.1 (1974), 1-7.

In March 1932 appeared the first of a remarkable series of periodicals composed exclusively of highly original articles written by a single author who gave his name as Peter A. von Budberg and simultaneously—in Cyrillic letters—as Baron Peter Budberg. So began the public career of a brilliant and to some an enigmatic scholar. It does not appear that the precocious publisher of these papers ever used either his title or the un-American spelling of his name again. We knew him as Peter Alexis Boodberg, an adaptation of Pyotr Alexeievich Budberg.

Family tradition has it that the earliest appearance of the surname is in the archives of the city of Mainz under the year 1003. At that time the title was held by Baron Cuno. One of the baron's noble descendants emigrated to Estonia in the thirteenth century and established the Baltic branch of the family there. In 1721, when Peter I of Russia obtained his "window on the Baltic" by the annexation of Estonia, the proto-Boodbergs became Russians. They remained a family of soldiers into the twentieth century.

Peter Boodberg was born in Vladivostok on 8 April 1903. At the outbreak of World War I he was a cadet in a military school in St. Petersburg. His sister says of him at the age of eight: "He drove us all crazy by reciting the names of all the battleships of *every* nation, their tonnage, length, armament and so on." Military disasters and domestic upheaval closed the school in 1915, and Peter was sent with his brother Alexander to Harbin for safety.

In Manchuria he turned from the study of strategy to the study of philology. He attended high school and began at the same time to instruct himself in the Chinese language. When the wave of revolution reached the Far East he was studying at the University of Vladivostok, separated from his family. But out of a background of Teutonic Knights and soldiers for the Czar came no fighter for or against the Bolsheviks. Peter Boodberg had the misfortune to be a "moderate," under attack by both student factions, the Reds and the Whites. What did survive of his knightly heritage was a deeply ingrained sense of honor, courtliness and loyalty which came to distinguish his whole career as scholar and as human being. He was utterly a man of peace.

In the summer of 1920 he came to San Francisco, where he was rejoined by his family in the following year. He enrolled at the University of California at Berkeley and obtained an A.B. in Oriental Languages in 1924. In the same year he began his graduate studies. He also began his long career as a teacher with the title of "Assistant in Oriental Languages." A typical course offering was "Elementary Study of the Chinese Written Language, Ancient and Modern." His studies followed the multifarious inclinations of his mind: not only Classical Chinese with the then Agassiz Professor, E. T. Williams, and Japanese with Y. S. Kuno, but also Assyro-Babylonian with Henry F. Lutz and Advanced Arabic with the formidable William Popper. Popper was Professor of Semitic Languages during this era, and his influence on Boodberg was as important as that of the more celebrated Arthur Ryder, Professor of Sanskrit, Chairman and only member of his distinguished department. So also was that of A. L. Kroeber of Anthropology. He came to know these men very well, and in the end his influence on them was as significant as theirs on him.

Boodberg earned his Ph.D. in 1930. A late trace of his military patrimony survives, characteristically, in this purely academic context. His doctoral dissertation, accepted at the University of California in Berkeley in June of that year, was entitled "The Art of War in Ancient China: A Study Based upon the *Dialogues of Li, Duke of Wei.*" It was also characteristic of the breadth of his interests and training that the committee in charge of his dissertation included only two members of his own department—one in Chinese and one in Japanese—but the real stars were Lutz, Popper and Ryder.

The years 1931 and 1932 were critical ones for the young scholar in search of a career. He held a two-month appointment at Berkeley with the title of "Lecturer" in the early fall of 1931. But after that—especially in January of 1932—he sent out a desperate flurry of applications for teaching positions at such universities as Chicago, Washington, Princeton, Cornell, Michigan, Wisconsin, Johns Hopkins and Pennsylvania. None of them was interested. Typical responses were: ". . . it is improbable that the University will be in a position to employ an instructor in Chinese within the very near future"; "We have no course in Chinese language and literature and are not in a position financially at this time to institute one . . ."; ". . . we have no openings in the fields you mention." Since then all of these universities have established respectable departments of Far Eastern studies, especially Chinese. But they had lost the chance of obtaining the young Boodberg. Berkeley hired him as Instructor in Oriental Languages on 1 July 1932, at an annual salary of $1,800. Soon afterwards his first publication appeared: "Discourses on Salt and Iron [*Yen T'ieh Lun:* Chaps. XX-XXVIII]."[1] It was nominally co-authored with his col-

1. *Journal of the North China Branch of the Royal Asiatic Society,* 65 (1934), 73-110.

leagues E. M. Gale and T. C. Lin, but his contemporaries report that it was primarily *his* creation.

In 1935 he was promoted to the rank of Assistant Professor. He was now teaching an array of courses on Classical Chinese along with one on "Chinese Lexicography and Bibliography" and an English language lecture course entitled "Chinese Civilization." These courses were classical in more than one sense. They came to dominate the tone of the department and raised the intellectual level of instruction and research beyond what it had ever been. Some of them are still given today, inherited by other men. But although these instructors have inevitably been influenced in some measure by Boodbergian rigor and by Boodberg's new ideas and methods, the courses are different from his unique and pioneering offerings. They are mutations, not mummies—but not necessarily better for that.

Boodberg's career came to be closely and finally identified with the burgeoning of humanistic studies on the Berkeley campus. The bare bones of a distinguished life in the University of California follow. He became an Associate Professor in 1937. He was awarded a Guggenheim fellowship in 1938-1939 for "foundation studies towards the reconstruction of archaic Chinese and studies of cultural inter-reactions between China and Central Asia." These two fields were to become his primary areas of research and discovery. In 1940 he became department chairman, inaugurating a new era—the era of true distinction for the Department of Oriental Languages. He was appointed full Professor in 1948. He resigned the chairmanship in 1950 in protest against administrative policies during the loyalty oath controversy. He was primarily responsible for the founding of the Western Branch of the American Oriental Society in 1951. He won a second Guggenheim award in 1956. In 1960 he succeeded Ferdinand Lessing as Agassiz Professor of Oriental Languages and Literature. He was awarded a third Guggenheim fellowship in 1963-1964 and in the same year became President of the American Oriental Society. He gave his presidential address at the annual meeting in New York on 8 April 1964. The title of the address was typical of his style: "The Stranger in our Midst." He described it as being ". . . about morphological and grapho-semantic aspects of the Classical Chinese . . . with some emphasis on the concept of negativity." He became Professor Emeritus in 1970, but was recalled to active service as irreplaceable. His health began to fail rapidly in 1972 and he died of a heart attack on 29 June of that year.

Boodberg's earliest contributions to scholarship consisted of a series of articles—all highly original and most of them in his special field of Sino-Altaica—which he published himself in a limited edition duplicated from his own elegant longhand script. The series was entitled *Hu T'ien Han Yüeh Fang-chu,* which may be rendered as "A Dew-Basin for the Han Moon in the Hunnish Sky." Thirteen sets appeared between March 1932 and March 1936. Unfortunately this luxurious array of little gems became known only to a narrow circle of friends and connoisseurs, and the complete series now seems to be irrecoverable. Typical titles, revealing, as do their contents, the scope of Boodberg's erudition and the daring solutions he offered to apparently baffling philological problems, are "A 'Turkish' Word in the Hsiung-nu Language," "The Royal Clan of the Avars," "Kumiss or Arrack?" These early essays, worthy of mature scholars, were the first public manifestations of Boodberg's preoccupation with what he styled "Global Sinology."

A typewritten report of work in progress in the Department of Oriental Languages, dated August 1944, states his ideal. It must have been written by Boodberg himself, although it modestly attributes the ideal to all members of the department equally. The influence of Pelliot and the "French school" of sinology appears plainly in it: "The Oriental Department and the scholars associated with it have always approached the study of China on the principle that the development of that nation can be rightly understood only as an integral part of that of the Eur-Asiatic continent. This 'global' approach reflects itself particularly in the interest paid to linguistic, historical and cultural relations of ancient and medieval China with its steppe neighbors and through them with the Eurasiatic 'Far West'." He was deeply committed to this ideal, and also to the belief in the value of sound philological analysis. Accordingly much of his own early work was devoted to making painstaking annotated translations from Chinese accounts of their neighbors to the north and west. Most of these were never published. This expansive approach, totally opposed to the commonly accepted assumption that Chinese history and literature could be studied as self-contained entities—the ideal of the mandarinate—transformed the Department of Oriental Languages in Berkeley completely. There were other manifestations of his special influence. He was instrumental in bringing Otto Maenchen-Helfen to Berkeley to teach the archaeology and art of the peoples of Central Asia in the broadest possible context, exploiting sources ranging from Greek to Chinese. He also found a place for Leonardo Olschki, an Italian humanist and specialist in Dante and Marco Polo, who enlivened the history of medieval cultural relationships between Europe and the Far East. He became the patron of Michael Hagerty, formerly of the U.S. Department of Agriculture, who analyzed early texts on Chinese domesticated plants. He actively promoted the study of non-Chinese Far Eastern languages; for instance, he led Richard Rudolph, who later became Professor of Oriental Languages at U.C.L.A., into the study of Manchu texts; he encouraged the study of Vietnamese under Diether von den Steinen; he brought Mary Haas, a specialist in Thai and American Indian languages, into the department; he himself offered instruction in Malay. Boodberg saw all of these offerings not merely as useful services to the University—and ultimately to the nation—but as essential to the development of a correct attitude towards the study of Asian literature and civilization as a complex organism with interdependent parts, whose study in isolation could be as dangerous as studying the human personality in terms of the nervous system alone, as if the endocrine glands did not exist. It follows necessarily that he was a staunch opponent of the common assumption that language study could be justified chiefly as providing tools for other disciplines.

Boodberg's international reputation began in 1936 when his first publications in Sino-Altaica appeared in the newly created *Harvard Journal of Asiatic Studies*.[2] These were sets of refined models of sophisticated philological research in areas either entirely neglected, or else devastated by the guess-work of amateurs. Typical titles from these collections of brilliant essays are "The Bulgars of Mongolia," "Theophylactus Simocatta on China," and "The Altaic Word for 'Horn' in the Political Nomenclature of the Steppe." It was during this period that Arthur Waley, already a recognized master, wrote to the young instructor "I read your article on the language of the T'o-pa with great admiration."[3] Even the Chinese linguist Lo Ch'ang-p'ei wrote to him in some perplexity—this was much later, in 1946—asking for information about the identification of the Chinese forms of old Asian place-names, such as those that are now known to represent Samarkand, Cambodia, etc.: "It seems to me that you are the only qualified scholar I have met in this country to help me in this field." At the same time, Boodberg's competence in these areas was beginning to have its effects on students at Berkeley. In 1939-1940 he inaugurated a course entitled "Introduction to the Study of Manchu and Mongol Texts," and in 1942 he delivered a lecture under the auspices of the Graduate Division on "Turk, Aryan and Chinese in Ancient Asia," an address whose scope and competence were at that time a complete novelty, not only in Berkeley but in America. There were byroads from this kind of research, such as the one that led him to the discovery of the methodological principle of stichometry in ancient Chinese texts—a potentially valuable tool for textual criticism.[4]

The continental approach to Far Eastern studies was never abandoned, as many writings, lectures and colloquia, both formal and informal, attest.[5] But meanwhile Boodberg was developing another of his passionate interests, which came gradually to dominate his professional life. This was the study of

2. "Two Notes on the History of the Chinese Frontier," *Harvard Journal of Asiatic Studies*, 1 (1936), 283-307; "The Language of the T'o-pa Wei," *Harvard Journal of Asiatic Studies*, 1 (1936), 167-185; "Marginalia to the Histories of the Northern Dynasties," *Harvard Journal of Asiatic Studies*, 3 (1938), 223-253; 4 (1939), 230-283.

3. Undated letter from London; from internal evidence, written about 1937.

4. First outlined in "The Coronation of T'o-pa Hsiu," *Harvard Journal of Asiatic Studies*, 4 (1939), 240-252 (a subdivision of "Marginalia") and elaborated in "Notes on Isocolometry in Early Chinese Accounts of Barbarians," *Oriens*, 10 (1957), 119-127.

5. See for instance "Three Notes on the T'u-chüeh Turks," *Semitic and Oriental Studies, Presented to William Popper* (University of California Publications in Semitic Philology, 11, Berkeley, 1951), pp. 1-11, composed of three studies on transcultural and multilinguistic problems; also "An Early Mongolian Toponym," *Harvard Journal of Asiatic Studies*, 19 (1956), 407-408.

the early history of the Chinese language and script, a field in which he became an unrivalled and —except locally—unrecognized master. The public aspect of this innovative scholarship was initiated by a brief flurry of controversy in professional journals. The crux of the matter was the true nature of the Chinese script. An exchange of articles between Boodberg and H. G. Creel of the University of Chicago was provoked by Creel's publication in 1936 of a defense of the "ideographic" theory of the Chinese script.[6] Boodberg's reply appeared in the *Harvard Journal of Asiatic Studies,* which was at this time also being hospitable to his Sino-Altaic studies.[7] This study, crowded with new insights and stimulating conjectures, supported the view, now adopted almost universally, that Chinese graphs did not and do not represent "ideas" or "concepts" but stand for words and morphemes, and that many of their components have hitherto unsuspected phonetic values. In short, they constitute a *logographic* system. His clear statement of the historical foundations of his position appeared later in the departmental report of 1944:

> "The application of the principle of logography to the study of Chinese, enunciated over a hundred years ago by Peter Du Ponceau—as against the sterile concept of the ideographic character of the Chinese script—opens up a vast new field for investigation."

Rejoinder and surrejoinder followed in the pages of *T'oung Pao,*[8] but the death-blow had already been dealt to quaintness and amateurism in the study of Chinese characters. Boodberg's professionalism continued to attack wobbly traditions for the rest of his life.

Meanwhile he was engaged in the completion of a major work which represented the thought and study of years. He seems to have finished it during his 1938-1939 sabbatical year. This was almost certainly a study of binomial expressions in old Chinese: pieces of such a work survive in typescript. Although he apparently thought it ready, Boodberg withdrew the work from publication. From that time on he published very little in professional journals. Nonetheless he continued to refine his novel ideas about the history of the Chinese language. Piles of new materials accumulated dust on the shelves of his study. An example of methods he found fertile and almost axiomatic is his belief that a large proportion of the rhyming binoms in Chinese represented dimidiations—lexicographical restorations of vanishing initial consonant clusters spelled out in bisyllabic form, akin to but different from the traditional *fan-ch'ieh* system of representing the pronunciation of words that typifies medieval and modern Chinese dictionaries. Related to this was his belief that paronomastic

6. H. G. Creel, "On the Nature of Chinese Ideography," *T'oung Pao,* 32 (1936), 85-161.

7. "Some Proleptical Remarks on the Evolution of Archaic Chinese," *Harvard Journal of Asiatic Studies,* 2 (1937), 329-372.

8. H. G. Creel, "On the Ideographic Element in Ancient Chinese," *T'oung Pao,* 34 (1939), 265-294; P. A. Boodberg, " 'Ideography' or Iconolatry?", *T'oung Pao,* 35 (1940), 266-288.

definitions were valuable guides to etymology. Virtually the only beneficiaries of his later creative work in this field were a few of his superior students. Probably most of his discoveries will ultimately appear only as remnants, filtered through their minds.

Boodberg's preoccupation with graphics continued unabated to the end of his life, almost to the exclusion of other concerns—even problems in Altaic philology. However, his novel hypotheses and the results that they engendered were treated by many of his Sinological contemporaries—if they received any reliable reports about them at all—with indifference and, in some instances, with abhorrence.

He soon returned to a manner of publication characteristic of the beginning of his career. In the summer of 1954 he began to turn out a new series of brief but richly informed articles. Each was carefully designed to fill only a single typewritten page. He entitled the series *Cedules from a Berkeley Workshop in Asiatic Philology.* These were mimeographed and distributed among a favored few. This second series of miniature jewels was much broader in subject matter than the "Dew-Basin" sequence. It was distinguished by the presence of a number of beautifully reasoned contributions to Chinese literary criticism, including "On Crypto-Parallelism in Chinese Poetry" and "On Latent Predicates in Chinese Poetry." His masterly—but to the uninitiated often perplexing—translations of T'ang poems had a greater vogue among professors of English and creative writers than they did among more tradition-bound professors of Chinese. They contain constellations of ingenious neologisms, intended to communicate strange images in a precise way. He believed firmly that creations of this sort were still as much the privilege of humanistic scholars as they had been in early centuries, although he was well aware that in the twentieth century the right to their invention seemed to have been abandoned by default to social and natural scientists. Since he made few concessions to weakness in classical languages or the shrinking of educated imagination, some of these publications tended to put off other Chinese specialists who did not share his tastes. He assumed that all cultivated men were familiar with the available stock of Greek and Latin roots and would readily accept such coinages as "teknarch" and "cheiromastic," to say nothing of respectable but rare English words he occasionally resurrected, although these last at least might easily be traced in Webster or the *O.E.D.* His predilection for such novelties is reminiscent of the writings of his fellow countryman Vladimir Nabokov, whose pages are sprinkled with such expressions as "pavonine sun," "favonian week" and "phocine mamma."[9] Happily the appropriateness of the Boodbergian exploitation of the resources of English is now beginning to be accepted in advanced Sinological circles. Joseph Needham, for instance, has found it a scholarly necessity

9. To be found in *Lolita.* See Granville Hicks on this point in *Saturday Review,* 28 January 1967, p. 32.

to render old Chinese technological terms in this manner, and gives us such useful words as "eremotic," "plerotic," "patefact" and "subdite." Precision may yet triumph over conservatism.

Boodberg's interests and capabilities also extended to biography and philosophy. An example of the latter is a short but fundamental article which attempted to clarify the true meanings of key terms in traditional Chinese philosophy and ethics—in particular to rid them of misleading overtones given them by the conventional English stereotypes used by almost everyone to translate them.[10] As to biography, it appears that a very important study—virtually a life work—has been lost to scholarship. This was a biography of Confucius that would have embodied the results of the most rigorous critical methods and the most modern philological knowledge. Boodberg's description of it as early as 1942 as "a major biography of the Sage" was almost certainly accurate. Inspired by his enthusiasm, the Department of Oriental Languages recommended to Robert Gordon Sproul, President of the University of California, that there be an official celebration of the 2500th anniversary of Confucius' birth in 1948-1949. The celebration never took place, but Boodberg offered a course on "The Life and Times of Confucius" in 1948, and as a result of taking this course the present writer can testify that the book would have been both revolutionary and definitive. The project was kept alive for many years: in applying to the Guggenheim Foundation in 1963 Boodberg referred to "the revision of a monograph on the life and times of Confucius." But the manuscript cannot now be found anywhere. It is also reported that he was preparing a masterly study of the *Lao tzu*. No trace of this survives, although an introductory note was published as a short but dense article.[11]

Boodberg also dedicated much time and effort to the production of exact notational systems for the romanized representation of Chinese characters.[12] An early drive in this direction appeared as one of his *Cedules* in 1956 with the title "Towards a Philological System of Notation for Chinese Characters." Typically he employed Graeco-Latin neologisms to describe the Chinese graphs and their segments. He saw his coding not only as a way of introducing precision into a traditionally imprecise field, usually left to amateurs, but also as "a basis for the tentative comparison of the semasiological range of Sinitic culture with that of the Mediterranean world."[13] But despite the rigor with which he devised and used these new terms they have not come into use beyond

10. "The Semasiology of Some Primary Confucian Concepts." *Philosophy East and West,* 2 (1953), 317-332.

11. "Philological Notes on Chapter One of the *Lao tzu*," *Harvard Journal of Asiatic Studies,* 20 (1957), 598-618.

12. Foreshadowed by two romanized orthographies, styled UCI and UCJ, which appeared in the short-lived *University of California Publications in East Asiatic Philology* in 1947. These were more rational and sophisticated than other systems in common use, and were unusual in taking historical change into account. They were not adopted by his contemporaries.

13. Application for a Guggenheim grant in 1963.

the immediate circle of his students. The familiar, old-fashioned systems remain triumphant.

Boodberg was a magnificent teacher. To compensate for the paucity of his publications in the latter part of his career, many of his original contributions to classical scholarship in Chinese are likely to persist and become widely disseminated, even if sometimes diluted or compromised, through the work of men and women who learned from him. Even on the elementary level he disdained the customary but outdated methods of language teaching derived ultimately from the methods employed by the Chinese gentry to transmit orthodox interpretations of the "Classics" to uncritical pupils. His syllabi were highly original and valuable.[14] They actually prepared students for the complexities of the literary language—for instance the study of parallel structure in poetry—and also to understand linguistic glosses on early texts and other technical apparatus essential to their proper interpretation. As a result, his students were on the average much more sophisticated than those trained by other Sinologists.

Boodberg was also noted, locally at least, as a popular lecturer and a significant contributor to general education. His course "Chinese Civilization," which he offered for many years, was a service to the university at large. Requiring no knowledge of the Chinese language, it attracted hundreds of students, many of whom emerged from it—although somewhat dazed—with their critical faculties remarkably sharpened and their knowledge of the thought and civilization of the Far East immensely enhanced. His stupendous erudition never baffled, injured or overwhelmed even the most innocent of them. They loved it. Comparable to this was a course he developed somewhat later, called "Great Books of Eastern Asia." It covered the literature and philosophy of India, Japan and China. His comprehension of and familiarity with these subjects was remarkable. For instance, he displayed an understanding of the innermost secrets of Japanese literature and Buddhist philosophical texts that could be envied by men of high repute who specialize in these fields. This course too was a truly popular one—even during a period of student protest and criticism of professional teaching.

Boodberg always tried to convey to audiences of non-specialists a sense of what problems were truly significant in his own field—or fields. As Chairman of the Department of Oriental Languages he organized two "Research Convocations" on Oriental subjects which, he hoped, would bring the results of new and original research to a much wider audience than usual.[15] These were magnificient series of lectures given by all members of the department, then in its heyday, including not only Boodberg himself, but also Lessing, Chao, Haas, Olschki and others. They were great successes, and the instructors and stu-

14. Notably *Exercises in Chinese Parallelism* (University of California Press, 1943) and *Introduction to Classical Chinese* (University of California Press, 1951).
15. Held on the Berkeley campus in November 1948 and May 1949.

dents who attended them are not ever likely to forget the excitement they generated. He was also one of the founders and for most of its life the guiding spirit of the Colloquium Orientologicum, a monthly assemblage of Bay Area scholars in every discipline related to Asia to announce and discuss their newest research. He gave a personal series of lectures which he styled "The Moil of Translation" in 1960. He described his purpose in these words: "A series of informal lectures and discussion on principles of Chinese semantics and grammar; essays on the traditional Chinese verbalization of experience with emphasis on *Wort-und-Sache* analysis and on *le mot juste* in translation." A typical title is "On Chinese things and matter, pattern, organic principle and law: poetic pedantry and Hopkinsiana." All were richly informed by his mastery of world literature and the deep sense of his mission—the raising of the level of scholarly sophistication in Far Eastern studies.

During the second half of his career Boodberg seemed to feel that his discipline was everywhere veering, with some significant exceptions, away from old-fashioned amateurism towards new-fangled opportunism. He recorded his disappointment about the deplorable state of "philological humanism" in Chinese departments throughout the country, and he commented on the "intimidation" of sinological scholars by "the organizational inroads of advocates of 'group' and 'integrated' research."[16] He became increasingly pessimistic about the prospect that the standards he had striven for so valiantly would ultimately triumph.

Boodberg deplored the computerization of academic life, and would sometimes ironically sign letters to administrative officers with his "employee number." He detested IBM cards and disdained to fill out questionnaires. He regarded all such devices as dehumanizing. He even rejected all dependence on indexes and concordances: one should have memorized the Classics and be sufficiently familiar with other major contributions to literature and history to be able to dispense with such crutches. A scholar needed only a good mind, good books, and good conversation.

Despite his pessimism, he remained convinced to the end of the rightness of his attempts to bring about a revolution in the study of the Chinese language and its literature through a fusion of traditional humanism with daring innovation. He claimed for himself—proudly—only the title philologist. He was, in fact, a philosopher in the best and most honorable sense of the term, in whom erudition and imagination were perfectly balanced. Indeed the tragedy of his life was that only a very few persons—chiefly his students and a small following of literary and historical scholars in other fields—were even partially aware of the great significance of his thought on fundamental problems. He came to believe that the world was not ready for his ideas. Perhaps it was not. In the end a large portion of the vast and fertile resources of his mind has been

16. Report to Chancellor Kerr on his sabbatical leave in the fall of 1956, dated 4 June 1957.

withheld from the scholarly world because of his diffidence, his perfectionism, and ultimately his bitterness. It would be a serious mistake to assume, as some of his contemporaries have assumed, that he was merely an eccentric or a crank. He was far from that. He was a great scholar.

But Boodberg was much more than a great scholar. He was a lordly man. He was on intimate terms with the history and literature of mankind. While he adhered to the strictest standards of intellectual honesty, he always showed himself as a courteous and compassionate gentleman to whom harshness, meanness and condescension were all equally alien—indeed repellent. He followed a code of personal honor and loyalty that is almost unknown in our times. He never expected others to conform to it. It was enough that he be true to himself. He was.

Selected Works of Peter A. Boodberg

Turk, Aryan and Chinese in Ancient Asia*

        Geological accidence made of Eurasia a single continental
mass. But the same tectonic forces which shaped it as one unit,
conspired in spacing the four great riparian centers of ancient
civilisation in such a way that one, the greatest of them, the
Yellow River valley civilisation of China, found itself separated
from its western sisters by a series of forbidding topographical
obstacles, unrivaled on this earth in length, height, and precip-
itousness.

        But even before he had begun his self-recorded history,
even ere he had learned to ply the sea in ships, man contrived to
circumvent or overcome these obstacles and succeeded in linking
the western and eastern seats of his civilisation with the
slender threads of two long and winding trails. It is an ironic
commentary on 30 centuries of culture and material advancement
that today the great nation which grew out of the small beginnings on the banks of the Huang-ho finds itself depending in its
struggle for existence on the same precarious and still
undeveloped trails, the now famous Burma road and the desert
track of Turkestan.

        The early history of China's land communications with
India, Western Asia, and the Roman world still contains many
blank pages, but what we have learned of it makes one of the most
fascinating chapters in the story of human exploration of the
planet. Our perception of China is even today considerably
affected, if not distorted, by distance and optical parallax. It
is not surprising, therefore, that our ancestors dwelling by the
sunny Mediterranean gave two different appellations to the
wondrous land beyond a thousand horizons, according as they
approached it from the south or from the north.

        The name of the Chinese terminus of the southern route
from the west, through India and Burma, later traversed chiefly
by sea, changed but little through the ages and appears in
western documents as Chin, Sin, or Θιν, the original form of our

[* P.A.B.'s unpublished lecture presented in 1942 at the
University of California, Berkeley. No. 36. -- Ed.]

word China. The Chinese terminus of the northern desert and
steppe road winding across the plateaus of High Asia was known
as Serica or the land of the Seres, a name later supplanted by
that of Tabgač or Cathay.

We use the word terminus advisedly, for in the early
period of intercourse the western world, Pagan, Christian, or
Moslem, knew China only, so to speak, at her anodic and cathodic
electrodes; it was more conscious of a mighty current of energy
emanating from a vast electrolyte at two given points than of the
spacious body lying between. In fact, a careful study of our
sources reveals that either of the two names for China was but an
appellation of one of her marginal territories, of an appendix to
her organic structure, of a vestibule to the main edifice, rather
than that of the great hall itself. The core of China remained
long unknown. Its inaccessibility in spite of the few tantaliz-
ing glimpses of its wonders which western man traveling for
business or enlightenment, in the flesh or in fancy, succeeded to
obtain through the two portals gave rise to a legend which to
this day haunts the western mind. In many a tongue, beguiling an
idle hour or seeking surcease for despair in a shred of hope that
a better and a juster world can be found on this earth, western
minstrels sang the praises of the orderly and peaceful land of
the Seres. To many, the far-off dwelling place of this wondrous
people peacefully governed by just laws and temperate wisdom must
have seemed to be a kind of Island of the Blessed, where all the
cruel antinomies of existence are resolved. Crafty trader and
informed statesman may have known better, but to the escapists of
those days the fair land of the Seres, the friends not only of
peace, but of life itself (as wrote in the 5th century Moses of
Chorene, the Armenian), must have played the same role that the
lost continent of Lemuria or Shangrila performs for their modern
counterparts.

The road leading the prospective western pilgrim to the
land of his dreams was long and tortuous. Between him and Chin
lay the terrors of the Erythrean Sea, its storms and moving
islands, its roc birds and sirens. Perils, indeed, but also the
thrills and adventures that our own incurable romanticists
associate with East of Suez and the Road to Mandalay.

Should he choose the northern caravan route through the
steppes, the vade mecum of the day would warn the pilgrim of the
great waterless wastes and sky-high mountains lying ahead, of the
sand and snow storms which Boreas would unchain against him. But
greatest of all the trials awaiting the traveler would be his
encounter with the great company and mighty army of Gog and
Magog--to paraphrase the Bible--and all the many peoples riding
upon horses, the number of whom is as the sand of the sea, the
unholy hosts of the land of darkness stretching to the Northeast.

A legend widely current in Hellenistic, Christian, Jewish, and Moslem traditions conceived those turbulent nations beyond the pale of civilisation as kept in restraint by a mighty wall built on the confines of the civilised world by the great hero of the western Οικουμένη , Alexander the Great. This magic wall, said the legend, would withstand all shocks of assault from the outside until the hour of the end of all things draws near. Then will Gog and Magog and their hosts break through its gates and descend upon sinful humanity. Every time a so-called barbarian invasion burst the barriers of the Roman world both learned and unlearned were tempted to recognize in the invaders the Gog and Magog of the legend. Thus, at various occasions, Scythians, Huns, Alans, Turks, Khazars, Magyars, and Mongols have been identified with the ravaging hordes from beyond the Wall, whose invasion was to usher in the Last Days.

The legend of the enclosed nations seems to reflect the wonder and vague disquiet that the citizens of settled communities of the Western part of Eurasia felt when brought in contact with pastoral-nomadic societies of the central portion of the conti-nent, a world of a strangely fluid economy, uncertain social traditions, of sudden formation of large political units and as sudden disintegration thereof, and often one of strange, hitherto unheard tongues.

Geographically, this land of Magog, to give it its traditional appellation, is well defined. It constitutes the great rectangularly-shaped region of steppes and semi-deserts stretching from the Carpathians to the West to the Khingan Mountains in the East, extending over some 90 degrees of longitude and 10 to 15 degrees of latitude in its widest places. Geo-politically, except for moments of sudden bursts of activity when its inhabitants dazzled the world with their grandiose alarums and excursions which shattered empires on the confines of the area, it marks an enormous white spot on the historical maps of Eurasia. Linguistically, it enfolds the domain of the distinct language group, comprising Turkish and Mongolian dialects, to which we give the name of the <u>Altaic</u> family of languages.

In discussing tonight certain aspects of the historical role of these Altaic pastoral nomads I speak as a Philologist, rather than as a historian or anthropologist. The three epithets I am using--Aryan, Turk, and Chinese--refer first of all to linguistic distinctions. It is needless to elaborate before an American audience that by Aryans your lecturer does not mean representatives of that recently discovered master race whose chromosomes stamp them as the lords of creation, endowed with the wisdom of a Merlin, the purity of a Parcifal, and the courage of a stuka bombing pilot. By Aryan we simply understand members of well-known historical societies whose dominant speech was one of the so-called Indo-European languages and who recorded their

experiences in one of those tongues. Being no specialist in the
art of juggling physical characteristics, such as a long head,
blond hair, and blue eyes, in such a way that they would mys-
teriously begin to spell out various virtues of the psyche, I
prefer to use the term in what is, I believe, its only proper
context, that of linguistic distinction. Similarly, by the term
Chinese we understand the Chinese-speaking and Chinese-writing
and historically well-defined communities of Eastern Asia. As to
Turks or "Altaics," to use the convenient term encompassing both
Turkish or Mongolian-speaking peoples, it is one of our objec-
tives to sound a warning against the misuse or anachronistic
application of the term, as currently employed in practically all
literature on the subject of Central Asia. The name Turk, of
obscure meaning, is of late origin as a so-called ethnic designation. Both in the East and in the West it became widely known
only in the 6th century A.D. While documents written in Chinese
or in the oldest of the Indo-European languages date back many
centuries before the Christian era, the sharp and martial speech
of the Turks or of the Mongols can be traced back at most not
further than the 2nd or 3rd centuries A.D.

It is true that a few earlier fragments of what is
supposed to be Turkish as reconstructed from Chinese transcriptions sound as if they might be described as having a genuine
"Altaic" ring, but all of them represent such vocables as proper
names, titles, or designations of objects of material culture the
history of which is obscure or complex enough to make us suspect
that they form part of a lingua franca, current through all that
part of Asia, and transcending the limits of a particular
language group. It is often asserted that the Hsiung-nu, the
earliest nomadic group known to us on the Chinese frontier where
they appear about 250 B.C., were Turks. This assertion is primarily based on the single word tngri 'heaven', 'god', which is
common, true enough, to all Turco-Mongol dialects of Asia, but
even that term is believed by competent and independent authorities to be of non-Altaic origin. Additional support for the
hypothesis is adduced from fragments of languages spoken by
tribes which are described by Chinese historians some 400 to 500
years later as descendants of the Hsiung-nu. The linguistic and
ethnic situation in the particular historical environment from
which the evidence is culled was, however, very complex,
suggesting a long antecedent period of intra-group mixture, and,
in the final analysis, the Turkish character of the Hsiung-nu
speech is based on three assumptions: first, one of a continuous
linguistic tradition projected into the past; second, the assumption that the fully developed Turkish language which we know from
actual written documents of the 7th and 8th centuries could have
reached its maturity and individuality only after centuries of
evolution from a supposed proto-Altaic or Turco-Mongol parent
language; and third, that the origin of Altaic, as the dominant
speech of the pastoral nomads of Central asia, must be shrouded

in the mists of the remotest past, as its distinctness from
Chinese on one hand, and Aryan on the other, reflects the primeval juxtaposition of the world of nomadism to that of settled
civilisation.

       The danger of speculation on the first assumption without
the support of concrete evidence is well illustrated by the
following now almost forgotten page from the Asiatic chapter of
19th-century scholarship.

       At the time of and several centuries following the forma-
tion of the Russian state in the 9th century A.D., the steppe
regions North of the Black Sea have been continuously occupied by
Turkish-speaking nomads who began to yield to the advance of the
Russian farmer only by the end of the 18th century. Early investigators of the remote past of that section of Eastern Europe,
applying in reverse, so to speak, the principle "once Turkish,
always Turkish," sought to find Turkish elements in the fragments
of the language of the Scythians as described by Herodotus, and
their successors the Sarmats and Alans who had occupied the
region during several centuries before and after the beginning of
the Christian era. The investigations have failed completely.
Modern scholarship has now widely accepted as conclusive the
evidence that the Scythians spoke an Iranian, i.e., Aryan tongue
and that the great crescent of nomadic peoples extending from the
Lower Danube through Southern Russia to the Transcaspian steppes
formed, at least linguistically, part of the great western Aryan
cultural complex.

       Similarly, the two great regions of Central Asia that we
know as Russian and Chinese Turkestan are not, as the name would
imply--Turkestan meaning land of the Turks--an ancient abode of
Turkish-speaking peoples. The archeological discoveries of the
past generation have clearly demonstrated that in the first
centuries A.D. and for at least three centuries prior to the
beginning of our era the oases and steppes of both divisions
were occupied by populations of Aryan speech. Turkish began to
infringe upon this Aryan territory not earlier than the 8th
century A.D.

       Thus, at the time of China's emergence as a great
continental power in the 2nd century B.C., the Aryan world
extended far into Central Asia. Aryan-speaking nomads controlled
the steppe regions and Aryan-speaking sedentary communities
occupied the string of oases in the desert sections far to the
east of their present habitat to the very confines of China
itself. Increasing evidence seems to indicate that even on the
frontiers of China in districts that are now predominantly
Chinese, Aryan had once been spoken and colonies from the Far
West with names familiar to the readers of the Classics had
stretched to the very banks of the upper Huang-ho. It appears,

in fact, that under the Seres, as described by Ptolemy and Pliny
in the first two centuries of our era, we must understand not the
Chinese, but inhabitants of those colonies of Aryans at the end
of the desert road of Central Asia, and in Serica we must see the
easternmost Ultima Thūle of our own ancient world, rather than a
land entirely extraneous to the Aryan cosmos. We may even assert
that these Aryan outposts at the extremity of the trail extending
all the way from the Mediterranean to the frontiers of the Chinese
world focussed on themselves the attention of Western geographers
to such an extent that the great country beyond remained in the
penumbra. We are not suggesting, naturally, that this failure
on the part of the Aryan to transcend his geographical and linguistic limitations was due to racial antagonism or inability to
bridge a gap in language continuity. The explanation of the
above curious state of affairs is to be sought in the physical
and human geography of the region. This marginal territory where
Aryan and Chinese joined hands, the Northwestern tip of China
proper, is a country of semi-oases consisting of patches of land
suitable for intensive irrigational agriculture with large
stretches of poorer soil lying between, suggesting a symbiosis of
settled and semi-nomadic pastoral societies. While to the north
the great wall of China rose to delineate clearly the frontier
separating the Chinese world from the steppe and the desert of
Mongolia, no such definite line could be drawn in the Chinese
Northwest. The early Chinese undoubtedly penetrated sporadi-
cally and in isolated groups beyond the Yellow River at Lan-chou,
but while the main body of the Chinese agricultural society had
not yet reached the limits of its natural expansion which were
identical with those of the zone of intensive agriculture, the
Chinese had no incentive to integrate this marginal country with
what was then China proper. Between the Chinese settled
communities and those of the Aryans of Central Asia there
existed a territory inhabited by groups of marginal nomadic or
semi-nomadic peoples, both Chinese and Aryan. One of the latter
is known to us by name; these were the Yüeh-chih, in archaic
Chinese zngut-tia, a name curiously reminiscent of Σκυθαι
Scythians.

Thus, even though the gap between the settled communities
of the East and West was not great, they were separated by an
intervening insulating element of nomadic groups. Many vexing
problems still face us in the reconstruction of the archaic
pronunciation of Chinese characters, but it is with some degree
of surety that our word Serica can be recognized in archaic
Chinese ser-kia or ser-t'ia, the name of a locality on the upper
course of the Yellow River. Now the same archaic Chinese compound ser-kia, a disyllabic word that does not seem to be
Chinese but represents rather the transcription of a foreign
vocable, was found in addition to designate, curiously enough,
four different products, two of them of undoubted Chinese origin,
plain silk and an aromatic and dye plant, the third a typical

article of nomadic economy "felt cloth", and the fourth, in a labialized form of our word, ser-bia, the metal buckle-clasp or fibula, a characteristic piece in the nomad's apparel. We thus have in Serica, to apply here a terminology brilliantly developed by Owen Lattimore in Inner Asian Frontiers of China, a territory "not yet Chinese," yet mortgaged to the Chinese in the future; a land where Chinese products were easily available, yet one potentially open to the rise of a new norm of existence distinct from that of the Chinese agricultural complex.

In order to prepare ourselves for the correct interpretation of the epoch-making events of the 2nd century B.C. which determined the history of Asia for centuries, and incidentally to dismiss as invalid the third of the assumptions discussed a few minutes ago, it would be well to review a few of the principles established by Mr. Lattimore in his novel and strikingly illuminating re-analysis of the development of Chinese society and its marginal territories.

Those of us who have for many years studied Ancient China do unhesitatingly welcome Mr. Lattimore's solution of the problem of the so-called barbarians which are represented in the ancient texts as living side by side with the Chinese within China itself. Mr. Lattimore demonstrates that we should consider them as "not yet Chinese," rather than "non-Chinese." That is, he fully confirms the view held in the past by several sinologists that the two groups were distinct not in language or race, as in cultural level. He further suggests that the more culturally advanced Chinese in their territorial expansion which brought more and more desirable land under intensive cultivation forced the retreat of their less lucky brethren into districts unsuitable for the full development of a settled economy, thus, so to say, progressively "barbarizing" them. When the Chinese began to reach the limit of their agricultural expansion to the North, China's marginal population, still "not yet Chinese," rather than "non-Chinese" and which had originally subsisted on a mixed economy basis, was pushed off the rim of the domain of Chinese intensive agriculture into the wastelands, steppes, and deserts of Mongolia, where, in order to survive, these groups had to adopt a highly specialized form of economy, pastoral nomadism. A new norm of existence was thus developed: that of pure nomadic society, an extreme phase of activity, polar to that of intensive agriculture. The "not-yet Chinese" then became non-Chinese. The pure pastoral nomadism of Mongolia grew thus as a highly specialized order of society incidental to the full development of the Chinese norm of life and did not exist from the beginning of time, either as an inevitable stage in the evolution of civilization or as a world totally extraneous to China and genetically unrelated to her.

The nomadic society of the Hsiung-nu that made its appearance in Mongolia about the third century B.C. was at the

time unique. Insofar as we are able to judge the meager archeological evidence available in regions of pastoral nomadism in
other parts of Central Asia, this form of economy was usually
preceded by one of mixed or settled civilisation. We may also
point to the testimony of Herodotus on the life of the ancient
Scythians, the earliest inhabitants of the steppe known to us, a
testimony which leaves no doubt that theirs was a mixed "cowboy"
economy practised in the vicinity of settled communities of
considerable size, rather than one of pure nomadism. The groups
of herdsmen tending their flocks near the Aryan oases of Central
Asia were likewise semi-nomadic, and not specialized nomads.
Only in Mongolia, on the Northern frontier of China, did the
prerequisites for the creation of absolute nomadism obtain: the
disappearance of a pre-historic agriculture too weak to develop
into extensive farming, soil and climatic conditions too unfavor-
able for intensive agriculture, and the high pressure from an
adjacent thickly populated zone of irrigational farming, which
was constantly barbarizing its own fringe by forcing marginal
groups to abandon their mixed economy and to adopt a specialized
culture of clearly steppe character.

The history of the Chinese frontier cannot, therefore, as
Mr. Lattimore shows, be interpreted as a perennial struggle of
two primevally juxtaposed worlds, but should be understood as the
conflict of China with a new historical force, suddenly emerged
on its fringe, a monster in a large part of China's own creation.

It is thus likely that prior to the appearance of the
Hsiung-nu on the North China frontier the only barbarians, using
barbarian in the sense of people of a language distinct from that
of the Chinese, were the Aryans. With Mr. Lattimore's further
analysis of these frontier relationships and his explanations of
China's policy in her expansion into Central Asia we cannot
unfortunately agree. His theory of the development of Chinese
society is, we believe, applied in too narrow and rigid a fashion
in interpreting the policies of the Han empire. He thus under-
estimates some very essential factors operating at the top of the
Chinese social pyramid and the manifold activities of Chinese
statesmen and military commanders in Inner Asia are explained by
him as determined by a mere negative desire to keep frontier
populations in the Chinese orbit. He seems to admit, however,
the decisive influence that the events of the end of the second
century B.C. had on the re-orientation of Chinese imperial policy,
though he does not recognize a change in its fundamental character.

We shall part, therefore, at this point with Mr. Lattimore, and return to Serica, for it is there that we shall find a
solution of the secret of the Han empire's penetration into
Central Asia. As we have observed, for some time prior to the
rise of the Hsiung-nu the Chinese had been in peaceful contact
with an Aryan semi-nomadic people, the Yüeh-chih or Zngut-tia,

who were established in the Serica region. Some time after 180
B.C. the Hsiung-nu confederacy struck at the Yüeh-chih and
obtained control of the region, forcing a large part of the Yüeh-
chih to remove westward along the T'ien-shan mountains as far as
Sogdiana and Bactria where they founded a large state adjoining
Parthia. The Hsiung-nu were now not only a general nuisance on
the Northern frontier of China, but had flanked the Chinese continental position and broken off China's contact with their
congenial neighbors to the west. There is absolutely no way to
circumvent the testimony of the Chinese sources that when, under
the great Wu Ti, the Chinese in a mighty effort which required
long and carefully planned preparations broke through this Hsiung-
nu blockade in the Northwest and launched a series of campaigns
into Central Asia, their primary purpose was to re-establish
contact with the Yüeh-chih. Numerous passages in Chinese historical documents testify that trade interests determined these
campaigns as much as considerations of national defense. One
must guard oneself, however, from committing the mistake of
interpreting, as is sometimes done, these trade interests in
terms of China's possessing a great surplus of that precious
commodity silk, or some other products, and being anxious to
dispose of it in foreign markets.

Contemporary Chinese texts reveal to us a more complex
situation. In the country as a whole there was no pressure to
inaugurate or increase the export of any surplus. The articulate
section of Chinese agricultural society, the landed gentry, whose
double role of landlords and bureaucrats made them guardians of
what they conceived to be the public weal, had no interest in
foreign trade. Their philosophy of life and conception of the
state was rooted in the norm of existence prevailing in the
microcosmic unit of a Chinese county with its concentration of
population in the most intensively cultivated centers and its
short range trade. Equitable control of irrigational facilities
and proper storage of surplus grain against a possible failure of
crops were the chief duties of administration. The macrocosm of
the nation, composed as it was of self-contained cells, contributed no new problems, except those of collecting the tribute-
tax and creating a system of transportation, definitely limited
to the conveyance of this tribute-tax to the metropolitan districts. Most of Chinese literature being the product of that
class, some investigators, notably Mr. Lattimore, have made the
natural mistake of overemphasizing their point of view and
deducted from the endless repetitions of the essential points of
the economic philosophy of the scholar-gentry found in Chinese
writings on political science that this philosophy lay at the
cornerstone of Han imperial policy. A more detailed study of
texts and of the sequence of events shows, however, that this
reiteration of principles by the scholar-bureaucrats was
necessitated by the existence at the Han capital of a counter-
movement and of groups and interests sharply differing in their
views on economics and national policy.

Time does not allow a full discussion of this interesting conflict. It suffices to say that the texts supply us with abundant evidence on the following points:

1. While the Imperial Han government and subsequent Chinese governments were always ready to offer fervent lip service to the principles of national economics as outlined by the class of literati, the immediate interest of court circles who enjoyed the usufruct of the tribute-tax accumulated at the metropolis made them anxious to dispose of the surplus available to them in exchange for foreign luxuries.

We possess for the period long lists of these luxury products of foreign lands. Among them we find horses--especially superior horses from West Turkestan--furs of sables, foxes, and marmots, imported jade, felt carpets and rugs, corals, crystals, asbestos, carnelian and other semi-precious stones--all, according to contemporary sources, obtained from the Far West or North of Asia through the western neighbors of China, in exchange for a few pieces of silk and other Chinese commodities supplied to the capital by the country.

2. In operating this exchange the court circles had the support of a not insignificant class of metropolitan middlemen and merchants, with a philosophy and a rapacity quite different from those of the short range trader of the interior.

3. While numerically small, these cliques exercised a tremendous influence in matters of foreign policy. With them, as with the petty chieftains of the border through whom the barter was carried on, considerations of prestige weighed heavier than economic factors. In their hands a few thousand pieces of silk, or a boxful of trinkets manufactured by the skillful Chinese artisans which could bring them in return a vast store of foreign novelties became a powerful lever of policy. The advantage in exchange was always on their side, for the petty kings of the western oases and the chieftains of smaller nomadic hordes were seldom powerful or shrewd enough to bargain successfully with the Chinese. The situation was immediately reversed, however, following the formation of the far flung Hsiung-nu confederacy. Through a blockade of the Chinese frontier the chieftains of the nomads could demand a better bargain for themselves. But even a slightly more equitable arrangement of the barter would appear as extortion to the metropolitan clique. The opposition of the bureaucratic literati class would not permit them to go too far in demanding or enforcing a larger supply of revenue from the native Chinese tribute-tax payers. They could use, however, the influence they exercised on the government to pursue a foreign policy favorable to the maintenance of their comfortable standard of living. Only too often, a fact overlooked by many investigators, they were the central government.

The phrase "trade" should not, therefore, be interpreted in terms of a major trade expansion directly affecting the economy of China as a whole. The court and metropolitan circles in whose interests the Han government launched its extensive campaigns were quite satisfied in leaving the actual movement of goods in the hands of outside middlemen and trade-carriers provided the rate of goods-exchange was overwhelmingly favorable to them. The only way to insure this and to eliminate the danger of a nomadic monopoly trusting on foreign goods was to establish Chinese influence along the oasis route of Central Asia in such a way that the Hsiung-nu would be prevented from diverting the flow of goods to the steppe route. For the Hsiung-nu chieftains, on the other hand, after their failure to hold their flanking advance on the upper course of the Yellow River, it became necessary, in order to regain their position for bargaining power, to break through at some point of the Chinese line now extended far to the west. This they repeatedly attempted to achieve at the Turfan passes where a gap in the T'ien-shan made it possible to exercise pressure on the northern oases now subject to the Chinese. Thus both Chinese and Hsiung-nu were pushing westward along parallel courses: the Chinese trying to anchor, so to say, their western flank to the firm bed of settled Aryan communities strong enough to resist the encroachment of a steppe society, the Hsiung-nu bent on preventing it and forcing the re-orientation of either the Chinese or the latter's natural Aryan allies towards the steppe.

I shall not weary you with the details of the struggle. The first race to the West ended in the middle of the first century B.C. with the defeat by the Chinese of a Hsiung-nu group which attempted to extend its control over the Oxus terminus of the Chinese oasis route. It is to be remembered that the Hsiung-nu movement westward was in no way a migration. It was essentially conquest through the extension of service and tribute exactions to neighboring peoples, the spread of a political system and a technique of a unique norm of life based on a reasoned antagonism to the sedentary order of society. This reasoned antagonism arising as it did from the peculiar conditions on the Chinese frontier, could not be maintained for long. The necessary heterogeneous composition of nomadic empires, the greater security that the mixed economy on the marginal lands of settled civilisations promised individuals and groups within the nomadic society, the various and often conflicting forces of attraction exercised by widely separated centers of gravity, all conspired to make the unity of such empires ephemeral. This unity could only be preserved by the strenuous efforts of energetic leaders who managed by operating along internal lines of communications between two centers of sedentary civilisations, to eliminate their competitors and enforce, primarily upon China, their demands for a monopoly as trade carriers.

In refusing these demands, the Chinese metropolitan trust had only two courses of action open to them: (1) to use the military resources of the Empire to establish a line of communications along the oasis route independent of the steppe, and defendable against the nomads even at considerable cost to the fundamental Chinese economy, or (2) to attempt through bribery and active support of potential rivals of the supreme ruling group of the nomads to break their unity. Significantly enough, such rivals were usually sought and found in the western part of the nomadic confederation, farther from China. Thus both methods of combatting the menace of the steppe resulted in forcing the nomads to extend their political control farther and farther to the West. Without a western anchor of their own at some point on the trans-asiatic front of sedentary communities, the steppe society of Mongolia lost its raison d'être and could only submit to Chinese control and reconcile itself to a marginal existence.

The Chinese way of life created on its periphery a new political, economical, and even ethical norm, a new force in the history of Asia. Having come into conflict with the new force on matters of trade monopoly, the Chinese government tried to shake loose the incubus by extending its frontiers westward along the natural front of sedentary or tame marginal societies. Instead, it carried the incubus on its back; with every step it made westward it gave an additional push to the spread of this new nomadic force in the same direction.

A working hypothesis can now be formulated. If the nomads on the fringe of China were originally "not yet Chinese" who were gradually forced to adopt pure nomadism due to the consolidation of China which culminated in the building of the Great Wall, these potential then actual "pure" nomads belonged to the Chinese linguistic group. They had, however, for neighbors the semi-nomadic mobile fringe of the Aryan settled communities on the frontiers of China whose nomadization was undoubtedly not so extreme as that of the tribes in Mongolia. Along the Ordos fringe and in the Serica region the Chinese nomads and the Aryan nomads intermingled freely. It is in that region that the originally Chinese nomads finally severed the last link that bound them to the Chinese cultural complex--the tie of language. Among the fragments of their speech that we can identify some four or five hundred years later, a few words can be recognized as Turkish or Mongolian, but as many of them show unmistakable identity with either Chinese or Aryan. When we first noticed this about five years ago we were intent on demonstrating the existence of Altaic as a distinct linguistic group, and were inclined to dismiss the nomadic words with a Chinese ring or Aryan association as loan-words foreign to the fundamental Altaic background. Accumulating evidence makes this view untenable. At present the distribution of these early fragments of words among the three groups is such that we may legitimately raise the question whether that nascent

Altaic vocabulary was not after all a mixture of Chinese and Aryan.

In grammar and morphology Altaic occupies an intermediary position between analytic Chinese and synthetic Aryan, Mongolian leaning more to Chinese, Turkish towards Aryan. An interesting avenue of linguistic investigation thus opens itself to us. Could it be possible that the Altaic linguistic group which is historically so closely bound with the economy of pastoral nomadism originated at the same time with this new norm of life? Rather than being a form of speech whose origin is to be sought in a dim pre-historic past, could it be a lingua franca first used by the mixed Aryan Chinese nomads of the fringe of China and spread slowly to the west with the movement of the Hsiung-nu?

I repeat again, there is no question of mass migrations, but rather of movements of small groups, numbering at most ten thousand men. To see in the Hsiung-nu foray into the Aral steppes a migration of a considerable part of the Hsiung-nu people westward, as do so many historians who attempt to link that group with the Huns who 400 years later invaded south Russia, is impossible. The Chinese sources of the period which in spite of their terseness give us a remarkably complete picture of the tribes extending from the Yellow River to the Aral Sea, yield no information whatever on a large body of Hsiung-nu living in this vicinity during those centuries prior to 375 A.D. The tempting identification of the Huns with the Hsiung-nu, a theory that has haunted the imagination of every student of Eurasia since Chinese records became accessible to our historians, is therefore too hazardous and is based in the final analysis on mere phonetic resemblance of the two names and the undeniable, but rather superficially interpreted, evidence that the movements in the steppe region occurred regularly in the general direction from east to west. It has also been pointed out in this connection that it is only after the eruption of the Huns into the Pontian plains that we find the Aryan nomadic crescent supplanted by Turkish-speaking tribes. If the Huns were Turks this linguistic revolution is to be attributed to them.

The disappearance of Aryan tongues in the steppe and the substitution of Turkish dialects for them was, however, a process consummated rather late, probably not before the ninth century. In the light of the documents accessible to us it would be unjustified to ascribe it, as is usually done, to a big migratory wave or even a succession of waves of Turkish invaders coming from some inexhaustible reservoir of remote Asia.

In the first place, this reservoir of Mongolia could never be considered inexhaustible. At no time, if we evaluate correctly the testimony of Chinese historians, could the steppes

and deserts of Mongolia support, especially in the state of absolute nomadism, more than two million people, and most of the
historically known migrations were those of numerically small
groups.

Secondly, our investigators are too prone to base their
belief in the Turkish character of certain nomadic groups on the
single evidence of a tribal name or the designation of a confederacy. Often that single fact is offered as evidence, in rebuttal to the testimony of some ancient historian that the people in
question spoke a language different from Turkish, the statement
being dismissed by a sneer that these scholars of the past could
not have been well versed in linguistic distinctions. Conscious
of this pronounced defect in the method of most students of the
steppe region, we proceeded to investigate the meaning of these
supposedly ethnic Turkish designations. This excursus was
rewarded with rather curious results:

1. In no case was such a tribal name found to be represented by what may be called a primary ethnic appellation.

2. Several of them were ascertained to connote "mixed",
"hybrid", "mongrel".

3. Most of them proved to be stereotyped terms designating the group's constitutional organization, for instance,
union of so many clans or tribes, such and such division of a
larger confederacy with which the tribe in question was bound by
political and economic rather than racial or linguistic ties.

Especially frequent are numerical designations such as
the Eight, the Five, the Forty. These numerical terms are, it is
true, in most cases Turkish, but their vague character in itself
suggesting multiplicity of origin and merely organizational unity
in no way permits us to pronounce ourselves on the character of
the language spoken by the tribe. Another widely used term is
represented by the root uχur, which appears in several phonetic
variants such as ïβïr, avar, uχuz, mog'er--all of them authenti-
cated in turkish dialects in the meaning "horn", which must have
early acquired the connotation of "horde", "chief", "tribal
division." The particular application of this term "horn" brings
us, indeed, back to the Hsiung-nu who, the Chinese historians
tell us, were divided into "ten horns" or ten "divisions", but it
is obvious that we cannot seek to identify remnants of the Hsiung-
nu in every tribe called "horns" or so many horns.

The predominance and wide use of the term indicates, however, a survival of Hsiung-nu political nomenclature. Some of
the strongest of the confederacies of the steppe adopted as their
name the term "ten horns" signifying by it, we believe, that they
aspired to perform the same grandiose role that that great nomadic

society once played on the frontiers of China. Thus, if it is
still problematical that the European Huns spoke Turkish, their
name is, in our belief, inspired by a turkish terminology. Hun
or Hon is, we think, nothing else but the turkish term hon "ten"
not necessarily suggesting a large representation of Turks in the
confederacy, but merely indicating a turkish inspiration for its
formation.

Another interesting example of the application of a
Hsiung-nu functional but not ethnic term originating on the
frontier of China to a situation thousands of miles away presents
itself in the case of the term Bulgar as used to designate important semi-nomadic groups in East Russia. Three groups of Bulgars
are known to us: one in the corner of the Pontian steppes north
of the Caucasus, the other on the upper Volga, and the third on
the lower Danube. Historians of Eastern Europe have been aware
of the undoubted derivation of that name from the root bulɣa
"mixed", "hybrid", "mongrel". Abundant evidence points that the
hybridization that produced the Bulgars could have occurred only
on a marginal territory such as that of the Volga-Don region, yet
a search is kept up for Bulgars as such in the depth of the
Asiatic steppes. We even hesitate to reveal that the Chinese
have recorded the same term Bulgar as a designation of the de-
nomadized Hsiung-nu on the Chinese frontier, Hsiung-nu who had
adopted the Chinese mode of life and by the sixth century A.D.
were largely Chinese-speaking; we hesitate to do so in fear that
some champion of the migratory theory should jump at the chance
to write an exciting epic on the migration en masse of the ancestors of the modern Bulgarians from the Huang-ho to the Danube.

In short, then, we suggest that the gradual spread of the
Turkish dialects from east to west was originally one of political nomenclature, stimulated by the movement of small organizing
units of fifth columnists, if you please, representing the
interests of chieftains directing the formation of a new order,
of a nomadic society intent on circumventing the Chinese or
Chinese-Aryan strategy of keeping the empire's communication
along the oasis line of Central Asia. Their movement was ever
westward for it was parallel if not synchronous with that of the
Chinese further south. Whenever the Chinese frontier line was
firmly anchored to the eastern tip of the landfast Aryan communities of Western Asia, the Turkish strategy prescribed in the
case of failure of a breakthrough against either of them to seek
the establishment of a terminus of their own at the end of a
purely nomadic steppe route further westward, at the Caspian
Gates, or on the eastern frontier of Rome. It must be remembered,
however, that this strategy did not involve changes in or fundamentally affecting the elementary life of the masses of the
nomadic society. It was essentially a policy of its upper layers,
of the "horns" and chieftains who with their select, well-trained
and mobile stormtroopers could both conceive and execute such

grandiose plans. The Aryan nomads on the fringe of the Roman and
Persian empires were, on the other hand, definitely marginal
societies with no interests beyond their purely local ones, and
unaware of the big issues considered or the stakes involved in
the complex political game played in Inner Asia. Those of them
who recoiled before the small but purposeful Turkish groups
retreated, to their second line positions nearer to the center
of their mixed economy; others allowed themselves to be weaned
from their marginal existence and were incorporated into larger
confederacies which, created by Turks, were necessarily known
under Turkish names and eventually adopted Turkish speech.

With the exception of the empire of the T'u-chüeh Turks
in the second half of the sixth century and that of the Mongols
the plan of the nomadic control over highways on a transcontinental scale originally conceived by the Hsiung-nu during the first
phase of their rivalry with the Chinese empire did not material-
ize. As the plan envisaged as one of its prerequisites the
location of headquarters near the Chinese frontier, the enormous
extension of lines of communications and the delegation of power
thus made necessary often precluded the possibility of effective
control along the entire caravan route.

The strong incentive that the nomads received for putting
their plan into execution from the activities of the Chinese
which immediately provoked their parallel action could not continue to inspire effectively the central headquarters once the
Chinese goal in the west was reached, and that goal was West
Turkestan. Further to the West the situation would to a great
degree depend not only on China, but on Persia. The secondary
headquarters of the nomads in the western T'ien-shan would then
take up the operations. Instead of a transcontinental problem,
however, these would often present themselves to them as only a
half-continental question, involving the line of communications
between the nexus of Chinese-Persian trade and the Danubian
frontier of the Roman empire along the Caspian and Pontian
steppes. This line of communication was fully organized by
Turkish chieftains only in the sixth and seventh centuries of
our era.

This situation is best illustrated in the events of the
sixth century, when the grand Hsiung-nu plan was revived by the
T'u-chüeh Turks.

The organizing clan of this federation originated in the
melting pot on the upper Yellow River. For several generations
they served as smiths to the Juan-juan, which formed in the fifth
and in the first part of the sixth centuries a great federation
in Mongolia. In 550 this clan who, probably owing to their occupation as metallurgical workers, were aware of the ties that
bound the life of the steppe to that of the South and were

conscious of the manifold currents permeating it, rose against
their masters, wrested from them the leadership over the welter
of tribes along the Mongolian route from North China to the Oxus,
and founded a confederation of their own. This confederation is
known to the Byzantines as Τοιρκοι a name registered in their own
inscriptions of some 200 years later as Turk and to the Chinese
as T'u-chüeh, or in archaic Chinese Tʿuət-kʿiᵂət. While the confederation was a polyglot one, it is undeniable that the inscriptions first deciphered by the genius of the Danish scholar V.
Thomsen some forty years ago are couched in a pure Turkish dialect. It is, however, unwise to do as is usually done, and to
make on the basis of this evidence the assertion that Turk was
then an ethnic designation of a numerous people. It is even
doubtful that Chinese Tʿuət-kʿiᵂət represents, as was suggested
by Paul Pelliot, a Mongolian plural form Türküt "Turks"; in fact,
the various versions of the Chinese sources on the subject can
best be reconciled on the supposition that the term represents
the transcription of doxut 'the helmetmakers' or toquz 'the nine'
--again, as we see, functional and not ethnic appellations.

     The organization of the Turks seems to have been from the
very beginning one based on two centers, an eastern headquarters
in the steppes adjacent to the Chinese frontier from which center
they exercised a constant pressure on China, then torn by internal dissensions, and a western one in the proximity of the
entrance from Mongolia into the Aral plains. It is the western
division that is known to us through the records of Byzantium,
which entered into diplomatic relations with their khans in the
sixties and seventies of the sixth century.

     As early as 531, according to Procopius, Justinian the
Great, emperor of the Romans intent on freeing Byzantium from
dependence on the Sassanians of Persia for their supply of silk,
dispatched to the Himyarites and Aethiopians, that is, to peoples
at the southern entrance of the Red Sea, an embassy urging them
to organize for their profit and that of the Romans the transportation of silk by sea so as to break the Persian monopoly on
this lucrative commerce. Justinian had thus plans to abandon the
Serica route in favor of that of Sin. The Sassanians naturally
took steps to prevent it by countermeasures.

     The southern sea route of Sin enters here as competing
with that of the Seres. We believe that this was primarily
determined by the events in China. When Northern China, after a
period of disintegration in the fifth century, achieved a new
unity under the dynasty of Topa, a group of Sinicized Turkish
nomads, the Central Asian line of the North Chinese empire found
again its anchor in semi-nomadic groups, originating again at the
Eastern extremity of the T'ien-shan but founded in a confederacy
embracing chiefly Aryan-speaking nomads and settled communities
of the western part of Chinese Central Asia, as well as some pure

nomadic groups to the north or northwest. The former are known
to us as the Hepthalites, the latter as Avars or Uẏur. When after
520 the Topa dynasty went into decline and sank into civil strife
and disunion, the tie between Tabγač as North China was then
known, and their allies in the west was weakened. Southern China
meanwhile was entering a short period of prosperity under the
founder of the house of Liang under whom China's maritime communications received considerable stimulus. Between 530 and 550,
therefore, the Sin route to the west achieved a brief prominence
which it may have retained even for a decade or two subsequently.

It is at this moment that the Turks par excellence enter
upon the scene and attempt to re-organize the northern caravan
route. They overcome the Hepthalites and then the Avars, and
offer to the Persians to enter into a trade agreement on the
question of silk. The Persians, who had meanwhile shifted their
trade route to the south, refused the offer and the Turks, enraged, sent in 567 their famous embassy to the court of Justinian
where they proposed an alliance to the Romans. This démarche led
to a lively diplomatic exchange between the two powers lasting
for several decades, and although full concord was not established
between them they repeatedly acted in concert in wars against the
Sassanian empire, and Turkish organization was steadily spreading
into the Caspian and Pontian plains.

Northern China was, however, recuperating, and from about
577 started again on its westward march. Through Chinese in-
trigues the eastern part of the Turkish confederacy was made to
disassociate itself from the western one, and eventually submitted to China. The turn of the occidental Turks came a few decades
later.

For one hundred years, however, the Turks had dominated
the Eurasiatic plains and had been engaged in consolidating their
cells, particularly in the western part towards the Volga and
south Russia.

It is interesting to speculate in this connection whether
in this they were not following through in a less violent way the
trail blazed two hundred years previously by the Huns.

The fourth century is one of the most obscure periods in
the history of Central Asia, but we are, however, in possession
of the detailed facts as regards China. The beginning of the
century marks a disintegration of central power in north China
followed by a movement of marginal groups into China proper. The
empire maintains itself in southern China, and just as in the
sixth century China's communications with the West are maintained
after 320 by the Sin maritime route. If the Huns were Turks in
their organization, we might have in their eruption into Russia a
movement trying to consolidate the plains on a Rome-Persia axis.

The geopolitical web of relationships in the Pontian steppes presents a problem in itself, complicated as it was by a set of communications running from north to south. But we cannot resist the temptation of pointing out the following interesting illustration of the use of Turkish terminology in the toponymy of Russia in the ninth century, a use which throws a flood of light on the role of the Turks in the control of trade routes extending even to waterways. The Khazars, who at that time dominated the country from their center on the lower Volga, spoke according to the Arabic geographers a language different from that of the Turks, yet the political-economic terminology of their state was Turkish. Thus in the names of their strongholds we can identify the Turkish term sam, a regular dialectical variant of common Turkish yam 'road', 'control post-station'. Observe now the distribution of these strongholds: Sambatas, identified with Kiev on the Dnieper, Samkerč on the Cimmerian Bosporus, Samburtas on the Volga leading into the country of the Burtas, Samender on the road to Persia--four stations giving them efficient control over the whole region. The complexities of trade relationships are furthermore suggested by the names of two other strategically located places: Tamtarxan on the Taman peninsula opposite Samkerč, and Astarxan at the mouth of the Volga. The second part of the names is without any doubt turkish tarxan 'tax exempt', 'free of duty' (Tam and As being respectively the ancient names of the Black and the Caspian Seas). According to recent investigations, it is at the first free port that the growing rivalry between the Khazarian commercial trust and their chief ninth-century competitors, roving bands of a trading rabble known collectively as Rus, came to a head. The clash finally resulted in a breakthrough by the Rus, led by Varangians, of the Khazarian tariff system both on the Dnieper and the Volga, and the establishment of the Russian state.

Incidentally, the term tarxan is known to us in Chinese transcription as early as the second century A.D., and is found also in the Aryan languages of Central Asia. Its antonym tamγa 'tax', 'duty', which survives to this day in Russian, is met with again in Chinese transcription in a text of the sixth century as the name of Bogdo-ula, the great mountain overshadowning the Turfan pass. The Chinese text implies that the majestic peak acquired the prosaic name of Customs Mountain from the location nearby of tariff-collecting agencies of the T'ieh-lê Turks who dominated at the time the trade route north of the T'ien-shan.

To recapitulate, we have attempted to indicate that prior to the third century B.C. the Aryan world extended along thin lines of oases fringed by semi-nomadic societies far into Central Asia to the westernmost tip of China. That on the outskirts of both these worlds a new nomadic society was born whose leaders entered into a struggle with the central Chinese government for monopolistic rights over luxury and prestige trade, and that the

incidents of that struggle led to the spread of a politico-
economic vocabulary in the language of that nomadic group far
beyond its original limits. That the displacement of Aryan dialects by that spreading language through groups of leaders whose
dream was to establish control of the steppe routes created an
illusion of migratory waves from east to west through the width
and breadth of the ocean of Central Asia, and that the comings
and goings of Gog and Magog were not produced by climatic changes,
racial antagonism, struggle for pasturelands, or sheer love of
war and plunder, but by a planned restlessness carrying in it
organization and intense purposefulness, but an organization due
to the character and wide geographical range of its activity
subject to quick changes, and easily affected in its orientation
by the policies of the government of the greatest and largest of
all Euro-Asiatic communities, the empire of China.

Though necessarily summarizing, I have tried in drawing
my conclusions to take cognizance of every detail of the history
of the steppe known to me. The foregoing analysis may differ in
broad lines of interpretation with that of Professor Teggart in
Rome and China, but the inspiration is his and whatever small
laurels we may earn in at least suggesting new avenues of approach
to the solutions of the historical mysteries of Central Asia we
gratefully and respectfully lay at his doorstep. For a complete
solution of the problem of Central Asia we must await a competent
analysis of the historical, archeological, and linguistic aspects
of the past of the third great region of Eurasia, that of the
northern forest belt from the fringe of which the nomads undoubtedly drew much of their resources in material and manpower.
While that fringe remained open to them and they themselves acted
as intermediaries between the population of the forest and the
great civilisations of the south, the nomadic way of life had a
function, a purpose, and in moments of determined organization
and drive, a glorious, if ephemeral, future. Far from being a
drone of humanity, the Turk played a necessary role in history--
a role not devoid of grandeur. He welded together, at least
linguistically, Central Asia into one unit, and thus incidentally
pointed the way to the Slav in the latter's march through the
forest to the Pacific Ocean. When the Slav reached his own Serica
on the frontier of the Celestial Empire and the landfast civilisations of China and the West joined hands both north and south
of the great steppe rectangle, the sun of the Central Asiatic
Turk tipped slowly beneath the horizon.

The encirclement of Gog and Magog by the settled peoples
of Eurasia is today completed. Never again will the banner of the
Turk be raised in answer to the unvoiced command of the eternal
blue heaven. The ringing names of Bumun and Temüčin, the founders
of the great Altaic empire, will fade on the rocks of High Asia,
and no Khan will shatter the peace of the steppe with a mighty
summons to his warriors. No more will the sound of the Tartar

flute strike terror in the hearts of Chinese or Slav, Persian or Roman. If Gog of the land of Magog ever takes to horse again and rides through the Magic Wall, even the hour of Armageddon will be past and it will be only to answer Gabriel's last earth-shattering trumpet call, for then time will be no more.

Comments on "Some Great Books of the Oriental Traditions"

Approaches to the Oriental Classics:
Asian Literature and Thought in General Education,
ed. W. T. de Bary, Columbia University Press,
New York, 1959, pages 166-170.

Speaking as a representative of the Pacific "backwaters" of America, I should like to call your attention to certain problems that appear to be of major importance to some of us at Berkeley, particularly in connection with the great task of incorporating the essence of the Chinese classics into the thesaurus of the Western tradition. My remarks will center around the theme of what I am inclined to call "linguistic imperialism." I feel that unless our Occidental societies accompany their all-in-all graceful retreat from attitudes of imperialistic arrogance in the political and economic fields by some effort in the direction of readjusting their linguistic sights and of cultivating a greater capacity for linguistic and philological resilience under the impact of the tremendous volume of cultural and literary information that is coming to us from Asia —the noble project of expanding our humanistic tradition to a truly global scale is doomed to failure. Assimilation of new information implies in-corpor-ation of new material into one's native structure and hence—as stated here by one delegate yesterday—that structure's transformation. No wonder that a task of such magnitude should evoke repeated expression of pessimism as regards our qualifications for such an undertaking.

All of the great languages of Asia have shown in the past few decades an amazing resourcefulness in successfully incorporating into the very fiber of their linguistic structure most of our scientific and technological notions. We of the West should be able to match this impressive achievement of the Asians by an equally creative, imaginative, and bold utilization of the vast riches of our own linguistic heritage in fashioning "new terms" for "new ideas" as we attempt to absorb some of Asia's humanistic thought.

The task is enormous, but not necessarily hopeless. Within the great Mediterranean family, the languages of Europe have for centuries lived in symbiosis. Ever since the Romans found it imperative to recast many of their linguistic conventions in the irradiating light of Greek experience, there has been constant interplay, inter-friction, interborrowing, and crossfertilization among the linguistic members of the Western division of the Indo-European family. The cultural partnership of the European world and the Semitic civilization has also been of sufficient duration to permit the absorption of a considerable number of Semitic "logoi" into our system of thought. The most summary survey of the Western "international" vocabulary would reveal at least 3,000 viable Arabic words (from "algebra" and "alcohol" down to "zenith"), and innumerable felicitous phraseological creations of Hebrew poets have subtly transformed the diction—and even syntax—of every European tongue through the translation of the Bible. The Sanskrit language, a sister tongue of Latin and Greek, has contributed a not insignificant list of important technical terms, albeit not as viable as the Arabic ones, to our common vocabulary.

As for the two great civilizations east of India, we may observe with some satisfaction that Japanese loanwords begin to be increasingly noticeable in English, but the magnificent contributions of the Chinese mind to human thought remain locked to us—linguistically speaking. Chinese monosyllables are not easily incorporated into foreign idiom when kept encased in the sarcophagi of our transcriptions which are notoriously irregular, uncertain, and confusing. It is not an exaggeration to say that the richness of the Chinese vocabulary—vocabulary remarkably monolithic and homogeneous among the great vocabularies of mankind—remains **entirely untapped and is at present practically inaccessible to the general humanist.** The problem of translating classical Chinese involves, moreover, a larger issue transcending that of diction. Of all possible human grammars, the structure of classical Chinese appears quite incommensurable with that of the Indo-European tongues. Let us consider for a moment the glosso-philosophical idiosyncrasies of Indo-European. Our language builds up subtle distinctions by means of those elusive and ineffable little particles called prepositions (used not only syntactically, but as morphological formants, in such pregnant terms as "co-gnition," "perception," "pre-conception"). Our nominal categories are saturated with notions of number and gender (grammatical "sexualization" of inanimate things and abstract words has undoubtedly exercized great influence on the pronounced tendency toward excessive personification in Western tradition). Our verb is a complicated network of such categories as past, present, future (our tense system), perfect and imperfect (aspect of action), mood and voice, person, number, and gender (in conjugation), and the hybrid forms of the infinitive and participle. Finally, one may hazard the supposition that the

Indo-European civilizations would never have developed their sophisticated ontological philosophies without the assistance of the mighty midget, the Indo-European ontological verb "to be."

Classical Chinese operates without all these paraphernalia. There are in classical Chinese no real prepositions; Chinese nouns and pronouns have no gender or number; the classical Chinese verb cannot be differentiated according to the twelve categories enumerated above and can hardly be distinguished in its monolithic structure from the Chinese noun. Classical Chinese lacks a verb covering the enormous territory encompassed by our "to be."

I must, therefore, in all frankness and honesty say—speaking as a philologist with long experience in studying classical Chinese texts and worrying over that problem of incompatibility of the two linguistic traditions—that while historical narrative, some technical and scientific texts, and novels have been with some measure of success transposed from the original Chinese into European languages, the more subtle kinds of writing, particularly poetry and what goes under the name of philosophy in China have never been translated, but only twisted and distorted in Western idiom through the imposition of our own linguistic idiosyncrasies, both in diction and syntax, upon the Chinese creation. Before we can translate Confucius or the writings of any other Chinese sage, we need to make a tremendous creative effort of devising out of the rich linguistic resources of our tradition a large number of calqued terms which would render in our idiom the contour of the Chinese etyma effectively and meaningfully, fully digesting and assimilating the underlying notions, and refraining from superimposing the so-called nearest, haphazardly chosen, and usually idiosyncratic, albeit elegant English equivalents. We need to work hard on simplifying our grammatical structure, cutting it to the bone, so as to approach as nearly as possible the austere simplicity of the original. And we should have enough faith in the wondrous flexibility of our linguistic heritage to deem such an experiment not only possible, but fruitful. It may take an entire generation even to begin the essential work and it will require a large cadre of workers. It may demand the enlistment of every one of us, the professional philologist, the creative teacher, the imaginative writer, the poet, the artist, and every devoted humanist.

May I, at this point, take issue with Professor Hahn's insistence on the prerequisite of technical linguistic competence in the original documents for teachers of foreign literatures. I have underlined in a preceding passage the abysmal failure of the representatives of competency in my own narrow field and, as a delegate from a monstrous academic institution that can afford to employ a linguistically competent interpreter in every major literary field, I should like to say a few words in defense of the small college where foreign literatures are often taught in translation by non-specialists, yet effectively and imaginatively. The great and rich centers of professionalism would do well to remember more generously the great educational and humanistic accomplishments of those often self-sacrificing workers and concentrate more—whenever criticism is the order of the day—on cases of professional negligence within their own ranks. Not that I would advocate closing our eyes to existing tensions in our field: tensions between professional and amateur, tensions between disciplines, and even within a given discipline. Our academic societies would often benefit from a more candid recognition of the existence of those inevitable tensions. The infinite loneliness of scholarship—of which Mr. Bokhári spoke last night—will always remain an individual problem for every one of us. But we can all join in one great task, that of humanist teachers trying to impart to our students our partial awareness of the lights shining in Asia. "He who can warm up the old and acknowledge the new, may be termed a teacher," said Confucius, and "teacher" in Chinese also means "musical leader"; a leader of a symphony or chorus, and one of many voices.

The Semasiology of Some Primary Confucian Concepts

Philosophy East and West, 2.4 (1953), 317-332.

Intercultural cross-pollination, natural or artificial, has long been a recorded phenomenon of human history, but at no time in the slowly developing tragicomedy of mankind, until the eschatologically accelerated denouement of our era, have microsporic mists of multilingual and multicultural origin so densely pervaded the atmosphere. The resultant cultural hay fever threatens to become endemic throughout the globe. How much real cross-fertilization has thereby been accomplished even the most astute of our cultural geneticists would be reluctant to say. Students of the Orient can, however, point to startling mutations produced in the lexicons of the great literary languages of Asia through the insemination of the proliferous Greco-Latin gametes of the Occidental scientific vocabulary. Their conjugation with native cells has indeed resulted in the spectacular growth of truly international protoplasts. Thanks to this hybridization, whatever be the obstacles that still remain to retard free linguistic communication between two scientists coming from opposite corners of the earth, each has at his disposal a rich supply of universally viable lexical plasma that can be easily transfused, without danger of incompatibility, from one intellectual blood stream into another.

For the humanist, however, linguistic barriers still stand as inviolable as if they were property lines of demarcation between cultural autarchies. Proud of his own heritage, often to the point of self-sufficiency, the humanist—who is essentially a "philo-logist," that is, a lover of his native *logos,* or, at best, of that of his cultural area or subcivilization—is loath to permit the infiltration of the tiniest logospore of foreign extraction into the well-guarded precincts of his native literary tradition. In moments of magnanimity or spiritual weakness, he concedes the possibility of admitting a few such spores, but only for the purpose of observation in the test tubes of his botanical laboratory. They may sojourn there under quaint labels in some semilearned transcription, transliteration, Romanization, or Latinization, or "in the native character," so that their exotic origin, and suspected virulence, could be easily apprehended by visiting minors or other innocents. Under no circumstances can these cells be allowed to come into mixogamous contact with the jealously protected gynoecia of the carefully nurtured word-plants of his native soil. The risk of having the beautifully laid-out garden turn into a jungle of linguistic hybrids and neological monstrosities is too appalling, and the unhappy asthmatic horticulturist rededicates himself anew to the desperate holding action against the clouds of coryza-laden pollen drifting from beyond his cultural horizon.

In contrast, pragmatists and opportunists that they are, the scientists all over the world blithesomely continue to condone, encourage, and practice linguistic miscegenation. Greek cytoplasts in various histological disguises permeate patterns of Chinese tissues; Latin compounds mutate on the spur of the moment into Sino-Korean aggregates; Indonesian prefixes and suffixes digest, phagocyte-like, some Anglo-Dutch terminological bacterium, while various Asiatic semantemes link themselves in farandoles faithfully reproducing the zigzags and swirls of the latest nomenclature of atomic fission or fusion. This linguistic cellular or nuclear activity is as lively as that which took place many centuries ago when the same vocables, roots, and particles broke their traditionally set and serried ranks under the impact of the flood of new thought unleashed on the Far East by the sorcerer's apprentices, the missionaries of the gospel of Gautama Buddha, in that fateful era when Cathasia experienced the only other cultural cataclysm that can be compared with the revolution now being brought about by the incursion of Western scientific thought and practical technology. Meanwhile, the humanist world of the sunset lands seems to be slumbering on a bed of faded laurels, the laurels of the Greco-Roman transfiguration of Europe's autochthonous tongues. It often gives the impression of locking itself into a literary provincialism no longer virile, no longer proud, but petulantly asthenic and only listlessly aware of the thunderous drama of verbal concourse being staged in Asia.

Not that many of the spiritual offspring of the Mediterranean cosmos have not knelt in worship, in both proper and improper circumstances, before the altars of known or unknown Asiatic deities. Not that staunch Western pioneers have not explored the philosophical gardens and courtyards of the East and have not tenderly transplanted many fruit-bearing plants to their Hesperian arboreta or have not piously preserved in the herbaria of their ponderous academic publications many a wilted flower of auroral learning. Not that part of the wisdom of far-off Asia has failed to find recognition, often refurbished with appropriate or even supernumerary accoutrements, in the thesaurus of our tradition. Not that the transposition of Eastern thought into Occidental linguistic harmonies has not been occasionally effected with good taste, in a judicious combination of healthy conservatism and bold innovation. Not that certain idioms of the Far East have been unable to gain sporadic currency in calqued form in some Western vernacular. Not that some stray Oriental word has not won full citizenship in the lexicon of the West, even to the extent that its ulterior provenience is now completely forgotten. But it often seems that Western linguistic tissues show a lack of flexibility in responding, in a creative philological way, to the series of electrical shocks to which they are subjected through the now almost habitual contact with the tide of thought-particles streaming from the vast regions beyond the rim of the historical sphere of influence of our monotheistic psyche and our classical heritage. Resilient and vigorous as ever in response to inner stimuli, our language appears to have lost faith in its own resources, in the wondrous flexibility of its word formation and derivation, and in the rich heterogeneity of its tradition to exercise controlled imagination in seriously attempting to absorb into its very fiber the novel, stimulating, and fruitful notions with which the world beyond the Pamirs confronts us in the turbulent present and which it conjures before us out of the long shadows of its past, so fertile with brooding thought.

We can scarcely afford to allow these conceptual monads to remain as unassimilated foreign bodies freely, idly, and unproductively circulating through our spiritual organism. The furious pace with which the internationalization of scientific thinking and terminology is taking place throughout the world must be accompanied by some, however timid, endeavor in the direction of the universalization of humanistic thought. Without necessarily dislocating the delicate patterns of our traditional linguistic growth, we could surely essay, with some profit and edification, a few systematic and controlled experiments in the ingrafting of seemingly alien concepts on our linguistic texture. Healthy neology is not incompatible with literary norm, while mummification of foreign terms in the sarcophagus of transliteration, with no gesture whatever toward the courtesy of translation, is as often the symptom of a latent xenophobia as an evidence of cautious and precise scholarship; and a well-executed calque is not necessarily to be condemned without hearing as a counterfeit caconym and denied probation as literary tender.

This paper is venturing to launch a pilot balloon in an attempt to estimate how the wind blows as regards the incidental incursion, through the permeable sections of the Sinological curtain, of ferment-inducing fragments of the traditional Confucian glossology into the realm of our philosophy of human nature and moral polity. It is proposed to subject to a test several terms in the vocabulary of the Chinese sage by grafting their connotational tissues in such lesions on the integument of English vocables as a decent respect for the integrity and norms of English philological tradition would permit one to incise. The object of the experiment will be to effect a more perfect organic union of the two linguistic usages in the hope that the resultant radical Anglicization of the Chinese concepts would find some consideration side by side with heretofore suggested or current English renderings. In a sense, it is but a plea for broadening the scope of that facet of the complex art of translation which forms the subject of hermeneutics, the discipline exordial to all exegesis, whether that of our own traditional scriptures, sacred or profane, or that of the classics of another civilization.

The methodology we shall follow may be characterized as that of philo-logical semasiology, which combines the meticulousness of scientific observa-tion and computation in establishing the range, frequency of occurrence, and environmental reflexes of a given logoid with a naïve but unshakable belief that within the diffuse and viscous cytoplasmic mass of its connotations there lurks an ascertainable and definable etymonic karyosome. To that belief is to be added the conviction that, once the nucleus of a Sinitic word is delineated with reasonable precision, a patient search through the rich catalogue of the contour forms of the etyma of our Mediterranean heritage would finally yield a silhouette of sufficiently congruous perimeter; that such a demonstration of the community of human experience would make the superposition of the latter on the former and the resulting coincidence of detail significant enough to lift the experiment out of the category of idle philological legerdemain; and that this exercise in cultural stereoscopy would bring into focus many a latent particular of the original outline. Without further preliminaries, then, I should like to proceed to the con-sideration of some of the most fundamental notions in Confucianism and suggest a few new renderings for them to test the validity of the method.

Translators of the Chinese classics are not necessarily betrayers of the originals, but most of them produce parallactic displacements of the model from the ideal historiocentric point of view. Though few interpreters of Confucius—and this goes for Chinese as well as Occidental exegetes—fail to sense the historical significance of some of the terms of social relationship used by Confucius, yet, in their understandable admiration for the Master and in their justifiable concern for an effective universalization of his mes-sage, they too often indulge in pious distortions. Bolstered with the belief that consistency is but a virtue of petty minds, they repeatedly yield to the exigencies of contextual adjustments by varying their renderings of key locutions, and thus produce successive out-of-focus pictures frequently incom-patible with the monocular vision of an undeviating historical stance.

Thus *chün-tzŭ* 君子, the prime sociological term used in Confucius' educational and ethical doctrines, though defined within a reasonably well-delineated area of connotations, has not yet received full semantic evalua-tion or been subjected to a thorough hermeneutic test. In English translations of *The Analects* and other Confucian texts, a tradition of multiple render-ings was established by James Legge,[1] under whose inspiration the term is variously construed, now as "the princely man," now as "the superior [or wise, or true] man," now as "the [perfect] gentleman" or "the scholar and

---

[1] In the first two volumes of *The Chinese Classics,* 5 vols. (Hongkong, 1861–72), comprising the translation of the Confucian *Four Books.*

gentleman," or even as "the prince [sovereign, ruler]." All translators feel that the term, literally "lord's [or prince's] son," must have originally been a title of nobility which, in the mouth of Confucius or that of some predecessor of his among the moralistic teachers of the sixth century B.C., came to denote a man of moral breeding, a person of culture and education. The parallelism with the evolution of the English term "gentleman" is indeed close enough to warrant consistent translation of *chün-tzŭ* as gentleman. Two reservations, however, must be made to that rendering. First, the Chinese term is a syntactic or dependent compound (of the type *tatpuruṣa*, in the precise terminology of the Sanskrit grammarians), while the English word is an adjectival compound (type *karmadhāraya*). The nature or pattern of the construction cannot be ignored here in view of the existence in ancient Chinese of the period of several analogical compounds such as "duke's son," "duke's grandson," "king's son [or grandson]," "king's man," etc., used first as titles and later as surnames. Second, while "gentility" is implicit in the Chinese word, our derivative "gentleness" is, as we shall see later, associated with quite another term in Chinese. Effort must be made to avoid the overlapping of the concepts, particularly in view of the tendency of many interpreters to mollify, on the one hand, the rough feudal character of the era, and to underemphasize, on the other, the significance of the social revolution through which Chinese communities were passing during the age of Confucius.

From the texts of the period, a strong case could be built in favor of a theory that the *chün-tzŭ* were "lordsons" indeed, that is, perennial sons of lords, in the sense that they could never, or hardly ever, become real lords. In other words, they were in all likelihood juniors of the noble families who, for one reason or another, such as enforcement of primogeniture, concubinary origin or bastardy, or political or economic accident leading to loss of patrimony, were forced to become *déclassés* or subsist on the bounty of their luckier relatives. It is even possible that "son," the second term in the Chinese compound, had already acquired in the language of the Chou period its later function of an enclitic of diminutive or even pejorative value, corresponding to our suffix −"ling" or −"kin." The lordsons may thus have been derisively called "lordlings" or "lordkins" by the optimates of that time.

To my mind, there is scarcely any doubt that Confucius himself was a natural "lord's son" (possibly one of Baron Mêng-sun, his first patron). As such, he became the intellectual champion of the cause of the "lordlings." His ethical and social doctrine can best be construed as having its message directed to those restless *déclassés* of his generation. He seems to have taught them to bear their half-title proudly, to consider it a badge of honor, a heraldic baton or bar sinister, a mark of the emergent moral nobility of the unprivileged gentleman, and to have enjoined them to formulate for themselves a philosophy that would permit them to operate as a class-conscious "third estate," immediately below the royal clans and the great patrician families. Repeatedly he put before them the example of those sages of the recent and remote past who had had the right, or had been offered the chance, to become lords in fact, but who had voluntarily chosen the status of lordlings through abdication from title and position and had thus humanized themselves by "unnobling" their persons. It is significant in this connection that the young Baron Mêng-sun, traditionally said to have been Confucius' first pupil, was a concubine's son, though one who eventually inherited his father's rank and title. Furthermore, the only time Confucius seems to have been involved directly in the politics of his native state was during the stormy period of 505–497 B.C., when the state of Lu was shaken by a revolution against the three barons who had formed a triumvirate over the dukedom and the impotent puppet, its hereditary duke, a revolution led by the dissatisfied juniors and bastards of the three baronial lines.

When given a chance to participate in affairs of state, Confucius' disciples were taught to serve devotedly and to lead their rulers into paths of righteousness; when out of position, to live nobly in poverty and to carry the message of aristocratic form to which they had been born into a wider range of society and to become teachers and molders of men in whatever walk of life the vicissitudes of the time placed them. Confucius himself seems to have been ever ready to extend his teachings to all newcomers, including the new class of "lordlings" by courtesy, the parvenus emerging from the lowest gentry or commonalty. The main tenets of his system of moral philosophy and civil polity can best be clarified by a close semantic analysis of a few of the key terms repeatedly occurring in the most authentic source of Confucian wisdom, the *Lun Yü* (*The Analects*).

We may begin with the Chinese word *chêng* 政, habitually translated "government," "to govern." This rendering can be accepted as doing no violence to the Chinese trend of thought only through the tour de force of dissociating the English term from its Greco-Latin etymon *guberno*, "to steer [as a helmsman]," on the one hand, and the Chinese vocable from its graphic and phonetic connaturality with *chêng* 正, "right," "correct," on the other. The two Chinese words have always been homophones, and the former contains the latter as the etymonic part of its graph. No Chinese, therefore, could, or still can today, enunciate or write the one without evoking the other. That the etymology was fully present in Confucius' mind is indicated by *Analects* XII.17, where the sage emphatically uses "correct" to define "government." "To rule means to regulate" is the nearest approach to the original achieved by English translators of the passage. What Confucius wanted to say is best expressed in Latin: *regimen est rectitudo* with *corregimen est correctio* as an overtone. In fact, if we could only accept *corregimen* as an English equivalent of the Chinese word for "government" (cf. Spanish *corregimiento*), Confucius' ambivalent attitude toward the concept would immediately become clear to us. The positive sense which he gives to *chêng* in the above passage is matched, without real contradiction,

by the pejorative connotation he instills into the word in *Analects* II.3.
There, *corregimen* is definitely equated with correction, in the sense of
"compulsory bringing to a standard," a semantic value which appears in
one of the archaic derivatives of the primary *chêng* (with determinative
No. 60 added), "to compel submission." If *corregimen* is too violent a
neologism to countenance, we should still insist on "regimen" as the only
semantically adequate English rendering of the Chinese term. According to
Confucius and most ancient Chinese moralists, *corregimen,* that is, effective
government, was to be achieved in a happy medium between the correctness
of the rulers and correction of the subjects, and a twofold rectification,
rather than helmsmanship, was stressed as the fundamental principle of
polity.

We can now move on to the consideration of the term *tê* 德, perhaps
the most significant word, next to *tao* 道, in ancient Chinese macro- and
microcosmology. The standard translation for it is "virtue," both in the
sense of inherent quality and in that of moral excellence, but with the
validity of the traditional rendering somewhat shaken by Arthur Waley's
insistence on interpreting it as "power." Indeed, it is believed by many
scholars that the term originated in the mytho-magical period of Chinese
speculation when *tê* was conceived as a kind of *mana*-like potency inherent
in substances, things, and human beings, a potency which, on the one hand,
made them true to their essence, and, on the other, made possible their
influencing of other entities. It appears often as if it had been imagined
as a kind of electric charge permeating the thing in question, waxing or
waning in accordance with some mysterious law, and capable of being
transmitted, in the case of living beings, from one generation to another.
Contrary-minded students of ancient Chinese philosophy dispute this interpretation as rather narrow and possibly anachronistic, and point to the fact
that *tê* had early acquired, at least in Confucian literature, ethical connotations close to our "virtue," that is, as moral, and only rarely amoral or
immoral, efficacy. They find, therefore, no quarrel with rendering *tê,* almost
invariably, as "virtue." Philologists are, however, troubled by the absence
in the Chinese term of any connotations reminiscent of the Latin etymon
vir, such as manliness and virility. They remind us that *tê* is free from any
contamination with sexual associations and differs in that from its great
counterpart, *tao,* the Way, which, in one or two expressions, such as
jên tao 人道, "the way of men and women," is suggestive of sexual activity.
Other recommended translations, such as "energy" and "essential quality,"
seem also inadequate from the same etymological point of view. "Essence"
is especially treacherous, for one of the cardinal peculiarities of the Chinese
language is the absence in it of any term or set of terms even remotely
congruent with the enormous linguistic and philosophical area covered by
the etymon and the derivatives of *esse* and of "being" in Indo-European
languages.

A graphophonetic analysis of the Chinese character will, I believe, lead us to a solution of this dilemma of translators. *Tê* is composed of a semantic determinative indicative of movement and a phonetic-etymonic element consisting of the graphs for "heart" 心 and "upright," "direct" 直. The latter word, though graphically distinct, is a remote cognate of *chêng*, "correct." In its ancient pronunciation this word, now read *chih* 直, was a homophone of *tê* and is undoubtedly the etymon from which *tê* was originally derived. "Upright" or "erect" seems to be the fundamental meaning of the word as evidenced by several derivatives (now written with the addition of various semantic signals), such as "hold upright," "to raise," "to plant," "to erect," "to place or set." Since our term *tê* contains an element suggestive of movement which appears in many other Chinese characters where it has the function of endowing the etymon with connotations often conveyed by the Latin prefix "ad-," one would hazard the guess that we have here a word close to "arrect" in meaning, possibly overlapping somewhat with Latin *insitio,* "to implant." While "insititious [ingrafted] potency" could doubtless serve as a compromise between the notion developed in our argument and that favored by Waley, I would be inclined to lean toward "arrectivity" or "arrectitude," and "arrective" as an adjective, to denote the abstract Chinese term. Thus, two essential semasiological elements of the graph would be satisfactorily accounted for. It remains now to suggest that connotation of the term which is supplied by the third element, "heart," which to the Chinese connotes, as it does to us, the "innerness" of the state or process involved. One of the good Latin understudies for *tê* is *indoles,* "natural disposition or character," which could perhaps be Anglicized as "indolescence" or "indultitude," but which overemphasizes the root meaning "to grow." It supplies us, however, with a useful formant, *indu,* the old form of the Latin prepositional prefix "in-," which has the merit of being distinctive enough to avoid confusion with the "in-" of negation. Whatever be its chances for survival in English lexicographical environment, I should like to submit the neologism "indarrectitude," "indarrectivity" as an almost exact equivalent of the Chinese term in its threefold aspect. For those allergic to excessive Latinity, one may suggest "enarrective," "enrective," "arrective," and "rective" as the second-best choice, with the abstract noun to be formed with either the suffix "-ness" or with "-ity." A distinction could further be established between the passive and active connotations of *tê.* Thus, the new word "enrective" would define itself as follows: having the inner power or quality to be straight, in the sense of having an invariable direction (the typical example of *tê* in ancient China was the downward-flowing tendency of water), of keeping true to one's essence or normal state or function; having the power to be right, upright, proper, virtuous, or good in the positive sense. Arrective would be defined as having the power or property of arousing, inciting, animating, or of communicating or causing rectivity or enrectivity. *Tê,* then, as a noun, can best be translated as "enrectiveness," "enrectivity," "enrectitude," in the passive sense of inherent quality; and as "arrectivity," in the active sense of the power to influence others, such as that of an effective substance or individual. For the Chinese, *tê* was always understood as potent, but not coercive, and as arrective, rather than corrective. Conceived in most cases as inherent, *tê* is sometimes described as an acquired quality, and it is significant that the word was often defined by the Chinese scholiasts by a homonym *te* 得, "to acquire" "to obtain." This is frequently dismissed as an idle pun of the glossologists, but one could easily demonstrate, through scores of ancient texts, that it was widely accepted as a paronym of our term. Since one of the good equivalents of that second *tê* is the Latin *apiscor,* I would suggest that "indarrectitude" came to connote, by dint of association with it, "indeptitude," i.e., "inner aptitude," as contrasted with vulgar "acquisitude."

Finally, a slight overtone: the most ancient graph of that component of the character *tê* which means "arrect" depicted an eye surmounted with a straight line. This graph is reminiscent of another composed of an eye surmounted with a fork-like object of uncertain significance meaning "to inspect." Our graph for "upright," "arrect," is also defined by the most ancient dictionaries as "to see straight." Thus, there was somewhere in the etymological background of our *tê* a connotation suggestive of "direct inspection," of "looking straight at things," which is exactly the etymology of our own "intuition." It may be worth while to review some ancient Chinese texts, particularly Taoist ones, with the hypothesis in mind that, at least in one of its facets, *tê* approached a function quite close to the concept of intuition.

Our next word, *li* 禮, the cardinal term of Confucian "cultimonious" polity, is relatively easy to define through semantic analysis. It has been variously translated: propriety, ritual (religious and social), cult and culture, worship, ceremony and ceremonial, etiquette, decorum, decency and refinement, urbanity, courtesy, rules of proper social usage or conduct, customary rules of living, polite traditional deportment, good manners, social order, *convenance, bienséance, Sittlichkeit,* formality, good form. With the exception of the last, none of these renderings approaches in meaning the concomitants of the semantic nucleus of the Chinese term or fits every occurrence of the word in the ancient texts. As is well known, the character *li* 禮 is composed of two elements: the so-called radical (semantic determinative) for "rite," "worship of the numina," appearing in most graphs relating to religious belief and ritual practices, and a "phonetic" part representing a vase or ritual vessel. The only other common Chinese character with the same "phonetic" is *t'i* 體, "body," "human body," "to embody," "embodiment," "form" (its radical is "bone," "skeletal structure").[2] This

[2] On the phonetic relationship between the two words, see Bernhard Karlgren, *Grammata Serica: Script and Phonetics in Chinese and Sino-Japanese* (Stockholm: BMFEA, 1940), No. 597.

would seem to indicate that for the ancient Chinese this particular word for "vessel" connoted something like "morphon" and, in a way curiously parallel to the use of *skeuos* in Greek and of "vessel" in our own scriptural language, served as a metonym for "human body." "Form," that is, "organic" rather than geometrical form, then, appears to be the link between the two words, as evidenced by the ancient Chinese scholiasts who repeatedly used *t'i* to define *li* in their glosses. Another favorite paronym for *li* is *ti* 第, "order," "series," "sequence." From the above we must deduce that, for the ancient Chinese, *li* was a concept situated somewhere near the point of intersection of notions that we could express by such words as "corporate form," "worshipful acconformation," "formal accorporation," "eumorphosis," "social co-ordination," or "corpor-ordination." It would seem that "Form," with a capital, to be understood as ritual form, social form, or good form, and so qualified whenever occasion would require, serves best as the simplest equivalent of the Chinese term.

As the code of behavior of the Chinese gentleman, *li* was elaborate and punctilious, yet allowed for some improvisation within the framework of traditional standards, conceived on occasion as variable and as growing toward greater perfection in time. In this it contrasted sharply with *hsing* 刑, the system of corporal, chiefly mutilatory, punishments by means of which the plebeians, the inarticulate mass of the people of ancient China, were "corrected" or "patterned" by their masters. It is interesting to note that the term *hsing* had a range of connotations closely paralleling those of *li:* (1) "form" or "mold," (2) "vessel," a kind of soup kettle, (3) "outline," "[two-dimensional] figure." The three words are exact homophones of *hsing* and were anciently often designated by the same character. In contradistinction to *li, hsing* appears to be thought of as crudely schematic, rather than morphological, as a matrix that was set and fixed, and changed only infrequently and reluctantly, and as a sort of Procrustean framework stamping the people into conformity. Rather than a system of "acconformation," it must be described as one of ruthless "accompagination" through the cut and cast of coercive punishments. No element of spirituality entered into it, for it was savagely corporal, rather than corporate, a quality reserved for the civilized pattern of the *li*.

The four terms discussed above, *chêng, tê, li,* and *hsing,* are well contrasted in the context of *Analects* II.3, for which we should like to offer the following strictly literal translation: "The Master said, 'Lead the way for them with [corrective] regimen, and compose them with [corporal] compagination, and the people will shirk and have no sense of shame. Lead the way for them with [arrective] Enrectitude, and compose them through [corporate] Form, and they will have a sense of shame and will thus be brought to pattern.' "

We have now reached a point in our discussion where we can tackle the mooted problem of the two most difficult and crucial terms in the Confucian moral system, the famous concepts of *jên* 仁 and *yi* 義. The first of these has been examined anew by Professor Dubs in the first issue of this journal, in an article entitled "The Development of Altruism in Confucianism," but with little attention paid to the semasiological aspect of the question.[3] Commonly accepted renderings of the Chinese word include: benevolence, human-heartedness, perfect virtue, true manhood, altruism, the Good or Goodness (capitalized; a well-reasoned suggestion by Arthur Waley), humaneness, and humanity. Only the last two do justice to the etymology of the Chinese term. *Jên* 仁, "humanity," is not only a derivative, but is actually the same word, though in distinct graphic form, as the common Chinese vocable *jên* 人, "man," *homo*. This is no mere pun, as Professor Dubs believes; the consubstantiality of the two terms is part and parcel of the fundamental stratum of Chinese linguistic consciousness, and must be reflected somehow in the Occidental translation. Unfortunately, the English abstract nouns which immediately suggest themselves as proper renderings, that is, "humaneness," "humanity," and "manhood," have acquired too specific connotations in English usage to be considered adequate. It must be observed in addition that the term *jên* in Confucian texts is used not only as a noun and an adjective, but also as a transitive verb, and the above words do not easily yield themselves to this role.

Waley's hypothesis that *jên* 人, "man," did not originally refer to mankind in general, but only to members of one's tribe, group, or clan (*gens*), is substantiated to a certain degree by pre-Confucian texts. We cannot follow him, however, in adopting "goodness"—to be capitalized as "Goodness" to distinguish it from the common quality of "goodness" designated by the Chinese word *shan* 善—as a translation of *jên*, "humanity," but there is no doubt that *jên* possessed the same connotations as our words "gentle," "gentleness," and "gentility," all derived from the Latin *gens*. The notion of gentleness as softness in a primary sense, rather than as a quality characteristic of the gentleman, is, however, more deep-seated and is probably inherent in *jên*, as evidenced by a host of its etymological relatives. *Jên* belongs to a group of Chinese words with a somewhat peculiar initial, archaic *zny-* or *nzy-*, normally giving us *j-* or *n-* initials in modern Chinese. Irrespective of their finals, all words having that initial appear to be derived from the same etymonic nucleus and to be conveying as words such notions as can be expressed in English by the following terms: softness, weakness, mildness, pliancy, lenity, comity, tenerity, mansuetude, forbearance, the quality of being soft but tough, slender, graceful, complaisant, patient and tender, tolerant, yielding, and coddling (in both senses of the English "coddle": to treat tenderly and to "tenderize" by cooking). This can be

[3] PHILOSOPHY EAST AND WEST, I, No. 1 (April, 1951), 48–50.

easily demonstrated by a brief consultation of any Chinese dictionary on the entries under such characters (some forty or fifty of them) as are pronounced *jên, nên, jan, nuan, juan, jang, jao, jo, no, jou, jui, jun, jung, niao.* It is important to note here that one of the characters, pronounced *ju* 儒, is the technical term designating Confucianism and Confucianists as a class. Most students agree that *ju* 儒 must have originally meant "weakling."[4] A semantic study of the homonyms of the *ju* series would suggest as a more precise and specific equivalent "fondling" (in both English senses of "baby" and "fool"), "coddling," "manikin." In the light of our discussion of the term "lordling," it is also significant that another *ju* 孺 (with the determinative for "child"), "baby," was used in ancient Chinese historical texts with the implication that it was a term reserved in the court language of the Chou period for the designation of an heir presumptive born of a concubine, rather than of a first wife.

In the attempt to find a suitable rendering for *jên* 仁, one must also bear in mind the graphic structure of the character. *Jên,* "humanity," is represented by a graph comprising *jên* 人, "man," and two horizontal strokes to its right, usually interpreted as being the Chinese character for "two," suggestive of the idea of duality. The phonetic function, if any, of that element is not clear; one should note, however, that, curiously enough, the Chinese word for "two" had archaically the same *zny* initial as *jên.* We are inclined to hazard here a new hypothesis of the origin of the character in substitution for the traditional half-hearted analysis of the graph. It is well known that on Chinese bronze inscriptions of the Chou Dynasty the character *tzŭ* 子, "son," has often a little ditto sign in the form of two horizontal strokes added to it to express such phrases as "son's son," "son after son." It may well be that Confucius, or some predecessor of his, had borrowed that graphic convention from the vocabulary of the inscriptions to endow the common graph for *jên,* "man," with a special meaning, perhaps in an attempt to instill into the graph, representing a word in a language devoid of a specific category of plurality, a contrasting singular-plural connotation, such as we would express in English by "man among men," and had then sublimated it by making it a key locution in his moralistic system.

It is my belief that the primary etymology of *jên,* "humanity," cannot be successfully conveyed in English, short of creating a neologism, on the prototype of the German *Menschlichkeit,* such as "manship," "manshipful," and "manshipfulness." If this be favored, there would be no difficulty in using the first noun as a verb, on the analogy of "to worship," as some Chinese contexts would require. In addition, to bring into focus the plurality implied in the Chinese graph, one could employ as a Latin synonym of "manship" a term such as "homininity" (with "hominine" and "hominate," as corresponding adjective and verb), that is, a derivative from *homines,* rather

---

[4] For recent literature on the subject, see H. G. Creel, *Confucius: The Man and the Myth* (New York: John Day, 1949), chap. XI, "The 'Weaklings,'" and Notes.

than one from the singular *homo*. The same result could be achieved by the retention of the traditionally acceptable "humanity" modified by the addition of the prefix "co-," which would serve the double purpose of distinguishing the word, on the one hand, from the European connotations not present in the Chinese term, and endowing it, on the other, with the necessary dual-plural overtone emphasized in the above discussion. "Co-humanity," "co-human," "co-humanize [oneself]," would also seem to satisfy the other semantic factor present in the Chinese term, the notion of pliant accommodation to others and identification with humanity of the commoner sort. Indeed, as can be seen from *The Analects*,[5] Confucius refused to grant the possession of the virtue of *jên* to most of his contemporaries. He unreservedly conceded it to a few worthies of antiquity whose common characteristic seems to be capacity for renunciation, the yielding of one's rights and prerogatives, and for a kenotic emptying of themselves of princely preconceptions and extraordinary privileges. Some of them seem to have attained the ideal through a spectacular flight from the responsibilities of a throne about to be inherited by them into a mountain wilderness (as in the case of the celebrated Po-i and Shu-ch'i), or into a frontier territory, as did T'ai-po, the legendary founder of the peripheral state of Wu, and Chi-tzŭ, the cultural hero of Korea.

Our last term, *yi* 義, is usually translated righteousness, right conduct, justice, loyalty, morality, and duty. Its secondary values are: "public," "patriotic," "adopted," "sense," "meaning." The most popular rendering is "righteousness." The Chinese word hardly connotes anything approaching that Old Testament virtue, nor has it any etymonic connections with such root words as "right," *jus, lex, mos, debeo, publicus,* etc. This has been noted ever since the first attempts to transpose Chinese into Occidental languages, but the search for an adequate equivalent has always been hampered by the inability, both on the part of Chinese and Westerners as well, to explain the evolution of either the graphic or the phonetic nature of the term. It was only after the revolutionary researches of B. Karlgren[6] into the phonetic structure of archaic Chinese that it became possible to establish that the word, in its phonetic contour 2,500 years ago, was a near relative of, if it was not directly derived from, the Chinese pronoun of the first person, "we" or "I" 我, the graph for which forms one of the two component parts of the character *yi* 義. The other graphic component, "sheep" 羊, appears as the common denominator of two other primary Chinese words: "beautiful" (*mei* 美) and "good" (*shan* 善). We are inclined to believe that, in all the three, "sheep" is a "graphic synecdoche" for "savor, saporous" (as mutton, the rankest of all meats), the name of a quality which the Chinese extended to cover other abstractions, in a way reminiscent of the manner

[5] Contrast particularly *Analects* V.7 and V.18 with VII.14 and XVIII.1.
[6] Culminating in *Grammata Serica*. For the words in question, see No. 2 in that work.

in which the ancient Latins are supposed to have broadened the range of the connotations of *sapio* from "taste" to "wisdom." "Sheep" can thus be dismissed as a semantic signal, and full attention must be concentrated on the first element as the real etymon of the word. As we have done with previously discussed words, we must also take cognizance of the ancient Chinese paronomastic glosses as clues to what the Chinese believed to be the nearest homonyms of the term. The most persistent of these is *yi* 誼 (same tone and archaic pronunciation but a different character), "suitable," "congruent," "proper," "ought." The obvious link between these and "we" or "I" is the Latin *proprius,* covering the connotations "not common with others" (that is, *our* own), "personal," "characteristic," "appropriate," "constant." It is a pity that many English translators of the Chinese classics have insisted on rendering *li* 禮, "Form," as "propriety" and have thus prevented the latter English term from being applied, as it should have been, to render *yi* as "[moral] propriety." We could, perhaps, circumvent this difficulty by translating *yi* as "compropriety," to parallel our "co-humanity" for *jên.* Indeed, *yi* seems to be contrasted to *jên,* in the works of Confucius and Mencius, as operative in a narrower sphere of obligations, that of one's immediate loyalties to family, elders, feudal lords, companions, fellow-clansmen, in short, to the "we" group, rather than in the realm of broader human contacts encompassing the "you" and "they" groups. To coin another term, then, *yi* seems to have meant something like "nostritude," "nostrate consuetude" (hence the meaning "patriotic"), as against the "vestritude" implied in *jên* (it is noteworthy that the Chinese words for "you" or "thou" belong to the group of words with the same *zny-* archaic initial). *Yi* may also be interpreted as "selfshipfulness," but is not to be confused with selfishness, as it called for devotion and self-sacrifice for a "nostrate" cause, a noble and virile ideal, and yet fell short of "manshipfulness," which transcended the interests of the small nostrate circle; it was also felt to be a "congruence" of action and function, hence the meanings "properly adapted," "adopted," "sense," "meaning" (as of words). To sum up, it would seem to me that most Chinese contexts would become perfectly clear if *yi* were translated "selfshipful compropriety" or "proper selfshipfulness."

In the contrast between these two words as defined and used by Confucius and Mencius is best seen their original and significant contribution to the development of moral ideals in their time. Both sages appear intent on bringing home to their contemporaries the lesson that, however elevating and traditionally satisfying "nostrate" comproprieties and loyalties may have been for the denizens of the small city-states of the early Chou period, in the fluid society of their time old clan-morality could hardly cope alone with the problems of the day. To them, the decencies of civilized life appeared as having their only chance for survival in the realization on the part of both "lordling" and commoner of their "co-humanity" with their neighbors, immediate and remote, for—and I believe they saw it clearly—war, social unrest, and increasingly complicated economy were molding before their eyes a new world in which, theoretically at least, "all within the four seas were brothers."[7]

Without entertaining too much hope that the Anglicizations of the six or seven Chinese idioms discussed here will be readily accepted by professional translators, we commend them, nevertheless, to the attention of Occidental exegetes of the scriptures of Asia. The orismological technique outlined in the preceding pages is, we believe, based on cogent hermeneutic principles and is worthy of wider and more systematic application in the analysis of Chinese and other linguistic material stemming from beyond the realm of the Semito-Aryan *logos.* Our generation, so desperately at grips with the problem of overcoming communication barriers between the major subcivilizations of the world, may yet find that judicious wordmongering across literary frontiers is one of the most potent weapons against glosso-philosophical isolationism.

[7] *Analects* XII.5.

HU T'IEN HAN YÜEH FANG CHU

胡天漢月方諸

筆則筆

削則削

大事書之于策

小事簡牘而已

Berkeley, California

1932

Selections from

HU T'IEN HAN YÜEH FANG CHU

The following articles are selected from P.A.B.'s
personally published serials. They were originally
typewritten or handwritten, and reproduced by some sort
of mimeographic process.

These are P.A.B.'s earliest publications, and are
clearly the work of a brilliant and bold intellect.
However, they must also be regarded as a sort of
'juvenilia', for some of them anticipate later more
mature publications, while others are experimental and
were later rejected by the author. An example of the
latter is the series "The Glottology of Proto-Chinese"
in <u>HTHYFC</u> numbers 12 and 13, a preliminary hypothesis on
the evolution of the early Chinese language that P.A.B.
later discarded; it is not reprinted here.   --Ed.

Abbreviations used by P. A. Boodberg*

(compiled by A. P. C.)

A	<u>Shih Chi</u> 史記
AFM	P. M. Melioranskij, "Arab-filolog o mongol'skon jazykĕ," <u>ZVOIRAO</u>, XV (1903)
AM	<u>Asia Major</u>
B	<u>Ch'ien Han Shu</u> 前漢書
C	<u>Hou Han Shu</u> 後漢書
CBD	<u>Chinese Biographical Dictionary</u> 中國人名大辭典

---

*My thanks to Professor Nicholas Poppe for his help in identifying
the Russian and German references.   -Ed.

CR	Chinese Review
D	San Kuo Chih 三國志.
DRAN	Dokladï Rossiĭskoĭ Akademii Nauk
E	Chin Shu 晉書
F	Sung Shu 宋書
G	Nan Ch'i Shu 南齊書
GBD	H. A. Giles, A Chinese Biographical Dictionary
H	Liang Shu 梁書
HTHY(FC)	Hu T'ien Han Yüeh Fang Chu 胡天漢月方諸
I	Ch'en Shu 陳書
IAN	Izvestija Akademii Nauk (see also IIAN)
IIAN	Izvestija Imperatorskoj Akademii Nauk
J	Wei Shu 魏書
JA	Journal Asiatique
JSFO	Journal de la Société Finno-Ougrienne
JSFOu	the same as JSFO
K	Pei Ch'i Shu 北齊書
KD	B. Karlgren, Analytic Dictionary of Chinese and Sino-Japanese
L	Chou Shu 周書
M	Sui Shu 隋書
N	Nan Shih 南史
O	Pei Shih 北史
P	Chiu T'ang Shu 舊唐書
Q	Hsin T'ang Shu 新唐書
R	Chiu Wu Tai Shih 舊五代史
S	Wu Tai Shih Chi 五代史記
SBAW	Sitzungsberichte der Berliner Akademie der Wissenschaften, Philologisch-historische Klasse
SBPAW	probably the same as SBAW
SPAW	Sitzungsberichte der Preussischen Akademie der Wissenschaften (probably the same as SBAW)
T	Sung Shih 宋史
TC	T'ung Chih 通志.
2TC	Hsü T'ung Chih 續通志.
TCNPCYTP	Tung Chin Nan Pei Ch'ao Yü Ti Piao 東晉南北朝輿地表

TP	T'oung Pao
TPHYC	T'ai P'ing Huan Yü Chi 太平寰宇記
TPYL	T'ai P'ing Yü Lan 太平御覽
TSCC	Ku Chin T'u Shu Chi Ch'eng 古今圖書集成
TT	T'ung Tien 通典
U	Liao Shih 遼史
UJ	Ungarische Jahrbücher
V	Chin Shih 金史
W	Yüan Shih 元史
WHTK	Wen Hsien T'ung K'ao 文獻通考
YHCHTC	Yüan-Ho Chün Hsien T'u-Chih 元和郡縣圖志
ZIOOE	probably an error for ZIRGOOE
ZIRGO	Zapiski Imperatorskago Russkago Geografičeskago Obščestva (subdivision on anthropology is ZIRGOOE)
ZIRGOOE	Zapiski Imperatorskago Russkago Geografičeskago Obščestva, po Otděleniju Étnografii
ZIVAN	Zapiski Instituta Vostokovedenija Akademii Nauk (This superseded the ZKV, which in turn superseded the ZVOIRAO)
ZKV	Zapiski Kollegii Vostokovedov (see also ZIVAN)
ZVO	same as ZVOIRAO
ZVOIRAO	Zapiski Vostočnago Otdělenija Imperatorskago Russkago Arxeologičeskago Obščestva (see also ZIVAN)
16 Kg.	Shih Liu Kuo Ch'un-ch'iu 十六國春秋
16 Kg. Chi Pu	Shih Liu Kuo Ch'un-ch'iu Chi-pu 十六國春秋輯補
АФМ	see AFM
ДРАН	see DRAN
ЗВОИРАО	see ZVOIRAO (see also ZVO)
ЗИВАН	see ZIVAN
ЗИООЭ	(ZIOOE), probably an error for ZIRGOOE (q.v.)
ЗИРГООЭ	see ZIRGOOE (see also ZIRGO)
ЗКВ	see ZKV
ИАН	see IAN
ИИАН	see IIAN (see also IAN)
*	prefixed to titles of books known only indirectly

[Preface to <u>HTHYFC</u>, number 1, March 1932]

    The title of this publication, <u>Hu T'ien Han Yüeh Fang</u>
<u>Chu</u>, which can roughly be translated "The Mirrorings of
the Chinese Moon in a Barbarian Sky", has been suggested
by the often recurring passages in Chinese poems describing
'the watch on the wall', where the moon appears as the
symbol of civilization and home, and the cold winter sky
is pictured as unhospitable as the wastes of the North.

    The <u>Hu T'ien Han Yüeh Fang Chu</u> will be devoted to the
study of Chinese documents relating to the cultural and
political history of Central and Eastern Asia. Half of
the publications will be reserved for annotated translations of selected biographies from the Dynastic Histories.

    The present number begins the series of biographies of
famous Chin dynasty barbarians. Glossaries will be appended
to the last issue of the series.

    It is hoped that this "journal" will be made a trimestrial
one.

                         Peter A. von Budberg

                         Баронъ Петръ Будбергъ

Days and years of the Chinese sexagenary cycle are designated by numbers from one to sixty

Western dates on margins of notes

	子	丑	寅	卯	辰	巳	午	未	申	酉	戌	亥
甲	1		51		41		31		21		11	
乙		2		52		42		32		22		12
丙	13		3		53		43		33		23	
丁		14		4		54		44		34		24
戊	25		15		5		55		45		35	
己		26		16		6		56		46		36
庚	37		27		17		7		57		47	
辛		38		28		18		8		58		48
壬	49		39		29		19		9		59	
癸		50		40		30		20		10		60

HTHYFC, 1 (March 1932)

T'ieh-fu Liu Hu

鐵弗劉虎

J 95

T'ieh-fu Liu Hu was a scion of the Southern shan-yü's and grandson of Ch'ü-pei 去卑, Left hsien wang 左賢王.

E 130 and 0 93 write Wu 武 for Hu 虎. The character Hu as the ming of Li Hu 李虎 (T'ang T'ai Tsu), grandfather of Li Yüan 李淵, was taboo at the time of the composition of these two works.

Also known as Wu-lu-ku 烏路孤. A nephew of Liu Mêng 猛, the chief of the Northern horde, he resided north of Lü-ssŭ 慮虒 in Hsin-hsing 新興.

The Northern horde—one of the five hordes into which Ts'ao Ts'ao 曹操 divided the Southern Hsiung-nu (E 97, E 101). 0 93 writes Ssŭ-i 虒意 for Lü-ssŭ.

He came to be known as t'ieh-fu, a term by which Northmen designate the son of a Hu 胡 father and a Hsien-pei mother.

0 93 and that clumsy forgery* Shih-liu kuo ch'un-ch'iu 十六國春秋 explain the term t'ieh-fu as follows: 北人謂胡父為鮮卑母為鐵弗 which does not make much sense and is undoubtedly a corruption of the above passage in J 95. It was later further corrupted into : 北人謂父為鮮卑，謂母為金鐵弗

'Northmen say Hsien-pei for father, and T'ieh-fu for

---

* [An amendment from HTHYFC, number 2. —Ed.] In HTHYFC 1, I refer to the Shih-liu kuo ch'un-ch'iu as a clumsy forgery. The adjective used applies really only to the defective edition of that work in 16 ch., contained in the Han Wei ts'ung-shu, a copy of which was kindly lent to me by Mr. Michael J. Hagerty. Since then I have been able to consult the real Shih-liu kuo ch'un-ch'iu in 100 ch., a reprint of the 1781 edition by Wang Jih-kuei 汪日桂. Although the work is undoubtedly a Ming forgery, it was rather well reconstructed from then existing fragments of Ts'ui Hung's original work and can by no means be termed clumsy. Apologies are hereby offered humbly to the manes of the Ming scholar or scholars responsible for the reconstruction.

mother'. This last reading was adopted by the <u>Tz'u</u>
<u>Yüan</u> and <u>CBD</u>.

I fail to see where K. Shiratori in his "Sinologische
Beiträge... Über die Sprache der Hiung-nu und der
Tunghu-Stämme," <u>ИИАН</u>, 1902, vol. XVII, 2, p. 06, gets
his authority (he quotes Ho-lien P'o-p'o's 赫連勃勃
biography J95, E 130) for equating 鐵伐 (=鐵弗) with
a supposed <u>Hsiung-nu</u> word meaning 'iron.' Both J 95 and
E 130 make it plain that P'o-p'o changed his surname
from T'ieh-fu (which apparently had the unpleasant
connotation of 'métis') to T'ieh-fa, which was given a
meaning more consonant with P'o-p'o's aspirations by
means of the <u>Chinese</u> transcription. T'ieh-fa was made
to mean 'smiting with iron' through the use of two
Chinese words; the sources give us no direct evidence
that we are here in the presence of the transcription
of a <u>Hsiung-nu</u> word meaning 'iron'.

When Mêng died and his son Fu-lun 副崘 sought refuge with
the T'o-pa, Hu's father Kao-shêng-yüan 誥升爰, also known as
Hsün-tou 訓兜, succeeded Mêng as leader of the clans.

272   E 3: 8th year of T'ai-shih, 1 mo.: Repeatedly defeated
           by Ho Chêng 何楨, Mêng is slain by Li K'o 李恪
           leader of the Left horde.
           093 writes Kao-shêng-yüan's name 誥汁爰.

420   E 130: Hsün-tou was canonized by Ho-lien P'o-p'o as
           Yüan Huang-ti 元皇帝. 兒 for 兜 in E 130 is
           apparently a misprint.

Hu first attached himself as vassal to the T'o-pa, but when
his tribe gradually increased in numbers he rose up in arms and
rebelled on the border. T'o-pa Yü-lü uniting his forces with those
of Liu Kun 劉琨, governor of Ping 并 chou for the Chinese, punished
him.

310   J 1, 0 1: 3rd year of Mu 穆 (T'o-pa I-lu 猗盧) Ti's
           reign: Hu raising a host in Yen-men 雁門 supported an

invasion of Hsi-ho 西河 by a chieftain of the White
horde 白部 with an attack upon the Yen-men and Hsin-
hsing <u>chün</u> held by Liu Kun. The latter came to beg help
of I-lu who sent his younger brother's son Yü-lü 鬱律
to his assistance with 20,000 horses. First crushing
the White horde, they put to the sword Hu's encampments.
Gathering what he could after the disaster, Hu fled
westward; crossing the Ho 河 he sought refuge in
Shuo-fang 朔方 .

Liu Hu fled. Seizing Shuo-Fang he submitted to Liu Ts'ung
劉聰. The latter in consideration of the fact that Hu was a
member of his house conferred upon him the titles of North-tranqui-
lizing 安北 general, Inspector 監 ... 諸軍事 of the Hsien-pei
forces, and Lieutenant-general of the Ting-ling 丁零中郎將 .

According to E 130 Liu Ts'ung enfeoffed him also as
duke of Lou-fan 樓煩 . After he had seized by force
Ssǔ-lu ch'uan 肆盧川 Hu was defeated by I-lu and fled
beyond the frontier. There is no mention of a raid by
Hu between 310 and 318 in any of the sources: it seems
therefore that the defeat suffered by Hu which is
referred to by E 130 must be that of 318 and was really
inflicted by Yü-lü.

He re-crossed the Ho and attacked the Western horde. Turning
against him Yü-lü inflicted upon him a serious defeat. Hu retreated
and fled beyond the border.

318   J 1, 0 1: 2nd year of P'ing-wên's 平文 reign: Liu Hu
         is seriously defeated in a raid upon the Western horde
         and escapes almost alone. His younger cousin Lu-ku 路孤
         submits with his clan and receives in marriage a
         daughter of Yü-lü (J 1 for the last statement). Cf.
         Liu K'u-jen's biography.

In the beginning of Shih-i-chien's 什翼犍 reign Liu Hu
again made raids upon the Western Horde. Shih-i-chien despatched
an army to drive him off. Seriously defeated, Hu died.

341   J 1, 0 1: 4th year of Chao-ch'êng's 昭成 reign, Winter,

10 mo.: Liu Hu raids the Western frontier. His forces
are crushed by an army sent against him and he barely
escapes with his life, dying soon after. He is succeeded
by his son Wu-huan.

420   E 130: Canonized by Ho-lien P'o-p'o as Ching Huang-ti
           景皇帝.

<u>HTHYFC</u> 1 (March 1932)   Liu Wu-huan
                                      劉 務 桓
                                      J 95

Son of Liu Hu. Also known as Pao-tzu 豹子. Succeeding his
father in the leadership over the clans, he sent an envoy to offer his
submission to the T'o-pa.

342   J 1, 0 1: 4th year of Chao-ch'êng, 10 mo.: Liu Wu-huan
           first comes to offer his submission. He is given the
           daughter of Chao-ch'êng in marriage.

He began to muster the various clans and became the champion of
the hordes. He then entered into a secret understanding with Shih Hu
石虎, who conferred upon him the titles of North-pacifying 平北
general and Left <u>hsien wang</u>.

-349   E 130: ... and <u>shan-yü</u> of the Ting-ling 丁零單于.

Upon his death he was succeeded by his younger brother O-lou-t'ou.

356   J 1, 0 1: 19th year of Chao-ch'êng, 1 mo.: Liu Wu-huan
           dies and is succeeded by his younger brother O-lou-t'ou.

My copy of J has 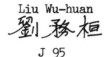 obvious misprints
for 務桓死其弟關陋頭
Wu-huan's sons were apparently retained as hostages at
Shih-i-chien's court.

418   E 130: Ho-lien P'o-p'o's grandfather Wu-huan is
           canonized as Hsüan 宣 Huang-ti.

<u>HTHYFC</u> 1 (March 1932)   Liu O-lou-t'ou
                                      劉 關 陋頭
                                      J 1, J 95, 0 1

J 95 and 0 93 write the name O-lou-t'ou, while J 1 and 0 1 omit the second character of the name.

356   J 1, O 1: 19th year of Chao-ch'êng, 1 mo.: O-t'ou
           succeeds his brother Hu-huan and secretly plans to rebel.
           J 1; 2 mo.: Shih-i-chien moves westward to the Ho
           and sends envoys summoning O-t'ou to submit peacefully.

357   It is possible that Ho-la-t'ou 賀賴頭 , the shan-yü
           of the Hsiung-nu who submitted to the Yen in 357 with
           35,000 of his followers (16 Kg. 27), is to be identified
           with Liu O-lou-t'ou. This move must have occurred in the
           summer of the year.

358   J 1, O 1: 21st year: The majority of O-t'ou's people
           revolt and flee eastward across the Ho. The ice breaks
           when they are half over. Later (Or the remainder of?)
           the host submits to O-t'ou's elder brother's son Hsi-
           wu-ch'i. Shih-i-chien sends the twelve sons of Wu-huan
           who were at his court back to the horde in order to stir
           up enmity between the various Hsiung-nu chieftains. All
           the clans join Hsi-wu-ch'i and O-t'ou, left without
           resources, submits to the T'o-pa, who accord him the
           same treatment as before (?).

HTHYFC 1 (March 1932)

Liu Hsi-wu-ch'i

劉悉勿祈

J 1, J 95, O 1, O 95

       Son of Wu-huan. With his eleven brothers hostage at the T'o-pa
court. Succeeds to wrest from O-lou-t'ou the leadership over the horde.

359   J 1, O 1: 22nd year, 4 mo.: Dies and is succeeded by
           his younger brother Wei-ch'ên.
           J 13, O 13: When Hsi-wu-ch'i was being sent back to his
           horde, Shih-i-chien's consort, née Mu-jung 慕容 , warned
           him against his brother, the wily Wei-ch'ên, and predicted
           the extinction of his family.

HTHYFC 1 (March 1932)   Liu Wei-Ch'ên

劉 衡 辰

J 95, 0 93

Third son of Wu-huan. Succeeding his brother Hsi-wu-ch'i, he
sent his son with presents to the T'o-pa court.

359   J 1, 0 1: 22nd year of Chao-ch'êng's reign, 4 mo.:
           Hsi-wu-ch'i dies and Wei-ch'ên succeeds him. J 1: 8 mo.:
           Wei-ch'ên sends his son to the court with tribute.

Shih-i-chien gave Wei-ch'ên his daughter in marriage.

360   J 1, 0 1: 23rd year, 6 mo.: Shih-i-chien's wife, née
           Mu-jung, dies. 7 mo: Wei-ch'ên arrives to be present
           at the funeral and requests a marriage alliance, which
           is granted.

361   J 1: 24th year, Spring: Wei-ch'ên sends an envoy to
           court with marriage presents.

Entering into a secret understanding with Fu Chien 苻堅 , he
was made by the latter Left hsien wang, and dispatched an envoy to ask
permission to hunt in Chien's inner lands from spring to autumn, which
request Chien granted. (J 1:) Wei-ch'ên then carried into captivity
over fifty families from among Chien's border residents and offered
them as slaves in present to Fu Chien. Declining the present, Chien
sent them back.

360-361   E 113: Wei-ch'ên, Left hsien wang of the Hsiung-nu, sends
           an envoy offering to surrender to Chien and requests ...
           etc. Chia Yung 賈雍, the hu-chün 護軍 of Yün-chung 雲中
           sends his ssŭ-ma 司馬 Hsü Pin 徐斌 to make a surprise
           attack upon Wei-ch'ên and despoil him. When he hears
           of this, Chien is indignant, impresses upon the guilty
           officers the necessity of dealing kindly with the "bar-
           barians," and orders that Wei-ch'ên's property be re-
           turned to him and that he be treated with all possible
           consideration. Thereupon Wei-ch'ên came to dwell within
           the borders and continued to send tribute according to
           agreement. Fu Jung 苻融, however, pointed out to

Chien the danger of allowing the Hsiung-nu to settle within the borders of the Empire and advised that they be removed to lands beyond the frontier. Chien followed Jung's advice.

365   J 1, 0 1: 28th year, 1 mo.: Wei-ch'ên plans to rebel and crosses the Ho eastward. Chao-ch'êng chastises him and Wei-ch'ên flees in terror.

Wei-ch'ên then turned against Chien, in all earnestness returned his allegiance to the T'o-pa, and rose up in arms against Fu Chien. The latter sent his chien-chieh 建節 general Têng Ch'iang 鄧羌 to punish him. Wei-ch'ên was captured, but when Chien came in person to Shuo-fang he appointed Wei-ch'ên duke of Hsia-yang 夏陽 and leader of the clans. Because Chien restored him his kingdom, Wei-ch'ên reattached himself to Fu Chien; although unremittently he continued to send tribute to the T'o-pa, he showed great lack of respect.

365   E 113: Ts'ao Ku 曹穀, Right hsien wang, and Wei-ch'ên, Left hsien wang, rose up in rebellion and at the head of 20,000 men attacked the districts from Hsing-ch'eng 杏城 southward. They encamped at Ma-lan shan 馬蘭山. Wu-yen, the So (-t'ou) barbarian 索虜烏延, and others also rebelled and made common cause with Ts'ao Ku and Wei-ch'ên. Chien put into the field his best troops. Generals Yang An 楊安 and Mao Sheng 毛盛 were placed in command of the van. Huo 活, Ts'ao Ku's younger brother, who opposed them at T'ung-ch'uan 同川, was defeated and slain by Yang An together with some 4,000 of his men, whereupon Ts'ao Ku surrendered. Yang An then proceeded against Wu-yen, who was defeated and slain, while Teng Ch'iang attacked and captured Wei-ch'ên at Mu-kên shan 木根山. However, when Chien came in person to Shuo-fang from Ts'ung-ma ch'êng 驄馬城, wishing to treat the barbarians kindly, he made Wei-ch'ên duke of Hsia-yang and placed him in command of the tribes.

365   E 8 puts the revolt of the two Hsiung-nu leaders in the seventh month of 365.

365   J 1: 28th year, 12 mo.: Fu Chien sends an envoy with "tribute."

366   J 1: 29th year, 5 mo.: Yen Fêng 燕鳳 is sent as envoy to Fu Chien. This exchange of envoys is undoubtedly to be linked with Wei-ch'ên's activities.

Setting out to punish him Shih-i-chien seriously defeated him and deprived him of six or seven tenths of his tribesmen. Wei-ch'ên fled to Fu Chien, who sent him back to Shuo-fang accompanied by troops to garrison it.

367   J 1, O 1: 30th year, 10 mo.: Chao-ch'êng starts on a campaign against Wei-ch'ên. As the ice on the Ho had not yet solidified, a crossing is achieved by means of reed mats spread upon the thickening ice. Wei-ch'ên, caught in a surprise attack, flees westward with his kinsmen. The T'o-pa capture most of his men and return loaded with prisoners and several tens of thousands of horses, cattle, and sheep.

373   J 1: 36th year, 5 mo.: Yen Fêng sent on a mission to Fu Chien.

374   J 1: 37th year: Campaign against Wei-ch'ên, who flees southward.

375   J 1: 38th year: Wei-ch'ên seeks assistance from Fu Chien.

During the last year of Chao-ch'êng's reign Wei-ch'ên guided Fu Chien in an invasion of the southern frontiers of Tai. The T'o-pa troops were disastrously defeated. Chien then divided Tai into two hordes: all territory west of the Ho was attached to Wei-ch'ên, that to the east of the Ho, to Liu k'u-jen (as related in Yen Fêng's biography).

376   J 1, O 1: 39th year: Fu Chien sends his <u>ta ssŭ-ma</u> 大司馬 Fu Lo 苻洛 with 200,000 men together with generals Chu T'ung 朱肜, Chang Tz'u 張蚝, and Têng Ch'iang to invade the southern frontiers of Tai along different routes.

E 113: Fu Lo with 100,000 of Yu 幽 chou's troops is sent against Shê 涉 -i-chien, king of Tai. Generals

Chü Nan 佢難 and Têng Ch'iang with 200,000 horse and foot are also sent out: one from the east through Ho-lung 和龍, the other from the west through Shang 上 chün, with orders to effect a junction with Fu Lo at the Tai ordo.

J 1, 0 1: 11 mo.: The White and the Tu-ku 獨孤 hordes oppose them and are defeated. Liu K'u-jen, the chief of the Southern horde, flees to Yün-chung. Shih-i-chien sends him back with 100,000 men to meet the invaders. He is defeated at the mountain range of Shih-tzǔ 石子 . Shih-i-chien flees to the north of Yin-shan 陰山 . He is hard pressed there by the Kao-chü 高車 and forced to return to Yün-chung, where he dies in the 12 mo. Cf. Liu K'u-jen's biography.

377　　J 2, 0 1: Chien recalls his troops and appoints Liu K'u-jen and Wei-ch'ên to gather together the scattered tribes, dividing the authority over Tai between the two.

J 24, 0 21: On the death of Shih-i-chien, Fu Chien wished to remove his grandson Kuei 珪 to Ch'ang-an 長安. Yen Fêng, however, advised Chien that Tai be divided between the two Hsiung-nu; K'u-jen being brave and wise, and Wei-ch'ên crafty and cruel, and the two hating each other, one would keep the other in check until the time when it would be possible to restore to the young boy his grandfather's throne.

Later Chien made Wei-ch'ên Western <u>shan-yü</u>, regent 督攝 of the different peoples of Ho-Hsi 河西 , and fixed his residence at the city of Tai-lai 代來 .

377-384　　Cf. Liu K'u-jen's biography.

When Mu-jung Yung 慕容永 seized Ch'ang-tzǔ 長子, he appointed Wei-ch'ên special deputy 使持節 commander 都督 of the Ho-hsi forces, great general, and <u>mu</u> of Shuo-chou, with residence in Shuo-fang. Yao Ch'ang 姚萇 also sent an envoy to seek his friendship and appointed him special deputy commander of the Pei-shuo 北朔 forces of various barbarians, great general, great <u>shan-yü</u>, <u>wang</u> of Ho-hsi, and

<u>mu</u> of Yu chou.

386   This must have happened in the last months of 386 or a
       little later. O 93 numbers among the titles conferred
       upon Wei-ch'ên by Mu-jung Yung that of <u>wang</u> of Shuo-fang.

       For several years he continued to harass and raid Tai.

386   Wei-ch'ên is mentioned in the 10 mo. of that year in
       connection with the troubles that accompanied the res-
       toration of the T'o-pa dynasty: J 2, O 1: Shu-sun
       P'u-lo 叔孫普洛, chief of the Northern horde, and
       twelve others together with some Wu-huan 烏丸 flee
       to Wei-ch'ên. So, a little later, does K'u-tu 窟咄,
       the pretender to the T'o-pa throne. He is murdered by
       Wei-ch'ên (J 2, 15, O 15).

389/390 According to J 103 and O 98, Yün-ho-t'i 緼紇提,
         chief of the Western Juan-juan, betrayed Wei and joined
         Wei-ch'ên. This must have occurred in 389 or 390, and
         explains the series of campaigns that T'o-pa Kuei had
         to undertake against the Juan-juan before he could
         concentrate his forces against Wei-ch'ên. (Cf. also
         <u>HTHY</u> 2.)

         It seems also (<u>16 Kg.</u> 85) that **just before his downfall Wei-
         ch'ên entered into amicable relations with Mo-i-kan.**

390   J 2, 83A, O 80: 6 mo.: Wei-ch'ên sends his son
       Chih-li-ti 直力鞮 to make a raid on the Ho-lan 賀蘭
       horde which is surrounded. Ho No 賀訥) sends his sub-
       mission to Kuei and begs assistance. 7 mo.: Kuei
       advances to Yang-shan, whereupon Chih-li-ti retreats.

       During the Teng kuo 登國 era Wei-ch'ên sent his son Chih-li-ti
with a host of 80 to 90,000 men to make raids upon the Southern horde.
With an army of but five to six thousand men, T'o-pa Kuei found himself surrounded by him. Kuei formed a square **wagenburg** with his
chariots, and now fighting, now advancing, inflicted upon Chih-li-ti
a serious defeat south of T'ieh-ch'i 鐵岐 mountain. Chih-li-ti
barely escaped on his horse. Over 200,000 head of cattle and sheep
were captured.

391   J 2: 6th year of Têng kuo, 7 mo.: Wei-ch'ên sends his
son through Ku-yang 綑陽 pass; he advances to Hei
ch'êng 黑城 .

11 mo., 15: Wei-ch'ên sends his son Chih-li-ti to raid
the Southern horde. 16: Kuei moves out against him.

19: Chih-li-ti's army is defeated south of T'ieh-ch'i
mountain. His stores, wagon train, and 200,000 head of
cattle and sheep are captured.

Following up the victory and hotly pursuing him, Kuei invaded
Wei-ch'ên's state, crossing the Ho southward at the Chin 金 (Golden)
ford in Wu-yüan 五原 . The resident population rose up in turmoil
while his tribesmen scattered, and Kuei was able to press on to
Wei-ch'ên's residence, Yüeh-pa 悅跋 city. Wei-ch'ên and his sons
fled in terror.

391   J 2: 28: Kuei reaches Yüeh-pa.

Kuei then sent his light horse generals in pursuit along
different roads. Yüan-chien 元虔 , duke of Ch'en-liu 陳留 ,
reached Pai-yen 白鹽 lake in the south where he captured Wei-ch'ên's
family. General I Wei 伊謂 reached Mu-kên shan and made prisoner
Chih-li-ti and all his men. Wei-ch'ên alone succeeded to escape, but
was killed by some of his subordinates and his head was sent to Kuei's
headquarters. Over four million head of horses, cattle, and sheep
were captured.

391   J 2: Kuei sends his generals in pursuit. Chih-li-ti
is made prisoner (29).

12 mo.: Wei-ch'ên's body brought to headquarters is
decapitated. His youngest son Ch'ü-chieh 屈孑 escapes.
Kuei's train arrives at the Salt lake. The booty in-
cludes 300,000 head of famous horses, Wei-ch'ên's
treasury, etc. Over 5,000 of his kinsmen are executed
without distinction of age.

Before the disaster the waters of the Ho became blood-colored
and the omen greatly upset Wei-ch'ên. Indeed, upon his death all his
relatives were executed and their bodies were thrown into the river.

420   Wei-ch'ên was canonized as Huan 桓 Huang-ti. His wife was surnamed Fu 苻 , possibly a daughter of Fu Chien. J 15, O 15 credit the finding of Wei-ch'ên's body and the sending of his head to the capital to T'o-pa I 儀 , <u>wang</u> of Wei 衛.

HTHYFC 1 (March 1932)   Liu K'u-jen

                             劉 庫 仁
                            J 23, O 20

<u>Tzu</u> Mo-kên 沒根, also known as Lo-ch'ui 洛垂. A man of the Tu-ku horde and kinsman of Liu Hu's. Distinguished himself in his youth by his courage and sagacity. His mother was a daughter of Yü-lü.

It is quite probable that K'u-jen was the son of Wu-ku, Liu Hu's cousin who surrendered to the T'o-pa in 318.

Shih-i-chien gave him a girl of the T'o-pa clan in marriage and made him chief of the Southern horde. In the 39th year of the Chien-kuo 建國 era, when Shih-i-chien died a violent death and T'o-pa Kuei had not yet established himself on the throne, Fu Chien made K'u-jen <u>Ling-chiang</u> 陵江 general and <u>kuan-nei hou</u> 關內侯, ordering him to divide with Liu Wei-ch'ên the authority over the hordes.

376   Shih-i-chien died a violent death... All the J sources (cf. J 1, 15, 24) imply that Shih-i-chien was murdered by his son Shih-chün 寔君 , whereas E 113 gives the story of his being surrendered to Fu Chien by one of his sons and transferred to Ch'ang-an where Chien made rather unsuccessful attempts to initiate the old man into the mysteries of Chinese civilization. Cf. E 9: Fu Lo attacks Tai and captures its king She-i-chien. This discrepancy will be discussed in the translation of the T'o-pa annals.

All territory west of the Ho was put under Wei-ch'ên's supervision, lands eastward under that of K'u-jen. Thereupon 'Empress' Hsien Ming 獻明, taking with her young Kuei and the princes of Wei 衛 and Ch'in 秦 , left the Ho-lan horde to dwell under his jurisdiction. K'u-jen performed his duties with all faithfulness, never allowing the vicissitudes of fortune to force him to depart from his mandate. He gathered together and comforted the scattered tribesmen, treating them with great solicitude and justice.

377-   J 2, 0 1 (Cf. J 25, 0 22) mention particularly Chang-sun Sung 長孫嵩, and Yüan T'a 元他, two chieftains of the Southern horde, who joined K'u-jen. J 2, 0 1 quote K'u-jen as repeatedly telling his son that in his opinion Kuei was predestined to restore the old glory of Tai.

Thereupon Fu Chien made him kuang-wu 廣武 general and conferred upon him the privileges of standards, drums, and parasol 幢麾 鼓蓋 making him equal in station to the nobles of the Empire (J), while Wei-ch'ên was placed below him in rank. This so incensed Wei-ch'ên that he (killed Fu Chien's governor of Wu-yüan and — J) rebelled and attacked K'u-jen's Western horde. K'u-jen defeated him (and pursued him for more than a thousand li northwest of Yin-shan, capturing his family and depriving him of his host. — J).

(J 23:) In the west K'u-jen made a campaign against the K'u-ti 庫狄 tribe, captured their livestock, and removed the tribesmen to Kan-sang ch'uan 乾桑川 .

Fu Chien gave him for wife a woman of the Kung-sun 公孫 clan, supplying her with a rich dowry. J 23: K'u-jen also paid a visit to Chien who added to his titles that of chen-wei 振威 general.

377-384   A study of all possible sources has so far failed to yield sufficient material to give more precise dates for these events.

Later, when Mu-jung Ch'ui 垂 besieged Fu P'ei 丕 in Yeh 鄴 and sent his general P'ing Kuei 平規 to attack in Chi 薊 Wang Yung 王永, Fu Chien's governor of Yu chou, K'u-jen sent his wife's elder brother Kung-sun Hsi 希 to Yung's assistance. P'ing Kuei was seriously defeated. (J 23:) The victors slaughtered some 5,000 of his men who had surrendered. Pursuing their success, they moved straight to T'ang-ch'êng 唐城 where they clashed with Ch'ui's son Lin 麟 .

Meanwhile K'u-jen was taking steps to raise a host in order to go to Fu P'ei's assistance. He called forth the troops of Yen-men,

Shang-ku 上谷 , and Tai, and encamped at Fan-chih 繁時.

Formerly Mu-jung Wen 文 and others who were to be removed to Ch'ang-an, but who had fled and joined K'u-jen's horde, were constantly nursing plans to escape eastward. Their opportunity now came during this expedition as they knew that discontent was rampant in the army. They attacked K'u-jen during the night. (J: K'u-jen sought refuge in the stables, but was captured and) slain by Mu-jung Wen, who fled to Ch'ui on K'u-jen's best horses.

When he heard of K'u-jen's fate, Kung-sun Hsi fled to the Ting-ling.

384   J 2, 0 1 place these events in the last months of 383 (7th year of T'ai-Tsu Tao-Wu 太祖道武 [i.e., T'o-pa Kuei]; 二 in J 2 is a misprint for 七). According to E 9, however, Ch'ui attacked P'ei in the 2 mo. of 384. K'u-jen's expedition and his death took place, therefore, in the early part of 384. On K'u-jen's predilection for fine horses, see J 29, 0 20, biography of Hsi Chin 美斤. Chin's father Tan 觕 who was in charge of the Tai horses found once that Liu K'u-jen had stolen an especially fine horse named Kua-liu 馬咼騮. His attempt to recover it led to a fist-fight between the two, and Tan was forced to flee to Wei-ch'ên.

<u>HTHYFC</u> 2 (April 1932)   Liu Chüan

劉 眷

J 23, 0 20

Younger brother of Liu K'u-jen. Succeeded his brother as regent. The <u>TCNPCYTP</u> 3 writes 頭眷 T'ou-chüan for 眷 . I have not been able to locate the authority on which this reading is based. It is quite plausible, however, as <u>chüan</u> frequently appears as the last character in polysyllabic Hsien-pei or Hsiung-nu names and doubtless represents some common ending in one or both of these languages.

384   10 mo.:(J 2, 0 1). For date see K'u-jen's biography.

     Chieh-fo 絜佛 , chieftain of the White horde, rebelled and
Chüan found himself too weak to punish him. He therefore invited
Chang Tz'ŭ, governor general of Ping-chou for Fu Chien, to attack
Chieh-fo. The latter was defeated.

     Chang Tz'ŭ was stationed in garrison at Ping chou (E 123,
<u>16 Kg</u>. 42), but Wang Têng 王騰 was apparently governor
general (E 115).

     Chüan also defeated the Ho-lan horde at Shan-wu 善無 , and
Tzŭ-wu 肺渥 the Juan-juan chieftain at I-ch'in shan 意親山,
capturing several hundred thousands head of cattle and sheep.

     His son Lo-ch'ên 羅辰 warned him against his nephew Hsien,
but Chüan disregarded the warning. Later when he moved his flocks to
Niu-ch'uan 牛川 he was killed there by Hsien.

385   See Liu Lo-ch'ên's biography.

     J 2, 0 1: T'ai-Tsu's 9th year: Chüan is murdered by
K'u-jên's son Hsien.

     J 13, 0 13: Liu Chüan's daughter became T'ai Tsu's
wife (she is known under her posthumous title as Hsüan
Mu Hou 宣穆后).

<u>HTHYFC</u> 2 (April 1932)   Liu Hsien
                         劉顯
                         J 23

     K'u-jên's son. His original name was Ch'ou-fa 醜伐 .

     Having murdered Chüan, he assumed the regentship and prepared
to rebel.

385   J 2, 0 1: T'ai-Tsu's 9th year: Hsien plans rebellion.
     A certain merchant named Wang Pa 王霸 who had learned
     of the plot warned T'o-pa Kuei of the impending danger
     by pressing his foot in the crowd. Kuei returned home
     with all speed. Liu-chüan 六眷 , the son of Liang
     Kai-pên 梁蓋盆 , a former chieftain, also sent
     posthaste a secret message to Kuei through the inter-

mediary of Mu Ch'ung 穆崇 . Kuei gathered around him
Chang-sun Chien 長孫犍 , Yüan Ta, and other former
retainers. In the 8 mo. (J 2) he arrived at the Ho-lan
horde. That very day Hsien sent men to murder Kuei.
Besides Liang Chüan (= Liu-chüan) J 13, O 13 also mention
Kuei's aunt who was married to K'ang-ni 亢埿 , Hsien's
younger brother, as one of the persons who warned Kuei
through 'Empress' Hsien-ming. The latter arranged her
son's escape while she plied Hsien's henchmen with drink.
Hsien wished her to pay for this with her life, but she
fled to K'ang-ni's home where for several days she was
kept hidden in "the gods' chariot" 神車 .
The "gods' chariots" among the Hsien-pei were apparently
similar to the carts described by William of Rubruck
as in use among the Mongols: "...tamen faciunt de filtro
imagines defunctorum suorum, et induunt eas quinque
pannis preciosissimis, et ponunt in vna biga vel duabus,
et illas bigas nullus audet tangere..."
She was finally spared through the entreaties of K'ang-
ni's family and fled to rejoin her son when turmoil broke
out in Hsien's horde.

When Kuei succeeded to his grandfather's throne, Hsien fled
from Shan-wu southward to Ma-i 馬邑 . His kinsman Nu-chên 奴真
came with his tribe, to declare himself Kuei's vassal.

386   J 2 places these events in the 3 mo. of the 1st year
                 of the Teng-kuo era.

Nu-chên requested then that his elder brother Chien 犍 who
resided with the Ho-lan horde be summoned that he might yield the
chieftainship to him. Considering it just, Kuei allowed Chien to
become the leader of their tribe. Having had for a long time been
dependent on Ho Na, Chien held him in high regard and sent his
younger brother Ch'ü-chin 去斤 with presents of gold and horses
to Ho Na. The latter's younger brother Jan-kan 染干 said to
Chü-chin: "We have generously treated you brothers, and it is meet
that, now that you have succeeded to the chieftainship, you come and

follow us." When Ch'ü-chin asked Nu-chên about it, the latter
replied: "Our fathers have for generations been loyal vassals of the
T'o-pa. It was my ambition to remain as faithful in the discharge of
my duties as they had been; that is why I yielded the chieftainship.
Now, being devoid of principle, you wish to rebel and become traitors
to our lord." Thereupon he killed Ch'ü-chin as well as Chien.

    Hearing that Nu-chên had murdered his elder brothers, Jan-kan
came with his horsemen to chastise him. Nu-chên fearing him sought
refuge with T'ai-Tsu, taking his horde with him. Kuei went out to
meet him in person, and sent a messenger to upbraid Jan-kan and stop
him. In gratitude Nu-chên offered his younger sister for Kuei's
harem; Kuei accepted.

386   These events must have been taking place between the
                3rd and the 8th month of the year while Hsien was con-
                centrating his forces at Ma-i.

386   J 2: 4 mo.: T'o-pa Kuei changes his title to that of
                King of Wei. 5 mo.: Hou-ch'ên 侯辰 , chieftain of the
                Hu-fo-hou 護佛侯 horde, and Tai-t'i 代題 , chieftain
                of the I-fu 乙弗 horde, rebel and move away. Kuei
                refuses to pursue them. In the 7th month Tai-t'i and
                his horde surrender; a fortnight later, they rebel again
                and flee to Liu Hsien. K'ang-ni makes raids on Nu-chên's
                horde.

                J 2, 0 1: 8 mo.: Hsien sends K'ang-ni to welcome
                Kuei's uncle, the pretender K'u-tu 窟咄 , who is
                supported by Mu-jung Yung in his claim. Hsien himself
                follows with his host and comes to harass the southern
                border of Wei, whereupon unrest breaks out among Kuei's
                followers. Kuei flees across the Yin-shan to the Ho-lan
                horde; sends messengers to Mu-jung Ch'ui asking for
                help. Mu-jung Ho-lin 慕容賀驎 is dispatched to his
                assistance. In the 10th month the allies defeat K'u-tu.

    Later Kuei moved against Hsien at Ma-i, pursued him to Mi-chai
獨澤 where he inflicted upon him a crushing defeat.

387   J 2, 0 1: 2nd year of Têng-kuo, 6 mo.: ...Hsien flees

southward to Mu-jung Yung. All his tribes join Wei.

J 24, 0 21: At that time Liu Hsien was in possession
of extensive lands and had strong troops; he boasted of
being the lord of the Northmen. Then dissension broke out
among his brothers. "Hsien is a man of great ambition,"
said Chang Kun 張袞 to T'o-pa Kuei. "It is time now
to take advantage of his family troubles to fall upon him
with the help of Mu-jung Ch'ui. His defeat is assured
once we attack him simultaneously from east and west."
According to 16 Kg. Chi Pu 44, Mu-jung Ch'ui joined the
expedition against Hsien because the latter stole the
horses sent by the Juan-juan to Ch'ui.

The original source of this statement is unknown to me.
There is a possibility that the Juan-juan were here
confused with Liu Wei-ch'ên (see next paragraph). Wei-
ch'ên was at the time in amicable relations with the
Juan-juan, and the horses may have been sent to Ch'ui
by the Juan-juan through the intermediary of Wei-ch'ên.
Be it as it may, it is apparent that Hsien's downfall was
brought about by his interference with Mu-jung Ch'ui's
horse supply.

Liu Wei-ch'ên, who entertained friendly relations with Mu-jung
Ch'ui, sent to the latter 3,000 horses. Ch'ui dispatched Mu-jung
Liang 良 to escort the herd. Hsien attacked Liang and took the horses
away. Ch'ui was wroth and sent his son Lin 麟, and his elder brother's
son Chieh 楷 to punish him. Hsien fled to the mountains west of Ma-i
馬邑西山 . Lin pursued him with light horse, whereupon Hsien fled
to Mu-jung Yung in Ch'ang-tzŭ. All his host surrendered to Lin who
removed it to Chung-shan 中山 .

387   Nothing further is recorded about Hsien. According to
           16 Kg. Chi Pu 44, his brother K'ang-ni was made Wu-huan
           Prince 烏桓王 and placed in charge of the 80,000 tents
           of Hsien's followers who had been removed to Chung-shan.
396   J 2: 1st year of Huang-shih 皇始, 6 mo., 10: Three
           armies under general Wang Chien 王建 and others are

sent against Liu K'ang-ni, governor of Kuang-ning 廣寧
for Mu-jung Pao 寶． He is beheaded, and his tribe is
removed to P'ing-ch'eng 平城．

HTHYFC 2 (April 1932)   Liu Lo-ch'ên
劉 羅 辰
J 83A, 0 20

Native of Tai. Third son of Liu Chüan. Elder brother of
"Empress" Hsüan-Mu.

According to J 23, he was Chüan's second son.

An alert and resourceful man, Lo-ch'ên said to his father,
"My cousin Hsien is a harsh and inflexible man. It would be wise to
eliminate him as soon as possible." Chüan did not heed the advice.

J 23: "In your two former campaigns," said Lo-ch'ên
to Chüan, "the enemy you had to face was not your most
important one. 比來行兵所向無敵心腹之疾
He should be eliminated first of all." "Whom do you
mean?" asked Chüan. "My cousin Hsien. This harsh and
inflexible man will rebel sooner or later."

On T'o-pa Kuei's accession, Lo-ch'ên joined him with his
horsemen. Every time he heard of a sinister plot laid by Hsien he
duly reported it to Kuei, who greatly loved and distinguished him.

Lo-ch'ên's biographies recount here briefly the story
of Hsien's defeat at Mi-chai, but make him flee to
Mu-jung Lin instead of to Mu-jung Yung.

He was appointed chief of the Southern horde and took part in
the pacification of Chung-yüan 中原． For all his achievements he
was made duke of Yung-an 永安 and for military prowess promoted
chêng-tung 征東 general and governor general of Ting 定 chou.

On his death he was given the posthumous title Ching 敬．

His descendants continued to serve Wei.

HTHYFC 2 (April 1932)   Ho-lien P'o-p'o

赫連勃勃

E 130, J 95, O 93, 16 Kg 66

16 Kg. begins P'o-p'o's history with that of his progenitors from T'ieh-fu Liu Hu down to Liu Wei-ch'ên,
which is substantially that of J, and which has been
translated in HTHYFC 1. E supplies a short account of
the same events, attention to which has already been
drawn in notes to the translation.

Third son of Liu Wei-ch'ên.

According to J and O his original name was P'o-p'o.
Ch'ü-chieh 屈孑(J) or Ch'ü-kai 屈丐 (O), which in the
language of the North meant 'low, vile' 卑下, was a
nickname given him by T'o-pa Kuei.

After Wei-ch'ên's defeat and death P'o-p'o fled to Ch'ih-kan
T'o-tou-fu 叱干佗狀, chieftain of the Ch'ih-kan horde.
391   The name of the tribe is written Hsieh-yü 薛于 or
Hsieh-kan 干 in J and O; the name of the chieftain
T'ai-hsi-fu 太悉伏 and T'a-tou-fu 他斗伏 in 16 Kg.
P'o-p'o was then 10 years old.

J 103: The usual encampment of the Hsieh-kan horde was
between the Three Cities 三城. At the approach of the
T'o-pa army which had just destroyed Wei-ch'ên, T'ai-
hsi-fu, the leader of the horde, tendered his submission
and was comforted and appeased by T'ai-Tsu. After the
latter's return home, Ch'ü-kai found refuge with the
horde. Hearing of it, T'ai-Tsu sent an envoy with the
order that Ch'ü-kai be delivered to him.

T'o-tou-fu was about to send P'o-p'o to the T'o-pa when his
elder brother's son A-li 阿利, who had been stationed in garrison at
Ta-lo ch'uan 大洛川, heard of it, returned posthaste home, and
admonished his uncle as follows: "Any human being would release a
sparrow or some other little bird which throws itself at his mercy;
so much more should we help this man P'o-p'o, who, having lost family

and country, has laid his fate in our hands, by facilitating his
escape if we cannot take the risk of protecting him! To send him away
in bonds would be most inhumane." T'o-tou-fu, however, refused to
follow his advice, fearing that the T'o-pa would hold him responsible.
Thereupon A-li secretly dispatched a party of strong men to re-capture
P'o-p'o on the way and sent him to Po-to-lo Mo-i-kan 破多羅沒奕于
duke of Kao-p'ing 高平 and vassal of Yao Hsing 姚興 of Ch'in.

> J 103 gives a slightly different version of these events:
> T'ai-hsi-fu had P'o-p'o brought before the T'o-pa envoy
> and said: "I would rather share the fate of this
> hounded man than suffer him to be delivered over to you."
> On his refusal to surrender P'o-p'o, T'ai-Tsu in great
> wrath personally took the field against T'ai-hsi-fu.
> The latter was at the time engaged in an attack upon
> Ts'ao Fu-yin 曹覆寅; taking advantage of the fact that
> the Ch'ih-kan forces were away, the T'o-pa army sacked
> T'ai-hsi-fu's city, and, carrying off his family and
> treasures, returned home. T'ai-hsi-fu pursued them, but
> was not successful in overtaking the enemy.   Thereupon
> he also fled to Yao Hsing. His people were removed by
> the T'o-pa.

393   According to J 2 all this happened in the 8 mo. of the
            8th year of Teng kuo. The Ch'ih-kan chieftain's name is
            there written T'ai-hsi-fo 佛. Cf. also O 1.

Mo-i-kan gave him his daughter in marriage. P'o-p'o grew to be
eight feet five inches tall and ten spans around the waist. He was
astute and clever by nature, heroic in appearance, and ingratiating
in manner. He greatly impressed Yao Hsing, who treated him with
exceptional civility, conferring upon him the title of hsiao-ch'i 驍
騎 general, and then adding that of fêng-ch'ê tu-wei 奉車都尉.
In important deliberations on state and military affairs Yao Hsing
constantly showed P'o-p'o preference over deserving and trusted advisors.

"P'o-p'o is a heartless fellow," said Yung 邕 , Hsing's younger
brother, to Hsing. "It is dangerous to attach him too closely to
oneself. It is an object of considerable worry to me that your

Majesty lavishes so much affection on that man." "P'o-p'o," replied
Hsing, "possesses talents which will make him a leader of his age.
Why should I be prevented from making use of his ability in uniting
the Empire with his help?"

Shortly after, he promoted P'o-p'o to the post of <u>an-yüen</u> 安遠
general and enfeoffed him as marquis of Yang-ch'uan 陽川 , sending
him to assist Mo-i-kan in keeping guard at Kao-p'ing. He also proposed to adjoin to him all the various barbarians of Erh- (or San-)
ch'eng 貳, 三城 and Shuo-fang together with the 30,000 men of Wei-
ch'ên's former host, and send him in command of reconnoitering
detachments in preparation for an invasion of the T'o-pa kingdom.
Yung again protested bitterly; when Hsing asked him how he could be
so sure of P'o-p'o's bad character, Yung replied: "P'o-p'o is negligent
in giving the king his due, cruel and greedy in his management of the
host; having no kin or deep attachments, he lightly comes and lightly
would go away. If you trust him beyond a certain limit, he will
surely prove in the end to be a danger on the border." Hsing thereupon abandoned his project.

Some time later P'o-p'o was made special deputy <u>an-pei</u> 持節
安北 (North tranquilizing) general and duke of Wu-yüan 五原 , and
was sent to keep guard at Shuo-fang with five hordes of San-chiao 三交
Hsien-pei and 20,000 tents of various barbarians.

401   J 2: 4th year of T'ien-hsing 天興, Winter, 12 mo., 48:
                 An order of the king directs Tsun 遵 , <u>chêng-hsi</u> 征西
                 general and prince of Ch'ang-shan 常山, to chastise
                 with 50,000 troops Mu-i-yü 木易于 (= Mo-i-kan),
                 chieftain of the Po-to-lan horde 破多蘭.

402   J 2: 5th year, 2 mo., 50: Tsun reaches Kao-p'ing in
                 An-ting 安定. Mu-i-yü and Ch'ü-kai with several
                 thousand horse abandon their country and flee. They are
                 pursued up to Wa-ting 瓦亭 in Lung-hsi 隴西. The
                 booty captured includes their wagon train and stores,
                 over 40,000 horses; over 3,000 camels and long-tailed
                 oxen 犛牛; 90,000 cattle and sheep.

Soon after when T'o-pa Kuei sent back to Ch'in T'ang Hsiao-fang 唐小方, the Ch'in general formerly made prisoner by the T'o-pa, Hsing's advisers proposed that Ho Ti-kan 賀狄干 be restored to Wei. A thousand excellent horses were then sent to the T'o-pa as ransom for Ti Po-chih 狄伯支, which T'o-pa Kuei accepted. Hearing that Ch'in had again entered into relations with Wei, P'o-p'o was enraged and made preparations to rebel.

> T'ang Hsiao-fang and Ti Po-chih were among the forty Ch'in commanders captured by the Wei forces in the great defeat of the Ch'in in the 10th month of 402 (J 2, J 95, E 117, 16 Kg. 56, 0 1). Ho Ti-kan had been kept prisoner at the Ch'in court since Yao Hsing's accession (J 28, 0 20).
>
> According to J 95, Hsing's campaign of 402 had been undertaken in retaliation for the T'o-pa raid upon Mo-i-kan and P'o-p'o. After they had fled to Ch'in-chou 秦, Hsing placed Mo-i-kan in garrison at Shang-kuei 上邽 and sent P'o-p'o to Shuo-fang, as has been said already. (TCNPCYTP 4.)

At that time Shê-lun 社崙 qaγan of the Juan-juan Hsien-pei of Ho-hsi sent 8,000 horses as a present to Yao Hsing. As soon as they crossed the Huang-ho and arrived at Ta-ch'êng 大城, P'o-p'o seized them. He then assembled all his host, numbering over 30,000 men, and on the pretext of making a battue at Kao-p'ing ch'uan, he moved against Mo-i-kan, attacked him by surprise, and killed him, incorporating Mo-i-kan's host into his own so that its number was swelled to several tumens.

407   In the 5th mo. of the year according to 16 Kg. 57.

In the 6th month of that year P'o-p'o proclaimed himself Heavenly King 天王 of Great Hsia 大夏 and Great Shan-yü, promulgating a general amnesty within his domains. He adopted Lung-sheng 龍昇 as the designation of the new era of his reign and established a complete hierarchy of offices. Considering the Hsiung-nu as descendants of the emperors of the Hsia dynasty, he called his kingdom the Great Hsia. His chief appointments were: His eldest brother Yu-ti-tai 右地代, Chancellor and duke of Tai 代; his next elder brother Li-hou-ti 力侯提, generalissimo 大將軍 and duke of Wei 魏; Ch'ih-kan A-li, Lord Grand Secretary 御史大夫 and duke of Liang 梁; the latter's younger brother A-li-lo-yin 阿利羅引 <u>chêng-nan</u> general 征南 and <u>ssǔ-li chiao-wei</u> 司隸校尉; Jo-mên 若門, <u>shang-shu ling</u> 尚書令; Ch'ih-i-chien 叱以軬建 <u>chêng hsi</u> 征西 general and <u>shang-shu tso p'u-i</u> 尚書左僕射; I-tou 乙斗, <u>chêng-pei</u> 征北 general and <u>shang-shu yu</u> 右 p'u-i.

407 E 10, J 2, 0 1 give the correct date. E 130 writes I-hsi 義熙 2nd year, which would correspond to 406.

In the 10th month P'o-p'o attacked the Hsieh-kan and two other Hsien-pei hordes, defeated them, and forced the surrender of several <u>tumens</u> (or ten odd thousands).

He then proceeded to attack the Ch'in garrison north of San-ch'êng (the Three Cities) and beheaded the Ch'in generals Yang P'ei 楊丕 and Yao Shih-shêng 姚石生. P'o-p'o's officers urged him to fortify himself in his present advantageous position, but he refused to follow their advice. Again they presented the following argument: "If Your Majesty entertains the hope of re-organizing the world and of taking possession of Ch'ang-an in the south, he would first firmly plant the root of his empire so as to set his people's minds at rest and give them a point of rally; then only can the Great Undertaking be brought to consummation. Kao-p'ing is a very fertile valley and naturally well fortified; it is well suited to become Your capital." "My lords," replied P'o-p'o, "you only know your A's (其一) and do not know your B's (其二). My Great Undertaking is but in its initial stage; my adherents and my host are not numerous enough. Yao Hsing is still the hero of the hour, and his captains still obedient to his commands: one cannot yet hope to seize Kuan-chung 關中. Now, if I concentrate all my forces in one city, they will all unite against us, overwhelm us with their superior numbers, and our downfall will be only a matter of time. But if we, with our clouds of horsemen, keep moving here and there, swift as the winds, attack them unawares, strike at their rear when they rush to the assistance of the van, strike at the van when they succor the rear, and harass them so much

that they will begin to desert their posts, then we shall be able to
devour Ch'in at our leisure. In less than ten years the country north
of the mountains (嶺北) and east of the river (河東) will be in
our possession. We shall wait until Yao Hsing dies; then we shall in
time capture Ch'ang-an. I have already outlined a plan of making
prisoner that boy, Yao Hung 姚泓, who will succeed him. In days
of old Hsien-yüan 軒轅 (i.e., Huang-Ti, the Yellow Emperor) also
had no permanent residence for over twenty years; we shall not be the
only ones to do so."

He thereupon engaged in a series of raids upon the districts
north of the mountain range (Ling-pei) with the result that no walled
town in the region dared to open its gates even in daytime. When
this was reported to Yao Hsing, he sighed and said: "Things have
come to this because of my failure to heed the advice of that
youngster!"

E 130 and 16 Kg. Chi Pu 66 try to explain the words 黃兒
as being the nickname of Yao Yung (see above). As
correctly pointed out by the Ch'ien-lung editors of E,
黃兒 is a common term meaning 'baby, infant.' As a
variant of 黃口 it finds a perfect equivalent in the
French blanc-bec.

At the time when he assumed royal dignity, P'o-p'o had tried
to conclude a marriage alliance with T'u-fa Jou-t'an 禿髮傉檀.
Jou-t'an refused. Enraged, P'o-p'o moved against him with 20,000
horse. From Yang-fei 楊非 to Chih-yang 支陽 he ravaged the
countryside 300 li in extent, killing and maiming over 10,000 men;
he then turned back, driving before him 27,000 captives and several
tumens of cattle, horses, and sheep. Jou-t'an started in pursuit
with his army.

407   In the 11 mo.

"Heaven endowed P'o-p'o with a strong, indomitable nature,"
said Chiao Lang 焦朗 , one of Jou-t'an's captains, to his master.
"Troops led by a man of his stamp are ordered and disciplined. One
cannot deal lightly with such a one. It would be dangerous to
attempt a straight attack against him, for he is now leading soldiers

anxious to get home with the booty they drive before them, and who
would fight eagerly for it. Better let us cross to the northern
bank from Wen-wei 溫圍 and hasten to block their crossing at Wan-hu
tui 萬斛堆, where by building a fortified camp we can hold them by
the throat. This stratagem is the surest road to victory."

> For this passage cf. also TPYL 314.

"P'o-p'o," angrily said another of Jou-t'an's captains named
Ho Lien 賀連, "is leading a flock of ravens, the scum saved from
the disaster that had nearly overwhelmed him. Devoid of loyalty,
breeding hatred, he was merely lucky in having achieved so much. Now
that his cattle and sheep block the road, his treasures are piled in
mountains, the oppressed rabble among his soldiers will begin to
dispute, carried away by covetousness, and he will be unable to retain
his grip on his host to offer us real opposition. As soon as our big
army overtakes them, they will collapse and disintegrate completely
(土崩瓦解). Why should our army try to avoid such an enemy
and make him believe that we are weak? Our soldiers are in high
spirits; we should hasten in pursuit of the enemy."

"I have already decided for the pursuit," said Jou-t'an.
"Anyone offering further remonstrances will be beheaded." When
P'o-p'o heard of Jou-t'an's decision, he was greatly elated; in the
lower defile of Yang-wu 陽武下峽 he ordered that trenches be dug
in the mountain and the chariots be (half?) buried (鑿陵埋車) so
as to obstruct the road.

> These fortifications and the burying of the chariots
> (under snow?) were apparently not so much for the purpose
> of impeding the progress of the enemy, as for serving
> notice to P'o-p'o's own soldiers that there would be
> no further retreat.

Jou-t'an sent forward his sharpshooters to begin the attack;
one arrow hit P'o-p'o in the left shoulder. P'o-p'o then launched
his troops in a counter-attack, crushingly defeated Jou-t'an at
Po-ching 百井, and pursued him for more than 80 li, killing and
wounding whole tumens of his soldiers and decapitating a dozen of his
generals. The heads of the slain were piled up to make a ching-kuan

京觀 (a τρόπαιον), which was named "The Tower of Skulls" 髑髏臺.
          Cf. also 16 Kg. Chi Pu 64 and TPYL 314, 177.

          Returning to Ling-pei, P'o-p'o also defeated Yao Hsing's
general Chang Fo-shêng 張佛生 in the plain of Ching-shih 青石原,
capturing and slaying 5,700 men.

> 16 KG. 89 gives substantially the same account of Jou-
> t'an's defeat. Six or seven tenths of his most famous
> and bravest knights perished in the disaster. Jou-t'an
> himself nearly fell into the enemy's hands while fleeing
> to Nan-shan 南山 with the few horsemen that remained
> with him.

                    (To be continued)*

HTHYFC 1 (March 1932)

A 'Turkish' Word in the Hsiung-nu Language

The works of Wei Wên-Ti (Ts'ao P'ei 曹丕) preserved in Chang P'u's 張溥 Han Wei Liu-ch'ao Pai-san Ming-chia Chi 漢魏六朝百三名家集 contain a short essay on Han Wu Ti. The following curious passage occurs in it: 刈單于之旗．勦閼氏之首． 探符離之窟．掃五王之庭

"He (Wu-Ti) cut down the shan-yü's standards, smote the yen-chih's head, probed the fu-li's burrow, and swept the ordo of the five kings."

The complete translation of this essay will appear in the next number of this series.

Fu-li (KD 44, 534 b'ịu-ljiĕ) undoubtedly represents a Hsiung-nu word, a title of some dignitary. It appears first in Chinese literature in Wu-Ti's eulogium of his famous general Wei Ch'ing 衞青 in A 111 and B 55, where the Martial Emperor in his enumeration of Wei Ch'ing's achievements says: "He chastised the p'u-ni and destroyed the fu-li" 討蒲泥．破符離． According to the commentator Chin Shao 晉灼, p'u-ni and fu-li are titles of Hsiung-nu princes; according to Yen Shih-ku fu-li is the name of a pass 塞; Ts'ui Hao 崔浩 also identifies it (it is hardly possible that an inanimate object could be the complement of 討) with a northern pass. Our text would tend to support Chin Shao's explanation as the complete parallelism of the four sentences requires that fu-li be some kind of title. The "probing of the burrow" seems to indicate at the same time that fu-li was also understood to be the name of some beast.

There is no doubt that we are here in the presence of the old 'turkish' name for 'wolf' (ﺑﻮﺭﻯ , büri, böri, börü in Eastern Turkish dialects) which appears in Chinese transcription in a slightly different form 附離 (KD 44 b'ịu) in L 50, O 99, Q 215A to designate the bodyguard of the qaɣan of the T'u-chüeh whose standard was decorated with a golden wolf's head. L 50:...旗纛之上施金狼頭仕衞之士謂 之附離夏言亦狼也 (Cf. Parker, "The Early Turks," CR, vol. XXIX, p. 122, note 45, p. 165, note 99.)

The word ﺑﻮﺭﻱ is already attested in the Orkhon inscriptions where it appears in the phrase:𐰴𐰣𐰢:𐰴𐰍𐰣:𐰽𐰽𐰃:𐰋𐰇𐰼𐰃
akaŋïm kaɣan süsi böri täg ërmiš (П. Мелиоранский,
"Памятникъ въ честъ Кюлъ Тегина," ЗВОИРАО,
vol. XII, 2-3, p 67), 'my father, the kagan's army was
as wolves...' (Denison Ross' version of V. Thomsen's
translation, <u>Bulletin of the School of Oriental Studies</u>
vol. V, 4, p. 865).

The equivalence of 附離 with ﺑﻮﺭﻱ (in the T'u-chüeh language)
has been recognized for some time (see E. Chavannes, <u>Documents sur</u>
<u>les Turcs...</u>, p. 220 n.), but it is the first time, I believe, that
the word can be definitely established as being a term of the Hsiung-
nu vocabulary through a text as early as the 3rd century A.D. (Ts'ao
P'ei died in 226).

The origin of the word ﺑﻮﺭﻱ is obscure. Attempts have been
made to derive it from 'Indo-european' roots (Cf. e.g. *Korsch in
<u>Thomsens Festschrift</u> who derives it from ir. *<u>bairaka-</u>; Blochet in
"Le Nom des Turcs," <u>Revue de l'Orient Chrétien</u>, vol. XXVI, p. 193)
but they are far from convincing. It is well known what an important
role the wolf played in the mythologies and genealogies of the peoples
of Central Asia: the Wu-sun (A 123, B 61), the Kao-chü (J 103), the
T'u-chüeh, and the Mongols (Bürte Činoa ᠪᠥᠷᠲᠡ᠍ᠴᠢᠨᠣᠠ 'Gray Wolf,'
Chingiz Khan's ancestor). Neither the word nor the legend are
necessarily 'turkish' (cf. P. Pelliot, "A propos des Comans," <u>JA</u>,
1920, p. 138), but belong rather to the primeval cultural heritage
which all the peoples of Asia seem to share in some degree.

The Mongolian word <u>činoa</u> (< činᵖa?) can, I believe, be
already attested for the T'o-pa Wei period. The list of
T'o-pa Hsien-pei surnames given in J 113 contains several
polysyllabic names of tribes which, at the time of the
adoption of Chinese monosyllabic surnames, were apparently translated into Chinese instead of being simply
apocopated. One of these is 叱那 , *či(t)nǎ, which
was transformed into 狼 lang (=wolf). Cf. 宥連 (KD
251, ji̯ə̯uᵖ < g-ui̯) with its Chinese equivalent 雲 yün,

'cloud', which makes one think of mongol ͡ᠥᠬᠦᠯᠡᠨ egülen.
Although names of tribes cannot really serve for purposes
of determining the linguistic relationship of the Hsien-
pei, as nomadic 'empires' generally incorporated within
their fold entirely alien peoples, other evidence inclines us in favor of considering the Hsien-pei as
predominantly of 'turco-mongol' stock rather than
'tungusic' (a theory which P. Pelliot has been advocating
for some time).
Note also that the Chinese word 纛 (phonetic d'uok, KD
645) above   is apparently a transcription of turkish
طوغ , تُوغ , mongol ᠲᠤᠭ tuy. The history of this word,
however, can not be exhausted by this brief statement.
It seems to be one of those words whose Chinese history
should be determined by a study of the oldest records of
China's conflict with the 'Werewolves'.

HTHYFC 1 (March 1932)

Some Tentative Etymologies

In an important note on Mount Ütükän ("Neuf notes sur des questions d'Asie centrale," TP, XXVI, pp. 212-219) Professor Pelliot has tentatively established the following two equations: P'o têng-ning-li = *Bod (?) tängri and Ütükän = 'the goddess of Earth.'

Although in his argument Pelliot seems to favor an original *BOD (with undetermined vocalization), he does not altogether reject a possible reading of *BOR for 勃. I venture to suggest that we have here again the root of the Central-Asiatic word for 'wolf'. But what connection has Ütükän or its peak *BOD with wolves or werewolves?

The T'ai P'ing Yü Lan, chüan 812, offers the following anecdote which indicates a certain relationship between the two:

Just before the defeat of the Hsieh-yen-t'o, a traveller came to beg food from a Hsieh-yen-t'o householder (or chief?). The latter introduced him into his tent and ordered his wife to get some food ready for the guest. As the wife glanced at the stranger she noticed that he had a wolf's head. She rushed to tell the neighbors about it, but when the latter arrived to look at the monster, he had already devoured his host and was gone. They formed a posse and pursued him to Mount Ütükän. Two men whom they found there, on being informed of the purpose of the posse, said: "We are supernatural beings. As the Hsieh-yen-t'o are about to be extinguished, we have come to take them." Seized with fear, the posse fled. Eventually the Hsieh-yen-t'o were defeated near Mount Ütükän.

初薛延陀之將敗也有一客乞食於主人主人引入帳令妻具饌其妻顧視客乃猿頭人也妻告隣共視之猿頭人已食主人而去相與逐之止鬱督軍山見二人追者告其故二人曰我則神也薛延陀當滅我來取之追者懼而退走薛延陀竟敗於鬱督軍山.

The original story in the T'ang Shu?

This story leaves no doubt as to the fact that the 'spirit' of Mount Ütükän was originally a wolf (could Ütükän be identical with one of the numerous Wolf Mountains or Mountain Ranges, 猿山, of the

Chinese annals?). This wolf could very well be the she-wolf who was
believed by the Turks to be the ancestor of their race (note in this
connection the appearance of <u>two</u> men in the above story — the divine
pair of progenitors?), and *BOR, the mountain dedicated to her in
her aspect of 'Mother Earth'.

 Ütükän itself I would conjecturally connect with mongol ütügü
ᠥᠲᠦᠭᠦ 'womb'. This etymology has its difficulties which at
present I am unable to explain satisfactorily. <u>El ötükän quti</u>
(Pelliot, <u>op. cit.</u>, pp. 218-9) would then mean 'the womb of
the nation'. The Chinese character 地 'earth', often explained
as being composed of 土 + 也 'womb', would offer here an
interesting parallel.

 *BOR <u>tängri</u> as a sacred mountain and as a god could be brought
together with the sacred mountain Burqan (不兒罕山, بورقان), near
the Onon, where Bürte Činoa (note the re-appearance of a wolf character) and Goa Maral, as the Mongol progenitors, settled. The name of
this ancient divinity could have been early adapted by the Uiɣurs for
the designation of Buddha, <u>burqan</u> in uig. and mong. (a reverse
borrowing is of course out of the question, cf. Pelliot, <u>op. cit.</u>),
while its doublet, Ütükän (in this case we have here to deal with one
and the same divinity) remained as a name for 'Mother Earth'.

 The obscure 他人水 T'a-jen shui of L 50 (Pelliot, <u>op. cit.</u>,
pp. 214-5) can perhaps be somewhat clarified by the supposition that
人 has been substituted under the T'ang for an original 民 (a taboo
character). Could 他民 T'a-min represent then *Taβin تانين or perhaps
*Tamir?

HTHYFC 1 (March, 1932)

Wolf, Horse, and Dragon in Eastern Asia

The two preceding notes are part of a series covering certain investigations carried on by the author over some period of time, and which can be best characterized by the above title. Quite conscious of his shortcomings, aggravated by the fact that a great number of important philological works, especially on the Turkish and Mongolian languages are at present inaccessible to him, the author feels that the hypotheses which presented themselves in the course of these investigations should be approached only after such a series of minor philological notes, every one of which might be judged on its own merits.

To avoid misunderstanding of the general trend of his investigation, however, the author feels it necessary to determine more clearly his position. Neither Iranophile nor Turanomaniac, he inclines in his sympathy more to rigid linguistic protectionism than to the policy of free trade which permits some mischievous words and phonemes to travel under clever disguise from the Baltic to the Pacific. He feels, on the other hand, that the role of the Central Asiatic nomad as the Great Middleman between peripheral cultures has been greatly minimized; that Advertising, to carry our metaphor further, as one of his essential characteristics has been greatly discounted; that in the processes of Asiatic cultural history the natural order has often been reversed: that the Thing in many cases followed the Word; Trade, the Flag.

HTHYFC 1 (March 1932)

<u>Mongol *odčin = odčigin, 'youngest son'</u>

On page 214 of Blocket's edition of the <u>Ta'rīh mubarak-i</u>
<u>ghāzāni</u> (<u>Histoire des Mongols: Successeurs de Tchinkkiz Khagan</u>,
E. J. W. Gibb Mem. Series, vol. XVIII, 2), Rashīd ed-Dīn gives the
etymology of اوتچیکین *otčigin, a comparatively common name among the
early Mongols. Two Otčigins are especially well known: Daritai
Otčigin داریتی اوتچیکین , youngest brother of Yesugei Bagatur, and
Temuge Otčigin تموكه اوتچیکین , fourth and youngest son (by the first
wife) of Yesugei and brother of Činggis. Otčigin is translated by
Rashid خداوند آتش 'master of the fire' and is decomposed into
tk. <u>ot</u> 'fire' and <u>tigin</u> (<u>tegin</u>) 'prince' (ar. امیر), the compound
becoming a common nickname for the youngest son in the family who,
according to Mongol custom, inherited the parental home and was
indeed 'the master of the (home-)fire.'

Cf. D'Ohsson, <u>Histoire des Mongols</u>, II, p. 3 and K'o
Shao-min's, <u>Hsin Yüan Shih</u> 柯劭忞, 新元史 ch. CV:
帖木哥斡赤斤烈祖幼子. 少太祖六歲. 國
語謂主竈曰斡赤斤. 幼子受父母遺產當
主竈. 故凡幼子稱斡赤斤. 人因稱帖木
哥為斡赤斤那顏
"T'ieh-mu-ko Wo-ch'ih-chin was the youngest son of Lieh-
Tsu (Yesugei), six years T'ai-Tsu's junior. In Mongol
they used the word <u>wo-ch'ih-chin</u> to designate 'the
keeper of the hearth.' As the youngest son inherited
the belongings of his parents, he became thereby the
keeper of the hearth. Therefore the youngest sons were
commonly named <u>Wo-ch'ih-chin</u>. It is for this reason
that people called T'ieh-mu-ko Wo-ch'ih-chin Na-yen
(*Odčigin Noyan)."
All this based on Rashid ed-Din?

This etymology was declared to be "fantaisiste" by Blochet
who proposes to see in Wo-ch'ih-chin the transcription of mongol
üčüken ﻭﺟﻮﻛﻦ 'little, small' (<u>loc. cit</u>. note e; cf. also note 1,

pp. 94, 95; basing himself apparently on D'Ohsson's [loc. cit.]
utdjukén 'cadet').   This equation of Wu-ch'ih-chin with ücüken is
repeated by F. E. A. Krause (following *J. J. Schmidt's Seneng Secen?)
in his Cingis Han: Die Geschichte seines Lebens nach den chinesischen
Reichsannalen, Heidelberg, 1922, note 232.

In his note on survivals of the fire-cult in the Mongolian
language ("Пережитки култа огня въ монгольскомъ языкѣ,"
ДРАН , 1925, p. 14; cf. also "Zum Feuerkultus bei den Mongolen,"
AM, 1925, p. 132) N. Poppe has made it clear, however, that odčigin or
odjigin (the second form would correspond to ﺍﻭﺗﺠﻜﻴﻦ given in some
manuscripts of Rashīd ed-Dīn) should indeed be considered as a compound of *od 'fire' and *čigin 'prince' (mong. čigin being a regular
equivalent of tk. tigin). Poppe's conclusion seems to have been
reached independently of Rashīd's etymology, as he makes no reference
to it nor to Blochet's or Berezin's (*История монголовъ, p. 97,
according to Blochet and Mírzá Muhammad, The Ta'ríkh-i-Jahán-Gushá,
Gibb Series, Vol. XVI, 1, p. 31) discussion of the problem. The
equivalence seems to be recognized at present as valid by Russian
orientalists (Cf. Vladimirtsov, The Life of Chingis-Khan, English
translation, London 1930, pp. 10, 35, 83, etc., where the mongolian
name is transcribed Otchigin).

It is to be noted that the Chinese 車斗 wo (KD 299 ·uât) never
transcribes mongol ü ⌇, but regularly o ⌇ (e.g. 轄讋 Onon,
轄亦剌 Oirai, 轄羅思 Oros, 轄月朵 ordo, etc.) while 赤介
ch'ih-chin (in the Mongolian period *či(k)-kin) could scarcely
represent anything else but a mong. *čigin. As to the final consonant
of od, ot, note the form T'o-to-yen Wo-t'i-ch'ih-chin 脫朵延轄愓赤介
(Blochet, Introduction à l'histoire des Mongols, p. 291) where the
phonetic complement 愓 t'i leaves no doubt as to the fact that 轄 wo
in the compound wo-ch'ih-chin was pronounced with a final dental.
Neither does Juwaynī's or Bar Hebraeus' (Ta'ríkh-i-Jahán, loc. cit.;
ﻣﺨﺘﺼﺮ ﺗﺎﺭﻳﺦ , Beirut 1890, pp. 390, 427, 428) transliteration,
ﺍﻭﺗﻜﻴﻦ *otigin, warrant reconstructing a mongol original ücüken
(cf. Мелиоранский, "Арабъ филологъ," ЗВОИРАО pp. 124, 160,
where ⌇ is transcribed ﺍﻭﭽﻜﻦ or ﺃﭽﻜﻦ).

T'ieh-mu-ko's name appears also in W 1 under the form Wo-ch'ên
or Wo-chên Na-yen 斡陳(真)那顏, which is apparently considered
by Krause (op. cit., notes 390 and 773) as a syncopated form of
ǔčüken noyan.   In the light of the etymology of odčigin this is
inadmissible. The form Wo-chên can, I believe, be best explained by
*odčin (a mong. form corresponding to tk. اوتــچى otči, cf. Rashid
ed-Din, loc. cit.) a word that could have existed parallel with odgan
and odčigin to designate the youngest son as the 'fire-keeper.' In W
the mong. nomen agentis suffix is generally transcribed 赤 ch'ih
(mong. či), but -čin (transcribed 真) is by no means unknown, especially in older words denoting the agent. The feminine suffix -čin,
-yčin (cf. Владимирцовъ, "Слѣды граматическаго рода въ
монг. языкѣ," ДРАН, 1925, p. 31) is also transcribed 真. In the
list of titles of the T'o-pa Hsien-pei given in G 57, most of which
can be explained by mongol or turkish parallels, 真 regularly
transcribes -čin.

A form *odči is also attested in W 118 under the Chinese
transcription 斡赤 wo-ch'ih. So-erh-ho 鎖兒合, the Chinese text
says, married the daughter (on her, see W 109) of Ögedei's son, prince
Wo-ch'ih 斡赤皇子. This prince is, without any doubt, to be identified with K'uo-ch'u 闊出, Ögedei's favorite son and the last to
bear the title t'ai-tzǔ 太子 (W 107). Though it cannot be shown that
K'uo-ch'u was the youngest son in the family (or the youngest son from
the first wife), the appellation given him in W 118 would tend to
indicate that at some time of his life he was the proud bearer of the
title of *Odči, the 'fire-keeper,' or Odčin Noyan, Prince of the Hearth.

The evidence, it seems to me, is sufficiently strong to warrant
the reconstruction of an old mongolian form *odči(n), co-signific with
the words odgan and odčigin.

HTHYFC 2 (April 1932)

"Amīr Ghalu"
(Additional note to "Mongol *odčin = odčigin, youngest son")

    In relating Baibars' embassy to Berke, Mufaḍḍal Ibn Abī-'l
Fada'īl (ed. E. Blochet, <u>Patrologia Orientalis</u>, vol. XII, 459–60)
mentions for the first time in his chronicle Berke's heir, Mengku
Timur (W – 忙哥帖木兒) in the following noteworthy passage:

و ليس له ولد و المشار اليه بولاية العهد بعده ابن اخيه و
يعرف بأمير غلو يعني الامير الصغير و اسمه منكو تمر بن طغوان
بن تسو قاأن بن باتو قاأن .

"He (Berke) had no son, and his designated heir-apparent was his
brother's son, called Amir ghalu, i.e., 'the little <u>amīr</u>', his personal name being Mengku Timur, son of Toghan, son of Tushu Khan, son
of Fatu Khan."

    It is to be noted, of course, that the genealogy of the Mongol
prince as given in this passage is quite faulty and is to be corrected
according to Blochet's footnote. Of greater interest is, however,
the curious nickname of the prince, which has considerably puzzled
the learned editor.

    While not presuming to be able to offer a complete and
definite solution of the problem, I am tempted to consider the expression امير غلو as a Mongol compound, half-arabicized by Mufaḍḍal
even before he had translated it. Indeed, if there be pre-supposed
a Mongol compound X A, in which A stands for some mongolian word
equivalent to <u>amīr</u>, given the Arabic translation of the compound as
'the little (young, younger) <u>amīr</u>', the author would naturally have
considered X to be an adjective and he would have, therefore, placed
it after the noun, following the rules of Arabic grammar; and much
more might that have been the case if <u>amīr</u> itself was the original
A in a hybrid half-Mongol half-Arabic compound.

    The original Mongol compound could have been, therefore, γalu-
(= غلو) A (= <u>amīr</u>, or a Mongol equivalent). <u>Qan</u> and <u>čigin</u> are often
translated by the Arabic <u>amīr</u>, but the regular Mongol equivalent of

the latter term is <u>noyan</u> (see e.g. Мелиоранский, "Арабъ филологъ," ЗВОИРАО, 1903, p. 152, where نوين = الامير). Ɣalu-noyan is a form that would yield us the necessary etymology by resolving <u>ɣalu</u> into <u>ɣal-un</u>, the genitive of Mongol <u>ɣal</u> 'fire', the final <u>n</u> of the genitive having easily been assimilated to the initial <u>n</u> of <u>noyan</u>.

This hypothesis, I believe, would solve the question satisfactorily. In <u>ɣal-u(n) noyan</u> 'prince of the fire' we find another Mongol title designating the youngest son as keeper of the hearth and as heir. (The use of Mongol <u>ɣal</u> vs. Turkish <u>od</u> in similar expressions [<u>ɣalaqan</u>, <u>ɣal-un qaɣan</u>] is well attested. Cf. Poppe, <u>AM</u>, 1925, p. 132.) The Arabic translation 'the little (young, younger) <u>amīr</u>' would in that case be entirely justified.

There is still the unlikely possibility that غلو is a mistake of the copyist for غن = غان, the Mongol diminutive ending, اميرغن <u>amirghan</u> being a doubtful hybrid form.

HTHYFC 2 (April 1932)

Dayan, Činggis, and Shan-yü

In his notable contribution to the medieval history of Asia,
"Les Mongols et le Papauté" (Revue de l'Orient chrétien, vols. XXIII-
XXIV), P. Pelliot adduces important material in support of his own and
Ramstedt's suggestion that the explanation of the heretofore obscure
title of the great founder of the Mongol Empire can best be found in
the supposition that in the word činggis we have a regularly palatalized Mongol form of the common-turkish *tinggis < tängiz 'sea, ocean'.
Pelliot's discovery of the fact that the early Ghenghizkhanids bore
the title of 'oceanic' (i.e., universal) khan (tk. talui nung Χan,
mo. dalai-in Χan) lends indeed considerable weight to his etymology.

No less weighty objections have, however, been raised to this
theory by B. Vladimirtsov in his "О прозвищь 'Dayan qaγan',"ДРАН,
1924, pp. 119-121, notably that tengis (unpalatalized) existed in the
Mongol language in precisely the same meaning of 'sea', and is
attested in the earliest texts. This objection does not, however,
envisage the possibility of tengis being a loan-word from the turkish;
such loan-words have been repeatedly pointed out in early Mongol and
'tengis' is quite probably one of those 'common-turkish' words
re-introduced into Mongol via an Eastern Turkish dialect.

Even if this be so, there still remains the question of how one
should explain the co-existence of the same word with one and the same
meaning but in two forms. One answer to that question would be that
činggis, having become part of the sacred title of the Great Khan,
the founder of the new empire, was taboo for ordinary use in its
common meaning of 'sea', and the turkish form tengis quickly supplanted
it in that meaning. Another way of answering the question would be
that činggis, although undoubtedly a cognate of tengis and still preserving the connotation of 'universal' as used in the title Činggis
Qaγan, had wider semantic affiliations, than one would derive from
the mere fact of equating it with tengis.

Some light may be thrown on this subject by a brief investigation of the root meaning of mo. dalai ᠳᠠᠯᠠᠢ , a synonym of tengis.

Dalai is related to Orkhon and Uigur talui (talui > dalai, talai —
with progressive vocalic harmony, > tului with recessive.　Cf.
P. Pelliot, "La version ouigoure de l'histoire des princes...", TP,
1914, p. 232) which is well attested in the meaning 'sea' in the
earliest documents (see e.g. Kül Tägin's Monument, Radlov, Ka,3:
taluiqa kičig tügmädim 'I nearly reached the sea').

In Uigur, however, there frequently occurs the expression
talui ögüz 'sea-river', which is commonly translated 'ocean' (cf.
Pelliot, op. cit., p. 237).　Doubtless such compounds are common in
Uigur, but it seems that in this expression talui has really the
force of an adjective qualifying 'river'.

Indeed, the root meaning of *TAL, *DAL in 'proto-turkish' was
apparently 'wide'(*Vambery, Etymologisches Wörterbuch der türko-
tatarischen Sprachen).　I am unable at present to check this statement
because necessary turkish dialectical dictionaries are inaccessible
to me, but I believe that sufficient evidence can be adduced in
support of this etymology.　(If I may be permitted to draw upon my
childhood memories, I may offer here from a meager stock of what I
believe to be Kirghiz words a word *tala meaning 'boundless plain,
steppe.')　The sea or the ocean were not directly known to the early
Turks.　The comparatively small inland bodies of water with which
they were acquainted were usually designated by the word köl, a term
never used in reference to the sea.　The above expression talui ögüz
would suggest that having come into contact with the ocean they named
it 'the boundless river', applying to it the epithet which they were,
perhaps, using to designate the boundless expanse of the steppe.
Talui became then 'the boundless one par excellence' and came to be
used alone in the meaning 'ocean, sea'.　(Cf. in this connection the
Chinese expressions designating the Yellow Sea, and in a wider sense
Okeanos, 大川 'the Great River', 無崖海 'the boundless sea.'
The root of tengis, *TENG is also possibly connected with *ENG
which in many turkish dialects has the meaning of 'wide' (e.g.,
osmanli انلى , اكلى , انكين , الكين 'wide', mo. eng 'id.').　Another
possible derivation, an extremely interesting one, is suggested by
J. Deny in his Grammaire de la langue turque, p. 648.　If tengri

'heaven, god', be traced to the same root (<u>tengri</u> has often been brought together with Sumerian <u>dingir</u> ⌄⌄ᚹ 'god', and is undoubtedly a "non-altaic" word. Cf. P. Pelliot, <u>TP</u>, 1928-29, pp. 215-6), the hypothesis receives additional support. Heaven, Earth (the steppe), and the Ocean are bound into a triad with their wide expanse, their boundlessness being their common semantic denominator.

The connotation 'universal' has, therefore, at least equal chances to be derived from the original meaning of 'boundless, extensive' which the words <u>činggis</u>, <u>tengis</u>, and <u>dalai</u> probably possessed, as much as from their probably secondary meaning of 'sea'. Before Pelliot's find it was usual to derive mo. <u>dalai</u> (in the sense 'universal') in <u>dalai lama</u> from Tibetan <u>rgya mcho</u> (of which it may or may not be a translation). Emphasis was naturally put on the Tib. <u>mcho</u> 'sea, lake' in order to explain the equivalence of the two terms. In the light of the foregoing, more, or at least equal attention must be paid to the first word of the Tibetan binom, the primary meanings of which are precisely 'width, size, wide, very extensive.'

If we accept this interpretation of the word <u>činggis</u> the title acquires additional and tremendous importance. Not only was Temujin by the mere fact of having the title conferred upon him given power to rule over the universe, but he was also associated to the Everlasting Blue Sky by sharing with it one of its epithets. (It is to be noted in this connection that the title was conferred upon him by the shaman Kökcü [<<u>kök</u> 'blue'?] or Teb tengri [on the probable significance of the name see В. Владимирцовъ, "Упоминание имени Теб-тенгри въ монгол. письменности," ДРАН, 1924, p. 116-7.]) What is still more important, the title assumed by Temujin was identical with that borne by the sovereign of the first historical empire in Mongolia, that of the Hsiung-nu. 'Vast, extensive' 廣大之貌 was in effect the translation given by the Chinese for the Hsiung-nu term <u>shan-yü</u> 單于 (B 94A). Furthermore, Pan Ku expressly says that this title of the Hsiung-nu Son of Heaven 撐犂 孤塗 was suggested by the 'vastness of the sky' 言其象天單于然也.

The equivalence of <u>činggis</u> and <u>shan-yü</u> was already suggested by Banzarov (in *"Черная Вѣра"?) according to H. Howroth "Some Notes on the Huns," Transactions of the VIth Congress of Orientalists, Sec. IV, p. 186.

It would be idle to speculate on the phonetic relationship of the words tengri 撐犁 and shan-yü as our knowledge of the pronunciation of these characters under the Han is still very imperfect. The circa 500 A.D. pronunciation as reconstructed by Karlgren tempts one, however, to trace them to one root:

撐 KD 1208 *ť'ɐng < t'-. Note the phonetic element.

尚 KD 856 *źi̭ang < ď-.

單 KD 968 *źi̭än < ď-. Note that yü, the second character in the binom, had apparently a guttural initial:

于 KD 1317 *ji̭u < g-.

Yü, on the other hand, is possibly a separate word, and not a mere suffix; at the same time it is not necessarily a Chinese loan-word as K. Shiratori would have it ("Sur l'origine des Hoing-nu," JA, 1923, p. 76), but again one of those old words of 'common Eastern Asiatic stock', the existence of which suggests itself as soon as one attempts to penetrate behind the veil that shrouds the history of the primeval relations of the Chinese world with that of the "Barbarians."

Although the Chi Yün 集韻 cannot be taken as an authority for the definition of primary meanings of such ancient characters as 于 yü, there is no doubt that Shiratori is right when he asserts that one of the fundamental meanings of yü was 'vast'. This fact is sufficiently attested by such 'enlarged" characters, which have 于 as a base, as 迂 'vast' and 訏 id., and, last but not least, 宇 yü KD 1317 ji̭u < g- 'canopy of heaven, space, vast, universe'. Not only is this word found in Chinese and Hsiung-nu, but also in the language of the Yü-wên 宇文 Hsien-pei. According to L 1, the binom Yü-wên meant 'lord of Heaven' (yü 'heaven', wên KD 1315 mi̭uən 'lord' 君).

The character yü 于 is, I believe, one of those in which a curious phonetic change is observable (note 于, 盂, 竽, 雩, etc. ji̭u < g- vs. 汙, 杅 ·uo). W. Simon has recently attempted to reconstruct in a series of similar words a final consonant. That this reconstruction is too hasty has been sufficiently made clear by Karlgren in

his exhaustive critique of Simon's work. At the same
time, although there is no doubt that it is impossible
to ascertain the nature of such a final with conclusive-
ness (as Simon does), there is nevertheless a certain
amount of evidence pointing to the fact that a consonantal
final or a glottal stop really existed in that series of
words. I hope to return to this evidence at some future
date. I will limit myself here to the indication of the
possible connection of our yü (in the name of the Yü-wên
Hsien-pei and the title of their eponymous ancestor) with
the title of the lords of the Keraits and the Karakhitai,
gur-, gür-khan, in which the first syllable has again
the meaning of 'universal' (cf. Pelliot, "Les Mongols...",
pp. 24-5).

We have thus a whole series of titles of sovereigns of nomadic
empires construed with the epithet 'universal', which term itself is
derived from different roots meaning 'vast', a qualifying term
applying equally to the three awesome Expanses of the universe, that
of the Sky, that of the Steppe, and finally that of the Sea.

Under the influence of various reasons, religious taboos,
Buddhistic cosmology, the Okeanos myth, or the Chinese concept of
the 'Four Seas' 四海, the 'Sea, Ocean' motif finally prevailed. It
is then that we find the nomadic world borrowing foreign words for the
expression of one of their own fundamental concepts. The last
instance of such borrowing is the title of Dayan, which, contrary to
Vladimirtsov (op. cit., p.119), who seeks a Mongolian etymology for
the word, I am inclined to derive from Chinese ta yang 大洋
'Ocean'.

HTHYFC 2 (April 1932)

The Structure of the Yao Tien

There is no more fascinating subject of study when one attempts
to penetrate the mythological mists that envelop the genesis of the
Chinese world than the story of the Deluge of Yao; and among the
actors of the great drama recorded in the first chapters of the Shu
Ching, none is more important (as a central figure of a whole cycle
of legends) than the Great Yü, and none more mysterious than his
father, Kun 鯀. Yü the Great was 'the first successful barbarian.'
As such, he is a subject for the procrustean experiments of which
these pages form a record.

Before an investigation of his barbarian genealogy can begin,
it will be found necessary to devote one's attention to the analysis
of the structure and the history of the most important document
containing the story of the Great Deluge, the Yao Tien. I propose,
therefore, to devote a few notes to the elucidation of several
difficult points of the text.

I. Boxing the Compass with Hsi Ho

In his "Légendes mythologiques dans le Chou King" (JA, 1924,
pp. 1-100) Professor Maspero has admirably set forth and adequately
solved some of the mythological problems connected with the Yao Tien.
As Maspero has conclusively reasserted we have in the Yao Tien a
definite substratum of mythology, on the canvas of which the Chinese
euhemerists had woven their supposedly historical tale. Thus, at
some point of the history of the Yao Tien text, Hsi Ho 羲 和 ,
the mythological charioteer of the sun, was cleverly transformed
into two sets of astronomers, the beautiful and naive story of the
progress of the sun's chariot across the sky was pedantically marred
by equinoctial and equatorial lines, and scientific interpolations
gradually transformed one of the most important documents on Chinese
mythology and religion into "the primary source for the study of
ancient Chinese astronomy and astrometry."

After the miraculous transformation of the sun's mother and

his charioteer into four astronomers, the brothers Hsi and the
brothers Ho, each of these officials is assigned in the present text
of the Yao Tien (in the so-called 'separate' instructions to the
four Hsi and Ho) to one of the four cardinal points, where, in
addition to their duties towards the sun (the mythological character
of which is revealed by Maspero), they are entrusted with "the
regulation of human affairs" according to the seasons. The seasonal
changes in their effect on the human and the animal worlds are recorded in the present text in the following four sentences:

Spring: 厥民析 "the people begin to disperse" 鳥獸孳尾

Summer: 厥民因 "the people are more dispersed", 鳥獸希革

Autumn: 厥民夷 "the people begin to feel at ease", 鳥獸毛毨

Winter: 厥民隩 "the people keep their cosy corner", 鳥獸氄毛

The interpretation of the four characters 析, 因, 夷, and
隩, has always been recognized as forced, but all native euhemeris-
tic editors of the Shu Ch'ung agree in giving them the meaning which
is faithfully rendered by Legge as above. We are here, nevertheless,
in plain mythology. Had Maspero pursued his study a little further,
he would have, I am sure, discovered the mythological key to these
four characters, so much more so that it is in his notes on page 24
that this key is to be found. In retracing the myths describing the
course of the sun, Maspero quotes the Shan Hai Ching 山海經,
chapters XIV, XV, and XVI of which yield to us the names of divine
beings, the regulators of the winds, stationed at the four quarters
of the world. A parallel table of the names of these deities and
the four above characters leaves no doubt as to the fact that in the
"four activities of mankind" we have the names of the "Four Winds"
abbreviated and euhemeristically interpreted:

Spring (= East) 析 East Wind 析丹. 折 interchanges with 析.

Summer (= South) 因 South Wind 因乎.

Autumn (= West) 夷 West Wind 石夷.

Winter (= North) 隩 North Wind 鳧 or 宛. Note that 隩 = 奧 = 寏 = 宛

To be continued*

*[The sequel to this essay is in HTHYFC number 3, which I have never
been able to locate. --Ed.]

HTHYFC 13 (March 1936)

The Lion in China

The belief is generally held by occidental students of things
Chinese that the lion came first to be known in China during the
great period of expansion and commercial penetration into Central
Asia under the First Han dynasty and that the Chinese term for 'lion',
shih 師~獅 KD 839: ₂si, is a loan-word from some Iranian language
(possibly derived from some form related to Persian šer or Iranian
*šarɣ). In the light of the continuously accumulating evidence re-
vealing much earlier intercommunications between the valley of the
Huang-ho and Central and Western Asia, however, it would seem strange
that no information whatsoever was possessed by the Chinese in the
pre-Han era concerning the mighty king of beasts.

In their search for the Iranian original of shih, most scholars
interested in the question had overlooked entirely the fact that
hidden away in the Erh Ya there was another, undoubtedly more ancient
and probably indigenous, Chinese term for 'lion'. This is suan-i
猨貎 or 猨麑 <*suan-ngiei or *si̯uen-ngiei, described in the
text of the Erh Ya as "a light-colored tiger (or feline) which eats
tigers and leopards" 如虦貓食虎豹 and identified by the
earliest commentators with the Han 'lion' (獅子). The word is not
of isolated lexicographical occurrence. It is found in the first
chüan of the Mu T'ien Tzǔ chuan (ed. SPTsK, 7a) where the suan-i
(and the wild horse) are said to travel 500 li daily. The same
term in a different transcription 尊耳 *tsuən-ńźi or 酋耳 *dz'i̯əu-
ńźi we find in the I Chou Shu, ch. 王會解 (ed. SPTsK, VII, 8a) where
it designates an animal with a body of a tiger and a tail three feet
long sent as tribute by (Southern) barbarians from the country of
Shih-lin 史林. The native commentators of both these important
(doubtlessly pre-Han) works identify the animal with the shih-tzǔ
or 'lion'.

All the three forms give us an original *sun-ngi (or *tsun-ngi)
which immediately evokes the Lepcha name for 'lion', sung-(n)gi,

(which, like Tib. seng-ge, is derived from Sanskrit simha?). The
word must have been of considerable antiquity in southeastern Asia
and must have entered China from the south or southwest. It was
probably in a period when communications became disrupted that the
term disappeared from the Chinese vocabulary and the lion became
"linguistically" extinct in China until he was resuscitated under
another name during the Han period.

It appears that even in the later Chou period, immediately preceding the re-appearance of the lion as shih, the lion as suan-i
began to acquire fantastic characteristics in the minds of Chinese
unacquainted with the animal itself. The variant form of the lion's
name *tsun-ngi undoubtedly underlies the name of the mysterious animal tsou-yü 騶虞< *tsiəu-ngiu (also written 貙 / and /牙 *tsiəu-
nga) made famous by the short poem in the Shih-ching "Chao nan". The
fancy of the commentators left to the tsou-yü only his original
"tiger-like" appearance and long tail, but endowed the poor lion
lavishly with many of the attributes of his rival, the unicorn.

Finally, in the Shuo-yüan, the lion comes to life again in
still another form: 駁鱗< *siuěn-ngia (it is again described as
"eating leopards"). This transcription is of particular interest as
the compound is traditionally connected with the name of the Hsien-pei
buckle of "animal style" (cf. Sino-Altaica III.5).* The determinative 鳥 'bird' used in this transcription led to the belief that
the term applied to some mythical bird. The half-feline half-bird-
like monsters of the "animal-style" plaques must have suggested
this form.

<hr />

*[This refers to "The Hsien-pei Buckle", HTHYFC 10 (June 1935)
   -- reprinted in this volume. -- Ed.]

HTHYFC 5 (January 1933)

Sino-Altaica I

Linguistic Notes on Central Asia

I.1. The Royal Clan of the Avars

The ruling clan of the Juan-juan (Avars) bore, according to J 103 and O 98, the name Mu-ku-lü 木骨閭 (KD 643, 427, 586: muk, kuət, $_c$li̯^{w}o) or Yü-chiu-lü (KD 251, 401: i̯uk, ^{c}ki̯əu). It traced its origin to a former slave of the early T'o-pa. That slave's hair grew 'as short as his eyebrows' (齊眉), and his master named him mu-ku-lü, which meant 'bald-headed' (首禿). No 'altaic' word *muqu^l/$_r$u meaning 'bald' has been found so far. The alternative reading *˙uqu^l/$_r$u indicates, however, that we must have here one of those 'altaic' words in which an initial labial (p-, sometimes b-) > h-, ˙- , and that the original word underlying the Chinese transcriptions must have been (Chin. m- for 'tk.' b-, p-) *p̊uqů^{l}/$_r$ů ~ *h̊uqů^{l}/$_r$ů.

Now, among the mongol and tungus words with an ancient *p- (> mong. h-, manchu f-) listed by P. Pelliot ("Mots à 'h' initiale, aujourd'hui amuie," JA, 1925, 193-263) we find the word *hoqar (Мелиоранский, АФМ: هوقار = Ar. قصير 'short, defective'), representing probably an ancient 'turco-mongol' *hoqor (P. Pelliot, p. 245). The progenitor of the Juan-juan was not really bald, his hair was merely unusually short, and the name given by his master must doubtless be traced to ancient mongol root *poqor~*hoqor 'short'(-haired).

Yü-chiu-lü has been compared by Chavannes (Mission arch., Sept., 250; JA, 1897, 406) with Yü-chüeh-lü 嫗厥律 the name of a Northern tribe (10th century).

Another ancient 'mongol' word with a p-> h- initial can, I believe, be identified in the northern surname P'u-liu(lou)-ju 普六女 (KD 765, 563, 944: ^{c}p'uo, li̯uk, ńźi̯^{w}o) 普陋茹 (KD 570 ləu^ɔ). This surname was conferred by a Northern Chou emperor upon Yang Chung 楊忠 for his services to the dynasty (L 19, O 11, M 1). The Yü-wên probably spoke a 'mongol' dialect (cf. Note I.8), and

the original 'altaic' word represented by p'u-liu-ju was undoubtedly
a translation of the Chinese yang 楊 (in North China 'aspen' or
'poplar'). The mongolian term designating that tree, uliya-sun,
uli-sun, goes back to an original form with an initial *p-. (For
various 'altaic' forms of that word, cf. A. Sauvageot, Recherches sur
le vocabulaire des langues ouralo-altaïques, 20). P'u-liu(lou)-ju,
with Chin. *ńźi- representing as usual (cf. Note I.3) an y(i)-,
would be an excellent transcription of *puliyo- ~ *polyo-.

I.2. Menander's Ἐκτάγ

In a brief note on 'A Passage in Menander' ("Linguistic
Gleanings," Lunds Universitets Årsskrift, XIX, 1923, pp. 81-82) Hannes
Sköld has attempted to reconcile the interpretation of the name of the
Turkish qaγan's headquarters as given by Menander in the well-known
passage " ἐν ὄρει τινὶ λεγομένῳ Ἐκτάγ, ὡς ἂν εἴποι χρυσοῦν ὄρος
Ἕλλην ἀνήρ " with the testimony of the Chinese sources (as analyzed
in Chavannes' Documents..., pp. 236-7) concerning the same mountain.
The Chinese names of the place, 白山 Pai shan (= 'White Mountain')
and 阿羯 (田) 山 A-chieh(-t'ien) shan, do not ostensibly suggest
any turkish term for 'gold', while the first name Pai-shan seems to
be a perfect equivalent of a turkish *Aq taγ (White Mountain).
Chavannes (loc. cit.) had accordingly corrected Menander's 'Gold
Mountain.'

   H. Sköld now suggests that in the Chinese A-chieh is concealed
the turkish word aqča, Osm. aqčä ٱقچِﻰ which means both 'white' and
'money' (that is, χρυσίον ~ ἀργύριον vs. χρυσός).

> The antiquity of the word aqča seems to be attested. It
> occurs in the Orkhon inscriptions (cf. W. Radloff, Die
> Alttürkischen Inschriften, Neue Folge, p. 160) and in
> Cumanian (see Radloff, Sprachmaterial).

   If in the original turkish name 'White Mountain', Sköld continues, aq and aqča were used alternatively for the adjective,
Zemarchos may have confused the first term in the name of the mountain
with the word aqča in the meaning of 'money'; then through the

further confusion of χρυσός with χρυσίον, Menander derived his
etymology.

  Now, the Chinese <u>a-chieh</u> could not, in my belief, stand for
ag̃ča. The ancient pronunciation of <u>chieh</u> was either *ki̯ät or *ki̯ɐt
(for <u>fan-ch'ieh</u>: 居竭 or 居謁). The third element in the Chinese
name, 田 , <u>t'ien</u> (ancient pronunciation ᵈd'ien KD 998), (A-chieh-t'ien
being the reading of the <u>T'ang Shu</u>, cf. Chavannes, <u>loc. cit.</u>, also
p. 115) is also disregarded in Sköld's supposition. If the trisyllabic Chinese name be taken as the original transcription of a
turkish word, A-chieh-t'ien = *Â-ki̯ɐt-d'ien would appear to represent
*Akaltien (with the regular correspondence of Chin. -<u>t</u> = foreign <u>l</u> or
<u>r</u>, and Chin. <u>d</u> = tk. <u>t</u>) or *Aq-altïn, a good turkish form with the
meaning 'white gold'.

        In the last syllable one would rather expect for Orkhon
        Turkish <u>u</u> instead of <u>ï</u>, i.e., <u>altun</u> (commonly trans-
        cribed in chinese with 敦 <u>tun</u> for the last syllable).
        <u>Altïn</u>, however, is valid for most dialects.

  The Chinese A-chieh-t'ien shan standing for a turkish original
*Aq altïn taɣ would solve satisfactorily the riddle of 'Εκτάγ "without
convicting Menander of falsehood." Indeed, if *Aq altïn taɣ, the
'White Gold Mountain' rather than the 'White-gold Mountain', had
been the original turkish name of the emplacement of the qaɣan's
<u>ordo</u>, Zemarchos through Menander, recorded its more common name *Aq
taɣ (> 'Εκτάγ , the Chinese 白 山 , 'White Mountain') while in the
interpretation of the name he emphasized the 'gilded' part of the name
as naturally having more 'copy value'.

  In fact, <u>altïn</u> would seem to be an 'honorary epithet' of the
mountain as the turkish sovereign's headquarters rather than an
original part of the name. The original Aq taɣ, the old Pai-shan,
became through being chosen by the qaɣan for his residence an
Altun yïš.

        Cf. Marquart, <u>Über das Volkstum der Komanen</u>, p. 69, who
        prefers to place in <u>the</u> Altun yïš (the Altai) the qaɣan's
        residence rather than in the Pai-shan North of Kučă.
  It is, however, tempting to re-evoke Sköld's theory in

explanation of the name of the residence of Tardou (Τάρδου , the
Chin. Ta-t'ou達頭) qaɣan, also given by Menander as lying ...ʿκατὰ
δὴ τό ᾽Εκτὲλ ὄρος, δύναται δὲ τό ᾽Εκτὲλ χρυσοῦν.

Ektel (= gold) and Ektaq (= gold mountain) seem to be in the
interpretation of the Byzantine historian two compounds formed with
a common element Ek- or Ekt- 'gold'. If Sköld is right and this
element represents tk. aqčä, what word underlies, then, the second
syllable of the first compound, Ektel? One thinks immediately of a
possible form *Aqčä-äl, with Orkhon tk. äl 'people', 'folk', 'clan' as
the second element, but äl does not seem to have ever been used in
the sense of ordo, 'headquarters'. The same turkish element appears,
however, in Sarkel, the name of the famous Khazar stronghold on the
lower Volga, the 'White City' of the Russian Chronicles. This word
Sarkel has been since Klaproth's times explained as being a compound
of tk. sarï(ɣ) 'yellow', but čuvaš šura 'white', and *kel (čuv. kəl
'village, town'). (Cf. A. Samoilovich in Яфктичиский сборникъ,
1924, 99-102: *gil, *kəl in other turkish dialects.) Ramstedt (JSFOu,
XXXVIII, 1, 13) seems to find the same čuvaš term kəl in the name of
Esgil (ar.ﺍﺻﻐﻞ , ﺍﺻﮑﻞ), the ancient city of the Volga Bulgars.
It would be possible, however, to divide Sarkel into *Sark- (with k
representing the final guttural of sarïɣ) and -el (cf. čuv. jal(yal)
< tk. äl; cf. N. Poppe, ИАН , 1925, 40, 413).

I.3. Hsien-pei *yamɣu (?)

In the biography of Yang Chung 楊忠 (507-568), famous
general of the Northern Chou dynasty and father of Yang Chien (Sui
Wên-Ti), in L 19 and O 11, is related the following anecdote concerning
the origin of Chung's cognomen Yen-yü 揑于 :

> Once when he followed [Chou] T'ai-Tsu [O 11: Wên-Ti, i.e.,
> Yü-wên T'ai] to the hunt at Lung-mên, Chung single-
> handed faced a wild beast. Holding it around the body
> with his left hand he tore out the beast's tongue with
> his right. T'ai-Tsu greatly admired his courage and
> gave him the cognomen Yen-yü, which in the language of

the North (北臺) meant 'wild beast'.

'Wild beast' 猛獸 in this passage could stand for an original 猛虎 'fierce tiger'. The latter expression is regularly replaced by the former in all T'ang texts, 虎 having been taboo under that dynasty as the name of Li Hu, Li Yüan's grandfather. The character is either omitted by T'ang writers altogether (see, e.g., the name of Han Ch'in-hu, the Sui General. Cf. Pelliot, <u>AM</u>, 1927, p. 380) or another suitable character is substituted for it (so, frequently, 武: cf. <u>HTHYFC</u> I, l). It is hardly possible, however, that tiger could have been meant in our passage as the feat of tearing out bare-handed the tongue of such a beast would be unbelievable even of a <u>baghatur</u> of the 6th century. It is more probable that some other animal commonly hunted at Lung-mên was meant.

What original Hsien-pei word does <u>yen-yü</u> represent? One must here bear in mind that 干 yü is often wrongly written for 干 kan. We have thus two possible forms: *i̯ɐmg$\overset{i}{\hat{}}$u and *·i̯ɐmɣan (KD 241, 1317, 296).

The first word reminds one of Chinese 羬 or 麙 (KD 148 ɣam, but cf. P. Pelliot, <u>TP</u>, 1930, 195, for discussion of a possible palatalized initial), the name of a large sheep or goat (<u>Erh Ya</u>), a large steinbok or ibex (<u>Lei Pien</u>), and a fabulous goat-like animal (<u>Shan Hai Ching</u>). This character also appears in the binom 羬麌 'stag, buck' (KD 1284 ngi̯u). This last word, *·i̯amni̯u, would be an almost exact equivalent of the term under consideration. As its earliest occurrence is registered in the <u>Lei Pien</u>, it is quite possible that the Chinese binom represents a loan-word from Hsien-pei or a related language (cf. ma. <u>yanggir</u>, solon. <u>yaṇir</u>).

*i̯ɐmɣan, on the other hand, would point to mong. <u>imaɣan</u>, khal. yamā, tung. <u>imaɣan</u>, <u>yankan</u>, ma. <u>niman</u> 'goat'. Although Kazwīnī, Ibn al-Muhannā, and Kirakos (cf. N. Poppe, "Монгольския названия животныхъ..." <u>ЗКВ</u>, 1925, 197-8) give for <u>imaɣan</u> the form <u>iman</u>, the evidence of the dialects is in favor of a form with <u>Brechnung</u>, *yamān. At the same time, while mong. <u>imaɣan</u> and related turco-mongol forms seem to be limited to the designation of the domestic goat and do not refer to a 'wild beast' such as the steinbok (for which Kazwīnī gives the mong. <u>uqɣai</u>, Poppe *uqɣan), there is some

evidence that the word was also extended to the wild representatives
of the goat family (cf. e.g. turkm. umɣa 'mountain goat', Th. Korsch,
"O бытовыхъ словахъ...", ЗИРГООЭ, 1909, 545; ma. nimadum id.).

There was undoubtedly real danger in trying to wrestle with a
large steinbok at bay on an uncertain path. The tongues of sheep,
goats, and deer were considered by the Chinese and their neighbors
as one of the choicest parts of the game (羊舌 , 鹿舌) and Yang
Chung may have chosen a dangerous but original and quick way of
obtaining a relished piece of venison for the table of his lord.

The same turco-mongol word must underlie a common Hsien-pei
and T'u-chüeh name, transcribed by the Chinese Jan-kan 染干 (KD
643 ńźi̯äm), cf. T'u-fa Jan-kan in 16 Kg. 94, Ho-lan Jan-kan (HTHYFC
II, 3), and the T'u-chüeh qaɣan Jan-kan (P. Pelliot, TP, 1928-29,
203 and 215).

I.4. Lupus pilum mutat...

The common 'east turkish' word for 'wolf', büri, böri, seems
to have anciently been widely diffused through Central Asia. Well
attested in Orkhon Turkish, it appears also to have been used in
Hsiung-nu (cf. HTHYFC I, 16-17). It may have also existed in the
language of another people among whom a legend of wolf-origin was
current, namely the Wu-sun, witness the Wu-sun name fu-li 拊離
(KD 44, 534 ᶜp'i̯u-lji̯e̯) recorded in B 94b.

K. Shiratori's "Über den Wu-sun Stamm ...," Keleti Szemle, 1902,
has unfortunately been inaccessible to me for the past few years,
but to the best of my recollection the author draws attention to
the possibility of *böri being the original Wu-sun word represented
by fu-li. It is to be noted at any rate that the two Chinese
characters contain the identical phonetic elements which are used
to transcribe the Hsiung-nu or T'u-ch'üeh word.

As a variant transcription of the latter note 附鄰
fu-lin (KD 556 ᶜli̯ĕn) given in TPHYC 194 as a T'u-chüeh
word with the meaning 'wolf', where the explanation
that it was a name given by the Turks to certain of
their qaɣans for their bloodthirstiness 有時置附

鄰可汗〔附〕鄰狼名也取其貪殺為稱

is reminiscent of the phrase in Kül tegin's inscription
quoted in HTHYFC, loc. cit. Parker's'*lin khakhan',
"lin being the name for wolf" (A Thousand Years of the
Tartars, p. 132) is an oversight caused by the omission
of the second 附 in the Chinese text. For other transcriptions of the T'u-chüeh word, cf. possibly 步利設
= *böri šad? and 步離可汗 = *böri qaγan? (E. Chavannes,
Documents...) (步 KD 759 ꞏb'uo).

It is also possible that the same 'Altaic' word appears in the
ancient name of the lake Bar köl, P'u-lei 蒲類 (KD 762, 227 ꞏb'uo-
1jʷiꞏ), Bar köl being an old haunt of the Hsiung-nu as well as that
of the ancient kingdom of P'u-lei 蒲類 in East Turkestan. The
history of the name of the lake is complex (cf. P. Pelliot, TP,
1928-9, 251), but its latter (9th century) designation *Bars köl
'Tiger lake' (op. cit.) suggests that in popular remembrance the lake
was associated with a widely honored animal, the bars taking the
place of an original *böri (the tiger's rise in honor among nomadic
peoples begins to be pronounced about this time).

It has also been suggested by Parker (op. cit. 134) that the
word *böri was likewise in use among the Ho-lien Hsia Hsiung-nu. He
based his supposition on the phrase 夏言亦狼 in L 50 (cf. HTHYFC
I, 16) where he takes Hsia 夏 as referring to the Ho-lien (the Hsi
Hsia are naturally out of the question for a text as early as L).
While I believe that in the above passage Hsia designates the Chinese
and has nothing to do with the Ho-lien, I still think that the latter
can be invoked here in the person of the celebrated founder of the
dynasty, Ho-lien P'o-p'o (勃勃 KD 748 b'uət, in J and O; 佛佛
[fo-fo], KD 47 b'iuət, in F, G, and N). P'o-p'o or Fo-fo would
indeed be an excellent transcription of *bör-bör, representing
possibly an original *bör or böz-bör(i) = 'gray wolf'? (On my
speculations on another 勃 P'o < *BOR, see HTHYFC I, 18-19.)

In further support of the possibility of the connection
of Mt. Ütüken with wolves, I would like to call the
reader's attention to a passage in P 194a where it is

stated that after the defeat and capture of Chü-pi qaγan
車鼻 in 650 the remnants of his horde were settled by
the Chinese near Mt. Ütüken and the Lang-shan (Wolf
Mountain!) tu-tu-ship was established there to keep
them under control.

Beside the word *böri in its numerous Chinese disguises we
have attested as existing in Central Asia since the 4th century
another term for 'wolf', this one with apparently 'mongolian'
affinities, namely the word *činuo > mong. činoa, transcribed by the
Chinese 叱奴 (KD 1055, 674 ts'i̯ĕt-ᴄnuo).

> In HTHYFC I, 17, following an inferior text of the Wei
> Shu, I wrongly wrote 叱那 ; all the best editions have
> 奴.

The history of this 'wolf' like that of the 'Wolf Lake' is
complex (cf. P. Pelliot, JA, 1927[1], 286). The T'o-pa surname 叱奴
translated in J 113 into Chinese 狼 lang 'wolf' was apparently derived from the name of a tribe defeated by T'o-pa Kuei in 390 (J 2,
0 1). This tribe possibly belonged to the Kao-chü confederation, as
it was chiefly against the latter that the T'o-pa king was campaigning in that year, and was evidently early incorporated into the
T'o-pa empire.

> In the language of the T'o-pa themselves the word for
> 'wolf' appears to be *böri as incidentally pointed out
> by Parker (loc. cit.). The tzǔ 字 name of T'o-pa T'ao,
> third sovereign of the Wei dynasty, was Fo-li · 佛狸
> (KD 529 lji) which probably transcribes the same foreign
> word as fu-li, although the only indication as to the
> meaning of the compound is the 犭 'dog' determinative in
> the second character.

The binom ch'ih-nu 叱奴 appears in J twice more, once as the
name of a T'o-pa prince (J 15) and in the name of a Ho-hsi 紇奚
chieftain Ch'ih-nu-kên 叱奴根 (J 1, 397; J 28). L 9 records it
as the surname of one of Yü-wên T'ai's wives. The name of the Ho-hsi
chieftain represents undoubtedly a diminutive form of činoa with the

suffix -ɣan, -ken (KD 312 kən).

For a corresponding diminutive form of *bü̈ri in T'o-pa
cf. the name of a chief of the Ho-lan horde (J 28),
Fu-li-chüan 附力眷 (KD 495 ki̯ʷä̈n) < *bü̈rikä̈n.

Finally the same word for 'wolf' may underlie Chin. Ch'ou-nu
醜奴 (KD 460 tś'i̯əu) found in J 103, O 98, as the name of a
Juan-juan khan, and in the name of a rebel at the end of the Wei
dynasty, Mo-ssŭ 万俟 Ch'ou-nu (cf. L and <u>Hsi Wei Shu</u>). For Ch'ou
as a possible dialectical variation of <u>ch'ih</u>, cf. the name 叱伐
(J 103) <u>vs.</u> 醜伐 (HTHYFC II, 2).

One is also tempted to hazard the supposition that the same
'mongol' word is to be found in the clan name of the T'u-chüeh,
A-shih-na 阿史那. This hypothesis has been advanced before and
was rejected on the ground that the word činoa is not found in
Orkhon Turkish; the initial a- and š̌ for č̌ create additional difficulties. We must keep in mind, however, that the T'u-chüeh originally formed a part of the Juan-juan confederation and that the latter
apparently spoke a 'mongol' dialect. The T'u-chüeh tradition of
wolf-origin and the constantly recurring T'u-ch'ueh numerical pattern
of <u>ten</u> would indeed suggest that in their originally 'mongol' clan-
name we have the combination of a numerical and a theriophoric
element. A-shih-na (KD 414, 885, 647 ·âṣinâ) would equal *<u>ar-</u> < *<u>har-</u>
(the root of mong. <u>arban</u> 'ten', cf., however, Ramstedt, <u>JSFOu</u>, XXIV,
who considers <u>arba-</u> as the root, although he believes the second
syllable of gur<u>ban</u>, dör<u>ben</u>, nai<u>man</u> to be a suffix; but see Pelliot,
<u>JA</u>, 1925, 201) + č̌inoa (tk. š̌ < mong. č̌ especially after a liquid;
cf. also KD 526 on the peculiar ancient initial of 史 ṣl-, sl-),
**<u>ar-č̌inoa</u> = 'the ten wolves', the ten sons of the she-wolf. (For
numerical elements in nomadic clan-names, cf. Ligeti, <u>Die Herkunft</u>
<u>des Volksnamens Kirgis</u>.)

I.5. The 'Demigod' of the Ch'i-fu

According to a legend preserved in E 125 and <u>16 Kg.</u> 85, the
royal clan of the Ch'i-fu 乞伏 Hsien-pei traced its origin to a
mysterious youth found by some Hsien-pei tribes under the following
circumstances: Three Hsien-pei tribes, the Ju-fu-ssǔ 如弗斯(引)
-yin, <u>16 Kg.</u>), the Ch'u-lien 出連, and the Ch'ih-lu 叱盧 encountered during their southward migration an enormous reptile which
blocked their road on a mountain pass. They sacrificed to it and
prayed that it let them proceed on their way. The reptile vanished,
but in its place they found a young boy who was adopted by one of the
tribesmen, an old man of the Ch'i-fu horde. Growing to manhood, the
boy became a great warrior and was recognized by the four tribes as
their khan under the title of Ch'i-fu qaγan <u>T'o-to mo-ho</u> 託鐸
(<u>16 Kg.</u>: 譯) 莫何.

The Hsien-pei words T'o-to (KD 1159, 202 t'âk d'âk) are explained in the Chinese text as meaning 'neither god nor man', 'demigod'
非神非人之稱. We have here undoubtedly the turkish term *<u>taγdaqï</u>
'mountain dweller', '<u>Bergbewohner</u>'.   The worship of mountains is
well-known among the early Turks, and I think that the translation
of *<u>taγdaqï</u> by 'demigod' is sufficiently warranted: <u>Mo-ho</u> represents, of course, *<u>baγa</u>.

I.6. T'o-pa Hsien-pei— T'u-chüeh Parallels

1. Ïšbara. The Orkhon turkish word <u>ïšbara</u> (occurs in the inscriptions as a proper name only; meaning doubtful) has been for a
long time tentatively identified with the <u>Sha-</u>(or <u>Shih</u>)-<u>po-lo</u>(or <u>lüeh</u>)
沙 (姓) 鉢 (or 波) 羅 (or 略) of the Chinese texts. (On the
difficulty presented by the Chinese surd in <u>po</u>, cf. P. Pelliot, <u>TP</u>,
1928-9, 211.) The meaning of <u>Shih-po-lo</u>, according to the <u>T'ung
Tien</u> and the <u>TPHYC</u> 194, was 'brave, robust' 勇健 and the word was
one of common occurrence in the turkish onomasticon.

In my opinion the word is of purely 'turkish' origin, and
is apparently a compound of ïš (uig. ïš 'Unternehmen',

'Tat', cf. Bang, <u>SBPAW</u>, 1931, 480) and <u>bar-</u> 'to have,
to be such', and must have originally meant 'he of the
(mighty) deeds'. The same construction with <u>bar</u> would
appear in the title of qaɣan T'a-po 他鉢 (cf. P. Pelliot
<u>op. cit.</u>, 215), representing an original *Tapar < *tap-
ar or *tap-bar, where *tap- would have the meaning
'honor, adoration, service'. In this connection the 他
人 T'a-jên (cf. P. Pelliot, <u>loc. cit.</u>) or 他民 T'a-
min (KD 629 ᴄmi̯ĕn, with <u>m-</u> for tk. <u>b-</u>) river, where the
Turks congregated in the fifth month to worship the god
of Heaven, is to be remembered, for the Chinese transcription could be traced back to tk. *tapïn 'to worship'
(on the possibility of reading <u>t'a-min</u> for <u>t'a-jên</u>, see
HTHYFC I, 28). In this case, however, we would have a
transcription with a sonant for a surd!

Whatever be the meaning and the etymology of <u>ïšbara</u>, the word
itself appears to be much older than the Orkhon period. In the
form *<u>ïšbar</u> it may underlie the Chinese transcription Sha-mo 沙末
(KD 636 muât) found in the name of a Hsien-pei chief, Sha-mo-han 汗 ,
son of Chüeh-chi 厥機 (D 30). Although the identification presents certain difficulties, the Sha-mo-han may be the same person
as Sha-mo-(漢 mâk)-han, son of Li-wei, of early T'o-pa history
(J 1, 0 1), cf. Parker, <u>op. cit.</u>, 94, 97.

2. The T'o-pa Hsien-pei title of a high official (equal in
rank to the Chinese 二千石) is given in G 57 as <u>yü-jo</u> 郁若
(KD 251, 938 ˙i̯uk-ńźi̯ak). The T'o-pa word underlying the Chinese
transcription is undoubtedly to be connected with T'u-chüeh <u>yü-shê</u>
郁射 (KD 865 dź'i̯äk) which occurs on P 194 as part of a turkish
title <u>yü-shê šad</u>. Another transcription of the same title seems to
be 奥射 <u>ao-shê</u> (KD 7 ˙âuᵓ). Cf. Parker, "The Early Turks," <u>CR</u>
XXV, 173. The T'o-pa title was overlooked by K. Shiratori in his
study of T'o-pa words.

3. The well-known turkish title <u>tigin</u>, <u>tägin</u>, as well as
that of <u>ärkin</u>(?), can also be traced in T'o-pa. The first appears

in F 95 and G 57 as the title of most of the T'o-pa princes of the blood under the Chinese transcriptions 直勤 and 直懃 (KD 1220, 389 d'i̯ək-g'i̯ən). The same title appears in J 1 (390, 12) and J 103 in the name of a chieftain of the Ho-hsi 紇奚 horde 屋地鞬建 (KD 1285, 223, 373: *uk-d'i'ᵌ-g'i̯ən) *Oq tigin? (Cf. P. Pelliot, JA, 1920, 148, for an identical title several centuries later.) As to *erkin, cf. the T'o-pa title (corresponding to the Chinese shang shu 尚書, ssŭ-ch'in ti-ho 俟懃地何, which would normally be reconstructed *erkin tigä (or tägä), the meaning of the second part of the compound being uncertain.

Following the above title, G 57 gives the T'o-pa equivalent of Chinese 'governor of a province' (刺史) as mo-t'i 莫堤 *baɣ-dï or possibly *baɣ-idi. (Cf. orkh. tk. baɣ 'Volksabtheilung'.)

I.7. Hsiung-nu Notes

Among the many Hsiung-nu words, titles, and proper names pre-served in Chinese transcriptions in the early Chinese dynastic histories only a few can be identified with certainty as being 'turkish' or 'altaic'. A great deal of work remains yet to be done before the problem of the linguistic affinities of Hsiung-nu is definitely solved.

A good brief review of the question is contained in K. Inostrantsev's Хунну и Гунны, 2nd. ed., St. Petersburg, 1926. 'Turkish' equivalents are sure for Hsn. *tängri 'heaven', *büri 'wolf (cf. supra, Note 4), and *sü 'army' (Chin. 秀 KD 805 si̯əu'ᵌ). Cf. Ramstedt, "Die Stellung des Tschuwassischen," JSFO, XXVIII, 31, whose identification is undoubtedly to be preferred to Shiratori's (in "Sinologische Beiträge...," ИИАН, 1902, 6).

Most of the many conjectural equations of Hsiung-nu words with turkish terms have so far been rejected on grounds of insuffi-cient evidence, and rightly so, yet it is also true that a great

deal of information supplied by the Chinese sources, directly or
indirectly, has been overlooked or neglected. At the risk of adding
new material to the long list of discarded identifications, the
author would like to present herewith some conjectures suggested by
the contextual occurrence of the Hsiung-nu words in the Chinese
sources.

1. Hsiung-nu lu-li 谷蠡, title of Hsiung-nu princes (presumably
sons of the shan-yü) immediately following in rank the hsien
princes. The first character read regularly ku (KD 425 kuk) should
be pronounced, according to all commentators (notably Yen Shih-ku
B 94a), as = lu 鹿 (KD 576 luk). According to C 119, the hsien
princes (of the right and left) and the two lu-li princes (forming
the group known as the 'Four Horns' 四角) together with six other
dignitaries (the 'Six Horns') were all sons and younger brothers
of the shan-yü. The title, therefore, corresponds to that of the
turkish tigin-s (cf. supra, note 6) which was born only by the
princes of the blood, the oγul of the khan. *Lukli (蠡 KD 1136
ᶜliei) can be thus equated with *äl-oγglï (ä)loγlï 'son of the
äl' (the khan's clan).

2. Ku-tu 骨都, another Hsiung-nu title, occurring chiefly in the
compound ku-tu hou 侯. C 119 informs us again that this title was
borne by nobles of clans other than the shan-yü's (presumably of
the three great clans: Lan, Hsü-pu, and Hu-yen). The right and
left ku-tu hou took a prominent part in the administration (B 94a),
and, from what we know of nomadic life, we can safely suppose were
linked with the ruling clan by bonds of intermarriage. Ku-tu
(KD 427, 1187 kuət-ₜtuo) represents, therefore, we may assume with
a great degree of certainty, the common 'turkish' *qudu 'father-in-
law, relative by marriage', ('match-maker' in certain **dialects**).
In mong. qadum and other dialectical forms with final m, -m is
undoubtedly the possessive suffix of the first person.

3. The Hsiung-nu Clans. The shan-yü's clan bore, according to
B 94a, the name Luan-t'i 孿鞮, according to C 119 Hsü-lien-t'i

虛連題 . Three other powerful clans are mentioned by both
sources: Hu-yen 呼衍, Lan 蘭 , and Hsü-pu 須卜 (C adds a fourth:
Ch'ü-lin 丘林). It is interesting to note that in the name of
the shan-yü's clan we may have one of those 'altaic' words beginning
with a p > h (cf. supra, note 1), for Luan (KD 590 li$^{w..}$an) is one of
those Chinese phonemes where an initial 'labial + l' can be postulated with some certainty (cf. Karlgren, loc. cit., pl-, bl-, ml-?).
The original Hsiung-nu word may thus have been *Pli$^{w..}$an-d'iei <
*P^{o}riendi (as given by B). C gives us a hypothetical *H^{o}riendi
(KD 168 ʻχi^{w}o for 虛). It would be unsafe to speculate on the
meaning of the word, however, as the Chinese sources yield no indication as to the possible significance of the name (for 'altaic'
roots *POR, *POL, see Sauvageot).

> J. Németh in his studies of Pecheneg clan names (UJ, X,
> p. 27 ff., cf. Körosi Archivum, 219 ff.) has called
> attention to the predominance of color-terms in nomadic
> nomenclatures and has invoked Chinese sources (A 110,
> B 94a) to illustrate the division of clans according to
> the colors of their horses. Indeed, at the siege of
> P'ing-ch'êng the Hsiung-nu to the west of the city
> were mounted on white horses, on the east side, on
> gray (駹), in the north, on black (驪), and on
> bay (騂) in the south. It would be tempting to seek
> in the names of the Hsiung-nu clans the designation of
> some of these colors: Luan-ti <*P^{o}riendi 'black'?
> (cf. Sauvageot, op. cit., 14), Lan < *(a)lan ~ alaγ
> 'dapple', Hu-yen < *kü'är 'gray', Hsü-pu < *sipük?
> 'bay?'

4. In analyzing one of the names of the T'u-yü-hun, 'the barbarians
A-ch'ai 阿柴', P. Pelliot connects this name with a Hsiung-nu word
recorded in the Wei lüeh (D 30) in Chinese transcription 訾 tzǔ,
with the meaning 'slave' in Hsiung-nu. This word (represented by
a slightly different Chinese character 訾 [KD 1096 ʻtsie <-a,
ancient pronunciation identical with the preceding]) occurs in

Hsiung-nu names and titles comparatively frequently and, I believe, with the same meaning 'slave'. I have noted it in the following compounds: 呼盧/, title of a Hsiung-nu prince in B 94a; 伊育/, tribe of the Northern Hsiung-nu in C 120; 伊秩/, Hsiung-nu of the left horde (Yü Hai 152). The Hsiung-nu had special officials appointed for the administration of tribes 'enslaved' by them, and many of those tribes must have borne the name 'Slaves NN' or 'Slaves of NN'.

The same word (with an affix [?]離) occurs, I believe, in the name of one of the petty 'kingdoms' of the Chü-shih 車師, Wu-t'an tzǔ-li 烏貪訾離 *Ot'âm tsiạ-ljei. Now, in the enumeration of Hsiung-nu tribes in E 97 is mentioned the Wu-t'an 烏譚 *Od'âm (KD 969) tribe. The name of the little T'ien-shan horde might thus be hypothetically explained as meaning 'the slaves of the *Otâm'.

I.8. 'Barbarian' tzǔ 字

The tzǔ of many 'half-sinicized' barbarians recorded in the biographical sections of the histories of the North appear to be 'altaic' equivalents of their Chinese ming 名. One of the certain cases is the tzǔ of the Hu-lü Chin 斛律金 -- 阿六敦 A-liu-tun (K 17). A-liu-tun represents obviously *altun 'gold', translating the Turk's Chinese ming (金 'gold').

L 13 gives us the tzǔ of the twelve sons of Yü-wên T'ai, all of which end in t'u 突, which undoubtedly represents the mongol adjectival ending -tu, -tü. Thus: 統萬突 (L 4 'born at T'ung-wan'), 毗賀突 possibly = *bilgätü (L 12, cf. TP 1928-9, 229), 豆盧突 = *dörötü?

I.9. 'Horses and Sheep'

The T'o-pa Hsien-pei title 曷剌真 G 57, 3a (KD 73, 509) represents undoubtedly *atlačin 'horseman' from tk. atla 'to mount a horse'. We have thus again a purely turkish form in T'o-pa. The question of the early turkish form of 'horse' is, however, complicated and would require a special study (cf. T'u-chüeh 賀蘭 *alan

[T'ung Tien] where we would expect *ad, *at).

The name of a T'o-pa prince in F 95 庫仁真 *qoyinčin
(appearing also in Juan-juan, J 26) in all probability equals tk.
*qoy/n inčin 'sheep herdsman'.

I.10. Varia

1. In the TP, 1928-9, 185-7, Professor Pelliot, in discussing the
question of 'winter wheat' which was sown in Bamiyan according to
the testimony of Hsüan-tsang, expresses some doubt as to whether the
compound su-mai 宿麥 is attested for that early period. I find
the expression used in C 5 under the year 106 A.D., where a note
specifically states that 'winter wheat' is meant. Mr. M. J. Hagerty
has drawn my attention to a still earlier use of the compound in
B 6 under the year 120 B.C., where Yen Shih-ku's note also explains
it as 'winter wheat'. I have noted since that the Supplement to the
Tz'ǔ Yüan has an entry on su-mai with a reference to the passage
in B.

2. The old mongol title transcribed by the Chinese 熬羅字極烈
*Ōlo bögilä (TP, 1930, 24-25) can, I believe, be traced back to the
Kao-chü 侯婁匈勒 *Oləu bögle(k), J 103, which meant, according
to J, 'great Emperor' 大天子 . The same title appears probably
in the famous Hsiung-nu phrase (Shiratori, op. cit.) of the 4th
century in the transcription 僕谷 pu-lu (where 谷 is to be read
luk as in lu-li, cf. supra, note 7, 1). It designates there the
title of the Hsiung-nu king Liu Yao. Shiratori's equation with
*böd is more than doubtful (pu-lu < *böglük!)

HTHYFC 7 (1934)

Sino-Altaica II (December 1933)

II.1. Some Hsiung-nu Names

Among the names of the T'ieh-fu Huns whose biographies are
given in HTHYFC 1 and 2 several can be identified under their
Chinese transcription as common 'turco-mongol' words. These names
represent primitive appellations usually found in the nomadic onomasticon: names of birds, beasts, implements of war and peace, and
other familiar objects of the nomad's milieu. The origin of their
names is undoubtedly to be connected with the nomadic custom of
naming the new-born child according to the first object that strikes
the eye of the mother immediately after the birth of the baby (cf.
P. Pelliot, TP, 1930, p. 29).

Thus the name of Liu Lo-ch'ên, HTHYFC 2, 6 (羅辰 KD 569,
1197 ₒlâ-ₒẓiĕn) undoubtedly represents 'turco-mongol' lačin ~ način
'falcon', لاچين , also لاجين ; ma. usually ﺳﻤﺤﻖ , a name
especially common among the nomads due to the popularity of falconry
as a sport. Although lačin is not unknown in mongolian, it is
usually met with in an environment subject to turkish linguistic
influences (cf. Poppe, 3KB , 1925, 203; Pelliot, JA, 1927, 290-1).

The name of Liu K'u-jên, HTHYFC 1, 12-14 (庫仁 KD 431,
930: k'uoᵓ-ₒńẓien) must represent turco-mongol' qoyïn ~ qonïn
'sheep, ram', قوين , ﺳﻤﺤﻖ , the Chinese initial of the second
syllable transcribing equally well *yi- or *ñi-. In the transcription of 'turco-mongol' words ancient Chinese nẓ́- usually stands for
y- (cf. HTHYFC 5, 9); *qoyïn is therefore more probable.

> Cf. also HTHYFC 5, for K'u-jên-chên transcribing
> *qoyïnčïn 'sheepherdsman'. The personal names of some
> T'o-pa Hsien-pei, as given in F 95, are apparently
> derived from titles of dignitaries: thus K'o-po-chên
> 可博真 *qapaɣčïn 'porter', according to G 57, occurs
> in F 95 as the name of Yü 余 , son of T'o-pa T'ao.

The name of Liu Hsien's younger brother K'ang-ni (亢埿 KD 305,

659: k'âng²-_cniei, <u>HTHYFC</u> 2:2,5; <u>TCNPCYTP</u> 3 writes 可泥) no
doubt represents tk. <u>qangli</u>'chariot'. While there is nothing unusual
in having Chinese <u>n</u> transcribe a foreign <u>l</u>, it would be logical to
suppose that the original Hsiung-nu word underlying the transcription
is *<u>qangni</u>, a mongolized form of <u>qangli</u> with the regular change of
<u>l</u> > <u>n</u> following ng (cf., e.g., Vladimirtsov, "Монгольское
'ongniɣud'...", ДРАН, 1930, 220-1.)

These equivalences of the Chinese transcriptions with 'turco-
mongol' words are regular and can, therefore, be accepted with some
degree of certainty. Several other T'ieh-fu names offer interesting
material for conjecture, though none of them can be identified with
surety.

Thus Hsi-wu-chi 悉勿祈 (the name of Liu Wu-huan's son;
KD 782, 1278, 385: si̯ĕt-mi̯uət-_cg'i̯ei) may represent tk. <u>sipürgä</u> ~
<u>sibürgä</u>, osm. اسپورغ, mong. *<u>sipürgä</u> 'broom' (on the mongol form
cf. P. Pelliot, <u>JA</u>, 1930, p. 262).

The turkish or mongol original of O-lou-t'ou (<u>HTHYFC</u> 1 關
陋頭 *˙ât (阿葛反) KD 570, 1015: lə̯u²-_cd'ə̯u) also seems to
underlie other Chinese transcriptions phonetically almost identical
with the above: cf. Kung-sun A-liu-t'ou 公孫阿六頭, name
of a T'o-pa envoy to S. Ch'i (J 7a, H 85); Ho-lu-t'ou 賀虜頭,
name of a T'u-yü-hun prince sent to the T'o-pa court in 492 (J 7b);
see also a possible variant of the first name of Ho-la-t'ou (<u>HTHYFC</u> 2).

The possible original *<u>altu</u> ~ *<u>alutu</u> seems to be a 'mongol'
adjectival form in -<u>tu</u> from a 'turco-mongol' word meaning 'spotted,
piebald' and also simply 'horse', from which are derived tk. آل ,
الجه , and mong. <u>alaɣ</u> (Ibn al-Muhanna, АФМ , 122, آل) 'variegated, dapple'. Ho-lan, the name of a Hsien-pei tribe, is known to
mean 'dapple' (cf. Chavannes, <u>Documents</u>..., p. 56, 2; the original
of the passage in the <u>Shan-hsi t'ung-chih</u> quoted by Chavannes is to
be found in <u>YHCHTC</u> IV, 4a); the same word appears in the name of
another tribe of Turks called by the Chinese 'dapple horses' 駮馬,
the O-lo-chih 遏羅支く *<u>a(l)lači</u> (cf. Chavannes, <u>op. cit.</u>, p. 29,
4 and J. Németh, "Die petschenegischen Stammesnamen," <u>UJ</u>, v. 10, 32.)

Color-terms occur often in nomadic nomenclature (cf. <u>HTHYFC</u>

5: 23) and *alutu ~ *alatu may have been a common name among the
turks and mongols and, as the <u>T'ung tien</u> in its list of turkish words
translates <u>ho-lan</u> by 'horse', it may simply have meant 'horseman'.

In reference to the use of color-terms as proper names I would
here like to call attention to a 'turco-mongol' word appearing in
various Chinese disguises: 拾賁 F 77 (name of a T'o-pa), 拾寅 and
葉延 (T'u-yü-hun names), 什寅 (Ch'i-fu), and possibly 什翼犍,
all of which would well transcribe tk. <u>šipkin</u> ~ <u>yipkin</u> ~ <u>yipün</u> 'purple'.

II.2. The Stirrup in China

The introduction of the stirrup into China has not yet been
definitely dated. Some scholars (B. Laufer, M. Rostovtsev) believe
that it must have been known in China as early as the Han dynasty;
P. Pelliot, while not denying the possibility of the nomads introducing its use among the Chinese in the first centuries of the
Christian era, inclines more to the period 200–400 as better supported
by Chinese evidence from historical and linguistic sources (cf. <u>TP</u>,
1925–26, 259–262).

Indeed, as pointed out by Pelliot, the earliest occurrence
of the Chinese word for stirrup, têng 鐙 , is registered in the
biography of Chang Ching-êrh (second half of the 5th century; J 25,
N 45). For the north of China, however, this date can, I believe, be
advanced by a whole century.

In the biography of Wang Luan 王鸞 16 Kg. 65 (the <u>TPYL</u> 377
quotes the text as coming from the <u>San-shih kuo ch'un-ch'iu</u> 三十國
春秋), Luan is described as an unusually strong man who could
spring on horseback fully armed and without getting hold of the
saddle or the help of stirrups 不據鞍由鐙 . The text can with
certainty be dated as referring to c. 380 (the <u>San-shih kuo ch'un-</u>
<u>ch'iu</u>, ed. <u>Kuang-ya ts'ung-shu</u>, gives 399 A.D. as the date when Wang
Luan attracted the attention of Mu-jung Tê of Southern Yen).

Another passage from the same work quoted by the <u>TPYL</u> 358 may
contain another reference to the stirrup some fifty years earlier.

It appears from this quotation that in 400 A.D. (Hsien-ning II 咸寧 of the Hou Liang) An Chü 安攄, a Hu 胡 of Liang chou, broke into the tomb of Chang Chün 張駿 (for whom see HTHYFC 4:1) and stole from it, among many other precious objects, "a whip of coral, a chung (goblet) of carnelian, and a golden bridle-bit." The same story appears with more details in 16 Kg. 82 (the authenticity of the 16 Kg. text is proved by TPYL 359 where the short entry relating to the same event is given as coming from the original work of Ts'ui Hung).

It seems strange, however, that a goblet should be mentioned among horse trappings, especially as vessels are enumerated separately in the 16 Kg. list of the loot. It is quite possible that chung 鍾 is here a corruption of 鐙 têng 'stirrup', although TPYL 761 has chung in another reference to our text (quotation this time from a Liang chou chi). If this emendation be accepted, we would have here the earliest reference to the stirrup in China (Chang Chün died in 346 A.D.).

II.3. The Three Wizard Chiefs of the Ancient Kitans

The Ch'i-tan kuo chih 契丹國志 in its introduction to the history of the Kitans gives the story of three ancient wizards (or shamans) who ruled over the ancestors of the Liao. The first wizard left his yurta in human shape only to assist at sacrifices; otherwise he assumed the form of a human skull (髑髏) hidden under the yurta rug. The second had the head of a wild pig, and dressed in pig-skins; he also appeared in public only on important occasions. The third wizard possessed twenty sheep of which he daily devoured nineteen; the one remaining sheep was on the morrow miraculously transformed into twenty (of which nineteen were duly consumed, etc.)

The names of the three wizards are given in Chinese transcription as:

迺呵 Nai-ho

喝 (or 嚆) 呵 Ho-ho, and

畫里昏 呵 Hua-li-hun-ho.

The scanty evidence we possess concerning the Kitan language
seems to indicate that it was a strongly palatalized dialect of
mongol (cf. P. Pelliot, JA, 1920, 146-147). The names of the last
two wizards, in the light of the stories told about them, can indeed
be easily identified with mongolian words.

Thus, ho-ho $<$ *γâ-*k'â undoubtedly represents mong. γaqai
'pig' (cf. the form kaka, Poppe, ЗКВ , I, 198-9, P. Pelliot, JA,
1927[1], 282), while hua-li-hun-ho $<$ *χ^wɐ(k)-*li-*χun-*k'â must be
equated with mong. χari(n) qur(a)γa(n) 'twenty lambs' (cf. an-ch'un
transcribing altun 'gold').

As to the name of the first wizard, the Kitan word underlying
Nai-ho must doubtless be connected with Kitan nai 㐀丁 'head' (cf. also
逈 nai 'first') for which see Shiratori's "Beiträge...", ИИАН,
1902, 023.

    I would like to here take the opportunity of calling attention
    to two other Kitan words which offer interesting material
    for comparison with mongol: 口丁 p'o 'time', cf. mong. *hon $<$
    **ɸon 'year', and 渾脱 hun-t'o 'sack', cf. mong. *huquta
    'sack' (cf. Pelliot, JA, 1925, 218-9, 226, for the mongol
    forms).

[Sino-Altaica II.4 - not seen]

HTHYFC 8 (February 1935)

Sino-Altaica II

II.5. Ting-ling and Turks
(To the memory of W. W. Bartold)

In his Die historische Bedeutung der Alttürkischen Inschriften
(cf. esp. p. 9) as well as in his review of Chavannes' Documents
sur les Tou kiue..., ЗВОИРАО.XV, pp. 171-173, the late Russian
orientalist raised strong objections to the identification of the
T'ieh-lê 鐵勒 of the Chinese sources with the Tölis |Y N η of the
Orkhon inscriptions. His doubts as to the validity of this identification have been shared by other Russian scholars (Melioranski,
Aristov, G. Grum-Grzhimailo), but among the rest of European orientalists the supposed equation has received wide credence. The more
we advance, however, in the interpretation of Chinese documents
relating to the history of Central Asia, the more untenable becomes
this equation both linguistically and historically. In the light
of the consistent accuracy of the Chinese transcriptions of foreign
words, the theory that T'ieh-lê (KD 991, 523: t'iet-lək) stands for
Tölis and (another fatal hypothesis) that Yen-t'o 延陀 (KD 235,
1011: $_c$iän < d-; $_c$d'â) represents tk. Tarduš ϒϞβϞϠ is entirely
unacceptable.

It appears clear from the Orkhon inscriptions that the terms
Tölis and Tarduš are used primarily as designations of political and
geographical divisions in the great Turkish confederacy, and not as
ethnic or tribal appellations. This fact was completely disregarded
by Western investigators, especially on the Chinese side of the
problem, and the resulting confusion is well summarized in Bartold's
conclusion of his criticism of F. Hirth's identification of the Hsieh
Yen-t'o with the Syr Tarduš:

> "...we are thus [i.e., if we accept this more than doubtful
> identification -- P.B.] forced to come to the following
> conclusion: originally the Syr Tarduš formed a part of the
> Tölis, who were distinguished by the Chinese from the Turks--
> T'u-chüeh; they then entered into the T'u-chüeh confederacy
> under the name of Tarduš and formed in it a western division

to be distinguished from the T̄ōlis, the eastern division. We leave the reader to judge for himself the probability of such a state of affairs." [Translated from the Russian of ЗВОИРАО, XV, pp. 172-3.]

The T'ieh-lê under the name ch'ih-lê 敕 (KD 909: t'i̯ə̯k) 勒 were known to the Chinese long before the formation of the T'u-chüeh confederacy and were always considered by the Chinese historians as a group belonging to the old Kao-chü federation. J 103 and O 98 (history of the Kao-chü) state that the original name of the confederacy was Ti-li 狄歷 (KD 117, 537: d'iek; liek) and J 103 adds (the O 98 text is undoubtedly corrupt): 北方以為敕勒諸夏以為高車丁零 which can only mean: "in the North they are termed Ch'ih-lê and by the Chinese Kao-chü ['High Cart'] Ting-ling". (Hyacinth's: "...уже на съвкрѣ прозваны гаогюйскими динлинами." Собрание овѣлѣний, I:2, p. 248, is based on the defective O 98 text.) It is clear that the Chinese considered the binoms: Ting-ling, Ti-li, Ch'ih-lê, and T'ieh-lê as the transcription of one and the same foreign word used as a designation of a political organization in the northern part of the steppe belt, and registered, faithfully as usual, the various changes the word underwent through the centuries (cf. Parker, Thousand Years..., pp. 123, 195, 196; Parker's fanciful etymologies are, of course, to be disregarded).

The literature concerning the Ting-ling, who appear in the Chinese sources as early as the pre-Christian era, is already considerable, especially in Russian, and the author hopes to be able to present in the future a review of the theories offered by scholars in attempts to solve this puzzling problem. Here he would like to emphasize one unmistakable point that stands out in the historical and linguistic evidence which can be gathered from the seemingly conflicting Chinese statements concerning this group of nomads. It appears evident from the Chinese sources that the most notable characteristic of the Ting-ling and their successors was the use of carts. It would seem, therefore, that underlying the various transcriptions from Ting-ling (KD 999, 558: ‿tieng-‿lieng) to T'ieh-lê (*tiel-lək) is a 'turco-mongol' or 'altaic' term meaning 'cart'. It is possible that such a term is the ancestor of mongol tenggelig

'cart axle' and turkish   تاليقه (> russ. telega, > magy. talyiga
'cart'), later supplanted by qanglï and araba. The term 'cart' may
have been used as a designation of all tribes distributed along the
northern trans-asiatic route which were competing as trade-carriers
with the peoples of the central mongolian pack-animal route.

The T'ieh-lê must thus be finally divorced from the Tölis.
Where are we to find, then, the Chinese transcriptions of the all
important names Tölis and Tarduš? As has been repeatedly suggested
by the Russian orientalists and finally effectively stated by Professor I. A. Kliukin in his "New Data concerning the Tardushi..."
(in Russian), Bull. of the Far Eastern Branch of the Academy of
Sciences, 1932, in the Chinese designations of the major divisions
of the Turks: The Western (西) T'u-chüeh and the Eastern or Northern (北) T'u-chüeh, and in the Chinese transcriptions of the names
of qaɣan Ta-t'ou (Ταρδου) and qaɣan T'u-li.

Kliukin's argument is unfortunately weakened by his untenable
hypotheses on the Chinese renderings of the turkish names isbara and
yamtar.

As to the turkish etymology of tölis and tarduš, it should be
sought, in my opinion, not so much in geographical terms or appellations of khans as in some such roots as 'original, parent' (for the
Tölis group) and 'branching, emigrant' (for the Tarduš group). Cf.
possibly uig. töl- 'Nachkommenschaft' and tart- 'ziehen', tardïl-
'herausgezogen werden.'

II.6. Some 'turco-mongol' words in geographical names
of the 9th century

In his note on 'Un mot mongol sous les T'ang' (TP, 1928-29,
pp. 250-252) Professor Pelliot has called attention to the fact that
the Yüan-ho chün hsien t'u-chih, the well-known geographical work of
the 9th century, contains several names of places in Northern and
Western China which are given in their local designations side by
side with the Chinese names, and has identified in one of those
designations the mongol word ɣucin 'thirty'.

The following five 'barbarian' names of northwestern localities

given in the YHCHTC, the K'uo ti chih, and the TPHYC seem to me also
to yield good 'turco-mongol' equivalents.

1. YHCHTC III, 4b (ed. T'ai-nan ko ts'ung shu) K'o-lan 可藍
(KD 414, 376: ᶜk'â-ᴄlâm) hill, also called Tu-lu 都盧 hill (KD 1187,
579: ᴄtuo-ᴄluo). Although no Chinese equivalent is given it would be
safe to suppose that the two 'barbarian' names are synonymic and the
original names underlying the Chinese transcriptions, *qalam and
*turu go back to tk. qal- 'to remain' and tur- 'to stay, to remain.'

2. Ibid. III, 5a: Chi-t'ou hill 笄頭, also called Po
(or Pu)-lo 薄(簿)洛 (KD 764: b'âk [or ᶜb'uo]; 411: lâk). The
meaning of Chinese chi-t'ou is 'coiffure, headdress' and the foreign
word underlying po-lo must have been *baklak ~ *boklak or *bokdak,
l- often serving in this period to transcribe turkish d-. It is
possible that we have here the famous word bogtak which according to
Mohammedan and Christian medieval sources designated the peculiar
headdress of mongolian women.

3. Ibid. III, 16b: K'u-li 庫利 (KD 431, 527: k'uoᵔ-ljiᵔ)
river. K'u-li, says the Chinese text, meant 'slave' 奴 in the
language of the Chi Hu 稽胡. The transcription represents obviously
tk. qul 'slave'.

4. Ibid. IV, 11b (TPHYC 38, 5b): Ch'i-yin 乞銀 (KD 332,
312: k'i̯ət-ngi̯ĕn) valley, ch'i-yin meaning in Chinese 驄馬 'piebald or dapple horse'. Possible mong. ﻌﻌﻌ (AⱣM, 149)
'dapple bay'.

5. K'uo ti chih III., 3b: Po-ku-lü 薄骨律 (KD 764, 427,
1321: b'âk [or ᶜb'uo]-kuət-li̯u̯ĕt), the barbarian name of 靈州
Ling (= 'magical')-chou. Most probably *bögü-uluš 'magic land'.

II.7. Mount Tamga

In the description of the kingdom of Kao-ch'en 高昌 in the
Sui Shu (M 83, cf. O 97) we find the following passage;

北有赤石山　山北七十里有貪汗山
夏有積雪此山之北鐵勒界也

"North (of Kao ch'ang) is situated the Ch'ih shih ['Red
Stone'] mountain. 70 li north of that mountain is Mount
T'an-han on which [even] in the summer there is accumulated snow. North of the mountain is the frontier of
the T'ieh-lê."

This mountain is without any doubt to be identified with the
Boghdo-ula massif, the most conspicuous mountain covered with eternal
snow in the region north of Turfan.

The Chinese transcription T'an-han 貪汗 represents an ancient
*Tamɣan (KD 386, 296: ₜt'âm-ɣân⁾ < g'-) which must stand for the
'turkish' word tamɣa 'seal, stamp, brand', a word already attested in
the Orkhon inscriptions. The Sui Shu text indirectly confirms this
derivation and suggests, in my belief, an explanation for this
curious name.

Although the word tamɣa occurs in ancient turkish chiefly in
the meanings of 'seal', 'cattle brand', it must undoubtedly have early
acquired the meaning of 'customs-stamp, duty' as evidenced by its
use among the Mongols, from whom it was borrowed by the Russians in
the form tamɣa > tamožnya 'customs, customshouse' (cf. bulg. damga
'stamp').

The T'ieh-lê frontier was immediately north of Mount T'an-han
and the latter must have been an important frontier landmark. If
the identification of the mountain with the Boghdo-ula be accepted,
the foot of T'an-han must be considered as an ideal site for a customshouse blocking the passes to the south. We know from M 83 that Kao-
ch'ang was at this time subject to the T'ieh-lê, who maintained in
Kao-ch'ang toll-gatherers who "levied customs-duties on all the
trading Hu passing in either direction [through Kao-ch'ang] and sent
[the revenue] to the T'ieh-lê..." The merchants crossing from or into
the territory of Kao-ch'ang would undoubtedly pay the toll either at
Ku-ch'êng or at Urumchi, and one can thus well understand how the
Boghdo ula, rising majestically to the south of those cities, would
acquire in this period the "sinister" name of "Customs Mountain."

The name T'an-han appears twice more in the Chinese sources:
once as the name of a turkish khan, T'an-han qaɣan, a vassal of

Sha-po-lüeh, deposed by the latter about 583 (M 84), and as the name
of a mountain which became the residence of Ch'i-pi Ko-ling, khan of
the T'ieh-lê (ibid., cf. Chavannes, Documents..., p. 95). In both
cases T'an-han must, I believe, be identified with *Tamɣan. *Tamɣan
qaɣan may well have derived his name from his office of custumarius
and it appears from the story of his conflict with Sha-po-lüeh that
his residence was somewhere in the Eastern T'ien Shan. The identification of the T'an-han mountain of M 84 with the T'an-han mountain
north of Kao-ch'ang and with the Boghdo ula presents no difficulties.

One is also tempted to identify with Mount *Tamɣan, Boghdo ula,
the Tamaɣ ïduq ↓ⵣ ⵏ ⵟ ⵉ ⵢ ⵣ   (which can also be read *Tamɣa ïduq)
of Bilgä qaɣan's inscription (29, 10). There is nothing that would
make it impossible for Bilgä's battle with the Qarluq to have taken
place in the vicinity of Beš balyq.

II.8. The Language of the T'o-pa

The histories of the Southern Chinese dynasties, notably the
Sung Shu (F 95) and the Nan Ch'i Shu (G 57), have preserved a considerable list of T'o-pa words, titles, and names in polysyllabic
transcriptions which apparently faithfully reproduced the T'o-pa
Hsien-pei originals. In the Wei Shu these terms are either translated into Chinese or so disfigured by condensation into genteel
Chinese monosyllables that it is often an arduous task to identify
by means of those names even well-known historical actors who are
mentioned in both sets of sources.

In the list of T'o-pa generals who appear in the letter of
T'o-pa Hung to a Sung transfuge (F 95) most of the names can be
identified and their corresponding 'sinicized' forms are found in
the Wei Shu. Among these generals is mentioned the T'o-pa t'ai-wei
Chih-chin Chia-t'ou-pa-yü-chih 直勤賀頭拔羽真, who is
without any doubt to be identified with Yüan Ho 源賀 who was
appointed t'ai-wei in 466, 3 (J 6).

The biography of this prominent individual (J 41, 16 Kg. 90)
yields us all the necessary clues for the identification of his name

in its barbarian form. Yüan Ho was the son of T'u-fa Jou-t'an 傉檀 and had sought refuge with the Wei after the destruction of 秃髮 his father's kingdom. Acknowledging the original relationship (源) which united the T'o-pa and the T'u-fa, T'o-pa T'ao conferred upon him the surname 源, Yüan. This was apparently tantamount to accepting the fugitive prince as a member of the Imperial Clan and explains the title chih-chin (≃ tk. čigin 'prince of the blood') which F 95 gives him.

The prince's original personal name was P'o Ch'iang 破羌 (≃ 'smiting the Ch'iang') and Ho 賀 , the name under which he is known in history, was given him by the T'o-pa for his distinguished service in campaigns against Kan-su barbarians. "Having chosen a personal name," said T'o-pa T'ao, "a man must strive to realize its meaning [in his deeds]. How can yours be improved upon?" Whereupon T'ao conferred upon him the name Ho.

In the light of the evidence supplied by F 95, it is clear that Ho, the name given in J 41, is only a sinicized monosyllabic abbreviation of Chia-t'ou-pa-yü-chih (駕 chia and 賀 ho being interchangeable characters), which must have been the T'o-pa name conferred upon the hero by the Emperor.

Chia-(Ho-)t'ou-pa-yü-chih would represent in the pronunciation of c. 500 A.D.:

駕 KD 342   ka² or γa²〈g'-
頭 KD 1015 ₒd'əu
拔 KD 750   b'ᵂat
羽 KD 1320 ᶜjįu〈g-
直 KD 1220 d'įək〈d'-

With γ- representing the turkish 'aleph' which the Chinese heard in vocalic anlaut, Chinese d' = tk. t, and final Chinese -t (δ) = tk. r or l, we get:

*atu bälgü täg — tk. at 'Name, Ruf,' bälgü 'Zeichen, Attribut', täg 'wie, gleichwie',

a phrase in perfect turkish 'a name as well as an omen', a phrase the meaning of which tallies perfectly with the above story of the circumstances under which Yüan Ho got his new name.

Added to the evidence collected chiefly through the efforts of
Professor Pelliot, this turkish phrase in the mouth of a T'o-pa
emperor should, I believe, definitely tip the scales in favor of a
turkish origin of the T'o-pa, and may, I hope, serve to destroy once
and for all the myth of their tungusic affinities.

II.9. An Early Example of the Use of the Animal Cycle among 'Turco-Mongols'

In a note on "Le plus ancien exemple du cycle des douze animaux
chez les Turcs' (TP, 1928-29, 204-212), Professor Pelliot has established that the earliest example of the use of the Animal Cycle
among the Turks is to be found in the letter of Sha-po-lüeh qaγan
to the Sui Emperor, where the year 584 (K'ai-huang IV, chia ch'ên
甲辰 , 41st of the cycle of 60) is designated in the preamble to
the letter by the character 辰 of the duodenary cycle which
corresponds to the Dragon in the Animal Cycle.

We possess, however, an even earlier instance of the use of
the Animal Cycle in a 'turco-mongol' environment, with even more
specific designation of the year by animal terms (and not by the
corresponding Chinese cyclical characters). This is to be found in
L 11 and 0 57, in the letter of the mother of Yü-wên Hu 宇文護 ,
nephew of Yü-wên T'ai, to her son, where, in the story of the early
hardships suffered by the family of Yü-wên Hao 顥 , we find the
following passage:

> ...Formerly, [at the time when we were] residing at
> Wu-ch'uan chên 武川鎮 I gave birth to you [and your
> two] brothers: the eldest [being born in the year]
> pertaining to the rat, the next [in the year] pertaining
> to the hare, and you [in the year] pertaining to the
> serpent.

The biographies of Yü-wên Hu (L 11) and his elder brother
Shih-fei 什肥 (L 10) state that the latter was 16, and the former
11 years of age when their father Hao was killed in battle. As
Hao's death must undoubtedly have occurred in 524, the two sons were

born in 513–514 and 508–509 respectively. The year 508 was a <u>wu-tzŭ</u>
戊子 (25th) year of the Chinese sexagenary cycle corresponding
to a rat year in the Animal Cycle, while 513 was a <u>kuei-ssŭ</u> 癸巳
(30th) year corresponding to the serpent. Yü-wên Tao 導, the
second son, coming between Shih-fei and Hu, must have been born in
511 (辛卯 <u>hsin-mao</u>, 28th), a hare year.

The above seems to indicate that the Animal Cycle must have
been in use not only among the Yü-wên, but also among the T'o-pa
Wei, who were in control of Northern China until the middle of the
sixth century.

II.10. Ötükän Revisited

<u>Ötüken,</u> the name of the Waldgebirge which was the holy land of
the Orkhon Turks and the residence of their khan, appears in Chinese
transcription under the following forms (cf. P. Pelliot's note in
<u>TP</u>, 1928–29, p. 213):

1. 烏德鞬 KD 1288, 981, 373: ͨ·uo-tək-ki̯ən
2. 於都斤 KD 1323, 1187, 385: ͨiᵂo-ͨtuo-ͨkiǝn
3. 鬱督軍 KD 555, 908, 508: ·iuət-tuok-ͨkiuǝn
4. 乞督軍 for 乞 Pelliot suggests reading 紇 *ɣuət,
   but one would rather think that the original character
   was 乙 ·iět, which is often interchanged with 乞 .

After Pelliot's and Vladimirtsov's (<u>DRAN</u>, 1929, pp. 133–136)
studies, there is no doubt that the name Ötükän must be connected
with mong. <u>ötügen</u> ~ <u>etügen</u> 'Mother Earth'. The etymology of the
turkish word still remains obscure. The following suggestions have
been made (see Pelliot, <u>op. cit.</u>, pp. 217–218):

1. <u>ötü</u> 'choisir, élire'⟩ 'geliebte' (Radloff)
2. <u>ütkin</u> 'tranchant' (V. Thomsen)
3. <u>ötü</u> + (<u>qan</u> ⟩ <u>ken</u>) 'Durchgangsgebirge' (W. Bang)

To these must be added Vladimirtsov's tentative mongol etymology:

4. mong. <u>ötügen</u> < <u>ötüg</u> 'humus'< √*<u>ötü</u> (<u>op. cit.</u> p. 134).

In the light of the testimony of the Chinese sources which
link Mount Ötükän with another important turkish place of worship,

the T'a-jên (or T'a-min, cf. <u>HTHYFC</u> 1:28; 5:17-18) river, I would
suggest that the etymology of the names of both places be sought in
an epithet describing their function as national shrines. Indeed, if
we accept the emendation <u>min</u> 民 for <u>jên</u> 人 and read the tk. name of
the river *Tapïn or *Tabïn ('river of) worship', a synonym suggests
itself to explain on the same basis the etymology of Ötüken. We
find in uïghur the root *ötü- from which are derived <u>ötün</u> 'erbitten,
ehrerbietig tun, darbringen', and <u>ötük</u> 'Bitte, Wunsch'.

   None of these words have been attested so far for Orkhon
turkish. It seems to me, however, that the last word, <u>ötük</u> (observe
a variant <u>itüg</u>, <u>SBAW</u>, 1931, I, 480) occurs in an obscure passage of
Bilgë Khan's inscription (X, 39; Radloff, p. 67):

            ylbčï dgü sbï ötgi klmz.

   At first translating the puzzling <u>ötgi</u> ⌐ᘓᚼ⋈ by 'von dort'
(ötägi), Radloff finally interpreted it as a derivative of <u>öt-</u>
'bezahlen' (?) and translated the whole passage: 'von ihnen kommt
nicht ihr Gesandter, ihre gute Nachricht und ihre Bezahlung...'
(p. 213). It would make much better sense to read <u>ötüg</u> ~ <u>ötük</u> 'Bitte'
(+ the possessive <u>-i</u>), especially since the combination <u>ötüg saw</u> is
well attested.

   Mount Ötüken may thus have meant 'mountain of prayer', a designation parallel to that of the sacred 'river of worship.'

   If we accept this etymology of Ötüken, we should not be surprised
if the same word were found in still earlier 'turco-mongol' material,
such as proper names of Hsien-pei (one should hardly expect a shaman-
istic believer to dare assume the holy name of 'Mother Earth', if
such was the meaning of Ötüken from the earliest time). It is thus
quite possible that <u>ötüken</u> underlies the Chinese transcriptions of
the following Hsien-pei names:

1. 樹竹犍 (KD 1249: ·iuᵊt-t̯iuk-kiɐn) D 30, III c. A.D.

2. 郁豆眷 (KD 251, 1015, 495: ·iuk-ᶜd'əu-ki^{W}än) F 23;
   G 25 (s.a. 480) name of T'o-pa Chia 嘉 , J 18.

3. 郁都甄 (*·iuk-tuo-kien) T'o-pa surname, J 113.

HTHYFC 9 (May 1935)

Sino-Altaica III

III. 1. Avars and Kermikhiōns

In Sino-Altaics II.1, "Some Hsiung-nu Names", attention was
called to a 'turco-mongol' word which underlies the following
Chinese transcription of a barbarian name common in the nomadic
onomasticon of the third to sixth centuries:

1. T'o-pa: 什翼犍 KD 876, 199, 373: $\acute{z}\underset{\frown}{i}$əp-i͜ək-ki͜ɐn (J1)
2. 拾賁 KD 71, 709: $\acute{z}\underset{\frown}{i}$əp-puən (F 77)
3. T'u-yü-hun: 拾寅 KD 71, 283: $\acute{z}\underset{\frown}{i}$əp-$_{c}$i͜ĕn
4. 葉延 KD 225, 235: (d)iɐp-$_{c}$i͜än (J 101)
5. Ch'i-fu: 什寅 KD 876, 283: $\acute{z}\underset{\frown}{i}$əp-$_{c}$i͜ĕn (J 99)

To these I would now add:

6. T'o-pa:(于)什門 KD 876, 609: $\acute{z}\underset{\frown}{i}$əp-muən (J 87)
7. T'u-fa: 思復犍 KD 813, 54, 373: $_{c}$si-b'i͜uk-ki͜ɐn (16 Kg 86)
8. Yü-wên: 涉亦干 KD 759, 187, 296: $\acute{z}\underset{\frown}{i}$ɐp-i͜ɐk-$_{c}$kân (16 Kg 24)
9. T'o-pa:(陸)什寅 $\acute{z}\underset{\frown}{i}$əp-$_{c}$i͜ĕn (J 30)
10. Wu-huan: 蘇僕延 KD 823, 760, 235: $_{c}$suo-b'uok-$_{c}$i͜än (Đ 30)
11. Ta-hsi: (建美):什伏代 KD 876, 46, 960: $\acute{z}\underset{\frown}{i}$əp-b'i͜uk-d'âi (L 29)

and possibly

12. Hsien-pei: 沙莫干 and 沙末干 $_{c}$sa-mâk-$_{c}$kân and $_{c}$sa-muât-$_{c}$kân (cf. Sino-Altaica I.6)

All these forms undoubtedly transcribe the 'turco-mongol'
word *šipkin ~ *yipkin ~ *yipün 'red, crimson, purple' found in
different dialects in the following transcriptions:

Uigur: yipin, yipün, yipkin, yäbkin, yupün, yübün, šipkin
(Bang, SPAW, 1931:1, pp.333-4, 500, 514)

Kumanian: ipchin 'violetus' (Radloff, 18)

Early mongol: *ǰibiyin < *ǰibi'in, ǰibigin (see P. Pelliot,
JA, 1930, 249-50, for discussion of these forms).

Turkish of Ibn-Muhannā: ایپکن (cf. Pelliot, op. cit.) and

یبون (3KB.III, 234) 'mauve' which S. Malov un-

justifiably changes into   ببون bibün (?)

The first nine Chinese transcriptions are absolutely regular
and faithful renderings of the 'turco-mongol' word in its three
essential forms *ǰibigin ~ *šipkin > *šipün, the Chinese initial ź-
representing the initial 'altaic' ǰ- or š- rather than yi-, for which
one usually finds Chinese ńź- (cf. Sino-Altaica I.3; II.1).

The *yipün form of the turkish word for 'crimson' can, however,
be found under another Chinese disguise. The 'altaic' color-term
underlies, I believe, the Chinese transcription of the name which
the Juan-juan (Avars) chose for themselves at the time of the
formation of their confederacy, i.e., Jou-jan:

柔然 KD 942 ˏńźi̯ au< ń- ; KD 929 ˏźńi̯än< ń-
with ńź- transcribing y- and the final of ńźi̯əu representing a -w-
or -β-. we get **yiβyän ~**yipyän, which could possibly represent
the Avar pronunciation of the common 'altaic' *šipün ~ *yipin.

The transcription is, however, slightly irregular and we
possess, moreover, no direct testimony from Chinese or Western
sources that the name of the Avars was in any way associated with
the terms 'red', 'purple', or 'crimson'.

Indirect evidence is, however, available. The name ῎Αβαρεις
was in some way connected by John of Ephesus with the way the Avars
dressed their hair (Marquart, Streifzüge, 43), while the chiefs of
the Yü-chüeh-lü who possibly represented the last remnants of the
Juan-juan confederacy wore, according to the Chinese traveller Hu
Ch'iao, purple bags over their hair (cf. Chavannes, JA, 1897, 406,
and Sino-Altaica I.1).

Marquart has also successfully shown that the term Kermikhions
(Κερμιχίων-,῾Ερμηχιόν-), which, according to the Byzantine historians, was a Persian designation of the Turks, is a compound of
pers. kerm 'worm' and the ethnic appellation Hyaonas. Accepting
Marquart's explanation, Chavannes (Documents... 232) has proposed
to see in the Kermikhions the Avars or Pseudo-Avars, and has evoked
in this connection the well-known story of J 103 that their original

name Jou-jan was changed by T'o-pa T'ao to Juan-juan 蠕蠕 KD 946
ᶜńźi̯ᵂⁱⁱan-ńźi̯ᵂⁱⁱan 'wriggling like <u>worms</u>' (cf. Pelliot, <u>JA</u>, 1920, 144
for the Southern Chinese forms).

The term <u>kerm</u> (Ssk. <u>kṛmi</u>) has, however, interesting semantic
connotations. It was apparently early applied to the designation of
the <u>coccus ilicis</u> and its product, crimson dye. In some ancient
indo-european form (Ssk. <u>kṛmijā</u>, soghd. <u>karm'īr</u>, arm. <u>karmir</u>) it
passed as a color-term into Hebrew כַּרְמִיל 'crimson' (II Chron..
2.6, etc.) and through the medium of persian and ar. [قرمز]
into all European languages (fr. <u>cramoisi</u> > eng. <u>crimson</u>). For the
same semantic development, cf. lat. <u>vermiculus</u> > fr. <u>vermeil</u>; russ.
črъvь > črъminъ 'crimson' (cf. Marquart, <u>UJ</u>, IX, 91-94).

Now, in his observations on the history of the term, Marquart
(<u>op. cit.</u>) quotes a middle persian text where the word <u>kalmīr</u> is
applied as an epithet to the hosts of the Turks (...Turk i̯ kalmīr
'die Türk, die roten...'). Although not noted down by Marquart,
the connection of this designation with the appellation Kermikhions
seems obvious. The persian sources appear thus definitely to
associate the invading nomads with a term designating a red or
crimson color.

If the designation <u>Kermikhions</u> was understood in the Near East
to mean <u>Crimson</u> Khions as well as <u>Worm</u> Khions (<u>kerm</u> ~ <u>kermez</u>) we
would have here a clue to the otherwise obscure renaming of the
Jou-jan by T'o-pa T'ao. The turbulent Jou-jan (< *Yipin 'Crimson
[ones]') appear in the light of the preceding to be nicknamed the
'Wriggling Ones' (Juan-juan) by a pun of the T'o-pa sovereign
("The Jou-jan [Vermillion Ones] are <u>juan-juan</u> [vermiculating]").

> Observe that associations of 'insects' (虫) with 'red'
> are not unknown to the Chinese: 蜎 蜎 'wriggling
> worms' <u>vs.</u> 縕 'dark red', 緟 'orange red'; 燸
> (same phonetic as in <u>juan-juan</u>) 'fiery color'; 赨 = 彤
> 'red'.

Finally, one is tempted to connect the original name of the
Avars (<u>yipin</u> ~ <u>yipün</u>) with the rather obscure <u>župen</u> ~ <u>yopan</u>, the
designation of the <u>chiefs</u> of the (Pseudo-) Avars who ruled over the

Slav communities of Europe (cf. Peisker, in <u>Cambridge Medieval History</u>, II, pp. 443 ff.).

III.2. "Une génération de gens qui s'appellent Argon..."

In its description of T'o-pa Hung's campaign against the Juan-juan, G 59 mentions a certain Chia-lu-hun, 駕鹿渾, prince of P'ing-yüan 平元, who was in command of the T'o-pa army. The same individual appears in G 57 as Fu-lu-ku Ho-lu-hun 伏鹿孤 賀鹿渾, duke of Chü-lu 鉅鹿 and governor of Hêng 恒 chou, and is stated to have been one of the leaders of the 496 rebellion against T'o-pa Hung.

According to J 113, the T'o-pa surname Fu-lu-ku was later abbreviated into Lu 陸. The T'o-pa official described by G 57 and G 59 is thus unquestionably to be identified with Lu Jui 陸叡, son of Lu Li 麗, who, according to his biography in J 40:

1. commanded the T'o-pa army sent against the Juan-juan in 492,

2. bore from 466 to 492 the title prince of P'ing-yüan 平原, and from 492 to his death that of duke of Chü-lu,

3. perished in the conspiracy of 496 together with Mu T'ai 穆泰 (who had just succeeded him as governor of Hêng-chou) and other high officials (J 27).

It is noteworthy that Lu Jui succeeded his father Li in the title of Prince of P'ing-yüan when he was a little over ten years of age, probably in 466, immediately after the execution of I-hun 乙渾, at whose hands Li had perished in 465. Jui's mother was a former concubine of T'o-pa Huang and was undoubtedly given in marriage to Li as a reward for the important role he played in the counter-revolution of 453 which placed T'o-pa Hsün on the throne. If Jui, who was 11-13 years of age (十餘歲) in 466, had been born about 453, it might be possible that there existed some doubt as to which of the two husbands of the Lady Chang 張 was his real father.

The high position occupied by Lu Jui at the court suggests, in fact, that he was a bâtard prince.

The mystery of his origin or, à la rigueur, the fact that he was born of the union of one not of royal blood with a 'lady of the palace', may, indeed, offer an explanation of Lu Jui's 'barbarian' name. Ho (or Chia, cf. Sino-Altaica II.8)-lu-hun (KD 342, 576, 508) gives us an original *Aluɣun or *Aruɣun. In the light of the foregoing observations, it would not be unreasonable to suppose that in *arɣun we have the earliest transcription of the 'turco-mongol' term for 'métis, bastard' which appears in Marco Polo as a designation of some half-breeds (cf. Pauthier, I.214-217; Yule-Cordier, I.290-292; P. Pelliot, JA, 1927[2], 265n).

The same word may underlie the following T'o-pa/Chinese transcriptions:

長孫渴侯 Chang-sun Ho-hou (< *Arɣu), another prominent actor in the events of 453,

劉渴侯 Liu Ho-hou, J 87,

庵渾海 the Lu-hun (< *(A)ruɣun) lake, J 103,

渴渾川 the Ho-hun (< *Arɣun) river, 16 Kg 86, and possibly the name of I-hun 乙渾 himself. This personage who exercized great influence at the T'o-pa court and was undoubtedly closely connected with the Imperial family is strangely ignored by the Wei Shu. There is evidence, on the other hand, that the series of coups d'état following the death of T'o-pa T'ao were occasioned by the struggle for power among the illegitimate sons and grandsons of that sovereign.

The term *arɣun re-appears, in my belief, a century later in the cognomen of the famous Kao Huan 高歡 founder of the fortunes of the Northern Ch'i house. His tzǔ (字), according to K 1, was Ho-liu-hun 賀六渾, another regular transcription of *Arɣun. His bearing the cognomen 'métis' is, I believe, explained by the fact that, although a Chinese by blood, he was raised on the frontier among Hsien-pei and his family undoubtedly belonged to that generation of cultural 'métis' which inhabited the fringe of the mongol steppes (cf. K 1: 神武既累世北邊故君其俗遂同鮮卑.

Indeed, the 'melting pot' of Central Asia, especially in the marginal lands adjacent to China, must have produced, since the dawn of history, whole generations of such "gens qui s'appellent Argon", and one wonders if we should not find the same term *aryun underlying the names of two such marginal peoples, one known to us from the Chinese sources, the other, from Western ones. From the description of the Wu-huan 烏桓 in D 30 (their great reverence for their mothers, their ethnic instability and cultural susceptibility) one might indeed infer that they were "Argons". The Οδαρχωνίται (pseudo-Avars) of Theophylactus Simocatta were also a tribe of mixed origin and were, therefore, in the language of the Steppes, *Aryun.

III.3. Some Early 'Turco-Mongol' Toponyms

1. The TPHYC 152 in its description of the Fan-ho 番和 hsien region in Liang chou mentions a river named T'u-mi-kan, the valley of which was a favorite pasture-land of Hsiung-nu hordes. T'u-mi-kan 土 (or 吐) 彌干 (KD 1129: ᶜt'uo, t'uoᵓ; 13: ᶜmjịa; 294: ᶜkân), adds the text, means 'bone marrow' in Hsien-pei which name was given to the river for the richness of the soil in its vicinity:
鮮卑語骨髓為吐彌干言此川土肥美如髓遺故以名之.
The Hsien-pei term is undoubtedly the ancestor of mong. čimügen— 'bone marrow'. The vocalization of the word as it can be reconstructed from the Chinese transcription presents, however, certain difficulties, for t'u-mi-kan would pre-suppose an original Hsp. *tümiken or *tumiqan.

One might consider, of course, 吐 t'u as a corruption of 叱 ch'ih (KD 1055: ts'ịet, with the final -t quiescent as in *činua 叱奴, cf. HTHYFC 1: 17; 5: 13-15: Yüan-ch'ao pi-shih I, la 赤那. This would yield us a form *čimigen.

One must keep in mind, on the other hand, that the mong. written i in the complex ji-, či- is only an orthographic peculiarity in such cases when the evidence of the dialects points to the existence of another archaic vowel. E.g., mong. jirüken 'heart', but kh. ʒwrw̆X̌, ord. DžureᵏX̌e, bargu-bur. zwrX̌ě, tk. yürak

وراك . The dialectical forms of čimügen (kh. č'v̌mv̌G, ord.
ts'ömögö, bargu-bur. sümüG) also indicate the presence of ü or ö
in the first syllable.

      The antiquity of these vocalic variations due to
Brechnung may possibly be attested by some Chinese
transcriptions of Hsien-pei names, e.g., Chiu-liu chüan
就六眷 (KD 252: dz'i̯əu; 563: li̯uk; 495: ki̯^{w}än⁾) vs.
Chi-lu-chüan 疾陸眷 (KD 1049: dz'i̯et; 573: li̯uk),
name of a Tuan Hsien-pei chief, J.103, O 98. Possibly –
*jürüken ~ *jirüken.

    Mong. čimügen has always been, tentatively, equated with tk.
sünggük 'bone, knuckle'. We should, therefore, consider our
*tümigen (or *tümägen) as a 'proto-mongol' form. I would hesitate,
however, to dismiss entirely the possibility that we have here a
common 'turco-mongol' or early turkish form.

    2. K 17 (biography of Hu-lü Chin 斛律金) and K 27 (bio-
graphy of K'o-chu-hun Yüan 可朱渾元) yield us two toponyms
which might be traced back to mongol originals. These are Wu-su
tao 烏蘇道 'the Wu-su road' (in Shan-hsi) and the Wu-lan 烏蘭
ford (near Wei 渭 chou). Wu-su (KD 1288, 823: *·uosuo) = mong.
usun < *husu (cf. TP, 1931, p. 118, for confirmation of h- initial
and later Chinese transcription Hu-su 斛速), while Wu-lan (KD 512:
·uolân) = mong. ulaɣan <*hula'an (AФM, هولون , cf. JA , 1925[1],
pp. 223-4). If these equivalences of the Chinese transcription
with mong. toponymic designations be accepted, we should have here
the earliest (6th century) occurrence of pure mongol forms. I have
not been able, however, to identify geographically the *'River'
road and the *'Red' ford.

III.4. Ta-lo-pien Le Gros

    In its enumeration of the ten most important T'u-chüeh titles
the T'ung Tien 197 contains the following passage:

...其勇健者謂之始波羅亦呼為英賀弗肥麤
者謂三大羅大羅便酒器也似角而麤短體貌

似之故以為 號此官特貴惟其子弟為之 ...

"Their brave men [the T'u-chüeh] call shih-po-lo, also
they name them ying-ho-fu. The fat and gross are termed
san-ta-lo. Ta-lo-pien is a wine vessel; it resembles the
chio 角, but is shorter and grosser; [men] are given
this title because the shape of their bodies resembles
it. This office (官!) is especially honorable as it is
assumed only by sons and younger brothers [of the ruler]."

The TPHYC 194 reproduces this passage faithfully but reads 賢
服 hsien-fu for 賀弗 ho-fu. The T'ung Tien text is here considerably garbled and presents some difficulties chiefly due to haplo-
graphy (cf. HTHYFC 5: 11), while in the above title both texts
have erroneous readings for *莫賀咄 = *baɣatur.

The phrase 謂三大羅 大羅 使酒器也 is obviously
haplographically corrupted. 使 pien (KD 732: ₍b'iän) is here without
any doubt the turkish suffix ـمن, ـمان -man, män (= 'similar to,
like', cf. Deny, Grammaire..., ₰ 519, rem. 1, ₰520) as it appears in
our text a few lines below in 珂羅便く珂羅 = *qara 'black' (黑).
In the original text 便 must have followed the first ta-lo, while 三
is unmistakenly a lapsus calami for 之 chih which is syntactically
necessary after 謂. The reconstructed phrase should thus read:
...謂之大羅便大羅酒器也 "[The fat and gross] are termed
Ta-lo-pien [i.e., ta-lo-like]. Ta-lo is a wine vessel."

Indeed, Ta-lo-pien is well known to us as a proper name, that of
A-po 阿波 qaɣan Ta-lo-pien 大羅便 (cf. M 84; Chavannes, Documents...), Sha-po-lüeh's cousin and son of Mu-kan. But what turkish
word does Chin. ta-lo (KD 952: d'ăiˀ, t'ăiˀ; 569: ₍lâ) represent?

One might be tempted to seek in ta-lo the original form of
turco-mongol čara 'drinking cup', attested in early mongol (cf. JA,
1930, 262-3 察剌) and in kitan (*sara 撒剌 U 116, cf. Shiratori,
ИИАН,1902, O 24). The evidence of the turkish dialects where čara
is current speaks, however, against the possibility of tk. *tara >
mong. *čara.

The solution, I believe, lies at the end of another, and more
difficult road. K 15 and O 54, in the biography of Tsu Ting 祖珽,

an official of Northern Ch'i who appears to have been suffering from
kleptomania, relate the story how Tsu Ting at a banquet offered by
Kao Huan to his officers stole a golden <u>p'o-lo</u> 叵羅 by concealing it
under his hat. All Chinese authorities agree in interpreting <u>p'o-lo</u>
(KD 24: ᶜp'uâ-lâ) as 'winecup' 酒巵. This foreign designation of
a drinking vessel appears, I believe, in other Chinese transcriptions,
notably 頗羅, (KD 721: ᶜp'uâ), 破 / (p'uâˀ), and 波 / (KD 753:
ᶜpuâ). (For these, see Chavannes, <u>Documents</u>..., pp. 119n, 139n, 310.)
In all cases it seems to designate some sort of vessel. A similar
word (strongly palatalized 匹裂 *piäliä) occurs in kitan (<u>Ch'i-tan
kuo-chih</u> 24) with the meaning 'wooden pitcher' (cf. <u>JA</u>, <u>loc. cit.</u>,
for wooden čaras).

The <u>po-lo</u> 破羅 mentioned in M 83, O 97 (cf. Chavannes, <u>op.
cit.</u>, 139n) applies to an object which formed part of a golden
statue, one of the chief idols in the kingdom of Ts'ao 曹 in Sui
times. Though undoubtedly a foreign term, <u>po-lo</u> is used in the
description of the statue as a word well familiar to the Chinese
reader of the 7th century and must be identified with other <u>po-lo</u>
mentioned in contemporary sources. We may, therefore, come to the
conclusion that it designated the drinking cup or rhyton which most
of the stone statues found in the 'Scythian' steppe belt are represented as holding, and which, in addition to the short sword hanging
on the thigh, is the most distinguishing feature of those crude
sculptures.

The 'turkish' term designating the stone statue is known to us
from the Orkhon inscriptions in the form <u>blbl</u> ∕S∕S which can be
vocalized (cf. Radloff, I, 234) as <u>balabal</u>, <u>balbal</u>, <u>balabyl</u>, etc.
The term does not seem to be turkish and may have been inherited by
the Orkhon Turks from their predecessors, the Juan-juan. In the
lengthy discussion carried on by P. Melioranski and Th. Korsch concerning the origin of russ. <u>bolvan</u> (болванъ) 'dummy', 'idol'
(Извѣстия Отд. Русск. Яз. Имп. Акад. Наукъ, VII.2 [1902],
274-284; VIII.4 [1903], 2-32; X.2 [1905], 68-81), Melioranski
demonstrated (successfully, in my opinion) its turkish connection
and its relationship to tk. <u>balaban</u> بالابان while Korsch defended

stoutly the derivation of the slavic term from pers. pāhlāwān.

The evolution of the word presents itself to my mind as follows
(I supplement and disagree with Melioranski in some details, while
agreeing with him en gros):

> *balaban = 'large and squat'
> > 1. *balbal 'crude stone figure representing a
> >   squatty man' > bolvan.
> > 2. a thickset, squatty bird>a species of falcon
> > 3. a drum
> > 4. a thickset dummy>a 'Falstaff'>braggart

Now, as to the origin of *balaban ~ *balaman itself, it seems
that, in the light of the Chinese material discussed above, we have
a semantic convergence of two associated ideas, closely linked
through their referential value to 1. a specific object (the stone
figure), and 2. its most significant feature (the drinking vessel).
Indeed, if *bala ~ *pala meant 'drinking vessel', the squatty stone
figure (*balabal) would have acquired its name both from its 'pot-
bellied' appearance and from the fact that it was represented as
holding such a vessel. Thus, while *bala(ban)(-man) may have meant
'bala-like', *balabal may be due to an enlarged and developed double
association of *bal 'squatty figure' + *bala 'vessel', i.e., *balabal
= *bala-bal = the *bal with a *bala?

*Balaman may indeed underlie some Chinese transcriptions of
barbarian names, such as that of P'o-lo-mên 婆羅門, khan of the
Juan-juan (J 103, 0 98; KD 753: ᵢb'uâ; KD 609: ᵢmuᵃn) generally
identified with *Brahman, and that of Yü-wên Pa-pa-ling-ling 拔拔陵陵
(Q 71b; KD 750: b'wat; 560: ᵢliᵃng).

But in what relationship does ta-lo 大羅 'drinking vessel' of
Ta-lo-pien stand with our *bala? We may be faced here with the same
problem that confronts us in the name of the founder of the T'u-chüeh
empire, which is Bumyn 〉ㄆㄒ𝔧 in the Orkhon inscriptions, but is
given in the Chinese sources as T'u-mên 土門, *Tumyn. One might
suppose, on the other hand, that if the original reading in Ta- 大
lo-pien had been P'o- 叵 -lo-pien , the rare character p'o 叵 was
altered by some copyist into ta 大 . Whatever be the explanation,

the connection of ta-lo and ta-lo-pien with p'o-lo and *balaban is
very suggestive and too striking to be easily dismissed.

    As has been observed above, the words *balbal and *bala-
ban are probably vestiges of an earlier, pre-turkish
civilization in Central Asia. The cup and the sword
are mentioned already by Herodotus as being two of the
most important sacred objects of the Scythians, and they
re-appear as such, according to the Chinese sources, among
the Hsiung-nu. One wonders if we should not seek for the
original of the puzzling Hsiung-nu name of their sacred
sword 徑路 <*kinglak? (B 94b) in the Scythian
ἀκινάκης, lat. acinaces, and whether in *bala is
not hidden an Iranian form of φιάλη.

HTHYFC 10 (June 1935)

Sino-Altaica III (continued)

III.5. The Hsien-pei Buckle

According to D 30 the Hsien-pei 鮮卑 derived their name from
the Hsien-pei mountain (situated apparently in the modern province
of Jehol).

The binom hsien-pei appears, however, as early as the period
of the composition of the Elegies of Ch'u. The commentators of
the "Great Summons" agree that hsien-pei in that text means 'girdle-
clasp', and Chang Yen 張晏 (3rd century A.D.) adds: "hsien-pei is
the name of an auspicious animal on the kuo-lo 郭洛 girdle which
the Eastern Hu love to wear." (Cf. Erkes in AM, I, 78.)

Hsien-pei undoubtedly represents the transcription of some
foreign word. It appears already in the form 師比 shih-pi in the
Chan kuo ts'e in connection with the activities of the famous king,
Wu-ling of Chao, celebrated for the introduction of barbarian customs
and dress into his kingdom. In A 110 the same word is written hsü-
pi 胥紕 and designates a golden girdle-clasp. B 94a refers to
the same object as hsi-pi 犀毗. For other variants of the same
term, see P. Pelliot, TP, 1928-29, pp. 141-144.

In most of the Chinese transcriptions of the term we thus find
the first character designating some animal: shih 師 'lion';
hsi 犀 'buffalo' or 'rhinoceros'; hsien 鮮 'venison', 'name of
a fabulous beast in the country of the Northeastern Barbarians'
(cf. 朝鮮, 鮮于 , and 鮮卑 as the name of a people, all of
which are located in the Northeast). The characters hsien-pei, etc.,
represent thus an attempt on the part of the Chinese to transcribe
a foreign word indicating at the same time its significance or the
form of the object referred to.

As shown by Pelliot, the barbarian name of 'the buckle' (which,
as one may infer from the above observations undoubtedly was an
'animal style' buckle, plaque, or hook), as well as that of the
people, can be traced through the Chinese transcriptions back to an

original *Särbi (<u>TP</u>, 1921, 331; <u>TP</u>, 1928–29, 142). The Hsien-pei
must have been known to the Chinese as wearers of 'animal-style'
buckles, or, if the etymology of D 30 is correct, may have derived
their name from a locality known towards the end of the Han as a
center of trade in Siberian 'animal-style' decorations. The 'turco-
mongol' original of both names must be sought, in my opinion, in
mong. <u>serbe</u> ～ 'hook', 'agraffe'.

III.6. The Language of the T'o-pa (II)

Our knowledge of the language of the T'o-pa Hsien-pei is
chiefly derived from the fragmentary material culled from the <u>Wei
Shu</u> (J) and F 95 and G 57. Through the efforts of K. Shiratori and
P. Pelliot, the following equivalences have been established between
Chinese transcriptions and reconstructed T'o-pa titles and words:

1. 可孫 (G 57; K. Sh., ИИАН, 1902, 018) < *qasun ~ *qatun
   'Empress'
2. 比德真 (G 57; K. Sh., <u>op. cit.</u>, 016; P.P., JA, 1925[1],
   254–5) < *<u>bitigčin</u> 'secretary'
3. 可薄真 (ibid.; cf. Sino-Altaica II.1, for variant /博/)
   < *<u>qapayčin</u> 'doorkeeper'
4. 乞萬真 (G 57; K. Sh., 017; P.P., <u>ibid.</u>) < *kälmärčin
   'interpreter'
5. 咸真 (G 57; K. Sh., <u>ibid.</u>; P.P., TP, 1930, 194–5)
   < *<u>yamčin</u> 'postman'
6. 豆盧 (K. Sh., 018) < *törü 'law'

To these may be added the following tentative reconstructions by the
present writer:

7. 庫仁真 (HTHYFC 5:25; Sino-Altaica II.1) < *<u>qoyinčin</u>
   'sheepherder'
8. 曷剌真 (ibid.) < *<u>atlačin</u> 'horseman'
9. 直勤 (HTHYFC 5:14) < *<u>tigin</u> ~ *<u>tägin</u> 'prince of the blood'
10. 賀賾拔羽直 (Sino-Altaica II.8) < *atï bälgü täg
    'nomen atque omen'

(See also <u>HTHYFC</u> 5, <u>passim</u>, for other much less certain equivalences.)

For most of the other T'o-pa words studied by K. Shiratori, restorations proposed by the learned Japanese sinologist are more than doubtful. Thus, T'o-pa *ho-jo* 賀若 'treu und rechtschaffen' is restored by him as *kajiak*, while according to the usual methods of Chinese transcription, we should reconstruct the T'o-pa word as

11. **ayaγ*, most probably from tk. (uig.) *ayaγ* 'Ehre, Verehrung'. The same tk. word must underlie *A-jo* 阿若, name of a Juan-juan chief (J 43); *A-jo-kan* 阿若干, T'u-yü-hun name (*16 Kg*. 85); and T'o-pa Jo-kan *Nei-i-kan* 若干內亦干 (F 95; this T'o-pa general is without any doubt to be identified with Ho-Shun 賀純 mentioned in J 28). The three Chinese transcriptions yield us respectively the forms: **ayaγ*, **ayaγan*, and **(a)yaγan*. The word may be of considerable antiquity as we find in Hsiung-nu the form *jo-t'i* 若鞮, C 119, Chin. 孝 'pious' (< **(a)yaγ-*ti*, apparently a Hsn. suffix).

12. T'o-pa *hu-lo-chên* 胡洛真 < **ɣuraqčin* or **ʾurayčin* (Pelliot, *JA*, 1930, 261) 'title of officer who girded (the ruler?) with the sword' 帶仗. K. Shiratori takes *hu-lo* as the T'o-pa word for 'weapons' and attempts to connect it with tk. *qïlïč* 'sword' and Hsn. **kinglak*. In *hu-lo* we have no doubt the old Hsn. word 郭洛 *kuo-lo* < **q^waraq* (cf. Pelliot, *TP*, 1928-29, 143-4) 'girdle', as the T'o-pa *nomen agentis* must have meant 'he who girds', 'the (royal) girder'.

13. The parallel T'o-pa title of the officer 'who carried aloft the (ruler's) clothes' (擔衣人) given in G 57 as *p'u-ta-chên* 樸大真 (KD 760: p'åk; < **boγdačin*?) has not been studied by Shiratori. In the light of the above etymology of *hu-lo-chên* it would be tempting to identify in *p'u-ta-chên* the officer in charge of one of the most important pieces of 'turco-mongol' apparel, the *boghtaq*, a headdress the wearing of which was in ancient times not exclusively limited to women.

The evolution of the word *boghtaq* demands a special

study. It probably underlies the name of the Mu-jung 慕容 tribe of the Hsien-pei and is to be probably traced to Chinese pu-yao 步搖.

14. T'o-pa chih-chên 直真 'official of the interior' 內左右 has been connected with tk. ič 'interior'. Chinese chih 直 goes back, however, to an ancient *täg, KD 1220 d'i̯ək< d'- (cf. Sino-Altaica II. 8) and the T'o-pa form should be, therefore, reconstructed into *tägčin. In order to under-stand the T'o-pa term one must bring it together with its parallel title, that of the 'officials of the exterior', which was, according to G 57

15. wu-ai-chên, 烏矮真 (KD 1288, 1306: ˛uo-ᶜ·âi) < *'u'ai-čin or *uɣaičin. In a tribal organization like that of the T'o-pa we should expect the terms 'interior' and 'exterior' to be used in the sense of 'agnatus' and 'cog-natus' respectively, and the titles *tägčin and *uɣaičin must in all probability be connected with tk. täg 'Geschlecht' (cf. tägin 'prince of the blood') and tk. uq 'id.' (cf. orkh. uɣuš 'Vasall, Klient[?]').

16. A-chên 阿真 'kitchen' (G 57) undoubtedly connected with tk. ašči 'cook'. Shiratori's equation of T'o-pa 阿付真 fu-chên with *baɣurči is tempting, but before it is accepted, many obscure pages in the history of the latter word will have to be clarified (cf. P. Pelliot, TP, 1930, 26-27).

17. Chê-hui-chên 折潰真 (KD 1185: t́śi̯ät; 456: ɣuâiʾ < g'-) 'official who goes out on behalf of the ruler to receive pleas and accusations' 為主出受辭人 (Shiratori: 'ein Mann welcher um des Herrn willen den Gruss erwidert'). Both interpretations are possible. If mine be accepted, one would be tempted to connect the T'o-pa term with mong. ǰarɣači 'bailiff' or ǰarɣuči 'judge'.

Two other possible mongol (and not turkish, as we have now the right to expect when dealing with T'o-pa material) equivalences present themselves for two remaining T'o-pa titles:

18. 契害真 ch'i-hai-chên < *kitgačin 'executioner'. From
    mong. kituga (АФМ , 146 كتُكا) 'sword'?

19. 拂竹真 fu-chu-chên < *füt(t)ükčin (but cf. Pelliot, JA,
    1925, 255) 'lower officials of the posts'. Cf. mong.
    üdekčin (< üde < *hüde 'to accompany', cf. op. cit. 234)
    'escort'.

The last three correspondences are, however, doubtful.

III.7. Juan-juan Notes

Of the language of the Juan-juan, vestiges of which (chiefly
proper names and titles of rulers) are preserved in J 103 and O 98,
only two words have been identified with surety. These are (K.
Shiratori, ИИАН, 1902, 019) 可汗 k'o-han < *qaɣan, and ch'ih-lien
敕連 < *tägrien 'holy' (cf. tk. tägri ~ tängri 'heaven', 'god').

Although most of the titles of the Juan-juan rulers are translated in the above sources, only very few of them yield to analysis,
and even those that can be equated with corresponding 'altaic' terms
present difficulties, both of phonetic and semantic character. The
following brief notes may, I hope, be found of some interest.

1. 他汗 t'a-han, title of Juan-juan khan, = Ch. 緒 hsü 'to
succeed'. Most probably < mong. daɣa ~ daɣan 'to follow, to succeed'.

2. 受羅部真 shou-lo-pu-chên < *syur/laβučin = Ch. 惠 hui
'favor', chên < čin being (as in T'o-pa) a nomen agentis suffix; the
Juan-juan term meant probably 'one dispensing favors'. *Syuraβu
is undoubtedly to be connected with mong. (and tk.) soyurɣa 'to
favor' (on which see Pelliot, "Le vrai nom de 'Seroctan'," TP,
1932, 52).

3. Ch'iu-tou-fa 丘豆伐, title of the first khan of the Juan-
juan. Fa 伐 occurs often in old Chinese transcriptions of 'altaic'
words and doubtless represents some common suffix. The Chinese
translation of this title 駕馭開張 seems to mean '(he who)
inaugurates and holds the reins (of government)'. *Küdü apparently

must be connected with mong. kǖtül-, kǖdül- 'to set into motion', 'to manage' (cf. kǖtülbüri 'reins').

4. Ai-ku-kai 譪苦蓋 (khan's title) = Chin. 姿質美好 'fine and handsome in appearance'. *Arquqai (cf. KD 73) < mong. arūqan, arūqatai 'good-looking'?

5. Among Juan-juan titles of dignitaries often appears the combination ch'ü-fên 去汾 (KD 491, 29: ᶜk'iᵂoꜛ < -b; ᵇb'iuǝn). E.g.: 去汾比拔; 去汾屋引叱賀真; 莫何去汾李具列; 莫何去汾俟斤丘升頭 (observe 莫何 = *baɣa? and 俟斤 = *erkin? entering into some of the titles). *Kōbun < mong. kōbegün 'son, youth' (cf. Vladimirtsov, DRAN , 1930, 163, for the use of the mong. term as a title).

6. Parallel with the above term we find in Juan-juan the corresponding turkish word oɣlan 'son, prince', in Chinese transcription wu-chü-lan 烏句蘭 < *ogulân (e.g., Wu-chü-lan Shu-shih-fa 樹什伐). The word *oɣul ~ oɣlan may have been known already in Hsiung-nu (cf. HTHYFC 5:21) and possibly underlies also the name Ho-lien 赫連 (KD 76, 551: χɐk-ₗliän) adopted by T'ieh-fu Liu P'o-p'o as a surname for his direct descendants (cf. HTHYFC 3).

In its mongol plural form, *oɣlus, it possibly re-appears in Hu-lü 斛律 (KD 1014, 1321: ₓɣuk-ₗliuět), name of (a) a Juan-juan ruler, (b) a clan among the Kao-chü, and (c) a T'ieh-lê clan.

Curiously enough, in K 4 s.a. 555, *oɣul appears in Chinese transcription as yü-chü-lü 郁久閭 in the Juan-juan name 俟利ⅠⅠ 李家提 which doubtless represents *Äl oɣlï Li Chia-t'i. If the family name of the Juan-juan royal clan could serve, even accidentally or incorrectly, to render in Chinese transcription the term *oɣlï ~ *oɣlu, it must have been approximating it very closely in sound. In such a case, the hypothesis advanced in HTHYFC 5:1-2 concerning the etymology of the royal Juan-juan surname must be revised.

7. Juan-juan Mi-o 彌峩 < *minga is undoubtedly connected with Kao-chü *mingatu 彌峩突 and mong. minggan 'thousand'.

III.8. T'o-pa Hsün, Heir of Line

According to G 57, T'o-pa Hsün 濬 (440-453-465), son of
T'o-pa Huang 晃 (428-451) and fourth sovereign of the Wei dynasty,
bore the cognomen (字) of Wu-lei chih-chin 烏雷直勤 , i.e.,
Wu-lei tigin.

The biography of the T'o-pa prince (J 5, 0 2) yields, I believe,
an explanation of his title. Hsün was greatly loved by his grandfather, T'o-pa T'ao (409-424-453), who conferred upon him the title
(號) of 'Imperial Grandson of the Line' 世嫡皇孫. This information must lead us to believe that in the Chinese transcription
Wu-lei (KD 1288, 520: ͨuo-luâi) is concealed the turkish term urï
(orkh. 𐰆𐰺𐰃) 'son', 'male', cf. uruɣ 'Same, Nachkommenschaft' (v. JA,
1925[1], 237 for other 'altaic' forms).

Here again the T'o-pa word finds a parallel in the language
of the Hsiung-nu. Khan Hu-han-hsieh's sons succeeded him in the
order of the following diagram:

```
        H.-h.-Hs  +  Chief Wife              H.-h.-hs  +  Secondary Wife
      ⌒‾‾‾‾‾‾‾‾‾‾‾‾‾‾‾‾‾‾‾‾‾‾‾‾‾‾⌒          ⌒‾‾‾‾‾‾‾‾‾‾‾‾‾‾‾‾⌒
        1 X      2 X     5 X      X            3 X        4 X
```

Now, successor number 5, with the accession of whom the throne reverted to the elder line, is known as Wu-lei jo-t'i Khan 烏累 (KD
522: ljiᵉ) 若鞮 which can be tentatively reconstructed into *urï
(a)yaɣ-tï, i.e., 'Pious Heir of Line'.

III.9. T'u-chüeh Notes

1. According to one of the versions of the origin of the T'u-
chüeh preserved in L 50 and 0 99, the first ancestor of the T'u-chüeh
was a certain I-chih-ni-shih—tu 伊質泥師都 (KD 272, 1227, 659,
893, 1187: ͨi-t͡śiᵉt(< t́-)-ͨniei-ͨsi-ͨtuo). It may be possible that
in the first four characters of the name we have the transcription
of tk. il tiris ~ äl täräs 'he who collects the äl together', and
in -tu the 'mongol' adjectival ending, perhaps a vestige of Juan-juan
influence in early Turkish (cf. the 'mongol' plural ending in t quite

common in Orkhon turkish and appearing in the very name of the T'u-
chüeh < *Türküt). It is noteworthy also that the title äl ügäsi
(Ch. 頡于伽思,) 'glory of the äl' discussed by F. W. K. Müller
in parallel with that of äl täräs (Uigurica, II, 93-95) is present
already in the sixth century in the official title of Sha-po-lüeh's
son qaɤan 頡伽施多那都藍, the first three characters of which
are a good transcription of *Äl (ü)gäsi.

2. The name of the mountain where the fourth son of I-chih-
ni-shih-tu settled is given in 0 99 as Pa-(L 50 Ch'ien)-ssǔ Chu-chê-
shih 跋(跋)斯處折施. As the river Ch'u-chê 處折 is mentioned
as the place where the third son settled (this river is possibly to
be identified with the *Čuš[?] Ⲭ〉人 of the Orkhon inscriptions),
there is no doubt that the tk. name of the mountain should be reconstructed as *Baš *Ch'u-chê-si 'the source of the Ch'u-che river'
(with -si the tk. possessive suffix of the status constructus).

3. The tenth of the grandsons of *Äl-tärästü who was chosen
leader of the T'u-chüeh tribes after winning a jumping contest (the
ten sons of Ta-êrh 大兒 having agreed to recognize as chief the one
among them who jumped highest 'against a tree' 向樹) was named
A-hsien 阿賢 (KD 369 ɣien) šad (Chin. 設). His name should be
unquestionably reconstructed as *Aɤin< aɤ 'to rise up'.

4. One of the sources of 0 99 disagrees with L 50 and later
texts as to the successor of T'u-mên (Bumyn, *Äl qaɤan) and names
as such his younger brother A-i 阿逸 (KD 880, 1132: i̯et< d- ~
*si̯ět) qaɤan instead of his son K'o-lo, I-hsi-chi khan. I believe
that the confusion was caused by failure to distinguish between
T'u-men's successor as one of the "Four Qaɤans" and his successor as
supreme leader of the Turks. In such a case A-i may well have represented *Äsit-, i.e., *Äsit(mä) ᚾᛇᚺᛁᚢ ~ *Istämi.

III.10. <u>Farderie à la turque</u>

In <u>TP</u>, 1930, 253-4n, Professor Pelliot expresses some doubt
as to whether tk. <u>al</u> 'red' is attested in the most ancient period
of the existence of the turkish language, and briefly mentions the
possibility that <u>al</u> (cf. pers. آل 'red') might be an old Iranian
loan-word in turkish.

Whether an original 'altaic' word or a loan from Iranian, <u>al</u> is,
I believe, found in a 'turco-mongol' linguistic milieu as early as the
third century B.C., namely in the language of the Hsiung-nu.

For many years scholars interested in the investigation of the
Hsiung-nu language have been endeavoring to discover the linguistic
relationship of the Hsiung-nu term <u>O-shih</u> ~ <u>Yen-chih</u> 閼氏 which,
according to the Chinese sources (A 110, B 94a) was the title of the
consort of the Hsiung-nu <u>shan-yü</u>.

Every investigator has tried diligently to equate <u>yen-chih</u>
with some turkish, mongol, tungusic, or finnish word meaning 'woman'
or 'wife'. The only reason I can find for this strange self-imposed
limitation for conjecture as to the meaning of the word is Liu Pin's
劉攽 note in B 94a where this commentator boldly asserts that <u>yen-
chih</u> was nothing else but 'the appellation given by the <u>shan-yü</u> to
his <u>wife</u>' and strongly criticizes Yen Shih-ku for translating the
term by 'Empress'.

There is, indeed, no indication whatever in the Chinese sources
that <u>yen-chih</u> meant 'wife' or 'woman'. On the other hand, the <u>So yin</u>
(Ssǔ-ma Chêng's) commentary to the <u>Shih Chi</u>, after a preliminary note
on the pronunciation of the word, gives us a clear indication as to
what the Chinese considered to be the meaning of <u>yen-chih</u>.

Let us review briefly the evidence. <u>O-shih</u> 閼氏, according
to all commentators, should be pronounced as if written 焉支 <u>yen-</u>
<u>chih</u>, <u>shih</u> as 氏 (= 支) in the name of the Yüeh-chih 月氏 , and
閼 <u>o</u> as 曷 <u>ho</u> (KD 73: γât < g'-) was pronounced <u>in T'ang times</u>, i.e.,
with the transcription value of *'<u>al</u> or *'<u>ar</u> (< γaδ). In other words,
when Yen Shih-ku takes the trouble to 'spell out' <u>o</u> 閼 through the
<u>fan-ch'ieh</u> 於連反 > *'ien, he is clearly indicating what should have

been, in his opinion, a correct pronunciation of the character in
Han times, if this character transcribed the same foreign sound
which, in his time, was transcribed by 曷 *γaδ; that is, the learned
Chinese commentator is quite aware of the fact that while foreign
-l and r were in his time regularly rendered by final -t, in Han
times the same sounds were represented in Chinese transcription by
final -n.

Moreover, as evidenced by the fact that the So-yin quotes the
fragment of Hsi Tso-ch'ih's 習鑿齒 (Chin dynasty scholar, E 82)
letter to a king of Yen where the author speaks of the connection
of o-shih with 烟支 yen-chih and by the insistence of all the commentators on equating o-shih with yen-chih 焉支 , the Chinese seemed
to be sure that the Hsiung-nu called the wife of their sovereign by
the same term with which they designated 'rouge' derived from the
'red lan' 紅藍 plant and the mountain which was the chief source of
this plant, that is yen-chih 焉支 , 燕支 , 胭脂 臙支 , etc.

"We lost our Yen-chih 焉支 mountain (to the Chinese)," ran
an old Hsiung-nu song preserved in a fragment of the Hsi ho chiu-shih
西河舊事 ,"and caused our wives and daughters to be without color
in their cheeks." There is thus no doubt that the Yen-chih mountain
derived its name from its chief product, the yen-chih rouge manufactured from the juice of the 'red lan' and used by the Hsiung-nu
women to beautify themselves.

The story of yen-chih 'rouge' on Chinese soil is a long one,
and it is not the purpose of this note to review it. Neither do I
wish to marshal at present all the texts which offer additional
proof of the identity of o-shih with yen-chih. I would limit myself
to indicating an interesting survival of the original connection
between the name of the Yen-chih mountain and the term 'red'. In
his article on the name of the Hsi Hsia kingdom (ЗИВАН,II, 3,
129-150) N. A. Nevsky gives the Hsi Hsia characters designating the
Yen-chih mountain 𗫂 𗉚 (sentence 51). The first character unmistakably contains the element 𗉚 which undoubtedly meant 'red' in
Hsi Hsia (cf. op. cit., sentence 12 and Hsi Hsia 𗉚 [= 'metal' +
'red'] 'copper' 銅, Han Fan Ho Shih... 12b).

The T'ang pronunciation of the Hsiung-nu term for 'rouge' and 'wife of the sovereign' was as we have seen above believed to be correctly reproduced by 閼支 which would give us a hypothetical *·alči. The first syllable in the light of all the evidence appears to be tk.(?) *al 'red'. The Han transcription offers some difficulty as it would presuppose an original *yäl for 焉 , but o 關 with its final -t of T'ang times and an undetermined final (phon. 於 KD 1323: ₂·i^wo₃, ₂·uo) in Han times, could well represent in the third century B.C. a Hsiung-nu *al. In 支 *či we may possibly have a 'mongol' feminine ending, the whole term thus meaning 'the red (rouged) one', 'the beautiful lady', a name quite appropriate for the designation of the wife of the sovereign.

Granted the existence of the 'turco-mongol' term *al 'red' in this early period, one wonders if we should not find it attested later in Hsiung-nu and Hsien-pei onomasticons. I am inclined in this connection to review the etymology proposed in Sino-Altaica II.1 for the numerous *altu ~ *alutu appearing as names of nomads and consider the form *altu as a masculine 'mongol' adjectival form of *al 'red'. L 50 offers, I believe, indirect substantiation of this interpretation. Mu-han qaγan 木汗 , the great leader of the Turks, whose proper name was Ssŭ-chin 俟斤 (< erkin?), was also called Yen-tu 燕都 . His face, adds the text, was very broad and very red in color. We may thus have in Yen-tu < *yältü, possibly <*altu, a nickname, 'the rouged one', by which the khan had become known in addition to his personal name.

HTHYFC 11 (September 1935)

Sino–Altaica IV

IV.1. Sarag and Serica

> ...Ye scrybe his slender China
> yarnes unravells...
>
> —H. Yule, Cathay

In the JA, 1927, pp. 138–141, Professor Pelliot suggests that
the sūl سُول , given by Qudāma (9th–10th centuries, cf. de Goeje,
Bibl. Geogr. Arab., v. VI), together with Khumdān خمدان , as the
names of the two great cities of China, reputed to have been founded
by Alexander the Great, be read as *Sarag سرگ and identified with the
the *Sarag ܝܣܪܓ of the Syriac inscriptions on the Nestorian monument
of Hsi-an-fu. As mentioned by Pelliot, this emendation had first been
proposed by J. Marquart in his Streifzüge, p. 502. Marquart suggested
sūl = سُورگ *šarag = Syr. Šarag (the monument has, however, Sarag)
= Greek Sērikē.

The entry Saraga = Lo-yang found by Pelliot in a Chinese-
Sanskrit vocabulary of the T'ang period leaves no doubt as to the
fact that Sarag is to be identified with Lo-yang 洛陽, the great
eastern capital of China, while Khumdān, Syriac *Kūmdan, doubtless
is another name for Ch'ang-an 長安, the western metropolis, the
two equivalences having long been suspected by all the interpreters
of the Nestorian stela.

In discussing the possible relation of *Sarag to Sērikē, Pelliot
hazards the supposition that the last syllable of *Sarag may be connected with 洛 lo < ancient lâk. The name of Lo-yang should,
however, be left out in considering any possible Chinese original for
Sērikē since that designation for China (Northern China) was already
current in the West in the pre-Christian era, while Lo-yang became
the capital of the mighty empire of the Seres only in the first
century A.D. In the following pages the writer hopes to offer a
solution to this difficult question, in which, while Sarag is kept

distinct from <u>sericum</u>, the name of the great city of China is revealed as closely bound to the designation of the chief product of the
Han Empire.

Lo < <u>Lâk</u>, the ancient name of the city (洛邑) of Lo-yang,
can, I believe, be linked still closer with *Sarag ~ Saraga through
an investigation of the possible archaic pronunciation of <u>lâk</u>, KD 411.
Lo < <u>lâk</u> belongs to a class of Chinese characters representing words
with an initial consonantal complex *<u>kl-</u>, *<u>gl-</u>, the existence of
which is certain for archaic Chinese. Without going exhaustively
into the difficult problem of the nature of these initial consonantal
groups or prefix formations, a problem demanding the skill of a
phonetician and Sino-Tibetan comparatist, the writer would like to
call the attention of scholars to a curious consonantal shift in
the "phonetic groups" with initial *<u>kl-</u>, *<u>gl-</u>. Many of these groups
or series exhibit, as shown in the following table, the material
for which has been assembled both according to the "phonetic series"
method and on the basis of synonymy, an interchange of *L~*G (guttural)
~*S (dental-supradental-palatal) initials.

*L-	*G-	*S-
1. 立 KD 524 li̯əp	泣 k'i̯əp	颯 *sâp 霋 *źi̯əp < d- cf. 霝霅霅 .
2. 林 KD 555 li̯əm	禁 ki̯əm	森 643 si̯əm
3. 婪 KD 555 lâm < *kl-		syn. 饞 *dz'am KD 1170 / syn. 婥 *ts'âm
	Ph. 今 ₌ki̯əm ←	syn. 貪 ₌t'âm KD 386
4. 婁 KD 572 ₌ləu, ₌li̯u	簍 ₌g'i̯u	數 KD 919 ˙si̯u˙
5. 屚 KD 588 li̯u	屨 ki̯u˙	
及 KD 322 g'i̯əp	及 interchanged in compounds with 羣 (cf. 1 and 磼 *lap!)	馺, 馺, 颯, 靸 *sâp ~ si̯əp
6. 侖 KD 583 ₌liuĕn / 巒 KD 590 ₌luân	昆, 囷, 圓, 圜, 亘, etc. *kuən ~ *g'wan	cf. 揌 suən in the 1341 group, *s- vs. *g'- in 841.

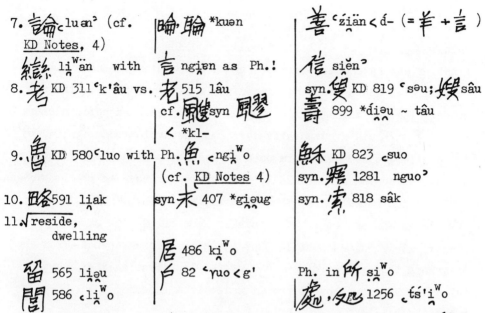

7. 論 ₍luan⁾ (cf. 崘,輪 *kuen   善 ⁽ẑiän ⟨ d- (= 羊 + 言)
KD Notes, 4)
� liᵂan with 言 ngien as Ph.!   信 siĕn⁾

8. 考 KD 311 ⁽k'âu vs. 老 515 lâu   syn. 叟 KD 819 ⁽səu; 嫂 sâu
cf. 颮 syn 飂   壽 899 *d̂ieu ~ tâu
⟨ *kl-

9. 魯 KD 580 ⁽luo with Ph. 魚 ₍ngiᵂo   鮻 KD 823 ₍suo
(cf. KD Notes 4)   syn. 寠 1281 nguo⁾

10. 略 591 li̯ak   syn 末 407 *gi̯eug   syn. 索 818 sâk

11. √ reside, dwelling   居 486 ki̯ᵂo

留 565 li̯eu   戶 82 ⁽yuo ⟨ g'   Ph. in 所 si̯ᵂo

閭 586 ₍li̯ᵂo   處,処 1256 ₍ts'i̯ᵂo

Examples could easily be multiplied. Within the KD 411 各~
洛 *klak group we can ascertain a similar shift of *kl (also *ng-
in phonetic compounds 峇,頷,諮 = *ngak) to an *S initial in the
following synonymic equations:

1. 駱 lâk = 驣 KD 1013 t'âk
2. 烙 lâk = 灼 KD 860 t̂śi̯ak ⟨ t̂-
3. 胳 kâk = 腋 KD 224 *zi̯ak
4. 鉻 lâk = 髟 *tuk
5. 閣 kâk = 杙,橝 *diek *śi̯ak
6. 跉 luo-g = 途 1322 ₍d'uo
7. 酪 lâk = 澤 (Shih Ming) 202 *d'ɐk

Finally the name of the river Lo 洛, from which Lo-yang derives
its name, is phonetically equated in Kuang-Ya IX with 繹 202 i̯äk ⟨ d-
(cf. 釋 śi̯äk).

It would seem, therefore, possible to reconstruct for most *kl-
phonetic groups, including the 洛 lâk (~ Lo-yang) series an archaic
*skl- ~ *sgr- consonantal complex with an evolution similar to
Tibetan sgr-, i.e., sgr ﹥ śr- ﹥ r- or ﹥ d-. The pronunciation of
洛 lâk in archaic Chinese could thus have been *śrak, from which
was derived Sanskrit Saraga and Syriac Sarag.

In trying to trace ser-, sericum back to a Chinese original,

scholars have mostly limited themselves to expressing a hope that
Chinese 絲 KD 614 ₍c₎si 'silk threads' would some day reveal a lost
final -r and have completely disregarded all other Chinese terms
for 'silk'. *Sarag = Loyang immediately singles out from the mass
of soieries the term 絡 lâk, containing the same phonetic element
as Lo 洛·絡 is a comparatively common equivalent of 緊 944 si₍ₐ₎ʷoꞋ
'écru silk', the usual term used to designate (together with 繒)
the silk exported or paid as tribute by the Chinese to the Hsiung-nu.
絡 lâk has as relatives the following synonyms: 紬 253 *d'i̯ǝug,
繹 *śie <-a, and 繪, 纅 *śi̯äk. Even if 絡 lâk had no s-
prefix, it is quite possible that the silk became known to China's
neighbors through the binom 絲絡 *si-lâk 'fine silk and écru'
(cf. also another known binom attested from an early period, 絲縲
*si li̯u < *si gli̯u).

> The expression 絲絡 is indicated in the Tz'ŭ Yüan as
> occurring in the Yi Chou Shu 汲冢周書. This, however,
> is a mistake as the best available editions of that work
> (so, e.g., the Ssŭ-pu ts'ung k'an ed., ch. 3, 6a) read
> 綌絡 KD 127, 501 ₍c₎f'i-k'i̯ɐk and the passage refers
> obviously to hemp or dolicho 葛 cloth (cf. Shih Ching,
> 周南,葛覃). f'i (note the *χ ~ *s shift in the
> KD 127 phonetic series) was the name of the finer kind
> of cloth, k'i̯ɐk, that of the coarser, offering thus a
> parallel to 絲絡.

If Lo 洛 lâk < *Srak and equals Sarag, the Central-Asiatic
designation of Lo-yang, the conjectural equation Khumdân = Ch'ang-an
receives fresh support, and its solution can be considerably speeded
by postulating that Ch'ang-an, just as Lo-yang, became known to
Central Asiatics under an older, perhaps not less glorious, name.
Khumdân is, indeed, an almost perfect transcription of the ancient
Ch'in-Han name of the city, Hsien-yang 咸陽 : KD 148 ₍c₎γam < g'
(but cf. TP, 1931, 67, where Karlgren proposes -ǝm, ǝm for archaic
Chinese in this series) + 陽 KD 214 ₍c₎i̯ang < d- = *g'ɐmdang.

IV.2. Kumiss or Arrack?

In his review of A. Conrady's <u>Alte westöstliche Kulturwörter</u>
("Zu dem frühesten Verbindungen zwischen China und dem Westen,"
<u>Deutsche Literaturzeitung</u>, 1926, pp. 1959–62; cf. also <u>Philology</u>
<u>and Ancient China</u>, pp. 138–139) Professor Karlgren has questioned
Conrady's hypothetical derivation of Chinese <u>lo</u> 酪 < *lâk < **klâk
~ glâk (KD 411) 'sour milk', 'a Hsiung-nu drink' from the indo-
european root for 'milk' *<u>galak</u>- > gr. γλάκος. Karlgren proposes
instead to consider **glâk > *lâk as a loan-word from a North-Asiatic
('Altaic') language and connects the Chinese term with *<u>araq</u>, one
of the most widely diffused cultural terms, and one which, next to
the word for tea, can claim to be truly international.

In the sense of 'alcoholic drink', 'brandy', *<u>araq</u> exists in
some form in every major European language, is current all through
Asia both along the Northern land (nomadic) 'cultural highway' and
along the Southern (Indian Ocean) 'diffusion route', and in its
linguistic range it encompasses hundreds of variations from the
French argot term <u>riquiqui</u> to Ainu <u>arakke</u>. It is generally supposed
to be derived from ar. <u>araq</u> عرق 'sweat', 'exudation' as used in
the well-known term عرق التمر 'spirituous liquor from the sap of
the date-palm'. It was introduced into European terminology
chiefly through East Indian traders who found the word widely in use
among the population in contact with Moslem culture. The form
*<u>aragi</u>, with the final –<u>i</u>, which seems to underlie many of the
European variations of the term, must have been derived, however,
from a turkish final –i form.(cf. B. Vladimirtsov, "Арабския слова
въ монгольскомъ," <u>ЗКВ</u>, V, 75–76).

Believing (on the basis of Hsiung-nu [2nd century B.C.] **^{a}rak)
in the 'altaic' origin of the term, Karlgren dismisses the arabic
etymology of *<u>araq</u> < ʿ<u>araq</u> 'sweat', etc., as a late folk etymology
for an ancient tk. term which found its way into the Arabic environment, from where it spread all through the world (in Northern Asia,
however, the diffusion was achieved independently within the 'Altaic'
domain). That the Chinese represented Hsiun-nu *^{a}<u>rak</u> by **glâk is

explained by Karlgren by the fact that in archaic Chinese there
apparently existed no simple phoneme *lâk (as most <u>ancient</u> *lâk are
derived from <u>archaic</u> *glâk, *blâk, etc., consonantal-complex-phonetic
groups) and by the influence of a purely Chinese word **glâk 'sour
sauce' represented by the same symbol 酪 .

Kumiss, the most widely used form of liquor among the nomads,
as well as Hsiung-nu 酪 **glâk, were, however, <u>fermented</u>, rather
than <u>distilled</u> drinks. Karlgren does not explain how the two terms
could have been confused. He overlooks the fact that while *<u>araqï</u>
is common among the nomads of Northern and Central Asia, it always
designates a distilled drink, often, it is true, prepared from mare's
milk, but always distinguished from fermented kumiss. In turkish
*<u>araqï</u> does not seem to be attested before the Moslem period.

The Hsiung-nu loan-word 酪 **glâk, thus, cannot, in my
opinion, represent *<u>araq</u>, the arabic origin of which can hardly be
doubted. In the light of what has been said in <u>Sino-Altaica</u> IV.1,
concerning the archaic pronunciation of the phonetic group 各 and
the <u>Shih-Ming</u> 'phonetic etymology' of 酪 **glâk = 澤 KD 222 *d'ɐk,
we can reconstruct for 酪 the following archaic forms:

1. **Sglak ~ Sgrak
2. **drâk ~ **dlâk
3. **^{o}glak ~ **^{o}grak, with ^{o} representing a possible
   archaic consonantal or vocalic prefix.

The third form could well represent mo. <u>uɣuraq</u> 'substance
épaisse, visqueuse', 'amouille' derived apparently from <u>uɣu</u> 'to drink'.
The history of the word is, however, complex, and in a turkish, and
not mongol, milieu, we should expect *<u>uɣuz</u> (cf. Pelliot, <u>TP</u>, 1930,
256-257).

The second form **dlâk ~ **drâk yields us an excellent 'altaic'
equivalent *<u>taraq</u> 'sour milk', 'curds and whey', from which are
derived russ <u>tvorog</u> 'cottage cheese', bulg. <u>tvarog</u>, pol. <u>twaróg</u>, etc.
In turkish dialects it is met with only in tatar; this led some
scholars to believe that it represents, therefore, a slavic loan-word.
Such authorities as Peisker, Korsch (cf."О бытовыхъ словахъ..."
ЗИООЭ, XXXIV, p. 538), Miklosić, and Vámbéry (the latter on the

basis of jag.? <u>turaq</u> and magy. <u>turó</u>) consider it as a genuine turkish
word. In mongolian it is attested in the form <u>taraq</u> ᠲᠠᠷᠠᠬ 'lait
caillé' and occurs already in Ibn Al-Muhannā's vocabulary in the
form طراغ = اللبن 'milk' (_AΦM_, 139). لبن can, however, also mean
'curds and whey.'

As there is no doubt that Hsiung-nu 酉各 designated <u>fermented
milk</u>, and not a distilled drink, the derivation of **glak from
*<u>araq</u> must, I believe, be abandoned.

IV.3. Notes on 'Ibn Al-Muhannā'

In his study of the then anonymous manuscript entitled كتاب
ترجمان فارسى و ترى و مغولى "An Interpreter of Persian,
Turkish, and Mongol" (p. III, dealing with the Mongol language,
ЗВОИРАО, v. XV, 1904, pp.76-171) P. Melioranski left two mongol
words, the arabic equivalents of which are quite clear, unexplained.
These are:

المحجّل اليد = قار يلا '(a horse) with white forelegs', p. 114

and المحجّل الرجل = كل يلا '(a horse) with white hindlegs', p. 116

For the first, Melioranski suggested a hybrid 'turco-mongol'
form قارى آلا ; in the first word of the second compound he rightly
recognized the mongol word <u>kül</u> ᠬᠥᠯ 'leg'.

يلا *<u>yalā</u>, which puzzled the editor so much, is undoubtedly a
bad reading of بلا ~ بُلا *<u>bulā</u> as the expression <u>kül bulaq</u> ᠬᠥᠯ ᠪᠤᠯᠠᠬ
'horse with white hindlegs' is well attested in mongol, cf. Kowalewski,
2597, as a synonym of <u>čaɣan šigere</u> 'id.' قر يلا should likewise be
read قر بُلا *<u>ɣar bula</u> 'horse with white forelegs' (lit. 'hands'—
mo. <u>ɣar</u> ᠭᠠᠷ , cf. Melioranski, p. 140, البد = قار . It is
interesting to note that the mongols apparently designated the
forelegs of a horse in the same way as the Arabs, i.e., by the word
hand, بر ~ <u>ɣar</u>, a usage not attested in late mongol.

As to the word <u>bulaq</u> > *<u>bula'</u>, the semantic value of which is
not clear in Kowalewski, it doubtless is connected with the <u>bulaq</u>
of the common turkish <u>alan-bulan</u> ~ <u>alaq-bulaq</u> 'variegated'. Its

relation to tk. bulɣa- will be discussed in a following note. Bulaq
in all probability underlies mo. hulaɣan 'sable'.

АФМ , 133: mo. جَلَوُو = المملوك 'slave' (cf. جلا وُو = الشابّ
'youth'), both of which must equal mo. ǰalaɣu ~ ǰala'u ﭑﺣ﮲ 'youth',
evokes Hsiung-nu 貲虜 *tsi̯a-luo (luo ⟨archaic *lX̣uo? if 虍 is
'phonetic'), cf. HTHYFC 5, and Pelliot, TP, 1920–21, p. 325.

АФМ , 113: حمار وحش = ڤولكبا 'wild ass' similarly might go
back to Hsiung-nu 驒騱 *dʼa-ɣiei (the instability of the final –n
in KD 968 單 suggests a final –l, –r in this series)⟨ **dâlɣiei
'the name of a wild horse in the Hsiung-nu country', considered by
the Chinese to be a kind of mule.

HTHYFC 13 (March 1936)

Sino-Altaica IV (continued)

IV.4. "La lengnée de celz Argon"

In Sino-Altaica III.2 the supposition was hazarded that we have
in the name of the Wu-huan 烏桓 (or 烏丸, **uoɣuan) the earliest
Chinese transcription of the 'altaic' term *arɣun (Marco Polo's
argon) which all through its long career in the North-Asiatic world
always appears to have carried the connotation 'métis', 'bastard'.

After the Wu-huan disappear as a distinct political organization
about 210 A.D., we find them mentioned as forming part of the T'o-pa
confederacy during the latter's first rise to power (c. 220–275).
J 113, in its short preface describing the early T'o-pa organization,
states moreover that Wu-wan 烏丸 was the collective designation of
the vassal tribes of the T'o-pa which were divided into Northern and
Southern hordes with two great chieftains exercising control over
them. G 57 yields us the T'o-pa name of those chieftains which was
wu-ai-chên 烏矮真 ⟨**uo-·âi-t͡si̯ĕn ⟨ **ŭɣaič̆in, apparently a
derivative -č̆in form of *ŭɣan.

The 'turco-mongol' root underlying these transcriptions is
probably orkh. uq 'Geschlecht' (cf. also uq 'to submit', uyuš 'vassal'
'tribe') although it is also possible that Chinese ·uo 烏 may stand
for *uru- (tk. -r- in intervocalic position is often quiescent, cf.
N. K. Dmitrijev, JRAS, 1927, pp. 521-527) and there is thus a faint
possibility that ·uoyuan is derived from *uruqan < *uruq 'relatives
on the maternal side', which would well correspond to Chinese wai 外
in 外左右 which translates wu-ai-chên.

> A form *(u)ruqan may underlie Lu-kuan 祿官 < *luk-kuan,
> the name of one of the youngest sons of Li-Wei 力微,
> the founder of the T'o-pa confederacy. In the light of
> the evidence which points to the predominantly 'turkish'
> and not 'mongol' character of the T'o-pa language, I
> would discard the proposed equation Li-wei < *liᵊk-^{W}Gei <
> **uruq ügei advanced in the preliminary draft of this note.

Uruq is undoubtedly a cognate of urï 'offspring', but has early
been specialized as indicating 'descendants through the mother' and
may thus possibly form the basis of *aryun < *åryun < **uruyun.

IV.5. T'an-shih-huai the Great

In the Shigaku Zasshi (recently made available to me) v. XXI,
9, Sept. 1910, pp. 15-16, Professor Shiratori, who was then pursuing
his investigation into the origin and language of the Tung Hu 東胡,
'Eastern Hu', suggests mo. *tangsuk 'marvelous' as the etymological
basis for the interpretation of the name of T'an-shih-huai 檀石槐,
the great founder of the empire of the Hsien-pei in the 2nd century A.D.

As a basis for his etymology, Shiratori invokes the D 30 story
of T'an-shih-huai's birth. T'an-shih-huai's father, campaigning with
the Hsiung-nu, left his wife at home for three years. On his return
he found in his yurt a little son whose appearance the mother explained as the result of a marvelous conception produced by the fall
of a hailstone into her mouth during a storm; hence the hero's name
—'marvelous'.

Now, T'an-shih-huai, KD 967, 883, 460: ꞓd'ân, *d̪i̯äk, *g'^{W}ai can

in no way represent *Tangsuk. Shiratori forgets to mention that the
irate 'father' did not believe his wife, who, in fear for the life
of the boy, had him <u>secretly reared</u> in the home of relatives (or
'her majordomo' 家令 ?). Chin. -<u>n</u> representing -<u>l</u> or -<u>r</u>, we have
in *<u>dând'ak</u>^w<u>ai</u> an absolutely regular transcription of mo. *<u>daldayai</u>
< <u>dalda</u> 'hidden, secret'.

IV.6. Hsiung-nu Titles

In <u>Sino-Altaica</u> I.7 the author attempted to interpret the
Hsiung-nu title 骨都侯 <u>ku-tu-hou</u> (borne by relatives of the <u>shan-yü</u>
on his wife's side) as containing the common turkish term *<u>qudu</u>
'father-in-law'. It appears now that most of the Hsiung-nu titles
of dignitaries originally represented terms designating the family
relationship of those who held them to the supreme ruler of the
Hsiung-nu.

The titles of Hsiung-nu princes appear in the Chinese sources
in the following forms:

A. <u>The Four Horns</u>:
1. Right and Left <u>t'u-chi</u> 屠耆 (translated by Chinese <u>hsien</u> 賢), B. 94, C 119, E 97
2. Right and Left <u>lu-li</u> 谷 (pr. 鹿) 蠡 (B 94 and C 119) or <u>i-li</u> 亦 蠡 (E 97)

B. <u>The Six Horns</u>:
1. Right and Left <u>jih-chu</u> 日逐
2. Right and Left <u>wên-yü-ti</u> (or -<u>tu</u>) 溫禺鞮 (or 犢) (B and C) or <u>yü-lu</u> 於陸 (E)
3. Right and Left <u>chien-chiang</u> 漸將 (B and C) or <u>chien-shang</u> 漸尚 (E)

C. <u>Dignitaries of families other than that of the shan-yü</u>
1. Right and Left <u>ku-tu-hou</u> 骨都侯 (C)
2. Right and Left <u>shih-chu</u> 尸逐

D. <u>Other dignitaries</u>: <u>Jih-chu ch'ü-chü</u> 日逐且渠 and <u>tang-hu</u>
當戶. E 97 further supplies the <u>shuo-fang</u> 朔方, <u>tu-lu</u> 獨鹿,
<u>hsien-lu</u> 顯祿 and <u>an-lo</u> 安樂.

1. T'u-ch'i < *d'uo-g'ji has often been equated with tk. *toghrï ~ *toghru 'virtuous'. I would prefer *toɣï or *toɣlï 'well born'.

2. Lu-li < *luk-liei or i-li < *i̯ăk-liei = tk. *oɣlï or (ä)loɣlï 'the sons of the ăl (the reigning clan).'

3. Jih-chu < *ni̯et-d'i̯uk = tk. *(i)ni-toɣ 'born of the younger brothers'. Ch. *ni̯et may represent an old plural of ini 'younger brother', *inis ~ *inid.

4. Yü-lu < *·uo-luk (E 97) = tk. uruq 'maternal relatives'. Wên-yü-tu < *·uən-ngi̯u-d'uk (B and C) may represent *urï-ngu-toɣ, *urï 'offspring' (cf. Note 4), *toɣ 'born', and *ngu some sort of 'altaic' suffix.

5. Chien-chiang < *tsi̯ăm-tsi̯ang, possibly = *(a)či-m-čă-ng with áči 'uncle', -m possessive suffix of the first person, -čă 'from', *áčimčă-ng 'of my uncle's issue?'

        Cf. T'o-pa I-chan 乙旃 *i̯ĕt-tśi̯än (a surname later translated Shu-sun 叔孫 'uncle's descendants') < *áči-n.

6. Shih-chu < *și-d'i̯uk = tk. *(i)ši-toɣ 'born of the iši (woman ~ sister)'.

7. Tang-hu < *tâng-g'uo possibly contains tk. element *ata-ng 'father's'.

The remainder of the titles I have not been able to explain.

As to the title of the sovereign of the Hsiung-nu, shan-yü 單于, the meaning of which was, according to the Chinese sources, 'vast, extensive' (cf. HTHYFC 2), it is undoubtedly derived from the 'turco-mongol' root *dal ~ *del which forms the basis of mo. delge 'to spread', delger 'spreading', delgegü 'extensive', shan-yü representing, in the Han period, a faithful transcription of *delgü.

It is also to be noted that it is possibly the tk. root toɣ 'to bear', 'to be born' which underlies the well-known Hsiung-nu surname Tu-ku 獨孤 < *d'uk-k'uo (the supposed Chinese ancestor of the Tu-ku clan, made prisoner by the Hsiung-nu, who married a 'barbarian' woman 'who bore him a son on the Ku mountain'; it appears that the Chinese commentators attempted to indicate in this story the Hsiung-nu etymology of Tu-ku).

IV.7. T'ieh-fu Hsiung-nu Names (II)

1. In <u>Sino-Altaica</u> II.1, I advanced the hypothesis that Lo-ch'ên 羅辰 ‹ lâ-ẑi̯ĕn, the name of a Hsiung-nu chieftain, represents 'turco-mongol' <u>lačin</u> لاجين ~ لاچين 'falcon', a word which is attested in mongol in the form <u>način</u> ﻧﺎﺟﻴﻦ. It had escaped my attention at the time that the name of the same individual is recorded in the <u>Wei Shu</u> in the mongol form also.

According to the biography of Liu Lo-chên translated in <u>HTHYFC</u> 2, he was the <u>third son</u> of Liu Chüan, younger brother of Liu K'u-jên. It was his sister who became the first consort of T'o-pa Kuei. Now, in J 23 (Liu Hsien's biography), cf. <u>HTHYFC</u> 2, p. 3-4, we find that the lady Liu, whom T'o-pa Kuei married in 386, was the younger sister of Liu Nu-chên 奴真 and was offered in marriage to the young T'o-pa prince by Nu-chên in gratitude for Kuei's aid against Ho-lan Jan-kan. Nu-chên is introduced in J 23 as a <u>kinsman</u> 族人 of Liu Hsien and is said to have had <u>two elder brothers</u>, Chien 犍 and Ch'ü-chin 去斤 (in other words, he was a third son). From the story of Nu-chên's relations with Liu Hsien and with the Ho-lan on one hand, and that of his loyalty to T'o-pa Kuei, which led to his sister's marriage to the latter (coupled with the fact that we know of only one Lady Liu among Kuei's wives), on the other, we can deduce but one conclusion: that Nu-chên and Lo-ch'ên are one and the same individual. The genealogy of the chieftains of the Liu (Tu-ku) horde presents itself, therefore, as follows:

Liu K'u-jên   — elder brother of   Liu Chüan

Liu Hsien 顯   1. Chien 2. Ch'ü-chin 3. Nu-chên 4. Lady Liu
                                        (Lo-ch'ên)

Nu-chên 奴真 (KD 674, 1194: ₍nuo-₍tsi̯ĕn) must thus represent the same 'turco-mongol' word as <u>Lo-ch'ên</u> 羅辰 lâ-ẑi̯ĕn ‹ *<u>lačin</u>. Nu 奴, as we have seen, appears in transcriptions of the 'mongol' word činoa ~ čonoa 'wolf'(cf. <u>HTHYFC</u> 5: 13-15) where it represents the syllable -noa ~ -nua. We must remember, moreover, that as a 'phonetic' 奴 is often read *<u>na</u> ~ *<u>nja</u> and that it is thus quite

possible that in the fourth to sixth centuries A.D. the compound
nu-chên was read *noa-čin ~ *njačin ~ *način which would represent
mo. način 'falcon'. As J 23 (in which both forms of the name occur)
seems to be a genuine chapter of the Wei-Shu, its author, Wei Shou,
either did not suspect the identity of Liu Nu-chên with Liu Lo-ch'ên
or (a more plausible explanation) made use in his compilation of two
sources, one of which recorded the name of the Hsiung-nu chieftain
in its 'turkish' form, the other in its 'mongol' variant.

It is to be noted that J 83A which contains the full
biography of Liu Lo-ch'ên is a spurious chapter of the
Wei Shu.

2.   In HTHYFC 5: 14-15, attention was called to the Chinese
transcriptions of two 'turco-mongol' terms which record the vocalic
fluctuation between -ï- and -o/u- common in turco-mongol, i.e.,:

1. 叱奴 < *činoa vs. 醜奴 < *čonoa
2. 叱伐 < *či-b'i^{w}ɐt vs. 醜伐 < *čo-b'i^{w}ɐt

Ch'ou-fa 醜伐 ts'iɐu-b'i^{w}ɐt, which was Liu Hsien's Hsiung-nu
name (cf. HTHYFC 2: 2), undoubtedly represents *čobar. The parallel
form *čibar (> 叱伐) gives us the clue to the meaning of the
Hsiung-nu name. Ch'ih-fa 叱伐 appears in the P'ien Ya 駢雅
ch. VII, as the transcription of an 'altaic' term designating the
color of a horse. Both transcriptions are doubtless attempts to
render the 'altaic' term for 'dapple-gray' which appears in jag.
čubar, tüm. čibar, kaz. čuwar, mo. čoχor, ma. cohoro 'gray, dapple,
dapple -gray, truité' (P. Pelliot, TP, 1930, 325). The 'altaic'
word passed as a loan-word into Russian where it is recorded (with
the same meaning) in the form čubar- > чубарый.

3.   The name of one of Lo-ch'ên's (Nu-chên's) brothers, Ch'ü-
chin 去斤 (KD 491, 385: ᶜk'i̯^{w}oʾ-ₑki̯ə̯n) can also be easily reconstructed into its original 'mongol' form. In its list of T'o-pa
surnames J 113 states that Ch'ü-chin as a surname was changed into
Chinese 艾 ai 'artemisia' >'blue-gray' > 'old man'. *k'i̯^{w}o -ₑki̯ə̯n
would, indeed, be an excellent transcription of mongol köke
'blue' (which applied to designate the color of a horse generally

equals 'blue-gray'; cf. also kᵖk <u>kökšin</u> 〰️ 'old man').

The <u>P'ien Ya</u>, <u>loc. cit.</u>, quoting the <u>Yü P'ien</u> and the
<u>Kuang Yün</u>, yields us another term which probably re-
presents an 'altaic' designation of the color of a horse.
This is 駮騿 po-han < *b'uât-ɣân, 'a large horse of the
barbarians'. Possibly related to mo. <u>baraɣan</u> 'dark', 'of
a black color'.

IV.8. 'Barbarian' Boots

In the <u>TP</u>, 1928-29, 141, n. 1, Professor Pelliot called attention (in reviewing Wang Kuo-wei's work <u>Hu fu k'ao</u> 胡服考) to a
foreign term designating 'boot' which underlies Chinese 鞲鞠 *sâk-
*d'âk (also written, according to <u>Shih Ming</u> 3, 速獨 *suk-*d'uk).
The term appears to be 'altaic', but cannot be identified with any
word meaning 'boot' in 'turco-mongol'.

The hypothetical *saɣdaq can, however, be linked with an
'altaic' term through a more complicated chain. In <u>Shuo Wên</u> 3A we
find another binom, also ostensibly a foreign term, meaning 'boot' ~
'shoe', 鞈沙 *kap-*ṣa (also written 韐韠 *kap-*ṣa). The 'altaic'
word underlying this binom is undoubtedly related to the 'turco-mongol'
root *qabsa- ~ *qabča- 'to cover', 'to clothe' (recorded in mong.
<u>qubčasun</u> 'clothes' and doubtless derived from the root *qab- ~ *qob-
√'hollow'). The same stem appears in another binom 鞲鞈 *kau-*tṣ'a
< *qəβ-ča? -'quiver' (箭室) originally probably 'covering (~ con-
tainer) for arrows'. (Cf. also tk. <u>qubur</u> > russ. кобура 'pistol-
holster' and mong. <u>qoɣor</u> ~ <u>qoɣur</u> ~ *qoβur > <u>qo'or</u> 'quiver'.)

In other words, it seems as if in 'proto-turkish' the root *qab
~ *qob√'hollow' ~ 'cover' served as a versatile source for the derivation of designations of various 'vestments' for human beings as
well as for their implements (cf. tk. <u>qabuq</u> قابوق 'covering' <u>vs.</u>
قاوق <u>qauq</u> ~ <u>qawuq</u> 'headgear', <u>qab</u> 'sack', etc.). It appears also
that the same root was current in the palatalized form *keb- from
which are derived 'turco-mongol' *kebis 'rug, carpet' and tk. *keβis
'boot'. It may have, indeed, been the latter which served as the

original of 鞈 鞡 *qabša ~ *kabša.

In the light of the preceding, therefore, it would not seem to be rash to compare *saɣdak ~ *suɣduk 'boot' with 'turco-mongol' saɣadaq 'quiver', 'covering for the bow' < √*saq- 'to protect'? and with mo. suɣuli 'to put arrows into the quiver', suɣut 'to pull out', suɣul 'id.' *Saɣadaq ~ *suɣduk as a term designating 'the boot' would thus be derived either from a root meaning 'protect by covering' or a related one ambivalently meaning 'put in' ~ 'pull out'.

The above discussion raises again the question of a possible ultimate relationship between 'Altaic' and Chinese (cf. 夾 kap 'to squeeze' vs. mo. qabči 'id.' and 韇 d'uk < KLuk 'quiver' vs. qoɣor).

HTHYFC 11 (September 1935)

Sino-Tibetan Notes

1. Some Tibetan Names of Bovidae in Chinese

Among the many Chinese terms designating bovine animals and classified under Det. No. 93 there appear several words undoubtedly Tibetan in origin or representing common Sino-Tibetan prototypes.

1. Ch. 犙麣 pr. 逵 $*gi^{w}_{\wedge}əγ$ 渠龜 (on the final consonant of the second word, cf. Karlgren, TP, 1931, $ki^{w}_{\wedge}əγ$), designating a big, heavy ox found in Min-shan 岷山 and in the Shu country. It is recorded that in 318 A.D. a native of Shang-yung 上庸 (Northwestern Hupeh) shot one of those oxen and obtained from it 30 piculs of meat. Undoubtedly identical with 犙, 犥 $*ngi^{w}_{\wedge}əγ$, mentioned already in the Erh Ya, 犥 is most probably to be connected with Tib. yag 〈 yyag ཨགགས 'yak'. The same Tibetan term may underlie Chinese 犥 $*b'_{\wedge}ăk$ or $*p'i^{w}_{\wedge}ok$ 'a large humped ox', cf. Tib. p'o-yyag 'male ox'.

2. The well-known Chinese term fêng-niu 封牛 'humped ox' is without doubt to be equated with the Tibetan designation of the wild yak, ₒbrong འབྲོང་, mod. pr. ḍong. That 夆 KD 31 $_{c}b'i^{w}_{\wedge}ong$ and 封 KD 33 $_{c}pi^{w}_{\wedge}ong$ (the phonetics of 犙 and 犚, the Chinese name of a wild humped ox, attested already in the Han dynasty) were pronounced in archaic Chinese as $*bl^{w}ong \sim *br^{w}ong$ is evidenced by the the following:

封 $*_{c}pi^{w}_{\wedge}ong$, another name of Lung-mên 龍門 KD 585 $_{c}li^{w}ong$ (KD 585 had an archaic $*kl-$ $*bl-$ initial, cf. especially 龐 $_{c}b'ăng$ and 朧 $*b'ung$).

封 and 峯 $_{c}pi^{w}_{\wedge}ong$ are undoubtedly connected semantically with 壟 $li^{w}_{\wedge}ong$ (all three words meaning 'mound') and 隆 KD 584 $_{c}liung$ (Ph. KD 351 夅 kăng$^{?}$) 'high'.

Chin. 蜂, 逢 $_{c}p'i^{w}_{\wedge}ong$ 'bee, wasp' = Tib. bung-ba $\sim$ sbrang-bu 'bee'.

This correlation is further substantiated by the existence in

Chinese of a word for 'wild yak' which registers the Tibetan phonetic evolution ₔbrong > ḏong. This is 牛庸, 豿庸 , archaic *dⁱ𝚠ong, a term already occurring in Ssǔ-ma Hsiang-ju's "Shang-lin fu" (note that the famous poet was a native of Ssǔ-ch'uan) in the meaning of 'large humped ox' and equated by all scholiasts with the 犎 *ₔbrong.

A similar Ssǔ-ch'uan black ox 'producing fine yak tails' is 犛 . When designating an animal the word has two pronunciations: *mⁱ𝚠ong and *lji (= 里 , cf. KD Notes 2 for a *bl- in this group). There is no doubt that we have here the Tibetan terms ₔbrong 'male wild yak', ₔbri 'female wild yak'.

3. In 犘 *ma (a large <u>black</u> ox from Ssǔ-ch'uan) and 牻 *miɛ̌n (a large <u>black</u> ox of Western China, also 牅 *p'iän) we have possibly the elements of Tib. <u>ba-men</u> 〔Tibetan script〕'wild ox', <u>Bos gavaeus</u>, identified by Vladimirtsov (<u>DRAN</u>, 1924, p. 118) with the 'Beyamini' of Marco Polo (Yule, II, 52n).

4. In Chinese 牨, 牛网 *ₔkâng 'bull' (cf.𠃐 Ph. k'âng, but pr. lâng; observe also that KD 1300 ᶜ mⁱ𝚠ang must be Ph., and not co-signific, in 岡 = 网 + 山, a *kl- *bl- consonantal complex existing undoubtedly in the Chinese word for 'mound') is hidden Tib. <u>glang</u> 'bull'.

5. A *kl- *bl- initial attested in 睦 mⁱuk ~ 坴 lⁱuk which forms the 'Phonetic' of 賣 KD 1336A *dⁱuk justifies us in equating Chinese 犢 d'uk 'calf' with Tib. <u>p'rug</u>, pr. t'ug, 'calf'. Cf. <u>Shih Ming</u> XIX where 犢 d'uk = 睦 mⁱuk.

2. Archaic Chinese *Bl- ~ *Br-

As established in the preceding note, the Tibetan word ₔbrong > ḏong 'wild yak' appears in Chinese, in the archaic forms *bl𝚠ong ~ *dⁱ𝚠ong, as a term designating a wild humped ox. The Sino-Tibetan root thus underlies the following Chinese characters:

1. 犎 ᶜ pⁱ𝚠ong < *bl𝚠ong
2. 牛庸 *ₔdⁱ𝚠ong KD 263
3. Add also 童 ~ 犝 KD 1149 ₔd'ung, name of a large

wild ox supplying 'yak-tail standards', found in the
country of the Southwestern barbarians (C 117) The antiquity of the word is attested by its occurrence in the
I Ching, hexagram N 26, as well as in the Erh Ya.

The same Sino-Tibetan term for 'wild ox' must form the basis
of Chin. 旄 601 ᵨmâu 'yak's tail, standard' (幢 *ᵨd'ằng 'stream-
er'!) and 氂 in its reading ᵨmâu 'id.' (cf. the preceding note
for the equation 犛氂 = ₒbrong ~ ᵨbri).

If ᵨmâu (possibly < *ᵨmâu-g) be identified with ₒbrong, we
would have a good basis for the explanation, in the light of Sino-
Tibetan comparative linguistics, of the Chinese generic terms for
'cattle'. These are:

1. 牛 ᵨngi̯ə̯u 'ox', cf. KD Notes 4, for the presence of
an l- in Anlaut.

2. 牡 ᶜmə̯u 'bull', 'male of animals'
Rarer synonyms: 特 d'ək
牬 *p'ə̯u
犦 *p'ầk
牰 *•ə̯u, *ɣə̯u
㸶 *•ə̯u

3. 牝 ᶜb'ji ~ ᶜb'i̯ĕn 'cow', 'female of animals'
4. 牧 mi̯uk 'tend cattle'

The last word, mi̯uk, seems to indicate an archaic *-g in the
whole KD 673 group. 牧 mi̯uk also appears in the Erh Ya as the name
of 'an ox with a black belly', parallel to 牰 *d'i̯ə̯ug 'an ox with
black eyes'. 土 ᶜt'uo ~ ᶜd'uo is Phonetic in 牡, according to the
Shuo-wen. The final -k of the two synonyms d'ək and pầk substan-
tiates further a final guttural. The evidence leads us thus to
reconstruct the evolution of the archaic Chinese word for 'bull' in
the following fashion:

'Proto-Chinese' **brə̯ug > arch. **brə̯uᵍ > 1. anc. mə̯u > 2.
anc. d'ək 'bull'; and >1. anc. mi̯uk > 2. anc. d'i̯ə̯ug 'black ox'
**brə̯ug is undoubtedly a variation of ₒbrong ~ Chin. **blᵂong
~ **brᵂong > **d'ung.

As to ᶜb'ji ~ ᶜb'i̯ĕn, it appears to be nothing else but the

Chinese counterpart of Tib. <u>ₒbri</u>. The evidence is supplied by the following:

1. 尾 ᶜmjʷei 'tail
   氂 ꜀lji 'horse's tail' } synonyms of 旄 and 犛,

in other words, <u>ₒbri</u> 'yak-tails' vs. <u>ₒbrong</u> 'yak-tails'.

2. 牝 ᶜb'ji ~ ᶜb'i̯ĕn, in the sense of 'mate, companion' ~ 比 pji 'match, double' belongs to a series of words, the root of which undoubtedly possessed a **<u>bl</u>-initial complex. Thus, cf.

並 KD 742 ᶜb'i̯ʷeng
并 KD 741 ꜀pi̯äng } 'double' and 兩 542 ꜀li̯ang 'id.'

With the regular change of **pl ~ **pr > d'-, t'-, we have:

量 574 ꜀li̯angᵓ 'even, to weigh' (Ph. 重!) <u>vs.</u> 重 1270 *d'i̯ʷong 'double'

平 743 ꜀b'i̯ʷang 'even' <u>vs.</u> 稱 (cf. 秤) 1206 *t́'i̯əng 'balance'

3. 牝 ᶜb'ji ~ ᶜb'i̯ĕn is also a synonym of 麗 540 lieiᵓ ~ ꜀ljie̯ 'mate', 'couple' and of 馬吝 *li̯ĕn 'mare', 'female' (observe that 文 muən is <u>Phon</u>. in 吝 li̯ĕn).

Archaic **brong and **bri ~ **brien did thus represent not only two words designating the 'wild bull' and the 'wild cow', but were applied also to the designation of all male and female animals forming couples. We find an amazing correlation with these ancient Sino-Tibetan forms in the old Chinese names of the dragon:

'Male dragon' 龍 li̯ʷong < **blʷong (the existence of a *bl- ~ *kl- initial is well-attested in this group.)

'Female dragon' 螭 *t'i̯a, but <u>Phon</u>. 离 KD 533 ꜀ljie̯ < *꜀lji̯a̯, also written 彲 *t'i̯a, but <u>Phon</u>. ꜀ljie̯, plainly indicative of **bl- ~ *-br- > t'- evolution. (Observe also that 麗, especially in the compounds 驪 and 鸝 ~ 離, means '<u>black</u>'.

Two common archaic designations of the mysterious Chinese dragon thus go back to Sino-Tibetan *<u>ₒbrong</u> ~*<u>ₒbri</u> which had undoubtedly the meaning of 'a pair of black wild animals' > 'wild ox'.

3. Wild Ox, 'Archaic' Monsters, and T'ao-t'ieh

(To the memory of Benjamin March)

Sino-Tibetan *brong-bri* 'wild ox', as has been suggested in the
preceding note, formed the nucleus of a far more extensive semantic
cluster than one would have supposed. The wild ox was the most
widely distributed species of wild life with which the primitive
population of Southeastern Asia came into contact, and in the term
designating it was preserved the original undifferentiated Sino-
Tibetan 'semantic atom', a referential complex with the meaning 'wild'
⟶ 'wild animal' ⟶ 'couple'.

Amazing as it seems, we find this original root underlying
almost all Sino-Tibetan terms designating animals, especially wild
ones. The differentiation of the root proceeded along the lines of
a phonetic evolution, the clearest case of which we possess in Tibetan
*S]BR ~ *S]GR- > ŚR- > D-, T-.

Indeed, it is only in the light of this phonetic 'law' and the
progressive differentiation of an original *S]BRONG ~ *S]BRI that
almost all puzzling problems of Indo-Chinese linguistics in connection with the names of animals can be explained. (The reader is here
especially referred to the vast material on the subject assembled by
Laufer in his study "The Si-Hia Language," TP, 1916, pp. 1-128.)

As may have been noticed, in many of the Chinese words with a
*bl- initial the *bl- is interchanged with *GL-, while one of the
earliest differentiated forms of *BRONG appears to be *BRAU-g. *BRI
~ *BRIA ~ *BRIEN offer no great phonetic difficulties. Bearing in
mind the phonetic 'law' *S]BR > *S]GR > *ŚR > T-,D-, we can now tabulate
the following evolution of *BRONG ~ *BRI in the names of various
animals:

1. Indo-Chinese *S]BRONG 'insect', 'reptile'

    a. 'insect': Tib.: bung-ba, sbrang-ba 'bee'

                     bong 'small insect'

          Ahom: mling 'firefly'

          Siam.: meng 'insect'

Chin.: 蜂 ₌pi^w ong < *bl- 'bee'

蝱 ₌mang 'gadfly'

蠓 ₌mung˙ 'flies'

蠅 ₌ieng, Ph. mɐng! 'fly'

Tangut: 夢積 mêng-tsi 'fly'

b. 'reptile': Tib.: sbrang 'worm'; sbrul > dul 'snake';   brug
'dragon' (cf. oprog 'pasture', Chin. 牧 miuk
'id.'); k'lu 'naga serpent'

Indo-Chinese (Gyami): *śre

Chinese: 龍蝘 li^w ong-t'ia < *blong-blia (cf. 麗
< *śria); 龍 ~ 虹 (g'ung 'rainbow', ori-
ginally 'dragon', as established by L. C.
Hopkins) < *glung; 它 d'a ~ 蛇 d'ia 'serpent'
< **blia?

Tangut: 沒魯 mo-lu < *bru? 'reptile'; 疲 mang
'serpent'

*S]BR- > *D: Chinese: 蟲 d'iung 'insect', 'reptile'

2. Indo-Chinese *S]BRONG 'horse'

Burmese, etc.: *mrang

Bunan: śrangs;   Kanaurī: śang

Tib.:   giling 'strong horse'; rkyang 'wild horse'
rta *bra? 'horse'

Tangut: 領羅 ling-lo < *bling-bla? 'horse'

Chin.: 馬 ma < *bra? 'horse'

Mongol: morin 'horse'

3. Indo-Chinese *S]BRONG ~ *S]GRONG 'tiger'

Lepcha: sa-t'ong 'tiger'

Tib.: stag < *sbrag? 'tiger'; tung-nga 'three
year old tiger'

Chin.: 虎 χuo < *gluo, as evidenced by the use
of 虍 as Ph. in 盧, 虜, etc., luo. Cf.
Fang Yen VIII for ancient dialectical words:
李父 *lji-b'iu (~ Manyak lêphê 'tiger');
伯都 *pek-tuo (for 伯 < 百 'hundred', cf.
Tib. brgya). Also the 楚 Ch'u state term for
'tiger' *t'uo 虓鬼 or * uo-t'uo 烏 /.

Mon-Khmer: *kla; Tangut: 勒 lê.

4. *S]BRONG ~ *S]BRIA likewise underlies the Sino-Tibetan terms for:

   a. 'camel' Chin.: 駱駝 d'ak-d'a < **brak-bra
              Tangut: 浪能 liang-nêng < **brang-breng (cf.
              能 Tang. 'two', 浪 'couple' = Chin. 雙
              *sâng 'id.')

              Tib.: rnga-bong 'id.'

   b. 'bear'   Chin.: 熊羆 g'i̯ung-b'ai < **brung-brai 'bear'
              Tangut: 領 ling < **bring 'id.'

   c. 'wolf'   Chin.: 狼 lâng
              Tib.: spyang
              Tangut: 勒 lê

   d. 'hare', Chin.: 兔 t'uo
              Tangut: 蕈詑 lê-wo
              Shan: pang-lai 'hare'

   e. 'fox'   Chin.: 狸 li < *bri (cf. KD Notes, 2)
              Tang.: 能 nêng < *breng

This investigation of the ramifications of this microcosmic ~ macrocosmic phoneme could be pursued almost indefinitely, but a detailed review of the phonetic changes of the words, as they appear with amazing regularity all through the Indo-Chinese world, will have to be postponed until a future note. Here the writer would like to present the evidence which reveals *S]BRONG ~ *S]BRI as the phonetic-semantic key to Chinese mythology.

We have established that *S]BRONG ~ *S]BRI underlies most of the Chinese words for 'couple' (of wild animals) ~ 'male and female'. In the guttural variation of the same root we see the basis of Chinese:

   雄 g'i̯ung < *GRONG 'male'
   雌 ts'ia < *GRIA 'female'

and the underlying roots of the names of all monsters of Chinese mythology also reveal themselves as connected with the *BR- ~ *GR-phoneme; (for an enlightening analysis of the complex problem of ancient Chinese mythology the reader is referred to Marcel Granet's

<u>Danses et Légendes</u>). Thus *BRONG ~ *BRI 'male and female ox',
'dragons', 'bears' are absolutely identical with the following monsters
of mythology:

1. 魍魎 *mi^w ang-*liang < *BRANG-BRANG (observe that both
<u>Phonetics</u> 罔 and 两, 'net' and 'two' have archaic *bl-)
'monsters of the hills and rivers'.

2. 重黎 *d'i^w ong-lji < [BR>D]ONG-[B]RI (黎 li 'black'!)
ancient monsters whose chief was 蚩尤 *t'i-*giəuɣ 'an ox-like
monster'. Cf. 重黎 Chung-li's connection with 夔 K'uei,
minister of music under Shun, who is in turn associated with
夒龍 *BRONG; K'uei ~ 犁夔 *gi^w əɣ (cf. Note 1) is the <u>yak</u>. Cf.
also 鍾馗 *d'i^w ong-*giəuɣ 'protector from all demons', himself nothing but a <u>k'uei</u> 'yak' (夔一足也,which see
Granet, <u>op. cit.</u>, 506-507).

3. 女丁(~姮)娥 *GRANG-NGA 'goddess of the moon', 'hare
in the moon' (cf. supra).

4. Most of the monsters connected with the Deluge Story, such
as 驩兜 *GRUAN-TƏG and 共工 *GRONG-GRONG, an early
differentiated form of *BRONG-*BRUA-N ~ *BRUAI, appear in KD 22:

   a. 番 c b'i^w ən 'footprints of wild animals'
      c p'i^w ən 'barbarians', cf. 蠻 *bluan
   b. 膰 c b'i^w ən 'roast sacrificial meat'
   c. 幡 c p'i^w ən 'banner', cf. 旂, 幢

The root, 'graphically' speaking, is here 田 c d'ien, which was
a polyphone as evidenced by 畝 c məu, 苗 *miau (cf. the monsters <u>San
Miao</u> 三苗) and 畾 luai, the original forms being *Brien (cf. 天
t'ien 'sky' vs. 旻 miěn < *brien 'sky'), *Breu, and *Bruai. This
last meaning 'thunder' (cf. Tib. ə brug 'dragon', 'thunder') immediately
explains the connection of most of our monsters with thunder and music
which runs like a red thread through all the myths (cf. also 彭 <
*BRANG, 震 *ȶien < *BRIEN, 霆 c d'ieng < *BRENG, 霹靂 *BREK-BREK
'thunder, noise of thunder').

Finally, it is through a form *GRAU-*GRIEN (~ *BRIEN) that we
can best understand the designation of that puzzling motif of ancient
Chinese art, the <u>t'ao-t'ieh</u>.

饕餮 t'âu-t'ien (or t'iet)

Note that t'âu has as its Phonetic 號 *g'âu which, in its turn, contains the phonetic element 虎 *GLUO ~ *GRUO 'tiger', while t'ien 'greedy' must necessarily be derived from an archaic *GLien as shown by its synonyms 婪 lâm < *klam 'greedy', 歉 kiem < *kliem, and 貪 t'âm Ph. 今 ₍kiəm < *kliəm. The t'ao-t'ieh < *GRAU-GRIEN is, then, in the light of the above discussion, just another form of *BRONG-BRI and combines, in this capacity, the meanings "wild animal - sacrificial animal - couple (-divine couple, heaven and earth?) - the beast of thunder." At the same time it shares with any other *BRONG-BRI the latter's peculiar characteristics. A universal symbol, it provided universal protection against the evil powers of nature and secured, on the other hand, all possible blessings. In one word, it was the Chinese Logos, the truly universal word, the beginning of all things.

As the author well realizes, the above theory of the *BRONG-BRI raises a thousand questions concerning the 'paleontology' of human speech and necessitates a further discussion of the theory of the genesis of language from an original single and undifferentiated sound. As 'altaicists' would undoubtedly have noticed, it also gives rise to the problem of an ultimate relationship between Sino-Tibetan and 'Altaic'.

HTHYFC 13 (March 1936)

4. Archaic final -S

The nineteenth chapter of the Erh Ya mentions an animal called mêng-sung 蒙頌 (KD 611, 475: *mung-zi^{w}ong). Kuo P'o's commentary supplies a variant name mêng-kuei 蒙貴 (KD 456: *mung-kj^{w}ei⁼), and describes the animal as being similar to a wei 蜼 (a small, long-tailed monkey), purplish black in color, catching rats and mice better than a cat, and being a native of Indo-China, where (add other commentators) it is often domesticated.

From the description, as well as the name, there is hardly any doubt that the animal is the mongoose (Herpestes griseus), the English name of which is derived from some Indian or Indo-Chinese language (cf. Marathi mangūs, Kanarese mungisi). If the second form given by

Kuo P'o be taken as a faithful Chinese transcription of an ancient Indo-Chinese loan-word (possibly some such form as *mungus), the question arises whether 貴 KD 456 kj^{w}ẹi² did not possess, in the archaic language, a final -S, ancient kj^{w}ẹi² being possibly derived from **kj^{w}ẹs.

This supposition can, I believe, be substantiated by the following: 1. at least in one case, KD 456 used as a phonetic is pronounced *ɣuət : 潰 ɣuâi² < g'-, but cf. Chi Yün: 胡骨切 *ɣuət > **ɣuəδ (in the T'ang dynasty). 2. 繢 ɣuâi², a synonym of 繪 ɣuâi² 'embroidery', undoubtedly had a final *-d (indicated by the tone and such synonyms as 絹 *kuət ~ ɣ^{w}at).

In the light of the preceding, we can now easily identify the Tibetan parallel of Chinese 貴 kj^{w}ẹi² 'value', which is ·k'os 'worth', 'value', 'importance'; *ɣuâd (繪,繢,絹), on the other hand, can be identified with Tibetan ·god 'to draw', 'design', 'decorate'.

Finally, KD 427 骨 kuət which is the phonetic of 絹 appears to be connected with its Tibetan relatives through the following chain:

1. 骨 kuət ~ *kuəδ 'bone' is phonetic in 㲉,猾,搰, 滑 *kuət ~ *ɣuət ~ *ɣ^{w}at, all meaning 'disorderly', which would indicate an archaic *KL- (cf. HTHYFC 12) which is further evidenced by its own phonetic 冎 KD 435 ᶜk^{w}a < *KL-, cf. 䯏 *lâ.

2. The ancient form of 體 ᶜt'iei 'body' was 骵, 髏 possibly read *kuət < *kl-, *Klues > *kliei > *t'iei.

3. Tib. bkod (< ·god) 'frame', 'body', 'figure'; rus 'bone'; lus 'body'.

Another final -s in archaic Chinese appears, I believe, in KD 615 米 ᶜmiei 'rice' which has always been conjecturally compared with Tibetan ·bras 'rice'. That the initial mi- of the Chinese word goes back to a *BL- is evidenced by 米 miei being phonetic in 類 *luâi² which, in turn, serves as phonetic in KD 227 類 lj^{w}i² (米 and 頁 are not co-signific as Karlgren implies). 類 *luâi² is also phonetic in 瀨 *luâi² and 籟 *luâi. The latter, it is to be noted, is a synonym of 戾 KD 530: liei and liet, and a final -d ~ -δ ~ -s?

is further substantiated by the following:

1. 潀頪 *luâi⁰ is also read *luât 拉捋切and is a synonym
of 酹 luâi< -d, luât 'libation'.

2. In the meaning 'similar' 类頪 ljʷi⁰ is read *luĕt 來聿切 ;
cf. also 樏頪 *ljwi⁰, a synonym of tsïäi⁰ < -d < *TSL-d 祭 'sacrifice', and for *BL- 类頪比也 .

The Tibetan -s of gnyis 'two' is likewise made apparent in
ancient Chinese 二   KD 8:   ńźi⁰ 'two' through its synonym 次 KD
1095: ts'i⁰ 'second' which must have had a final -ᵹ ~ -s as indicated
by 朳次, 木咨 *tsiet: 前迭切 .

Cedules from a Berkeley Workshop in Asiatic Philology (with Postscript by S. H. Chen)

Cedules Reprinted 1969

Tsing Hua Journal of Chinese Studies, 7.2(1969), 1-39.
*[This is a selection of 26 "Cedules" from the complete group
of 54 (see # 24). The original serial numbers of the 26
reprinted here are: 001, 005-009, 012-013, 017-034. —Ed.]

1

On Crypto-Parallelism in Chinese Poetry

Most students of Chinese prosody would readily agree that a disciplined inquiry into the principles of stylistic parallelism is propaedeutical to all translation work, for in Chinese, a language innocent of morphology, clarity of thought and intelligibility of syntactical relations are often dependent on rigid adherence to word-order patterns, particularly so in the poetic style with its paucity of kommatic particles. Yet few translations reflect adequately the more intricate cases of parallelistic construction, and fewer still show an awareness of what may be called crypto-parallelism. We may illustrate the point with Tsu Yung's quatrain "CHUNG-NAN (famous mountain range south of Ch'ang-an, the capital), GAZING AT THE REMNANT SNOWS" which reads as follows (characters below):

L 1: *Chung*	*nan*	northern slope	mtn range	flourish
L 2: Amassed	snow	float	cloud	tip, edge
L 3: Forest	beyond	brighten	fairing (sky)	color
L 4: City	within	increase	sunset	cold

The close *parallelismus membrorum* of the second distich is evident, but most readers would take the first as non-parallel and treat L 1 & 2 as nominal sentences, perhaps with 1.5 serving as a half-hearted predicate, somewhat in this fashion: "How luxuriant is the N. slope of Chung-nan, with its massed snows at the edge of floating clouds" (so do the Japanese translators). They would maintain that 1.1-2, being a proper name, cannot be // to 2.1-2, and that 1.3 is definitely a substantive. If so, they would have overlooked two important rules of parallelism: a) it is the function of the second line of a distich to give us the clue for the construction of the first; b) a common noun // to a proper name can subtly revive the concrete connotations of the latter. 'Northern (properly 'shadeward') slope', if // to 2.3, may function as a verb: 'to overshadow'. In fact, viewed in the light of L 2, all the words in L 1 (with the exception of 'range') appear to be bifunctional: 1-2 is a proper name, but at the same time, as // to 2.1–2, a descriptive phrase (*Chungnan* means 'to end in the south'); 1.3 is the predicate of the line ('overshadows') and concurrently the attribute of 'range'; 1.5, // to 2.5, is a noun, but is also apprehended as a verb on first reading. This character has the same classifier as 2.1, the etymonic 'grain', and the juxtaposition of the two graphs is doubtlessly intended to bring out their dormant primary meanings, namely 'budding, as ears of grain', and 'to stack up, as grain'. Finally, the key role played by 1.3 should draw our attention to 3.3 and 4.3, as predicates of their lines, and make us note their etymology. After a few trials, a careful translation may succeed in reproducing most to these features. We feel that the following rendering does at least partial justice to the original in its vocabulary and the interplay of parts of speech at pivotal points:

> Chung-nan, full-ended south, shadows its shadeward range, florescing—
> The ricked snows afloat the tags of fleeting clouds,
> Moon-brightening, beyond the forest-line, the hue of fairing scuds,
> But here, within these city-walls, aggrading the sunset chill.

終南陰嶺秀, 積雪浮雲端, 林表明霽色, 城中增暮寒.

Workshop Fund 1, in memoriam Edward T. Williams.

2

Philology in Translation-Land

Recent readings in translations of T'ang quatrains have left us immersed in deep sadness in the face of the lack of philological acumen, the critical shallowness, and the self-centered irreverence towards great poetry exhibited by would-be competent writers seeming unable to resist the lures of precocious publication. Wang Wei's *Deer Wattle* (*Hermitage*), presented *anglice* in skeletal form below, is a particular victim of a score of mistranslations:

L 1: Empty	mountain	not	see	men
L 2: Only	hear	men	talk	echoes /R/
L 3: Reverse	sunlight/shadow	enter	deep	forest
L 4: Again	shine	green moss *shang* /R; provisionally untranslated/

L 1 & L 2 having paraphrased themselves, most of our dragomans bog down on L 3.1, an epithet they frequently suppress, unaware of how aptly it describes the 'antistrophic' motion of the rays of a setting sun creeping into a grove in a direction opposite to the one they had followed at sunrise. But it is in the persistent rendering of L 4, by some such sentence as "And shines again *upon* the green moss", that all translators known to me (including, alas, modern Chinese and Japanese authors) betray their listless misconception of the whole poem. To interpret *shang³* (L 4.5: rhyming, hence homotonic, with L 2.5: *hsiang³*, 'echo'), without a blush, as if it were the postposition *shang¹*, 'on', 'upon', is a philological misdemeanor, notwithstanding the claims of some scholiasts that the tonal distinction is occasionally ignored; or else an unwarranted calumny imputing rhyme-tagging to the poet (a preposition is already implied, *more sinico*, in the verb 'to shine'). The supposedly irregular tone-pattern of the piece might be invoked in justification. Yet its orthodoxality is readily demonstrable in a diagram subjoining the standard tonal sequence to that of Wang Wei (level tone /-/; oblique /^/; optional /⌒/):

$$⌒_⌒ \, ^\wedge_-/⌒_{--} \, ^\wedge \, ^\wedge/⌒ \, ^\wedge \, ^\wedge_{--}/⌒ \, ^\wedge \, ⌒_- \, ^\wedge/$$
$$⌒_{--} \, ^\wedge \, ^\wedge/⌒ \, ^\wedge \, ^\wedge_{--}/⌒ \, ^\wedge \, ⌒_- \, ^\wedge/⌒_- \, ⌒ \, ^\wedge_-/$$

It is clear that Wang Wei must have first conformed to the traditional prosodic scheme, then simply transposed L 4 to head the tetrastich, thus bringing into focus his tritotonic rhymes and warning his reader to watch for a rondeau effect, his L 1 now reverberating as a putative L 5. As distinct from *shang¹*, 'upon', *shang³* meant 'to go up', and the poet—and renowned painter—must have depicted here one of the ever-wondrous aspects of sunset: its glow slowly ascending a mountain to its very top and fading into the void. A still inadequate, yet philologically correct, rendition of the stanza (with due attention to grapho-syntactic overtones and enjambment) would thus read:

> The empty mountain: to see no men,
> Barely earminded of men talking—countertones
> And antistrophic lights-and-shadows incoming deeper the deep-treed
>   grove
> Once more to glowlight the blue-green mosses—going up
>   (The empty mountain...)

空山不見人 • 但聞人語響 • 反景入深林 • 復照青苔上 •

Workshop Fund 5, in memoriam Michael J. Hagerty.

3

On the Translation of Chinese Binoms

Translators from the Chinese show a curious reluctance to attempt a systematic treatment of Sinitic compound phthegms, as distinct from monosyllabic morphemes.

Echoic binoms which abound in Chinese poetry suffer particulary from cavalier handling. Illustrative samples may be taken from that much-translated first song of the *Shih ching* (on the English renderings of which, including the better-founded, philologically speaking, versions by Legge (L), Karlgren (K), and Waley (W), see R. E. Teele, *Through A Glass Darkly: A Study of English Translations of Chinese Poetry*, Ann Arbor 1949):

1. *yao³-t'iao³* /A/, a typical rhyming homotonic binom; homosematic in that the hemiphthegms have the same graphic classifier (No. 116: 'cave'). Usually glossed by lexicographers as a unit. Here, the locus classicus, Han scholia draw fine distinctions between the components suggesting that the proton is descriptive of a woman's quiet temperament, the deuteron, of her beauty. Their equations, perforce couched in 'Basic Chinese', are paraphrased, rather unimaginatively, in basic English terms: 'modest, retiring' (L), 'beautiful and good' (K), 'lovely' (first stanza), 'shy' (W). This notwithstanding the fact that the phrase is not part of the elementary Chinese vocabulary. If scholiasts are to be followed, one is at a loss to understand what prevented the translators from using 'coy-and-comely', which would be more exact and would better echo, in its alliterativeness, the original. Now, elsewhere in literature, the compound occurs as a phrase descriptive of valley landscapes or architecture and is universally interpreted to mean 'secluded and loculated'. This is confirmed by cognates. We suggest a simple solution for the problem: 'cloistered-and-coved' (< 'cove', recess, secluded valley), alliterative and applicable equally to shy beauties, orography, and buildings.

2. *chan³-chuan³* /B/, a homosematic (No. 159: 'wheel'), homotonic synonymic binom. Translated simply 'to toss' or 'to turn'. The deuteron is the common word, the proton is obsolescent. We suggest: 'to throw (in the obs. sense of 'revolve, as a wheel')-and-turn', or 'to tourn-and-turn'.

3. *ts'en¹-tz'u¹* (arch. *ts'jəm-ts'ja*) /C/, a homotonic, alliterative, adverbial or predicative binom. Defined as descriptive of irregularity of line. Paraphrased: 'in patches' (W), 'of varying length' (K), 'here long, there short' (L). The binom has a close phonosemantic analogue in our 'zigzag' (adv.). In somewhat American English, 'jag-jog', 'jagged-and-jogged' would be a quite legitimate, self-explanatory rendering.

4. *tso-yu* /D/, an antonymic, complementary compound. 'Left and right' (adj. & adv.), but also, as every tyro knows, 'those on the left and right', 'attendants and acolytes'. In our text the term is amphibolous, probably deliberately, and appears three times in the construction: L & R, verb, pronominal object. It could be adverbial; all versions are positive it is. Yet it could also be nominal. A translation which overlooks the ambiguity is guilty of partiality. Solution: translate 'left-and-rightward', leaving to the reader the choice of interpreting this as an adverb or an adjectival noun in the plural.

A 窈窕   B 輾轉   C 參差   D 左右

Workshop Fund 1, in memoriam Edward T. Williams.

4

Shih Ching 1, a Re-Translation

The interpretations of that renowned classic range between two extremes: the Han scholiasts saw in it a paean extolling the virtue of Wen Wang's queen who self-effacingly kept searching for worthy maidens as additional consorts for her lord and instilled in them the same high-mindedness towards their rivals; sober moderns treat it as a simple folksong with two themes, the longing of a lover for his bride and an allusion to lustration rites with water-herbs (so Waley). The over-sophistication of the first view seems to strike a false note, although one can hardly overstress the polygynous character of ancient Chinese marriage customs after Marcel Granet's revealing studies. To accept wholeheartedly the second is to impute pathological perversity to those early commentators. Obviously, the original Chinese must have been sufficiently ambiguous to permit either interpretation. The following re-translation, which we believe to be syntactically and etymologically faithful, attempts to render the text's amphibology:

> "*Cwen-a-cwen*", the dove hawks
> Resting on the River's isle.
> So cloistered-coved the maiden(s) prim
> The lordling ('s) fained (–) for compart.
>
> Jag-jog, culls of rowèd-cress,
> Left-and-rightward stream such;
> So cloistered-coved the maiden(s) prim,
> To wake or drowse, but seek such.
>
> Seeking such—and getting not,
> To wake or drowse, lie prone in thought,
> And heart-away oh, heart-away oh,
> To tourn-and-turn, and 'verse to side.
>
> Jag-jog, culls of rowèd-cress,
> Left-and-rightward cull such;
> So cloistered-coved the maiden(s) prim,
> (With) lute and cittern friend such.
>
> Jag-jog, culls of rowèd-cress,
> Left-and-rightward pluck such;
> So cloistered-coved the maiden(s) prim,
> (With) bells and timbals glee such.

L1: Note the slightly suggestive Anglicized spelling of the onomatopoetic *kuan-kuan*. The bird of prey referred to here is unidentifiable, but its bisyllabic name contains the word *chiu*, 'turtle-dove', hence 'dove hawk'. L2: 'Resting': *tsai* is a verb, a mere preposition would not do. L3: See CBWAP 6; *shu* means 'beginning', 'tidy', 'nice', not 'good'; hence 'prim'. L4: For 'lordling', cf. *Philosophy East and West*, 2:4.321–322; *hao* is either the verb 'to be fond of' or the adjective 'fond'; *ch'iu*, mistranslated 'mate', means 'match', i.e. either 'mate' or 'rival'; it is this word that made possible the abstruse Han interpretation of the piece. L5: See CBWAP 6; *hsing*, 'duckweed', but etymol. 'herb growing in rows'; *ts'ai*, 'edible greens', etymol. 'culled herbs', hence 'culls'. L6: See CBWAP 6; *liu* is worrying commentators and translators unnecessarily: it is patently 'to stream' (causative), as water-herbs eased into the current preparatory to plucking. We use 'such' as a non-committal equivalent of *chih*, 'him, her, them, it'. L11: *yu*, 'longing' (unfortunately overworked in being equated to a dozen Chinese terms). Its sematic (No. 61: heart) suggests 'heart-away' // to 'far-away'. L14: 'cull', to // 'culls'. L18: 'pluck', mostly mistranslated; the etymonic is *mao*, 'to depilate', of plants: 'to tear away from stalk and root'. L18: 'glee' happily straddles the two meanings of *lo/yüeh*, 'music' and 'joy', 'give joy', 'enjoy'.

Workshop Fund 6, in memoriam Marcel Granet.

5

On Chinese *ts'ing*, 'blue-green'

For a language so homogeneous and so isolationist (in the sense of admitting to so few loanwords), Chinese is rather rich in color terms. A serious student of Chinese literature should be able to name on the spur of the moment some 30 monogrammatic chromatonyms, with graphs for 'black', 'red', and 'purple' heading the list with no less than 7–8 each. At this point lexicological memory would begin to falter. Only two or three synonyms for 'white' would be conjured. An erudite might succeed in recalling an additional word for 'yellow' (besides *huang*), or retracing a lonely classical counterpart to our 'brown'. A lexicographer would then be prone to launch into a dissertation on the peculiarity of the Chinese chromatic vocabulary (by no means an idiosyncrasy, though, for Chinese shares here a feature characteristic of other linguistic milieus) in having several words covering the spectrum of 'blue-green-purple-gray-black', with a none too clear—and but slowly emerging—differentiation. In the same breath, he would reminisce on the vexations endured in the contextual translation of these terms only one of which, the relatively modern word for 'blue' (*lan*, 'indigo-blue'; as a dye, derived from the Ch. woad-plant, a species of Polygonum), is unambiguous enough to present no exermeneutic stumbling-blocks. The primary chromatonym for 'blue-green-gray', *ts'ing*[1] /A/, is of considerable semantic interest. Like our 'green', it seems to be a cognate of 'to grow', Ch. *sheng*[1] /B/, which enters into the composition of the protograph; and like Gr. *chlōros<chloe*, 'chlorine', it refers above all to the color of vernal growth (in the cosmological color-scheme, it symbolizes the east, spring verdure, and youth). It does not show, however, an affinity with 'yellow', as do some IE analogues, and corresponds more to Gr. L. glaucous, 'bluish-green'. As an attribute, it may be rendered cerulean, azure, perse, leek-green, peacock-blue, cyaneous, bice, verdigris, gris, or livid, but it rarely designates 'yellowish green' and lighter shades of green, such as citrine, lime-green, reseda, or lettuce-green. These are commonly described by *lu* /C/ which has, as do dozens of other chromatonymic characters, the classifier No. 120, 'silk', indicative of its origin as the name of a tint in the ancient textile-tinctorial sub-industry of the great sericulture complex. Applied to greenery, then, *ts'ing* stresses its 'glaucophyllous' tinge; *lu*, its chlorophyllous aspects. The pleochroic diapason of *ts'ing* (and occasionally that of *lu*) is such that we have no choice but to translate it, according to context, with hyphenated forms: 'blue-green' (as vegetation), 'clear-blue' (as the sky), 'bluish-gray' (as a cloud, or smoke), 'bluish-black' (as hair); reserving 'green' and 'virid' for *lu*. As a phonogram, *ts'ing* produced several graphs of great semasiological import: *ts'ing²* (/D/; with C061: 'heart'), 'feeling, emotion, passion'; *ts'ing¹* (/E/; C085: 'water'), 'clear, pure'; *ts'ing¹* (/F/; C119: 'rice-grain'), 'fine, refined, subtle'; 'sperm, semen'; 'quintessence'; 'vital spore in some object or substance surviving its ostensible decomposition', hence often 'spirit, wraith'; *tsing¹* (/G/), 'quiet'; *ts'ing³* (/H/; C149: 'word'), 'to request'. One is tempted to treat all these graphs as originally related and express the bond between them by the word 'quick' (alive, vigorous)>'to quicken', as an English analogue of *sheng*, the protoglyph of which /I/ may well have represented a 'quickset' plant; and to etymologize their derivation thus: 'feeling'<'heart-quickening'; 'clear'<'quick-and-clear'; 'essence'<'quick-germ'; 'quiet'<'unquickened', 'quick-still'; 'to ask'<'to quicken verbally'. The overtone of 'quickening' is noticeable for TS'ING in poetic usage and I would favor translating it as 'quick-blue'(-green,-gray,-black).

A 靑 B 生 C 綠 D 情 E 淸 F 精 G 靜 H 請 I 坒

Workshop Fund 2.

6

On Latent Predicates in Chinese Poetry

Of all European languages, English enjoys the greatest commensurability with Chinese in its morphology and syntax. This gives English translators an enormous advantage over their continental confreres, but—by the same token—places them under heavier obligation to exercise all their resources in diction and taxis so as to achieve the closest possible approximation to the original, a goal frequently beyond the powers of those whose tongue is burdened with the impedimenta of

IE grammatical distinctions alien to Chinese, such as gender, desinence, and a strict differentiation between verbal and nominal forms. This obligation is, unfortunately, ignored by most translators who persist in encumbering their versions with supernumerary syntactical paraphernalia. Thus we find in them an almost universal horror of an alleged vacuum in every ostensibly verbless stichos and a feverish urge to fill it—with the first verb that comes to their mind. Yet a naive student of Chinese literature could easily quote scores of famous Chinese lines which in faithful word-by-word translation would be as free from any taint of avant-gardiste subversion of the Queen's English as Browning's: "The grey sea and the long black land;/ And the yellow half-moon large and low;/ And the startled little waves..." Let us take as an example a distich from one of Tu Fu's well-known poems (characters below):

> *Wei* (n. of a river)   north   spring   sky   trees (overtone: 'screen')
> *Chiang* (*the* Stream) east   sun/day sunset clouds

Strict parallelistic construction, with five substantives in each line, and no verb in sight; patently, two prepositional phrases that may be soberly read:

> (For me:) North of the Wei, the trees against the spring sky,
> (For him:) East of the Stream, the clouds at the sunset of the day.

Instead, the latest English rendering (W. Hung, *Tu Fu*, p. 51) paraphrases: "Now as I *look upon* the spring trees north of the Wei,/ He *is probably watching* the evening clouds east of the Chiang..." Forke's German version (*Dichtungen der T'ang-und Sung-Zeit*, p. 66) is by far more economical, yet still verbal: "Im Norden des Wei die Bäume/ Im Frühlingskleide *stehn*,/ Und östlich vom Kiang die Sonne/ In Wolken *will untergehn*". Even in German, and even under the self-imposed handicap of rhyme, a faithful translator could have avoided the gratuitous use of finite verbs. Thus, he could have written (with apologies for my bad German doggerel): ...die Bäume/ Am Frühlingshimmel rein/... die Wolken im Abendsonnenschein; or managed to hammer out some similar prepositional phrases with: ...dicht/ ...Abendsonnenlicht, or ...Kranz/ ...-glanz, ...Borten/ ...dorten, ...Band/ ...Rand, usw., usw. The original is, however, much more sophisticated in its overtones. As we have already pointed out (CBWAP 001), one of the potent Chinese poetic devices is positional bifunctionalism. Besides the obvious prepositional-phrase construction, another syntactical interpretation could be read into the distich, provided that interpretation is kept on the level of suggestion and is not over-stressed; that of construing each stichos as a verbal sentence: locative phrase, subject, predicate, object. The fourth word in each line would then acquire an overtone: 'sky' to be read *sotto voce* as 'to sky' (to send or impel skyward); 'sunset', as 'to sunset' (to darken or color, as at sunset). Granted this, no other European language but English could successfully reproduce the subtle amphibology:

The Wei and northward, springtime—skies—arbory,
The Stream and orient, the day-suns—sunset—clouds.

渭北春天樹, 江東日暮雲

Workshop Fund 3.

7

On Allotonic Overtones in Chinese Poetry

The problem of allotonic overtones in T'ang poetry is as little studied as that of crypto-parallelism. Witness another of Wang Wei's celebrated quatrains /A/:

L 1:	Alone	sit	dark	bamboo-thicket	inside
L 2:	Thrum	lute	again	long	whistle R
L 3:	Deep	forest	man/men	not	know
L 4:	Bright	moon	come	mutual	shine R

With minor variations, all 12 translators known to me rephrase: "I sit alone in the dark bamboo-grove/ I thrum my lute and sigh/ In the deep forest no one knows me/ Only the moon comes to shine upon me/". A fair rendering, as translations go, with four commonplace departures from the original: 1) The usual IE prosopocentric travesty of the infinitival mood of the Chinese (with 7 'me', 'my', 'I' in one version; 6 'ich', 'mir', 'mein', 'mich', in another). 2) The misrendering of the key word in the poem, 'whistle' (apparently deemed to be *mauvais ton* for a poet) by 'sigh' ('sing, hum, croon, seufzen, jauchzen', even 'shout'). 3) The common omission of 'again' and 'long'. 4) The pedestrian resolution of the challenging ambiguity L3 (what is the object of 'know': the poet, the grove, the whistling, the moon?). The clue to an understanding of the tetrastich lies in its anomalous tonal harmonics (cf. CBWAP 5) which may be seen through the collocation of its mode /WW/ with the standard scheme:

WW: ^ ^ _ _ _ ^ / _ _ ^ _ ^ / _ _ _ _ ^ _ / _ ^ _ _ _ ^ /
SS: ⌣ ^ _ _ _ ^ / ⌣ _ ^ ^ _ / ⌣ _ _ _ ^ ^ / ⌣ ^ ^ _ _ /

WW shows 5 tonic irregularities: L2.4: *ch'ang²*, 'long' (_ for ^); L2.5: *hsiao¹*, 'whistle' (^ for _); L3.5: *chih¹*, 'know' (_ for ^); L4.3: *lai²*, 'come' (_ for ^); L4.5: *chao⁴*, 'shine' (^ for _). Three of these are ditonic characters which may be read and construed in the requisite tone: *ch'ang²* as *chang³*, 'to prolong'; *chih¹* as *chih¹* (i.e. as=*chih⁴* /B/, not 'wisdom', but 'recognize', 'acknowledge',=*shih¹* /C/); *lai²* as *lai¹*, 'to induce to come'. The rhyme-words are, however, monotonic. Doubtless, the poet intended them primarily as loxotones (oblique in tone), but he also meant to puzzle his reader who—if at all sensible to prosodical canons—was likely to misread the words at first as homeograms of the proper tone. Now, *hsiao¹* and *chao*[1] have each two common platytonic (level tone) homeograms: *hsiao*[1], 'Panpipe', and *hsiao*[1], 'sough' (as the wind); *chao*[1], 'bright light', and *chao*[1], 'to summon' /D & E/. In Chinese tradition, Panpipes (also called *lai*[1] /F/) were believed to conjure the magic aeolian music of nature (t'ien- (ti-)-lai). Lastly L 3 & L 4 are crypto-parallel. All that is needed to reveal the parallelism is to read L 3.3, 'man', as a verb 'to man' ('to furnish with man/men', 'to make manlike', // to L 4.3, 'is /caused to /come'). Note further (in the translation below): 'to longwhile'—to be taken either as *v.t.* or *v.i.*; 'celate': the most comprehensive term covering the range of L 1.3 ('den-dark, ensconced, latebrous, occult, arcane, Hell-dark, to encell (incarcerate)'; the reiteration of 'moon' in L 4 reflecting the graphic gemination in Chinese (// to that of 'trees' in L 3), and the emphatic position of 'bright' for the double entendre: 'bright'=a) luminous, b) intelligent. Enjambement *à discrétion.* (..) for overtones.

> All by one's lone, to sit within the celate bamboo-bosk,
> ' To thrum the lute, once more to longwhile whistling
>   (for a Pandean sough)—
> The deep-treed grove—manned—not to acknow—
> The moon, moonbright, is come—aspectant—to glowlight
>   (a glow invoked...)

A 獨坐幽篁裏, 彈琴復長嘯, 深林人不知, 明月來相照. B 智   C 識   D 蕭簫
E 昭招 for 嘯照   F 籟

Workshop Fund 5.

8

On Fishing Snow

In this cedule I wish to confess to twenty years of academic treason: two decades of grudging admiration for the clumsy and sometimes pathetic, but always honest and sincere attempts of the late Florence Ayscough to metaphrase Chinese poetry verbatim. Her grasp of Chinese grammar may have been infirm and her enthusiasm for the graphic analysis of characters as unbridled as Ezra Pound's. Yet her scripts show recognition of a primary responsibility of a translator, the search for diction in some degree commensurate with that of the original; perhaps also a deeper respect for great poetry than is evident in the product of so many of us, staid academicians, who dismiss her efforts with an indulgent smile. Her work often betrays her innocent fallibility; ours, as often, unfaithfulness to our knowledge. Imagine Mrs. Ayscough—in her 'Tu Fu Period'—re-translating Liu Tsung-yüan's memorable RIVER SNOW:

L 1:	Thousand	hills	: birds'	flight	cut-off /R/
L 2:	Ten-thousand paths		: men's	footprints	extinguished /R/

L 3: Orphan   boat   : straw-cloak bamboo-hat old-man
L 4: Lonely   angles : cold   river   snow   /R/

This unwieldy 'pony' would happen to be a better translation of the tetrastich than the 7 or 8 current periphrases rather nonchalantly produced by unquestionably competent men.   Diction: Mrs. A. would have striven, in her gauche way, to hit the right semantic key for every word.   Pundits omit or add words *ad libitum*. Taxis: Mrs. A. would not have been too sure of her syntax, but would have at least refrained from tampering with the striking alignment—in favor of idiomatic clichés.   Common misfeasance of translators: in LL 1 & 2, they invariably emasculate the two rhyme-verbs by reading: 'not a bird flying', 'not a trace of men'.   Though all cognizant of the poet's Buddhistic bent, they undiscerningly slur over the verb 'extinguish', 'put out, as a fire' (the graph actually contains the elements 'fire' and 'water'), with its Buddhist subauditur of 'release through extinction'.   By contrast, they supply in L 3 some flabby verb: 'there is' (an old fisherman who...) 'sits', 'lies in', etc.   Either L 3.1 or L 4.1 is dropped or toned down, on the pretext of tautology; L 3.3–4 often omitted as superfluous local color.   The uniform interpolation of the preposition *'in'* after 'angle' in L 4 is insensitive and untenable. Translators seem oblivious of the tradition (both Buddhist and Taoist) of philosophical angling—without bait or hook—(the sole exception is Soame Jenyns imaginative enough to consider the possibility in a footnote), not only as "The Contemplative Man's Recreation", but as a symbolic monition on the vanity of life's fuss and flurry.   There is little doubt that the poet intended us to read the last three words as the *direct* object of 'angle', and that the desolation of the scene and the implied parable (the flakes of ego extinguished in the flow of eternity) were underlined by him in the nominal (non-verbal), bead-like parallelistic structure of the distich (LL 3 & 4).   Finally, one need not share Mrs. A.'s predilection for discovering graphic overtones in every word to note the significance of the sematic (C094: 'dog') in L 4.1, 'lonely', contrasted with L 3.1, 'orphan' (C039: 'child').   Lexicographers assert that the term referred *imprimis* to the 'singleness' of a shepherd dog.   We should not hesitate, therefore, to translate it emphatically 'cur-lonely' (English 'cur', originally 'shepherd dog').

A thousand hills: bird-flights cut short,
A myriad paths: men's track damped out;
An orphan-boated, strammel-coped, straw-hatted gaffer
Cur-lonely angling—the chill—Stream—snow...

千山鳥飛絕, 萬徑人蹤滅; 孤舟簑笠翁, 獨釣寒江雪.

Workshop Fund 7, in memoriam Mrs. Florence Ayscough McNair.

9

Syntactical Metaplasia in Stereoscopic Parallelism

The essentials of Chinese syntax may be reduced to two simple rules: 1. 'Modificative precedes principal', 'M—P'. 2. The normal order of the main members of the sentence is: 'subject (often latent)—predicate—object'; in our terminology: 'G—F—E—D—C': 'gerent' (subject)—'factor-functive' (a bivalent term designating either a 'pre-predicate' /factor/ or a 'finite predicate', an intransitive verb terminating a syntactical unit /functive/—'effective' (a transitive predicate)—'destinate' (object)—'complement'. Among syntagms preposed to a gerent ('G'), we may have a 'hypothematic' ('H'), the 'logical' subject of discourse, not infrequently a preposed destinate repeated later on, in its normal post-predicate position, in the form of a 'resumptive' pronoun ('R'); or a 'topological' ('T'), that is a topotactical term or phrase indicative of the location of the action in space or time. As the Chinese language has no genuine prepositions, but only topological nouns (postpositive) and verbs (prepositive), used mostly in nude juncture, it is not always easy to distinguish a hypothematic from a topological. As a principal, the first member of the main syntactical body may also be preceded by a modificative ('M'), and we often face the problem of weighing the relative merits of an 'H' vs. 'T' vs. 'M' interpretation of the head item of a sentence. Thus the sequence BOAT MAN..., or BOAT INSIDE (topological noun) MAN..., beginning a sentence might mean: 1. "As for the BOAT, the MAN..."/ As for the INSIDE of the BOAT, the MAN..." 2. "In the BOAT, the MAN..."/"INSIDE the BOAT, the MAN..." 3. "The BOAT—MAN..."/"The MAN INSIDE the BOAT...", that is it might be construed as: 1. H—G, or 2. T—G, or 3. M—G. In the translation of Chinese prose, common sense and the context will prescribe the choice among the three possibilities. In poetry, however, where key syntagms are often called upon to perform more than one function, the architectonic subtleties of parallelistic syntaxis frequently present a situation demanding the closest analysis of the structure of the poem as regards the interplay of 'H'/'T'/'M'. One would presuppose that in formal parallelization, once the poet's intention in the basic stichos (BS) of a parallelized distich (DS) is ascertained, the syntaxis of the basic should be faithfully mirrored in the parastichos (PS). This seems to be a safe rule to follow. We did so in our translation of the first DS of RIVER SNOW (CBWAP 013) by reading: BS "A thousand hills:..."//PS "A myriad paths..." (H//H), ignoring for the moment what may be called the principle of 'stereoscopy' in parallelism. Indeed, parallelism is not merely a stylistic device of formularistic syntactical duplication; it is intended to achieve a result reminiscent of binocular vision, the superimposition of two syntactical images in order to endow them with solidity and depth, the repetition of the pattern having the effect of binding together syntagms that appear at first rather loosely aligned. Structurally, 'H'/'T'/'M' represents a progressive scale of juncture, and the parallelistic juxtaposition of 'H' to 'H' should have the stereoscopic effect of elevating the reiterated 'H' in the PS (its appositive function having lost its novelty) to the status of 'T'. From that point of view, a better rendering of the hemistichs would be: BS "A thousand hills..." (H); PS *"On* myriad paths..." (T). A premature 'TT' construction (*"Above* the hills...//*On* the paths...") would be too prosaic, and would not give us the satisfaction of re-experiencing the 'build-up' step-by-step, first viewing the panorama presented by the poet from one syntactical angle, then from another, and fully savoring the stereoscopic aftersensation or afterimage.

> *Workshop Fund 9, in memoriam Dr. Helen B. Chapin whose over-enthusiastic, yet sensitive and suggestive, graphic analysis of RIVER SNOW (**Leaves from a Western Garden** 1:3, Mills College, 1938) is commended to the reader.*

10

On 'H'/'T'/'M' Progression in Quatrains

Chinese quatrains (4S) may be composed of free, non-parallel stichoi, but usually one of the distichs (DS) is parallelized; occasionally, both; and, in addition, crypto-parallelism may often be inferred. The second DS of RIVER SNOW (CBWAP 013 and 017) seems to be crypto-parallelized, even though—at first glance— BS 2, the noun BOAT cannot be treated as matching its alleged parastichic PS 2, ANGLING, a verb.

> BS: orphan (adj)/BOAT (n)/mino (straw-cope, n/adj)/bamboo-hat
> (n/adj) old-man (n)
> PS: lonely (adv)/ANGLING (v)/chill (adj)/Stream (n/adj)/snow (n).

One of the interesting features of this 4S is the undeniable parallelism, both syntactical and semantic, in the opening words of the stichoi, each line beginning with what one is tempted to call a 'logistic' ('L'), numerant term: "thousand"// "myriad"//"orphan"//"lone". A little facetiously perhaps, one might symbolize the semantic parallelism in this form: $L/10^3/..., L/10^1/..., L/1/..., L/1^2/...$ Granted this, one would further notice that the pre-caesural part of the third line (S3.1–2) is strictly parallel to those of SS 1 & 2: "thousand hills"//"myriad paths" //"single boat", each unit consisting of 'logistic'+'univocal' (our term for 'noun'), L—U. This peculiar "2 1/2" stichic parallelism is not uncommon in 4S and is unquestionably a deliberate stylistic device. It seems designed to create for the reader the effect of progressive syntactical juncture leading up to a climax at the critical, veering point (the caesura of S 3), where a new thought, expressed in a new grouping of words, is introduced into the poem. The question now arises as to how are the precaesurics of SS 1, 2, & 3 to be construed: as H/H/H, T/T/T, H/H/T, H/T/T/, or as H/T/T>M? The first two choices, quite legitimate in prose, are too battological for poetry; the second two possess some merit in syntactical progression; but it is the fifth which accounts best for the effect of stereoscopy in SS 1 & 2 and subtly carries the progression into S 3. Instead of interpreting S 3.1–2 as a 'hypothematic' (*Lo*, an orphan boat...), or a 'topological' (*In* an orphan boat...), we should, I believe, express the progression by turning BOAT into a modificative of the following syntactical unit. From the 'univocal,' word-class, BOAT would have to shifted to the 'adjectival' class. Chinese adjectives are in our terminology 'vice-verbals', or 'work-words' ('W', 'W'=VV), for syntactically they may function as verbs ('V') being directly predicated to nouns as 'F' or 'E'. In modificative position, they can often be translated by English participials or gerundials. In this case, BOAT may well be rendered BOATED or BOATING; the 'U' becoming thus a 'crypto-W', can now match the 'V' ANGLING. The syntactical scheme of the 4S is then to be diagrammatized as follows (with 'x' marking parataxis, 'y', (h)ypotaxis, and '/' indicating 'or'):

(LU) H	:	U	x/y	UG		VF
(LU) T	,	U	y	UG		VF
(LW) M	:/,	(U	x	U)	x/M	UG
(LV) E	-	(W	y	U)	y/x	UD

    The reader will remember that 'G' is 'gerent' (subject); 'F' is for 'functive'; 'D', 'destinate' (object); 'E', for 'effective'.

In a slightly different version from that in CBWAP 013, the 4S would read:

    A thousand hills: bird-flights cut short;
    On myriad paths, men's tracks damped out;
    And orphan-boating, a mino'ed, bamboo-hatted gaffer (*or*: a mino,
        a bamboo-hat, a gaffer)
    Cur-lonely angling the chill Stream—snow...

Workshop Fund 6.

11

Translations, Hyperbatic and Hyperbathetic

The Cedules dealing with problems of translation from the Chinese are directed exclusively to the author's coreligionists and cosectarians, the members of the teaching profession. I have no advice or comfort, and above all, no criticism to offer to free-lance translators of whose beliefs, motivation, and habits I am, as a pedant, totally ignorant. A pedant I take to be: 'a self-disciplined and disciplinarian disseminator of painfully acquired knowledge to the young'. His decalogue begins: "Thou shalt not, without apology, attempt to avoid an issue which thou hast taught thy disciple to face squarely". Now, pedants who call themselves philologists have a short and simple confession of faith: 'Grammar = Order = Beauty'. This naive credo sustains them through endless hours of drudgery spent in scribbling palimpsestic paradigms, and serves them as a potent incantation for dispelling phantasmagorias conjured by the solecistic sprites who haunt them in the night. But judging from the 2000 pages of translation of Chinese poetry carefully read in the past year, the philologist's credo is not too efficacious in withstanding the wiles of the pixies flittering in the interlinear spaces of Chinese verse. One of our articles of faith has always been that hyperbaton in Chinese is so rare as to be practically nonexistent. To our amazement, the 2000 pages showed almost 300 cases of hyperbaton construed from the original, and not reflecting the translators' stylistic predilections. Full of alarm, we consulted the texts; in not one single case did we find the inverted construction justified. We must sorrowfully conclude that philologists are in the habit of mislaying their gramarye when flirting with the Chinese muse, or else that one of the mottoes of 'traductory' politics in *Paris vaut bien une messe*. As Exhibit A, we offer one of Tu Fu's charming quatrains:

Tardy	sun	:	mountains	Stream	beautiful
Spring	wind	:	grass	flowers	fragrant
Mud	melt	:	fly	swallow	*tzu* (enclitic)
Sand	warm	:	sleep	Mandarin drake & duck	

All translators of high or medium competence known to me read the post-caesural halves of DS 2: "...swallows fly" // "...ducks sleep", obviously convinced that Tu Fu was indulging here in trite inversion in the mode of European poetasters. They show no inkling of an elemental rule of Chinese syntax: 'neuter verbs become causative by taking an object' ('a functive may become positionally effective'). The structure of the 4S is translucent ('z' marking a 'zygomatic' noun; '/', 'vergent on'):

W	U	(H)	:	(U	x	U) G	WF	
U	U/W	(M)	,	(U	x	U) G	WF	
UG	W	(F)	,	VE	(U		zU) D	
UG	W/V	(F/E)	–	VE	(U	x	U) D	

Some notes on diction: 'beautiful' is one of 17 common words with that meaning; its specific overtone 'pair' must be stressed in view of the 'pairing' of objects throughout; 'Mandarin ducks' are symbols of conjugal felicity; sexual binomization is hence imperative. 'Melt', 'to vapor', // to 'wind', should evoke one of its special meanings: 'NE breeze of spring', the 'Favonius' or 'Zephyr' of China. 'Warm': etymonic overtone: 'drag', 'lag', 'lax'; 'fragrant', graphical etymology: 'grain'+'sweet'. *Tzu*, cf. 010. With all the philological points of commisure marked, the 4S translates itself:

> A slow-paced sun: the hills, the Stream are paired in beauty;
> Spring-breezed, both herb and bloom scent—grain-like—sweet;
> The mudflat, zephyr-steamed, sends Master Swallow flying,
> The sands lax warm and drowse the duck and drake in mated sleep.

Workshop Fund 2.

12

Prolegomenon to *Lao Tzu* 1.1 : TAO

Whenever cautious scholars decide, usually *à contre coeur*, to take TAO, the basic concept of Chinese macro-& micro-cosmology, out of the cereclothes of transcription, they favor rendering it as "WAY", "*THE* WAY". This anglicization (with the corresponding L. "via", F. "la Voie, and G. "der Weg") is said to be semantically acceptable insofar as TAO is used, in non-philosophical texts, in the concrete sense of 'way' 'road', 'method', and is 'synonymous' with LU, 'road', 'route', 'path', combining with that synonym to form the dvandva TAO—LU, 'road' (attested already in Han times). Since on the religio-philosophical or religio-emotional level TAO operates as a counterpart of our trionym 'VIA—VITA—VERITAS', "*THE* WAY" would seem to be quite adequate for the purpose of registering its overtones without resorting to semantically inappropriate—and glossophilosophically dangerous —paraphrastic terms, such as GOD, NATURE, REASON, LOGOS, FIRST CAUSE, WORLD-LAW, UNIVERSAL PRINCIPLE, etc. Graphically, the digram TAO $<*d'\hat{o}g$ /A/ is clearly analyzable as being composed of two hemigrams: the semantic 'signal' or determinative 'to go', 'proceed', 'make steps' (C162, interchanging in the ancient scription of TAO with C144, 'to go', 'to act', 'march in formation', L. *ago*/B/), and the phonetic, or more correctly etymonic, *shou*<*šjôg*, 'HEAD' (C185, /C/). Phonetically, the alternation of initial stop and spirant presents no difficulty: compare *t'ao*<"*t'ôg* vs. *shou*<*šjôg*, KGS 1073 and 1099, in both of which *shou* (C041, serving as an allogram of *shou* C064) is the phonetic /D/. Now, if 'HEAD' is the etymonic of TAO, its semantic contour would not be coincident with that of the etymon embodied in the IE root VAG—, VEH—, 'move', 'carry', with its offshoots from VIA, WAY to 'vehiculum', 'wain' 'wagon', Gr. *ochos*. From this point of view, a better analogue of WAY would be Chinese LU, 'road', with its homeograph and homophone LU, 'wain' /E/, while TAO would connote 'HEADway', or 'proceeding AHEAD'. Furthermore, when we translate TAO as "WAY", we work on the assumption that the Chinese etymon is primarily a nominal one, and that the use of TAO as a verb—of which there are numerous examples in non-metaphysical literature, e. g. *Analects* 1.5, 2.3—is denominative: 'to show the WAY', hence 'to lead, (in that sense, TAO is now pleiomorphically enlarged with C041 /F/). The sematic C162 is, however, much more common as a determinative in graphs representing dynamic, verbal notions than in those of static, nominal significance, and one is inclined, therefore, to give the verbal aspect of the etymon precedence over the nominal one. Thus, the dynamic overtone of TAO could better be rendered in German by the pairs: 'bewegen', 'Bewegung,; 'leiten' and 'Leitung' (than by 'Weg'); and in Japanese, by 'michibiku' and 'michibiki', than by 'michi'; while in the Latin range of associations, PROCESS (and even AGENT) would be nearer to TAO than 'via'; and in Greek, one should think of TAO as an ARCHEGETIC (or 'hodegetic'), rather than a METHODIC principle. In English, we would advocate the use of LODE ('way, course, journey, leading, guidance'; cf. 'lodestone' and 'lodestar'), the somewhat obsolescent deverbal noun from 'to LEAD'. The etymonic 'HEAD' can then be effectively expressed in English by 'LODEHEAD' or 'HEADLODE'. In the light of this analysis of TAO, the supposedly copulative synonym-compound TAO— LU, 'road', traditionally interpreted as 'road I+road II', appears to be a descriptive compound, simply meaning 'LEADING road'. In disposing of this particular dicephalous monster of an 'elucidative' dvandva, I feel happy indeed to be able to join, albeit as a mere skirmisher, Prof. George Kennedy in his merry battle of 'debunking' the inflated linguistic myths which clutter our textbooks of Chinese (see his *Wennti*, No. 8).

A 道 B 辶; 行 in 術 C 首 D 討守; 寸＝手 E 路辂 F 導

Workshop Fund 1, in memoriam Edward T. Williams.

13

The Necessary Nuisance of Grammar

According to the canons of Chinese syntax, the rhematic sequence "EAT ENVOY" can have only two meanings: "(X) ATE the ENVOY", as in a not inconceivable report of a fatal outcome of an embassy to an anthropophagous potentate; or "(X) FED the ENVOY" (i. e. CAUSED the ENVOY to EAT), as reflecting normal diplomatic protocol. A novice translating Chinese historical prose would not survive for long the fulminous bolts of critics should he attempt to read the rhematic as a hyperbaton: "The ENVOY ATE". Nor would a reviewer tolerate his translating the unadorned two-word tale, even with the support of knowledgeable extra-textual commentaries, as: "The ENVOY PARTOOK of a five-course supper and went to bed at 10 p. m." Such is the artless design followed by us all in the translation of Chinese prose: a statement is carefully parsed in accordance with simple grammatical rules, then soberly anglicized, with a minimum of improvization, and but slightly garnished with the expletives made necessary by English idiom. In the translation of poetry, however, grammar seems to be relegated to a second place, even by experts, the vain tricks of intuition are given free rein, and dark hints adumbrated by commentators are allowed to creep into the text and are enlarged upon in haphazard fashion, often at the expense of syntactical patterns lucidly outlined by the poet. Thus we find as meticulous and experienced a translator as the late von Zach interpreting the line discussed in CBWAP 019, freely inverting a predicate adjective in the first hemistich and construing a hyperbaton in the second, as (*Tu Fu's Gedichte*, Harvard ed., 393): "...im warmen Sande schlafen die Mandarinenten", instead of: der Sand ist warm und einschläfert (die M. Ente und den Enterich)... In the following examplarily parallelized DS, the same translator parses correctly the BS, then proceeds to mutilate the PS, apparently unwilling to recognize the transitivity of its verb:

> BS sky G: black F: shut E: spring M: court D
> PS earth G: pure F: 'to roost' E: dark M: fragrance D/ and
>   reads (*op. c.* 93):

> Der schwarze Himmel umschliesst den frühlingsfrischen Hof/auf dem reinen Klostergrund wachsen duftende Blumen (die jetzt unsichtbar sind)..., with 2 inversions, 1 travesty.
> Prof. W. Hung, an even more distinguished scholar and TU—FU'ist, reads in the same vein:

> Darkness in the temple yard has shut off all spring colors/But the fragrance of unseen blossoms floats in the quiet enclosure/(*Tu Fu*, 107)...

Now, to use 'roost' transitively, in the sense of 'bring to roost', 'give a resting place to', may be bold, but so is Tu Fu's positional use of *hsi*, 'to roost', normally a neuter verb in Chinese. The poet's intention is crystal-clear and the DS should read:

> The sky, grown black, occludes the vernant courtyard,/The earth is quickened pure and roosts dark-hidden fragrancies...(On the translation of 'pure', cf. CBWAP 008).

Again commentary-conscious, both translators shy away from another PS verb in the DS:

> BS guardpost M: drum G: cut asunder E: men M: going, traveling D
> PS border M: autumn G: 'one' E: wildgoose M: voice, sound D

> Die abends gerührten Trommeln der Wachttürme lassen den Verkehr der Menschen aufhören/ hier an der Grenze hört man dann im Herbste nur noch den Schrei einer einzelnen Wildgans (*op. cit.* 184). The watch-tower

drum has sounded to close the road to traveling/ I hear a lone wild goose's cry in the autumn skies of the frontier (*Tu Fu*, 143)

In prose, neither would have any difficulty in parsing 'one' as a transitive verb: 'to unify', 'to single' (as = 'to make one', or 'single out one by one', even 'to monotone').

> The guardpost's drumming severs human traffic,
> The border's harvest-tide 'singles' the voices of the geese.

Workshop Fund 3.

14

On Chromatographic Effects in Chinese Poetry

The rich spectrum of Chinese chromatonymy, multilined and multibanded, has not received the attention it deserves. Most chromatonyms are not too well defined in our dictionaries, and translation equivalents are chosen haphazardly according to context, with little consideration paid to semantic nuances. Among the many Chinese color-terms crying for simple and effective rendering is the adjective TS'UI <*ts'jwəd* (C124, 'feathers', as sematic,+*tsu*<*tsjwət* as phonetic) /A/, 'vivid green-blue-purple-black', originally descriptive of the glossy iridescent plumage of the kingfisher, TS'UI being the second hemiphthegm of the dissyllabic name of the Asiatic kingfisher (*Halcyon*), FEI—TS'UI /B/. 'Kingfisher-green' (-blue, -black, -brown) is an awkward polysyllabic way to translate TS'UI which may describe women's penciled eyebrows as well as foliage. With due regard to the fact that kingfishers in Chinese literature were probably both *Halcyoninae* and *Alcedininae*, is there any reason why we should not use the term ALCEDINE (from L. *alcedo*, 'kingfisher') to designate exactly what TS'UI connoted to the Chinese? ALCEDINE is a handsomely tailored word, sonorous and precise, yet broad enough to be safely applicable as a color-epithet to a variety of things. Speaking of chromatonymy, we often underestimate the strong chromato-aesthetic associations ingrained in the Chinese mind as a facet of their traditional pentadic cosmology. I refer to the automatic correlations between their pentad of colors and the 'Five Elements' in spacetime: Wood-GREEN (blue)-east-spring; Fire-RED-south-summer; YELLOW-center-midsummer; Metal-WHITE-west-autumn; Water-BLACK-north-winter. Take the following 4S by Tu Fu:

> BS couple: (numeral adjunct): yellow: oriole:: call: TS'UI: willow
> PS one: line: white: egret:: ascend: TS'ING (cf. CBWAP 008): sky
> BS window: hold: western: mountain range:: thousand: autumn: snow
> PS gate: moor: eastern: *Wu* (lower Yangtse):: myriad: miles: boat

Diction: S 1.1-2, *liang-ko*, is a deliberate colloquialism; it would not do to translate it 'zwei' or 'two'; it is a vernacular 'a couple of'. LI, 'oriole' is a word with several scriptions, all of them glossed as : 'bi-colored', 'brown-and-yellow', 'black-and-yellow'. In MING, 'call' (graph='mouth'+'bird'), note the graphic echo of C196, 'bird', in 'oriole' (where the particular LI phonetic used is the LI 'pair' of CBWAP 018). LU, 'egret', is a homotonic homophone (and homeograph) of LU, 'path', and LU, 'dew'; in Chinese folklore, the white egret PAI LU is the harbinger of PAI LU, the 'white dew' of autumn, while the oriole symbolizes spring's evanescence, the all too swift transition from the black solstice of winter to the yellow one of summer. S 3.2, 'hold', lit. 'hold in the mouth', an apt figure for a window framing a landscape. 'Moor' is graphically: C085, 'water'+'white' as phonetic. 'Myriad miles' is to be capitalized as the P. N. of a 'bridgeport' near Ch'eng-tu (see the excellent topographical documentation in Prof. Hung's *Tu Fu*, 160 ff.). Color symbolism in the 4S: *S 1*: Spring: GREEN willows, orioles (from winter-BLACK to late summer-YELLOW; *S 2*: Spring-BLUE skies, but an ominous note of autumn (dew-WHITE egrets); *S 3*: In autumn-WHITE-west, (GREEN) mountains capped with (WHITE) snow; *S 4*: Towards the spring-GREEN-eastern region of Wu, boats moored WHITE. Translating the 4 S with a 5th line to underline its idiopathy:

> A couple of orioles—paired yellow-black—birdcalling willows
>   plumed with alcedine,
> A line of egrets—a path of dewy white—ascending quickblue skies,
> Where windows hold embouched the Western Range, snows of a
>   thousand harvests,
> And gates moor white the Eastern Wu, the boats of Myriad Leagues
> (The bridgeport of my autumn in the recurrent vernant green...)

A 翠　B 翡翠　C 兩個黃鸝鳴翠柳. 一行白鷺上青天. 牎含西嶺千秋雪. 門泊
東吳萬里船.

Workshop Fund 7.

15

On the Verbal Use of Topochronological Univocals

Any Chinese univocal ('U',=noun) may positionally become a vice-verbal or a verb; one cannot, though, always be able to quote an appropriate passage to prove the point in a specific case. Thus, in answer to a challenge to demonstrate that *shan*, 'mountain', a natural univocal, could function as a verb, this writer succeeded to produce but one quotation from the vast literature of China, *viz.* the phrase *'shan chih'* (E —RD), "(X) 'mountained' it", i.e. "piled it (=grain) in mountain-like heaps". Topochronological univocals, such as 'time', 'day', 'evening', 'night', are found, however, quite frequently operating as verbs, but the usage is oftentimes overlooked by translators, the idiom not being properly lexiconized in foreign dictionaries. Yet, already in the Classics, we have *shih*, 'time', effectively used as a verb 'to time' (as in English: 'he timed his visit'), in *Analects* 17.1; and in the commentaries to *Spring and Autumn*, *jih*, 'day', frequently appears in the rhematic phrase *pu jih*, "(X) did not 'day' (i.e. 'date') it (=the event)". There are many striking illustrations of such verbalization of topochronologicals in T'ang poetry; e.g., in the following 4S by Shen Ch'üan-ch'i:

> North: *Mang*: hills: top:: seriate: tomb: grave-lot/
>   (M—U) y U—U: M/E (UxU)/D
> Myriad: old: thousand: autumn:: appose: Lo (yang): walls
>   L—U x/y L—U: M/E (UyU)/D
> Walls: inside: day: 'evening':: chant: bells: rise
>   U—T/H M—U/E: (Ux/yU) VF/C
> Hill: top: barely: hear:: pine: cedar: voice
>   U—T M—E: (UxU) UD/C

North-*Mang* is the great cemetery N. of Loyang. Note the anadiplosis or epanaleptic enjambment in S2.7–S3.1. The second DS is parallel and we must, therefore, consider the topochronological 'evening' not in a 'T' sense (i.e. as 'evenings', adv.), but as a verb 'to eventide', 'to tide the evening (in/for)', as//with 'hear'. 'Chant-bells' may be taken paratactically: 'songs and bells'; normally, it means: 'carillon-bells'.

> Hilltops of Northern Mang: seriating tombs and blocks of graves;
> A myriad elds, a thousand harvests: apposing Loyang's city-walls,
> And walled within, adays, to evetide for cantilena bells to rise,
> Atop the hill, barely to hear the pines and cedars(') call.

We have a similar problem in one of Wang Wei's picture-poems:

> Autumn: hills:: gather: remnant: glowlight
>   MU/T UG: E (M—U)D
> Fly: bird:: pursue: forward: mate
>   MW UG: E (M—U)D
> Motley: 'alcedine':: *'time'*: divide, distinct: bright
>   MW UG: T/E (WxW) F/D or C
> Evening: mist:: have-not: place, abide: place, where
>   MW/T UG: E (Ux/yU)D

Notes on diction: LIEN, 'gather', 'lay up', 'glean'; I think that Wang Wei describes here, as in the 4S of CBWAP 005, the evening sunlight creeping up the mountainside. 'Alcedine' is bifunctional here: = 'alcedine color', and = TS'UI—(wei), 'hillside' or Fr. *'amqnt'*, uphill. LAN<*LAM, 'mist', graphically: 'mountain', C046, +*BLAM, 'wind', as etymonic; hence, *aura montium*, 'aura of the hilltops', 'mountain fog or vapor', 'WINDGAP-mist', rather than merely 'mist'. The key word in the 4S is S 3.3: at first, it appears to be an adverb, 'seasonally', 'at times', modifying the vice-verbal phrase 'distinctly-bright', 'party-clear and bright'. As we parse S4, we note the parallelization of 'time' with the V 'have-not' and become conscious of its function as a verb.

> The hills, at harvest-tide, gleaning the remnant glowlight,
> The birds, aflight, pursuing vanward mates;
> Amont, the motley alcedine tides the distincter bright,
> And evening windgap-mists have not a where of place.

Workshop Fund 6.

16

On Colloquialisms in Tu Fu's Poetry

One of the pronounced defects in most of the existing translations of Tu Fu, from the philological point of view, is their failure to do justice to the poet as a stylist, more particularly their negligence in rendering properly his masterful contrasts of formal classical construction with the bold use of colloquialisms. However subtle the motivation for the shift, a not too profound syntactical parsing will often reveal the poet's stylistic intention. Take, for instance, the second DS of his "Moonlit night, thinking of the cadets of the family-cote (= 'my younger brothers')". Cf. 021 for DS 1.

Dew: starting-from: present: night: white/Moon: it-is: old: parish: bright/
S 2.2, *shih*, is a morpheme that should immediately alert a philologist. In the classical language it functions as 'this', 'such', 'yea', 'truly'; but in the vernacular of the post-Han period it begins to serve as a copula, possibly following the evolution: 'this'>'this (is)'>"*t*is'>'(it) is'. In S 1, one should note the loose insertion of a whole phrase, 'from to-night on', between the subject, 'dew', and its predicate, 'white'. The reference is to the White Dew Season, one of the Twenty-Four 'Articles' (*tsieh*, 'arthra', 'divisions') of the Chinese year (see W. Hung, *Tu Fu*, 142, for a careful dating of the poem on this basis). The sequence 'old-parish-bright' is as colloquial as 'hometown-familiarity', or "that 'mother-used-to-bake' flavor". Yet no competent translator ever attempts to approximate the homely forcefulness of the DS:

W. Bynner & K. H. Kiang: "the dews tonight will be frost/...
How much brighter the moonlight is at home!" (*The Jade Mountain*, 150).   Von Zach, *TF's Gedichte*, 184: "Glänzender Tau erscheint
von heute Nacht an (*Liki* I, 373);/der Mond strahlt so helle wie
in meinem alten Heimatsland".   W. Hung, *Tu Fu*, 143: "The White
Dew Season begins tonight/The moon is not as bright as I used to
see it at home".

If translators would only follow the philological principle of letting the text
speak for itself, the DS would read, without violent transposition or unnecessary
frills:

The dew, from to-night on, "dew-whitens"/The moon, it be "old-
parish-moon—like" bright.

Here is another of Tu Fu's famous lines, persistently misconstrued and quoted
ad nauseam as an example of 'brilliant inversion', whereas it is again a case of a
'*shih*' colloquial construction.   The poet describes the aftermath of a disastrous
battle:

Blue-black: *shih*: beacon: smoke:: white: *shih*: bones

It is a melancholy commentary, indeed, to note how low the esteem of grammar must have fallen among sinologists when a grammatical subject (hence, a
substantive) followed by a copula-like *shih* is taken as an inverted predicate, in
contumacious disregard of all syntactical laws, ancient and modern; for our most
experienced translators read:

"Schwarz ist der Rauch der Lagerfeuer, weiss die Knochen der
    Gefallenen" (von Zach, 88)
"Black is the smoke left over the camps, and white are the bones
    of our dead" (W. Hung, 102)

The DS in which the line occurs presents a dream-like vision of the scene of
desolation after the battle, and the tragic, dreamy stillness is underlined stylistically by the absence of verbs (except *shih*, which retains, however, much of its
pronominal force):

And the snows of the hills, and the ice on the river:
    the eventide all sough-and-swish,
And *the* blue, that's the smoke of the beacons;
    and *the* white, that be bones (of the dead).

A 露從今夜白，月是故鄉明
B 山雪河冰晚（var. 野）蕭瑟. 青是烽煙白是骨

17

Semantics, Chromatics, and Grammar

Another of Tu Fu's great pentametrical quatrains, the companion piece to the stanza translated in CBWAP 019, may serve to illustrate several principles of Chinese poetic diction and taxis already discussed or alluded to in the Cedules. The 4S reads:

> The Stream (= Yangtse): emerald-green-blue:: birds: cross over: white
>
> Hills: blue-green (TS'ING):: flowers: wish, will, about to: blaze
>
> Present (adj.), this: spring:: look, watch: again: pass by, trespass
>
> What (interr. or indef.): day:: *shih* (cf. CBWAP 024): return home: year

DICTION: Chin. *PIK*, usually translated 'blue', 'green', 'emerald''—graphically a compound of C112, 'rock', C096, 'jade', both sematic, and C106, 'white', 'candid', as phonetic—designated originally some kind of bluish or greenish jasper or chalcedony. To bring out the phonosemantic associations of *PIK* without committing oneself as to the exact chromatic shade (the term is applied equally to the color of the sky as to that of water or greenery), it should, perhaps, be rendered ' JADE—CANDID' or 'JASPIDEAN. S 1.4, *Yü*: 'to cross over, exceed, excel, transcend'. The key word in the 4S is S 2.5, JAN, 'to burn, blaze, inflame, incend'. Its scription has C086, 'fire', as sematic; the character having been 'borrowed' at an early date to represent the homonym JAN, 'thus', '-like', '-wise' (adverbial postfix), an additional C086 is written on its left to re-activate the primary meaning. We have no way of knowing whether Tu Fu used the simple or the pleiographic scription. It is tempting to believe that the defective form stood in the original text to challenge the reader's interpretative skill in the alternative of reading S 2.4–5 as 'wish to blaze', or 'are lust-wise' (an unlikely, yet possible 'first' reading). S 3.5 KUO, is a dyotonic word; as a platytone: 'to be passing through, pass by, undergo, experience'; as a loxotone: 'to go beyond, exceed, transgress, trespass (spatially or morally)'. The prosodic scheme requires a loxotone here. TAXIS: The parallelization of the first DS presents several problems. The pre-caesural hemistichs may be interpreted: 1. as 'H' (hypothematic'): "As for the emerald of the Stream..."; 2. as 'T' ('topotactical'): "Across (against, above) the green of the Stream..."; 3. as finite utterances paratactical with the second hemistichs: "The Stream is jasper-hued; the birds..."; 4. as 'H D', 'hypothematic preposited destinates' of the post-caesural sentences (GFE), 'the blue of the Stream' and 'the green of the hills' to be taken as preposited objects of the verbs 'to whiten' and 'to set ablaze'. The last interpretation is particularly attractive in view of the ever-present cosmic-seasonal connotations of the Chinese chromatic terms. 'Blazing with fire' immediately suggests FIRE—RED—SUMMER, the waning green of spring about to be supplanted with the red of summer. The connotative force of JAN in this context could be approximated by our word ESTUATE, 'aestuate' (Lat. aestuo, 'be warm, to glow, burn, seethe', a cognate of ESTIVATE, 'aestivate' ('to pass the SUMMER, L. aestivo, aestas). This subauditur illuminates the entire 4 S and makes us notice the flash of WEST—WHITE—AUTUMN in S 1, thus underlining the ephemeralness of the EAST—GREEN—SPRING scene. We do not believe this is over-interpretation; the 4S (as that of CBWAP 022) was written by Tu Fu in the 'autumnal' years of his homeless existence. Finally, it would not do—as most translators have done—to invert the highly original order of 'day' and 'year' in S 4. We translate, therefore:

> The Stream's jaspidean: the birds, transcendent, white;
> The hill's quick-green: the flowers fain to estuate;
> But for the nonce, the spring: to watch,—again, to digress on
> Unto whatever day it be a homeward-turning year
> (For this lone passer, occident...)

Workshop Fund 4.

18

A Neglected Aspect of Chinese 'Epistemology'

The semantic configuration of the Chinese words *chih* (platytone) and *chih* (loxotone) that we translate by 'to know' and 'knowledge, wisdom' is best ascertained through graphic etymology. The important and unmistakable elements in the two graphs /A/ are 'mouth' and 'to speak, say' /B/. The Chinese terms seem to emphasize, then, 'judgment by word of mouth' and lack those perceptually concrete associations that are still felt in the various European words designating 'knowledge': KNOW and GNOSCO, with their suspected connections with roots referring to physical ability (Eng. *can*, Ger. *kennen* vs. *können*, Eng. *ken*, L. *gigno*, 'to procreate'); WISDOM (Eng. *wit*, traceable to the I E root VID—'to see'); COMPREHENSION (i.e. 'grasping together'); UNDERSTANDING and EPISTEME (clearly associated with the root 'to stand'); SCIENCE (from *scio*. 'cleave, divide'), etc. Most of our translations of primary Chinese texts do not sufficiently emphasize the highly significant fact—doubtless noticed by all serious students of the literature of ancient China—that 'knowing' is predominantly concerned with what may be defined as "acquaintance WITH", rather than "knowledge ABOUT", as "knowledge through CONFRONTATION", rather than "knowledge through COMPREHENSION (i.e. 'encompassing'); perhaps even as mere "*AC*knowledgment" or "*RE*cognition". The most persistent—one is tempted to say 'connatural'—object of "knowing" is MAN, MEN. Throughout its history, Confucianism remembered the

Master's definition of "knowledge", *Analects* 12. 22: "On (Fan Ch'ih's) asking the meaning of knowledge, the Master said: "Know your fellow-men" /C/. This precept to the effect that "the proper knowledge of mankind is man" became one of the strongest ethological elements in Chinese civilization, while linguistically the association of the two terms is reflected in a dozen of Chinese synonyms meaning 'friend' /D/. To express it in another way, there is in the Chinese concept of "knowledge" a peculiar unidimensionalism suggestive only of movement to and fro, in a direct line, which is best rendered by our prefix '*a-*' as in "acknow", "acknowledge", or by the Latin *ad-*, as in "agnize", "agnition". It seems deficient in the 'two-dimensional', aspects of the process of knowing which appear to be implied in the "flanking", enveloping connotations present in the European prepositions: UNDER, as in 'understand'; EPI, as in 'episteme'; CON, as in 'comprehension', 'co-gnition', 'concept'. We are convinced that CHIH, 'know', was felt essentially as 'acknow-ledgment', i. e, as the establishment of distinctions by word of mouth, and never encouraged coming, so to say, to grips with the object of knowledge, of 'grasping', 'taking hold of it', while the 'prehension' element in 'apprehend', 'compehend', 'per-cept', and 'con-cept' almost forced Eurpean thought to develop in the direction it did. In China, 'knowledge' seems to have been kept on the level of 'formal avowal', correlated or contrasted with 'action' barely enjoining encompassing, probing into, and dissecting objects of knowledge, which in the West produced eventually both the glory and the tragedy of Occidental epistemology. It would be interesting and instructive to subject the hypothesis developed here to a test by re-translating some of the important Chinese texts dealing with the problem of 'knowledge' by substituting the formal term AGNITION (i. e. acknowledgment) for 'knowledge' as a rendering for CHIH whenever there is danger that the uninitiated reader might mistake CHIH-knowledge for the epistemologically pregnant term COGNITION. Confining oneself to the *Analects*, one could, for example, reduce to its proper perspective the famous controversial passage in *An.* 11. 11, usually rendered: "While you do not know life, how can you know about death?", and read: "Not yet acquainted with the living, how can you become acquainted with the dead?"—bearing in mind that the preceding parallel passage speaks of "serving men" and "serving their spirits". Agnition or recognition of specific entities and duties was the subject of discussion, not the cognition of the abstractions called in our language 'life' and 'death'.

A 知 智   B 口 日   C 知人   D 故 知, 知交 etc.

Workshop Fund 5.

19

Diction and Poetic Unity

One of the finest of Meng Hao-jan's poems, "Home at the Southern Mountains at the Eve of the Year" (included in the 300 Poems of T'ang), has been competently, but too paraphrastically translated by Hans Frankel (in *Biographies of Meng Hao-jan*, 1952, p. 13). The diction of the octet deserves closer analysis. We translate verbatim & membratim:

> Northern: pylon, gate:: stop, desist: raisé, rise: documents
> Southern: mountains:: return home: battered: hut.
> Not (verbal): talent:: bright: lord (of household or state): discard
> Many, much: sickness:: ancient, heretofore: men: rare, scattered.
>
> White: hair:: urge, press: year(s): old(ness)
> Quick-green:YANG, 'sunward slope':: press near: year-period:
>   do away with; steps
> Ever, continually: embosom:: melancholy: not (verbal): slumber
> Pinetree: moon:: night: window: void.

We may begin by mentioning that in a mettlesome article on the "Difficulty of Translation" (*Studies in Chinese Thought*, pp. 263–285), unfortunately marred by hastily contrived bits of criticism of the work of various translators from the Chinese (most of them identifiable, but ungallantly unnamed), Achilles Fang somewhat petulantly takes exception at Frankel's rendering of *ming chu*, S 3.3–4, as 'illustrious ruler'. In Fang's opinion, "the phrase always refers to the intelligence of a ruler", and H. F. was wrong in trying to improve upon the traditional cliché: 'wise ruler'. As a scholar of integrity and competence, Dr. Frankel stands in no need of defence or patronage—on such an ostensibly puny issue—yet Frankel happens to be correct and Fang woefully wrong. 'Illustrious' (personally I prefer 'illuminate') is right on two counts: semasiologically, *ming*, 'bright', refers to the relative brightness of the moon; in the context of the poem, 'wise' is more than inappropriate. The full force of S 1.2 seems to have been overlooked, on the other hand, by both translator and critic. While we all know that 'gate' means here the northern pylons of the palace where petitions were presented, etymologically the word means 'gaping' 'hiatus', and is also used as 'waning (of the moon)'. The poet chose the word deliberately and subtly echoes it in S 8. The anecdote concerning Emperor Hsüan Tsung's displeasure at the third line of the poem may be fictitious as shown by Frankel, yet it is *ben trovato*, for the double entendre of the piece is plain: my cycle of life may be coming to an end in spite of the promise of rebirth implied in the approaching spring; is the waning cycle of the dynasty under a 'moon-bright' ruler the prelude to a new glorious spring, or a steady irremediable decline like mine ? S8 has been misconstrued by Frankel, I believe: 'night' must be a verb, 'to haunt at night', not a topochronological adverb. His emendation of 'window' to 'hall' (S8.4) would weaken the poem. The last line is an 'echo-picture' of the waning moon in the gaping frame of the casement as the symbol of waning sovereignty standing between the two pylons of the 'gaping gate' of the palace.

> The Northern Hiant-Gate has sisted the upraised writs,
> And Southern Mountains wend one home: a battered hut.
> Untalented: offcast of an illuminate state-lord,
> And many-illed: sparse of the goodmen of the heretofore.
>
> White hair now urges on the agedness of years
> As quick-green Sunwardness compels the period's stoop,
> And ever-bosomed here, heartvexing slumbers not
> Whenas the pinetreed moon nights the casement's void
> (Hiant...waning...)

Workshop Fund 1, in memoriam Edward T. Williams.

20

Self-Criticism in Eighth Century China

In the bleak winter of A. D. 756, at the height of An Lu-shan's rebellion, Tu Fu, his heart torn by the news of the successive defeats of the loyalist troops, wrote several moving poems full of personal and civic anguish. One of them is an octastich the fine prosodic points of which have been rather mishandled by translators (abbrev.: TLs):

> Battle: cry (as in mourning), wail:: many: new: ghosts
> Melancholy: hum:: lonely, 'cur-lonely': old: 'gaffer'
> Tangled, turbulent: clouds:: droop low: thin: sundown
> Hasty, urgent: snow:: dance: whirling, turning: wind
> Ladling-gourd: discard:: jug, bottle: have-not: *LUK* (untransl. for the
>   moment)
> Brazier: keep, enquire:: fire: resemble: red
> Several: province, shire:: flow: 'ebb': cut asunder
> Melancholy: *TSO*, 'sit':: just, 'rightwhile': write: void.

The opening DS is tricky: 'many' and 'lonely' are not inverted predicates as naively believed by TLs, but positionally causative verbs: 'to more', 'to make lonely'. LUK (with C085, 'water'), 'vitreously clear', 'n. of a river in Hunan', is polychroic. Some take it for its homonym LUK (same phonetic, C120), 'virid'. F. Ayscough translates, therefore, correctly—but noncommittally—'clear green' (in quotation marks), while other TLs studiously try to avoid calling wine (the obvious contents of the jug) 'green'. R. Wilhelm has a fantastic reading: "In der Blumen-vase ist das Grün gestorben". *Luk* can also be treated as an allogram of LUK (C085+C198), 'to strain liquids', 'decant', 'to dredge'; as a noun, 'decantate'? It may also refer to LUK-wine (same character, or with C164), a wine made in Hunan with the 'vitreously clear' water of the LUK river. S 8 is the key stichos of the piece. The allusion it contains is ponderously spelled out by von Zach: "Ich bin voll Sorge und schreibe gerade Zeichen in die Luft (wie einst Yin Hao...)". The reference is to a scholar-general (4th cent.) who, having been disgraced and cashiered after suffering a defeat, never complained aloud, but kept writing in the air the four characters: "Tut-tut, the uncanny affair!" The commentators who diligently hunted down the allusion for us are not too clear on its relevance, being content to have proved once more Tu Fu's erudition. TLs improvise: Forke (scholastically precise): "Betrübt sitz' ich zur Stunde/Schreib Zeichen in den Wind/(footnote: "Tu Fu schreibt seine Gedanken in die Luft"); Wilhelm (avoiding the issue): "Zögernd wohnt das Heimweh im Gemüt"; Ayscough (analyzing, *more suo*, the character 'melancholy' as being composed of 'autumn' and 'heart'): "I sit in autumn grief: verily it is futile to send a letter"; W. Hung (enigmatically): "Preposterous! Preposterous!". The secret of the line lies in the word TSO. Contextually, it means of course 'to sit', but the above allusion immediately evokes its common idiomatic meaning: 'to be incriminated'. Tu Fu, always the earnest citizen, felt at the time personally responsible for the disasters and was yearning to participate in the strategic planning of the campaign against the rebels, know-ing that some of his scholar-friends were then in command of the imperial troops. Their defeat was his; a dark hour indeed—for scholarly generals.

> A battle keening mores the newer ghosts,
> A heartvexed drone solens an olding gaffer,
> As raveled clouds droop a tenuous null-of-day
> And urgent snow goes dancing with the whirling wind.
> The ladling-gourd—discarded: the jug holds naught of 'vitreate',
> The brazier—kept inquired: the fire is but dissembling red;
> And with the ebb and flow of news from sundry shires now severed,
> To sit, heartvexed and criminated, just writing despatches in the void
> (A General of Letters, self-cashiered...)

Workshop Fund 7.

21

On the Virtue of the Infinitive

Translators (TLs) of Chinese verse into European languages have to face two harsh philological facts: the absolute genderlessness of the language and the almost

total absence of pronouns in the Chinese poetic style. The problem is a difficult
one to cope with, even in 'genderless' English (which still retains a threefold
distinction of gender in the pronoun of the third person singular). The Gordian
knot is usually disposed of by the Macedonian method. The translator wields his
mighty sword of contextual decision and lets the chips (or bits of the thong, to be
mytho-historically exact), in the shape of 'idiomatic' HE, SHE, IT, HIM, HER, I,
ME, WE, US, etc., fall where they may. The resulting product may be quite
satisfactory as a paraphrase; as a translation, that is as a purported mirror-image
of the original, it often is a cruel or grotesque distortion. To avoid this, TLs
should exercise the greatest caution in the use of pronouns, especially those indicative of gender (& number), even in cases when the sex of the referent is unmistakable, as in countless Chinese poems on the theme of the abandoned lady of the
palace. Let but one SHE infiltrate the text, and the whole pronominal tribe will
follow suit. Witness this famous 4 S by Li Po, a TLs' favorite:

> Beautiful, fair : person :: roll up : pearly : curtain, screen, 'cascade'
> Deep : TSO, to sit :: pucker : moth-like : ant-like : brows
> Only : to see :: tears : trace, scar : damp
> Not (verbal) : know :: heart : resent, hate : who

Most existing translations reproduce essentially the versions by H. A. Giles &
R. Wilhelm:

> A fair girl draws the blind aside
> And sadly sits with drooping head;
> I see her burning tear-drops glide
> But know not why those tears are shed

> Die Schöne rollt den Perlenvorhang auf,
> Sitzt in der Ecke, faltet ihre seidnen Brauen.
> Ich seh' die feuchten Tränenspuren nur,
> Doch wem sie böse ist, vermag ich nicht zu schauen

The two competent TLs managed to reduce the use of pronouns to a minimum
(2 in English, 4 in German); doubtless they would have had about the same number
had they given us a meticulous prose version of the 4 S. The use of 'I', 'ich', 'you',
or 'we' in S 3 is wellnigh obsessive: Forke: "Ich möcht' wohl wissen..."; *White
Pony*: "I see in the corner of her eyes..."; Ayscough & Lowell: "One sees only...
We do not know..."; Bynner and Kiang: "You may see...", etc. The introduction
of an outside observer in S 3 seems to be the standard practice in European (and
modern Chinese & Japanese) interpretations. While possible, it is neither plausible
nor quite *comme il faut*, poetically or ethologically. Who is the Peeping Tom of
S 3? The poet? A chance passer-by? With all due allowance for poetic license,
we must remember that the prudish conventions of polite Chinese literature would

not have tolerated such invasion of the privacy of a highborn or high-placed lady in her penetralian seclusion, even by such gay blades as Li Po. The interpretation is at best a tertiary one. The original is much more subtle. When it is translated without supernumerary pronouns, the primary—but not necessarily exclusive— meaning of the poem becomes apparent. The lady is truly alone, sitting disconsolately, probably looking at herself in a mirror, as ladies are prone to do, in China as elsewhere, trying to find the reason for her fall from grace. The 'who' of S 4 is not her husband or lover whose identity is unknown to the Peeping Tom, but her rival. TSO, 'to sit', as in our previous Cedule, has an overtone of 'feeling incriminated'.

> The fair one: to roll up the pearl-cascading screen,
> And deep within, to sit—deep-criminated—plying antennal brows,
> Only to see the damp of tear-made scars,
> And not to know the hearted hateful—Who?...
> (The fairer one...)

Workshop Fund 2.

22

'T'/'M' Parallelism Once More

One of The Three Hundred Poems of the T'ang, a heptametrical quatrain by Liu Fang-p'ing, again on the theme of the abandoned lady, prompts us to return to the problem of syntactical metaplasia discussed in Cedules 017 and 018, particularly to the criteria determining the construction of a 'hypothematic' element beginning a sentence as a 'T' (a topological prepositional phrase) or an 'M' (modificative of the subject).

> Gauze : window : sun, day : fall, drop :: to steep, gradually : yellow : dusk
> Gold-en : room : have-not : man, person :: to see : tear : scar
> TSIK : MOK : empty : courtyard :: spring : wish, will : late (of time)
> Pear-tree : blossoms : fill, suffuse (C085, 'water') : not (adv.) : open : gate

As a sample of existing translations, those of Bynner & Kiang and Prof. A. Forke:

> "With twilight passing her silken window, / She weeps alone in her chamber of gold; / For spring is departing from a desolate garden, / And a drift of pear-petals is closing a door." (*Jade Mountain*, p. 95) "Vom Fenster aus sieht man sinken / Die Sonne. Der Abend graut. / Die Spuren ihrer Tränen / Hat niemand im Goldhaus geschaut. / Lenz stirbt. Aus dem öden Palaste, / Da tönt kein Laut

hervor. / Die Birnbaumblüten fallen; / Verschlossen bleibt das Tor."
(*Dichtungen der T'ang-und Sung-Zeit*, p. 100).

DICTION : TSIK—MOK, 'lonely, desolate, still' (etymonic of deuteron : MOK,
'no one'), is a common echoic descriptive binom (cf. CBWAP 006). These binoms
function as vice-verbals, but may be preposed, as *predicates*, to their subjects, a
characteristic they share with predicates followed by the kommatic particle *yi*, the
only two cases where hyperbaton is normal in Chinese. The construction is
reminiscent of : "So fresh and green (is) the...", "Rare indeed (is)..." "Golden
Room" is an allusion. The background tale may be synopticized in one sentence :
"I shall love the little princess dearly," said the young prince, "and keep her all to
myself in a pretty golden room." The last two words of the 4S are very vivid
graphically : 'gate' is a pictogram of a gate with two folding doors; 'open' is the
same pictogram with a horizontal line inside, presumably representing a bar, and
'two hands' lifting it.   TAXIS : At first glance, the opening DS should be read :
"Through the gauze window, the sunset steeps the yellow dusk, / In the golden
room, no one sees the tear-scars", with the first two words in each stichos taken
as 'T'. This is, however, an inferior reading : the parallelism is rather weak and
unoriginal, with 'have-no one', a strong verbal phrase reduced to a substantive (in
Chinese, 'no one' can be expressed by a single word : MOK); the "Golden Room"
allusion is sufficient to suggest 'splendid isolation', and expatiation seems redundant;
no stereoscopic progression is achieved. We think that the parallelism of the DS
has a subtler purpose. The appearance of a verbal in S 2.3 to match a noun in
S 1.3 suggests the possibility of interpreting the latter ('sun, day') as a verbalized
topochronological : 'to mark day after day', with 'fall, drop' as its object. This
may be taken in its attested meaning of 'an eavesdrop', i. e. 'anything dropping
from the eaves', in this case, the syntactical object being indebted semantically to
its verb and to the standard compound 'sun-set' : 'the eavesdrop of the sun'. At
this point, 'sunset' and 'no one' yield their function as grammatical subjects to the
logical subject of the poem, the abandoned lady herself, with the 'T' phrases
becoming 'M' phrases descriptive of her movements : window -mirror? -yard—gate.

> Gauze-windowed, day-telling sunfalls, steeped in yellow dusk,
> And golden-roomed, to habit no one to see the tear-made scars;
> And still-and-null the vacant courtyard; the spring is fain to tardy
> Pear-blossoms to suffuse the ground—so as to open not the gate
> (The gate unbarred...)

Workshop Fund 3.

23

On Indo-European Prosopocentricity

A reader of the Cedules finds "prosopocentricity" (a term we used to describe the habit of translators of injecting 'idiomatic' personal pronouns into a Chinese text) 'awkward and annoying'. We agree : an awkward and annoying word indeed—for an awkward and annoying practice. The idiomatological use of IE finite verbs with their pleonastic pronoun-subjects and inevitable retinue of pronominal objects and possessives may be justified in verbating Chinese prose, but it is definitely out of place in the translation of Chinese poetry markedly allergic to pronomination and eschewing most "empty words". A striking example of this problem in translation—and of the futile discussions the hasty solution thereof engenders—is found in Tu Fu's epistle to his elder contemporary and friend, Li Po (usually dated A. D. 745) :

> Antumn : come : respectant : regard::still : wind-tossed : tumbleweed
> Not-yet : attain : cinnabar : sand-grain : : ashamed before : Ko : Hung (an alchemist)
> Sore : drink : mad : sing : : vain, empty : span : day
> Fly : upward, rise : "traipse-:-tail" : : for-sake-of : whom : cock, rooster, male

Von Zach reads : "Als ICH DICH im vergangenen Herbste aufsuchte, triebst DU noch umher wie Distelwolle im Winde./Da es DIR noch nicht gelungen war, des Lebenselixiers habhaft zu werden, schämtest DU DICH vor Ko Hung./ DU verbrachtest die Ziet ausschliesslich mit anhaltendem Trinken und wildem Singen./ Wem nützt wohl *Dein* hochfliegender Stolz und kühner Eigensinn?" (with 8 supernumerary pronouns; Ayscough and Lowell have: one WE, four YOU, three YOUR. Prof. W. Hung (*Tu Fu*, p. 38) censures previous traductors for their use of the pronoun of the second person which, in his opinion, makes the poem "sound as if the elder poet were being chided as a worthless boy". He effects himself a party-per-pale compromise by inserting WE in the first DS and translating the second:

> "I drink, I sing and I waste days in vain/Proud and unruly I am, but on whose account?"

In the well-documented biographical part of his work, however, we find no specific evidence that Tu Fu shared at the time Li Po's braggadocianism or his Taostic and alchemistical propensities (on which see A. Waley's *Li Po*), or had to "chide" himself on that score. The problem is not in the text, but in our labored rendering of Chinese verbals (infinitival and gerundial in character and free of the puny accidents of person and tense) as finite verbs. While the poetic message is addressed to a particular person, couched as it is in 'infinitival' terms, it becomes a timeless and personless expression of the creed of defiant Bohemianism. Much more puzzling is the structure of the second DS, its adroit alignment greatly admired by the Chinese critics who are a little baffled by the strict parallelism of the first hemistichs contrasted with the freer syntax of the post-caesural halves. 'Cock' is unmistakably verbal :'to act rooster-like'; but which is the verb in S 3: 'span', or 'day'? At first, we naturally parse : 'vainly to span the days' (adv.-verb-object). Then we begin to wonder : can 'day' be verbalized to match S 4.7? We are tempted to construe : 'vainly spanning (=reaching across space or time), to (live) day by day'. The poet challenges us to consider the problem and find a solution. Happily, in English at least, one can devise a construction approximating the amphibology of the original and its stereoscopy :

> With harvest-tide acoming, aspectant in regard : as ever, a windtossed tumbleweed,
> To have, as yet, unreached those miniate granules : shamefast before Ko Hung—the master alchemist—
> And sorely to drink, and madly to sing, in vacant spanning day-by-day,
> To fly aloft, thrashtail and swagger, and play the cocker for whosesoever sake (And let life's autumn come...)

Workshop Fund 8.

24

On the Semasiology of Chinese 'Poetry' and 'Thought'

A few years ago, in a full-bodied article, thoughtful and thought-provoking, Prof. S. H. Chen (*The Beginnings of Chinese Literary Criticism*, in SEMITIC AND ORIENTAL STUDIES, A Volume Presented to WILLIAM POPPER, pp. 45–63) subjected to a penetrating analysis the earliest Chinese definitions of 'poetry', particularly that of the *Shu*, "*shih yen chih*", which he translates "poetry expresses purposiveness", and that of Lu Chi, "*shih yüan ch'ing...*", translated "poetry born of pure emotion..." Much of the discussion hinges on an excellent graphosemantic investigation of the affinity of the words *shih*, 'poetry', and *chih*, 'purpose'. As the study was centered on the evolution of Chinese literary criticism and was only indirectly concerned with the validity of our traditional renderings of Chinese terms, Prof. Chen did not question the orthology of equating *shih* with 'poetry'. Now, whatever our anti-etymologists may say, 'poetry' in Mediterranean tradition still retains much of its etymological force, with connotations, such as 'creative making', 'a creative power or act or *Gefühl* of any kind', ranging far beyond the field of literature. The Chinese term whose 'rationale' (in Prof. Chen's terminology), i. e. the semantic element in the graph representing the vocable in the Chinese script, is 'WORD', on the other hand, can hardly be employed outside the domain of letters. No Chinese could speak, for instance, of the *'shih* of nature'. I do not imply, of course, that *shih* meant only 'versification'. The term was as pregnant in overtones as 'poetry', but along different semantic lines. The ETYMONIC of the word, as Prof. Chen has shown, was an affine of *chih*, 'purpose'. Pursuing the investigation a little further, let us note other relatives of *shih* and *chih* (word-family *KGS* 962): SHIH (with C009), 'to wait upon'; CH'IH (C064, 'hand'), 'to hold'; CHIH (C157, 'foot'), 'to hesitate'; SHIH (C072, 'sun'), 'time'; TAI <*təg* (C118), 'grade, degree'. As soon as we substitute INTENT for Prof. Chen's 'purpose', the semantic diversity of the list can be reduced to a common denominator in a root analogous to L. tendo, 'stretch', and teneo, 'hold' : INTENT' 'to at-TEND' ('wait upon'), 'to mainTAIN' (hold with hand), 'to move pedeTENTOUSly' ('hesitate'), TIME, TEMPUS (suspected by some to be a derivative of TENDO, as a 'time-stretch'), L. pedeTENTIM, by degrees'. Our attention is now directed to a sixth century paronomastic gloss of 'poetry' (in Liu Hsieh's *Wen hsin tiao lung*, one of the most remarkable texts in all Chinese literature and, next to the *Lao Tzu*, the most challenging for a translator). In ch. 6, Liu Hsieh equates *shih* with CH'IH, 'to maintain', 'sustain', apparently defining 'poetry' as 'WORD-TENOR' as contrasted with 'HANDTENOR' (cf. Eng. 'tenor' = ,holding on a course'; as a musical term : 'the voice which took and held the principal part'). Following Liu Hsieh's suggestion, we can render Prof. Chen's formula 'poetry expresses purposiveness' with greater semasiological percision as : 'WORD-TENOR spells INTENT'. It is further likely that the sematic of *shih* is not YEN, 'word', but its synonym SSU< *dzjəg*, reflected in the graphs *KGS* 968 and 972j 'utterance', 'speech', 'indictment', semantically analogous to our 'dit', 'dite', 'indite', 'dight' (Ger. *dichten*), and that both hemigrams are to be considered etymonic. *Shih* would have, then, connoted to the Chinese something that would be expressed by us as 'TENOR-DIT', 'TENOR-INDITEMENT'. As for Lu Chi's formula, *"shih yüan ch'ing"*, I think that by translating it "poetry born of pure emotion..." Prof. Chen does not do full justice to its bold metaphor. *Yüan*, 'to have affinity with', originally meant concretely 'hem, selvage' (note C120, 'thread'), and to me the definition means : 'WORD-TENOR' 'SELVAGES THE QUICKENING-of-the-HEART'. The versions of A. Fang and E. R. Hughes also ignore the metaphor.   The Chinese word *yi* (graphically C061 + C180, 'heart' + 'sound', 'tone'), translated 'thought', 'idea', was anciently defined as 'the emission of INTENT'. Its main derivation *yi* (+an additional C061) means 'to recall'. Paronomastically it is defined as 'repressing word-expression' (the homonym *yi*, 'repress' often interchanges with our *yi*). It would appear from the above that *yi* was semantically closer to our 're-flect' than to idea or thought, and that it could perhaps be defined as 'THE HEART'S ENTONE' ('inner tone', using EN- to avoid confusion with 'intone').

Workshop Fund 4.

25

On Tu Fu's Humour

The sly humour which enlivens some of Tu Fu's lighthearted poems has often been underestimated not only by translators, but even by commentators who have failed to note some of his delightful cranks and quips. We should like to draw attention in this connection to one of his poems, the 3rd of five octastichs entitled WILDERNESS AT HARVEST-TIDE, where the double entendre seems to have escaped the vigilance of TL or annotator:

> Propriety, LI : Music (as one of the polite arts) :: attack : my : shortcomings
> Hills : grove, woods :: induce : elation : CH'ANG (see Notes)
> Wag : head :: gauze : (official's) cap : aslant
> Expose to the sun : back :: bamboo : book, writing : glow
> Wind : fall, drop :: gather, garner : pinetree : TZU (here: 'seed')
> Sky : cold, chill :: split, carve : honey : room, receptacle, = — 'comb'
> Rare, spare : sparse :: small, minor : red : 'alcedine'
> To station : clogs, pattens :: draw near : minute : scent, fragrance

NOTES. S 2 has been badly misunderstood by TLs. Von Zach reads (p. 655) : "Ich möchte mit konfuzianischer Bilding (Riten und Musik) meine Mängel verbessern; / aber Berge und Wälder erfreuen mich so sehr, *dass ich jene für immer vergesse*". W. Hung (p. 246): "What I have learned of propriety and music should be helpful with my shortcomings; / Such beautiful hills and wood should give me feelings, *joyful and enduring*". Here we have no quarrel with the TLs' "prosopocentricity", for in S 1 we encounter one of the rare emphatic uses of a personal pronoun ('my', S 1.4); our objection to the renderings concerns their disregard of the parallelization of the first DS and their failure to underscore the clever use of CH'ANG in 2.5 // S 1.5. The latter word, TUAN, 'short', has an excellent analogue in the English 'shortcomings'; the perfect antonym is, however, lacking in English; we say : 'assets', 'good points'; but in Chinese, the contrast is expressed by CH'ANG, 'long', hence 'LONGCOMINGS'. KUNG, 'attack', had as etymonic KUNG, 'work, labor'; in this context, it expresses exactly our 'to belabor'. KUNG...TUAN, 'belabor shortcomings' is undoubtedly a waggish reference to the controversial passage in *Analects* 2.16 and its KUNG...TUAN (a homophone of TUAN, 'short', except for the tone), the famous "the study of strange doctrines is injurious indeed" (Legge). S 5.3–5 : Pineseeds were believed to contribute to longevity. S 7 presents a serious problem. 'Spare and sparse' form a binom which can, as such, be preposited as a predicate; but what does 'minor-red-'alcedine '(–green)' mean ? TLs extemporize : "Hier und da sehe ich kleine Blumen"; "Here and there, only a few red flowers are left". Annotators are silent. The key to the understanding of the phrase is to be found in the very first word of the octastich,

LI, 'propriety', 'good form'. Tu Fu is poking fun at himself for his disregard of the Proprieties while rusticating. LI evokes immediately the rich terminology of the several Chinese Books of Leviticus, which Tu Fu, as a Chinese gentleman and classical scholar, must have had at his fingertips. HSIAO HUNG 'minor red' was a well-known allogram of HSIAO KUNG, 'minor mourning (clothes)', where KUNG is a homeogram of KUNG, 'to belabor' (on 'minor mourning', see *Li Chi, passim*). We translate provisionally, recognizing that some additional points may have escaped us:

> Propriety and Polite Canor do belabor all the shortcomings that are mine,
> As hills and woods induce elating—'longcoming'—faculties :
> To wag the head—that formal gauzy cap will lob aslant,
> To bask the back—and in the sun, those bamboo writs will glow.
> Yet, come windfall-tide, to garner pineseeds (that longevous-making food)
> And in the chill of sky, to carve asunder honeycombs,
> When spare and sparse the alcedine in the lesser red of mourning,
> In stationed pattens, to make neighbors with the minim scent
> (Of autumn's world, so short of Culture..)
>
> *Workshop Fund 3.*

26
Two of Tu Fu's 'Last Poems'

The poems to be discussed were written in the spring of A. D. 768, some 32 months before his death (for Prof. Hung's excellent reasoning for dating the second piece, cf. *Tu Fu*, p. 256; *Notes*, p. 106). The first, a 4 S penned after a carousal, ends in a chuckle; the second closes on one of the most poignant notes in all literature. The 4 S is entitled ABRUPTED CROTCHET (Ch. for '4S') PROLATED UNDER THE MOON, ONCE MORE INVITING THE HON. PREPOSITOR OF SCRIPTURES LI (Chih-fang) TO DISMOUNT, AFTER HAVING SPENT THE NIGHT DRINKING IN A HALL OF SCRIPTURES. The bon mot of the piece is aborted by annotators & TLs.

> Lake : moon : forest, grove : wind :: respectant : partake : quickclear
> Maimed : jug (of wine) : dismount : horse :: once more : together : to tip
> Long (of time) : decide : wild : cranes :: such as : twin, *var.* frost :
>   hair on temples
> CHE–:–MO (coll. for 'no matter if') : neighbor : fowl : HSIA : fifth :
>   watch (of night)

The 4 S hinges on the word HSIA, 'under, down, get down, dismount', used four times in the text : 'under the moon', 'dismount' (*bis*), and in 'to HSIA the

5th watch'. The repetition is deliberate, preparing the ground for a word-play in S 4.5–7 : HSIA is the idiomatic verb for 'laying (an egg)'; KENG = 'watch' = 'encore' (Fr.<L. *ad hanc horam*):

> The moon of the lake and the wind of the forest partake, respectant, in the
>   quick & clear
> Half-mangled jugs command 'Dis—mount!'--for to be tipped once more
>   together;
> For wild-born cranes, of long decided, such with twin-frosted temple-
>   locks
> Should noways care that the neighbors' fowls be laying the fifth encore
> (The final watch of our revels 'in wind and moon'...)

BOSOM-THOUGHTS WRITTEN AT NIGHT, ON A JOURNEY :
Slender, thin : grass :: minim : breeze ; shore
Topple : mast :: 'cur-lonely' : night : boat
Stars : droop, *var.* 'to sue' :: level, plane : wild plain : broadening, separate
Moon : bubble, boil :: great : Stream : flow
Name, fame : how (rhet.), L. *num* : letters : stave, stanza, essay : be
    manifest
Office : ought, should : : old age : sickness : to sist
Windtossed : windtossed :: what : SO, a nominalizing zygomatic : resemble
Heaven : earth :: one : sand : gull, tern

The somber mood of the 8S is created by the verblessness of the first DS contrasted with 4 verbals in the second. The last hemistich of the 8S is usually anemically read : "...just a sand-gull", Tu Fu's marvelous diction and knowledge of his literary heritage being thus sadly underestimated. 'Sand' seems to be a supernumerary epithet, until we remember that it also means 'sand-grain'. In the light of the character's use as an allogram of SSU, 'raucous shriek of a bird' (*Li Chi* 10.1) and its juxtaposition with OU, 'gull', a perfect homophone of OU, 'to disgorge', Tu Fu's intention becomes clear:

> A slender-grassed and minim-breezèd shore,
> A topple-masted, lonely nighting boat,
> The stars sue down to the planing wild—outspaced,
> And the moon bubbles the greatened Stream—onflowing past.
> Can Fame in lettered staves be manifest
> When Office should for agèd sickness come to sist ?
> Windtossed and tossed, unto what semblance ?
> This : heaven, earth—and one sand-granule of a gull..one shriek
> (Disgorged into their silence..)

Workshop Fund 1.

愛 文 廬 札 記 小 跋

(代 中 文 摘 要)

卜弼德教授前數年間，覃思精心，作札記蓋近百篇，未嘗正式發表，只每篇親手謄寫複製若干份，按期分致同好傳觀。其論題廣，創旨多，閱者自可隨時仁智各見。但於其析理之深湛，發意之奇闢，則人口交碎。當時每有隔期不獲，則爭相索取者，久以希而愈珍。然迄未合帙，散佚可虞。予與先生有廿載餘同事之雅，深契之誼，恒苦勸其整輯出版。全稿廣涉亞洲語文，徵校琢磨，更及歐西古今文範。今幾經懇商，且數互嘲諧，始獲默許，以予所藏稿選其有關中國詩文者廿六篇付印。先生學術閎深，誨人不倦；而愛楮惜墨，自律摹嚴。坐與友生論學，時能片語而如發天機，於著文問世，則似淡以為餘事。謙德所至，即精心篇什，亦自均謂試驗。蓋以真理境界無限，語言亦難盡意，惟自以獨往精神造詣之，但求得之於心。故偶落言筌，亦常不以普通世間語出之。所成輒如提丹煉汞，深識者擇用其精，合劑而啖之，則啓益至宏；若徒望其形，囫圇而吞之，則非丹方之意，大藥之理矣。先生沖懷下問，囑付稿時加以評騭，因聊附短跋，以酬嘉命。至扴析毫末，抒發異同，詳焉則容待他日。原稿各自獨題成篇，無待撮述，故以跋稍代摘要。只譯總題，就古西所稱文字學之本意，簡遂曰 "愛文廬札記"，或副先生治學究極窮源之旨志。原稿每注自以其次貿力紀念某先賢者，亦排小字保留，以珍重其尚友之意云爾。

陳 世 驤 識

Proto-Bulgarian *ičirgü ~ ičürgü

In his study of "Altaic Elements in the Proto-Bulgarian Inscriptions,"
Karl Menges reiterates, with apparent approval (Byzantium 31:1.96-98),
the commonly asserted interpretation of Proto-Bulgarian ētzērgou ~
ēzourgou, title preceding and seemingly qualifying that of boila
'boyar', as a Turkic denominative adjectival form reconstructed as
*ičargü ~ ičarigü, corresponding to standard Turkish ičraki 'inner',
from icra ~ icari 'within'. Despite the phonetic difficulties presented by the Greek transcriptions—necessitating the supposition of
vocalic assimilation or syllabic reduction in the conjectural and
admittedly aberrant Turkic original—the assumption has been widely
favored as tending to substantiate a reference in De Caerimoniis
(pp. 681, 682) to "interior and exterior boyars" (hoi esō kai exō
Boliades) in the Bulgar khanate. Without prejudice to the theory
that such a division, not unknown for other Turkic tribes, may have
existed among the Bulgars (cf. F. Köprülü in Rev. internat. des
études balkan., 3.316-319), the possibility still remains, as already
pointed out in the notes to the Bonn edition, that this phrase, used
only in a ceremonial salutation formula, reflected purely Byzantine
terminology, meaning no more than "those at court and abroad." At
any rate, the importance attached to this lonely passage appears
somewhat exaggerated. Another etymology is both possible and legitimate for the title, one which would account perfectly for the
variable Greek spelling: namely, taking *ičirgü ~ ičürgü as a deverbal adjective-noun in -gü (cf. A. von Gabain, Alttürkische Gram-
matik, sections 115, 141) from the causative stem of the verb ič-
'to drink', ičir ~ ičür- (both forms are common), 'to make a pledge
to be drunk, an oath or vow taken'. Since ceremonial drinking as a
rite of renewing allegiance to the ruler is well attested among
Altaic nomads, it is earnestly suggested to Proto-Bulgarian specialists that they re-examine their material in the light of the possibility that certain nobles of the Bulgar khans' entourage may have
borne the title of 'propinating boyars', in their capacity of
trusted horcotic officers in charge of administering oath and potion
to their less-privileged sympotic colleagues. Compare, in this
connection, the function of kumyss-dispensing odači at the court of
Uzbek khans, described by W. Bartold in Zap. Imp. Geogr. Ob. Otd.
Etnogr., 34.305. After A.D. 811, Slavic chieftains in the Bulgarian
empire appear to have been granted the high honor of toasting their
sovereign with quaffs from a unique vessel: the silver-lined skull
of Emperor Nicephorus in which the great khan Krum, the conqueror of

---

*[These seven Cedules bear their original serial numbers. They are
not among the group reprinted in 1969 (No. 31). -- Ed.]

the basileus, <u>boastfully made them drink</u>. Our reconstruction of the title <u>ičirgü</u> lends particular significance to the closing phrase in Theophanes' paragraph (De Boor, 491) which tells the gruesome story: <u>pinein eis autēn tous tōn Sklauinōn archontas epoiēsen egkauchomenos</u>. The potable may have been kumyss, rather than wine, in view of Krum's alleged ampelophobic legislation (ap. Suidas, but cf. G. Kazarow, in <u>Byzan. Zeitschr.</u>, 16.255).

Workshop Fund 2, in memoriam Paul Pelliot

* * *

CEDULES FROM A BERKELEY WORKSHOP IN ASIATIC PHILOLOGY   003-540720

A Triplex Fusion in Ancient Chinese

One of the best-known fusions in Archaic Chinese is that of <u>pu-k'o</u>^{3} (archaic <u>pju(g)-k'â</u>), 'may not' [graphs A below], into <u>p'o</u>^{3} (arch. <u>p'uâ</u>) [B], with prospneusis of the initial of the negative <u>pu</u> through amalgamation with the guttural of <u>k'o</u> and synizesis of its atonic with the long vowel of the main word, and with the fusion carrying the tone of the latter. Now, <u>Chi Yün</u> 3.14 lists a character [C] <u>p'uâi</u> with the meaning 'may not.' This is undoubtedly a fusion of our fusion with a third element <u>-i</u>. It may well have been the kommatic particle [D] in its ancient, rather than archaic pronunciation, <u>ji</u> < <u>zjəg</u>, or the coverb [E], <u>i</u> < <u>zjəg</u>, which usually follows 'may' before a transitive verb (for both words, see <u>GS</u> 976). The fusion is again homotonic with its stressed components. Graph [C] is also entered in <u>Chi Yün</u> and <u>Kuang Yün</u> 3.15 with the reading <u>p'âi</u> (defined in the former dictionary as <u>pu-k'o,</u> and in the latter as <u>pu-k'eng</u>^{3} [F] (anc. and arch. <u>k'əng</u>, <u>GS</u> 882), 'not willing'. <u>P'âi</u> appears to be the fusion of the same three vocables, but with syncopic synaloephe of the vowel of the negative: <u>p'-(k')â-i</u>. Known only lexicographically, the graph is first found in <u>Kuang Ya</u> 4 A, in a list of negatives, all of them fusions. Among them we have <u>p'əng</u> [G], <u>CY</u> and <u>KY</u> 3.43, defined by the latter as <u>pu-k'eng</u>, and undoubtedly a synaloephic fusion of the two words: <u>p'-(k')əng</u>. Normally read <u>b'əng</u> in the meaning 'associate', [G] has also a secondary reading <u>b'uâi</u> < <u>b'wəg</u>, indicated already in <u>Shuo Wen</u> 8 A. It is further interesting to note that <u>CY</u> 3.15 gives [G] as a graphic variant of [C], in the reading <u>p'âi</u> < <u>p'əg</u>, and that the same <u>CY</u> section supplies us with a <u>k'âi</u> < <u>k'əg</u> value for [F], normally <u>k'əng</u>. This opens a new avenue of speculation: could [F] itself be a fusion of <u>k'o</u> with <u>neng</u> [H] (anc. <u>nəng</u>, arch. <u>nəg</u>), 'be able', 'possible'. The compound <u>k'o-neng</u>, 'possible', occurs in texts, but rather late. What militates against the hypothesis is the tone of <u>neng</u>^{2}, although <u>CY</u> and <u>KY</u> 3.43 register an unusual reading <u>neng</u>^{3}. Fusions with <u>k'o</u> as the first element are likely. An archaic one seems to me definite

in [I] k'an (GS 658: k'ậm < k'əm), 'able to bear', 'to sustain', which
must be a synaloephe of k'o and jen [J] (GS 667: ńʑjəm < njəm), 'to
bear'. In ancient Chinese the two words, though homotonic, were
classified under different rhymes (CY and KY 2.22 and 2.21), but in
archaic Chinese, as demonstrated by Karlgren, they had the same final
(see, en dernier lieu, Compendium of Phonetics in Ancient and Archaic
Chinese, BMFEA 26.243). If our conjecture concerning the fusion
nature of k'əng is confirmed, we would have in [G] a twofold triple
fusion: in the reading p'əng, a fusion of pu-k'o-neng; as p'âi (that
is as an allogram of [C]), one of pu-k'o-i.

A 不可 B 巨 C 佫 D 矣 E 以 F 肯 G 倗 H 能 I 堪 J 任

Workshop Fund 3, in memoriam Berthold Laufer.

*   *   *

CEDULES FROM A BERKELEY WORKSHOP IN ASIATIC PHILOLOGY   004-540801

Chinese Hsiāng, 'country-wick', and Ch'īng, 'grandee'

The characters representing these two important terms (archaic xjang
and k'jǎng, graphs [A] and [B] below) are paleographically identical,
both being derived from the protograph [C], indubitably a picture of
two men face to face with a dish of food between them (Karlgren, GS
714; also Creel et al., Literary Chinese, 2.314), enjoying a convivium
or syssitia. Two semasiological threads seem to be woven in the
graph: a) the etymon 'aspectant' (coram, con-, syn-, counter-, para-).
and b) that of 'food' (epulation, ritual meal). The first is well
attested in three cognates: [D] and [E] xjàng, 'facing towards',
'window' (said to have meant 'counter-foramen'), and [F] xjâng, 'echo',
'countertone'. In spite of the difference in the initials, one
wonders if we might not have here a distant affine of sjāng, sjàng
[G], the common word for 'aspectant'. The second is manifest in
xjâng [H], 'banquet or sacrificial refection', and xjâng [I], 'pro-
visions'. It would appear, therefore, that English 'country' (<contra-)
is a good fortuitous analogue for HSIANG, although 'parish' (<paroikos,
'dwelling side by side') reflects even better, in its socio-religious
overtones of 'parochialism', the 'isms and the emotional associations
conjured by the Chinese ku-hsiang, 'old country home'. Now, the
grandees called CH'ING cannot be identified with particular court
functions (cf. T. Itō, in Tōhōgaku Ronshū 1 [Feb. 1954],105-119) and
it is not unlikely that they originally were mere 'king's companions',
i.e., messmates in the ruler's companium. We may thus express the
grapho-semantic linkage between our two words with any pair out of
the following list of terms culled from the thesaurus of our own
glossological tradition: XJANG: country-wick, commune, parish,
convictorage, (con-)cenacle, coenository, syndeipnon; K'JANG: ruler's
companion, paroeciarch, convictor, (con-)cenator, coenosite, syndeipnos,

<u>syndaitor</u>. On further consideration, however, we feel that greater semantic emphasis must be laid upon the sacramental quality and redolence of the commensal occasion, for XJANG is undoubtedly a cognate of <u>xjâng</u> [J], 'to offer, or partake of, a dapatical sacrifice (for gods or ancestors)', and of <u>xjāng</u> [K], 'fragrant', 'redolent (as grain or tallow)', and [L], 'fragrant', 'incense' (of which [M], the central element in [C], is supposed to be the allogram). In our linguistic and cultural heritage the two notions are well blended in Greek <u>thyō</u>, 'to sacrifice', <u>thyoō</u>, 'to make fragrant' (whence <u>thyme</u> and <u>thymiam</u>). The nature of the ancient Chinese village community may thus be best conveyed by some such word as *SYNTHYTERY (a community of <u>syntheters</u>, 'persons offering a redolent sacrifice in common'), while K'JANG grandees may well have been *SYNTHYSIARCHS (<u>synthysia</u>, 'sacrifice in common'), either as prepositors of communal sacrificial meals or as the ruler's companions at the sacrificial mess.

A 鄉 B 鄉 C ⿱ D 向 E 鬱 F 響 G 相 H 饗 I 餉 J 享
K 薌 L 香 M 皀

Workshop Fund 4, in memoriam Gustav Haloun.

* * *

CEDULES FROM A BERKELEY WORKSHOP IN ASIATIC PHILOLOGY   010-541001

Chinese TZU [A], 'child'

The "semantic diversities" of TZU^3 < <u>tsjəg</u> seem somewhat magnified as tabulated in Harvard-Yenching Institute's <u>Chinese-English Dictionary</u> <u>Project</u>, Fascicle 39.0.1, pp. 7-16, due perhaps to over-categorization and insufficient use of semasiological analogy. A simpler, more synoptical presentation of the etymon would be: CHILD: progeny, unborn child (as in "with child"), BABY; son (BOY, lad), daughter, youngster; OFFSPRING of animals, from the fetal stage on (inc. eggs, spawn); of plants: fruit, spec. seed, GRAIN, kernel, PIP, offshoot (from roots). CHILD OF A SOMEBODY: hidalgo, cadet, younker, young person, damoiseau, damosel. In compounds, reminiscent of Mac-, O'-, Fitz-, Pers. -<u>zade</u>. CHILDE, as in Childe Harold: proton in bisyllabic cognomina (<u>tzŭ⁴</u> [B]), esp. in the ancient period, with the deuteron synonymic with the first given name. E.g., Mencius' names: K'o (Axle-tree), TZU Yü (Childe Chassis); those of Confucius' beloved disciple: Yen Hui (Vortex), TZU Yüan (Childe Whirlpool). CHILDE > THANE (allied to Greek TEKNON, 'child'): title of distinction; feudal rank approx. corresponding to 'viscount', but two millennia older; thane, thaness; or—to coin a less ambiguous term—TEKNARCH. In direct address: Your (His, Her) Thaneship (sometimes: whimsically, familiarly, or in reference to things, more like 'Sirrah'). TEKNARCH,

teknagogue: person of learning or technical competence, master,
teacher (of young thanes?). When prefixed and suffixed to a P.N.
seems to have meant: TZU K'ung TZU, 'The (or 'our') thaneshipful
Teknarch K'ung'. TEKNARCHOLOGY: writings of the teknarchs, the third
division of Chinese literature. CHILD > GRAIN > PIP: grain-like
object; pip, as a marker in some games, MAN (as in chess); chit; spot.
CHILD > 'TO CHILD': v.t., to adopt or treat as a child, with
CHILDING-love (cognate of dz'jəg [C], 'enfanter', breed, dz'jəg
[D], 'love', storge, and of [B], in both senses); to beget, to spawn;
to behave as a child towards its parent; also adverbially; possibly
'TO PIP': to appear as a pip or spot. CHILD, BABY, babylike: of
objects subordinate to, encased in, or contrasted with a 'mother'
object (as in 'baby-sail'); spec.: phonetic hemigram vs. semantic
hemigram ('matrogram'); numerator of a fraction, as the child of
'mother' denominator; child of money usance: interest (either directly
from CHILD, as Greek TOKOS, or through 'proliferating', < proles).
CHILD > BOY > MAN: as the deuteron or teleuton of bi- and trisyllabic
appellations, occupational or descriptive, similar to -man, -boy, -er,
-ie, -y; as in 'boatman, cowboy, goalie, cabby, Fatty, Gabby,' etc.
CHILD > BABY > ENCLITIC SUFFIX: analogous to -kin, -ling, -let, -ole,
-cule, etc. Often no longer felt as diminutive, i.e. as much the -let
of 'bracelet' as that of 'streamlet', or the -ling of 'starling' as
that of 'duckling'. CHILD (in any of the above meanings: P.N. or
part of P.N. Note: the main derivative of our etymon tzu[4] [B],
'procreate', 'love', 'written (compound, digrammatic) character',
'secondary name given to an individual upon reaching marriageable and
procreating age', should be translated, in the light of the above:
TEKNOGRAM, TEKNONYM (-IC), or TOKOGRAM, TOKONYM. Etymological note:
Like the IE root of Latin filius (Greek thēlazō), TZU may have been
connected with an etymon 'to suck, suckle, abound'. Cf. dz'jəg [E],
'milch cow'. Its protograph may also have stood for a synonymous
root KU, KUG, XOG, as shown by the appearance of the graph in the
digrams: xŏg, 'filial piety', xôg, 'love', xəg < k'ung [F]; and through
synonymy: common words of the type KU ('colt', 'puppy', cub', 'calf'
[G]) and the phonogram KUK [H], phonetic in 'grain'; 'baby, nourish,
suckle'; 'nestling', 'milk a cow', 'egg-shell' (with sematics 115,
39, 196, 93, 'egg'). Cf. also the now current term hai < g'əg [I],
'child'.

A 子 B 字 C 孳 D 慈 E 牸 F 孝 好 吼 孔 G 駒 狗 物 H 殼 I 孩

Workshop Fund 4.

*   *   *

CEDULES FROM A BERKELEY WORKSHOP IN ASIATIC PHILOLOGY   011-541010

On Ancient Chinese Titles

The adoption of THANE, TEKNARCH as a translation of Chinese TZU (as a
title of nobility or eminence) should greatly facilitate devising more
precise renderings for other titles. Thus, while there seems to be no
need of tampering with the now prescriptive rendition of T'ien-tzu as
'Son of Heaven' in favor of 'Heaven's Thane', the manifestly inadequate paraphrase of both T'ai-tzu and Shih-tzu [A] as 'Heir Apparent'
could well be abandoned for the exact equivalents: 'Grand Thane (or
Teknarch)' and 'Aeval Thane'. It may seem, furthermore, advisable to
utilize the termination -ARCH as a convenient formant for a more
rigorous semantic reproduction of the well-attested connotations of
many ancient 'feudal' appellatives. It is rather incongruous to
speak of Chinese 'barons' of the 8th century B.C. Like TZU, the
term NAN [B] is etymologically transparent and means simply 'male',
'masculine'. Why not render it, then as ANDRARCH (< anēr 'male')?
Similarly, HOU [C] which we habitually translate 'marquis' or, in
broader contexts, 'feudal lord' means specifically 'man of the
target, or butt', 'archer'. ARCHER-LORD or SCOPARCH (< Gr./L. scopus,
'butt in archery') would emphasize much better the origin, temper,
and praxis of the ancient Chinese aristocracy who thought of themselves,
above all, as expert archers. The reader may see that I unreservedly
endorse the abjuration of denotational 'traductions' advocated by my
colleague Professor E. H. Schafer in a recent spirited article (FEQ
13: 251-260). The next titles, higher up the feudal scale, present
more of a problem. PO [D], 'earl', belongs to an etymon signifying
'eldest in a generation', 'paternal uncle', 'chief'. PATRARCH
(< patrōs, 'paternal uncle') is the best gloss, with PROTARCH a close
second choice. KUNG [E], 'duke', has no analogical connections
whatever with 'dux', but its etymology is not easy to determine. The
semantic nucleus is 'elder progenitor', 'sire', 'venerable one', but
adjectivally the term means 'public', 'pertaining to the public good'.
As such, it may be linked with a near homonym (with which it sometimes
interchanges) KUNG [F], 'common', 'together'. I should recommend, for
the present, COENARCH, COENARCHIC (< koinos, 'common', 'public').
WANG [G], 'king', 'prince', 'emperor' (of the Chou dynasty), may best
be metonymized as BASILEARCH. The etymology of WANG, like that of
Greek basileus, is unknown; it seems, however, to be a Sinitic word,
but the native scholiasts can suggest nothing better than association
with the homonym WANG, 'to go', and the far-fetched school-etymology
'king' = 'one to whom the people go'. Through a curious coincidence,
this parallels the attempts of the Greek grammarians to decode
basileus as some coadunation of bainō, 'to go', and laos, 'people'.
HUANG [H], 'emperor', 'august', is, on one hand, a cognate of WANG; on
the other, an affine of KUANG [I], 'bright glow', 'glory'. The upper
part of the graph, now written with the element 'white' [J], the Shuo
Wen interprets as being 'original' [K], while the protograph is
suggestive of the representation of a corona (of the sun), an aureole,

perhaps an anthelion. Since HUANG was traditionally applied to
the divine WANG of the highest antiquity, ARCHIBASILEARCH, ARCHI-
BASILIC (adj.) may prove to be hermeneutically acceptable, with ARGI-
(< argos, 'shining bright') as a paragram for the first element. For
TI [L], 'god', 'emperor', the logical option is THEARCH or DIARCH
(< dios, 'divine'); for HUANG TI, ARGIBASILIC DIARCH.

A 太 孑 世 好 子 B 男 C 侯 D 伯 E 公 F 共 G 王, 往 H 皇 I 光 J 白
K 自 L 帝

Workshop Fund 1, in memoriam Edward T. Williams

*   *   *

CEDULES FROM A BERKELEY WORKSHOP IN ASIATIC PHILOLOGY   014-54110

Imperial Aurigation in China

Among the various Chinese terms, twenty of them or so, that we translate, monotonously and unimaginatively, as 'Imperial', is the word
yü < ngjwo [A], used chiefly as a bound form to qualify, adjectivally
or adverbially, the belongings or actions of the Son of Heaven. The
dictionaries register the following meanings for the vocable:
1. to drive a chariot, commonly a quadriga; charioteering,
    charioteer.
2. to manage (the Chinese word retains stronger associations
    with the 'manège' of horsemanship than English 'manage' and
    is free of contamination with housekeeping 'ménage').
3. to proffer, to attend; to offer to the Emperor.
4. imperial (presence, action, possession, entourage, etc.).
5. imperial attendants, particularly women.
6. to withstand, to repel (then normally written with C113, [B]).
7. (traditionally read ya < nga): a. to invoke; b. to go to meet.
Textual examples, glossaries, and ancient graphic variants [C] attest
the primacy of the first meaning. The oldest allogram [C 1] is
composed of a kneeling figure and the protograph of wu < nguo [D],
'the seventh of the duodecimal series of cyclical characters',
presumably the picture of a beetle, beater, or pounder, Chinese ch'u
tsʻjwo [E] (the Shuo Wen says wu is phonetic in this character, an
indication of a possible *TSNG- initial in the phonetic group).
Another [C 2] is a digram of 'horse' and 'hand' (holding a whip?),
while the protograph of the modern form of yü contains in addition to
the 'pounder' and the 'kneeling figure' the classifiers C060
'to step forward' and C077 'to stop'. The right hemigram of the
modern scription [F] is explained in the Shuo Wen as forming the
graph hsieh, 'to unharness', with nguo as 'phonetic'. Hsü Shen
amplifies the observation with a note to the effect that the graph is

to be read as <u>hsieh</u>< <u>sjag</u>, 'to write' [G], in a dialectical pronunciation. No unusual reading of <u>hsieh</u> is known except that in <u>Shih</u> 214
where it must have had the value *<u>sjo</u> (it rhymes there with two words
in <u>-jo</u>).   Again Hsü Shen's statement makes sense only on the supposition of an original value of *(T)SNGO for <u>nguo</u>, 'beater'. The primary
meaning of our <u>yü</u>, then, appears to be 'to use a beater', or L. <u>pello</u>,
'to put in motion by beating or pushing', and its derivative <u>appello</u>,
'to drive towards', 'bring to a terminus', and <u>depello</u>, 'to drive
away, to put aside', or 'repel'. Meaning 7a may be the result of the
same type of convergence that we see in <u>appello</u> (<u>appellere</u>) 'to
drive', and <u>appello</u> (<u>appellare</u>),'to appeal'. We find here, then, the
Chinese monarch conceived as an appulsive agent impelling, or appelling
the chariot of state, or his subjects treated as a team of horses.
One might advance, therefore, as suitable translations for the imperial
<u>yü</u> the terms AURIGAL, ELATERIC, ELASIARCHIC (from Greek <u>elaunō</u>, 'to
drive a chariot', <u>elasis</u>, 'driving').   These would not, however,
convey the 'appulsive' connotations of the etymon. Better suggestive
of the highest authority in the political driver's seat would be the
compound CURULE-APPULSIVE or, in most adjectival contexts, simply
CURULE, CURULIAN; and for the verbal <u>yü</u>, TO APPULSE (i.e. 'to appel
something to') and 'to repulse' (6) would best serve the purpose. A
vivid idiom parallel to our 'backseat-driving' occurs in old Chinese
military texts (e.g. <u>Liu T'ao</u> 21) where undesirable interference by
the chief of state in the decisions of a field-general is described
as 'driving from within' [H].

A 御 B 禦 C 犯劉 D 午 E 杵 F 卸 G 寫 H 從中御

Workshop Fund 8, in memoriam Diether von den Steinen.

*   *   *

CEDULES FROM A BERKELEY WORKSHOP IN ASIATIC PHILOLOGY   016-541201

Chinese 'State' and 'Nation'

The term <u>kuo</u>, customarily translated 'state', 'country', 'kingdom',
'realm', 'nation', and even 'dynasty', shows no semasiological links
with the Chinese analogues of the etyma '<u>status</u>' — 'state', 'opposite
tract', 'king', 'homogeneous or connascent group', or 'powerful
dominion or sovereignty' which underlie the English vocables. The
derivation of <u>kuo</u>< *KWĔK appears to be clear-cut. Its scription [A]
is a pleiomorphic digram, the graph of the original etymon *GJWĔK [B]
being enlarged with the sematic C031, 'enclosure', 'periphery',
'ambit' (see <u>GS</u> 929). *GJWĔK with C032, 'soil', gives us <u>yü</u> <
*GJWĔK, 'territory, boundary, frontier, march'; with C085, 'water',
<u>hsü</u> < XJWĔK, 'moat'; with C120, 'silk', <u>yü</u> < *GJWĔK, 'seam'; with
C169, 'gate', <u>yü</u>< *GJWĔK, 'threshold' [C]. Indubitably the core of
the etymon is to be sought in such notions as: 'limen', 'limes',

'boundary', 'mark', 'mere, mear', 'circuitus civitatis', Gr. horos, horisma, ta horia, 'boundary line'. More distant relatives of our word undoubtedly are: kuo < *KWÂK, 'outer wall', 'enceinte of a city', 'rim'; yu < *GJŬK, 'enclosed garden or orchard', 'garth', hortus; and possibly huå < *G'WĔK, 'to delineate' [D]. The Chinese concept of 'state', then, put stress upon the horistic, territorial aspect of the state, rather than on its 'body politic', sovereignty', or its 'rex' and 'dominus'. IE etymologists may debate the possible remote relationship between Latin populus, plebs and Greek polis, or that of urbs and urvus, 'city circuit', but one can be reasonably sure, with the invaluable help of graphosemantics, that in China amburbial demarcation loomed as the determining factor in the formation of the concept of the ancient urbs or city-state over those of 'towered, fortified burg' (registered in the protograph of king < *KJÅNG, 'capital' [E]), 'township', *HJEP (C163, [F]), or plēthos of the populace (cf. Chinese shih and chao, defined as 'multitude', in the compounds KING-shih, KING-chao, 'metropolis'). The notion of 'authority', historically ingrained in the term, cannot be overlooked semantically, however, for demarcation naturally implies some authoritative horistic agency; and it is significant that early paronomastic glosses for *GJWEK, 'state', equate it with GJŬG, 'to have and to hold' [G]. Besides MARKLAND, MEARLAND, BOURNELAND, GIRDLAND, GIRTLAND, and LIMINARY as semantically appropriate terms for the translation of kuo, we should also suggest HORARCHY or HORIARCHY (in keeping with our advocacy of the utilization of the suffix -ARCH, -ARCHY in rendering the flavor of some ancient Chinese terms). For the nearest affine of kuo, yü, 'territory, frontier', MARCH and MARCHLAND appear satisfactory. In the famous historical name Hsi yü designating "The Western Regions" (Serindia), LIMITROPHES, in addition to MARCHES, might give even fuller expression to the traditional role of these oasis centers as food-bases for Chinese garrisons. The closest literary and emotional equivalent of our 'nation' is the Chinese binom kuo-chia (-kja, Sino-Japanese kokka), 'state (-/and) family'. 'Family' is a good reading, especially in view of the use of chia, analogously to Ciceronian familia, in the meaning 'sect, association, school of philosophers'. Its etymology is obscure except for the graphic connotation of 'fold', 'pen', suggested by the composition of the digram [H]: 'roof' + 'pig'. We propose HOMEFOLD and, for the undertone of 'authority', OECIARCHY (Greek oikia, 'house, household, family'; cf. oikēma, 'house', 'pen'). KUO-CHIA as 'nation', then, seemed to connote to the Chinese something like GIRDLAND AND HOMEFOLD or HOROECIARCHY.

A 國 B 或 C 域 淢 緎 D 闋 郭 囿 畫 E 京 F 邑 G 有 H 家

Workshop Fund 6

The Language of the T'o-Pa Wei*

Harvard Journal of Asiatic Studies, 1 (1936), 167-185.

In the second decade of the third century A. D., a century which proved to be so eventful in the history of China, when the wily Ts'ao Ts'ao 曹操, having triumphed over his chief rivals north of the Yangtse, was turning his attention to the great " Problem of the Frontier " and to the re-establishment of Chinese communications with Central Asia, there appeared in the northern marshes of Shansi a little tribe of nomads who were predestined to leave an indelible stamp on the life of the Middle Kingdom in the tragic centuries to come. Their fame was to spread through the entire continent from ocean to ocean, and they were to bestow upon China one of her many names.

Their advent passed almost unnoticed by the Chinese (so far as we can judge from contemporary sources) in the midst of the manifold problems that confronted Ts'ao's and his successor's chancellery in dealing with the complex relations existing at the time between China and the Hsiung-nu 匈奴, Hsien-pi 鮮卑, and Wu-huan 烏桓 nomadic organizations. Ch'ü-pei 去卑, then regent of the Hsiung-nu by the grace of Ts'ao, must have, however, reported to Yeh 鄴, the Chinese capital, about the pressure exercised upon his northern frontier by the newcomers.[1]

---

*Abbreviations used: Capital letters followed by Roman numerals indicate the Twenty Four Dynastic Histories (the 1902 reprint of the Ch'ien-lung 1739 edition by the *Shih-hsüeh Hui-shê* 史學會社) and chapter referred to, viz.: E—*Chin Shu* 晉書; F—*Sung Shu* 宋書; G—*Nan Ch'i Shu* 南齊書; J—*Wei Shu* 魏書; K—*Pei Ch'i Shu* 北齊書; L—*Chou Shu* 周書; O—*Pei Shih* 北史: 2P—*Hsin T'ang Shu* 新唐書. KD—B. KARLGREN, *Analytic Dictionary of Sino-Japanese*; pht.—posthumous title; tk.—Turkish; mo.—Mongol; ma.—Manchu; tk. mo.—" turco-mongol."

[1] O 53, 1 b, biography of P'o-liu-han Ch'ang 破六韓常 (cf. K 27, 1 b), has preserved for us the only mention of the early clashes between the T'o-pa and the Hsiung-nu. Ch'ang traced his ancestry back to P'an-liu hsi 潘六奚, younger brother of Ch'ü-pei, who was sent by the regent to stop the inroads of the T'o-pa, but was defeated and taken prisoner together with his five sons.

These invaders, known as T'o-pa 拓跋, formed at first part of the great
Hsien-pi confederacy under T'an-shih-huai 檀石槐[2] in the second half
of the second century, and possibly entered into the loose union of tribes
created about 225 by the Hsien-pi chieftain K'o-pi-nêng 軻比能. They
emerge as a distinct political entity under the "First Progenitor" (Shih-
tsu 始祖) of the future emperors of Wei, T'o-pa Li-wei 拓跋力微. In
248 Li-wei, heretofore subject to the Mo-lu-hui 沒鹿回 horde, murdered
its chiefs and became the supreme head of a nomadic organization numbering "over 200,000 bowmen" (J1, 1b). Ten years later, he established
himself on the Chinese frontier and entered into close relations with the
Ts'ao-Wei Empire. We shall find the T'o-pa in the welter of the great
movement of the "Barbarians" which caused the "Fall of the Chinese
Empire" half a century later, and see them achieve supremacy over the
entire North of China by 450 A. D.

It must have been prior to the rise of Li-wei that a group of T'o-pa,
known in Chinese history as the T'u-fa 禿髮, led by Li-wei's elder
brother P'i-ku 匹孤, detached itself from the main body and, skirting
the western bend of the Yellow River, proceeded southwestward into
Kansu, where they founded a kingdom of their own, the Southern Liang
南涼, which flourished from 397 to 414 and was destroyed by the Western
Ch'in 西秦. J 99, E 126, and *Shih-liu Kuo Ch'un-ch'iu* 十六國春秋,
ch. 88, in their account of the ancestry of the T'u-fa kings, do not mention the blood relationship uniting them with the T'o-pa, but from J 41
(biography of Yüan Ho 源賀, cf. *infra* § 20) and the brief genealogy of
the Yüan 源 family preserved in 2P 75 A, we know that this relationship
was recognized by the T'o-pa Wei rulers.[2a]

Who were, then, these T'o-pa or T'u-fa and what was the "barbarian
tongue" which resounded in their tents before they established themselves as rulers of China and exchanged it for the genteel Sinitic monosyllables? Before attempting to reconstruct and analyze their name, the
author would think wise to pass in review the fragmentary vocabulary
material of T'o-pa which has been preserved to us in the Chinese sources.

Our knowledge of the T'o-pa language is chiefly derived from titles
and proper names that can be culled from the *Wei Shu* and from two of
the histories of Southern Chinese dynasties, primarily F 95 and G 57.
Proper names have not heretofore been studied, while it is mainly through

---

[2] KD 967, 883, 460: *d'ân-d'iäk-g'wai* < mo. *daldaɣai*—"secret," "hidden"? Cf.
the story of his birth and childhood, *San Kuo Chih*, 30.

[2a] The genealogy of the two branches of the T'o-pa presents itself on general

the efforts of Professors Kurakichi Shiratori and Paul Pelliot [3] that the following equivalences have been established between Chinese transcriptions and reconstructed T'o-pa titles:

1. *K'o-sun* 可孫, *KD* 414, 833: *k'â-suən*—"title of the T'o-pa Empress," G 57. Tk. **qasun~qatun* ⟨ *qaɣatun*—"wife of the sovereign

lines as follows:

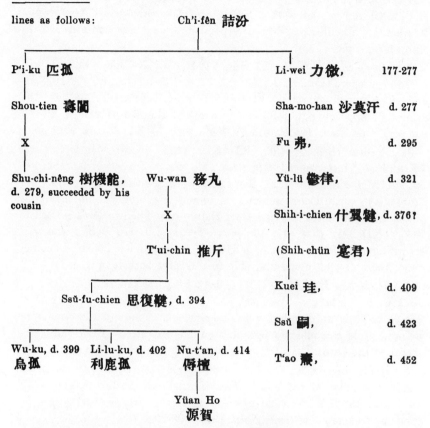

The reader might be surprised that Shih-chün 寔君 is designated as the father of Kuei. The author has been forced, however, to accept this conclusion and will sometime undertake to demonstrate this correction of the *Wei Shu*.

[3] SHIRATORI Kurakichi, Über die Sprach der Hiungnu und der Tunghu-Stämme, *Bulletin (Izvestiia) de l'Academie Imperiale des Sciences* 1902, vol. 17. 2, pp. 015-018, henceforth quoted as *Izv.*; Über die Sprache des Tung-hu Volks (Pt. VI and VII), *Shigaku Zasshi* 史學雜誌 22. 11 and 12, pp. 1-24 and 1-27, quoted as *SZ*. PELLIOT's occasional observations are scattered in numerous brief notes in *JA* and *TP*, as indicated in the text of this article.

(khan)," which is found in Tʻu-chüeh Turkish as *kʻo-ho-tun* 可賀敦 KD 342, 1143: *kʻâ-γâ-tuən* < *qaγatun* (L50, 1a), and in Tʻu-yü-hun as *kʻo-tsun* 可脅, KD 1112: *kʻâ-tsuən* (*ibid.*), cf. K. Shiratori, *Izv.*, 15, 18, and *SZ*, 22. 5, 75-84, also P. Pelliot, *JA* 1930, 260. *-tun, -sun, -tsun* may be a feminine suffix which re-appears in Hsien-pi *a-ma-tun* 阿麽敦 KD 1,593: *ʼâ-muâ-tuən* < **aβaγatun?*—" mother " (L 11, 2a, cf. O 57), cf. Tʻu-yü-hun *mo-ho* 莫何, KD 638: *mâk, muo-g-γâ* < **(a)baγa*— " father." This suffix possibly corresponds to the mongol feminine suffixes *-lun, -tani, -tai*.[4]

2. *Kʻo-po-chên* 可薄眞, KD 764, 1194: *kʻâ-bʻâk-tʻśi̯ĕn* < tk. *qapaγčin* —" door-keeper," *ibid.*; *Izv.*, 17; *SZ* 22. 12, 20; Pelliot, *JA* 1925, I, 255. The initial sonant of 薄 *bʻâk* offers no difficulty as we have the same title appearing in F 95 as the name of the Tʻo-pa prince Yü 余 son of Tʻo-pa Tʻao, in the form 可博眞, with 博 KD 50 *pâk* for *bʻâk*.

3. *Chʻi-wan-chên* 乞萬眞, KD 332, 1295: *kʻi̯ət-mi̯ʷɒn-tśi̯ĕn* < mo. *kälmärčin*—" interpreter," *ibid.*; *Izv., loc. cit.*; *SZ* 17-19; Pelliot, *loc. cit.* The Turkish form of the same word (with initial t- for k-) **tilmač(i)* > germ. Dolmetscher, russ. tolmač, may underlie the nickname of the ancestor of the Ho-lien Hsia Hsiung-nu, Tʻieh-fu 鐵弗 ~ Tʻieh-fa 鐵伐 (KD 991: *tʻiet*; 47, 16: *pi̯uət, bi̯ʷɒt*) Liu Hu 劉虎, who was, according to J 95, the son of a Hu 胡 father and a Hsien-pi mother (and, therefore, bilingual and able to interpret both languages?).

4. *Pi-tê-chên* 比德眞, KD 714, 981: *pji-*(or *bʻji*)-*tək-tśi̯ĕn* < tk. mo. *bitäkčin* or **pitäkčin*—" scribe," *ibid.*; *Izv.*, 16; *SZ* 11-14; Pelliot, 254-255. This word calls for no observations, outside of those made by Pelliot, while a whole monograph would be required to determine the origin (Chinese or Indo-European?) of tk. **bitig*—" writing." [5]

5. *Hsien-chên* 咸眞, KD 148: *γâm-*(<γɒm)-*tśi̯ĕn* < tk. *yamčin* > russ. yamščik—" rider of the post," *ibid.*; *Izv.*, 7; *SZ* 21-24; Pelliot, *TP* 1930, 192-195; B. Vladimirtsov, Zametki k drevne-tyurkskim . . . tekstam, *Doklady Akademii Nauk* 1929, 290-294.

---

[4] On which cf. Pelliot, *TP* 1932, 50-51, also B. Vladimirtsov, Traces du genre grammatical dans la langue mongole (in Russian), *Doklady Akademii Nauk* 1925, 31-34.

[5] If one pre-suppose that the chief of the Kirghiz was the proud possessor of a " secretariat," one could see in the obscure *mi-ti-chih* 密的支, KD 617, 860, 1212: *mi̯ĕt-tiek-tśi̯ɐ*, of 2P 217 B, designating the large tent of the Kirghiz ruler, a variant transcription of **bitigči*. It is through a strange lapsus that Father Hyacinth in his *Sobranie svedenii* . . . I: 2, 445, identifies this term with tk. *mesǧed* < ar. *masjid*—" mosque."

6. *Tou-lu* 豆盧, KD 1015, 579: *d'ạu-luo*—" to become loyal " (歸義) ⟨ tk. mo. *törü*—" law," " right," O 68, 1 a; *Izv.*, 18; *SZ* 7-8. The same word is found in Tou-lu-t'u 豆盧突, KD 498: *d'ạu-luo-t'uэt* (with the final *-t* quiescent)⟨ *törütü?, the cognomen of Yü-wên Chao 宇文招, prince of the Northern Chou, L13, 1 a.

Several other identifications proposed by Shiratori are tempting, but not conclusive; attention to some of them will be called when occasion demands. As to the following list of T'o-pa words, most of them have been discussed by the writer before; [6] they include, besides words identifiable through Chinese translations, many terms the meaning of which has been established through phonetic equivalences or their occurrence in " etymological " contexts.

7. The T'o-pa prince Jên 仁, prince of Yung-ch'ang 永昌 (J 17) is called in F 95 *K'u-jên-chên* 庫仁眞, KD 431, 930: *k'uo-ńźi̯ĕn-tśi̯ĕn*. Here again a prince of the blood is bearing a title of a dignitary. Although there is no clue as to the meaning of the T'o-pa word, the almost perfect phonetic equivalence makes it clear that we have here the turco-mongol term *qoyinčin~qoninčin*—" sheep-herdsman," Chinese initial *ńź-* transcribing equally well " altaic " *yi-* or *ńi-*. The root of this word, *qoyin~ qonin*—" sheep " appears, transcribed by the same Chinese characters, as the personal name of the Hsiung-nu regent of the T'o-pa kingdom from 376 to 383, Liu K'u-jên. [7]

8. The mo. term *aqan*—" elder brother," which is registered in the T'u-yü-hun language (cf. PELLIOT, *TP* 1920-21, 329) doubtless underlies the T'o-pa title *a-kan* 阿干, KD 396: *'â-kân* ⟨ *aqan, attested chiefly in the combination *nei a-kan* 內阿干—" *aqan* of the interior." Cf. J 15, biography of T'o-pa Tsun 遵 who bore that title, and 2 P 71 B, 15 a, where it is mentioned as a position held under the Wei by Yü-wên Hsi 宇文系.

9. *K'o-han* 可汗, *k'â-kân* ⟨ *qaɣan*. Although the title " Khan " is not mentioned in the texts as the one borne by the early T'o-pa rulers, we are justified in assuming that this was the case for the following reasons: in 310 T'o-pa I-lu 猗盧 is given in addition to the title of duke of Tai 代, that of great *shan-yü* 單于, which in Chinese texts of the period is a " learned " archaic equivalent of *qaɣan*; the T'o-pa Empress, as we have

---

[6] In *Sino-Altaica*, Series I-IV (privately mimeographed).

[7] Another Liu K'u-jên 庫仁 is mentioned in J 26, biography of Wei Chüan 尉眷, as one of eight high officials of the Wei, and the same element enters into the name of a Juan-juan chieftain, appearing on the same page.

seen, bore the corresponding feminine title *qaɣatun*. In the famous song
of Mu-lan 木蘭, which was undoubtedly composed in the North during
the time of T'o-pa domination, the Emperor is referred to as *k'o-han*.
The title, made famous by the Orkhon Turks, was probably derived by
them from the Juan-juan, who, in turn, must have borrowed it either
from the T'o-pa or the Mu-jung.

10. Most of the T'o-pa princes of the blood mentioned in F 95 and
G 57 are referred to as *Chih-chin* 直勤 (or 懃), KD 1220, 389 : *d'i̯ək-
g'i̯ən*. This is obviously the equivalent of *t'ê-chin* 特勤, KD 811 : *d'ək-
g'i̯ən*, which transcribes regularly in T'ang texts the Orkhon Turkish
tigin, tägin > mo. *čigin*—" prince."

11. *Chih-chên* 直眞, *d'i̯ək-tśi̯ĕn*—" chief officers of the interior " 內
左右, G 57. In *Izv.*, 16, SHIRATORI suggests tk. *ič*—" interior," basing
himself on the modern pronunciation of *chih* 直; in *SZ* 9-10, the no more
acceptable ma. *doko*—" lining " and other tungus forms. In order to
understand the T'o-pa term, one must compare it with the parallel title
of the " chief officers of the exterior," which was, according to the same
Chinese source :

12. *Wu-ai-chên* 烏矮眞, KD 1288, 1306 : *'uo-'âi-tśi̯ĕn* < *'u'âičin* or
'uɣaičin. Shiratori unwarrantedly alters *wu* 烏 into *niao* 鳥, KD 662 :
tieu, and adduces again Tungus forms (*op. cit.* 10-11). The Chinese
terms *nei* 內 and *wai* 外 mean also " *agnatus* " and " *cognatus*," respectively, and it is doubtless in those meanings that we must take the above
two expressions. *Tägčin* [8] must, thus, in all probability be connected
with the tk. root of § 10, found in Orkhon Turkish *täg*—" Geschlecht,"
while *'uɣaičin* is derived from tk. *uq*—" id.," a synonym of tk. mo. *uruq*
" family relations on the mother's or wife's side." We have further substantiation of this etymology in a passage in J 113, 1 a, where it is stated
that in the early T'o-pa organization various clans not directly related
to the T'o-pa but who joined their confederacy were collectively called
Wu-wan 烏丸, KD 1293 : *'uo-ɣuân*. The two chiefs appointed over such
Wu-wan must undoubtedly be the officials termed *'uoɣaičin*.

13-14. In its description of the Wei army during the campaign of 495,
G 57, 3 a, speaking of the retinue of T'o-pa Hung and the enormous
chariot in which he traveled, says that the chariot was surrounded by
曷刺眞槊多白眞眊 " lances of the *ho-la-chên* and yak-tailed standards
of the *to-po-chên*." KD 73, 509 : *ɣât-lât-tśi̯ĕn* yield us a T'o-pa form
atlačin, while KD 1006, 685 : *tâb'ɒk-tśi̯ĕn* gives *tabaqčin*. *Atlačin* is

---

[8] Cf. the proper name *t'ê-chên* 特眞 < *tägčin*, occurring in L 17, 2a.

obviously derived from tk. *atla*—"to ride on horseback" (cf., however, PELLIOT, *TP* 1930, 306-308, for the history of that word in turkish), **tabaqčin*, from tk. mo. *tabaq*—"ground, sole of the foot." It thus seems safe to suppose that **atlačin* and **tabaqčin* represent the T'o-pa terms designating "cavalrymen" and "foot-soldiers" respectively.

15. *Hu-lo-chên* 胡洛真, KD 91, 411: *γuo-lâk-tśi̯ên* < *γuraqčin* or *'uraqčin* (PELLIOT, *JA* 1930, 261)—title of "the officer who girded (the ruler?) with weapons" 帶仗人, G 57. Shiratori suggested at first (*Izv.*, 16) tk. *qïlïč*—"sword" and Hsiung-nu **kinglak* 徑路—"sword," but later (*SZ* 22. 12, 17-18) he attempted to connect the T'o-pa word with mo. *χorči*—"quiver-bearer," and with the tk. root **qur*—"encircle," "guard," "fortify,"[9] but trying to derive from it a meaning close to "weapons". (he repeats apparently his observations in his study of Mongol words in the *Korye Să, Tōyō Gakuhō* 東洋學報, 1929, XVIII, 149-244, cf. Pelliot's remarks, *JA, loc. cit.*). In spite of the initial *γ*- or *'*-, the word underlying this title must undoubtedly be connected with Hsiung-nu *kuo-lo* 郭洛, 廓落, 鈎絡, **qʷaγlaq* or **qʷaγraq* (also possibly **quraq*)—"girdle," on which see PELLIOT, *TP* 1928-29, 143-144, commenting upon Wang Kuo-wei's study of that word in the *Hu Fu K'ao* 胡服考.

As the T'o-pa *nomen agentis* was apparently understood by the Chinese as meaning "the (royal) girdler," **γuraq* (< **χuraq* < **quraq*?) must indeed go back to tk. **qur*—"encircle," "gird," and does not specifically refer to arms or designate any particular weapon.[10]

16. As to the T'o-pa word for "quiver," it might possibly enter as an element in another title which appears in F 25, 3 a and F 51, 1 a as the name of a T'o-pa general and governor of Yü chou 豫州, defeated by Liu Tao-lien 劉道憐 in the sixth month of 405. This T'o-pa leader can with surety be identified with Mu Ch'ung 穆崇 (J 28, O 20) who at the

---

[9] It seems that mo. *qor*—"quiver" is to be connected with tk. *qubur*—"holster" > russ. *kobur, kobura*—"*id.*," derived from the same root (either **qob*—"thick and round" or **qob*—"empty," "hole") as mo. *qo'ur ~ qour*, tk. *qobuz* > russ. *kobza*—"a kind of a guitar" (cf. PELLIOT, *TP* 1914, 258), and not from the root **qur*—"to encircle" which lies at the basis of orkhon tk. *qur*—"Gürtel," tk. *quřaq* > *qušaq*—"girdle."

[10] As to the T'o-pa word for "weapons," it must underlie another title appearing in F 95, 3b, *jo-k'u-chên* 若庫真, KD 938, 431: *ńźi̯ak-k'uo-tśi̯ên*, as the name of the T'o-pa governor of Yü 豫 chou in 448, who is, I believe, to be identified with Chang-sun Lan 長孫蘭 (J 26), governor of that province about that time. According to Lan's biography, he was in charge of T'o-pa T'ao's arms when following his Emperor in the latter's campaigns.

begining of the fifth century occupied the post of governor of Yü chou and died in the seventh month of 406 (J 28 and J 2). Mu Ch'ung was one of the trustiest supporters of T'o-pa Kuei and, at the time of the establishment of the Wei Empire, received the title of *shih-chung* 侍巾 and was appointed *t'ai wei* 太尉. It is possible that the name or title which is given him by the Southern Chinese history, *So-tu-chên* 索度眞, KD 818, 1128: *sâk-dâk-*(or *d'uo-g*)-*tśi̯ĕn* < **saqdaqčin* or **saqdučin* contains the tk. root **saq*—" bewahren," mo. *saki*—" to guard," and means " guardsman " (possibly " commander of the guard," *i. e. t'ai wei*).

The same root might underlie *So-kan* 索干 < **saqan* which is given in G 57, 2 b as the name of the capital of the T'o-pa. **Saqan* could indeed mean " watch," " guarded place " (cf. tk. *saqla*—" dwelling "), although it is also possible that it is simply a variant form of Sang-kan 桑乾, KD 769, 299: *sâng-kân*, the region of the Sang-kan river in Shansi, where the T'o-pa *ordo* was then situated.

*Saqdaq can, on the other hand, be connected with mo. *saγadaq*, tk. *sadaq*—" quiver " > russ. *saidak*—" quiver." Mu Ch'ung may thus have borne the title of **saγadaqčin*, an old Turco-mongol term for the later mo. *qorči*—" quiver-bearer."

17. *P'u-ta-chên* 樸大眞, KD 760, 952: *p'ȧk-d'âi-tśi̯ĕn*—title of the " officer in charge of (the ruler's) clothes," 擔衣人, G 57; SZ 22. 12, 14-15, where rather unsatisfactory mongol and tungus parallels meaning " to cover " are offered. In the light of the above etymology of *hu-lo-chên*, it would be tempting to identify in *p'u-ta-chên* the officer in charge of one of the most important pieces of turco-mongol apparel, the *boghtaq*, a head-dress the wearing of which was not in ancient times exclusively limited to women. The initial surd of *p'u* would then present the same problem as the initial of *pi* 比 in § 4. The history of the term *boghtaq* < tk. *boqtaq~boqta'* would require a special study (cf. PELLIOT, *JA* 1925, I, 222). It is most probably of Chinese origin.

18. *Chê-hui-chên* 折潰眞, KD 1185, 456: *tśiät-γuâi-tśi̯ĕn*, G 57, 為主出受辭人, which Shiratori translates (*Izv.*, 16) " ein Mann welcher um des Herrn willen den Gruss erwidert." It seems to me that *tz'ŭ* 辭 should be taken here rather in the judicial sense of " pleas and accusations." The T'o-pa term could then represent **jilγuâičin* < mo. *jiluγa(duq)či* —" administrator " < tk. mo. *jiluγa~jiluγu*—" reins "; possibly, although the vocalization of the T'o-pa term speaks against it, mo. *jarγači*— " bailiff " or *jarγuči*—" judge."

19. *A-chên* 阿眞, *'â-tśi̯ĕn*—a title entering into the designation of a part of the T'o-pa palace, the *a-chên* kitchen 廚, G 57. Shiratori is inclined (*SZ* 22. 12, 15-16) to interpret *a* 阿 as being a mistake for *fu* 附, KD 44: *b'iu*, which appears in the title *fu-chên* 附眞, equated by him with tk. mo. **baɣurčin*—" cook." The vocalization of the Chinese character does not, however, support this hypothesis. One would rather think that *'â-tśiĕn* represents the common tk. **ačin < aščin*—" cook " < *aš*—" food." [11]

20. In the list of Wei generals which appears in the letter of T'o-pa Hung to a Sung transfuge (F 95) is mentioned a T'o-pa *t'ai-wei Chih-chin Chia-t'ou-pa-yü-chih* 直懃駕頭拔羽直, who is without any doubt to be identified with Yüan Ho 源賀 who was appointed *t'ai wei* in the third month of 466 (J 6).

The biography of this prominent individual (J 41) yields us all the necessary clues for deciphering his " barbarian " name. Yüan Ho was the son of T'u-fa Nu-t'an 禿髮傉檀, last ruler of the Southern Liang, and had sought refuge with the Wei after the destruction of his father's kingdom. Acknowledging the original relationship which united the T'o-pa and T'u-fa, T'o-pa T'ao conferred upon him the surname Yüan 源 (= " origin," " -al "). This was apparently tantamount to accepting the fugitive prince as a member of the Imperial Clan and explains the title *chih-chin* 直懃 < *tägin*—" prince of the blood."

The young prince's original personal name was P'o Ch'iang 破羌 (= " smiting the Ch'iang "), and the name Ho 賀, says J 41, was given to him by T'o-pa T'ao for his distinguished services in campaigns against Kansu barbarians. " Having chosen a personal name," said T'o-pa T'ao in conferring the new name, " a man must strive to realize its meaning (in his deeds). How can yours be said not to correspond (*lit.* be untrue) ? " As Ho 賀 and Chia 駕 are often graphically interchanged, it seems clear that the *Wei Shu* name is only a sinicized monosyllabic abbreviation of *Chia-t'ou-pa-yü-chih*. KD 342, 1015, 750, 1320, 1220 give us *ɣâ-d'əu-b'ʷat-(g)iu-d'iək < *atïbälgütäg*, possibly, if the lost consonant of *d'əu* was still sounded in that period, < **atïɣbälgütäg*. In this Turkish phrase we can distinguish the elements: *at*—" name," *bälgü*— " omen," *täg*—" like," " as." In the light of the above story of the cir-

---

[11] *Ch'i-hai-chên* 乞害眞 *k'iət-ɣât-tśiĕn*—" executioner " might contain any of the numerous tk. mo. stems **KES*—" to cut," or mo. *kituga*—" sword." As to the remaining two titles *yang-chên* 羊眞—" high official " and *fu-chu-chên* 拂竹眞—" postmen of the lower rank " (cf. PELLIOT, *loc. cit.*) they do not yield to analysis. For the last, equations advanced by both Shiratori and the present writer seem to be unsatisfactory.

cumstances under which the name was conferred, it seems obvious that the emperor nicknamed the prince " *Nomen Atque Omen.*" The grammatical structure of the phrase is not, however, entirely clear. We can interpret it as *at-ï* (possessive suffix) *bälgü täg*—" his name (is) like an omen," although in that case we should expect *bälgü* to be in the instrumental case. There is also the faint possibility that in *at-ïγ* we have the accusative of *at*—" name," while *bʷat-(g)i̯u-d'i̯ək* might be a verbal form of *bäküt*—" to establish," or *bälgürt*—" to reveal." The phonetic equivalence would, however, be less good; in addition, the weakness of the *g-* in *(g)i̯u* suggests strongly *bälgü*~dial. *bälyü*.

21. According to both F 95 and G 57, T'o-pa Hsün 濬 (440-453-465), son of T'o-pa Huang 晃 (428-451), and fourth sovereign of the Wei dynasty bore the cognomen (*tzǔ* 字) Wu-lei *chih-chin* 烏雷直勤 i. e. " Prince Wu-lei," KD 520: *'uo-luâi tigin.* The biography of this T'o-pa prince (J 5, O 2) yields, I believe, an explanation of his title. Hsün was greatly loved by his grandfather, T'o-pa T'ao, who conferred upon him the title (*hao* 號) of " Imperial Grandson of the Line " 世嫡皇孫. *'Uo-luâi* doubtless contains the Turkish term *uri*—" son," " male descendant " (attested already in Orkhon turkish, cf. *uruγ*—" posterity ").

22. G 59 mentions a certain Chia-lu-hun 駕鹿渾, prince of P'ing-yüan, as commander of the T'o-pa army during a campaign against the Juan-juan. The same individual appears in G 57 as Fu-lu-ku Ho-lu-hun 伏鹿孤賀鹿渾, duke of Chü-lu 鉅鹿 and governor of Hêng 恒 chou, and is said to have been one of the leaders of the 496 rebellion against T'o-pa Hung.

According to J 113, the T'o-pa surname Fu-lu-ku was later abbreviated to Lu 陸. The official described in G 57 and G 59 is thus unquestionably to be identified with Lu Jui 陸叡, son of Lu Li 麗, who, according to his biography in J 40: a) commanded the T'o-pa army against the Juan-juan in 496, b) bore from 466 to 492 the title of prince of P'ing-yüan 平原, and that of duke of Chü-lu, from 492 to his death, c) perished in the conspiracy of 496, together with Mu T'ai 穆泰, J 27 (who had just succeeded him as governor of Hêng chou) and other high officials.

Jui's mother, the lady Chang 張氏, had been formerly a concubine of T'o-pa Huang and was undoubtedly given in marriage to Li as a reward for the important rôle the latter played in the counter-revolution of 453 which placed T'o-pa Hsün on the throne. Jui was thus the issue of a union between commoner and a " lady of the palace."

In the light of this evidence, it would not be unreasonable to suppose that in Jui's " barbarian " name, Ho-lu-hun 賀鹿渾 , KD 576, 508 : γâ-luk-γi̯uən, we have the earliest transcription of the Turco-mongol term *arγun—" métis," " half-breed," " Bâtard," the original of the well-known *Argon*—" half-breed " of Marco Polo (cf. PAUTHIER, 214-217; YULE-CORDIER, I, 290-292; PELLIOT, *JA* 1927, 2, 265, note).

23. The common turkish *tümän*—" ten thousand " forms without any question the original of T'u-wan 吐萬 , KD 1129 : t'uo-mi̯ʷɒn < *tümän, the name of a T'o-pa prince, a great-grandson of T'o-pa Kuei. The same two characters appear in the *T'ung Chih* 19, 9 b, as a Northern surname derived from the name of a Tai 代 tribe.

24. The T'o-pa surname Ch'ü-chin 去斤 , KD 491, 385 : k'i̯ʷo(-b)-ki̯ən, later changed to *Ai* 艾 (" artemisia," " old man "), is a good transcription of tk. *kök*, mo. *köke*—" blue." We have in this case an apparent attempt on the part of those responsible for the change to suggest, while simplifying the surname, the turkish original semantically. *Kök* forms undoubtedly the base of mo. *köksin*—" old man " (" blue-gray haired "? Ch. *Ai* 艾—" old man " < " moxa-haired," while " artemisia " suggests " sage-brush-colored " ~ " blue "). The same word Ch'ü-chin 去斤 occurs in the *Yüan-ho Chün-hsien T'u-chih*, ch. 3, as the Hsien-pi name of the Ch'ing 清 (" clear " ~ Ch. 青 *ch'ing*—" blue ") river in Shensi.

25. The original surname of Tou Pin 竇賓 , chief of the Mo-lu-hui horde who befriended Li-wei, was, according to J 113 and 2 P 71 B, 2 b, Hou-tou-ling 侯豆陵 or Ko-t'u-lin 紇突隣 , KD 79, 560 : γəu-d'əu-li̯əng ; KD 332, 498, 556 : γuət-d'uət-li̯ĕn. At the basis of this transcription lies possibly the common Turkish *qudu*—" father-in-law," the name of the Tou clan being undoubtedly derived from the fact of their inter-marriage with the early T'o-pa.[12]

26. Yu-lien 宥連 , KD 251, 551 : ji̯əu(< g-ui̯)-li̯än, Northern surname later changed into Ch. *Yü* 雲—" cloud," J 113, < mo. *egülen*—" cloud." The same Mongol word appears as a proper name in L 17, 2a in the transcription Yu-lien 祐連 , KD 150, pronunciation identical.

27. Ch'i-nu 叱奴 , KD 1055, 674 : tśi̯ĕt-(with the final -t quiescent)-nuo, Northern surname, later changed into Ch. *lang* 狼—" wolf," *ibid.* < mo. *činoa*—" wolf." Possible variant Ch'ou-nu 醜奴 , KD 460 : tś'i̯əu-nuo registering the mo. form *čono*—" id." [13] There is no evidence that

---

[12] The term *qudu* appears already in the Hsiung-nu language as a designation of dignitaries belonging to clans other than that of the *shan-yü*, the *ku-tu-hou* 骨都侯 . It is uncertain whether *hou* 侯 is here a suffix or the Chinese title *hou*.

[13] Both of these surnames may have been derived from the names of tribes of

both these terms were genuine T'o-pa surnames or words. There exists, on the other hand, some indication that the tk. word for " wolf," *büri*, is present in the cognomen of T'o-pa T'ao, Fo-li 佛狸, KD 47, 529: *b'įuət-lji*.

28. Among the genuine T'o-pa surnames, particularly arrests our attention that of I-chan 乙旃, KD 176, 965 : *'įĕt-tśiän*. This surname was borne by descendants of the uncle of T'o-pa Lin 隣, pht. Hsien 獻, the grandfather of Li-wei; later the surname was changed to Shu-sun 叔孫 (*shu* = " uncle "). The first part of the T'o-pa word contains without any question the tk. term *iči*—" elder brother," " uncle " (uig. *iči*, orkh. *äči*). **Ičin* or **iči-en* can be compared in structure with *tigin~tägin*, < *täg*, which contains the same derivative suffix.

29. Ho-jo 賀若, KD 938 : *γâ-ńźiak*, T'o-pa surname, explained in *T'ung Chih* 29, 7 b as meaning " upright in determination " 志正, most probably from tk. (uig.) *ayaγ*—" honor."

30. G 57, 2 b describes a religious ceremony performed by T'o-pa Hung in which the Emperor, prior to sacrificing to Heaven on a special altar, would ride, accompanied by his chief officers on horseback, around the altar once, while his retinue performed the same rite seven times. The ceremony was called " stamping 踢 the altar." *T'a* 踢, KD 958 : *t'âp*, might represent a genuine T'o-pa word, and not the Chinese " to stamp," " to tread on "; indeed, *t'âp* can be equated with the tk. root *tap*—" to worship," re-appearing possibly in the surname T'a-lu 沓盧, *t'ap-luo* (J 113), and in T'a-kan 沓干 < **t'apqan*, a proper name in J 30, 4a.

31. Another T'o-pa surname, Yü-tu-chin 郁都甄, KD 251, 1187, 278 : *įuk-tuo-kiĕn*, and Yü-tou-chüan 郁豆眷, KD 495 : *įuk-d'əu-ki̯wan*, the name under which prince T'o-pa Chia 嘉 (J 18) appears in F 23 and G 25, contains another important tk. root connected with the preceding. namely *ötüg*—" to pray," which underlies the name of Mt. Ötüken, the sacred mountain of the Orkhon Turks. On *tap* and *ötüg* as Turco-mongol idioms used at court functions cf. PELLIOT, *TP* 1930, 33, note.

32. Another Turco-mongol term of interest may underlie the surname A-fu-kan 阿伏干, KD 46 : *'â-b'įuk-kân* ~ Ssŭ-fu-chien 俟伏斤, KD 183 : *dẓ'i-b'įuk-ki̯ən* (but cf. PELLIOT, *TP* 1928-29, 225-229, for the archaic pronunciation of *ssŭ* 俟) possibly < mo. *ebügen*—" old man," " forefather." The same word under the first transcription occurs in

purely Mongol origin which had been incorporated into the T'o-pa organization. The identification of *yu-lien* and *ch'i-nu* was made by Shiratori and, independently, by the present writer in *Sino-Altaica* I.

F 95 as the name of a T'o-pa general who is in all probability to be identified with Wei Chien 尉建 of J 29, 2b. Cf. also the name of an important mountain in the old territory of the Wei, where T'o-pa Ho-nu 賀傉 fixed his capital in 342, Mu-kên shan 木根山, KD 643, 312: *mukkən < *ebügen?*

The above list contains most of the T'o-pa words that can be identified with some degree of certainty. Many tempting equivalences have been discarded on the ground of insufficient evidence,[13a] but the author feels that with further careful analysis of the texts of the Chinese dynastic histories and meticulous correlation of the Northern and Southern versions of many events of the period, we should be able to reconstruct a great deal of the lost language of the T'o-pa.

Thus far we have not touched upon the origin and the meaning of the name T'o-pa itself. In order to be able to analyze it properly, we shall find ourselves obliged to review in some detail the traditions concerning the origin of the T'o-pa preserved in the first chapter of the *Wei Shu*.

The T'o-pa traced the origin of their ruling house eighty-two generations back from T'o-pa Li-wei to the times of " Emperor " Shun. In writing his introduction to T'o-pa history, Wei Shou 魏收 [14] undoubtedly tried to correlate their traditions with Chinese chronology. His chronological scheme can, indeed, be reconstructed as follows, counting a generation as equal to 30 years (the usual number in Chinese sources) and marking the three crucial points of T'o-pa " pre-history ":

1. Shih-chün 始均, the reputed Chinese ancestor of the house, *circa* 2210 B. C., corresponding to the " Standard Chronology " date of Shun. 67 generations later brings us down to Mao 毛, pht. Ch'êng 成, who united under his leadership " 36 tribes 國 and 99 clans 姓," 2210-2010 (67 x 30) = *circa* 200 B. C., corresponding to the period of the great process of unification going on in Mongolia at the time of the formation of the Hsiung-nu Empire.

2. Counting 5 more generations (including that of Mao) until the time of T'ui-yin 推寅, pht. Hsüan 宣, under whom the first migration of the T'o-pa took place,[14a] gives us the date 50 B. C., which doubtless

[13a] Some of these, however, require special treatment, and the author hopes to return to them in the near future.

[14] For a clear and thorough account of Wei Shou and his work, see J. R. WARE, Notes on the History of the Wei Shu, *JAOS* 52 (1932), 35-45.

[14a] From their home in the extreme North to the shores of a " Great Lake " 大澤, a thousand li in circumference. The question of the location of that home and of the path of the T'o-pa migration constitutes a problem in itself. Accord-

corresponds to the period of the break-up of the Hsiung-nu organization
and the southern movement of northern tribes into the territory of the
Hsiung-nu.

3. With seven more generations we reach the reign of Lin 隣, pht.
Hsien 獻, *circa* 160 A. D., corresponding to the time of the formation
of the Hsien-pi confederacy under T'an-shih-huai. Lin proposes to migrate further south, but on account of his old age leaves the realization
of the project to his son, Ch'i-fên 詰汾, pht. Shêng-wu 聖武, between
160 and 190 A. D.

Under his leadership the T'o-pa start southward through impassable
mountain defiles. Discouraged by the difficulties encountered on the way,
they are on the point of abandoning the enterprise, when a supernatural
animal " resembling a horse with a bull's voice " leads them out of the
mountains. Ch'i-fên and his tribe occupy then " the old territory of the
Hsiung-nu." As the project of migrating south originated with the two
" Emperors " Hsüan and Hsien, adds the *Wei Shu*, both of them received
the nickname T'ui-yin 推寅, which in the language of the North has the
meaning of " boring through."

Through this word *t'ui-yin*, KD 1265, 283 : *t'uâi-i̯ĕn*, we can, I believe,
link the T'o-pa with one of the most important and interesting complexes
in the cultural history of Mongolia and the Asiatic continent which I
am tempted to call the " Gog and Magog Complex." [15] It constitutes a
problem of major magnitude and manifold ramifications of which only
certain linguistic aspects call for our consideration in this paper. The
nucleus of the legend in High Asia is composed of the following elements :

1. A tribe of metal workers is shut in a valley (or cave) in the mountains, accessible from the outside only through a narrow pass.

2. This tribe derives its origin or is otherwise connected with either a
wolf or a bull.

3. They multiply and come forth from their seclusion by boring their
way through the mountains.

---

ing to J 108: I and J 100, it was located northwest of the country of Wu-lo-hou
烏洛侯. There still existed in the middle of the fifth century an ancestral T'o-pa
temple in that region, as was reported to the Wei court in 443 by Wu-lo-hou
ambassadors.

[15] For the latest literature on the subject, cf. C. E. WILSON, The Wall of
Alexander against Gog and Magog; and the expedition sent out to find it by the
Khalif Wāthīq in 842 A. D., *Asia Minor* I, 575 *seq.*, and A. R. ANDERSON,
Alexander's Gate, Gog and Magog, and the Inclosed Nations, Cambridge, Mass.,
1932.

The essential motifs of the story occur in the legends of origin and
in the history of the T'u-chüeh Turks, the Kirghiz, and the Mongols,
while geographically it may be localized in the Tienshan-Altai nexus, in
the region of the Upper Yenissei, and the Orkhon-Tula mountain ranges.
The above elements of the legend, as they appear in the various versions,
can be schematized as follows:

1. T'u-chüeh Turks: Metal workers for the Juan-juan in a closed
valley where their ancestor took refuge; descendants from wolves (and
possibly deer, cf. *Yu-yang Tsa-tsu* 酉陽雜俎, ch. IV, 1b-2a) ; come forth
from the mountain to overthrow their masters.

2. Kirghiz: Live beyond the Kögmän mountains, accessible only
through a narrow defile (cf. Tonyukuk's inscription, 24-25) ; their country is rich in metals; descend from a bull (*Yu-yang Tsa-tsu, loc. cit.*) ;
issue forth to overthrow the Uighur Empire.[15a]

3. Mongols: Their ancestors locked in the Ergene-kün valley; their
ruling house tracing its origin to a wolf and a doe; come out of the
valley by melting the metal side of the mountain.

Linguistically the complex is connected with the following tk. mo.
roots and words:

1. *Kök*—" blue," " gray." a) The T'u-chüeh Turks designated themselves as *kök türk*—" the blue Turks," cf. also *kök büri*—" the gray wolf,"
their sacred animal. b) The ancestral cave of the Kirghiz was situated
in the Kögmän mts. (ch. Ch'ü-man 曲曼, KD 492, 595: *k'i^wok-muân*),
< *kök*—" blue," as evidenced by another Chinese name of the same moun-
tains, Ch'ing shan 青山—" blue mts." c) The version of the Gog and
Magog story by the Xth century arabic geographer Ḳudama is localized
in the region of Kokonor—" the blue lake." [16]

2. Various tk. mo. roots with the meaning of " round," " blunt,"
" ball " (the series exhibiting little distinction between vowels of the
" strong " series and the palatalized ones), such as: a) mo. *moqor*—
" blunt," *moγolčoq*—" ball," *müger*—" circle," *mügürik*—" small ball ";
moqor is related to *mungaq*—" stupid " < " blunt "? (cf. the folk-etymology of Mongol = " stupid," D'OHSSON, I, 42). b) mo. *kükel*—
" round," " ball," *kükü, kükel, küken*—" breast." [17] c) mo. *tügürik*—
" circle," *tuγuriq*—" id.," tk. *tägirmi*—" encircling," etc.[18]

[15a] It must have been ruins of cities devastated by the Kirghiz in 840 that the
mission of Khalif Wāthiq saw as it passed through Dzungaria two years later.

[16] Cf. M. J. DE GOEJE, *Bibliotheca Geographorum Arabicorum*, vol. 6, 206.

[17] Might we have in the obscure name of the mountain where Alexander the

3. Roots meaning "to cross a mountain," "to pass through," "to bore through": a) tk. *aš*—"to cross a mountain," *ašin*—"id"; it is most probably this root which is hidden beneath the Chinese transcription of the clan name of the T'u-chüeh Turks, A-shih-na 阿史那, KD 1, 885, 647: *'âṣinâ*, and A-shih-tê 阿史德, KD 981: *'âṣitək*.[19] b) mo. *toγol*— "to penetrate, pass through"; *toγolγa*—"to accomplish"; *tegüs, dügür*— "to accomplish," tk. *tükä*—"to finish"; *tök*—"to pour *out*"; mo. *čoγu* —"through"; *čoγul*—"to bore through"; *tolbur*—"a boring instrument" (cf. Tegüs—the name of one of the ancestors of the Mongols who found refuge in the Ergene-kün).

4. The last root is connected in Mongol with words designating metallurgical terms: *duγulγan*—"tin," "lead"; *duγulγa*—"helmet";[19a] *toγa, toγon, toγoγan*—"cauldron"[20] (in the *KÖK* series, cf. *kügürge*— "bellows," *kügürgede*—"to blow a fire").

TO'OL also underlies, in my belief, the name of the T'u-yü-hun 吐 谷渾, KD 425: *t'uo-kuk-γuən* (cf. PELLIOT, *TP* 1920-21, 323-331), also possibly *t'uo-luk-γuən* (as 谷 is often pronounced 鹿 *luk* in transcriptions of Northern names), corresponding to Thu-lu-hun, the Tibetan rendering of the name of that people. Note that the T'u-yü-hun were a tribe "migrating through mountains" and settled eventually in the Kokonor region.

Great built his wall against Gog and Magog in the "Pseudo-Callisthenes" story, μαζοὶ βορρᾶ, "the breasts of the North (cf. ANDERSON, *op. cit.*, 25), a half translation, half popular etymology of two elements of an original turkish compound in the wolf version of the legend (*kök*—"breasts" and *büri*—"wolf")?

[18] A form *tügürik* > *tü'ürik* > *türik* might, indeed, be the real etymology of the very name of the Turks.

[19] This etymology of A-shih-na is much to be preferred to that advanced by the writer in *Sino-Altaica* I, 15, where *'âṣinâ* is derived from *ar-činoa*—"ten wolves."

[19a] The above discussion suggests also a revival of the etymology of T'u-chüeh 突厥 (< *Türküt, as established by Pelliot) by *duγulγat the plural of *duγulγa*— "helmet." Cf. *T'ung Chih* 29. 15a, where the T'u-chüeh are referred to as 突厥窟, *d'uət-kiwət-k'uət* < *duγulγut?

[20] This word is, I believe, attested already in the language of the Mu-jung Hsien-pi and forms the base of: T'u-ho 徒河, 徒何, KD 1129: *d'uo-γâ*, the name of an important subdivision of the Hsien-pi on the Manchurian frontier, closely related to the Mu-jung. Thus Mu-jung Hui 慕容廆 is referred to in J 1, under the year 307, as the great *shan-yü* of the T'u-ho. As a variant of the name we have Tuan 段, KD 1135: *d'uân* < *toγan*; T'u-ho-chên 吐賀眞 *t'uo-γâ-tśiĕn*, name of a Juan-juan khan, J 103 (in F 95 菟害眞, KD 1132, 57: *t'uo-γât-tśiĕn*) < *toγačin*. T'u-chü-chên 吐屈眞, KD 427: *t'uo-kuət-tśiĕn*, the name of a river in the T'u-yü-hun country, is undoubtedly derived from the root *toγul*, as is the name of the river *Tula* < *Toγula*.

In the light of the above, the nickname of the two T'o-pa leaders T'ui-yin, ⟨ *t'uâi-i̯ĕn* ⟨ **tu'ayin*, assumes great importance. We see the T'o-pa as sharing in the common Turco-mongol tradition of tracing their origin to " Borers." Although there is no direct evidence of the early T'o-pa being engaged in metallurgical occupations, their practice, attested since the latter part of the IVth century, of determining the choice of consort by the success of a prospective candidate in casting a metal image of herself,[21] seems to indicate the existence of metal-working traditions in their midst.

It is in the same direction that, as it seems to me, we must look for an etymology of the name T'o-pa 拓跋, KD 883, 750: *t'ak-b'uât*. Already in *TP* 1912, 792, Professor Pelliot had suggested that in **t'ak-b'uât* we have the original of the early medieval designations of Northern China, tk. *Tabγač*, ar. *Ṭamghāj* طمغاج, Byzantine Greek Ταυγαστ. The metathesis of *b ~ β* and *γ ~ q* explains the Chinese **Taqbač* (with the final -*t* of *b'uât* representing tk. *č*).

The Chinese sources at our disposal give the following interpretation of the meaning of T'o-pa:[22]

1. J 1, 1: " lord of the soil ": " Huang Ti (the ancestor of both Chinese and " Barbarians ") became ruler by virtue of the soil (one of the Five Agents 五行) ; as in the language of the North they call " soil "—*t'ak* 拓, and " lord "—*b'uât* 跋, the T'o-pa adopted " lord of the soil " as their surname." [23]

2. As we have seen, the T'u-fa 禿髮, KD 1131, 750: *t'uk-pi̯wɐt*, are identical with the T'o-pa; the etymological explanation of their name should, therefore, help us to restore and to understand the original of *T'ak-b'uât*. According to J 99, the meaning of the compound T'u-fa was " covered with a blanket " or " (born) in a blanket," their eponymous ancestor having been born in this, rather natural, fashion.

---

[21] T'o-pa Kuei is said to have chosen by this method the daughter of Mu-jung Pao for his " Empress," while another of his wives, the daughter of Liu Chüan 劉眷, failed in the test.

[22] The etymologies given by the Chinese historians for barbarian names have often been discounted, unjustly so, for while the etymology might be fanciful, it nevertheless gives priceless phonetic hints as to the original word. One must say, on the other hand, that the Chinese historians (prior to the notorious Ch'ien-lung commission) have always been careful to qualify their statements with numerous *kai* 蓋, " it seems that . . . " and *huo yün* 或云, " according to some information. . . ."

[23] Cf. also *T'ung Chih* 29, 9a, where T'o-pa is considered to be an abbreviation of 拓后跋 *t'ak-γə̯u-b'uât*, and *b'uât* is interpreted as *shou* 受—" recipient " ?

3. A comparatively recent source, the *Chi-lan* 集覽 of the *Tz'ŭ-chih T'ung-chien Kang-mu*, ch. 16, under 270 A. D., insists that T'u-fa meant " slave."

4. Both T'u-fa (*t'u*—" bald," *fa*—" hair ") and the purely Chinese (*Nan Shih*) designation of the T'o-pa, So T'ou 索頭 (= braided heads ") might also contain some semantic indications (through some play on words) concerning the meaning of T'o-pa.

For the first interpretation, in the light of the Chinese meanings and division of words, tk. *baš*—" head," " lord " immediately suggests itself for the second element. The first part would then be the tk. root **top*— " soil " > tk. mo. *tobraq*, mo. *tobaraq, toburaq*—" *id.*" There is, indeed, a phonetic possibility that **Taβγač* could have been understood or interpreted folk-etymologically as **Taβγač* > *Toβ^wač* > *Top-baš*. Tk. *taγ ~ taγu* ~mo. *daβaγa*—" mountain," also meaning " Northland " might have entered into the etymological considerations of the historians, while **Tabaqči(n)* > *Taβqač(i)* (cf. *supra*, § 14)—" the ground-ers," " those of the soil " would offer an excellent tk. *-či* form of *tabaq*—" ground."

For the equation of T'u-fa < *t'uk-pi^wnt* with *Taqbač* we should postu-late the same metathesis of *k* and *p* as in *t'ak-b'uât* and reconstruct the form as **Tupqač*. The blanket of the nomad is, of course, his saddlecloth. The common turkish term for " saddlecloth " is *čapraq* (< *čap*[24]—" to cover ") whence eng. " shabrack," in mo. *toχom*, which would indicate an original **tap ~ top*. The Chinese etymology could thus have arisen from **Toβač* mispronunciation of *Tabqač* and a popular etymological associa-tion with a root **tap*—" to cover " > " saddlecloth " and an unconscious attempt to include paronomasically the root *toγ*—" to be born."

As to the *Chi-lan* explanation, it is obviously based on tk. *tapïγči ~ tapuqči*—" slave " < *tap*—" to worship," " to serve " (cf. § 30).

The association of the name of the **Taqbač* with the way they appar-ently dressed their hair also finds an explanation in tk. words very close phonetically to the first syllable of the T'o-pa name, namely: mo. *tuiba*— " braided hair," *toγorčaq*—" hair tied in a knot," tk. *tüpe*—" braid of hair left on the top of the skull " (the root of these words is semantically

---

[24] The root *čap*—" to cover," " to put on," exhibits in Turkish an interesting shift of the initial *č ~ t ~ q*, which has not so far been duly analyzed by " Altaists." Cf. mo. *qom*—" felt " *vs.* *toχom*; *qubča*—" to dress " *vs.* *jubčaγa, čuba*—" fur-coat," " coat "; also in *qaba*—" crack " *vs.* *taba, čaba*—" ib." This shift had al-ready been observed by Abū-l Ghazī who records it in *Qïpčaq* > *Čipčaq* (cf. PELLIOT, *TP* 1930, 280).

affiliated with the stem for " round " discussed above, as well as with
dobo—" protuberance "; curiously enough, we find in Mongol the word
kükel—" braided hair " (the root of which also seems to be linked with
the semantic series *KÖK* mentioned before). The second element would
again be *baš*—" head."

The variety of the etymologies, all of which, as we have seen, are justifiable on phonetic grounds and are based on a mispronunciation or mis-
interpretation of an original *Taβγač, suggests that the real explanation
of their name was suppressed by the T'o-pa, either because it evoked
their low origin or because of sacred associations. I am inclined to derive,
basing myself on the connection of the T'o-pa with the " Gog and Magog
Complex " outlined above, *Taβγač > T'o-pa from Turkish form of mo.
daβa-, *daβaγa-* " to cross mountains," " to make one's way through a
defile " (mo. *d-* often represents tk. *t-*, cf. mo. *daβaγan* ~ tk. *taγu*—
" mountain "), and interpret the name of the great T'o-pa Wei as
" *Transmontani*," " *Ultramontani*."

The T'o-pa vocabulary thus reveals itself as being essentially Turkish,
with a certain admixture of Mongol elements. Except in a few cases, where
pure Mongol terms can only be explained as reflecting the composite
nature of the T'o-pa confederacy, seemingly Mongol forms can always be
traced back to Turkish or proto-turkish originals. This conclusion may
sound bold. Admittedly an amateur in the field of " Altaic " linguistics,
the writer has primarily attempted to call the attention of specialists to
the " Case of the T'o-pa." The right of pronouncing the final verdict
belongs to Turkologists.

Two Notes on the History of the Chinese Frontier

Harvard Journal of Asiatic Studies, 1 (1936), 283-307.

I. Hu 胡 Colonies in Northwestern China under the Han

We are in August 155 A. D., the seventh month of the first year of the Yung-shou 永壽 era, according to the Chinese reckoning. The weakling Liu Chih 劉志 [1] is the Son of Heaven occupying the throne, but the reins of government are in the hands of Liang Chi 梁冀, omnipotent dictator and head of the wealthy and arrogant Liang clan; it is to him and his sister, the Dowager Emperess Liang, widow of Liu Pao 保, that the young Emperor owes his elevation to the throne. [2]

Following the death of the Dowager in 150, however, Liang Chi's power had begun to wane. Another of his sisters is the Emperor's consort, but she is childless, and a palace clique is already secretly plotting the dictator's downfall. [3] Drought, locusts, famine and epidemics are devastating the northern and central provinces of the empire. Banditry and general social unrest have been growing in intensity all through China, [4] and the " Barbarians " are restless on the frontiers. In the north, after a decade of peace on the Ordos front of the Han Empire, the Southern

---

[1] Pht. Hsiao Huan Ti 孝桓帝 of the Eastern Han, 132-147-167 A. D., *Hou Han Shu* 7.

[2] Liang Chi, d. 159 A. D., *Hou Han Shu* 64. Liang Na 妠, pht. Shun Lieh 順烈 Liang huang-hou, 116-132-150 A. D., *ibid.* 10B. [Read 35 for 45 as her age at the time of death, or 23 for 13 as her age in 128 A. D. when she entered the Emperor's harem; in the latter case she would be born in 106 A. D.]. Hsiao Shun Ti (pht. of Liu Pao) 115-126-144 A. D., *ibid.* 6.

[3] Liang Yung 瑩, pht. I-hsien 懿獻, (?)147-Aug. 9, 159 A. D., *ibid.* 10B. Exactly a month later, on Sept. 9, Liang Chi and his clan were overthrown and exterminated by the eunuch party.

[4] The seriousness of the situation is indicated by the fact that between 147 and 154 A. D. the Annals record at least six cases of usurpation of the imperial title by rebels in various parts of China.

Hsiung-nu are again sending raiding parties across the border. A repetition of the disaster of 140-143 A. D. threatens the population of the marches.

It was in May 140 A. D. [Yung-ho 5] that a chieftain of the Left Horde of the Southern Hsiung-nu, Chü-lung Wu-ssŭ 句龍吾斯,[5] broke the long period of amicable relations with the Chinese and, together with his clansman Chü-lung Chü-niu 車紐, rose in rebellion against the Han. Joined by the Right *hsien-wang* 賢王, they besieged Mei-chi 美稷 in Hsi ho chün 西河 and raided the entire northern frontier causing the removal of three administrative centers of border provinces into the hinterland.[6]

In their raids the Hsiung-nu were assisted by the Wu-huan 烏桓 and the Ch'iang 羌 and Hu 諸胡 of the Shensi uplands. Their combined forces, now numbering several myriads, threatened the metropolitan district of Ch'ang-an itself. Although Chü-niu, who had been made *shan-yü* by the rebels, was soon forced to surrender to the Chinese,[7] Wu-ssŭ and his allies continued their depredations. In September 142 A. D. Wu-ssŭ was joined in his rebellion by the *yü-chien* 奧鞬 T'ai-ch'i 臺耆 and the *chü-ch'ü* 且渠 Po-tê 伯德.[8] In the eleventh month of the next

---

[5] *Hou Han Shu* 6, 119. In ch. 6 Wu-ssŭ is referred to as " chief of the Chü-lung [tribe?] " 大人; in ch. 119 as " prince of Chü-lung " 王. Wu-ssŭ < *NGÀ-Si is a common termination in Hsiung-nu names. Cf. 烏鞮牙斯, 蠡知牙斯, 伊屠智牙師, 都塗吾西, 呼屠吾斯, *Han Shu* 94.

[6] The seat of Hsi-ho chün was removed to Li-shih 離石; that of Shang chün to Hsia-yang 夏陽; and that of Shuo-fang 朔方 to Wu-yüan 五原.

[7] He was made *shan-yü* in place of Hsiu-li 休利 who reigned under the title of Ch'ü-tê-jo-shih-chu 去特若尸逐 *shan-yü* 128-140 A. D. and was driven to commit suicide by the Chinese general Ch'ên Kuei 陳龜 [biography in *Hou Han Shu* 81, d. about 158; ch. 119 incorrectly makes him die in prison in 141] who accused him of laxity towards his subjects during the crisis. Chü-niu was defeated on Dec. 1, 140 A. D. and submitted to the Chinese with many Hsiung-nu dignitaries. A year later, however, two more *chün* are apparently overrun by the invaders, as the seats of An-ting 安定 and Pei-ti 北地 are removed to Fu-fêng 扶風 and Fêng-i 馮翊 respectively.

[8] *Hou Han Shu* 6 writes *yü-chien*; ch. 119 *yü-ti* 鞮. *Yü-chien* and *chü-ch'ü* are undoubtedly *Hsiung-nu* titles, but may have already been used as surnames. On July 24, 143 A. D. the Chinese government in its efforts to liquidate the rebellion appointed amid great pomp a Hsiung-nu prince named Tou-lou-ch'u 兜樓諸 as *shan-yü* [= Hu-lan-jo-shih-chu-chiu 呼蘭若尸逐就 *shan-yü*, 143-147 A. D.]. The festivities took place at the capital [where the prince had been residing as hostage], outside Lo-yang's western Kuang-yang 廣陽 gate. Liu Pao [Shun Ti] is said to have witnessed the games which accompanied the ceremonial of investiture from the Hu t'ao 胡桃 [= 'walnut,' *Juglans regia*] palace. Many of the Han palaces both at Ch'ang-an and Lo-yang, were named after plants [usually exotic ones] cultivated in their gardens. In his study of the introduction of the walnut into China [*Sino-Iranica*, pp. 254-275] Laufer expressed in conclusion (p. 263) the opinion that " . . . it is not probable that the walnut was

year, however, Wu-ssŭ was assassinated by *bravi* in the pay of the Chinese,
and in the spring of 144 A. D., with the defeat of the remnants of his
horde by the Chinese general Ma Shih 馬寔, peace was re-established on
the border.[9]

It is Tʻai-chʻi and Po-tê,[10] the old associates of Wu-ssŭ, that we find on
the war-path again eleven years later, and again Mei-chi is the first among
Chinese communities to suffer from their raids. Again the easternmost
of the Chʻiang tribes are up in arms ready to join hands with the nomads
of the North. Should the two groups of " Barbarians " succeed in effecting a union all the work of the preceding years is lost.

Fortunately for the Han, the post of *magister militum* of the " dependent state " of An-ting 安定屬國都尉 is held by the energetic Chang
Huan 張奐.[11] Unmindful of the protests of his pusilanimous subalterns,
Chang Huan, who has at his disposal but some two hundred men, moves
quickly to the Great Wall, and assembles under his command all the
available frontier guards. Having first detached a small force to delay
the Chʻiang, he occupies with his contingent a place called Kuei-tzŭ 龜茲,
thus preventing the Hsiung-nu from penetrating South and establishing
contact with their allies. As able a diplomat and administrator as he is
a soldier, Chang Huan soon wins the Chʻiang over to his side, turns in
force against the Hsiung-nu, defeats them in battle, and obtains their
submission.[12]

The quick and courageous action of the Chinese commander prevented
thus the repetition of the disastrous war of the forties. In the interpretation of this episode in the history of the Han frontier by some
western writers, Chang Huan's feat has, however, been magnified to
colossal proportions. The strategic center of operations, Kuei-tzŭ was
identified by them with Kucha [Chin. Chʻiu-tzʻŭ 龜茲, written with

generally known in China earlier than the fourth century A. D. under the Eastern
Tsin dynasty (265-419)." He rejects completely the testimony of the spurious
work *Hsi ching tsa chi* 西京雜記 which mentions walnuts as being grown in the
parks of Chʻang-an under the First Han dynasty. The above reference to a
" Walnut " palace would indicate, however, that that foreign tree was cultivated
at Lo-yang over a century prior to the earliest date conceded by Laufer.

[9] *Ibid.* 119. Cf. PARKER, Turko-Scythian Tribes, *China Review* 21, pp. 297-299.

[10] *Hou Han Shu* 7, *sub anno* 155, reads 左臺且渠伯德等.

[11] Native of Tun-huang, 104-181 A. D. In his youth he had served under Liang
Chi and probably owed him his position. At the time of the downfall of the latter,
he was saved only through the intercession of an old friend, Huang-fu Kuei 皇
甫規, 104-174 A. D. Biographies of both in *Hou Han Shu* 95.

[12] *Hou Han Shu* 95.

identical characters], the famous oasis city of Central Turkestan. Thus, in his account of the event, Father Wieger writes: "... T'ai-t'i chef hun, tente de soulever la Dzoungarie (12). Les K'iäng du Tangout (h) se disposent à faire cause commune avec lui ... ... [Chang Huan] fut d'une traite s'établir à Koutcha (m) empêchant ainsi toute possibilité d'une jonction entre les Huns (19) et les K'iäng (h)." [13] L. Aurousseau [14] cites Chang Huan's exploit as evidence of the Chinese being in control of Kucha in the fifties of the second century. Both authors neglect to explain how Chinese troops could have been transported with such lightning rapidity from the marches of Shensi to the heart of the "Western regions" and how the occupation of Kucha in Turkestan would have prevented the union of Huns and Tibetans.

Neither suspected the existence of a second Kucha. The unfortunate mistake was caused by overlooking an important note by the Chinese commentator Li Hsien 李賢 [15] immediately following the mention of Kuei tzŭ in ch. 95 of the *Hou Han Shu*. In this note we are informed that the name of Ch'iu-tz'ŭ [so reads the phonetic gloss for the two characters 龜茲, 音丘慈] designated a hsien in Shang chün 上 [in modern NE Shensi]. Li Hsien adds that, according to the *Yin-i* 音義 of the *Han Shu*, the place derived its name from the fact that it was inhabited by people from the state of Kucha [龜茲國 in Turkestan] who had surrendered to the Chinese and settled there.

The *Yin-i* referred to by Li Hsien is that of Yen Shih-ku, the well known annotator of the Han history, found in *Han Shu* 28 B, where Ch'iu-tz'û is enumerated among the *hsien* sub-divisions of Shang chün and is described as follows: "Seat of the *magister militum* of the 'dependent state'; has an office of the salt [administration]. According to Ying Shao 應劭 [16] the name is pronounced Ch'iu-tz'ŭ. [Yen] Shih-ku says: 'It is said that ... [follows the above explanation of the origin of the city's name in a slightly different wording from that of Li Hsien:

---

[13] *Textes Historiques*, 1922 ed., pp. 750-751. The numbers and letters in parentheses refer to map X of Wieger's atlas. In an effort to link the situation with Kucha in Turkestan he makes out the rebels to be Northern Hsiung-nu in Western T'ien shan, hence "la Dzoungarie."

[14] À propos de l'article de Sylvain LÉVI Le 'tokharien B,' langue de Koutcha, *TP* 1914, pp. 391-404. On p. 398: "Koutcha est occupée à l'automne de année 155 ... par ... Tchang Houan. ..." Aurousseau refers the reader to *Hou Han Shu* 95 and *Tzŭ-chih t'ung-chien pu-chêng* 53.

[15] 651-684 A. D. Pht. Chang huai 章懷. Sixth son of Kao Tsung of T'ang and, from 675 to 680, his heir apparent. *Chiu T'ang Shu* 86, *T'ang Shu* 81.

[16] *Hou Han Shu* 78. Flourished in the last third of the second century A. D.

龜茲國人來降附者處之於此故以名云]. *Hou Han Shu* 33 likewise mentions the 'dependent state' of Ch'iu-tz'ŭ as an administrative subdivision of Shang chün, and Li Hsien again calls attention to it in a note to *Hou Han shu* 4 under the year 90 A. D. [Yung-yüan 2] on the occasion of the re-establishment of the offices of *magistri militum* of the 'dependent states' of Hsi-ho and Shang chün.[17]

We possess, however, a still earlier reference to the Kucha of Shensi and the origin of its name in the *Shui ching chu* 水經注 of Li Tao-yüan 酈道元 of the Northern Wei[18] and are not thus entirely dependent on the T'ang scholiasts for this important information on the existence of a Kuchean colony in Northern China. Describing the course of the Shê-yen 奢延 river in northeastern Shensi, the *Shui ching chu* repeatedly mentions Ch'iu-tzŭ hsien 龜茲 and states specifically that it acquired its name from a settlement of Hu from Kucha who had surrendered to the Chinese 縣因處龜茲降胡著稱 [ed. *Ssŭ-pu ts'ung kan* 3, 18b-19a].[19]

The evidence seems to justify the supposition that sometime during the Han dynasty, presumably after the great conquests under Wu Ti, a colony of Kucheans had come to establish themselves in Northern Shensi under the terms of a treaty concluded by them with the Chinese, as one may infer from the continuance of the colony in the semi-independent status of a *shu-kuo* 屬國[20] until practically the end of the Second Han. As

[17] Five *shu-kuo* were established by Wu Ti in the autumn of 121 B.C., at the time of the surrender of the Hun-yeh 昆邪 prince of the Hsiung-nu, *Han Shu* 6. They are usually believed to be the 'dependent states' of An-ting, Shang *chün* [with the administrative seat at Ch'iu-tzŭ], T'ien-shui 天水, Wu-yüan, and Chang-yeh 張掖. An-ting and T'ien-shui were not established as provinces until 114 B.C. and Chang-yeh as late as 111 B.C. It is thought by some, therefore, that the five provinces were the old frontier commanderies of Lung-hsi, Pei-ti, Shang chün, Shuo-fang, and Yün-chung. Cf. Notes of Ch'ien-lung editors to ch. 6. The offices of Chinese military commanders for these 'states' were abolished under Ai ti, 6 B.-C.-1 B.C.

[18] d. 527 A.D. *Pei Shih* 27; *Wei Shu* 89, cf. ch. 42. Ying Shao, Li Tao-yüan, and Yen Shih-ku all had had considerable experience with frontier affairs, and each exercised in his generation some influence on the shaping of the government's foreign policy. Their testimony has, therefore, considerable value.

[19] If the Shê-yen river is to be identified with the present Wu-ting 無定 ho in Shensi, Ch'iu tzŭ may have been situated in the vicinity (probably to the NW) of Mi-chih hsien 米脂. Most Chinese historico-geographical works agree that the 'dependent state' was located within the limits of Yen-an 延安 fu. Wang Hsien-ch'ien is, however, inclined to place it much further north, to the N. of Yü-lin hsien 榆林.

[20] Cf. Yen Shih-ku's definition of a 'dependent state'; 不改其本國之俗而屬於漢故號屬國。

hundreds of other communities it must have been engulfed in the cataclysm of the fall of the Han and the subsequent Great Barbarian Invasion. The *Shui ching chu* passage would suggest that it was still alive
under the Wei, but had lost most of its importance as we hear no more
of it under the succeeding dynasties.[21]

The Kucha of Shensi was not an isolated case of a " Western " colony
flourishing on the very frontier of China. Another colony from an oasis
kingdom of the " Western Regions " existed in Shensi in close proximity
to the Han capital. The evidence is again supplied by Yen Shih-ku in
a note to *Han Shu* 96 B, 4a, where he observes that the Wên-hsiu 温宿
mountain range which rose to the north of Li-ch'üan hsien 醴泉 in Yung
chou 雍 was named after people from the kingdom of Wên-hsiu in
Chinese Turkestan who had settled or had pasture lands allocated to them
on that range in the time of the Han dynasty.[22]

The earliest mention of Li-ch'üan is in the Sui geography (*Sui Shu*

---

[21] One should not overlook the possibility that the Shensi Kucha might have
existed even prior to Wu Ti's time. The existence of a Kuchean colony in Shang
chün throws interesting light on the suggestion advanced already by Hsüan-ying
(VII c. A. D.) that the famous Ch'ü-ch'an 屈產 [KD 493, 1167: *k'iuət-san*] in
Shansi, where famous horses were bred in Ch'un-ch'iu times, ['cf. *Tso chuan*, Hsi
2] is another transcription for Kucha (Küsän). Cf. PELLIOT, Tokharien et
koutchéen, *JA* 1934, p. 72, note. Ch'ü-ch'an was believed to be situated near
Shih-lou 石樓 mountain in Shansi, not very far across the Huang ho from where
the Shensi Kucha lay. The whole problem of horse-breeding regions in Western
Shansi and on the Shensi-Kansu border demands special treatment. The Chinese
northwest was famous for its horses since the time of Fei tzŭ 非子, the ancestor
of the house of Ch'in. To mention but a few passages indicating that the breed
of horses raised in that region was associated with the West, I would call attention to *Shui ching chu* 3. 20b which mentions a " Dragon Source " 龍泉 where
were bred horses as good as the " heavenly horses of the T'ien lake ' 滇池天馬
(Issyk kul?); *T'ai-p'ing huan yü chi* 150 describes in E. Kansu a " Dragon
Horse Source " 龍馬泉 where mares produced (after drinking of the water of
this source) hairless colts which grew up within the year to resemble the horses
of Ta yüan 大宛 (Fergana). The same work, 151, 3b, quotes a doggerel verse
current in Wei chou 渭 which extols the virtues of its pasture lands. The
" dragon horses " of Kucha are well known ['cf. PELLIOT, *op. cit.*], and it is not
impossible that long before Wu Ti's conquest Western horse-breeders were plying
their trade in the northwestern marches of China. *En passant*, I should like to
note that the word *lung* 龍 ' dragon ' as an epithet applied to a horse may mean
nothing more mysterious than ' dapple ' [it is then read *mang* < *blang ~ blung?].

[22] Cf. *T'ung Tien* 192. 8b and *Ts'ê-fu yüan-kuei* 958. 5a. In the latter read
令 for 今 and 此 for 北. For Yen Shih-ku's . . . 本因漢時 . . . it has . . .
本前漢時 . . . , which is perhaps to be preferred because of the repetition of
因 a few characters later. Wên-hsiu was situated in the region of modern Aqsu.

29). A Wên-hsiu 溫秀 range (also called 三陽山) is referred to in that chapter in a note on Li-ch'üan hsien. The instability of the graph for the second part of the binom Wên-hsiu [溫秀 ～溫宿～ 溫修] [23] would be a supporting indication that we have here to deal with the transcription of a foreign name.

Besides the two " Aryan " colonies in Shensi there are reasons to believe that there existed on the Chinese border a third colony from the " Far West," this time located in modern Kansu. In the list of *hsien* dependent on the prefecture of Chang-yeh we have in *Han Shu* 28B a Li-chien hsien 驪靬, which re-appears again in *Hou Han Shu* 33, but is listed among the subdivisions of Wu-wei chün 武威 in *Chin Shu* 14.[24] It is undoubtedly the same name that underlies the transcription Li-kan 力乾 mentioned in *Sui Shu* 29 as one of the five *hsien* which were incorporated sometime during the last decade of the sixth century into Fan-ho hsien 番和 in Wu-wei chün. It is tempting to see in the name of this administrative subdivision of a western Chinese province a variant transcription of Li-chien 犂鞬 [*Hou Han Shu* 118, *Chin Shu* 97] Li-kan 犂軒 [*Wei Lüeh*, in *San kuo chih* 30, *Han Shu* 96A], or Li-hsien 黎軒 [*Pei Shih* 97 ＞ *Wei Shu* 102], which is one of the names under which the Roman Orient (Ta Ch'in 大秦) was known to the Chinese of the Han dynasty.

In *Han Shu* 96 [biography of Chang Ch'ien] Li-kan 犛軒 appears in the list of western countries to which were sent Han envoys after the opening up of the Great Silk Route. In his note to the text Fu Chien 服虔 of the Second Han dynasty [25] identifies it with our *hsien* in Chang-yeh. Yen Shih-ku [whose note follows], equates it positively with Ta Ch'in, but, while condemning Fu Chien's statement, believes it nevertheless possible that the Li-kan of Kansu derived its name from the great country of the West: . . . 驪靬縣蓋取此國爲名耳驪犛聲相近。

The restoration of the original western name that underlies these transcriptions presents manifold and peculiar difficulties,[26] as does the identi-

---

[23] Cf. *Li-ch'üan hsien chih* 2. 3b, *Ch'ang-an chih* 16. 11b.

[24] Cf. *Shuo-wên chieh-tzǔ* 3A where Li-kan 麗軒 is also defined as a *hsien* in Wu-wei.

[25] Flourished at the end of the second century A. D. *Hou Han Shu* 109B.

[26] All the *li* used in the transcriptions are derived from archaic phonemes with initial consonantal complexes the exact nature of which it is difficult to ascertain; various indications point to a *KL or *BL- and, in the case of 麗 to *SL-. The problem deserves detailed consideration. The phonetic glosses in the above sources are confusing.

cation of the place with any district of the Roman East. At present, opinion among scholars on this question remains divided: some following de Groot and Herrmann [27] believe that the Chinese characters represent a transcription of Hyrcania,[28] others lean towards the suggestion made by Pelliot [29] that Li-kan should be equated with Alexandria. It would transcend the scope of this note to attempt even to review the complex evidence adduced in support of either hypothesis. Hyrcania or Alexandria,[30] or a *tertium quid*, the name of the little Chinese city on the desert road to the West, would indicate that an important Western community must have sent out its sons to the distant land of the Seres to imprint the name of the metropolis on an outpost of the Han Empire.

The above jottings on "Kucha," [31] "Wên-hsiu," and "Li-kan" in

---

[27] De Groot, *Die Westlande Chinas in der vorchristlichen Zeit*, p. 18; cf. HERR-MANN, *Atlas of China*, pp. 17, 26-27.

[28] Old Persian *vrkāna*, cf. E. HERZFELD, *Archaeologische Mitteilungen aus Iran* 4. 1, Oct. 1931, pp. 29, 31. For the Kansu Li-kan one might even think of Ptolemy's Ἀρραγάνα.

[29] In *TP* 1915, pp. 690-691.

[30] We are not, of course, thinking so much of the Egyptian Alexandria, as one of the numerous Alexandrias, founded by the great conqueror in the East (near Khōjend, Kābul, Merv, Kandahār, etc.).

[31] In connection with Kucha, I should like to discuss briefly a peculiar problem arising in the matter of Chinese transcription of foreign words, a problem that has received heretofore only passing mention. In *JA* 1934, pp. 74-103 Professor Pelliot has devoted considerable space to the elucidation of the question of what original central-asiatic term is represented by the Chinese transcriptions *chüeh-li* 爵離, *ch'üeh-li* 雀離 [KD 1126, 1265, 533: *tsįak-ljie* ⟨ -a var. 棃 *tsįak-lji*] and *chê-chüeh* 柘厥 [*tśįak-kįuət*, cf. KD 883, 503]. All these binoms represented the name of a famous temple in Kucha as well as that of a synonymous mountain-pass near that city.

The unknown Kuchean word undoubtedly meant, as established by Pelliot, 'spire' 'point,' and is compared by him with tk. *čäkür* which must have designated [as it appears clear from a Turfan fragment] the spire of a *stupa*. Pelliot dismisses for some reason the possibility of this word having an Indian origin and supposes that the term *čäkür* [and its 'tokharian' original] must have meant 'watch-tower' ∼ 'stupa' and thus could have been applied to designate both a temple and a pass, protected by watch-towers. Even if the mysterious word were 'tokharian,' I still would think that it is related to Sanskrit *çikhā* — 'point,' 'summit,' 'crest' ⟩ *çikhara*—'pointed,' 'summit of a mountain,' 'steeple,' 'spire,' 'tower of a palace or temple.' The semantic evolution of the Sanskrit word leaves nothing to be desired for an explanation of its application as the name of the above localities; while the initial may present some difficulty, the earliest Chinese rendering 爵離 *tsįak-*lja*, possibly *tsįǝk-*lja*, would be a reasonable transcription of *çikhara* ∼ *çekhara* or of its unknown 'tokharian' relative.

China throw an interesting light on the puzzling twins of Ptolemy's itinerary, Issedon Scythica and Issedon Serica. How many such X Scythicae, transplanted eastward by trade or war, became X Sericae only a further study of the sources will reveal. Our purpose has been to draw attention to the wealth of material hidden beneath the still virgin soil of Chinese historiography and to suggest that in the melting pot that was Northwestern China an " Aryan," linguistic if not ethnic, element may have played a not inconsiderable part.[32]

II. The Bulgars of Mongolia

September, 251 A. D. A century has passed and with it has vanished the glory that was Han. Bled by the incessant wars and revolutions of the past three generations, her population decimated, her wealth half gone, China is hopelessly split into three rival political entities. The house of Ts'ao Wei rules over the greater part of the Empire in the North,

---

One of the common compounds of *çikhā* — ' crest ' in Sanskrit is *çikhādhara* ~ *çikhādhâra* — ' crest-bearing ' which is often used as an epithet for crested birds, particularly the peacock. In transcribing a foreign word, the early Chinese scholars often selected out of several possibilities characters which, while rendering as faithfully as possible the foreign sounds, would at the same time suggest the semantic value of the original. Indeed, all three characters 爵, 雀, and 鸖 used in the ancient transcriptions of the Kuchean word are names of birds, the second term entering as an element into the Chinese designation of the peacock, *k'ung-ch'iao* 孔雀, while both *chüeh* and *ch'iao* are occasionally used in reference to tufted birds.

[32] It would be desirable to investigate carefully the genealogy of several historically prominent Chinese originating from the Western provinces of the Empire with a view to ascertaining whether under their ' sinitic ' surnames are not concealed names that would indicate that they were descendants of western colonists who settled in China. It is well known that most of the K'ang 康 of Chinese history trace their origin to Sogdian [K'ang-chü 居] emigrants, and that the clan An 安 derives its name from An-hsi 息 — Parthia. If we believe *Wei Shu* 30, An Shih-kao, the great Parthian Buddhist missionary, must have left descendants in China, as that source claims that An T'ung 同, an officer of the early T'o-pa, traced his genealogy back to An Shih-kao. The Kan 甘 clan, representatives of which played such a prominent role in Chinese exploration of the west [甘父 Kan Fu, Chang Ch'ien's guide, Kan Yen-shou 甘延壽, khan Chih-chih's conqueror, and Kan Ying 英, Pan Ch'ao's envoy to the West] and whose name is, I believe, reflected in the name of China's westernmost province, was probably of foreign origin. So possibly is the surname So 索 < *Sâk, borne by a distinguished Tun-huang family under the Chin dynasty. In several cases, when it is question of natives of the west, Chang 張 appears to be a sinicized form of Chih 支 < Yüeh-chih 月支 — " Indoscythian." Chang Huan, who was a native of Tun-huang, could thus have had foreign blood in him.

but again, as ninety-six years ago, at the helm of government, over-shadowing the Son of Heaven, stands the powerful figure of a majordomo. Ssŭ-ma I 司馬懿, the last of the great warriors of the period, has just breathed his last and left the management of the Empire's affairs and the tutelage over the Emperor to his son Ssŭ-ma Shih 師.[33]

Among his father's officers to whom the new dictator willingly lends his ear when considering matters of foreign policy, is one Têng Ai 鄧艾 [34] who is busy outlining to his master a plan for strengthening China's defenses in the North. The perennial problem of Hsiung-nu and Ch'iang is under discussion. A new process of unification has been tak-ing place among the Hsiung-nu and the age-old prescription of political dichotomy is indicated for them, lest the empire's northwestern communi-cations be endangered again.

In 215-216 A. D. Ts'ao Ts'ao, the founder of the fortunes of the Wei house, had divided the remnants of the Southern Hsiung-nu who had settled in the depopulated marches of the North into five hordes. Grazing lands were allocated to each of the hordes and each native chief was forced to share the control over his tribesmen with a Chinese resident.[35] The *shan-yü* remained a prisoner at Ts'ao's court, while his uncle Ch'ü-pei 去卑, a loyal vassal of the Wei, acted as regent.[36]

But Ch'ü-pei is now dead, the strict surveillance exercised over the chieftains has apparently been somewhat relaxed, and Liu Pao 劉豹, Right *hsien wang* and nephew of the last *shan-yü*, has been extending his authority over all the five hordes, not without opposition, however, from rival leaders.[37] Têng Ai now proposes to Ssŭ-ma Shih to split the

---

[33] Emperor Ts'ao Fang 芳 [as he was dethroned by Ssŭ-ma Shih, he has no pht.] 232-240-254-274 A. D., *San Kuo chih* 4. Ssŭ-ma I, 179-251 A. D., *Chin Shu* 1. Ssŭ-ma Shih 208-255 A. D., *ibid.*, 2. He passed on his post to his brother Chao 昭, 211-265 A. D., whose son Yen 炎, 236-265-289 A. D., became the first emperor of the Chin, *ibid.* 3.

[34] Died 264 A. D., *San kuo chih* 28.

[35] The Northern Horde, numbering some 4,000 tents, was settled in Hsin-hsing 新興 *hsien*; the Central Horde, 6,000 tents, in T'ai-ling 太陵 *hsien*; the Left Horde, 10,000 tents, in Tzŭ-shih 茲氏 *hsien* [many texts have incorrectly 泫 for 茲] near T'ai yüan; the Right Horde, 6,000 tents, in Ch'i *hsien* 祁; and the Southern Horde, 3,000 tents, in P'u-tzŭ *hsien* 蒲子. *Chin Shu* 97, cf. also G. UCHIDA 內田吟風, On the Five Tribes of Hsiung-nu in the Third Century A. D. (in Japanese), *Shirin* 19. 2, April 1934, pp. 271-295.

[36] *San kuo chih* 1; *Hou Han Shu* 119; *Chin Shu* 56.

[37] *San kuo chih* 24 [biography of Wang Li 王禮] mentions an important Hsiung-nu chief Liu Ching 靖 who, about 248 A. D., was steadily growing in power. I am not able to identify him, however, with any of the known chieftains.

Hsiung-nu anew by " making manifest Ch'ü-pei's meritorious services to the dynasty " through an appointment of his son to high office among the Hsiung-nu. Measures are also to be taken to stop the infiltration of the Ch'iang and Hu among the Chinese population of the marches. Fiat! [38]

It must have been in that year that Mêng 猛, the son of Ch'ü-pei, received the chieftainship of the Northern Horde.[39] In the same year to the aged Liu Pao was born a son predestined to revive the old glory of the Hsiung-nu and found a Hsiung-nu kingdom on the ruins of Ssŭ-ma's empire.

Thirteen years later we find this boy as a hostage at the Chinese court where he is winning the friendship, admiration, and support of many prominent officials.[40] Ssŭ-ma Chao has just taken another step in the policy of weakening the Hsiung-nu through a new division of hordes, and their number is increased to three.[41] About 266 A. D., the imperial Chin government creates a new subdivision, apparently at the expense of chief Liu Mêng. The latter raises the standard of rebellion in 271 A. D. and seeks support among the nomads of Mongolia. As in the case of Chü-lung Wu-ssŭ, however, his career is cut short by the sword of one of his followers bribed by the Chinese,[42] and his brother Kao-shêng-yüan 誥升 爰 supplants him as chief of the Northern Horde. Some years later Liu Pao, having died, is succeeded by his son, Liu Yüan 淵.[43]

The reconstruction of the genealogy of the Hsiung-nu royal house from the end of the second century on is rather difficult, and several problems present themselves in ascertaining the family relationship of the Hsiung-nu leaders during the period under consideration.

If we are to believe *T'ang Shu* 75B, Ch'ü-pei had little Hsiung-nu

---

[38] Cf. *San kuo chih* 28 for Têng Ai's report.

[39] In *Chin Shu* 57 [biography of Hu Fên 胡奮] Liu Mêng is, however, referred to as chief of the Central Horde. *Wei Shu* 95 specifically says, however, that he resided in Hsin-hsing, where, as we have seen, was situated the *ordo* of the Northern chieftain.

[40] Among them Wang Mi 王彌 *Chin Shu* 100, and Wang Hun 王渾 *ibid.* 42.

[41] *Chin Shu* 56 [biography of Chiang T'ung 江統, d. 310 A. D.; his lengthy report on frontier conditions was presented to the throne probably in the year 300].

[42] Liu Mêng's revolt lasted from the first month of 271 to the first month of 272 A. D., *Chin Shu* 3.

[43] *Chin Shu* 101, *Wei Shu* 95. Liu Pao must have died a very old man, as he could not have been born later than 195 A. D. It is curious that he had no son until about 250 A. D., and the sources would indicate that he died about 280 A. D. In the last year of Ssŭ-ma Yen's reign Liu Yüan was made, according to *Shih-liu kuo ch'un-ch'iu* 1, chief of the Northern horde [supplanting Kao-shêng-yüan?].

blood in his veins. The genealogy of the Tu-ku 獨孤 family contained in that source makes Ch'ü-pei to be the descendant of the Chinese prince Liu Chin-po 劉進伯 who had been captured by the Hsiung-nu and [having married a Hsiung-nu woman?] had begotten in captivity near Mount Ku [孤山下] a son named Shih-li 尸利.[44] Shih-li was made *ku-li* 谷蠡 prince by the *shan-yü* and given the surname Tu-ku.[45] Ch'ü-pei was his son or grandson. Supplementing this evidence with information supplied from *Hou Han Shu* 72, we obtain the following genealogy:

Liu Hsiu [Kuang-wu Ti of Han] 4 B. C.–25 A. D.–57 A. D.
|
Fu 輔, prince of P'ei 沛, ?–39–84 A. D. [cf. ch. 3]
|
Ting 定, ?–84–95 A. D. [cf. ch. 4]
|
Chêng 正, ?–95–108 A. D. [*T'ang Shu* 75 : Kai 丐]
|

Kuang 廣 ?–108–142 A. D.	I 廙
Jung 榮 ?–142–161 A. D.	Mu 穆
Tsung 琮	Chin-po 進伯
Yao 曜	Shih-li 尸利
Hsieh 契 c. 220 A. D.	Ch'ü-pei 去卑

Now the *T'ang Shu* text reads: . . . 尸利生烏利二子去卑猛猛生 etc. . . . In the language of the T'ang genealogists this can only mean

[44] There is no doubt from this story that the Chinese etymologized Tu-ku < *d'uk-kuo* as derived from tk. *toγ* — 'to be born.' The existence of this tk. root in Hsiung-nu would suggest that the mysterious ku-tu 孤塗 < *kuo-d'uo*, forming the second part of the title of the Hsiung-nu sovereign equivalent to the Chinese 天子 'Son of Heaven,' may be explained as resulting from an inadvertent transposition of the two characters *tu-ku < *d'uo-kuo*. The original Hsiung title corresponding to the Chinese transcription *ch'ang-li tu-ku* would then be *tängri toγu* — 'born of Heaven.' The latest attempt to explain the puzzling *ku-tu* [K. SHIRATORI, Sur l'origine des Hiong-nou, *JA* 1923, pp. 71-81] is not conclusive.

[45] Tu-ku is probably identical with Tu-ku-hun 渾, registered as a surname in *Wei Shu* 113 and is possibly related to Tu-ku 屠各 < *d'uo-kân* which was, according to *Chin Shu* 97, the name of the *shan-yü*'s clan. As 瓜 *k'ʷa, the phonetic of *kuo*, as well as 各 possessed an archaic *KL- in *Anlaut*, Tu-ku may possibly go back to *d'uo-*klo < tk. *toγlu*. Cf. Доуло, the clan name of the Danube Bulgars [cf. MIKKOLA, *Die Chronologie der türkischen Donaubulgaren*].

" Shih-li begat Wu-li, (Wu-li had) two sons, Ch'ü-pei and Mêng; Mêng begat, *etc.* . . . ," with an unexplainable omission of the repetition of the two characters 烏利. From *Wei Shu* 95 we know that Mêng was Ch'ü-pei's son, and not his brother.[46] We are thus forced to emend the text by inserting 生 'begat' after 去卑 and translate: " Shih-li begat Wu-li. His [Chin-po's, Shih-li's, or Wu-li's] second son Ch'ü-pei begat Mêng. Mêng begat. . . ." Liu Chin-po, as we are also informed by the same text, was Tu Liao 度遼 general at the time of his capture by the Hsiung-nu. The succession of Tu-Liao generals is uncertain only in the period from 141 A. D. to 156 A. D.[47] If we suppose that Chin-po was made prisoner in 155 A. D. at the time of Chang Huan's famous campaign [see *supra*], this would well correspond to his elder cousin's dates and would explain why Chang Huan had to take upon himself the task of stopping the Hsiung-nu movement south, the prevention of which was one of the duties of the Tu-Liao general.[48]

Pei Shih 53 refers, however, to Ch'ü-pei as the uncle of Hu-ch'u-ch'üan 呼廚泉 [*shan-yü* 195-216 A. D.] who was the son of Ch'iang-chü 羌渠 [*shan-yü* 179-188] and younger brother of Yü-fu-lo 於扶羅 [*shan-yü* 188-195]. This complicates matters considerably: 1. Yü-fu-lo, who died in 195, left a son [Pao], and hence could hardly have been born later than 179 A. D. 2. His father Ch'iang-chü who left two sons at the time of his death in 188, must have been born not later than 164 A. D. 3. Hence Ch'iang-chü's father could not have been Shih-li, if Shih-li was born about 156 A. D. The only way of reconciling the conflicting evidence of the sources is to suppose that Shih-li = Ch'iang-chü and Wu-li = Yü-fu-lo, and read the above passage of the T'ang Shu as follows: . . . " Shih-li begat Wu-li. [Chin-po's] second son Ch'ü-pei begat Mêng. . . ."[49]

---

[46] *Wei Shu* 95 calls Kao-shêng-yüan's son, Liu Hu, a nephew 從子 of Liu Mêng, and a grandson of Ch'ü-pei.

[47] We can re-establish with almost complete certainty the name and date of tenure of every Tu-Liao general from the time of the re-establishing of the office under Ming Ti in 65 A. D. until the war of 141. After the break, from 156 A. D. on, we have half a dozen names of Tu-Liao generals, but their order of succession is not at all clear from the sources.

[48] There is a faint possibility that Liu Chin-po's defeat and capture took place in 140-141 A. D. *Hou Han Shu* 119 speaks of Ma Hsü 馬續, then Tu-Liao general, as " resigning *again* " in the summer of 141 A. D. without mentioning, however, a former resignation. If Ma Hsü had, indeed, abandoned his post for a short time previously, due to some indecision on the part of the government during the crisis, Liu Chin-po could have undertaken his duties, been defeated in a rashly conducted expedition, and Ma Hsü resumed his post immediately after.

[49] In Wu-li we may have, however, not a name, but a descriptive title < tk. mo.

Whether Ch'ü-pei was the son or the grandson of Chin-po, there seems to be no reason to doubt his Chinese origin. If Ch'iang-chü was his elder brother [and is identical with Shih-li], he may indeed have been the *ku-li* prince whom Chang Huan wished to place on the throne following the Hsiung-nu raid of 166 A. D., a plan that would thus appear to have been put in effect by the government only thirteen years later. The Chinese origin of Ch'iang-chü may then explain the revolt of his subjects and his murder in 188 A. D., as well as the elevation to the throne by the rebels of a Hsiung-nu prince of another clan.[50]

We must not lose sight, however, of the possibility that the *Pei Shih* statement of relationship between Hu-ch'u-ch'üan and Ch'ü-pei is errone-ous, and that Ch'iang-chü's branch and that of Ch'ü-pei are only remotely connected, the former being a continuation of the old line of Hsiung-nu sovereigns.[51] In that case, the Hsiung-nu policy of the Chinese govern-ment during the third century can be explained as shrewd playing of the male line of descent against the female line, with support being given now to the one, now to the other.[52] The genealogy of the Hsiung-nu in the IIIrd and IVth centuries is presented, however, on p. 298 with greater emphasis on the first supposition outlined above.

Since the beginning of the century, Ch'ü-pei's line of Hsiung-nu had been brought into contact with the T'o-pa Hsien-pi in the North. His younger brother and his five sons had been made prisoners after a battle that marked the first appearance of the T'o-pa on the Chinese frontier;[53] Mêng's son Fu-lun found a refuge among them after his father's defeat; his son and grandson married T'o-pa princesses; so presumably did Kao-shêng-yüan. Thus whatever Hsiung-nu blood there flowed in their veins

---

uri — 'son,' 'offspring.' Cf. *HJAS* 1. 176; also *Han Shu* 17 where Wu-li 黎 appears as a Hsiung-nu name, and *ibid.* 94B where Wu-li 累, as a title of a *shan-yü* [the third son, but fifth successor of Hu-han-hsieh], seems to indicate that with him the throne reverted to an elder [and legitimate] line.

[50] The new *shan-yü* belonged to the Hsü-pu 須卜 clan, one of the three great clans from which the former *shan-yü* choose their wives. We do not know whether this new founded line endured for any length of time. *Hou Han Shu* 119.

[51] The change of the clan name of the Hsiung-nu sovereigns from Luan-t'i 攣鞮 [*Han Shu* 94A] or Hsü-lien-t'i 虛連題 [*Hou Han Shu* 119] to Tu-ku [cf. note 45] would indicate, however, that the male line of Hsiung-nu khans had become extinct.

[52] Until 216 A. D. the Chinese government supports Hu-ch'u-ch'üan; then Ch'ü-pei, apparently to the time of his death; then shifts its weight to the side of Liu Pao until 251 A. D.; leans again towards Ch'ü-pei's line; and then about 265-270 decides to support Liu Pao again.

[53] Cf. *HJAS* 1. 167, note.

became still more diluted with that of the Hsien-pi; the story of Ch'ü-
pei's branch is now closely bound with the history of the rise of the T'o-pa.
Mêng line is assimilated by them, while the house of the Ho-lien Hsia
赫連夏, founded by a descendant of Kao-shêng-yüan disappears, in 432
A. D. following a long struggle with the T'o-pa Wei, a century after the
Han-Chao dynasty established by Liu Yüan had come to an end at the
hands of another Hsiung-nu conqueror.[54] This mixed nature of our
Hsiung-nu is reflected, as we shall see, in their onomasticon.

Some ninety years after the fall of the Ho-lien Hsia we hear again of
the Shansi Hsiung-nu. They re-appear as a distinct political organization at the time of the break-up of the T'o-pa Wei empire under the name
Chi Hu 稽胡, when their chief Liu Li-shêng 劉蠡升 assumes in 525-
526 A. D. the title of khan.[55] Later we see them taking active part in
the wars between the Northern Chou and the Northern Ch'i.

Chou Shu 49 contains a brief description of the mode of life of these
Hsiung-nu from which we learn that they had become intermixed with
the Chinese settlers, were partly engaged in agricultural pursuits, and had
acquired some of the ways of their neighbors. Thus they raised hemp,
and even silk, as the male part of the population had begun to adopt
Chinese dress and funerary customs. They had, however, preserved their
language and some of the old mores [" loose morals " and typical nomadic
marriage customs are especially noted by the Chinese historian].

Our source informs us also that the name under which they are known
in Chinese history was but an abbreviation of their polysyllabic " barbarian " appellation which was Pu-lo-chi 步落稽, KD 759, 566, 1215:
b'uo-lâk-kiei [or *k'iei*].[56] The considerable emphasis placed by the Chinese
on the meticized character of these Hsiung-nu would indicate that it is
in their mode of life and mixed origin that we must seek an explanation
of this curious name unheard of in the previous centuries.

<hr/>

[54] For the history of the Han-Chao, cf. *Chin Shu* 101-103 and *Shih-liu kuo* . . .
1-10; for that of the Hsia *Chin Shu* 130, *Shih-liu-kuo* . . . 66-69; also *Wei Shu* 95.
[55] *Wei Shu* 9. They are also referred to as Shan Hu 山胡, " Mountain " Hu
and Hu of Fên 汾 chou.
[56] *T'ai-p'ing huan-yü chi* 34: Pu-lo-chi 部 [KD 756: b'uo]. Quoting the *Sui
t'u ching tsa chi* 隋圖經雜記, this source describes them in the quaint phrase
胡頭漢舌 "*Hu*-headed and Chinese-tongued," which would indicate that during
the last part of the sixth century Chinese had largely supplanted their native
tongue. Of the several words of the Chi Hu language preserved in Chinese
geographical works we can identify with surety only two: K'u-li 庫利 < *k'uo-li
< tk. *qul* — ' slave ' [Chin. 奴] and K'o-yeh 可野 < *k'â-zįa < mo. *qasiya* — ' fort,'
' enclosures ' [Chin. 堡].

Genealogy of Hsiung-nu Rulers in the III-IV cc. A. D.[1]

Chin-po? 進伯 [or Shih-li 尸利?]

Ch'iang-chü

羌渠 ?-179-188

Yü-fu-lo 於扶羅 ?-188-195

Hu-ch'u-ch'üan 呼廚泉 ?-195-216-?[8]

Pao 豹

Yüan 淵 c. 352-304-310

K'u-jên 庸仁 c. 319-383

K'ang-ni 兀颽 d. 396[9]

Hsien[8] 顯

Ch'ü-pei

去卑

Mêng 猛 d. 272   Kao-shêng-yüan[4] 誥升爰   N

Fu-lun[5] 副崘

虎 Hu d. 341

Lu-ku[6] 路孤

Wu-huan 務桓 ?-341-356   O-lou-t'ou 閼陋頭 ?-356-358-?

Chüan 眷 d. 385

Hsi-wu-ch'i 悉勿祁 ?-358-359   N   Wei-ch'ên 衛辰 ?-359-391[7]   N   N   N

Chien 犍 d. 386   Ch'ü-chin 去斤 d. 386   Lo-ch'ên 羅辰[10]   N   N

P'o-p'o 勃勃 381-407-425

P'an-liu-hsi

潘六奚

N   N   N

¹ This genealogical table is based on the following sources: *Wei Shu* 1, 23, 95, 83A; *Chin Shu* 57, 97, 101, 130; *Pei Shih* 1, 53, 93; *T'ang Shu* 75B; *Hou Han Shu* 119; *Shih-liu kuo ch'un-ch'iu* 1, 66.

² *Chin Shu* 57 writes Yü-mi-fu-lo 彌.

³ *Pei Shih* 53, incorrectly, Hu-ch'u-mao 貌.

⁴ For his name, cf. Kao-shêng-yüan 袁, n. of an affluent of the Yellow River in Shansi, *Shui ching chu* 3. 14a. It is possible that Kao-sheng-yüan is identical with Liu Hsüan 宣, Right *hsien-wang* and chief of the Northern Horde, who played an important rôle in establishing Liu Yüan as great *shan-yü* in 304. He was still alive in 308 and as we hear of the activities of Liu Hu only beginning with 310, it must be at this time that he died and that Hu succeeded to the chieftainship. Kao-shêng-yüan's place in the genealogy would also correspond to Yüan's designation as an avuncular grandfather 從祖 of Liu Yüan. Cf. *Chin Shu* 101, *Wei Shu* 95, *Shih-liu kuo ch'un-ch'iu* 1, 8.

⁵ It is possible that Fu-lun is identical with Fu-liu-t'un 伏留屯 who is mentioned in *Chou Shu* 16 as one of the 36 tribal chieftains under the first To-pa and as the ancestor of Tu-ku Hsin 信.

⁶ *Wei Shu* 1, *sub anno* 318, supports indirectly the *T'ang Shu* genealogy by calling Lu-ku a cousin 從弟 of Liu Hu.

⁷ Wei-ch'ên's name [KD 1308, 1197: *$gi^{u}\ddot{a}i$-$\dot{z}i\breve{e}n$*; *Sung Shu* 95 writes Wei-ch'ên 臣] represents undoubtedly mo. *geyiči ~ giyiči* — 'guest,' 'stranger.' A related mo. form *jočin* — 'guest' > so. mo. *jüči* 'id.,' name of Genghis Khan's son, appears in the T'o-pa onomasticon under the Chinese transcription Ch'u-chên 處真 < *tś'i^{u}o-tśi̯ĕn* [name of a T'o-pa prince] and Ch'u-chên 初真 < *tṣ'i^{u}o-tśi̯ĕn* [*Wei Shu*, ch. 30, name of the father of Lai Ta-kan 來大干, and *Chou Shu*, ch. 20, that of the father of Ho-lan Hsiang 賀蘭祥. For various forms of this word in tk. mo., cf. VLADIMIRTSOV, Сравнительная грамматика, p. 247.

⁸ In Hsien's 'barbarian' name Ch'ou-fa 醜伐 < *tś'i̯ou-b'i^{u}ɐt* we see tk. mo. *čubar* — 'dapple-gray.' The parallel form ch'i-fa 吡伐 [name of a tribal chief in *Wei Shu* 103] appears also in *Hsü Po-wu-chih* 4. 3a ['cf. *Pien Ya* 7] as the color-designation of horses presented to the Chinese court by Ta-yüan c. 742-755 A. D. and undoubtedly reflects the tk. mo. variant *čibar* — 'id,' the tk. mo. term exhibiting the same fluctuation of the vowel of the first syllable as mo. *činua ~ čonoa* — 'wolf' for which cf. *HJAS* 1. 177.

⁹ Possibly < tk. *qanglï* — 'cart.'

¹⁰ For Ch'ü-chin, cf. *HJAS, loc. cit.* Lo-ch'ên < *Lâ-ȝi̯ĕn* is identical with Nu-chên 奴真 < **nuo-tśi̯ĕn ~ *nja-tśi̯ĕn* of *Wei Shu* 23. The name of the Hsiung-nu chieftain was registered by the Chinese in the two variant pronunciations of the tk. mo. word for 'falcon,' *lačin ~ način.* His sister became the consort of T'o-pa Kuei. On her ritual murder, cf. J. R. WARE, An ordeal among the T'o-pa Wei, *TP* 1936, 207. It is to be noted that the custom of putting the heir-apparent's mother to death is probably a survival of the old nomadic tradition of killing the parents as soon as their son reached maturity and that the rule applied as much to the father as to mother. It is significant that most of the early T'o-pa rulers ended their lives at the hands of, or at least with the connivance of, their youthful sons. We have assembled a considerable number of texts, both western and Chinese, on the subject of the 'dying kings' of the steppes and hope to return to this interesting problem in the future.

B'uo-lâk-kiei yields us, indeed, a tk. mo. form *bulaqï which is un-doubtedly derived from the root √ *bul-, bula- < bulɣa ~ bulaq — 'to mix,' 'to become mixed.' This root is registered in Orkhon Turkish in the form bulɣaq — 'Mischung' [= Chin. 渾] and appears in almost all turkish dialects in derivatives with the meaning 'mixed,' 'muddy,' 'troubled'> 'rebellious.'[57] It is also found widely distributed in turkish in the alliterative binoms alaq-bulaq ~ alan-bulan — 'mixed,' 'variegated.'[58] In mongol besides the common bulanggir — √'muddy,' we find bulaq used as a term designating a horse spotted with white.[59]

As shown by J. Nemeth,[60] bulɣa underlies the name of the Bulgars, an ethnic designation which we find applied since the early Middle Ages to three distinct groups of peoples, one on the Upper Volga, one in the Euxino-Caspian steppes, and one on the Lower Danube, all of which, as is well known, were mixed peoples. In the case of the Volga and the Danube Bulgar, the mixture consisted essentially of turkish and slavic elements.[61] Each of these three great regions of Eastern Europe was

[57] Cf. particularly P. PELLIOT, "Les Mongols et la Papauté," pp. 322-323, J. MARQUART, *Die Chronologie der alttürkischen Inschriften*, p. 103. For an interest-ing example of use of bulɣaq as a proper name, see *Ibn Taghri Birdi's Annals*, ed. W. POPPER, 6. 273. The relation of our *bula to tk. bulan — 'elk' < mottled animal?' is problematical, cf. PELLIOT, *JA* 1925, I, p. 224. While there is no doubt that the medieval mongol compound il bulɣa meant, as established by Pelliot [Les Mongols . . . , *loc. cit.*] 'les peuples soumis et [les peuples] revoltés' the original significance of it may have been 'the il (nucleus, original tribe responsible for the creation of a confederacy) and the bulɣa (the heterogenous elements comprising the larger unit of the nomadic federation, the later 'ad-mixtures' to the nucleus).'

[58] On these alliterative compounds, cf. Н. К. Дмитриевъ, О парныхъ слово-сочетаніяхъ въ башкирскомъ, Изв. Ак. Наукъ, 1930, 501-522.

[59] Cf. kül bulaq, bulaq kül — 'a white-legged horse.' In the form bula the term appears in the mongolian vocabulary of Ibn Al-Muhannā. On pp. 114 and 116 of Melioranski's edition [Записки Вост. Отд. Имп. Арх. Общ., vol. XV, 1904, pp. 76-171] are found two mongol idioms قار ٸل and كل ٸل translated respectively: المعجل اليد 'horse with white forelegs' and معجل الرجل 'horse with white hind legs.' There is no doubt that for the unexplainable *yalā ٸل we must read ٸُل *bulā and transliterate both expressions *ɣar bulā, *kül bulā — 'with white hands [*i. e.* forelegs]' 'with white legs [*i. e.* hind legs],' mo. ɣar and kül corresponding exactly to ar. يد and رجل.

[60] In *Symbolae Grammaticae in honorem Ioannis Rozwadowski*, 2. 217-226, La provenance du nom *bulgar*. The derivation was first suggested by Tomaschek in PAULY-WISSOWA.

[61] The belief in a purely turkish origin of the Volga Bulgars has, I believe, been based on an undue emphasis on some passages in Arabic geographical works in which these Bulgars are referred to loosely as Turks. Shams al-Dīn al-

situated on the nexus of important highways, near trading centers where nomad met, bartered, hobnobbed, intermixed with settler.

The marches of Shansi on the banks of the Yellow and Fên rivers constituted exactly such a region. There converged the great Mongolian caravan routes connecting Central Asia with the Chinese internal system of highways and leading the traveler to the two capitals of China. There nomad met Chinese and Tibetan, and as we have seen, even " Aryan "; and there it was that the Hsiung-nu, with the loss of their political cohesion and the severance of formal ties that bound them to the life of the steppes, became definitely committed to the rôle of a ' marginal ' people. The Hun was now a ' Mischling,' a *Bulaq*, a Bulgar.

The term *bulγa ∼ bulaq* as a designation of a hybrid people may be of high antiquity, but space limits forbid detailed consideration of its origin at present.[62] I should like only to draw attention here to several cases of its use in the nomadic onomasticon. Among Chinese transcriptions of ' barbarian ' names scattered through the Northern histories we possess the following which are apparently based on derivatives of **bul*, *bulγa ∼ bulaq*:

1. Pu-lo-chi 步落稽 b'uo-lâk-kiei ⟨ **Bulaqï, Pei Ch'i Shu* 10; nickname of the Ch'i Emperor Kao Chan 高湛.[63]

Dimashqī [b. 1256 A.D.] reports, however, the answer of some Bulgars who passed through Baghdad on their way to Mecca, and who, when questioned on the meaning of " Bulgar," responded: قوم متولدون بين الترك والصقالبة [ed. MEHREN, p. ٢٩٤], lit.: " a mixed people between the Turks and the Slavs," with *between* introducing the components of the mixture, rather than indicating the location of the people, cf. MEHREN's translation, *Manuel de la cosmographie*, p. 381. The name of the river Volga, from which " Bulgar " is often derived, originated itself from **bulγa*; cf. its other name Rōs which it owes to its being the scene of another ' commingling,' that of the Rus ⟩ Russians.

[62] In the *Ch'un-ch'iu* there appears [under the years 638 and 606 B.C.] a Jung tribe called Lu-hun 陸渾 ⟨ **liuk-γiuən* which was settled in the first of the above years in the watershed between the I and Lo rivers in Honan. Kung-yang's commentary writes, however, Pên-hun 賁 ⟨ **puən-γiuən*. As recently established by *Karlgren* [Word families in Chinese, p. 33] 賁 was pronounced in archaic Chinese *piar, b'iwər*; we have some grounds to believe, on the other hand, that 陸 *liuk* is derived from an archaic *BLuk. Both compounds thus may go back to **bulγun* or *bulγur*. Cf. *Shih Chi* 110, DE GROOT, *Die Hunnen der vorchristlichen Zeit*, 18, and TSCHEPE, *Histoire du royaume de Tsin*, 57-58. The syllabic phoneme *BLƏK is so common in archaic Chinese, forming the root of at least 10 phonetic series in which the semanteme ' mottled,' ' variegated ' is well attested, that the question naturally arises whether we do not have in √*bul-*, *bulγa-* a root common to Chinese and ' Altaic.'

[63] Pht. Shih Tsu Wu-ch'êng 世祖武成, 537-561-565-568 A. D., *Pei Ch'i Shu* 7,

2. Pu-lo-chien 步落堅 [KD 369: kien] < *bulaqïn, *Wei Shu* 74; name of a barbarian chieftain, no doubt from among the Chi-Hu.

3. Mo-kên 沒根 [KD 637, 312: muət-kən] < *bulqïn, the nickname of Liu [Tu-ku] K'u-jên, who was the son of Hsiung-nu and a T'o-pa princess.[64]

4. Mo-ko 沒歌 [KD 413: kâ] < *bulqa, possibly *bulγa, the name of a tribe which T'o-pa Shih-i-chien defeated in 364 A. D., *Wei Shu* 1. Here we may have *bulγa in the sense of ' revolt ' > ' rebellious.' On the other hand, it may be identical with

5. Mo-lu-hui 沒鹿回 [KD 576, 108: luk, γuâi] < *buluγai ~ *bulγai, a tribe related to the T'o-pa. Cf. *Wei Shu* 1, *sub anno* 220 A. D., ch. 13, also *HJAS* 1. 177.

6. Mo-ku 沒骨 [KD 427] muət-kuət < bulqut ~ *bulqur. Name of the murderer of T'u-fa Shu-chi-nêng, *Wei Shu* 99.

7. Fu-li-chüan 附力眷 [KD 44, 523, 495: b'iu-liək-kiʷän] < *bul(i)-qïn, name of a chief of the Ho-lan horde, *Wei Shu* 2, *sub* 397, cf. 28.

8. Fu-lo-han 扶羅韓 [KD 41, 569, 299: b'iu-lâ-γân] < *bulaγan, name of a Hsien-pi chief, *San kuo chih* 30. This transcription may represent mo. bulaγan—' sable.' The latter word, however, may in itself be derived from bulγa—' mottled ' [animal] > ' sable ' — bulaγan.[65]

9. Finally, several transcriptions of the name of two T'o-pa clans registered in *Wei Shu* 113 and *T'ung Chih* 29:

a. Pu-lu-ku 步陸孤 [KD 573, 426: b'uo liuk-kuo]; Pu-lu-ku 步鹿孤 [b'uo-luk-kuo]; Pu-liu-ku 步六孤 [KD 563: b'uo-liuk-kuo] < *buluqu ~ *bulqu.

b. Pu-lu-kên 步鹿根 [b'uo-luk-kən] and Pu-lu-chin 步鹿斤 [KD 385: b'uo-luk-kiən] < *bulqïn.[66]

Pei Shih 8; cf. A. PFIZMAIER, Nachrichten aus der Geschichte der nördlichen Thsi, p. 3, in *Denkschriften of the Vienna Academy*, 1884. He was the ninth son of Kao Huan and the fourth sovereign of the Northern Ch'i dynasty. The fact that at the age of eight he was betrothed by his father with a Juan-juan princess may explain his nickname.

[64] K'u-jên had a third name, Lo-ch'ui 洛垂 < lâk-źʷie < *alaγči? K'u-jên represents undoubtedly tk. *qoyin ~ qonin — ' sheep ' [*HJAS* 1. 171]. The history of the latter word in tk. mo. is of peculiar interest cf. latter tk. qozï vs. mo. quča, quraγan < quřaγan ~ quzaγan? Compare with the last the Chinese transcriptions of a T'o-pa surname: 庫若干 ~ 俟官 < *quźyaqan. Might, then, 賀若 which we equated with *ayaγ in *HJAS* 1. 178 represent tk. *arïγ — ' pure,' ' honest '?

[65] On which see PELLIOT, *JA* 1927, I. 283 and *BSOS* 6. 562.

[66] The second member of all these triliteral compounds (liuk, luk, lâk) may represent nothing but the -l- of the ' altaic ' original as in the case of A-liu-tun

The above ending *ku* is apparently the same that appears in Tu-ku 獨孤 [cf. note 44] and in Wu-lu-ku 烏路孤 [KD 577 : *'uo-luo-kuo*], the transcription of a name found frequently among the nomads. This name was borne by the Hsiung-nu chief T'ieh-fu Liu Hu,[67] the son of a Kao-shêng-yüan and a Hsien-pi woman. In Wu-lu-ku [as well as Lu-ku, the name of K'u-jên's father] we may have a T'o-pa nickname derived from the tk. mo. term *uruq* — 'family,' 'relative by marriage,' cognate of both *uq* — 'family,' 'clan' and *urï* — 'offspring,' 'seed.'[68]

The exact relationship of these roots with another 'altaic' term designating the offspring of a mixed marriage, the celebrated appellation *argon* (<*arγun**ărγun*?) of Marco Polo, can be established only by specialists. We have previously called attention to an early transcription of this term in *Ho-lu-hun* 賀鹿渾 ⟨*γâ-luk-γi̯uən*, the name of a prominent T'o-pa official of the fifth century.[69] It reappears in the cognomen of Kao Huan 高歡[70] which was, according to *Pei Ch'i Shu* 1, Ho-liu-hun 賀六渾 [*γâ-li̯uk-γi̯uən*]. Huan's nickname is undoubtedly explained by the fact that, although a Chinese by descent, he was raised on the frontier among Hsien-pi, his family having for generations resided in marginal territory.

I am inclined, moreover, to see the same 'altaic' term in the following transcriptions :

1. 阿鹿桓 [KD 1, 841 : *'â-luk-γuân*], a T'o-pa surname, *Wei Shu* 113.

2. The name of the Wu-lo-hou 烏洛侯 [*'uo-lâk-γəu*] tribe, *ibid.* 100, also called Wu-lo-hun 渾.

3. The name of the Lu-hun 鹿渾 [*luk-γi̯uən*] lake in Mongolia, *ibid.*

阿六敦 ⟨ tk. **altun* — 'gold' which appears in *Pei Ch'i Shu*, ch. 17 as the 'barbarian' cognomen of Ho-lü Chin 斛律金 [Chin. 金 = 'gold']. Cf. PFIZMAIER, *op. cit.* pp. 48-53. Some of these transcriptions may also reflect mo. *bülü* — 'family' [maternal line], *bülüken* — 'weak,' and *bülük* — 'company,' 'troop.' The relation of the last to Chinese *pu-lo* 部落 deserves special investigation.

[67] The interpretation of T'ieh-fu is still uncertain [cf. *HJAS* 1. 170]. Shiratori's suggestions, *Izv.* 6 and *SZ* 22: 12, 1381, are not satisfactory. As a mere possibility, cf. mo tataburi — 'hybrid.'

[68] *Uruq* appears probably in Hsiung-nu *yü-lu* 於陸 ⟨**'uo-li̯uk, Chin Shu* 97. I am inclined to believe, with Ligeti, that from *uq ~ oq* is derived, as a plural form, the name *Oγuz ~ Oγur*.

[69] *HJAS* 1. 176-177. Pu-lu-ku Ho-liu-hun's biography [*Wei Shu* 40] contains the amusing anecdote of his future father-in-law, who was otherwise quite pleased with the groom, complaining that his prospective son-in-law had an impossibly polysyllabic name.

[70] Pht. Shên-wu 神武 Ti, 496-547 A. D. *Pei Ch'i Shu* 1-2, *Pei Shih* 7.

103, and the Ho-hun 渦渾 [*'ât ~ *âr-ɣi̯uən*] river, *Shih-liu kuo ch'un-ch'iu* 86.[71]

4. Finally, in the name of another hybrid marginal people, the well known Wu-huan 烏桓 [*'uo-ɣuân*] or Wu-wan 烏丸 [*'uo-ɣuân*], *Hou Han Shu* 120, *San Kuo chih* 30, cf. also *HJAS* 1. 172.[72] The Wu-huan, as all Chinese sources bear witness, reckoned their descent on the mother's side only, or, in nomadic terminology, recognized essentially the *uruq* as the only social unit in their organization. The restoration of the original represented by " Wu-huan " is difficult. Normally going back to *'uo-ɣuân*, the bionom could also be read **âr-ɣuân*.[73]

In connection with *bulaq ~ bulan*, our attention is drawn to tk. *alaq ~ alan*, the second form of which appears in the name of the Ho-lan 賀蘭 [KD 512: *ɣâ-lân*] Hsien-pi tribe.[74] This tribe played a consider-

---

[71] Cf. the name of the river Argun in present Mongolia. Possibly also Orkhon. The relation of Orkhon to *Warkhonitai, the real name of the Pseudo-Avars [suggested by Marquart] and the possible connection of both with *argun constitutes a problem in itself, to which we hope to return soon.

[72] Of the language of the Wu-huan only one word can be identified with surety. This is *chü-chüeh* 句決 < **ki̯u-ki̯ʷet* — 'braided hair' [*San kuo chih* 30] < mo. *kükül* — '*id.*' On this word in mongol cf. PELLIOT, *JA* 1930, pp. 258-259.

[73] That KD 1288 烏 *'uo* possessed in the archaic language a final consonant is suggested by the following: a) *'uo* in the meaning 'what,' 'how' is undoubtedly the cognate of 安 *'ân*, 曷 *ɣât*, and 害 *ɣât* which, together with 何 *ɣâ*, probably go back to ***ɣâr*; b) both *'uo* and its original form 於 built phonetic derivatives, notably with classifiers 75, 86, 169, which are pronounced **'ât **'uət* [cf. 安 *'ân* with Nos. 85, 64, 30 and 64, all pronounced **'ât*]; c) 烏 itself was, according to an early scholiast, quoted by Yen Shih-ku in *Han Shu*, ch. 96, pronounced **an* in the transcription of the name of a Turkestan kingdom. Cf. *TP* 1936, pp. 276-280, where Professor Pelliot explains this gloss as based on an original reading of 焉 *'i̯än* instead of 烏 in pursuance of his theory of the graphic confusion of these two characters. In the course of his able argument, Pelliot does not, however, take cognizance of the fact that 焉 *'i̯än* could itself go back to **'i̯är*, especially in the transcription of a foreign word [cf. 安 in 安息 < **Arsak*]. *'i̯än*, as is well known, is a synonym, and undoubtedly a cognate, of both 安 and 於, and is sometimes pronounced 夷 **i ~ iei*; *-i ~ -n* in *Auslaut* indicates strongly an archaic *-r*; we suspect that in the case of the Chinese transcription of the native name of mod. Qarashahr [Yen-ch'i 耆 <*i̯än-g'ji*] *yen* transcribes indeed a foreign phoneme with *-r* and it is in a central-asiatic root **yär- ~ *yör-* that we should look for an etymology of the old name of the oasis city; its Sanskrit name *agni* — 'fire' is probably a translation of the local designation which was possibly 'shiny' ~ 'fiery.' One should also note that 烏, in the light of the above discussion, is probably a cognate of 燕 *yen* < *'ien* — 'swallow,' both being derivatives from **'ier ~ *'ien* — 'black,' 'dark.'

[74] Cf. Ho-la 賀賴 < *ɣâ-lât*, the name of one of the nineteen tribes of Hsiung-nu that crossed the frontier into China in 287 A. D., *Chin Shu* 97. In **alat* we un-

able rôle in the history of the early T'o-pa and was closely related to them through a series of marriage alliances that continued all through the fourth century.[75] Its name is said to be derived from that of a mountain chain [undoubtedly the modern Ala (< Alaɣ) shan]. According to the Chinese, the Ho-lan mountains were thus called because of the variegated grass covering their slopes which from afar presented the appearance of a coat of a mottled or dapple horse.[76]

It was an established tradition among the Chinese historians to derive the name of a nomadic people from the name of a mountain which marked their place of habitat. There is scarcely any doubt that the derivation occurred in the reverse order, the tribe giving its name to the locality. We have abundant evidence, on the other hand, to indicate that all through the steppe region tribes often derived their appellations from the color of their horses.[77]

Alan as the name of a tribe would suggest that their horses were dapple. It is significant that in the short T'u-chüeh vocabulary preserved in the *T'ung Tien* 197 the Turkish term for 'horse' is transcribed *ho lan* 賀蘭 < *alan*, while, from the linguistic material of the Orkhon inscriptions, we should expect *at*. The dapple coat of a horse, whether piebald, skewbald, or striped, is obviously the result of the crossing of various breeds. Like

---

doubtedly have a 'mongol' plural in -*t*, a regular formation from a singular in -*n*. An interesting case of an irregular -*t* plural is found in the Chinese transcription of the 'barbarian' name of a cave in Lung-chih 龍支 *hsien* (Kansu). According to *T'ai-p'ing huan-yü chi* 151. 10a, it was inhabited by fairies and avoided on that account by the local Ch'iang and Hu who called it T'ang-shu 唐述 < *d'âng-*źiuet which in their language meant 鬼 'ghost,' 'supernatural apparition.' *d'âng-źiuĕt* represents undoubtedly *tangsut* a 'mongol' plural of tk. mo. *tangsuq* — 'wonder,' 'supernatural thing.' It is with the latter term that K. Shiratori [*SZ* XXI, 1017-1018], followed by FANG Chuang-yao [*Hsien-pi yü-yen k'ao* 鮮卑語言考, *YCHP* 1930, pp. 1440-1441], has attempted to equate the original of "T'an-shih-huai" [on which, cf. *HJAS* 1. 168]. See also notes 77, 80.

[75] To-pa I-huai, Shih[-chün], and Kuei married Ho-lan women, while daughters of Yü-lü and Shih-i-chien became the wives of Ho-lan chiefs. The struggle between the Ho-lan and the Mu-jung hordes for domination over their T'o-pa relatives explains many an upheaval in early Wei history.

[76] See *T'ai-p'ing huan-yü chi* 36. 14a, *Yüan-ho chüan-hsien chih* 4. 4a; CHAVANNES, *Documents* ... p. 56 note.

[77] Cf. the name of a Turkish tribe, the Po-ma 駮馬 [Chin. 'dapple horses'] which was also known as O-lo-chih 遏羅支 < '*ât-lâ-tśie* < tk. *allači* [CHAVANNES, *Documents sur les Tou-kiue* ... p. 29, n. 4], or Ho-la 曷剌 < '*ɣât-lât* < tk. *allat* [*T'ung Tien* 200, 10b; *T'ai-p'ing huan-yü chi* 200, 2a, where it is specifically said that *ho-la* meant 'dapple' in T'u-chüeh]. Cf. also the *alakčin* tribe mentioned by Abu'-l-ɣāzi [J. NÉMETH, Die petschenegischen Stammesnamen, in *Ungarische Jahrbücher* 10. 32].

horse, like man; in the life of the steppes, a mixed breed of horses indicates strongly a mixed breed of men. The T'u-chüeh confederacy, controlling at the height of its power the entire stretch of highways that linked China with the West, must have intensified the interbreeding of horses of subject tribes, both consciously, for improvement of the stock, and incidentally, by promoting contact among various tribes, until 'dapple' supplanted in the common terminology the generic term 'horse.'[78]

The convergence of so many terms into single concept 'mixed' should not astonish one. 'Commingling' is indeed the big moment in the historical life of the steppe. Names of nomadic organizations, as well as those of individuals, are built up according to limited number of principles. In the predominant majority of cases they go back to words designating:

1. Birds, beasts, implements, and other familiar objects of the nomad's milieu: in tk. mo *lačïn, qoyïn, noχai* — 'dog,' *γaqai* — 'pig,' *qanglï etc.*, are especially common.[79]

2. Terms of relationship, such as *uruγ, qudu, aqan, oγul.*[80]

3. Official titles; in the case of a tribe, the position of its chief at the khan's court may give the tribe its name. Such are *tilmač, qorčin.*[81]

4. Geographical position or relationship of the individual tribe in respect to a larger unit.[82]

[78] Like **bulaq, alan* may not be a Turkish word originally. The *alan* horses of the Middle Ages may be the same as the 'dragon horses' of antiquity [see note 21] and we must look to Western Turkestan for their place of origin. It is tempting also to seek in *alan* the origin of the ethnic designation Alani.

[79] Articles of apparel gave names to two of the greatest nomadic unions: Hsien-pi 鮮卑 < *Särbi [cf. PELLIOT, *TP* 1921, 331, Karlgren, *op. cit.*, pp. 29-30] is undoubtedly derived from the name of the animal style buckle or fibula so common among the nomads [cf. mo. *serbe* — 'agraffe'] while Mu-jung 慕容 was originally, according to *Chin Shu* ch. 108, the designation of a special form of headgear. Cf. also Pelliot's note in *TP* 1930, p. 49.

[80] *Oγul* appears in a 'mongol' plural form **oγlut* in the name of the Hu-lü 斛律 < *γuk-ljuĕt* clan, found among the Kao-chü and also the T'ieh-lê, while the clan name of the Ho-lien is probably based on *Oγlan* [cf. also Juan-juan Wu-chü-lan 烏句蘭].

[81] Cf. J. NÉMETH, Zur Kenntnis der Petschenegen, *Kőrösi Csoma Archivum* 1. 219-225; *TP* 1930, p. 30; one of the earliest cases on record is that of the Hsiung-nu title *chü-ch'ü* [cf. *supra* note 8] which became the name of the royal clan of the Northern Liang [see *Chin Shu* 129].

[82] *E. g.* the Qurīqan tribe of the Orkhon inscriptions probably owes its name to its western position in respect to the center of the turkish confederacy: cf. *qurïγaru* — 'backward,' 'westward'; the Su-ho 素和 tribe of Hsien-pi to its

5. The color of the tribe's horses.[83]

6. The number of clans or tribes composing a federation, which is then simply called " the Eight," " the Forty " etc.[84]

7. Finally, as we have seen, ' mixture,' ' association of heterogenous elements,' ' hybrid.' [85]

Whatever aristocratic ideals or tendencies may have existed among individual nomadic clans, ' hybridization' was never conceived by the nomad as an evil in itself. The constant formation and desintegration of enormous confederacies promoted inter-breeding in the steppe and especially on its fringe, on the frontiers of the great peripheral civilizations of China, Persia, and Rome. Intermarriage, in peace and war, repeatedly created mixed racial types and individuals who often were, in the words of the Venetian, *plus beaulx hommes que les autres mescréans et plus sages* and who as often obtained *la seigneurie* over their pure-blooded relatives.

The ' mongers ' of Central Asia have always been ' mongrels.' It would seem, therefore, that for a better understanding of the history of the steppe, emphasis should be laid not on ascertaining the location of the ' original home ' of this or that group of nomads, but on investigating the emplacement of this or that politico-geographical crucible from which, mixed with other ingredients, it emerged on the historical scene; not on the study of " the path of migration " of, let us say the Bulgars, from " their ancestral home in Central Asia," but on the analysis of the interplay of forces which produced the *bulɣa* — ' mixture,' without which there could have been no Bulgars.

position to the left of the center [cf. *T'ang Shu* 217B, where Su-ho is translated by Chin. 左]. Distinction is often drawn between the nucleus of a nomadic union and the ' federati,' or occupants of the original pastures and the ' emigrants.' Thus the name of the Tartar is probably derived from tk. *tat-* on which see THOMSEN, *Turcica*, in *Samlede Afhandlinger* 3. 102-105, while the terms *Tölis* and *Tarduš* of the Orkhon inscriptions are based on the second distinction.

[83] See note 77 and J. NÉMETH, *op. cit.* As shown by Marquart in *Über das Volkstum der Komanen* [cf. Pelliot's review of this work in *JA* 1920]. Polovtsĭ [the Russian name of Kumans; germ. Falben] is derived from *palóvyi* — ' fallow,' possibly from the color of their horses. I am inclined to interpret their tk. name as *Qum-man* — ' sand-like,' ' sand-colored ' and كمن انى *quman-aty* [MARQUART, *op. cit.* 58, 64] as ' with sand-colored horses.'

[84] Cf. especially LIGETI, Die Herkunft des Volksnamens Kirgis, *Körösi Csoma Archivum* 1. 369-383.

[85] Another great semi-turkish political organization which derives its name from a term meaning mixed [again one of great antiquity on the Asiatic continent] is that of the Khazars. On the root *Kas, cf. MARQUART [Markwart], Woher stammt der Name Kaukasus? in *Caucasica* 6, esp. p. 29.

Marginalia to the Histories
of the Northern Dynasties

Harvard Journal of Asiatic Studies, 3 (1938), 223-253.
Harvard Journal of Asiatic Studies, 4 (1939), 230-283.

I. THEOPHYLACTUS SIMOCATTA ON CHINA

As is well known, the Byzantine historian Theophylactus Simocatta (VI-VII cc. A. D.) devotes a paragraph of the seventh book
of his *Historiae* [1] to the description of a great kingdom in eastern
Asia which, as has been universally recognized, can only be China.
The information contained in that paragraph, so justly characterized by G. F. HUDSON [2] as "the most intimate glimpse of
China in European literature before Marco Polo," was undoubtedly obtained by the Byzantines from the Turks and is inserted
by Theophylactus into his account of the growth of the Turkish
power in Central Asia as revealed by a diplomatic communication
from the Turkish khan to the court of Constantinople. [3]

This all-important source for the history of Asia during the last
part of the VIth century provides us with the following fifteen
items of information concerning the Middle Kingdom:

1. The country, its people, and its chief city are called Taugast,
Ταυγάστ. [4]

2. The ruler (κλιματάρχης) of Taugast is termed Ταισάν which is
said to mean son of god (υἱὸς θεοῦ).

3. The kingdom is not disrupted by disputed succession, the
latter being hereditary in the family of the ruler.

4. Worship of idols, just laws, and temperate wisdom characterize the inhabitants.

---

[1] 7, 9. Ed. BEKKER, *Corpus Scriptorum Historiae Byzantinae,* v. 46, Bonn 1834, pp.
286-288. Ed. DE BOOR, Leipzig 1887, pp. 260-262.

[2] G. F. HUDSON, *Europe and China,* London 1931, 127.

[3] *Historiae,* 7, 7-8, translated by CHAVANNES, *Documents sur les Tou-kiue occidentaux,*
246-249.

[4] Taugast is referred to by Theophylactus for the first time in 7, 7. On the curious
mistranslation of the passage corrected by CHAVANNES, cf. *op. cit.* 246-247, n. 5.

5. A law enjoins men from wearing gold ornaments, although gold and silver derived through commerce abound in the country.

6. The country is divided in two by a great river forming the boundary between two nations, one wearing clothes dyed black, the other, red (κοκκόβαφος).

7. In the time of Emperor Maurice (582-602), the "black-coats" crossed the river, conquered the "red-(ἐρυθρός) coats," and became masters of the whole empire.

8. The city of Taugast was founded by Alexander the Great after his conquest of the Bactrians and Sogdians.

9. In the city the ruler's women ride in gold chariots drawn by an ox. The women of the nobles use silver chariots.[5]

10. The ruler of Taugast is attended at night (κατεπαννυχίζετο) by seven hundred women.

11. The women mourn the sovereign with shaven heads and in black clothes, and are forbidden to leave the vicinity of his tomb.[6]

12. A few miles away from Taugast is another city called Khubdan (χουβδάν), also said to have been built by Alexander.

13. Two rivers flow through it lined with cypresses.

14. The people of Taugast trade with the Indians[7] and possess many elephants.

15. They rear silkworms and excel in sericulture.

Repeatedly quoted and referred to as a mixture of fact and fiction, the text has never been critically examined in the light of Chinese sources. Most investigators still rely on the briefly annotated translation of the text by H. YULE[8] and limit themselves to repeating his observations which, though quite adequate for a non-sinologist of his day, are misleading when used unjudiciously.

Our analysis might best begin with items 6 and 7, of which the latter, besides providing us with an approximate dating for Simocatta's information, is taken by all commentators as referring to a

---

[5] In the text the last statement follows No. 10.

[6] In the text No. 11 follows No. 12, seemingly indicating that the tombs of the rulers are located in Khubdan, and not in Taugast.

[7] Northern Indians, described as having become white from living in the North. Undoubtedly a reference to the inhabitants of Eastern Turkestan.

[8] *Cathay and the Way Thither*, London 1866, pp. L-LII.

most important event of Chinese history, the re-unification of the northern and southern parts of the empire in 589 A. D. after almost three centuries of disruption.[9]

While, as we shall see later, the passage in question may contain a faint echo of the great campaign of 589 and the establishment of the Sui as masters of the whole of China, in the text of Theophylactus No. 7 is so closely bound with No. 6 and so dependent on it that the interpretation of one hinges absolutely on that of the other. Now reference to the distinct colorings of dress in the two contending nations is usually passed over in silence by students of Theophylactus or dismissed as a mere fable in the telling of which that much-maligned Byzantine scholar is supposed to have taken great delight. The present writer has long suspected that this part of Simocatta's tale, far from being an invention or a vague generalization on the various types of dress affected in different parts of the vast Chinese empire,[10] might be an exact description of the color of military uniforms worn by the contending armies. Search through Chinese texts for the substantiation of this supposition has been long and weary, information cropping up in rather unexpected places and being conspicuous by its absence in the obvious sources, treatises on military organization.

Cuneus cuneum . . . We shall begin by confronting the supposed fable with a would-be idle tale. *Sui shu 23, Wu hsing chih,* relates that CH'ÊN Shu-pao 陳叔寶,[11] the last ruler of the Ch'ên

---

[9] Cf. HUDSON, *loc. cit.*, who, for some reason or other, gives 588 A. D. as the date of the conquest. Sir Percy SYKES (*The Quest for Cathay,* London 1936, p. 61) is apparently merely paraphrasing Hudson, but carelessly writes: . . . " the men of the *south* side crossed the river and, defeating the men on the *north* side, became supreme. Here we have an account of the struggle between the Sui and Ch'ên dynasties which ended in the unification of China under the Sui dynasty in 588." (The italics are mine.) It is no wonder that after such cavalier treatment Theophylactus appears to the above writers as a mere ' recorder of gossip ' (HUDSON) or a ' recorder of tales ' (SYKES).

[10] Cf. YULE, *op. cit.*, n. 4. As we shall see later, however, YULE, with his usual acumen, was on the right track, and had he had access to the Chinese sources, undoubtedly would have solved the problem.

[11] Born Dec. 10, 553; ascended the throne Feb. 20, 582. Made prisoner by the Sui troops in Feb. 589, he died at Ch'ang-an Dec. 16, 604. *Ch'ên shu 6, Nan shih 10.* He has no posthumous title and is known merely as the " Last Ruler," Hou Chu 後主' of Ch'ên.

dynasty, once had a dream where he saw his capital surrounded by men dressed in yellow. Deeply affected by the vision, he had all the orange trees growing near the city walls destroyed, unaware, adds the text, that the dream portended the siege of his capital by the *yellow-robed* army of the Sui. True or false, the story carried a point undoubtedly appreciated by contemporaries. The point of the tale was that CHʻÊN Shu-pao was neither demented nor unmindful of the danger presented to his empire by its powerful neighbor in the north. He did not immediately associate the " yellow men " surrounding his capital with Sui soldiers because (as was undoubtedly understood by those who read or heard the story) he was in the habit of associating his enemy's armies with some other color. Indeed, it was only a few months before his accession to the throne that the newly established Sui emperor,[12] supreme lord of the entire north, decreed that the official color at his court should be red and the color of his army's uniforms, yellow.[13]

We have not been able to ascertain the color of the uniforms of the Chʻên soldiers, but in their color pattern the Chʻên followed the Liang,[14] whose official color was *red* (for ensigns and flags) ; [15] otherwise colors varied according to year, season, and probably point of the compass, as was usual in a tradition-bound Chinese milieu. In the campaign of 589 A.D., therefore, there were " yellow-coats " (the Sui) invading the territory of the red-bannered [16] southern empire, and not " black-coats " conquering an army of red-robed warriors.

The histories of the Northern Dynasties supply us, on the other

[12] Yang Chien 楊堅, pht. Sui Wên Ti (541-581-604 A. D.), *Sui shu* 1-2, *Pei shih* 11, ascended the throne March 4, 581.

[13] *Sui shu* 1, 12. The edict was promulgated July 21, 581. On August 22, the Emperor appeared for the first time in a yellow uniform. It must have taken several months before the change could be put into effect throughout the empire.

[14] *Sui shu* 12.

[15] Supplanting green which was the color of the banners of the preceding dynasty of Southern Chʻi. *Sui shu* 10. 1a.

[16] If the Chʻên followed in any way the usual scheme of cosmological colors, they would have adopted as their distinctive color, yellow or white, which correspond to earth and metal, either of which follows red fire in the order of elements. Yellow would have been preferable to white, the color of mourning.

hand, with numerous bits of evidence that black and red (of at least two different shades) were the official colors of the uniforms of the two Northern states of Chou and Ch'i, successors, respectively, of the western and eastern Wei, which had carried on from the first third of the sixth century a bitter struggle for supremacy over northern China. This rivalry ended in 577 A. D. with the conquest of the red-coats of Ch'i by the black-uniformed armies of Chou. Shortly after, on March 4, 581, the Sui officially supplanted the Chou, but did not change the established form of military dress until some four months later. The testimony of the Chinese sources contains both sober fact and faithfully recorded phantastic stories of colorful (ὡς ἔπος εἰπεῖν, as Theophylactus would say) portents.

We shall first paraphrase a passage from *Pei Ch'i shu 2, Pei shih* 6, which gives an account of the last campaign of Kao Huan 高歡, the powerful major-domo of the Eastern Wei. On October 3, 546 A. D. Kao Huan broke the armistice that had reigned for three years (spring 543-546) between the two hostile halves of the Wei empire. Establishing his headquarters at Chin-yang 晉陽, he made preparations for descending the valley of the Fên. In the ninth month (sometime after October 11) he laid siege to the city of Yü-pi 玉璧 [17] which barred his road to the west. Yü-pi, ably defended by Wei Hsiao-k'uan 韋孝寬,[18] successfully withstood a series of fierce attacks, and some two months later, Kao Huan, disheartened and sick, was forced to abandon the siege and the campaign, having lost in the undertaking some 70,000 men.[19] On February 13, 547, he died.[20]

---

[17] Situated in the vicinity of modern Chi-shan 稷山, on the Fên river, Shansi.

[18] *Chou shu* 31, *Pei shih* 64, 509-580 (died Dec. 17, according to *Chou shu* 8).

[19] 20-30% of his army (*Chou shu* 2); 40-50%, according to *Chou shu* 31.

[20] On the *ping wu* day of the 1st month of Wu-ting 5 of Hsiao ching Ti of Eastern Wei, *Ch'i shu* 2, *Chou shu* 2, *Pei shih* 6, *Wei shu* 12, *Pei shih* 5. In the 2nd month of Ta-t'ung 13 of Wên Ti of Western Wei, according to another entry in *Pei shih* 5. The discrepancy is explained by the fact that news of his death was suppressed and mourning was officially proclaimed only on July 19, 547 (*Ch'i shu* 2) or July 22, 547 (*Wei shu* 12), the difference of three days to be disregarded as the first gives us the beginning, the second, the end of the period of court mourning, Kao Huan left particular instructions to his son not to make an official announcement of his death until he was sure to be in full control of the situation in Eastern Wei. The news must

The disastrous end of that brief campaign had been vainly predicted to KAO Huan, says the *Ch'i shu*, by one of his officers, Ts'AO Wei-tsu 曹魏祖. Besides, KAO Huan passed unheeded another warning. Ever since the beginning of the wars between the eastern and western Wei, it had been observed that prior to the start of a campaign black and yellow Formicidae would stage a battle in phalanxes under the walls of Yeh, the capital of the eastern Wei. Prognosticators considered that the black ants represented the western Wei whose military uniforms were black, and the yellow ants the eastern Wei whose troops dressed in yellow. The populace used to predict the outcome of a campaign on the basis of the ants which triumphed. On that occasion the yellow ants had been exterminated, presaging dire results for KAO Huan's undertaking.

Pei Ch'i shu 49, *Pei shih* 89, supply us with another story. During the Mang-shan 邙山 campaign in the spring of 543 A.D., KAO Huan had in his service a Taoist by the name of CH'I-WU Huai-wên 綦母懷文.[21] That worthy pointed out to KAO Huan that, the latter's banners being red, he had little chance to prevail against the black ones of the Western Wei (black being the color of the water element which conquers the red of fire) and suggested that they be changed to yellow ones (yellow earth being triumphant over water). KAO Huan followed his advice and ordered the banners dyed in ocher.[22]

Liang shu 5, under Ch'êng-shêng 3, relates that in the sixth month of that year (on August 12, 554) a black vaporous emanation in the form of a dragon appeared in the palace. *Sui shu* 23 repeats the story, adding that black being the color of the Chou,

---

have leaked out, for Hou Ching 侯景 of whose loyalty KAO Huan was especially doubtful, rebelled on February 18, and surrendered to the Western Wei (*Ch'i shu* 3, *Wei shu* 12, *Pei shih* 5). It would appear from *Wei shu* 108, 4, 8a that it was the Wei emperor who betrayed the secret.

[21] The *Ch'i shu* text appears to be the primary source, as KAO Huan is referred to by his temple name, Kao-tsu, and the Eastern Wei army is spoken of as 官軍, "the government army."

[22] Ocher yellow 赭黄, probably an orange shade of yellow, produced by dyeing the originally red silk yellow. The text adds that the banners became known as Ho-yang 河陽 banners.

the portent presaged the subsequent terrible invasion of Liang by the northerners. The same *Sui shu* chapter tells us that in 547 dragons were observed fighting in a river, after which a white dragon fled south pursued by a black one. The latter was recognized as a symbol of Hou Ching, the traitorous adventurer then in the service of the western Wei, who in the autumn of that year surrendered to Liang Wu Ti.[23]

According to the same source, in 568 A. D. the death of a yellow dragon, found in a tree and inadvertently wounded by a wood-cutter, presaged the death of the Ch'i sovereign in that very year.[23a] In 576 they observed in Ch'i a desperate fight between a *red* serpent and *black* one resulting after several days in the death of the red serpent. The fall of Ch'i followed the next year. During the same twelvemonth a black dragon fell down from the sky and died in Chou, indicating clearly that the end of the Chou themselves was near. In both passages the editors are careful to indicate that the colors symbolize the respective dynasties. In 573 in Ch'ên black clouds were interpreted as predicting a victory for the Chou, which supposedly followed in the next year.[24] In 577 in Chou (*Sui shu* 23) three animals resembling water buffaloes were observed, one yellow, one red, one black. The black ox and the red one had been fighting for a long time, when the *yellow* one gored the black from the side so that it died. After this the yellow and red animals disappeared into the river. Again the text explicitly states that the yellow ox symbolizes the yellow uniforms of the Sui, while the red one stands for their flags. Judging from the context (the black ox fighting the red one), the red animal symbolizes the Ch'i as well. On March 27, 580, record

---

[23] He had been in the service of the Western Wei less than six months. For his biography see *Liang shu* 56, *Nan shih* 80.

[23a] That of KAO Chan, the "abdicated ruler" of Ch'i. The "dragon" was probably some rare lizard.

[24] Scattering, the clouds formed shapes resembling pigs. According to *Sung shu* 33, the pig is the symbol of the barbarians of the North. The Chou victory is said to be that of WANG Kuei 王軌 (*Chou shu* 40) over the famous and heretofore seemingly invincible WU Ming-ch'ê 吳明徹 (*Ch'ên shu* 9) of Ch'ên. There must be some mistake in dating, however, as WU Ming-ch'ê's defeat took place in 578 A. D. (*Chou shu* 6, *Ch'ên shu* 5).

the annals of Chou (*Chou shu* 7), adjutant birds perched in front
of the recently completed T'ai chi 太極 palace in Lo yang, while
near Yung chou a black dragon was seen fighting a red one, the
combat resulting in the death of the former. There is no doubt
that in the mind of the historians the red dragon and the red
caruncles on the adjutants' heads were portents of the inevitable
triumph of the Sui. The maniacal last emperor of the Ch'i, *Pei
shih* 8, *Pei Ch'i shu* 8, used to have fortifications erected and,
ordering people to dress in black and attack the forts, he would
shoot at them with arrows while pretending that they were Chou
troops.[25] During the reign of the same sovereign, a mad śramana
of Ch'i is said (*Sui shu* 23) to have been wandering about making
obeisances to black crows and insulting Buddhist monks, obviously presaging the extinction of the Ch'i by the Chou and the
persecution of Buddhism by the latter.[26]

The above evidence indicates sufficiently that between c. 543
and 577 the western Wei (Chou) and the eastern Wei (Ch'i)
troops were clearly distinguished by the color of their uniforms,
those of the first being black, and those of the second, red or
yellow, and that these color associations were firmly established
in ominal lore and in the popular mind. The color patterns
affected by the two rival Chinese states must have been well
known to the Turks who were in intimate contact with both
powers, and there is thus no doubt that the famous passage in
Theophylactus Simocatta's text refers primarily to events in
Northern China. The river dividing the two nations is thus undoubtedly the Yellow river, and not the Yangtse, as generally
believed, the "black-coats" are the Chou, and the "red-coats,"
the Ch'i.

The conquest of the Ch'i took place, however, in 577 A. D., a
year which would fall in the reign of Justin II, and not in that

---

[25] Literally, Ch'iang 羌 troops. Under the Northern Dynasties Ch'iang was a
popular name for the inhabitants of Shensi and whatever power occupied that territory.

[26] Yü-wên Yung 宇文邕 (Kao-tsu Wu Huang-ti of Chou 543-561-578 A. D., *Chou
shu* 5-6), an ardent anti-Buddhist and anti-Taoist, proscribed both religions and ordered
their statues and books destroyed (edict promulgated June 21, 574). The persecution
continued until his death, but both faiths were re-established in favor in 579 during
the reign of his son Yü-wên Pin 贇 (pht. Hsüan Ti, 559-579-580).

of Maurice. Two explanations of the discrepancy are possible. Simocatta's information came unquestionably from turkish sources, either from the famous letter of khan Tardou to Emperor Maurice [27] or from data collected for the Constantinople chancelleries by Byzantine ambassadors to the Turks. News of the conquest of Ch'i, which was completed in February-March 577, may have been conveyed by the Turks to Valentinus [28] who, as is not improbable, was still in territory controlled at that time by the Khan. If the account of the events of 577 had been included in Tardou's letter of 598, the Ch'i conquest may have been dated in the original document as having occurred in the time of the reigning Khan, *i. e.* Tardou. Now Tardou's reign being practically synchronous with that of Maurice (576-c.603 *vs.* 582-602),[29] it is possible that the Byzantine translators or commentators of the document substituted the name of the sovereign of the Romans for that of the barbarian ruler.

On the other hand, the conquest of Ch'ên by the Sui in 589 A. D. could not have passed unnoticed by the Turks. The story of Sui Wên Ti presenting to the Turkish ambassadors [30] his great general HAN Ch'in-hu 韓擒虎 [31] as the mighty conqueror of the empire south of the Yangtse has become famous in Chinese literature. Though it was only events in northern China that were of primary interest to the Turks, one might conceive that the latter also transmitted news of happenings farther south. One should, however, imagine the bewilderment of the Foreign Office at Constantinople on being informed that in a far-off land "black-coats," having disposed of "red-coats," turned red (or yellow) themselves

[27] This is a natural supposition based on the order of narration in the text of Theophylactus. It is not, however, binding, as the paragraph dealing with Taugast can also be interpreted as being an independent appendix to the substance of the khan's communication.

[28] According to Menander (ed. BEKKER and NIEBUHR, *Corpus* . . . , v. 19, Bonn 1829, 397-398), Valentinus left Constantinople sometime in 576. His journey to Ektel and back must have taken at least two years, probably more, as he was detained for a considerable time at the khan's court. Cf. CHAVANNES, *Documents* . . . , 239-241.

[29] On Tardou's dates, cf. CHAVANNES, *op. cit.*, 48-51.

[30] Probably in 591 A. D. when two important embassies from the Turks arrived at Ch'ang-an, *Sui shu 2*.

[31] Also called HAN Ch'in (the last character *hu* being taboo in T'ang texts), 538-592, *Sui shu 52*.

and subsequently proceeded to make war on some more "red-(or non-descript) coats," first crossing one mighty river from west to east, then a mightier one from north to south, etc. We cannot blame the poor clerks for being satisfied with the first half of the story and either dismissing the rest entirely or lumping the two accounts together and twisting their chronology slightly in the process.

It is thus more likely that Simocatta's account of Taugast deals fundamentally with northern China just prior to and immediately after 577 and describes primarily the state of affairs in Chou and Ch'i, most probably ante-dating the establishment of the Sui. Item No. 10 here becomes pertinent to our discussion. The enormous number of female attendants that Theophylactus attributes to the ruler of Taugast does not tally at all with what we know of the character and the court organization of Sui Wên Ti, the conqueror of Ch'ên. He is reputed to be the only monogamist among Chinese emperors,[32] and the number of palace women of rank during his reign did not exceed fifty before his wife's death in 601 A.D. and one hundred and twenty after that date.[33] It is true, on the other hand, that Chou Wu Ti, the Chou emperor under whom the subjugation of Ch'i was achieved, favored also stringent regulations limiting the number of ranking women attendants and is said to have curtailed the list at one time to no more than a dozen.[34] His successor, however, was as extravagant as the profligate emperors of Ch'i. He had his empire searched for the most beautiful women to be taken into the palace as concubines and attendants, built lavishly decorated quarters for them, and increased the number of ranks and titles for women to a hitherto unknown degree.[35]

---

[32] YANG Chien is said to have sworn to his wife, Empress Wên-hsien 文獻 (553-602), daughter of *Tu-ku* Hsin 獨孤信 (503-557, *Chou shu* 16) whom he married in 566 that he would never be unfaithful to her. He broke his promise but once, the unfortunate object of his affection being immediately murdered by the jealous empress, and took unto himself concubines only after her death. As TU-KU Hsin himself is said to have betrothed his daughter to YANG Chien, we seem to have in this case an interesting instance of child marriage. *Sui shu* 36.

[33] *Sui shu* 36, introduction.

[34] Cf. the end of his biography. Also edict in 11th month of 577, *Chou shu* 6.

[35] *Chou shu* 7. Cf. 5th month of 579.

On the side of the Ch'i, the last sovereign's (KAO Hui) insane extravagance in distributing ranks and official emoluments to his women has become proverbial in Chinese history. Over 500 palace ladies are mentioned as attending him at table or levee.[36] But it is in his father's (KAO Chan) biography that we find an indication that Theophylactus' information was amazingly accurate. It is again a supernatural story that supplies us with the evidence. In the third month of 565 A. D., relate *Pei shih* 8 and *Ch'i shu* 7, a ghost described as very corpulent, with face indistinct but with two white tusks protruding from his lips, appeared in the park of the imperial palace. The emperor himself saw it only in a dream, but the vision was attested by the seven hundred palace women attending the emperor at night.

Passing on to item No. 9 which describes briefly the chariots of the noble women of Taugast, we must note that the description agrees more with what little we know of the official regulations of the Ch'i (rather than the Chou). Chariots decorated with gold (gilding or inlay) were in common use at the courts of all dynasties; the minute regulations covering every type of vehicle and the pattern of decoration have been preserved in dynastic histories, and those of the period under consideration are found in *Sui shu* 10.[37] The Chou ceremonial is quite complicated; only some vehicles for women are said to be drawn by oxen, the majority of palace chariots being described as horse-drawn. For the Ch'i only few details are given, but among them we find that princesses of the blood (公主 kung chu) rode in varnished chariots, both chariots and oxen being decorated with gilt and solid silver. At the same time while gold decorations are said to be prescribed for chariots of officers of higher rank, those of lower rank could use only copper which would indicate that there existed a definite gradation in the use of different metals according to official position. The distinction that Simocatta's text draws between the women of the ruler and those of the nobles could thus well have been based on reality. In addition, according to the *Sui shu*, the regulations of the Wei[38] (on which those of Ch'i

---

[36] *Pei shih* 8, *Pei Ch'i shu* 8. [37] Cf. also as a convenient reference *T'ung tien* 65.
[38] Dating from 516 A. D., *Wei shu* 108, 4.

were based) allowed but one horse or ox for the chariots of nobles below the rank of *wang*; the Chou rules seem to have permitted the use of teams.

The use of gold for decorating men's chariots does not conflict with the supposed law which prevailed according to Theophylactus in Taugast (item No. 3), prohibiting men the use of gold ornaments, as it would seem that καλλωπίζεσθαι of the text applies only to personal adornment. We can find no mention in Chinese sources of such a law obtaining either in Chou or Ch'i, unless it refer to one of the insane regulations issued by the megalomaniac Chou Hsüan Ti (Yü-wên Pin) who ordered all his officers to remove the golden clasps from their hats, lest his own resplendent imperial majesty suffer from lack of contrast in adornment with the court surrounding him. With less probability we may have here an allusion to the activities of Hsüan Ti's father, Wu Ti (Yü-wên Yung) of Chou, a much more sympathetic character, but, as we have already noted, definitely inclined towards puritanism. He is said to have used no gold or jewelry personally, ordered the destruction of many elaborate palaces and buildings, notably in the conquered territory of Ch'i, and prohibited architectural decorations. There is, however, so far as we have been able to discover, no record of his having promulgated sumptuary laws regulating the personal appearance of his subjects. It is, however, not unthinkable that wearing no gold ornaments himself, he did not allow his officers to indulge in this extravagance.

Items No. 3 and No. 4 require no special comment. Worshipping of statues (ἀγάλματα) refers, of course, particularly to Buddhism which was stronger in Ch'i than in Chou, while undisputed (officially) succession, just laws, and σωφροσύνη of the inhabitants can be said to be natural clichés which nomads would use to describe a thickly settled, highly civilized, and orderly (even in those troubled days) country like China.

The name of the ruler of Taugast given in item No. 2 presents, however, unusual interest. Since the day of KLAPROTH ταισάν translated by the Byzantine writer " son of God " has been supposed to be a corruption (either by the author or a copyist) of Chinese *t'ien-tzŭ* 天子—" Son of Heaven." J. MARQUART, who was well acquainted with Theophylactus' work and quotes it repeatedly, boldly emended ταισάν into *τανσαι and even used this emendation as a basis for tampering with the transcription of a foreign title in Armenian.[39] YULE hesitatingly suggested T'ai-tsung 太宗,[40] the temple name of the great sovereign of the T'ang dynasty. As universally recognized, this is out of the question, as the T'ang emperor became known under that title only after his death in 649 A.D., and there is absolutely no evidence that Simocatta wrote (or even lived) beyond that date.

Now ταισάν represents a most faithful transcription of Chinese *t'ai shang* 太上, an imperial title with an interesting history and especially frequent in our period. The title *t'ai shang* was created by Liu Pang, the founder of the Han dynasty, for the purpose of honoring his father.[42] Between 300 and 630 A.D., Chinese histories register the following cases of its application as the title of an abdicated emperor, usually one whose son officially rules in his stead:

1. On February 4, 301, Ssŭ-MA Lun 倫 [41a] deposed the imbecile Ssŭ-MA Ch'ung 衷 (Hui Ti of Chin 259-290-306). On the next day, having imprisoned the fallen emperor in the citadel of Chin-yung, he conferred upon him the title of *t'ai shang: Chin shu* 4.

2. About January 400 A.D., Lü Kuang 呂光, ruler of Hou Liang 後梁, abdicated in favor of his son Shao 紹 and adopted himself the title of *t'ai shang*. He died a day or so later: *Shih-liu kuo ch'un-ch'iu* 81, *Chin shu* 10, *Wei shu* 2, *Chin shu* 122.[42]

3. On September 21, 471, To-PA Hung 弘 (Hsien-tsu Hsien-wên Ti 顯祖獻文 of Wei, 454-466-471-476) having abdicated in favor of his son, accepted the title *t'ai shang*, urged upon him by

[39] *Ungarische Jahrbücher* 9, 100-101.

[40] *Op. cit* (in note 8), L, n. 3, LI, n. 2. In order to justify his equation, Yule suggests that Theophylactus might have inserted the supposed name of T'ai Tsung at a time later than 628, the chronological terminus of his work.

[41] In 201 B.C., *Shih chi* 8, *Han shu* 1 B. Already in 221 Ch'in Shih Huang-ti had used the title to honor posthumously his own father Chuang-hsiang Wang 莊襄王 of Ch'in (249-247 B.C.), *Shih chi* 6.

[41a] Biography in *Chin shu* 59.

[42] Three years previously, nearing the sixtieth year of his life, Lü Kuang had assumed the title of *t'ien wang* 天王.

his officers as a suitable designation for the father of a reigning emperor. Lɪᴜ Pang's father's holding of the title was pointed out as a precedent. Tʻᴏ-ᴘᴀ Hung continued to be known as *tʻai shang* until his death on July 20, 476: *Wei shu* 6.

4. On June 8, 565, Kᴀᴏ Chan of Chʻi abdicated in favor of his son.[43] He assumed the title of *tʻai shang* retaining it until his death on January 13, 569: *Chʻi shu* 7-8, *Pei shih* 8.

5. On February 4, 577 Kᴀᴏ Hui of Chʻi, his son, who had abdicated his tottering throne to his son, was given the title of *tʻai shang*. He was captured 24 days later by Chou troops: *Pei shih* 8, *Chʻi shu* 8, *Chou shu* 6.

6. On April 1, 579, Yü-wᴇ̂ɴ Pin of Chou abdicated in favor of his son and assumed the title of *tʻien yüan* 天元 *huang-ti*, specially created for the occasion. It was apparently Pin's megalomania which made him dissatisfied with the traditional appelation. He spent the remainder of his life elaborating regulations and inventing fitting titles for his empresses and now super-exalted entourage and died in June 580.[44] It is quite likely that during this period his subjects and foreign ambassadors, unable to follow the wild vagaries of his title-obsessed mind, called him by the traditional name for " abdicated " emperors: *Chou shu* 7, *Pei shih* 10.

7. On April 2, 586, Sui Wᴇ̂ɴ Ti is urged through the petition of a certain Kᴀᴏ Tê [44a] 高德 to abdicate the throne to his son and assume the title of *tʻai shang*. He refuses to follow the precedent established during the two preceding dynasties and relinquish the responsibilities of his high office: *Sui shu* 1, *Pei shih* 11.[45]

8. On December 17, 617, Lɪ Yüan (the future Tʻang Kao-tsu), having captured Chʻang-an and set up a puppet regime with Yang Yu 侑 as emperor, conferred upon Sui Yang Ti, the reigning sovereign and father of the boy, the title of *Tʻai shang*: *Sui shu* 4-5, *Pei shih* 12.

---

[43] Prompted, it is said, by astrological considerations.   [44] See note 95.

[44a] Note that, judging from his surname, that individual was a member of the former royal clan of Chʻi.

[45] Observe, however, that Yᴀɴɢ Chien changes his *nien-hao* to 仁壽 *Jên-shou* in 600 when he was *sixty* years old and demotes his heir-apparent. He undoubtedly feared that he would be forcibly made *tʻai shang* because he had completed a full cycle of life. Hence, we believe, the *shou* " (continuous) long life " in his new *nien-hao*.

9. On September 3, 626, Li Yüan himself was forced to abdicate in favor of his son, Li Shih-min.[46] He was proclaimed *t'ai shang*, a title he continued to bear until his death on June 25, 635: *Chiu T'ang shu* 1, *T'ang shu* 1.

It is noteworthy that those of the *t'ai shang* who abdicated voluntarily in favor of young, or even infant, sons reserved for themselves the right to manage important affairs of state, especially matters of foreign policy. Thus, T'o-pa Hung as *t'ai shang* is mentioned as leading in the second and third months of 472 a military expedition against the Juan-juan and the T'ieh-lê; in the winter of 472-473 he again campaigned against the Juan-juan; in the 10th month of 473 he placed himself at the head of an army moving to suppress a rebellion in the south, and in the 10th month of 475 he held a military review, apparently staged for the benefit of Juan-juan envoys (*Wei shu* 7A). Kao Chan appears to have retained almost complete control over state affairs as the majority of edicts issued between 565 and 569, the first part of the nominal reign of his son, were promulgated in his name (as *t'ai shang*). Yü-wên Pin likewise seems to have ruled as *t'ai shang* as arbitrarily as he did before his abdication.

During the period that interests us there were, then, in Northern China three rulers who bore the title of *t'ai shang*: one in Ch'i from 565 to 569, another in the same state for a fortnight in 577, and one in Chou from April 579 to June 580. It is interesting to observe that it is under Kao Chan (particularly in his *t'ai shang* years) that diplomatic relations between Ch'i and the T'u-chüch Turks became intimate. Acutely conscious of the danger to Ch'i of an alliance of the Turks with the Chou, Kao Chan tried desperately to win the Turks over to his side. It appears that in the three last years of his life he succeeded, at least partially, in his purpose, for although the Chou continued on good terms with the Turks, the latter sent embassies to Ch'i in 566,

---

[46] Note again that Li Yüan, who was born in 566, was then sixty years old. His deposition was a foregone conclusion and it merely remained to decide who would be his successor. The murderous conflict between his sons was apparently provoked by the temptation which the tradition that a ruler should not attempt to continue on the throne beyond the appointed three score years offered them.

567, and 568, and there is no doubt that envoys of the Ch'i *t'ai shang* were active at the ordo of the Turkish Khan during the same years.[46a] During the last two years of Chou Hsüan Ti's (Yü-wên Pin) reign the Turks, while continuing diplomatic relations with the Chou, lent their support to the Ch'i pretender Kao Shao-i 高紹義,[47] cousin of the last *t'ai shang* of Ch'i, in his hopeless struggle against the *t'ai shang* of Chou. The Chinese title of "abdicated" emperors who exercised the real power behind the throne was thus well known at the court of the Turkish Khans. The appearance of that title in preference to *t'ien-tzŭ* (or its persian-turkish translation *baɣpur*[48]) in the text of Theophylactus may even give us a clue to the date of the composition of the abstract of information on China prepared by the Turks for the benefit of the Byzantines. The fresh memory of the state of affairs in Ch'i and of the latter's extinction, a *t'ai-shang* (prohibiting wearing of gold ornaments by men) on the throne, and the enormous size of the Taugast ruler's gynaeceum, all tend to indicate that the Turkish brief of information on which Simocatta's text is based, dates from the last years of the Chou dynasty, most probably from the period April 579-June 580.

Professor Pelliot was the first to recognize[49] that Taugast the name under which China appears in our text has its origin in the ethnic designation of the Turkish or Mongol speaking ruling class of the T'o-pa Wei dynasty, the **t'ak-buât* 拓跋 of the Chinese sources. The name is well attested in early Turkish and Central Asiatic documents in the form *Tabɣač* or *Tabqač*, which was also adopted by the Moslem sources.

A primary ethnic name has no etymology. If the social group it designates has had a history of any significance, an ethnic designation early becomes a whole system of linguistic associations

---

[46a] Because of interference by the Ch'i, the marriage of the Chou emperor with a T'u-chüeh princess was delayed from 565 to 568 A. D.: *Chou shu* 9.

[47] *Pei Ch'i shu* 12. He was the third son of Kao Yang. In 577 he refused to lay down arms before the Chou and fled to the Turks. The latter eventually sold him to the Chinese.

[48] On which see particularly G. Ferrand, L'élément persan dans les textes nautiques arabes, *JA* 1924, 243.

[49] *TP* 1912, 792.

of great complexity, pregnant with the memories and hopes of the bearers of the name, and conscious or unconscious reactions of their friends or foes, a magnetic field where forces of self- or mutual induction are constantly at work. Add to it sophisticated scholastic etymologizations which, as soon as they penetrate into the consciousness of the semi-educated, show great tenacity of life (one is almost tempted to say virulence), and we can well imagine how hopeless is any attempt at a simple, unilateral etymological explanation of a given ethnic name. No historically registered interpretation, on the other hand, is valueless, because in the majority of cases such an interpretation, however fanciful or scholastic, originated in the consciousness of a social group or class which, from within or from without, participated in the life of the ethnos bearing the name in question. In case of an ethnic name of considerable antiquity, we shall probably never be able to tell what particular significance such a name originally had, as it is quite probable that the majority of them originated in what one may describe as a henopoetical stage of linguistic development, and the means of research at our disposal can hardly enable us to penetrate beyond the veil of so-called "popular etymology." But for the historian and student of social institutions, after all, to know what people thought a name meant is much more important than to discover what its real significance had been once upon a time.

In *HJAS* 1, 180-185 we reviewed briefly some of the meanings ascribed to *Tabγač ∼ Taugast ∼ *Tʻak-buât. A few additional observations will further reveal the complexity of the problem. To sum up all the material from Chinese sources which the present writer has been able to gather, the name of the Tʻo-pa was given the following interpretations:

1. "Lords of the *Soil*" 土 which, from the context of *Wei shu* 1 where the interpretation is found, could mean: (a) the soil, as one of the Chinese cosmological elements, (b) the soil of the northland. Suggested Turkish forms: *tabaq-či*—"those of the soil," [50] *taγ-baši*—"lords of northland" (lit. mountains).

---

[50] It is not impossible that WEI Shou had also in mind mo. *tabuγat ∼ *tabuγač < √tabu—"five," the "soil" 土 being the fifth of the Chinese five elements.

2. "Slave." This meaning suggested by later Chinese commentators is apparently based on hints dropped by contemporary Chinese sources that the T'o-pa were in some way ashamed of their name as indicative of a low or servile origin. The Turkish original would be in that case *tapïɣčï*—"slave." [51]

3. The Chinese surname Ch'ang-sun 長孫 which was adopted by one of the branches of the T'o-pa clan and which might be translated as "honoring (lit. treating as elder) a grandson," would tend to indicate that some of the T'o-pa preferred to semantize their name as a combination of some form of *tap*—"to honor" + *ači* < **hači* [52]—"grandson."

4. "Braided heads" 索頭 is the usual designation of the T'o-pa in the histories of the southern Chinese dynasties. Possibly based on *tuɣ*—"tail" (which a braid of hair left on top of the skull resembles) + *baš*—"head," as indicated by another transcription of the T'o-pa name, T'u-fa 禿髮 **t'uk-pi̯ʷǝt* (= "bald" + "hair"). [53]

5. T'u-fa was also supposed to mean "covered" or "born in a blanket." The possible origin of this explanation is that **T'ak-buât* was interpreted as a Mongol compound of *toɣ*—"to be born" + *qubča*—"to cover." [54]

6. The fact that the sinicized T'o-pa adopted as their Chinese surname the word 元 Yüan—"original," while the T'u-fa had their name changed to 源 Yüan—"source" [55] (of a river), is another indication that the second syllable of the name T'o-pa was interpreted as containing the Turkish word *baš*—"head," but also "origin," "source of a river." [56]

---

[51] More specifically, "female slave." *Sung shu* 95 and *Nan Ch'i shu* 57 maintain that the T'o-pa were descendants of the Han general Lɪ Lɪɴɢ 李陵 who surrendered to the Hsiung-nu in 99 B.C. and married, according to *Nan Ch'i shu*, a Hsiung-nu woman named T'o-pa 托跋.

[52] On which cf. PELLIOT, Mots à H initiale dans le mongol, *JA* 1925, I, 202-203.

[53] Cf. Kurakichi SHIRATORI, The Queue among the peoples of North Asia, *Memoirs of the Research Department of the Tōyō Bunko*, 4. (1929), 1-70.

[54] The first element could also be *daχu*—"fur-coat" or *toχom*—"saddle-cloth."

[55] Cf. *HJAS* 1, 168.

[56] Several examples of the last in the Orkhon inscriptions. Possibly underlying the Chinese transcription *pa-ssŭ* 跋斯 **b'uât-sï* in 跋斯處折施山 of *Chou shu* 50. Cf. Грумм-Гржимайло, Западная Монголія и Урянхайскій край, vol. II, 209.

7. A purely Chinese and fanciful etymology is suggested by *Wei shu* 1, where the mythical ancestor of the T'o-pa who lived under the legendary emperor Yao won fame by driving out, 逐 *d'iuk*, the she-demon of drought, 魃 *b'uât*.

8. The metallurgical customs of the early T'o-pa and the legends which tell of their boring their way to civilization through mountains lead us to believe that their name was often interpreted as mo. *toᵝuɣači*—" metal-worker " or *dabaɣači*—" they who pass through mountains." [57]

The suggested " turco-mongol " etymologies would indicate that the metathesis of the guttural and the labial in T'ak-b'uât (*vs.* tk. *Tabɣač* which undoubtedly registers more or less faithfully the original " Altaic " name) is not accidental and that on the Chinese frontier *Tabɣač* was often sounded *Taɣbač* or even *Toɣbač*.

Applied by the Turks to the whole of northern China, the name of the T'o-pa was apparently used by them in the sixth century to refer also to the Chinese court and its seat. The proximity of Taugast to Khubdan indicated in No. 12, Khubdan unquestionably referring to the Ch'ang-an district,[58] leaves no doubt as to the fact that it is the capital of Chou that is described in the text of Theophylactus, no mention being made of Yeh, that of Ch'i.

The origin of the name Khubdan or Khumdan as referring to the great western metropolis of China has never been satisfactorily explained. We suggest that the name is a transcription of Chinese Hsien-yang 咸陽, arch. *g'ɒm-dang*,[58a] the name of the old capital of Ch'in and in our period still an important city (the seat of a *chün*) northwest of Ch'ang-an and situated at the confluence of the Wei and the Fêng (cf. in this connection No. 13). The respective situation of Ch'ang-an and Hsien-yang at this particular period is a complex question demanding detailed topographical study. There is no doubt, however, that of the two, Ch'ang-an was at the time farther from the banks of the Wei, and the

---

[57] Cf. *HJAS* 1, 179-183, 185.

[58] Khubdan is the Syriac Kūmdān of the Nestorian Monument and the Khumdān خملان of the Arabic sources.

[58a] Note that, as in *t'ai shang* > taisan, Chinese final -*ng* is rendered by foreign -*n*.

mention by our text of two rivers flowing through the city would apply to Hsien-yang better than to Ch'ang-an.[59] The only difficulty in the way of accepting the derivation of Khumdan from Hsien-yang is that it would presuppose the borrowing of the name sometime in the Han period, while Khumdan is not attested in foreign sources before Simocatta.

The reputed founding of the two cities by Alexander the Great, besides being the usual application of the Alexandrian Saga to a description of a distant foreign land,[60] has two rational explanations. The antiquity of the Hsien-yang district and the approximate date of its founding may well have been known to the informants of the Byzantines. Hsien-yang (and Ch'ang-an, the two together treated as one administrative district) being founded in 349 B. C., the brief Turkish " Baedeker " would have informed the Greeks that the city was some 930 years old in 580 A. D. A quick computation would carry a Greek scholar back to the time of Alexander the Great (with 20 years' approximation, it would give him 329 B. C., the date of the invasion of Bactria). The existence of foreign colonies in Shensi and Kansu[61] would further lend support to the Greeks' belief that the Macedonian's conquests extended as far as China. It is not unthinkable, at the same time, that the Turks themselves, acquainted with at least fragments of the saga of the great conqueror, would have confirmed the above natural supposition of the Greeks. This interesting question deserves, however, special consideration.

Of the remaining items on our list, Nos. 14 and 15 call for no comment, except that in the mention of elephants we have the first positive indication that the information of the Turks extended to districts south of the Yellow river, the wording of the text precluding the possibility that the elephants mentioned were

---

[59] There are many references in Chinese sources to willows lining the rivers and canals near Ch'ang-an and Hsien-yang, but we have found so far no mention of cypresses. *At spes non fracta.*

[60] Some three centuries later the Arabic geographer Qudāma repeats Simocatta's tale, mentioning two Chinese cities founded by Alexander, of which one is Khumdan. On the second, see PELLIOT, *JA* 1927, 138-141.

[61] Cf. *HJAS* 1, 283-291. As we pointed out, it is not impossible that one of those colonies was even named Alexandria.

only those received at the capital as tribute or gifts from the South.[62]

There remains only No. 11 which describes the mourning of the sovereign by his women. We would suggest that we have here an echo of the custom prevailing at the period according to which empresses, imperial concubines and other palace women, when ousted from the palace by the death of the emperor (or foreign invasion, as in the case of the Ch'i court, and other vicissitudes of life), often sought refuge [63] in Buddhist monasteries where, on taking vows, they would indeed have their heads shaven, would adapt black clothing, and remain usually in these sanctuaries the rest of their lives.

To sum up, despite several doubtful points that require further clarification, we have in the famous paragraph of Theophylactus Simocatta an amazingly accurate description of northern China at the close of the sixth century. So far as this particular peace of " reporting " is concerned, Theophylactus stands, in our opinion, completely vindicated of all charges of malicious or rhetorical distortion of his material and worthy, as a writer *vetus atque probus*, of our gratitude and attention, and of further unprejudiced and diligent study.

II. On the Use of the Animal Cycle Among " Turco–Mongols "

In his note on " Le plus ancien example du cycle des douze animaux chez les Turcs " (*TP* 26, 204-212) Professor Pelliot established that the earliest instance of the use of the animal cycle among the Turks is to be found in a letter of the T'u-chüeh Khan Sha-po-lüeh 沙鉢畧 [64] to the Sui emperor Wên Ti, where the year 584 A. D. (K'ai-huang 4, *chia-ch'ên*, the 41st of the cycle of sixty)

---

[62] Elephants were brought into China both through the southern ports and through Eastern Turkestan.

[63] Or were forced to become nuns. For empresses we have two such cases in Ch'i (*Ch'i shu* 9), four cases in Chou (*Chou shu* 9). Three of them were empresses of Hsüan Ti (Yü-wên Pin).

[64] Title of Shê-t'u 攝圖 who reigned from 582 to 587 (died on May 18, according to *Sui shu* 1).

is designated in the preamble to the khan's communication by the character *ch'ên* 辰 of the duodenary series which corresponds to the dragon in the animal cycle.[65]

We possess, however, an even earlier example of the use of the animal cycle[66] in a "turco-mongol" milieu with more specific designation of the year by animal terms (and not by the corresponding Chinese cyclical characters). It occurs in a letter written in the year 564 A. D. by Lady YÜ-WÊN 宇文,[67] *née* YEN 閻, to her son YÜ-WÊN Hu 護, regent of the Northern Chou.[68]

This letter, one of the most interesting human documents of the period, was composed at the instigation of KAO Chan 高湛, the ruler of the Northern Ch'i, under the following circumstances. About 563, YÜ-WÊN Hu, then at the height of his power, decided to put into operation against the rival kingdom of Ch'i a strategic plan of attack which had been originally conceived by YÜ-WÊN T'ai 泰, presumably just before the latter's death. It envisaged a simultaneous invasion of Ch'i territory by Chou troops from the south and west, and by the T'u-chüeh from the north. In the first two raids the nomads ravaged the frontier districts so seriously[69] that KAO Chan, much perturbed, was forced to open peace

[65] The official Chinese calendar, one must remember, was not adopted by the Tu'-chüeh until 586, *Sui shu* 1.

[66] CHAVANNES' study "Le cycle turc des douze animaux," *TP* 1906, 51-122, contains the completest information on the subject.

[67] The YÜ-WÊN appear to have been a Mongol-speaking clan. Their name, interpreted by *Chou shu* 1 as meaning "lord of heaven (or universe)," is probably to be restored as **ümün < *i̯u-mi̯uǝn*. *T'ang shu* 71 B ascribes to Yü-wên the meaning of "grass" and equates it with 俟汾 **i-b'i̯uǝn* (on the pronunciation of the first character, cf. PELLIOT, TP 26, 225-229). The Mongol word for "grass" being *ebü + sün* (-sün is undoubtedly a suffix), it is clear that the Chinese vacilliated between two forms **ümün* and **ebün* for the original of Yü-wên. This fluctuation of *ü ~ e* is indicated in many words of the Mongol written language. Among them we have *ümüne ~ emüne*—"front," "south." It is, therefore, quite possible that it is that word that underlies the Chinese transcription Yü-wên, the *Chou shu* explanation being based on the Chinese semantic connotations of "south": "south" > "facing south" > "sovereign" 南面. Cf. also *T'ung Chih* 30, 16a where the surname NAN 南 (= 'south') is said to have been changed under the Northern dynasties into YÜ-WÊN.

[68] *Chou shu* 11, *Pei shih* 57. Murdered on April 12, 572 (*Chou shu* 5); on April 16, according to *Chou shu* 11.

[69] The Turks were under the command of the Great Khan Mu-han 木杆 himself, the Chinese under TA-HSI Wu 達奚武 (504-570) and Yang Chung 楊忠 (507-568,

negotiations with the Chou and, in token of his good faith, proposed to liberate the female members of the YÜ-WÊN family who
had been kept as hostages in Ch'i for the past three decades. First
setting free one of the four paternal aunts of YÜ-WÊN Hu,[70] KAO
Chan detained for a while the last and most important hostage,
Hu's mother, and in order to influence more speedily the Chou regent's decision, he had a message written in the old lady's name
where she implored her son to effect her release and in touching
terms reminded him of the tragic experiences of their family since
the year 524 A. D.[71]

In the spring of that year there had flared up on the northern
marches of the T'o-pa Wei empire a rebellion which unchained
all the dormant subversive forces of the realm and started the
process of political disintegration that culminated, a decade later,
in the split of the Wei into two rival dynasties and caused
eventually the ruin and extinction of the house. Under the leadership of P'O-LIU-HAN Pa-ling 破六韓拔陵,[72] the rebels, consisting
chiefly of "barbarian" garrisons of the northern frontier posts
overran the important district of Wu-ch'uan 武川.[73] Among the
well-to-do families of the vicinity who strove to organize some
resistance to the plundering bands was that of a certain YÜ-WÊN
Hung 肱.[74] In a skirmish with a detachment of one of Pa-ling's

---

the biographies of both in *Chou shu* 19). The raids took place in the 9th and 12th
months of 563 (*Chou shu* 5) or 12th month of 563-1st month of 564 (*Ch'i shu* 7).
The timing and coordination of the military operations were not very successful, a
large contingent was defeated by the Ch'i, but the Turks, who turned up in full force,
mercilessly devastated the Fên valley. A harsh winter added to the sufferings of
the population.

[70] One of them, known as Princess Chien-an 建安長公主, had married HO-LAN
Ch'u-chên 賀蘭初眞 and was the mother of HO-LAN Hsiang. Another, the Princess
Ch'ang-lo 昌樂, married WEI-CH'I I-t'ou 尉遲俟兜 and was the mother of Ch'iung
迥 and Kang 綱 (*Chou shu* 20, 21). The one who was released in the 6th month of
564 (*Ch'i shu* 7) had married a Yang 楊.

[71] Finally released, she arrived at Ch'ang-an in November 564 where she died in
567 at the age of 80, having been spared the sorrow of witnessing five years later the
ruin of her last son and the extinction of her line.

[72] On his surname, cf. *HJAS* 1, 167, n. 1.

[73] Near modern Kuei-hua ch'êng, Sui-yüan.

[74] Pht. Tê 德 Huang-ti. Two of the leading families of the region were the HO-PA
賀拔 and the TU-KU. The YÜ-WÊN were allied with the first through marriage.

subalterns WEI K'o-ku 衛可孤,[75] Hung lost his eldest son Hao
顥,[76] Lady YEN's husband and Hu's father.   Two years later,
Hung, who had been forced to join fortunes with another rebel
leader HSIEN-YÜ Hsiu-li 鮮于修禮, himself perished together with
two other sons.[77] Only T'ai, the youngest son, and two grandsons,
Tao 導 and Hu, survived the debacle. T'ai, who had succeeded
in escaping from the meshes into which the family had fallen and
who was shrewdly making his career in the complicated political
situation of the day, managed to extricate eventually his two
nephews Hu and Tao, together with another nephew HO-LAN
Hsiang 賀蘭祥.[78] About 531, they joined him in Shensi and followed him in his climb to power. Lady YÜ-WÊN had not seen her
son since the day when he, " attired in a purple silk robe with a
belt decorated with silver," rode away to join his uncle.

" Formerly," begins her letter, " when (our family was) residing at Wu-ch'uan I gave birth to you (and your two) brothers,
the eldest being born (in the year) pertaining to the rat, the
second, (in the year) pertaining to the hare, and you, (in the
year) pertaining to the serpent. . . ." [79]

Now *Chou shu* 10 (biography of YÜ-WÊN Tao, the second son
of Hao) states that Tao died in the twelfth month of the first
year of Kung Ti of Wei, January 555 A.D., at the age of forty-
four.[80] This would mean that he was born in 510-511 A.D. 511

---

[75] *Pei shih* 9 writes 可瓌 *g'a-γωái, possibly < mo. γaqai—" pig." Cf. *Ch'i shu* 50
where the last character of the name KAO A-na-hung 高阿邢肱 is said to have
been pronounced as if written 瓌.

[76] Pht. Shao-hui 邵惠 Kung: *Chou shu* 10, *Pei shih* 57.

[77] HSIEN-YÜ Hsiu-li's revolt took place in the first month of 526 and he was killed
in the ninth month. From lady YÜ-WÊN's letter it would appear that YÜ-WÊN Hung
perished in one of the early skirmishes with government troops. Lien 連, the second
son, was killed with his father. The third, Lo-shêng 洛生, was executed by ÊRH-CHU
Jung, probably about 528.

[78] According to *Chou shu* 5 and *Pei shih* 10, Hsiang died on March 19, 562. He
was 48 at the time of his death (*Chou shu* 20), and was thus born in 515. Indeed,
his biography states that he was orphaned at the age of eleven, while in Lady YÜ-
WÊN's letter he is said to be younger than Hu.

[79] The passage is noticed in CHAVANNES' study, *op. cit.* (in note 66), 71, but no
observations are made on its significance.

[80] Computing, apparently, *à la chinoise*. We do not know, however, whether the
nomads followed the Chinese practice of reckoning the period of gestation as a full

was a *hsin-mao* year (the 28th of the sexagenary cycle) and a hare year in the cycle of twelve animals, which would tally perfectly with the statement in Lady Yü-wên's letter.

As to Shih-fei 什肥, Hao's eldest son,[81] the same source informs us that he was fifteen years of age at the time of his father's death which, as we know, occurred in 524. This would give us 509-510 for the date of his birth. The nearest rat year is 508 (the 25th of the cycle, *wu-tzŭ*). The discrepancy is not great and Shih-fei's age as given in *Chou shu* 10 must be considered as approximate.

The same slight difference is also found in the biography of Yü-wên Hu. As stated in his mother's letter, he was born in a year of the serpent, which would fall in 513 A. D. (*kuei-ssŭ*, the 30th year of the cycle of sixty). His biography says, however, that he was eleven years old at the time of his father's death and seventeen when Yü-wên T'ai summoned him to P'ing-liang 平涼 in 531. In her letter his mother states, furthermore, that he was twelve about the time of Hsien-yü Hsiu-li's defeat, that is in 526. Considering the figures cited as designating Hu's real chronological age, we get for the date of his birth 513, 514, 514 respectively, a very close approximation.

The animal cycle was, then, in use among people of nomadic origin living on the northern frontier of China about 500 A. D. It would seem, moreover, that it was not unusual at that period to adopt the animal cycle designation of the year as the name of a child born within that twelvemonth. One of the clearest indications of that custom is supplied to us by the *Yo-fu shih chi* 樂府詩集 ch. 86 (ed. *Ssŭ-pu ts'ung-k'an*, p. 7 ab). This work quotes a passage from a *Yo-fu kuang t'i* 樂府廣題 which refers to an order issued in 546 by Yü-wên T'ai on the occasion of Kao Huan's attack on Yü-pi.[82] Yü-wên speaks there of his archenemy as the rat or son of the rat 鼠子.[83] As we know

year of a person's life. It is not impossible that for less important individuals of nomadic extraction age was established in the usual way, counting from the year of birth.

[81] Killed by Kao Huan about 534. A filial son, he remained at Chin-yang with his mother: *Chou shu* 10.

[82] For this campaign, see *suprā*.

[83] It is not certain whether 子 is to be taken as meaning "son" or whether it was already used as a particle at this period.

from his biography, the founder of the Ch'i house died on February 13, 547 A. D. at the age of fifty-two. He was thus born in 496 A. D. which was a rat year (13th of the cycle, *ping tzŭ*).

We find another illustration of the custom in the history of the same house. In the biography of KAO Yang 高洋 (pht. Hsien-tsu Wên-hsüan Ti 顯祖文宣帝, 529-550-559 A. D.), second son of KAO Huan, *Pei shih* 7, we are told that among the several prophecies which forecast the length of his reign there was a ditty which ran: 馬子人石室三千六百日 "the son of the horse [will] enter the stone chamber [for] 3600 days." The text goes on to explain that the "stone chamber" refers to the Yeh palaces built in the fourth century by SHIH Hu 石虎 [84] (a pun on the character *shih*: (1) stone, (2) the proper name SHIH), and that "3600 days" gives the length of KAO Yang's reign.[85] The latter is called 馬子 "son of the horse" because he was born in a *wu* (cyclical character corresponding to the *horse* in the animal cycle) year.

A grave difficulty presents itself here. KAO Yang was born in 529 A. D. which was a year of the cock, the nearest horse year being 526. While the prophecy, probably postliminary, cannot be taken too seriously, it would be unsafe to dismiss offhand the specific explanation of the text that "son of the horse" refers to the emperor's birth in a *wu* (horse) year. KAO Yang died on November 25, 559 at the age of 31.[86] Making all possible allowances, he could not have been born before 528-529. At the beginning of his biography in *Pei-shih* 7 it is furthermore, said that he was born at Chin-yang 晉陽 of which his father became

---

[84] By some, at least, "stone chamber" must have been understood as meaning the grave.

[85] He actually reigned less: from June 5, 550 to September 25, 559, about 3300 days. *Pei shih* records also that when KAO Yang inquired of a Taoist from T'ai-shan how many years were granted to him, the fortune-teller replied: "Thirty." Later, Yang expressed to the Empress Li his fear that he would not live beyond the 10th day of the 10th month of his 10th year. He died, indeed, on that very day. The characters composing his *nien hao* T'ien-pao 天保 were said to be dissected into 一大人只十 "one great man only ten" which was supposed to be another indication of the length of his reign.

[86] Counting in the Chinese fashion. *Ch'i shu* 49, in an account of another prophecy gives him 32 (Chinese) years of age at the time of his death.

governor not before 528. On the other hand, as the family is said to have been in straitened circumstances 家徒壁立 at the time, it could hardly refer to the period when KAO Huan's star was well in the ascendency.[87] The possibility that KAO Yang was born in 526 is supported by the story contained in both *Ch'i shu* 4 and *Pei shih* 7 that just before his birth the room where his mother resided was lighted at night by a red glare.[88] Now *Pei shih* 6 and *Ch'i shu* 1 relate that when KAO *Huan* first came to join ÊRH-CHU Jung 爾朱榮 and followed him to Ping chou (of which Chin-yang was the administrative seat) he rented there a small room or hut 圍焦 [89] from a certain P'ANG Ts'ang-yen 厖蒼雁. The several supernatural manifestations observed near the hut by the landlord's family after KAO Huan took up residence in it included a red glare extending up to the sky. The hut was preserved as a shrine exactly in the state it was when the KAOS occupied it and was turned into a palace under KAO Yang. It is quite possible that the latter was thus honoring the place of his birth. It is not improbable, then, that KAO Yang's age at the time of his death is incorrectly given by the historians and that he died in his 34th, and not 31st year.[90] A solution of our difficulty, is, we believe, possible without convicting of falsehood either chroniclers or prophets. In explaining the term " son of the horse " the text of the *Pei shih* says: 帝以午年生故曰馬子 " the emperor being born in a *wu* year is therefore spoken of as ' son of the horse.' " In the context of the chapter 帝 " the emperor " obviously means KAO Yang. But was it necessarily so in the original document used by the historian? The second of KAO Yang's successors was his brother KAO Chan

---

[87] In the story of the flight of KAO Huan's family from TU Lo-chou 杜洛周 which must have taken place in 525-526, *Ch'i shu* 1 mentions among the children only KAO Chêng 澄 and a daughter.

[88] According to *Pei shih* 7, he owed to this supernatural manifestation, his Hsien-pi name which was Hou-ni-yü 侯尼于, meaning child of good omen 有相子. One might read the transcription 侯尼干 *i-ni-γân* and equate it with a hypothetical turco-mongol *hilγan*—" omen." Cf. PELLIOT, *JA* 1925, 243-244.

[89] Sometimes written with 標 *piäu* for 焦 *ts'iäu* indicating, in our opinion, a *BTS-intial in both phonetic groups.

[90] There is no evidence, however, that the text is corrupt in the passage where his age is given.

who came to the throne some two years after Yang's death.[91] Now
KAO Chan, who died on January 13, 569 A.D. at the age of 32
years (*à la chinoise*), was born in 538 which was a horse year
(55th of the cycle, *wu-wu*). It could well be possible that it is
KAO Chan who is to be understood as " the Emperor " of the text
(especially if we take the cynical view that the " prophecy " could
not have been composed until after Yang's death). The ditty
could thus be interpreted as reading: " Within 3600 days (after
the accession of KAO Yang, another ruler who is) a son of the
horse will enter the stone chamber." [92]

We may have a further chronogrammatic reference in another
ditty dating according to *Pei shih* 5, from the period of the Wei
emperors Hsüan-wu 宣武 and Hsiao-ming 孝明, that is 500-528
A.D., or taking the date ending the reign of the first and beginning
that of the second, 515 A.D. It was supposed to presage Yü-wên
T'ai's role in the downfall of Wei and ran as follows: " As a fox,
not a fox; as a badger, not a badger, the sallow-faced (?) son of a
dog [will] gnaw asunder the cord " 狐非狐貉非貉焦梨狗子齧斷索·
Wise interpreters, says the *Pei shih*, saw immediately in the cord
a reference to the T'o-pa (*i.e.* the 索頭 " corded [or braided]
heads ") and in the fox, badger, and son of the dog an allusion to
Yü-wên T'ai's cognomen which was Hei-la 黑獺—" black otter." [93]

In order to ascertain whether the above is just a vague allusion
to black otter or whether 狗子 " dog " or " son of the dog " is
chronogrammatic we must establish Yü-wên T'ai's date of birth.
This presents a problem. His biography in *Chou shu* 2 says that
he died on the day *i-hai* in the tenth month of the third year of
Wei Kung Ti which would correspond to November 21, 556 A.D.
He was 52 years old and was buried on the day *chia shên*, that is
but nine days later. This is improbable in the light of both
Chinese and nomadic customs and the practice of the day. About
two months were usually required to elapse between the time of

---

[91] On December 3, 561: *Chou shu* 7.

[92] The number of days in that case would be, of course, approximate.

[93] It is under that name that he is usually referred to in the *Ch'i shu*. The character
t'ai 泰 was taboo under the Ch'i as being the personal name of one of KAO Huan's
ancestors.

death (or the official announcement thereof) and the day of burial, unless the will of the deceased directed otherwise. Thus KAO Huan's death was announced on July 19, 547 [94] and the burial took place on September 19, 547; Hsüan Ti of Chou died on June 8, 580 and was buried on August 8, 580.[95] Now *Pei shih* 9 reads 50 instead of 52 for Yü-wên T'ai's age and has . . . 時年五十十 二月甲申葬 . . . "[he was] at the time [of his death] 50 years of age. On *chia shên* of the 12th month [he] was buried. . . ." The *chia shên* day of the 12th month of that year would correspond to January 21, 557, exactly two months after the day of Yü-wên T'ai's death. It is obvious that the *Chou shu* telescoped 五十 into 十二月 " 12th month " and, omitting 月, produced 五十二 "fifty-two." The *Pei shih* is thus correct and Yü-wên T'ai was fifty years old at the time of his death in 556. He was then born in 506-507. As 506 was a dog year (the 23rd of the cycle, *i hsü*) it is quite likely that T'ai was indeed nicknamed "son of the dog." In the early part of his biography, however, his age at the time of HSIEN-YÜ Hsiu-li's death which occurred in 526 is given as eighteen. This must be considered in the light of the foregoing as approximate or may be the result of a clumsy re-arrangement of the sources used by the historian.[96] The paragraph in question speaks of Yü-wên T'ai following his father in the latter's campaigns of 524-526, and T'ai's age as given could well refer to the first date 524, when T'ai would have indeed been 18 years old.

We have thus three cases of men born between 496 and 538 A.D.

[94] Cf. note 20.

[95] According to *Pei shih* 10, 11 and *Chou shu* 7, 8 he fell ill on June 8. YANG Chien, who was about to be exiled to Yang chou, "was summoned" to the palace to attend the emperor in his illness and on June 22 the latter died. *Sui shu* 1 gives June 8 as the day of the emperor's death and June 20 as the date of the proclamation of the news. It is quite likely, therefore, that Hsüan Ti was murdered on the very day YANG Chien arrived at the palace and his death was kept secret for a fortnight by Chien and his fellow-conspirators in order to gain time for arranging their affairs. Decrees issued within these 12-14 days were undoubtedly forged as all the sources indicate.

[96] The *Chou shu* text has 少隨德皇帝. . . . The character 少 (" in his youth ") appears already some 20 characters above and its repetition is incomprehensible unless the passage in question came from a source other than that of the preceding paragraph. *Pei shih* 9 omits the second 少.

who were known under chronogrammatic nicknames containing
animal cycle terms. The custom is, however, much older. In
the biography of SHIH Hu 石虎, *Wei shu* 95, it is said that the
great Hunnish warrior was seventeen years old in Yung-chia 永嘉
5, *i.e.* 311 A.D., this being the only clue that we have as to Hu's
date of birth. He was then born in 296 A.D. which was a tiger
year (51st of the cycle, *chia yin*). It appears, then, that SHIH
Hu (Hu—" tiger ") owed his personal name to his birth in a
cyclical year consecrated to the animal that symbolized military
prowess. So far as we have been able to establish this is the
earliest example of the use of the animal cycle in a nomadic milieu
and one of the earliest instances of the chronogrammatic use of
an animal term.

There exists a faint possibility that we have a similar use of
the animal cycle in the name of SHIH Hu's relative,[97] SHIH Lê
石勒. His personal name Lê, judging from the testimony of *Wei
shu* 95, appears to be an abbreviation of Pei-lê 䩡勒 **b'ʷâi-lək.*
As SHIH Lê's Chinese cognomen was Shih-lung 世龍 which contains the word *lung*—" dragon," it is not improbable that in
*b'ʷâi-lək we have the transcription of a " turco-mongol " word
meaning " dragon." One is tempted to compare it with the puzzling **blqsun* بلقسون (with *-sun* being obviously the well-known
Mongolian suffix) of Qazwīnī, and equated with " crocodile " in
the Qaitaq list.[98] Is the name chronogrammatic? SHIH Lê died
on August 17, 333 A.D. at the age of sixty, according to *Shih-liu
kuo ch'un-ch'iu* 13. He was born then in 273 or 274 A.D. The
first year was a year of the serpent. According to the same source,
SHIH Lê's death was portended in 333 A.D. by the fall of a large
meteor which left a trail resembling a serpent, as well as by the
death of a large snake following a two day long fight with a rat.

---

[97] SHIH Hu was adopted by SHIH Lê's father. He is also spoken of as *Shih Lê's*
nephew.

[98] See PELLIOT, Le prétendu vocabulaire mongol des Ḳaitaḳ, *JA* 1927, 1, 289. The first
part of the word may represent tk. *balïq*—' fish,' which in IBN MUHANNĀ's list of the
animal cycle terms takes the place of the dragon (cf. PELLIOT, *TP* 27, 17-18). *Balïq*
appears under the Chinese transcription 磨勒 *muâ-lək* as the name of a city in T'u-
chüeh territory (*TPHYC* 38), the place owing its name to the excellent fish that was
found in the nearby river.

In the same source is recorded, however, the appearance in a well of the capital of a black dragon which rejoiced SHIH Lê greatly. Now 272 A. D. was a year of the black dragon and it is possible that SHIH Lê, being born or conceived in that year, considered himself under that cyclical animal's special protection.[99]

Whether the chronogrammatic application of the animal cycle is of Chinese origin, or originated with the nomads is difficult to decide. For the period under consideration, we know only one case of such use of animal terms in the purely Chinese onomasticon. The biography of TS'AO Hu 曹虎, *Nan Ch'i shu* 30, indicates that that southern Chinese officer was executed in 499 A. D. at the age of "past sixty" 年六十餘. He could thus have been born in 438 A. D. which was a tiger year and may have been given his personal name Hu—"tiger" for that reason.

The same history of the Southern Ch'i gives in ch. 19 several cases of the use of animal chronograms in a prophetical ditty dating from the time of Tung-hun hou 東昏侯 (HSIAO Pao-chüan 蕭寶卷),[100] the last emperor of Nan Ch'i. The emperor is referred to as "wild pig" 野猪; he was, indeed, born in 483 A. D., a pig year. Liang Wu Ti (464-502-549) who overthrew him is spoken of as "dragon," and 464 A. D. was a dragon year. HSIAO Ying-ch'ou 蕭穎冑 462-501)[101] is alluded to as "tiger," 462 being a tiger year. The same ditty contains an unidentifiable reference to a 馬子 "(son of the) horse." The study of the chronogrammatic use of the animal cycle in China proper constitutes, however, a larger problem beyond the scope of the present investigation.

[99] It must be remembered that SHIH Lê, having reached the age of sixty, must have been in fear for his life as the custom of putting to death (or at least setting aside) rulers who had reached that age must have been a living tradition during the period. See notes 42, 45, 46.

[100] *Nan Ch'i shu* 7, *Nan Ch'i shu* 5. Also called Fei Ti 廢帝—"the deposed emperor." Murdered on December 31, 501 A. D., at the age of 19 (Chinese).

[101] *Nan Ch'i shu* 38.

3. The Altaic Word for "Horn" in the Political Nomenclature of the Steppe

According to the Northern Chinese historians,[1] the rulers of the powerful federation of the Juan-juan 蠕蠕 who dominated Mongolia during the fifth and the first half of the sixth centuries and who are generally identified with the "real" Avars of the Byzantine sources[2] bore the clan name Yu-chiu-lü 郁久閭 (anc. *iuk-$ki̯əu$-$li̯^wo$). This appellation is believed to be a variant of Mu-ku-lü 木骨閭 (anc. muk-$kuət$-$li̯^wo$), the nickname of the eponymous ancestor of the clan whose story is briefly recounted by the chroniclers in the opening lines of their history of the Juan-juan.

At the end of the reign of the T'o-pa "emperor" Li-wei 力微 (pht. Shên-yüan 神元, 174-220-277 A. D.),[3] runs the story, some raiding horsemen of the T'o-pa captured a young slave who could remember neither his clan nor his personal name and was nicknamed by his master[4] Mu-ku-lü. On reaching maturity, the youth freed himself from servitude and became a rider in the T'o-pa horde. In the time of I-lu 猗盧 (pht. Mu 穆, born between 267 and 277, ruled 308-316 A. D.),[5] Mu-ku-lü, threatened with execution for having been late for duty, escaped to Mongolia, where

---

[1] *Wei shu* 103, *Pei shih* 98; cf. *T'ung tien* 196, *T'ai-p'ing huan yü chi* 193; for the southern sources, cf. particularly *Nan Ch'i shu* 59, *Liang shu* 54.

[2] The identification is by no means certain, and the whole question deserves careful re-study.

[3] His dates we gave incorrectly in *HJAS* 1.169. The above are based on *Wei shu* 1, *Pei shih* 1. Father Hyacinth mistakenly identifies the Shên-yüan of *Wei shu* 103 with Khan Chieh-fên 詰汾. (Собраніе свѣдѣній . . . 206).

[4] It is difficult to say whether the T'o-pa master of the slave is meant, or a former one; more probably, the captor.

[5] Father Hyacinth again erroneously takes the Mu of the text as referring to Ssŭ-ma Tan 聃 (343-345-361 A. D.), emperor of the Chin dynasty, whose posthumous title was also Mu (*Chin shu* 8).

he assembled a band of fugitives like himself and thus founded the nucleus of the Juan-juan confederation.[6]

The reason for the nickname bestowed upon the young slave was, says the text, that " his hair was originally on a level with his eyebrows " 髮始齊眉, which may mean that the hair on his head grew as short as that of the eyebrows, or, possibly, that his hair, when loose, did not extend beyond the eyebrow-line, that is it was not more than two or three inches long.[7] He was accordingly named Mu-ku-lü which meant " bald of head " 首禿.[8]

The Chinese transcription does not evoke any of the known Altaic terms for " bald," [9] but immediately suggests, as pointed out already in 1903 by K. SHIRATORI (*Izvestiia Akademii Nauk* 1903, 018; discussed at greater length in *SZ* 22, 1383-1387),[10] Mongol *moχor ~ *moqor*—" blunt," " without horns " > *moχotur*— " hornless cattle " ~ Manchu *muχūri*—" blunt," " rounded," *moχolo* —" hornless." [11] Now both *moχor* and *moχotur* are usually used to designate deficiency of a normal body excrescence and besides horns are also applied to indicate absence or poor growth of hair in animals, especially as to the tail (cf. *moχotur* or *moχor segül*— " tailless," " short-tailed ").[12] As *moχor* and its derivatives are

[6] The original name of the confederation was Jou-jan 柔然, chosen as a designation for the horde by Mu-ku-lü's son Ch'ê-lu-hui 車鹿會. Possibly from Tk. *javčan*— " artemisia " > " artemisia-colored " > " purple."

[7] The first interpretation is more likely. Cf. the expression " to cut off hair to the level of eyebrows " 剪髮齊眉, *Wei shu* 102 (referring to customs of the Yüeh-pan). There is no reason to see in what was probably nothing more than an individual style of dressing hair (or a vitamin deficiency) a " gorilla-like morphological trait " as GRUM-GRZHIMAILO does in Западная Монголія 2, 174.

[8] The *T'ang lei han* 120, 4a, writes: 字之曰大百階木骨閭者首禿也. I do not know what to make out of the first three characters of the name. They appear to transcribe some such word as *tabaqai ~ *dabaqai*. Could it be a cognate of Mo. *dabaγan*—" mountain " with the semantic extension " top " > " head " ? Or is it a mistake for 大洛階 which would give Mo. *taraqai*—" bald " ?

[9] One of these terms, Mo. *qaljaγai*, is possibly transcribed by Chinese *k'o-lo-kai* 可洛峐, the name of a mountain in Kansu (*Sui shu* 53, *Pei shih* 73). Chin. 峐 means " bare hill."

[10] Cf. also the Chinese translation of SHIRATORI's study by FANG Chuang-yao, *Tung Hu min-tsu k'ao* 東胡民族考, Shanghai 1934, 145-154.

[11] The modern Mongol dialects have: *muhăr* (Buriat), *muχur* (Ordos), *MoGor* (Monguor).

[12] Chinese 禿 " bald " is used in the same sense in 禿尾 " hairless tail," but also " short-tailed," " tailless."

also registered in the sense of " dull " (mentally, spiritually), it would seem that the term was quite appropriately conferred as a name upon a queue-less youth stupid enough to forget his origin and appellation.

Whether Mu-ku-lü renders an old Mongol or an old Manchu form is difficult to decide.[13] The final vowel of the Chinese transcription would, at the present stage of our knowledge, favor Ma. *moχolo*. A more interesting problem is, however, raised by the Anlaut of our word. The *Wei shu* text implies that Mu-ku-lü and Yu-chiu-lü [14] were variant pronunciations of the same word. We must have here, then, an Altaic vocable exhibiting the highly significant fluctuation in initial sound: labial ~ aspiration ~ vocalic ingress, of which the so-called " Schmidt-Ramstedt Law " is the best known illustration.[15]

It is generally believed by those favoring the hypothesis of a proto-Altaic language, common ancestor of the Turkish, Mongol, and Tungus groups, that Altaic initial *p- had undergone the following evolution: [16]

$$\text{Altaic *p-}\begin{cases} \text{Turkish:} & > \text{'-} > \text{°-} \\ \text{Mongol:} & > \phi\text{-} > \text{h-} > \text{°-} \\ \text{Tungus:} & > \text{f-} \\ & \text{p-} \end{cases}$$

The list of correspondences, at least so far as the two Far Eastern branches of the family are concerned, is imposing, and

---

[13] We are not sure what language the Juan-juan spoke. Professor PELLIOT believes that they spoke Mongol. Naturally, the scanty evidence that we get from Chinese transcriptions of names and titles cannot be taken as conclusive in forming an opinion as to the language of the masses comprising the federation and can serve only as a clue to the speech of the ruling clan.

[14] The latter undoubtedly represents *h'uqul/ru* or *hükül/rü*.

[15] G. RAMSTEDT, Ein anlautender stimmloser Labial in der mongolisch-türkischen Ursprache, *JSFO* 32-2; P. SCHMIDT, The language of the Negidals, *Acta Univ. Latviensis*, 5. The discussion of the alternation was, I believe, inaugurated by SCHMIDT as early as 1898 in Der Lautwandel im Mandschu und Mongolischen (*J. of the Peking Or. So.*, 4).

[16] Elaborated to include Finno-Ugrian languages by A. SAUVAGEOT, *Recherches sur le vocabulaire des langues ouralo-altaïques*, Paris 1930. This work has been bitterly attacked by SHIROKOGOROFF in Ethnological and linguistical aspects of the ural-altaic hypothesis (*CHHP* 6), perhaps a little unjustly, though SHIROKOGOROFF's strictures on the validity of the " law " carry weight.

the restoration of an initial *h- for a series of ancient Mongol words where the *h- is invariably matched by a Tungus f- (or Goldi p-) is an important achievement in the field of Altaic linguistics.[17] In a few cases, however, the simplified theory of *p- > *φ- > *h- > °- is complicated by the sporadic appearance (in a given series) of words with initial *b- or even *m-. Thus, the hypothetical Altaic *palqa which produced regularly Ma. folχo— "hammer," Goldi *palua*—'id.,' Mo. *aluqa*—'id.,' is registered in Turkish as *balqa*—'id.,' where we should expect *alqa or some similar form without consonantal Anlaut.[18] Mongol *üniyär* (< anc. Mo. *hüni*, corresponding regularly to Shirongol *funi*)—"fog," "vapor" appears in a Sino-Mongol dictionary of the 14th century as *moniyar*.[18a] The theory of phonetic evolution does not account for such cases and it would seem at the present state of the investigation preferable to note carefully every instance of such phonetic alternation without committing oneself to upholding a strict phonetic law of evolution.[19]

The supposition that our word *mu-qul/ru ~ *huqul/ru exhibits such an alternation is supported by a study of its hypothetical original. Indeed, if we take the Manchu form of the term *moχolo* —"hornless" (corresponding to Mo. *moχor*), it appears to be a close relative of *foχolon*—"short," "deficient"~Jučen *fuχolo~ Mo. *oqor* < *hoqor (IBN AL-MUHANNĀ, خوقار *huqar*, so also the Leyden MS, *Izv. Ak. Nauk.* 1928, 76), Buriat *oχor*.[20] Remembering, on the other hand, our connotations "blunt"~"rounded," we must connect *moχolo* with Ma. *muχeliyen*—"round," *muχaliyan*— "ball," *muχeren*—"ring" (cf. Bur. *möχŏron*—"round," Mo. *möχoliq*—"id."). In Mongol the same root "round" is registered also in the palatalized form *müger, mügür*—"circumference," *mügürek, mügülik*—"little ball," "circle."

---

[17] Cf. particularly PELLIOT, Mots à *h* initiale dans le mongol, *JA* 1925, 193-263.

[18] Cf. PELLIOT, *op. cit.* 262-3, and 210-11, 224.

[18a] *Op. cit.* 238.

[19] Cf. additionally Ma. *falga*—"village" vs. Mo. *balγa-sun*—"city"; Mo. *burgi*— "to rise" (as smoke, dust) vs. Ma. *furgibu*—"to rise" (of dust); Mo. *horim, orom* (*op. cit.* 220) vs. *mör*—"trace," "path."

[20] PELLIOT, *op. cit,* 245; Г. Санжеевъ, Манчжуромонгольскія языковыя параллели, ИАН 1930, 702.

" Horn " and " blunt " lead us further to Mo. *mögere-sün~ bögere-sün*—" cartilage " > modern dial. *mögŏrs, möχŏrs, mügörs~* Turkish *bönüz*—" horn "; Jag. *münüz*, Kirg. *müyüz*, Osm. *boynuz* —'id.' [21] Finally to Altaic *püker*—" ox," " horned cattle " > Mo. *üker*—'id.' (< anc. Mo. *hüker* هوكر), Khalkha *uχχŭr*,[22] Chuvash *vəGə̂r, məGə̂r, moGor*; Turkish: Osm., Jag., Cum. *öküz*, Yak. *oγus*;[23] and Mo. *eber*—" horn," probably derived from *eger* > *eβer* (cf. Khalkha *ewer*).[24]

Underlying all these words is the root *BUGUR~*hUGUR~ *UGUR which apparently underwent the following semantic evolution:

$$\frac{\text{horn}}{\text{cartilage}} > \frac{\text{horned}}{\text{cattle}} > \frac{\text{short-horned, blunt}}{\text{hornless cattle}} > \begin{cases} \text{short} \\ \text{deficient} \\ \text{rounded} \\ \text{dull} \\ \text{stupid} \end{cases}$$

The most interesting connotation of the Altaic word for " horn " is found, however, in its use as a term relating to nomadic organization. According to *Hou Han shu* 119, the four greatest chiefs of the Hsiung-nu (the two *hsien* 賢 princes and the two *lu-li* 谷蠡 princes) were called the " Four Horns " 四角. Next to them came the " Six Horns " 六角 (two *jih-chu* 日逐 princes, two *wên-yü-t'i* 溫禺鞮 princes, and the two *chan-chiang* 斬將 princes).[25] All of

[21] Cf. POPPE, ДАН 1925, 19-22; also *Ungarische Jahrbücher* 9.110; RAMSTEDT, Az ɒ hang a mongolban . . . , *Nyelvtudományi közlemények* 1913, 233; POPPE, Skizze der Phonetik des Barguburjätischen, *AM* 7, 339. Cf. Chuvash *mə̂yraGa* < *mə̂graGa*— " horn," POPPE, ИАН 1925, 41.

[22] Monguor *fuGuor*, SMEDT & MOSTAERT, 104.

[23] On that series see Z. GOMBOCZ, Die bulgarisch-türkischen Lehnwörter in der ungarischen Sprache, *MSFO* 30, 111; PELLIOT, *op. cit.* 240; POPPE in ДАН 1925, 11.

[24] We believe that in some cases *üker* in Mongol has survived in the older meaning " hornless " > " bald," as in names of plants where it appears to designate beardless, awn-less varieties of grain: *üker arbai*—" beardless oats." Cf. also *mekir*—" n. of a plant," LAUFER, *TP* 31, 267-269, and PELLIOT's observations p. 269 n. *T'ung tien* 29, 14b translates our Mu-ku-lü as 青首禿. Whence the character 青? Could there have been some confusion in the mind of the author of the source which the *T'ung tien* used between the different meanings of the original T'o-PA word: 首禿—" bald " and 青稞 (*mekir?*)—" *Hordeum nudum* " ?

[25] None of these titles have yet been satisfactorily explained.

them were sons and brothers of the shan-yü; the other Hsiung-nu
ranks and offices mentioned by the Chinese sources were held by
chieftains belonging to clans other than that of the supreme ruler.[26]
There were thus no more than " Ten Horns " in the Hsiung-nu
organization. This is confirmed by the post-face of the same chapter of the *Hou Han shu* where Chinese victories over the Hsiung-
nu are described as having resulted in 破龍祠焚罽幕阬十角梏閼氏
the destruction of the Dragon Altar (the Hsiung-nu central place
of worship), the burning of their felt tents, the entrapping of the
Ten Horns, and the fettering of the *o-shih*[27] (the *shan-yü's*
consort).

This important text leads us to the solution of one of the most
puzzling questions in the history of Central Asia, the significance
of the term **uɣur, *ɣur, *ɣuz~*oɣuz* which appears with disconcerting frequency in so many supposedly ethnic designations
among the nomads. As our passage shows, the chiefs of the Hsiung-
nu, the oldest nomadic organization of the steppe known to us,
were collectively called by the Chinese the " Ten Horns," [28] undoubtedly a term translated from the Hsiung-nu language. The
confederation of the Western T'u-chüeh, as we learn from both
Chinese and Orkhon Turkish sources, was similarly termed the
" Ten Arrows," Tk. *On oq*, Chin. 十姓 or 十箭—the " Ten Clans "
(V. THOMSEN, *Turcica* 4-26; CHAVANNES, *Documents*, 27-28;
HIRTH, *Nachworte zur Inschrift des Tonyukuk*, 67-69). According to the Chinese, the designation originated in the custom of
each of the ten chieftains being presented by the khan with an
arrow.[29] While THOMSEN's argument is conclusive on the point

[26] Cf. DE GROOT, *Die Hunnen der vorchristlichen Zeit*, 56, but " Ecke " is hardly
the correct translation for 角.

[27] The Hsiung-nu word underlying this transcription is still doubtful. The title was
probably derived from an epithet, " the beautiful (lady) " < " the rouged one," as an
almost identical transcription renders the name of a plant from which rouge was
obtained by the Hsiung-nu.

[28] Whatever may be the real etymology of the name of the Hsiung-nu, our study
would suggest that **χiuən-iuk ~ *χiʷong-nuo* may have been interpreted folk-etymologically as containing Altaic **hon*—" ten " + **oq* or **uɣur*.

[29] The use of arrows as credentials, sending messages, etc., was wide-spread among
the nomads of the period. On an interesting case of such use, cf. *Wei shu* 28, biog.
of Mo T'i 莫題.

that *On oq* usually stood for "ten arrows," RADLOFF's opinion that the expression was sometimes understood as *on uq* "ten families" (rather than RADLOFF's "ten tribes," in view of Chin. 十姓) should not be dismissed, as *uq* is a term that would precisely cover the khan's family (~families) of which the chiefs of the ten divisions were undoubtedly members (cf. "Ten *šad*," Chin. 十設, a synonym of 十姓; the title of *šad* was borne by immediate relatives of the khan only).[30]

The close parallel between the two organizations, the ten divisions with both peoples being split into two groups, a "left" group of five, and a "right" one of five,[31] would strengthen the supposition that the old Hsiung-nu term "horn"~"chieftain"[32] survived in the political nomenclature of nomadic peoples long after the disappearance of the Hsiung-nu power. "Horn" came to mean simply "unit of organization," "division," "horde." In many cases its etymology was forgotten, but whenever large confederations of nomads were formed they called themselves by the traditional appelation * (B) UGUR—"horns"~"hordes," now in the compound form "so many horn-s," now in the combination of "horn" with a color term (white, yellow, black).[33] In every case the name reflected their constitutional organization, and never their ethnic consciousness.

It is interesting to note that the traditional term when used as the designation of such a confederation reflected the pronunciation

[30] The link between *On oq*—"Ten Arrows" and our hypothetical **On oɣur*—"Ten Horns" might be sought in a variant of the latter, **On oɣuz < *On oɣud*, that was interpreted as a Mongolian plural of *On oq*.

[31] Or, Eastern and Western, respectively. We suspect that whenever we have an organization of five hordes it represented originally one half of a larger confederation of ten units. Such appears to be the case of the five hordes of the Bulgars.

[32] We do not want to discuss here the other common connotations of "horn," strength, vitality, power, its religious symbolism, or the polarity of the meanings. The polarity of associations (strong : weak) can be interpreted by sociological factors, without going into "paleolinguistics."

[33] The use of the color term can be explained variously: (1) as indicating geographical location (black for north, red for south, yellow—center, white—west, and green (bluish) —east); (2) from the color of the horses; (3) as referring to class distinctions (white—noble, black—low-born).

of the word in different Turkish-speaking localities. We have it thus in the form *UGUR: [34]

1. In the name of Unugurs, Οὐννουγούροι of THEOPHYLACTUS,[35] Οὐνιγούροι of MENANDER, 'Ονόγουροι of PRISCUS, < *On uɣur— " Ten Horns," a nomadic confederation which appeared in Europe in the middle of the fifth century and whose constitutional organization was probably inspired by that of the Hsiung-nu.[36]

2. As the last element of the names Κουτρίγουροι and Οὐτιγούροι of AGATHIAS, the Cuturguri and Uturguri of PROCOPIUS.

3. In the Σαράγουροι of PRISCUS.[37]

4. The 'Ογώρ of THEOPHYLACTUS SIMOCATTA, generally believed to be the Uigurs.[38]

5. The Угры of the Russian sources.

6. In the name of the " Eastern Magyars " the *Bašɣirt* باشغرد *Bašɣird* بشغرد, *Majɣar* مجغر of the Arabic geographers.[39] The fluctuation of the middle radical between -*G- and -*NG- (as in *bögere ~ bönere*—" cartilage ") explains the form

7. UNGAR *vs.* Ugri ~ Ugor (Угры), the alternation making it unnecessary to derive the name of the Hungarian from *Onuɣur, unless, of course, it could be demonstrated that the Hungarians possessed an organization of ten divisions.[40] The labial initial of some forms of our etymon " horn " appears in the original name of the same people

[34] We limit ourselves to the most significant illustrations, without noting all the variants which can be easily ascertained by reference to the texts and to special studies.

[35] Whether Simocatta's Οὐννουγοῦνοι (Bonn, 284) is a mistake for Οὐννουγούροι, or a final -*n* variation of our root (cf. PELLIOTT, *op. cit.* 240) is difficult to decide.

[36] Cf. particularly J. MORAVCSIK, Zur Geschichte der Onoguren, *Ung. Jahrb.* 10. 53-90. Also J. SCHNETZ, Onogoria, *Archiv für slavische Philologie* 40. 157-160.

[37] Long recognized as being a transcription of *Sarï-ugur*—" the Yellow Ugur."

[38] And Οὐγούροι of MENANDER (Bonn, 301).

[39] The first element might well be, as supposed by J. NÉMETH, the numeral *bäš*— " five." For the latest review of the vexing question of the *Majɣar*, cf. MINORSKY, *Ḥudūd al-'Ālam*, London, 1937.

[40] On the ancient history of the Hungarians, cf. MACARTNEY's excellent work *The Magyars in the Ninth Century*, Cambridge 1930. Also H. SCHÖNEBAUM, *Die Kenntnis der byzantinischen Geschichtsschreiber von der ältesten Geschichte der Ungarn vor der Landnahme*, Berlin 1922; DARKO, Die auf die Ungarn bezüglichen Volksnamen bei den Byzantinern, *Byzantinische Zeitschrift* 1912, 472-487.

8. Magyar < *Mog'er (cf. Hetu Mogyer—" *Seven Horns," the seven chiefs of the Hungarian legend). We should expect, indeed, a labial initial in the Volga region, where the Magyars originated, on the basis of Chuvash *vәĝәr, mәĝәr*—" ox " < horn.[41]

9. The same labial sound reappears in Vengri~ Венгры, the slavic rendering of the name of the Hungarians.[42]

10. The vanishing labial explains also the form Pugur, the name under which the Ugur are mentioned in the chronicle of Michael Syrus (MARQUART, *Streifzüge*, 485).[43] In Mongolia, where on the basis of Mo. *eber*—" horn " it is not unreasonable to expect dialectically a labial for the middle radical, we have

11. The Avars, the ʼΑβαροι of the Byzantines, and the Обры < *Obĕr, of the Russian chronicles.[44] Finally, the z variation of *uɣur* (> *uɣuz*), valid for several dialects, clarifies

12. The name of the *Toquzoɣuz*—" Nine Oɣuz " < * " Nine Horns." Also probably the name of Oɣuz Khan, the great legendary hero of the Turks.[45]

---

[41] Cf. CONSTANTINE PORPHYROGENITUS, *De adm. imp.* 40, for Μεγέρη, one of the transcriptions of the name of the Magyars, which is registered by the emperor as the name of the third tribe of the Κάβαροι. On the difficult question of the relationship between the Magyars, the Κάβαροι, and the Κάγκαρ, cf. H. GRÉGOIRE, Le nom et l'origine des Hongrois, *ZDMG* 1937, 630-642. I am inclined to believe with Professor GRÉGOIRE in the identity of Kabar and Kangar. The Altaic alternation of -ng- with -β- ~ -w- (of the type that we find in Tk. Mo. *quwur* ~ Tat. *qowur* > russ. каурый — " isabella," " buff " (of horses); the relation of the Tk. Mo. word to Chinese *hua-liu* 驊騮 is problematical) makes it, however, unnecessary to presuppose a graphic metathesis in Κάβαροι. See note 46.

[42] For the various names of the Hungarians, cf. J. MELICH, Ueber den Ursprung des Namens Ungar, *Archiv für slavische Philologie* 38. 244-250.

[43] It is quite probable that the name of the Mongols (mongol ~ mongor) also goes back to our etymon. Traditionally the name is usually explained as meaning " dull," " weak " (D'OHSSON, *Histoire* 1.22).

[44] In the light of our hypothesis, RAMSTEDT's suggestion (Этимологія имени Ойратъ, Зап. Имп. Русск. Геогр. Общ. по отд. Этногр. 34. 547-548) that the name of the Oirat is derived from *ogir-, a root related to that found in the name of the Uïgurs, receives considerable substantiation. Cf. for the development of the middle consonant of our *eber* ~ *eger* in Monguor, SMEDT and MOSTAERT, Dictionnaire monguor-français 480: *uyer*—" corne."

[45] Cf. PELLIOT, Sur la légende d'Uɣuz-Khan en écriture ouigoure, *TP* 27. 247-258; W. BANG and G. RACHMATI, Die Legende von Oɣuz Qaɣan, *SPAW* 1932, 683-724; W. RADLOFF, Къ вопросу объ Уйгурахъ, 21-53. Oɣuz Khan's birth is obviously connected at the beginning of the legend with an ox.

If the above suggestions should find substantiation, we shall see ourselves obliged to revise several of our notions concerning the history of Central Asia. Instead of ethnic designations we shall have to deal with terms of political nomenclature reflecting essentially the form of the constitutional organization of nomadic groups. We believe that the dark mists obscuring the history of the steppe would be dispelled sooner if emphasis were laid on the study of the migration of political symbols rather than on that of hypothetical migrations of ethnic units, on the " alarums and excursions " of political groupings, rather than on the mythical meanderings of self-conscious ethnoses, each bent on propagating its particular linguistic or racial self.[46]

[46] It is not improbable that the same etymon, *horn ~ *horde, was current in eastern Europe in a form with an initial sibilant (cf. Old Bulgarian σίγορ ~ ШЕГОР—" ox " < *šγγur; J. MIKKOLA, Die Chronologie der türkischen Donaubulgaren, *JSFO* 30) and it is with that initial that it appears in *Bašγirt* and *Majγar*, as well as in the name Σάβιροι and the Σάβαρτοι ἄσφαλοι (on the latest hypothesis concerning the second part of the last term cf. H. GRÉGOIRE, L'habitat " primitif " des Magyars, *Byzantion* 13. 267-278). The alternation *h-* ~ *š-* (and *q-*, *k-* ~ *š-*) is well known in Mongol dialects.

To sum up, we believe that it would repay investigation to study the various ethnic names of early medieval Asia and Europe in the light of the hypothesis that the different " Gog and Magog " confederations of the Steppe called themselves merely *horns* > *hordes*, the primitive etymon appearing in the following forms: 1. UGUR: -ογουρ-, -γουρ-, угр-. 2. UNGUR: Hungar-. 3. BUGUR: Mogeri, Μεγέρη, Mu-ku-lü. 4. BUNGUR: Венгр-. 5. BAGAR: Magyar > Μάξαρ-. 6. ΑβAR < AGAR: Avar-, Обр- (cf. also the habit of the Russian chronicles of referring to the Turks as Агаряне —" sons of Hagar," " Ishmaelites," the Biblical allusion being possibly suggested by the homonym AGAR). 7. XAGAR ~ XANGAR: Κάβαρ-, Κάγκαρ-, *XAG'AR > χαξάρ- (cf. Mo. *qabar*—" nose," but also " *horn* ends of a bow "). 8. SABAR: Σαβαρ-, Sabir, also the Arabic name of cis- and trans-Uralian tribes: Ibir-Sibir. 9. UGUZ: -ογuz, Οὔξ.

Whether Theophylactus Simocatta's Μουκρί should be adduced here is doubtful. That name is apparently identical with Mukuri, the designation of Kao-li (Corea) which is found in a Sanscrit-Chinese dictionary. Cf. PRABODH CHANDRA BAGCHI, *Deux lexiques sanscrit-chinois* 77, 348. If, on the other hand the Avars are not identical with the Juan-juan, it may well be that Μουκρί refers to the latter, and is to be equated with our Mu-ku-lü.

In the case that *Mukri ~ *Mukuri really refers to Kao-li (very likely including Southern Manchuria) it would be interesting to ascertain whether the name is not related to that of the Mu-jung 慕容 (anc. *muo-g-*ziʷong) or Mu-yü 慕輿 (anc. *muo-g-ziʷo) who dominated southwestern Manchuria for over a century and whose name must have been well known to the nomads of Mongolia. *Mukzu ~ *Mukzü may indeed have been a z variation of *Mukuru. Cf. also the Mo-i 墨台 (anc. *Mək-d'i),

4. The Coronation of T'o-pa Hsiu

On July 21, 531, Kao Huan, ally and sworn brother of Êrh-chu Chao 爾朱兆,[47] found the moment propitious to utilize the growing tide of popular resentment against the Êrh-chu for purposes of his own ambition, and, throwing off all pretense of allegiance to their cause, took up arms against the dictators at Hsin tu 信都.[48]

Although forewarned of his plans,[49] Êrh-chu Chao and his cousins, distrustful of one another, allowed Kao Huan to gain time which he skillfully utilized, and it was only on September 5 that the cousins started a concerted movement of armies against Hsin tu. Craftily making use of the dissension in the ranks of his enemies, Kao Huan spread the rumor that he was secretly in accord with Chao and plotting in common with him the downfall of Êrh-chu Chung-yüan 仲遠 and Êrh-chu Tu-lü 度律.[50] The suspicious cousins, believing the report, withdrew from the campaign, and Êrh-chu Chao was for the moment left alone to deal with his erstwhile friend.

On October 31, to give an air of legitimacy to his undertaking, Kao Huan set up at Hsin-tu prince T'o-pa Lang 朗 as emperor,[51] and on November 9, he inflicted a serious defeat upon Êrh-chu Chao at Kuang-o 廣阿,[52] thus opening up the road for a march

the supposed surname of Po-i and Shu-ch'i, whose kingdom was traditionally located in Jehol; cf. also *Chou shu* 17, biog. of I Fêng 怡峯, who was a man of Liao-hsi and whose original surname was also Mo-I.

For *Mukuru, cf. additionally the "barbarian" surnames Mo-hu-lu 莫胡盧, Mo-hou-lu 莫侯盧, and Mo-lu 莫盧 (*T'ung chih* 29-30).

[47] *Wei shu* 75, *Pei shih* 48.

[48] Near modern Chi 翼 hsien in Hopei. He had come into possession of that city in the second month of the year. For the past several months Kao Huan had been manoeuvring for the best position from which to strike at the Êrh-chu. On his relations with other rebels, cf. S. Hamaguchi, 高齊出自考 Eine Forschung zur Herkunft von Kōsei, *SZ* 1938, 821-855, 1004-1040. We hope to be able to add some pertinent material to Hamaguchi's interesting study.

[49] By his lieutenant Mu-jung Shao-tsung 慕容紹宗 (501-549), *Pei Ch'i shu* 20, *Pei shih* 53.

[50] *Wei shu* 75, *Pei shih* 48.

[51] On the advice of Sun T'êng 孫騰 (481-548), *Pei Ch'i shu* 18, *Pei shih* 54.

[52] Near modern Lung-p'ing 隆平 hsien, Ho-pei. Êrh-chu Chao's forces outnumbered those of Kao Huan, who was at the time very apprehensive as to the outcome of his

on Yeh 鄴. That important city was taken after several weeks siege on February 8, 532, and on April 3, KAO Huan installed there the new sovereign. The movement was growing; already eastern provincial commanders were rallying to KAO Huan's cause.[53]

Realizing only too late the grave threat to their very existence that KAO Huan now presented, the ÊRH-CHU rushed all available forces towards Yeh. On April 28 an army of some 200,000 men under the command of ÊRH-CHU Chao, ÊRH-CHU Chung-yüan, ÊRH-CHU Tu-lü, and ÊRH-CHU T'ien-kuang 天光 [54] arrived under the walls of the city. Entrusting the defense of the citadel to FÊNG Lung-chih 封隆之, [54a] one of his most reliable lieutenants, KAO Huan with a field corps of about 2,000 horse and 30,000 foot soldiers entrenched himself at Han-ling 韓陵. [55] A night attack upon the city having failed (May 16), the ÊRH-CHU turned against KAO Huan's camp two days later. The battle ended disastrously for them; panic and treachery [56] shattered the ÊRH-CHU army; the defeat became a rout; and the four leaders sought safety in flight.[57]

Within a fortnight KAO Huan was master of the situation and in possession of Lo-yang, the capital. On June 6, both T'O-PA Kung 恭, the emperor set up by the ÊRH-CHU, and his own puppet ruler T'O-PA Lang, whom he had brought to the capital, were deposed, and KAO Huan made preparations to install a new emperor. His choice fell at first on T'O-PA Yüeh 悅, prince of Ju-nan 汝南, then living in Liang, whither he had fled in 528 at the time

undertaking. *Pei Ch'i shu* 16 and *Pei shih* 54 give the credit for persuading him to strike boldly to Huan's wife's nephew TUAN Shao 段韶.

[53] *Pei Ch'i shu* 1, *Pei shih* 6.

[54] *Wei shu* 75, *Pei shih* 48: 496-532.

[54a] *Pei Ch'i shu* 21, 485-545 A.D. He had a private score to settle with the ÊRH-CHU, as his father had been killed by ÊRH-CHU Jung.

[55] A hill NE of An-yang.

[56] HU-SSŬ Ch'un 斛椿斯 (*Wei shu* 80, *Pei shih* 49: 495-537) and CHIA Hsien-chih 買顯智 (also known as CHIA Chih; *ibid.*: 490-534), generals of the ÊRH-CHU, passed over to KAO Huan's side and, in order to save their own skins, prevented the organization of further resistance.

[57] Chung-yüan fled south to the Liang. T'ien-kuang and Tu-lü were beheaded at Lo-yang. ÊRH-CHU Chao managed to evade pursuit until early in 533, when, tracked down, he committed suicide.

of ÊRH-CHU Jung's 榮 [58] capture of Lo-yang and the merciless slaughter of members of the imperial court. When Yüeh arrived from the border where he was residing in wait for a possible chance to re-enter the realm, KAO Huan changed his mind. Informed that T'O-PA Hsiu 脩, prince of P'ing-yang 平陽, [59] was discovered hiding in the vicinity, he had him brought to his camp, and on June 13, Hsiu was proclaimed emperor in the eastern suburbs of Lo-yang.

In its account of these events, *Pei shih* 5 has preserved an interesting detail of the coronation ceremony which is not found elsewhere. It appears that an ancient rite which the T'o-pa had practiced at Tai [60] was revived on the occasion. Seven men, presumably high officials, for KAO Huan is said to have been one of them, held up (lit. " were covered by ") a black felt rug on which the new emperor, facing west, made obeisance to Heaven. Following the ceremony, the emperor proceeded into the city, where he received at the palace, in the customary Chinese fashion, the congratulations of the court: ...。。。即位于東郊之外用代都舊制以黑氈蒙七人歡居其一帝於氈上西向拜天訖自東陽雲龍門入．

This custom is well known in the coronation ritual of the nomads of Central Asia, and is especially well attested by western sources for the Mongol period of the 13-14th centuries. The Armenian HETHUM [61] describes it as a part of the ceremonial of Jenghis Khan's inauguration, mentioning the detail of the black rug and the seven chiefs supporting it. HETHUM's insistance on the sanctity of the " primer usaige " is significant enough to cite the passage in full: [62]

" Dont il avint que les VII chevetaines dessus només [63] as-

---

[58] *Wei shu* 74, *Pei shih* 48: 493-530 A. D. Murdered by T'O-PA Tzŭ-hsiu on November 1, 530 (*Wei shu* 10, *Pei shih* 5).

[59] See genealogical table of the T'o-pa which indicates the relationships of all these princes (at end of this article).

[60] That is in the fourth and fifth centuries, prior to the removal of the capital to Lo-yang by T'O-PA Hung in 494.

[61] Nephew of Hethum I, king of Armenia, author of *La flor des estoires de la terre d'Orient*, dictated in French to Nicolas FALCON about 1307.

[62] *Recueil des historiens des croisades: Documents arméniens* 2, 148-149; cf. BERGERON (La Haye, 1735 ed.), *Histoire orientale de Haiton*, 27-28; L. DE BACKER, *L'Extrême-Orient au moyen-age*, 163-164.

[63] The seven chiefs of the seven " nations " enumerated in the preceding paragraph:

semblerent le pueple des Tartars, et firent faire obedience e reverence à Canguis, e eaus firent ce meismes, comme à leur naturel seignor." [64]

"Après ce, les Tartars establirent un siege à miluec de eaus e estendirent un feutre noir sur terre, e firent seer desur Canguis. E les chevetaines des VII nacions le leverent aveu le feutre, e le mistrent sur le siege [65] e le nomerent Can; [et en] egenoillant soi, li fesoient tout honor e reverence, come à leur seygnor. De cele sollempneté que les Tartares firent à leur seignor en celui temps, nul ne se devroit merveiller, car, par aventure, il ne savoient miaus, ou il n'avoient plus bel drap sur quoi il feissent seoir leur seignor. Mès de ce que il ne ont volu changier leur primer usaige, se porroit l'om bien merveiller, qui ont conquis tantes terres e roiaumes, e encores tienent leur primer usaige. Quant volent eslire leur seignor, e j'ai esté II foiz à la eleccion de l'empereor des Tartars,[66] e ai veü coment tous les Tartars s'assembloient en un grant champ,[67] e celui qui devoit estre leur seignor faisoient seoir sur un feltre noir, e metoient un riche siege au mi d'eaus. E venoient les hauz homes et ceaus du lignaige de Changuis Can, e le levoient en haut, e le metoient aseoir sur le siege, e puis lui faisoient toute reverence e honor, come à leur cher seignor e naturel. Ne por seignorie ne por richesce qu'il aient conquises, n'ont volu changier leur primer usaige."

So far as we know, Oriental sources do not mention such a rite at Jenghis Khan's elevation to leadership over the Mongol hordes.

Tartars, Tangot, Eurach (read Eurath), Jalair (some MSS Jasan), Sonit, Mengli, Tebet.

[64] End of ch. 1 of Book 3. Some MSS. have as the title of ch. 2: Comment les Tartars firent et esleurent premièrement leur seigneur, et le nommerent Cam.

[65] . . . cum maximo tripudio et clamore . . . adds the Latin version (*Recueil,* 284).

[66] The BERGERON version (*op. cit.,* 28) omits the repetition of the description of the ceremony, apparently believing it redundant. The omission is unwarranted, as the significance of the repetition lies in the emphatic testimony of the Armenian eyewitness to the fact that the ritual as practised in the second half of the 13th century was exactly the same as that performed at the enthronement of the founder of the Mongol empire.

[67] One French MS, supported by the Latin version, mentions a richly decorated tent erected on the ground where the ceremony took place. In the *Pei shih* account the emperor is said to have awaited KAO Huan's pleasure in a felt tent.

There is, however, no reason to doubt HETHUM's testimony, as much of his work is based on information he obtained directly from the Mongols. Practised by nomadic rulers already some eight or nine hundred years before Jenghis Khan, the rite must have been part of the traditional ceremony of the inauguration of a khan, and the solemnity with which it was performed by the great conqueror's descendants would indicate that it was well sanctified by tradition.

According to SIMON OF ST. QUENTIN (in PLANO CARPINI IX, 10)[68] the ritual was followed at the coronation of Güyük in August 1246. The color of the felt is not given nor the number of the nobles who lifted the rug but Güyük's consort is said to have sat on the rug together with the khan during the elevation. As SIMON himself was not present at the coronation his testimony is but of secondary importance. The *Waṣṣāf*, on the other hand, testifies that the ritual was performed at the coronation of Hai-shan 海山 (pht. Wu-tsung 武宗, 1281-1308-1311). The details of the ceremony, as given by D'OHSSON (*Histoire des Mongols 2.* 528-529 n.), differ slightly from those noted by the Armenian historian for preceding enthronements: the color of the rug is said to be white, and while seven princes of the blood participate in the ritual, only four of them lift the khan up, while two others support him by the arms, and the last of the seven presents him with a cup of wine.

IBN 'ARAB-SHĀH (*Fākihat al-Khulafā*, Bonn 1832 and 1852, 234-235; Mosul ed. 1869, 234) describing the coronation of Mongol khans also mentions but four high officials اربعة النفس كلامير كبير who lift up the rug by the corners, but specifies the color of the felt as black.[69] Our last contemporary witness, SCHILTBERGER (*Travels*, Hakluyt Soc. 58, p. 48), states that the kings of Great Tartaria were raised at enthronement on a white felt three times, then carried around the tent and seated on the throne. The survival of the custom (invariably with a white felt and in most cases

---

[68] That section of Carpini's work is attributed to Simon by Vincent de Beauvais.

[69] I am indebted to Professor W. W. POPPER for the correct understanding of the passage describing the coronation.

with four men lifting the rug) has been observed among Turkish and Mongol tribes down to the present time.[70]

Prior to the Mongol period, we find some elements of the ceremony among the T'u-chüeh. According to *Chou shu* 50, at the inauguration of a new khan the highest nobles of his entourage raised him up on a felt rug making nine turns in the direction of the sun's movement, and at each turn the new khan's subjects made obeisance to him. The color of the felt and the number of men lifting the rug are not specified. It is probable, however, that the T'u-chüeh custom, if not borrowed from the T'o-pa, originated in the same milieu, and that the number of chieftains was also seven. Although nine and ten are arithmologically more important in the known customs of the T'u-chüeh, it is likely that the number seven was associated among them with an older constitutional tradition. In the famous letter of the T'u-chüeh khan to Emperor Maurice,[71] the khan calls himself in the preamble ὁ μέγας δεσπότης ἑπτὰ γενεῶν καὶ κύριος κλιμάτων τῆς οἰκουμένης ἑπτα. We are inclined to see in the " seven races " and the " seven climates " genuine Turkish expressions rather than *calques* of western origin. The division of the T'u-chüeh into eight μοῖραι mentioned by MENANDER [72] can also be interpreted as meaning seven traditional tribal groups plus that of the παλαίτερος μονάρχος 'Αρσίλας.

Returning to the T'o-pa ritual, one must observe that the number of men supporting the rug is based undoubtedly on the tradition that prior to their migration southward the T'o-pa under Khan Lin 隣 (pht. Hsien 獻, c. 160 A. D.) [73] were divided into seven hordes under seven chiefs, all elder and younger brothers of Lin. Together with Lin's own clan or horde, there were eight divisions; including two other divisions (of more distant relatives), the T'o-pa came to comprise altogether ten clans

---

[70] See Н. И. Веселовскій, Пережитки нѣкоторыхъ татарскихъ обычаевъ у русскихъ, Живая Старина 1912, 27-38. VESELOVSKY thinks that the Russian custom of " rocking " (качать) a person at the celebration of his promotion might be a survival of the Tartar rite of " elevation " on a rug (pp. 36-38).

[71] Theophylactus Simocatta 7. 7-9.

[72] Menander, Bonn 399.

[73] Cf. *HJAS* 1. 180.

族.[74] This division should not be confused with that into four hordes, of administrative and geographical origin.

As to the color of the felt, the testimony of *Nan Ch'i shu* 57 and *Sung shu* 95 is explicit that black was the official and most honored color among the T'o-pa.[75] That the emperor faced west during the ceremony is curious. Orientation to the east seems to have been the most prevalent among the nomads,[76] until supplanted by a southern orientation, probably under the influence of the Chinese. Northern orientation is not unknown, but a western one is not attested. A possible explanation in our case might lie in the fact that as the coronation took place in the eastern suburb of Lo-yang, the emperor faced west towards the capital where he was about to hold sway.

Our passage in the *Pei shih* raises incidentally another very interesting question. If we compare our text with that of *Wei shu* 11, we note that the description of the ceremony is inserted between 即位于東郊之外 and 自東陽雲龍門入 (*Wei shu* has 入自 東陽雲龍門) of the *Wei shu*, and comprises twenty-four characters. The number is highly suggestive in view of the fact that many ancient Chinese texts were characterized by a pronounced stichometry, the usual length of a line being twenty-two or twenty-four characters. The question requires a detailed study. We shall limit ourselves for the present to pointing out a few salient facts and significant illustrations.

It is well known that prior to the Han certain important texts such as the *Shu ching* were written on bamboo (or wooden) tablets 22 or 24 Chinese inches long. According to *Han shu* 30, LIU Hsiang believed that the tablets 22 inches long contained 22 characters, while those 24 inches in length comprised 25 characters (cf. CHAVANNES, Les livres chinois avant l'invention du papier, *JA*

---

[74] *Wei shu* 113.

[75] Prior to the removal of their capital to Lo-yang the T'o-pa ruled (according to the Chinese cosmological scheme) by virtue of the water element, whose color is black.

[76] The T'u-chüeh, Wu-huan, and Hsiung-nu, as is well known, oriented themselves towards the rising sun. So did the Juan-juan, according to a text which has, I believe, been overlooked heretofore: *Pei shih* 13, biog. of the Juan-juan princess, daughter of A-na-huai, who became the consort of T'O-PA Pao-chü. She died at childbirth in 540, aged 16 Ch.

1905, 1-75, esp. pp. 30-38), and used effectively his theory in his critical analysis of the *Shu ching*. If, however, tablets of 22 inches contained 22 characters, it is more probable that those of 24 inches long contained 24, rather than 25 characters.[77] Indeed, should we examine certain suspicious passages in the *Shu ching*, we would find that many of them number exactly 24 characters. Thus, in the *Yao Tien*, Yao's famous speech to Hsi Ho on the length of the year, a paragraph markedly differing from the rest of the chapter in its rhythm and style, is 24 characters long: (1) 帝曰咨汝羲暨和朞三百有六旬有六日以閏月定四時成歲.[78] The long speech of Kuei 夔 in *I chi* 益稷 (preceding another by the same person which is but a repetition of a passage in the *Shun tien*: 夔曰於予擊石拊石百獸率舞) contains from (2) 夔曰戛擊 ∘ ∘ ∘ to 鳳凰來儀, 48 characters, *i. e.* 24 x 2.[79] Similarly, the paragraph preceding the aforementioned passage of the *Shun tien* (3) 帝曰夔命汝典 ∘ ∘ ∘ 神人以和 = 48 characters. The one following the twelve characters, beginning 'Kuei said ' . . . , which may be considered an interpolation, (4) 帝曰龍朕聖 ∘ ∘ ∘ 朕命惟允 is 26 characters long; omitting 帝曰, which is not necessary if the passage is a continuation of paragraph 3, we have 24 characters.[80]

Again, the first part of chapter 20 of the *Lun yü*,[81] which has always been recognized as containing a jumble of passages taken

---

[77] Liu Hsiang's estimate is, however, not necessarily incorrect; there are, indeed, a few scattered paragraphs in the *Shu* that are 25 characters long.

[78] The corresponding passage in *Shih chi* 1 is only 13 characters long. Ssǔ-ma Ch'ien omits the preamble (7 chars.) and ∘ ∘ ∘ 有 ∘ ∘ ∘ 有 ∘ ∘ ∘ 成歲. On the supposition that the preamble is not necessarily a part of the text, we have 17 chars. forming the fundamental part of that paragraph. With the following eight chars. which close the first section of the *Yao Tien*, the paragraph would number 25 chars. in the *Shu*, 21 in the *Shih chi*. In the second part of the *Yao Tien*, we note the following stichometrical paragraphs: 1. 帝曰疇咨若時 ∘ ∘ ∘ 訟可乎—23 chars. 2. 帝曰咨四岳朕在位 ∘ ∘ ∘ 忝帝位—25 chars. 3. 曰明明 ∘ ∘ ∘ 如何—24. The section closes with two paragraphs, the first of 26, the second, 23 chars.

[79] Note that the passage coming just before the one in question numbers 22 characters: 帝曰迪朕 ∘ ∘ ∘ 象刑惟明.

[80] In addition we have in the *Shun tien*: 帝曰俞咨禹 ∘ ∘ ∘ 皐陶—24 chars. (so also in *Shih chi* 1); 帝曰契百姓 ∘ ∘ ∘ 在寬—21 chars. (22 in the *Shih chi*).

[81] The *Lun yü* is generally supposed to have been recorded on tablets 8 inches long (Chavannes, *op. cit.* 33). Cf. Forke, *Lun Hêng*, 456.

out of texts similar to the *Shu ching* in style and content, inserted in the original text of chapter 19 （子張）, can be paragraphed in the following manner: （5）堯曰咨爾舜。。。天祿永終: 24 characters.

Then follows an obvious interpolation or gloss of five characters 舜亦以命禹; next comes （6）曰予小子履。。。有罪不敢赦: 22 characters. This, together with the following paragraph, seems to be taken from a version of the present *T'ang kao* 湯誥 chapter of the *Shu*;[82] one or possibly two characters are missing before 曰. （7）帝臣不蔽。。。罪在朕躬; 24 characters.[83] （8）周有大賚 。。。在予一人: 24 characters.[84] Two paragraphs, the first of 31 characters, the other of 22 characters,[85] close the text.

These examples of stichometry in the *Shu* could easily be multiplied. But there is a far cry from Chou texts written on clumsy wooden tablets to chronicles put down on paper a thousand years later. How could the stichometry of the *Shu ching* and similar texts affect the material organization of the jottings of an historian of the sixth or seventh century A.D.? An examination of a printed page of the pre-revolutionary period would gives us the answer. Until recent times the outward appearance of such a page still preserved all the essential features of ancient texts written on tablets. Evenly written columns of a Chinese text each containing the same number of characters and separated from each other by thin vertical lines are but a reproduction of a row of tablets placed side by side for uninterrupted perusal.[86] The respectful elevation

[82] Cf. also *Mo Tzŭ*, ch. 兼愛, where the quotation of the second paragraph of T'ang's speech is closer to the *Lun yü* text.

[83] The corresponding section of the *T'ang kao* （爾有善。。。以爾萬方）numbers 22 + 20 words.

[84] The last 16 words of the paragraph come from the *T'ai shih* chapter of the *Shu*, where 12 characters intervene between the first and the second sentences composing the 16.

[85] Totaling altogether 53 characters. Note, however, that the five characters 信則民任焉 are omitted in the oldest versions, such as that of the stone Classics. Without these five characters the paragraphs would comprise 48 (24 x 2) words.

[86] It is quite possible that the custom of making a paper scroll for recording important documents by pasting together long and narrow strips of paper, which was current in the medieval Near East, is a survival of the Chinese conception of a page as a row of tablets glued together.

of some lines by one or two characters reflects the old uneven dimensions of the tablets, as 24 inch *vs.* 22 inch tablets. The title of the book on the margin is a survival of the practice of marking the title on the edges of tablets stacked up in a bundle,[87] while the black wedge mark placed on the margin one-fourth of the length of the page from the top edge (and sometimes also at a point marking the same distance from the bottom), the so-called "fish-tail" 魚尾, is undoubtedly the vestige of the notch on ancient tablets which held in place the string which kept the tablets together when tied.[88]

It is noteworthy that rolls of silk which supplanted tablets as writing material were in ancient China 24 inches wide.[89] It is reasonable to suppose, therefore, that when paper was substituted for silk, the traditional dimensions were preserved, at least for the most important documents, and that the length (in terms of number of characters) of the ancient tablets was reflected in the length of a line.

It could well have been thus that the chronicles of Wei were recorded on paper with columns containing 22-24 characters following the time-honored *Shu ching* pattern. Our passage numbering 24 characters formed such a line in the original source used by both the *Wei shu* and the *Pei shih* and, while omitted in the former text, was restored in the latter.

A study of the paragraphing of *Pei shih* 5 will further confirm the supposition. In the annals of Tʻo-pa Lang we have: (1) 二年春二月甲子以勃海王高歡爲大丞相卅國大將軍太師： 24 characters,[90] followed by (2) 及歡敗爾朱氏於韓陵四月辛巳帝於河陽遜位

[87] As is still done today when titles are marked on the edge of the *pên,* so that a particular *pên* can be located without opening the *tʻao.*

[88] Cf. Sir Aurel STEIN, Notes on Ancient Chinese Documents, *New China Review,* 3. 243-253.

[89] Cf. Sir Aurel STEIN, Central-Asian Relics of China's Ancient Silk Trade, *TP* 20. 130-141 (with additional notes by Professor PELLIOT).

[90] The date corresponds to March 1, 531. *Pei shih* 6, *Pei Chʻi shu* 1 mention KAO Huan's elevation to the posts of chancellor and generalissimo immediately following the date of the capture of Yeh (February 8). Note that both passages from 正月壬午○○○ to ○○○太師 number also 24 words. In *Wei shu* 11, where the appointment is given in greater detail, all the events of the second month are registered in a passage 44 chars. long.

於別邸: 22 characters,[91] then, (3) 五月孝武封帝爲安定郡王十一月殂於門下外省時年二十: 24 characters. Cf. the different wording of the same paragraph in *Wei shu* 11 which also contains the same number of characters, 24 from 五月 ○ ○ ○ to 二十. (4) At the beginning of the annals of the same emperor the paragraph 廢帝諱朗 ○ ○ ○ 明悟 numbers 24 characters in *Pei shih* 5. In the *Wei shu*, with slightly different wording, the same number.[92]

The annals of T'o-pa Hsiu begin with (5) 孝武皇帝 ○ ○ ○ 李氏, a paragraph 24 characters long (*Wei shu* has 21), followed by (6) 帝性沈厚 ○ ○ ○ 縣公, 22 characters (corresponding to *Wei shu*'s 23). Next come two paragraphs numbering 17 and 19 characters,[93] the latter parallel to an entry of 69 (23 x 3) characters in the *Wei shu*. The text continues with (7) 中興二年 ○ ○ ○ 遜大位, 21 characters (or 24, if we suppose that 安定王 stood after 廢帝 in the source used by the *Pei shih*), matched by 24 characters in the *Wei shu* (same content but different wording). Then, following the words 歡乃與百燎議, we have (8) 以孝文 ○ ○ ○ 而止: 23 characters (24, if we suppose that 歡 had originally been the subject of the sentence) parallel to 21 in the *Wei shu*.

With a rather loosely used 又—" also," *Pei shih* takes up the story of Hsiu's hiding, and we count in (9) 又諸王 ○ ○ ○ 五旬而 44 characters. The 而 supposedly linking this paragraph with the next, is not in good style, and it is reasonable to suspect some omission.

Continuing with the account of Hsiu's discovery by KAO Huan. *Pei shih* has a long section consisting of 26 + 26 + 26 + 26 + 9 characters[94] extracted undoubtedly from some *Ch'i chü chu* (Court

---

[91] Here the *Pei shih* is obviously summarizing a long account in its sources.

[92] The next sentence, omitted in the *Pei shih*, numbers 23 characters. The rather lengthy account of the first year of his reign (in the *Wei shu*) is summarized in the *Pei shih* in three paragraphs of 23, 26, and 23 words.

[93] That last number is rather significant, for in the *Wei shu* the enumeration of all the appointments T'o-pa Hsiu received after his enfeoffment (from 通直 ○ ○ ○ to 左僕射 inclusive) takes 76 (19 x 4) characters. These have been reduced to 19 in the *Pei shih*, making it appear as if, at one stage of the process of editing, four lines of a text written in columns of 19 characters had been condensed into one single column.

[94] Note that at the beginning of the fourth paragraph we have 使斛斯椿 ○ ○ ○

Journal) rather than from chronicles. Then follow in succession four paragraphs dealing with the enthronement: (10) 於是假 ○ ○ ○郭之外: 21 characters. (11) 用代都○ ○ ○拜天訖: 24 characters, or 23 if the last character be considered part of the next paragraph. (12) 自東陽○ ○ ○極前殿 23 (or 24) characters. (13) 羣臣朝○ ○ ○昌元年 22 characters.

In order to understand the re-arrangement of the different sources, one must compare the above section with the corresponding passage of the *Wei shu*[95] which consists of 戊子 (a) 卽帝位於東郭之外 (b) 入自東陽雲龍門 (c) 御太極前殿 (d): 22 characters. 羣臣朝賀禮畢昇閶闔門 (then omitting the long edict) 大赦天下改中興二年爲太昌元年: 24 characters.

This text the *Pei shih* supplemented with passages from an unknown source and re-arranged as follows: (1) The second line was reduced to 22 characters by the omission of 天下. (2) Date (a) in expanded form 永熙元年夏四月戊子皇帝[96] was inserted between sentences (b-c) and (c-d), thus producing our example 12. (3) The description of the elevation ceremony (24 characters) was inserted at point (b). (4) (a-b) was joined to the 14 characters 於是假廢帝安定王詔策而禪位焉[97] which probably formed the concluding sentence of the section from the *Ch'i chü chu* mentioned above. Altogether, the original 46 characters of the *Wei shu* were expanded into 90 (49 characters added and 5 omitted) or, in other words, to two original lines two more were added, and the text was re-arranged to form a continuous study.[98]

" (he) sent Ho-ssŭ Ch'un . . ." the name unnecessarily written in full, where on the basis of the preceeding we should expect Ho-ssŭ Ch'un's *ming* alone to be used.

[95] On the supposition that the *Wei shu* forms the basic text. The argument and the reconstruction would not be fundamentally affected, however, if the *Wei shu* paragraphs prove to be, as suggested above, an abridgment of an ulterior source.

[96] It is likely that the *Pei shih* is correct in omitting the date for the "elevation" ceremony and giving it only for the sitting on the throne in the capital itself, as the possibility is not to be dismissed that the "elevation" took place some time before the emperor's enthronement in the Chinese fashion.

[97] 廢帝安定王 "the deposed emperor (who later became) king of An-ting" comes obviously from a source which termed both Kung and Lang "deposed emperors," and hence had to specify which of them was meant. The *Pei shih* editors should have used *fei ti*, "the deposed emperor," alone, as Kung is termed by them *Chieh-min ti* 節閔帝. See *supra*, paragraph 7.

[98] Stichometry throws an interesting light on the processes followed by ancient

We do not imply, naturally, that a Chinese historian was obliged to use exactly 22 or 24 characters [99] to express a thought or record an event and was not permitted to shorten or expand paragraphs. But given the traditional length of a line and the instinctive tendency of an artist to arrange his material in conformity with the physical dimensions of his canvas, it is not surprising that paragraphing in a terse and flexible language like Chinese was conditioned by time-honored stichometry. We believe that the above examples are suggestive enough to give the stichometrical method of textual criticism a trial in disentangling the strands of the web that we call a historical text.[100]

Chinese scholars in editing or condensing a text. Take, for instance, the well-known passage in *Shih chi* 1 where Ssŭ-MA Ch'ien speaks of Shun's employment of the descendants of Kao-yang and Kao-hsin. In the present text the passage can be paragraphed as follows: $17 + 13 + 20 + 16 + 24 = 90$ chars. In a much completer form the story is found in the *Tso chuan* (Duke Wên, 18th year) and is paragraphed: $41 + 40 + 21 + 22 + 24 = 148$ characters. The only paragraph which is identical in both texts is the last paragraph (24 chars.). From the first paragraph a line of 24 chars. was eliminated from the *Tso chuan* text, leaving substantially the same 17 characters that we have in the *Shih chi* (substituting only 世得其利 for 天下之民). Another continuous line of 24 chars. was left out in the second paragraph; and the remaining 16 chars. were reduced to 13 by substituting 世 for 天下之民. The third *Tso chuan* paragraph was reduced to 20 by the omission of 以 before 至. The next paragraph of 22 chars. was reduced to 16 by the omission of 臣堯 at the beginning of the sentence and of 地平天成 at the end. The last omission is especially significant. The four paragraphs in the *Tso chuan* total 124 chars. If we suppose that these 124 chars. were recorded on tablets 24 inches long, they would require 5 tablets with 4 characters left over. Of these five tablets or lines, the *Shih chi* eliminated two (24 chars. of the first paragraph and 24 of the second), leaving $72 +$ the 4 surplus chars. Through editorial changes 6 of the 72 were eliminated within the paragraphs and the 4 surplus characters were discarded altogether. The total was thus reduced to 66 chars. which could conveniently be written in 3 lines of 22 chars. each. That the last was indeed the stichometrical pattern of that part of the *Shih chi* is indicated by the fact that in the following section (also apparently based on the same *Tso chuan* text) we have paragraphs 22, 21, 21, 21 chars. long. Note that the last paragraph (on the *t'ao-t'ieh*) was produced, by the elimination of 24 continuous chars., out of the corresponding paragraph of the *Tso chuan* (and six characters transposed from the remaining part).

[99] Observe that the numbers 22 and 24, as consisting of various combinations and multiples of 4 and 6, are numbers well adapted for purposes of paragraphing a Chinese text written in phrases of 4 or 6 characters each.

[100] Illustrations of the stichometrical form of the old documents are abundant in the earlier dynastic histories, and can be easily located through a comparison of variant

5. The Rise and Fall of the House of Yang

On May 15, 578 reports reached Ch'ang-an that the T'u-chüeh Turks had invaded Yu 幽 chou and were raiding the countryside.

renderings of events by two different sources, as in the case of the *Shih chi* and the *Han shu*. In reading Professor H. H. Dubs' translation of the *Han shu* annals I have noted numerous passages where a little stichometrical computation would throw considerable light on the history of the text and its relation to that of the *Shih chi*.

The very opening of the first chapter may serve to supply us with several examples. The paragraphing of the sources down to the words 丈夫當如此矣 (or 也, *Shih chi*) is as follows: *Han shu*: 15, 31 (+4?), 24 (-4?), 20, 21, 22, 23, 25. *Shih chi*: 22, 35 (+4?) 24 (-4?), 22, 22, 22, 23, 26.

Note that the sixth paragraph, where the *Han shu* does not specify the "wonderful sight" which appeared over Kao-tsu in the wineshops, while the *Shih chi* mentions a dragon manifestation over the drunken hero, is nevertheless exactly that same length in both sources. Again in both sources, the only paragraph that exceeds our limit of 20-25 characters is the second paragraph, precisely the one that we should suspect (it deals with the miraculous conception of Kao-tsu by a "dragon" 交龍). A skeptic might, indeed, suggest that the source used by both the *Shih chi* and *Han shu* originally ran: 嘗息大澤之陂夢與神遇是時雷電晦冥父太公往視則見交 (24 characters in the *Han shu*; 23 in *Shih chi*, omitting 父) meaning simply that Kao-tsu was the offspring of a "union (交) in the open field." I doubt very much if Professor Dubs' translation "came *to look for her*" is justified for 往視, as 視 does not ordinarily mean "to look *for*." The dragon could, of course, have played a part in another version of the story, but the possibility should not be overlooked that it was introduced into our paragraph from paragraph eight. Note, furthermore, that the first two paragraphs combined number in the *Han shu* 46 (15+31) characters, *i.e.* originally they comprised two lines, one of 22, the other, of 24 characters. This supposition is further strengthened by the fact that the *Shih chi* rendering of the first paragraph numbers 22 characters.

For interesting instances, cf. Dubs, pp. 72-76. On p. 72, we have the account of Kao-tsu despatching troops for the relief of his parents at P'ei and of measures taken by Hsiang Yü to prevent it. The account is 40 characters long, but the sentence 遣將軍○○○於沛, which is practically identical with the corresponding story in *Shih chi* 8, contains 24 characters. As to the *Shih chi* version it consists of two paragraphs each exactly 24 characters long: 令將軍○○○於沛 and 楚聞之○○○漢兵.

On pp. 72-73, we have, beginning with 陳餘○○ · and ending with ○○○代王, two paragraphs, the first of 22, the second of 24 characters. Next follows one of 25 characters. The last sentence of that paragraph occurs in *Shih chi* 8 as part of a paragraph 正月○○○父老 numbering 24 characters. The paragraph 使韓太尉 ○○○韓王 24), on p. 73, reduced to only 20 characters, is split up in the *Shih chi* by the interpolation of 24 characters: 於是置○○○河南郡. Another paragraph of 24, 使諸將○○○上塞 completes the page.

The events of the third month, on p. 75, down to the words ○ ● ○河南郡 (27

Fresh from his triumph over the Ch'i, the Chou emperor Yü-wên Yung prepared to send his veteran troops against the invaders,[101] and on June 13, Chou armies began moving towards the frontier. The emperor was about to place himself at their head, when, on June 17 he fell ill. Three days later on account of the aggravated condition of the sovereign, the order was issued to discontinue the

characters) correspond to another paragraph of 24 in the *Shih chi* 三月 ○ ○ ○ 河南郡. The next sentence, omitted in the *Shih chi* has 21 characters (with the preceding 27, the paragraph numbers 48). The following long story of the *San-lao* of Hsin-ch'êng is summarized by the *Shih chi* in 23 characters. The paragraph telling of Kao-tsu's proclamation of mourning for the Emperor I (ending with the words 告諸侯) numbers 23 characters in the *Shih chi*, 22 in the *Han shu* (in different wording).

The difficulty observed by Professor Dubs on p. 70 in the dating of the expedition against Yung, which *Shih chi* 8 says occurred in the "eighth month," seems to be solved by the application of stichometrical principles. In the *Han shu* the day "fifth month" is obviously part of the text for the first two paragraphs of the account (五月 ○ ○ ○ 陳倉 and 雍兵 ○ ○ ○ 雍地) each number 20 characters (including the 五月). In the *Shih chi* the three paragraphs (omitting "in the eighth month" 八月) number: 22 + 21 + 23 = 66, that is exactly three lines of 22 characters, indicating that 八月 is a later addition.

On p. 71, the paragraph 時彭越 ○ ○ ○ 梁地 is 24 characters long. The corresponding paragraph in the *Shih chi* 予彭越 ○ ○ ○ 大破之, 23 characters. The preceding paragraph (p. 70-71) numbers 43 characters. Altogether this section from 五月 ○ ○ ○ to 爲齊王 has: 20 + 20 + 17 + 43 = 100 characters, plainly indicating that it was originally recorded in 5 lines each containing 20 characters. The corresponding section of the *Shih chi* (with much additional material and including the P'ÊNG Yüeh paragraph) has from 乃陰令衡山王 ○ ○ ○ down to 頂羽大怒北擊齊: 16 + 28 + 23 + 21 + 23 + 21 characters, showing that it was written in lines of 22 characters. It is interesting to note that after the P'ÊNG Yüeh interlude (24) and another paragraph of 24, the *Han shu* returns to the 20 character line in 秋七月 ○ ○ ○ 降漢 (observe that, as in the preceding paragraph of 20, we have an exact date).

On page 81, beginning with 六月 ○ ○ ○ to ○ ○ ○ 十餘縣 we have 48 characters, corresponding to the same number in the *Shih chi* (without a different wording of the last sentence. That the next 11 characters are an interpolation (as suggested by Professor Dubs) is confirmed by the fact that the next line 於是令 ○ ○ ○ 乘塞 numbers 24 characters (23 in *Han shu*).

These examples can be easily multiplied. We shall end with one more significant illustration. The enthronement of King Huai is described in *Shih chi* 7 in two paragraphs, each of 24 characters: 乃求 ○ ○ ○ 所望也 and 陳 ○ ○ ○ 武信君. In *Han shu* 31, with different wording, we also have 48 characters; in *Shih chi* 8, from 聞陳王 ○ ○ ○ to 武信君, 25 characters (or 24, omitting either 聞 or 梁); *Han shu* 1 (again in a paragraph containing a date) covers the whole story in 20 characters.

[101] The frontier garrisons had been defeated and the commander of the Yu chou march, Liu Hsiung 劉雄, slain (*Chou shu* 29, 50).

elaborate preparations for the campaign.[102]   On June 21, while being transported back to his capital, Yung breathed his last.[103]

There is little doubt that, had that energetic ruler lived, the unification of the empire which he had inaugurated with his smashing victory over the Ch'i in 577 would have been carried to a successful conclusion sooner than it actually took place eleven years later under the succeeding dynasty.[104] The seasoned warriors and able generals of Chou, under the command of an emperor beloved by the rank and file, would have undoubtedly been successful, had the Turkish campaign been carried out, in administering a serious blow to the power of the T'u-chüeh, and might have thereby spared the frontier districts of China years of misery. As it happened, however, Yung's scepter passed into the hands of his maniacal son Pin who managed in the brief space of two years to destroy all his father had built.[105]

Officially, Pin abdicated the throne in favor of his young son on April 1, 579, but continued to rule the empire until June 580, when, upon his death, the control of the government slipped into the grasp of YANG Chien. On March 4, 581 YANG Chien deposed the boy Yü-wên Ch'an 闡 [106] and Northern China awoke to find a new dynasty ruling over its twenty-five odd millions of souls.

As Chinese dynastic changes go, the transition was rather sudden. Of all the great officers of Yü-wên Yung, YANG Chien was perhaps the least conspicuous, even though he was heir to YANG Chung, a general who had served the dynasty with great distinction, and had become himself Crown Prince Pin's father-in-law

---

[102] These included the commandeering of all horses and donkeys, public- and privately-owned, in the region " within the passes " (Kuan chung).

[103] *Chou shu* 6, *Pei shih* 10. It is possible that he died a day or two before, but that his death was not announced until June 21. Cf. *Chou shu* 40, biog. of WEI-CH'IH Yün 尉遲運, 539-579.

[104] The fate of the Southern Chinese Empire was sealed with the occupation of the Shu country in 553 by the troops of Western Wei under WEI-CH'IH Ch'iung. With the North united under one rule, the weaker South could never withstand a simultaneous attack from the plains and along the river from Szechwan.

[105] Yü-wên Yung was well aware of the defects of his son, and is said to have considered setting him aside. Cf. *Chou shu* 40.

[106] Consult genealogical tables of the Yü-wên family for every Yü-wên mentioned here (see end of this article).

in 573. The position occupied by the YANG family at the Chou court was certainly inferior to that of the LI 李 [107] and the WEI-CH'IH 尉遲, and his personal prestige incomparably lower than that of such military leaders as WEI Hsiao-k'uan, prince YÜ-WÊN Hsien, WANG Kuei 王軌,[108] or LIANG Shih-yen 梁士彥.[109] The posts he had occupied and the titles he had received since October 30, 573, when his eldest daughter YANG Li-hua 麗華 [110] was married to Pin, were no more important or high sounding than those of a dozen of his contemporaries.[111] And yet, within two years after Yung's death, this seemingly unpretentious man,[112] with no other claim to prestige than that of being the empress dowager's father, suddenly emerged as master of China and, crushing swiftly the opposition of men far greater than he, displaced the YÜ-WÊN on the throne.

Usurpation, in China as elsewhere, must, in order to be successful, follow time-honored rules and requires a complex technique. Traditional loyalties and old habits must be carefully managed and hearts and minds brought slowly to the acceptance of the coming change as inevitable. All through the history of China,

---

[107] LI Hsien 賢, LI Mu 穆 and their relatives. *Chou shu 25, Pei shih 59.*

[108] *Chou shu 40, Pei shih 62.* Often referred to as WU-WAN 烏丸 Kuei.

[109] 515-586 A.D. *Sui shu 40, Chou shu 31, Pei shih 73.*

[110] *Chou shu 9, Pei shih 14,* 561-609 A.D. Enfeoffed as Lo-p'ing 樂平 *Kung-chu* in 586. Died during Yang ti's western campaign. Her only child, a daughter, married LI Min 李敏, *Sui shu 37.*

[111] He was in command of one of the several armies sent against Ch'i in 575; commander of the third army in the Ch'i campaign of 576-577; on March 17, 577 he was made *tsung-kuan* of Ting 定 chou and on January 22, 578 tsung-kuan of Nan Yen 南兗 chou. It was only after YÜ-WÊN Yung's death that he received his first appointment at the court, as ta ssŭ-ma (September 14, 578). *Sui shu 38,* biog. of LU Fên, states incorrectly that he occupied the last post already under YÜ-WÊN Yung.

[112] The biographies of KUO Jung 郭榮 and P'ANG Huang 龐晃 (*Sui shu 50*) state, however, that about 577 YANG Chien confided to these two friends that he hoped some day to supersede the Chou on the imperial throne. P'ANG Huang even urged him to revolt at Ting chou, but Chien did not think the time ripe. What chances of success would an open insurrection have at the time? In order to answer that question, we must establish on what dissatisfied elements of the population ambitious plotters of the period based their hope of turning an uprising into a revolution. P'ANG Huang was an old retainer of YÜ-WÊN Chih 直, Yung's brother, who rebelled in 574, and P'ANG Huang had approached YANG Chien on his behalf as early as 562. It is likely that the persecution of Buddhism and Taoism which began in 574 afforded adventurers a good chance of organizing a movement of opposition to the government.

wise politicians contemplating a dynastic revolution painstakingly followed historical precedents which prescribed in details the gradual steps to be followed in such cases. They knew that the public must be convinced that the " virtue "[113] of the old dynasty is exhausted and that the vigor of the new house must fully manifest itself before the change is sanctified in the actual transfer of of the title of Son of Heaven.[114] History taught them that fifteen to twenty years were necessary for a prospective usurper to win, cajole, or buy lasting allegiance. How often in the troubled dynastic story of China, all-powerful dictators with the coveted imperial scepter within their grasp delayed with the final step of usurpation, and continued to honor outwardly some puppet of their own creation, hesitating to dispossess the moribund dynasty of the last visible vestige of power. Not infrequently, undoubtedly aspiring to emulate the example of the illustrious Wên wang, they left this task to their sons and limited themselves to setting the stage for the dynastic change.

Thus, the mighty Ts'ao Ts'ao, undisputed master of Northern China by 205 A. D.,[115] with the Han emperor completely in his power, contented himself with the titles of chancellor and *wang* and left to his son Ts'ao P'ei the honor of becoming the first emperor of the Wei. The three dictators of the Ssŭ-MA family, omnipotent since 249 A. D.,[116] with the deposition of the Ts'ao-Wei a foregone conclusion in everybody's mind, delay the seizure of the throne until 265, when the son of the last of the three establishes the new dynasty of Chin. Liu Yü,[117] founder of the

---

[113] Chinese *tê* 德—" energy," " power." *Tê* is conceived almost as a charge of electric energy accumulated by the ancestors of a house which keeps it " going " for a definite amount of time. As long as a dynasty continues to manifest the efficacy of its *tê*, any attempt to supplant it runs counter to the *t'ien tao* 天道.

[114] Continuous success in undertakings, military victories (especially over barbarians), recognition by elder sages, and enfeoffment as *wang* were generally considered necessary preliminaries.

[115] The last members of the Yüan 袁 family, Ts'ao's chief rivals in the North, were suppressed in that year. In 208, Ts'ao made himself chancellor. In 213 he is made kung, in 216, wang.

[116] In that year, Ts'ao Shuang 爽, the most dangerous of the Ts'ao princes of the blood, was put to death by Ssŭ-MA I, and his party completely crushed.

[117] *Sung shu* 1-3, *Nan shih* 1. Ascended the throne on July 10, 420. He was born on

Sung house, did not dispossess the last Ssŭ-MA (Chin emperor)
of the throne until 420, although he was certainly contemplating
and had ample opportunity for usurpation as early as 405.[118] Both
KAO Huan and YÜ-WÊN T'ai, in complete control of the situation
in Eastern and Western Wei respectively, the former for thirteen
years (534-547), the latter for twenty-two (534-556), bequeath
the task of establishing new dynasties to their sons. In the case
of HSIAO Tao-ch'êng,[119] founder of the Southern Ch'i dynasty, the
period of apprenticeship for the imperial throne was unusually
short, but in that instance the change was quickened by a struggle
for power among the members of a regency.[120] Having disposed
of his rivals, HSIAO Tao-ch'êng proceeded unhesitatingly to his
aim, no one daring to raise his voice in a *quo jure*.[121]

YANG Chien's hand seems to have been forced in a somewhat
similar manner. Whatever plans he may have had to make use
of his position as the emperor's father-in-law were seriously
jeopardized in the spring of 580. Sometime early in the year
YÜ-WÊN Pin became enamoured of a beautiful grand-daughter of
WEI-CH'IH Ch'iung who had recently become the bride of YÜ-WÊN
Wên 溫, a prince of the blood. The emperor having forced his
attentions upon the beauty,[122] her husband's father, YÜ-WÊN

the night of *jên-yin* of the third month of the first year of Hsing-ning 興寧 under Ai
哀 ti of Chin, April 16, 363. The *Sung shu* says he was 67 (Chinese) years old at
the time of his death, on June 26, 422. The *Nan shih* gives his age correctly as 60.
The "7" of the *Sung shu* is a dittographical lapsus due to the following 七月 "7th
month" (giving the date of burial).

[118] His task of deposing the Ssŭ-ma was facilitated by a previous unsuccessful
usurpation, that of HUAN Hsüan 桓玄.

[119] Pht. T'ai-tsu Kao ti, b. 427, ascended throne May 29, 479, died April 11, 482.
Nan Ch'i shu 1, *Nan shih* 4. Father WIEGER, *Textes historiques*, 1153, gives his age at
the time of death incorrectly as 54 (Chinese).

[120] The regency had been administering affairs since May 10, 472 in the name of
LIU Yü (born March 1, 463; asc. throne May 11, 472; died August 1, 477) and LIU
Chun (born Aug. 8, 469; asc. throne Aug. 5, 477; deposed May 26, 479; died June 23,
479). *Sung shu* 9-10; *Nan shih* 3. I cannot explain why *Sung shu* 10 says Chun was
13 (Chinese) years old when he died.

[121] The Liang who succeeded the Nan Ch'i belonged to the same HSIAO family. The
dynastic change did not thus involve a transfer of the heavenly mandate. The Ch'ên
inherited the empire in a time of internal turmoil and foreign invasion, and their case
is, therefore, exceptional.

[122] She was presented at court probably on the occasion of her marriage, or possibly
at one of the banquets given by the emperor. There was one given on April 1, 580.

Liang亮, unable to suffer the disgrace to his family honor, rose up in rebellion on April 2, 580.[123] The uprising was suppressed, Yü-wên Liang and his son, another Uriah, were put to death, and on April 19, Wei-ch'ih Ch'ih-fan 熾繁 [124] (such was the unfortunate girl's maiden name) was made fifth empress.[125] It must have been sometime during the next six weeks that Pin, determined to exalt his new love further and to eliminate Yang Chien's daughter, condemned, on some pretext or other, the latter to death. She was saved only by the intercession of her mother, *née* Tu-ku, who so insistently pleaded for her daughter's life that the emperor relented.[126]

The fortune of the Yang family hung, however, in the balance. Pin had never liked Yang Chien and had once threatened to extinguish his entire family.[127] On June 2, 580, Yang Chien was made *tsung-kuan* of Yang 揚 chou, an appointment tantamount to exile.[128] He delayed his departure [129] until June 8 when it became known that the emperor was desperately ill. Friends of Yang Chien issued a forged imperial order commanding his presence at the sovereign's bedside.[130] He appeared at the palace, and the same night, or sometime within the next few days, Pin

[123] At Yü 豫 chou, while returning from a campaign against Ch'ên (under the command of Wei Hsiao-k'uan), *Chou shu* 7, 10, 31.

[124] *Chou shu* 9, *Pei shih* 14, 566-595 A.D. Forced to become a nun, she later assumed the name Hua-shou 華首. Is she identical with the grand-daughter of Wei-ch'ih Ch'iung of whom Yang Chien became enamored sometime in the nineties and who was killed by the jealous Tu-ku?

[125] Pin had four "Heavenly Empresses." Lady Wei-ch'ih was made "Heavenly Empress of the Left" succeeding Empress Ch'ên 陳, who became "Heavenly Empress of the Center."

[126] *Chou shu* 9, *Pei shih* 14.

[127] *Sui shu* 1, *Pei shih* 11.

[128] According to *Sui shu* 38, however, Yang Chien himself sought a provincial post, probably in order to avoid further imperial displeasure, and the appointment was secured for him by Pin's favorite Chêng I. As the latter was one of the chief figures in the plot which gave Yang Chien his chance, it is likely that there was some secret understanding between them as to that particular move. Chêng I himself was appointed military commander of Shou-yang and was to join Yang Chien in an attack upon the Ch'ên empire.

[129] Because of illness, real or pretended.

[130] Chêng I and Liu Fang were mainly responsible for his being summoned. The efforts of Yen Chih-i 顏之儀 (523-591, *Chou shu* 40, *Pei shih* 83) and others who attempted to notify elder members of the dynasty were circumvented.

expired.[131] His death was kept secret while the conspirators urged YANG Chien to assume the regentship. Uncertain of his power, Chien hesitated, but finally yielded.[132] In his own words, the situation in which he found himself was illustrative of the adage " astride a tiger—unable to get off." [133]

Once he decided upon usurpation, YANG Chien proceeded swiftly and ruthlessly. On June 20, the five remaining sons of YÜ-WÊN T'ai, princes Chao 招, Shun 純, Shêng 盛, Ta 達, and Yu 逌 were summoned from their fiefs to the capital.[134] Three days later, with the exception of Empress Dowager Chu 朱,[135] mother of Ch'an, and, of course, YANG Chien's daughter,[136] Pin's empresses were forced to become nuns. On June 25, WEI Hsiao-k'uan was appointed *tsung-kuan* of Hsiang 相 chou to succeed WEI-CH'IH Ch'iung,[137] the most dangerous of Chien's potential rivals. Though suspecting that they were marching into a trap, the YÜ-WÊN princes, arrived at the capital on July 1,[138] and YANG Chien could

[131] Cf. *HJAS* 3.251, n. 95.

[132] LIU Fang, one of the chief conspirators, is said to have threatened to seize power himself had YANG Chien declined. At the moment Pin was still alive, though unable to speak, his tongue being paralyzed (*Sui shu* 38).

[133] According to *Sui shu* 36, the saying was used by YANG Chien's wife in a message she sent him urging him to assume control of the government. In *Sui shu* 78 (*Pei shih* 89) Chien uses it himself in a conversation with the diviner YÜ Chi-ts'ai 庾季才 (516-603) whom he consulted on the occasion. 獸 in the text stands for 虎—" tiger," a T'ang taboo. Cf. also *Sui shu* 38, biog. of LU Fên 盧賁, for YANG Chien's acknowledgment of his indebtedness to the conspirators and his admission that without LIU Fang, CHÊNG I, LIU Ch'iu, LU Fên, and HUANG-FU Chi 皇甫績 he would never have obtained power.

[134] Their appanages were created on June 30, 579 and the princes were ordered on the same day to proceed to their respective fiefs. YÜ-WÊN Chao's daughter's impending marriage to the T'u-chüeh khan served as a pretext for the summons (*Chou shu* 7, *Sui shu* 1).

[135] CHU Man-yüeh 滿月, 547-586, a native of Wu. She became wardrobe-keeper in the Chou palace, where she attracted the attention of YÜ-WÊN Pin, who was 12 years her junior. She changed her name to Fa-ching 法淨 on becoming a nun (*Chou shu* 9, *Pei shih* 14).

[136] YANG Li-hua approved her father's seizure of power, and he considered himself greatly indebted to her (cf. *Sui shu* 37, LI Min's biography). She was much perturbed, however, by his plans to usurp the throne and openly showed her disapproval of his intentions.

[137] Father WIEGER (*Textes historiques*, 1923 ed., 1225, 1264) reads incorrectly WEI-CH'IH Hui 迴 for WEI--CH'IH Ch'iung 逈.

[138] At least one of them, YÜ-WÊN Shun, was brought to Ch'ang-an under duress. Cf. *Sui shu* 54, biog. of TS'UI P'êng 崔彭.

now be sure that no rival of his could gain precedence over him by making use of the prestige of a member of the dynasty.

On July 7 (a *chia tzŭ* day, auspicious for pronunciamientos) WEI-CH'IH Ch'iung announced to his troops, as YANG Chien had feared, his intention of rescuing the YÜ-WÊN from Chien's designs, and openly rose against the self-styled chancellor. On the same day prince YÜ-WÊN Hsien 賢, the first victim of YANG Chien's ambition, was executed.[139] Fearing that Ch'iung might find an ally in WANG Ch'ien 王謙, commander of I 益 chou,[140] Chien despatched LIANG Jui 梁睿 [141] to relieve him. Within the next days, however, half of the empire was in open rebellion against the chancellor: YÜ-WÊN Ch'ou 冑 and WEI-CH'IH Chin 勤 [142] took up arms on August 12, SSŬ-MA Hsiao-nan 司馬消難,[143] the father of Ch'an's consort,[144] on August 21, and, finally, WANG Ch'ien on September 1. On August 24, YANG Chien barely escaped assassination at the hands of YÜ-WÊN Chao and YÜ-WÊN Shêng.[145] Both princes were forthwith executed.

YANG Chien's situation was indeed precarious.[146] Three of the most influential military commanders of the empire were mustering their troops for a march upon the capital.[147] LIU Fang 劉昉

---

[139] Hsien's plot to thwart YANG Chien's plans for usurpation was uncovered by Chien's kinsman YANG Hsiung 雄 (*Sui shu* 43: 542-612). The other princes were under constant observation. On August 8, they attended YÜ-WÊN Pin's funeral "escorted" by 6000 horse, led by YANG Hsiung.

[140] *Chou shu* 21, *Pei shih* 60.

[141] *Sui shu* 37, *Pei shih* 59, 531-595 A.D.

[142] Ch'iung's nephew, second son of WEI-CH'IH Kang 綱, Ch'iung's younger brother, *Chou shu* 20, *Pei shih* 62: 507-569.

[143] *Chou shu* 21, *Pei shih* 54. The son of SSŬ-MA Tzŭ-ju 子如, a great officer of the Ch'i, he had fled to Chou in 558. A sworn brother of YANG Chung, he was treated with great respect by YANG Chien who looked upon him as his uncle.

[144] SSŬ-MA Ling-chi 令姬, *Chou shu* 9, *Pei shih* 14. She later married LI Tan 李丹, a provincial governor under the Sui, and was still alive at the time of the composition of the above sources.

[145] For details, cf. biog. of YÜAN Ch'ou 元冑, *Sui shu* 40.

[146] One of his satellites, YÜAN Chieh 元諧 (*Sui shu* 40, *Pei shih* 73) compared Chien's position to that of an adobe wall 垣牆 in the midst of water. YANG Chien is said to have laughingly reminded him of the comparison after his triumph.

[147] In addition KAO Pao-ning 高寶寧, a former officer of Ch'i, rebelled in the Northeast, and together with the T'u-chüeh made ready to support YANG Chien's rivals.

and CHÊNG I 鄭譯 [148] to whom he owed his elevation showed
signs of becoming lukewarm towards his cause and both declined
to assume responsibility for the conduct of the campaign against
WEI-CH'IH Chiung, the chief of the " rebels." Generals whom he
had sent against Yeh, Ch'iung's stronghold, were employing dila-
tory tactics, playing for time and waiting whither the wind of
fortune would turn.[149] LIU Fang was already contemplating plac-
ing another YÜ-WÊN, prince Tsan 贊, Pin's brother, on the throne
and becoming dictator himself.[150]

But YANG Chien's luck held. In KAO Kung 高熲,[151] an adopted
member of the Tu-ku clan, he found a new confidant and a faithful and energetic servant who volunteered to undertake the task
of coördinating the armies of the northeast. His spies must undoubtedly have informed him of the inherent weaknesses of his
enemies.[152] They were acting as men of small ambition. At Yeh,
WEI-CH'IH Ch'iung, at odds with his own sons, entrusted the
management of affairs to local officers, many of them old subjects
of the Ch'i, who were naturally imbued with separatist tendencies
and thought little of the empire as a whole. Instead of moving
boldly on Ch'ang-an as he had been advised by KAO A-na-hung
高阿那肱,[153] WANG Ch'ien remained inactive in the fastnesses of
Shu. Ssŭ-MA Hsiao-nan, pressing but feebly his claims as the little
emperor's father-in-law, concentrated all his efforts on safeguard-
ing his rear by effecting an alliance with the Ch'ên empire.[154] To

[148] LIU Fang: *Sui shu* 38, *Pei shih* 74. CHÊNG I (540-591): *Sui shu* 38, *Chou shu* 35, *Pei shih* 35.

[149] Cf. *Sui shu* 60, biog. of Yü Chung-wên 于仲文, on how YÜ-WÊN Hsin, one of the chief generals, was persuaded to act more energetically by Yü Chung-wên's analysis of YANG Chien's virtues. Cf. also *Sui shu* 42, biog. of LI Tê-lin 李德林.

[150] CHÊNG I and LIU Fang's rôle in the *coup d'état* became known almost immediately, as both lost no time in making a display of the favors with which they were rewarded.

[151] *Sui shu* 41, *Pei shih* 72. Cf. *Sui shu* 37, biog. of LI Hsün 李詢.

[152] According to the biography of YÜ-WÊN Ch'ing 慶, *Pei shih* 57, YANG Chien had correctly estimated his rivals' worth as early as 579. He thought of WEI-CH'IH Ch'iung as a man of no great intellectual capacity, Ssŭ-MA Hsiao-nan, his " uncle " by adoption, he believed to be flighty, and WANG Ch'ien, downright stupid.

[153] Governor of Lung 隆 chou and former great officer of the Ch'i, who had been in a large measure responsible for their downfall (*Pei Ch'i shu* 50, *Pei shih* 92). *Chou shu* 21 writes incorrectly A-shih-na Huai 阿史那瓌 which would make him a T'u-chüeh Turk.

[154] LIU Hsiung-liang 柳雄亮 (*Sui shu* 47) was despatched by YANG Chien to Ch'ên

YANG Chien's immense relief LI Mu 李穆, who occupied the key post of commander of Ping 并 chou, after some hesitation decided to throw in his lot with the chancellor.[155]

By the first week of September the tide began to turn definitely in YANG Chien's favor. On September 11 WEI-CH'IH Ch'iung was completely defeated and committed suicide;[156] ten days later, SSŬ-MA Hsiao-nan, abandoning the struggle, fled to Ch'ên; and YANG Su 素,[157] the ablest of Chien's clansmen, defeated and killed YÜ-WÊN Ch'ou. Emboldened, YANG Chien deposed the SSŬ-MA empress (October 3) and conferred upon himself additional titles,

in order to circumvent Hsiao-nan's plans. LIU Chuang 莊 (*Sui shu* 66, *Pei shih* 70) performed the same task at the court of the king of Liang, vassal of the Chou. His estimate of the "rebels" was as uncómplimentary as that outlined above. Cf. *Chou shu* 48.

[155] *Chou shu* 30, *Pei shih* 59, *Sui shu* 37. The vacillating LI Mu was persuaded to join YANG Chien's cause by LIU Ch'iu 柳裘 (*Sui shu* 38) and his son LI Hun 渾 whom Chien despatched to him for the purpose. According to the son's biography, LI Mu sent him back to YANG Chien with a flatiron as a present urging him to use it to pacify the empire (to "pacify" and to "iron" are homonyms and homographs in Chinese). He is also said to have offered YANG Chien a golden belt with thirteen rings, one of the imperial insignia, thus signifying his assent to YANG Chien's plans of usurpation.

The above passage is one of the earliest references in historical sources to the "flat-iron" (by name, the object is known since Han times), *wei-tou* 熨斗 anc. *$iu\partial t$-$t\d{z}u$-g. Another is found in *Chin shu* 75, biog. of HAN Po 韓伯. We believe that the Chinese term was borrowed by the Turks who designate the flatiron by the word *ütüg* (Osm. *ütü*, with numerous derivatives), which appears already in Kašγari (BROCKELMANN, *Wortschatz*, *ütük*, but cf. RACHMATI's review of BROCKELMANN's work, *Ungarische Jahrbücher* 10, 450: read *ütüg*). From Turkish the word passed into Russian which has утюгъ. The final -*g* of the Turkish word would date the borrowing from Chinese as about the IV-Vth cc. A.D. when the Auslaut of *tou* 斗 was still sounded in the north of China. On the belt with thirteen rings, cf. WANG Kuo-wei's *Hu fu k'ao* 胡服考, also PELLIOT's review of that work in *TP* 25.

Another northern military commander whose defection might have proved fatal to YANG Chien, but who signified his adherence to the cause by arresting the envoy of WEI-CH'IH Ch'iung and sending him to Ch'ang-an was YÜ I 于翼, tsung-kuan of Yu 幽 chou. With LI Mu and YÜ I on his side, YANG Chien could count upon eventual victory. For YÜ I, cf. *Chou shu* 30, *Pei shih* 23, *Sui shu* 60.

On May 22, 607, LI Mu's services to the dynasty were commemorated with a sacrifice at his grave by emperor YANG Ti (*Sui shu* 3).

[156] How much YANG Chien feared WEI-CH'IH Ch'iung is indicated by the fact that he degraded Ts'UI Hung-tu 崔弘度 (*Sui shu* 74) for not killing WEI-CH'IH Ch'iung in time to prevent the latter from denouncing YANG Chien in a violent speech before his self-inflicted death.

[157] *Sui shu* 48, *Pei shih* 41. The rôle that this man played in the events of the next 25 years demands a special study.

tightening his control over the government on October 30. Three
days later Yü-wên Shun was executed and on November 18, WANG
Ch'ien's rebellion was completely crushed. A month later, the last
of the minor rebels was suppressed.

On January 3, 581 (*chia tzǔ*, the first day of the cycle) YANG
Chien signified his triumph by assuming the title of *wang*. A week
later, Yü-wên Ta and Yü-wên Yu, the last of the elder princes
of the blood, were put to death, and all preparation for usurpation
proceeded apace. Auspicious clouds appearing on February 6
prompted diviners to urge YANG Chien to ascend the throne, and
on the next *chia tzǔ* day (March 4) [158] the new dynasty came into
being. In the summer of the same year, the last surviving members of Yü-wên T'ai's family were liquidated, including the little
ex-emperor, Ch'an, who died, presumably murdered,[159] on July 10.

As one reads the chronicles of YANG Chien's reign, one gets the
impression from the passages where the emperor appears as a real
individual, rather than a pompous figurehead, that, for the first
few years at least, he could hardly believe his luck.[160] He never
forgot the desperate situation in which he found himself in July-
August 580. He realized that he had no great popular following,
that his house had had no time to establish fully its rights to the
empire, and that in the minds of many he had arrogated to himself the mandate of Heaven which could not have departed from
the Chou so soon after the manifestation of heaven's favor towards that house in the military triumph of 577.[161] Though sober-
minded himself, he began to welcome any testimony whatever to

---

[158] The day was selected by the diviner YU Chi-ts'ai. Precedents: Chou Wu wang
and Han Kao-tsu, who both ascended the throne on a *chia* day of the second month
of the year. The same diviner " noticed " the clouds.

[159] His death was, says tersely *Chou shu* 8, 隋志也 " the will of the Sui." Altogether, 59 Yü-wên princes were put to death and the main branch of the family was
exterminated without trace. Suggested by Yü Ch'ing-tsê 虞慶則 (*Sui shu* 40, *Pei
shih* 73: died 598), the executions were protested only by LI Tê-lin.

[160] He was much perturbed once early in his reign by a prediction of his Grand
Astrologer that his " fortune " would end within three years (or in the third year of
his reign?). Cf. *Pei shih* 63.

[161] As P'EI Su 裴蕭 (*Sui shu* 62, *Pei shih* 38) expressed it, on hearing that YANG
Chien had made himself chancellor: " Is it possible that Heaven should renounce the
Chou when the earth is not yet dry on the grave of the great conqueror Wu ti (Yü-
wên Yung)? " His remark is said to have so displeased YANG Chien that Su was
deprived of official position for five years.

the effect that his family was indeed predestined to the crown, and sycophant diviners eagerly seized upon this opportunity.[162]

The abundance of the most absurd testimonials as to signs and portents presaging his rise, horoscopic calculations, and far-fetched interpretations of trivial events as auspicious manifestations predicting a long reign for him and his dynasty, presented to the throne by sundry wizards and seers,[163] serves as a good indication of YANG Chien's uneasy state of mind and his lack of confidence in his fortune, especially after 586 when he was reminded by a serious plot against his power [164] how shaky was the foundation on which he had built his throne. There is also no doubt that his tolerance towards Buddhism and Taoism, which from 600 on becomes a definite predilection towards those creeds, had its inception in his hope to win adherents and at the same time to find in the divine hosts of their pantheons protection against the consequences of his hybris.[165]

---

[162] Cf. *Sui shu* 78, *Pei shih* 89, particularly the biographies of HSIAO Chi 蕭吉 and CHANG Ch'ou-hsüan 張冑玄; *Sui shu* 69, biographies of WANG Shao 王劭 (also *Pei shih* 35) and YÜAN Ch'ung 袁充.

[163] Thus his appointment as governor of Sui chou in 562 is said to have been portended by the clearing of the muddy waters of the Yellow river; the discovery of stones and tortoises with inscriptions predicting a long reign is duly recorded in 580; the appearance of white dragons is naturally interpreted as referring to YANG Chien since he was born in the year of the white cock (*hsin yu*, 541 A. D.); a white dragon triumphs over five black ones: the black dragons are, of course, either the five emperors of Chou (Yü-wên Chüeh, Yu, Yung, Pin, and Ch'an) or the five Yü-wên princes put to death in 580; YANG Chien should not have hesitated to take the throne immediately after Pin's death; the dates of the solstices hide deep significance, all indicating continuous prosperity, etc., etc. Astrologers went as far as reporting that his benign influence caused the lengthening of the gnomon's shadow!

Some physiognomists prided themselves on having discovered his high destiny long before 580. One of them, LAI Ho 來和, pointedly reminded him that in 575 and 576 he had had abundant opportunity to betray YANG Chien's secret to Yü-wên Yung, but had instead allayed the Chou emperor's suspicions. He and three others were handsomely rewarded for both perspicacity and discretion.

While it is true that Chinese sources record similar signs and portents at the accession of every dynasty, in no other case do the chronicles record such an intense interest on the part of the new emperor in this evidence of heavenly favor.

[164] The chief conspirators were LIANG Shih-yen, LIU Fang, and Yü-wên Hsin 忻 (*Sui shu* 40, *Pei shih* 60, 523-586) executed on October 16, 586 (*Sui shu* 1). Cf. *Sui shu* 38 (biog. of LIU Fang) for YANG Chien's long edict listing their crimes and justifying the punishment visited upon them. One must remember that earlier that year Chien had been urged to abdicate.

[165] His quick success in wresting power from the Chou had undoubtedly inspired

There was in YANG Chien's character a curious puritanical strain,
possibly fostered in him by his wife, but the ostentatious simplicity
of dress and manner that he affected cannot entirely be explained
by his natural sobriety and thriftiness. One feels in his moralizing
speeches an undertone of deep-seated fear that should he or members of his immediate family exercise too freely the privileges or
enjoy too completely the benefits of their position, fate would
speed up the inevitable turn downward of the wheel of fortune.
It seems indeed as if the dread of "the jealousy of the gods"
haunted YANG Chien through all his years as emperor.

Earlier in his life, again probably under the influence of his
wife, he had quarreled with his brothers.[166] After he became emperor, he repeatedly showed signs of being suspicious of his own
sons, accusing them of extravagance and of being too anxious for
coming into their inheritance. These suspicions were not entirely
unfounded. The life of Northern China was strongly affected by
the nomadic traditions of its Turco-Mongol conquerors. Among
those traditions was one which did not permit a ruler to continue
beyond a fate-appointed time,[167] and another, still more sinister,
which enjoined patricide as an almost religious duty.[168] YANG
Chien must have pondered over the significant fact that for the
preceding two hundred years only two emperors [169] (from among
those of the Wei, Ch'i, and Chou dynasties) had reached the age
of forty, his own age at the time of the usurpation, and that in
many cases the demise of an imperial father was not without the
connivance of his imperial son and heir.

---

some of his officers with the hope that, given a favorable opportunity, some one of them
would be able to duplicate YANG Chien's feat, but at his expense. In the edict mentioned in the preceding note YANG Chien accused, probably not without reason, LIANG
Shih-yen of paying heed to a physiognomist who predicted that he would become
emperor sometime after his sixtieth year. One of the reasons for KAO Kung's disgrace
was that his son dared to compare his father with SSŬ-MA I. As early as about 584
YANG Su's career was seriously jeopardized by his wife's denunciation that in a moment
of anger he had said that he might be emperor some day.

[166] See genealogy of the Yang family, below.

[167] Cf. the custom practised by the T'u-chüeh and the Khazars of half-strangling a
newly elevated khan and asking the dazed man how long he expected to reign,
subsequently murdering him if he exceeded the limit. We suspect that the same
tradition existed among the T'o-pa.

[168] The question of gerontoctony among the nomads, a custom attested already by
western classical writers, demands a special study.

[169] T'O-PA T'ao and T'O-PA Pao-chü who both lived to the age of 44.

The year 600, twentieth of his reign and the sixtieth of his life, marked the crisis in YANG Chien's relations to his sons. As early as 586 he had been urged to abdicate in favor of his eldest son Yung 勇 [170] whom, in the latter's capacity of heir-apparent, he suspected most of evil designs against himself. The relations of father and son had been strained since 591, when Yung's mother, a fanatical believer in monogamy,[171] accused her son of doing away with his chief wife for the sake of one of his concubines.[172] How YANG Kuang 廣,[173] the second son, skillfully used his parents' prejudice against his elder brother to further his own ends is too well known a story to be recounted here. We must insist, however, on the significance of the date of Yung's disgrace and Kuang's elevation in his stead, 600 A. D. In July of that year YANG Chien had completed a full sexagenary cycle (59 years in our reckoning) of life.[174] He must have suspected that in the belief of many of his subjects he should not attempt to exceed that, to them natural, limit.[175] A week after his birthday, his third son Chün 俊 died under exceedingly suspicious circumstances: his wife was accused of having poisoned him and was forced to commit suicide.[176] YANG Chien openly displayed great callousness at his son's funeral, performing the prescribed lamentations in less than perfunctory manner. Was he secretly glad of being rid of a prospective rival and was there more to Chün's death than we are led to believe by the sources? [177] In the tenth month of the same year, on November

---

[170] Cf. *HJAS* 3, 236.

[171] Her puritanism in this respect went as far as meddling in the family affairs of her husband's ministers. Cf. the biog. of KAO Kung, *Sui shu* 41.

[172] Lady YÜAN, Yung's consort, died on February 22, 591 (*Sui shu* 1). She was the daughter of YÜAN Hsiao-chü 元孝矩 (*Sui shu* 50). Yung's favorite concubine was Lady Yün, daughter of YÜN Ting-hsing 雲定興, *Sui shu* 61.

[173] Pht. YANG Ti, *Sui shu* 3-4, *Pei shih* 11. Ascended throne August 13, 604; murdered April 11, 618.

[174] He was born on July 21, 541.

[175] About 598, some Buddhist seers prophesied that YANG Chien would not live beyond 599, *Sui shu* 41.

[176] *Sui shu* 45, *Pei shih* 71. She was a sister of Ts'ui Hung-shêng 崔弘昇. The latter's daughter married YANG Chao, YANG Kuang's eldest son, who divorced her following her aunt's condemnation.

[177] The prince had been deprived of his official position and title on August 30, 597 for extravagance and wasting public funds. YANG Chien had repeatedly declined the petitions of several of his officers to reinstate Chün, and upon the prince's death,

20, Kuang's machinations against Yung finally accomplished their purpose. Yung was publicly degraded and he and all his sons were reduced to the state of simple subjects without rank or title. On December 13 Kuang was proclaimed crown prince. YANG Chien and his wife thought that they had nothing to fear from their favorite, who had shown himself to be a dutiful and pious son in the best Chinese tradition, and doubtless congratulated themselves on having left the critical year behind them. On February 4, 581 (three days before the close of the Chinese year) YANG Chien issued an edict which re-established Buddhism and Taoism as religions favored by the state by proclaiming that the defama-tion of Buddhist and Taoist images would be henceforth con-sidered a criminal offense.[178]

On September 15, 602 YANG Chien lost his life companion, the Empress Tu-ku.[179] Still suspicious of his sons, he lent a willing ear to the calumnies of YANG Kuang and on January 27, 603 he degraded his fourth son Hsiu 秀 on the accusation of black art practices against his father and his brother Liang 諒. In the manu-factured evidence Kuang skillfully involved the last brother by instilling into Chien's mind the belief that Hsiu considered Liang a rival worthy of a magic attack and, therefore, a potential equal to his father. With all his brothers out of the way, Kuang had now the field to himself and undoubtedly resolved to succeed his father at the earliest opportunity.[180] This presented itself in the summer of 604. YANG Chien was ailing,[181] and YANG Kuang was im-patiently awaiting his passing. An incident at the palace having revealed to the emperor the evil mind of his son, YANG Chien

ordered the latter's richly ornamented and expensive household objects to be burned and refused the request of Chün's retainers to erect a stele in his memory.

[178] On June 16, 603 (5 mo., 40, *Pei shih* 11; *Sui shu* 2, incorrectly, 4 mo.) an edict prohibited the slaughter of animals on YANG Chien's birthday (13th day of the 6 mo.).

[179] According to the sycophant WANG Shao she was an avator of Avalokiteśvara, and undoubtedly continued to protect him in the beyond.

[180] Although YANG Chien apparently did not suspect Kuang of treacherous designs, he lost his confidence in Kuang's chief supporter, YANG Su, who was denounced about that time by LIANG Pi 梁毗 (*Sui shu* 62).

[181] Both *Pei shih* 11 and *Sui shu* 2 say he fell ill on *i-mao* of the fourth month. Read " fifth " (June 22), as there was no *i-mao* day in the fourth month. On March 4 of that year he had retired to the Jên-shou palace, entrusting YANG Kuang with the management of current affairs. Note that 604 was a *chia-tzŭ* year, the first of the cycle.

came suddenly to the realization of his folly in playing into his designs.[182] With his plans discovered, no way was left to Kuang but to administer the *coup de grâce*. The *Sui shu* pointedly hints that on his orders YANG Chien was murdered in his bed on August 13, 604.[183]

A life beset by fear of retribution had ended and the uneasy conscience of a man who dared too much was stilled by death, but the curse of the family which presumed to gather the fruits of power before they were ripe descended upon the patricide.[184] The sources are suspiciously vague on the subject of YANG Kuang's relations with his sons. His eldest, Chao 昭, died in August 606,[185] a day before YANG Su, Kuang's *âme damnée*, whose death was undoubtedly ordered by the emperor,[186] who since his accession feared this unscrupulous man, the companion of all his crimes, and as Kuang well knew, a crafty and dangerous plotter. Did the

---

[182] After the death of his wife, YANG Chien elevated to the rank of *kuei-jên* his favorite among the women of the palace, the lady Hsüan-hua 宣華, a daughter of CH'ÊN Hsü 陳頊 (emperor Hsüan of the Ch'ên). According to her biography in *Sui shu* 36, *Pei shih* 14, YANG Kuang had as early as 589 formulated a plan to use her in furthering his ambitions and it is said that gifts from the prince influenced her to the extent of helping him in his campaign against Yung, the heir-apparent. At the time of YANG Chien's illness, YANG Kuang tried to make love to her. When she reported it to the emperor, the latter in his wrath against Kuang ordered that his disgraced son Yung be recalled, apparently in the intention to restore him to his rightful place as Crown Prince, but YANG Su and YANG Kuang prevented the order from being executed.

After Chien's death, the lady Ch'ên was forced to accept Kuang's attentions. She died about 606, at the age of 29 (Chinese). Her father, CH'ÊN Hsü was emperor of Ch'ên from February 5, 569 to February 17, 582 (*Ch'ên shu* 5, *Nan shih* 10); he died at the age of 52 (Chinese), and was thus born in 530. The *Ch'ên shu*, however, gives as the date of his birth August 6, 528 (7th month, day *hsin-yu* of the second year of *Ta-t'ung*). The *Nan shih* corrects *Ta-t'ung* to *Chung-ta-t'ung* which indeed give us the correct date 530, but there was no *hsin-yu* day in the 7th month of 530.

[183] Presumably by CHANG Hêng 張衡, *Sui shu* 56, *Pei shih* 74; cf. *Sui shu* 1. He was executed in 612.

[184] YANG Yung and his sons were put to death shortly after YANG Chien's death, and YANG Liang was killed in prison sometime in 605, after an unsuccessful rebellion. YANG Hsiu remained incarcerated all through Kuang's reign.

[185] On August 30 (*Sui shu* 3, *Pei shih* 12), the next day, according to *Sui shu* 59. Note that YANG Su was at the time t'ai shih of the Heir Apparent.

[186] Shortly before Su's death, YANG Kuang had him enfeoffed as Duke of Ch'u 楚, maliciously expecting the fulfillment of an astrological prediction that death would soon strike a great personage residing in that region. *Sui shu* 48 implies that Kuang intended to poison Su.

emperor suspect YANG Su of contriving his overthrow in favor
of his heir, and was the murderer of father and brothers a filicide
as well? A further study of the sources might elucidate that question. Kuang's second son Chien 暕 enjoyed a brief period of
favor,[187] but soon fell into disgrace, was suspected of harboring
secret designs against his father and was kept under close observation. The remaining members of the Yang family felt constantly
upon themselves the suspicious eye of the emperor. A cynic, YANG
Kuang tried to enjoy at least the years allotted to him by fate to
the full. He lived in real imperial style and remained in Chinese
history a notorious example of the regal spendthrift, a magnificent
and proud waster. When his ambitious and grandiose plans of
foreign conquest failed and the empire began to crumble under
his feet,[188] with a flippant *après nous le déluge,* he let his dynasty
and power crash to their doom, recognizing, with the ease of the
amoral individual that he was, that in the battle against fate man
is always worsted, and in the hour of his death he undoubtedly
let the responsibility for the ruin of the house rest on his father's
shoulders. When the news of his murder at the hands of Yü-wên
Hua-chi 化及,[189] a scion of the house that his father had overthrown in 580, spread through the disrupted empire, it startled no
one, for the masses instinctively know that Heaven's ways are
sure and the doom of retribution it visits on those guilty of hybris
is inexorable.[190]

6. ADDENDA AND CORRIGENDA TO MARGINALIA 1-2 AND GENEALOGICAL TABLES

We hasten to correct two mistakes committed in "Theophylactus
Simocatta on China," *HJAS* 3, 236:

1. For KAO Hui read KAO Wei. The character 緯, which served

---

[187] He was, however, never officially proclaimed crown prince.

[188] On Yang ti's reign and the disintegration of his empire, cf. Woodbridge BINGHAM,
Factors Contributing to the Founding of the T'ang Dynasty (Univ. of California doctoral dissertation, 1934) which, we hope, will soon be published in revised form.

[189] *Sui shu* 85, *Pei shih* 79. Killed on March 22, 619, *T'ang shu* 1. Four months
previously he had proclaimed himself emperor.

[190] The fate of the Yang is constantly used by Chinese historians as an illustration
of the principle of the dependency of the fate of a dynasty and the empire on the

as the personal name of the last sovereign of Ch'i, is now read Wei. Same correction on p. 233.

2. At the bottom of the same page, in the phrase: " the reigning sovereign and father of the boy," read *grandfather* for *father*.

Note 32 on p. 232 requires a more serious correction:

The age of the empress TU-KU (personal name Ch'ieh-lo 伽 羅,[191] pht. Hsien 獻) was incorrectly given, as we were misled by *Sui shu* 36 which says that she was 50 (Chinese) years old at the time of her death in 602. The correct figure is 59, as given by *Pei shih* 14. She was then born in 544 and was thus already of marriageable age at the time of her father TU-KU Hsin's death in 557. She was YANG Chien's junior by only three years.

The date of her birth is confirmed by *Sui shu* 78, biography of HSIAO Chi, where, in his report to the emperor, that diviner insists that the year 594 has especially auspicious chronological characteristics since the winter solstice falls on the day *hsin-yu* (58th of the cycle) which is also the cyclical designation of the year of the emperor's birth (541), while the summer solstice falls on *chia-tzŭ*, the cyclical designation of the date of the empress's birth, and 544 was precisely a *chia-tzŭ* year.[192]

The possible explanation of the mistake in the *Sui shu* (50 for 59) is that in the original source used by the compilers after the mention of the empress's death which took place in the *eighth* month, there followed some entry of a happening (such as an order

---

proper exercise of *tê* by the ruler, expressed so tersely in the saying 一人失德四海 土崩 (cf. postface of *Sui shu* 5).

[191] Anc. *g'ia-lá*, transcribing Sanskrit *kāla*. The binom usually designates agallochum or eaglewood perfume (the wood of the *Aquilaria agallocha*), Chin. *ch'ên hsiang* 沈香 and possibly represents the first two syllables of Sanskrit *kālāguru*—" black *aguru* (agallochum)." A term referring to incense or perfume would be quite appropriate as a girl's name, while " black " alone would hardly be suitable as a proper name for a representative of the fair sex.

[192] As 544 was a rat year, it is possible that the empress's birth within that cyclical animal's twelvemonth made her, in the opinion of witch doctors, particularly susceptible to the attacks of the malignant " cat demon " 猫鬼 which her half-brother TU KU T'o 陀 was accused of cultivating in his house and the exorcism of which was prohibited by imperial edict in 598 (*Sui shu* 1, *Pei shih* 11). On the magical practices of T'o's household, cf. *Sui shu* 79, *Pei shih* 61, and CHAVANNES, " Le cycle des douze animaux." It is to be noted that, according to the story, the " cat demon," to whose influence the empress's illness was attributed by the shamans, was exorcized on rat days.

issued by YANG Chien to select a proper burial place for his wife) dated the *ninth* month of the year. That is, the original text ran ran 八月。。。后崩於永安宮時年五十九九月。。。The compilers, omitting the "ninth month" entry, inadvertently dropped the "*nine*" of "fifty-nine" also. Cf. note 117 for a similar mistake in the *Sung shu*.

A further study of the documents enables us to make the following additions to the discussion of Theophylactus' testimony:

1. That the troops of Chou wore black uniforms is further attested by a passage in *Pei Ch'i shu* 11 (cf. *Pei shih* 52), biography of prince KAO Yen-tsung 延宗, where these troops investing Chinyang are compared to black clouds surrounding the doomed city on all sides. *Pei Ch'i shu* 10, biography of KAO Huan 渙, the seventh son of the founder of the house, says that one of the pretexts that his brother, KAO Yang, used for persecuting that unfortunate prince was that 七—"seven," his number in the chronological order of the brothers, was a homonym of 漆—"lacquer," one of the blackest substances. In this coincidence the perverted mind of KAO Yang saw an echo of the prophecy that "that which will destroy the KAO will be black-robed," a prediction which impressed the first sovereigns of the Ch'i sufficiently to make them dislike the sight of black-robed Buddhist monks. Again, in the letter of KAO Chêng upbraiding HOU Ching for his desertion in 547, preserved in *Liang shu* 56, that prince warns Ching of the futility of seeking help from the Black Ch'in 黑秦 under which are obviously understood the Western Wei of Shensi and their majordomo YÜ-WÊN T'ai.

Finally in *Hsi Wei shu* 23, biography of LI Shun-hsing 李順興, is recorded an anecdote, the original source of which we have not been able to ascertain. YÜ-WÊN T'ai, it is said, consulted LI Shunhsing at the time of KAO Huan's invasion of Shensi in 537 as to the outcome of the campaign and Shun-hsing replied with a little ditty in which he alluded to the Eastern Wei as a yellow dog and to the Western Wei as a black one.[193] The colors refer, says the text, to the yellow banners of the Easterners, and to the black color pattern affected by their Western opponents.

[193] The ditty ran: 黃狗逐黑狗，急走出筋斗，一個出筋斗，黃狗夾尾走 "a yellow dog was chasing a black dog, running fast and turning somersaults; one

2. That the princesses of Northern Ch'i rode in richly decorated chariots drawn by an ox is further confirmed by an entry in *Sui shu* 22. In the autumn of 576, runs the story, Empress Mu 穆, the consort of KAO Wei, on the eve of her departure for Chin-yang,[194] rode in her chariot to the northern palace to take leave of her mother-in-law, the Dowager Empress Hu 胡.[195] As she entered the inner gate of the palace, her "seven-jeweled" chariot sank into the ground without any apparent reason, the four feet of the ox becoming imbedded 牛沒四足. The wording of the passage implies that there was but a single ox pulling the empress's cart.

3. To the enumeration of instances of the use of the title *t'ai-shang* we must add the case of the father of the notorious Empress Hu, HU Kuo-chên 胡國珍 (*Wei shu* 83B, *Pei shih* 80: 439-518). Upon his death, on May 7, 518, the Empress-Regent, to all intents and purposes the real sovereign of the empire, had conferred upon him the title of *T'ai-shang* Duke of Ch'in 太上秦公, and upon her mother (*née* HUANG-FU 皇甫, died in 502), that of *T'ai-shang* Lady. On the long deliberations on the appropriateness of the titles, see *Wei shu* 78, biography of CHANG P'u-hui 張普惠 (468-525).

THE CHRONOGRAMMATIC USE OF ANIMAL CYCLE TERMS IN PROPER NAMES

To the cases discussed in "Marginalia 2" we are now able to add the following:

1. LIU T'êng 劉騰, the well known eunuch who played an important rôle at the Wei court in the first quarter of the sixth century, bore, according to his biography in *Wei shu* 94, *Pei shih* 92, the cognomen Ch'ing-lung 青龍. The *Wei shu* states, moreover, that he died in 523,[196] aged 60 (Chinese). He was thus born

turned a somersault and the yellow dog ran (away), its tail between the legs." I take the third line to be as vague in the original as in the tentative translation, as such vagueness is characteristic of the fortune-tellers' ditties.

[194] Apparently on September 29, 576, on which day, according to *Pei Ch'i shu* 8, the emperor proceeded to Chin-yang.

[195] The biographies of both empresses are found in *Pei Ch'i shu* 9, *Pei shih* 14.

[196] In the third month of the year. According to *Wei shu* 9, *Pei shih* 4, seemingly in the second month, but it is quite probable that in both texts some passage has been left out following the record of troubles with the Jüan-juan, noted down under the 22nd day (c. 16) of the second month. Immediately after the mention of LIU T'êng's death follows an entry dated the fourth month.

in 464 which was a *chia-ch'ên* year, corresponding to the green dragon in the animal cycle, and green dragon is precisely the meaning of Ch'ing-lung, LIU T'êng's *tzŭ*.

2. We have another " son of a dragon " in LU Ch'ang-hêng 盧昌衡 (*Sui shu* 57, *Pei shih* 30). That worthy died at the beginning of the Ta-yeh era, while en route to the capital whither he had been summoned to a post in the household of YANG Chao, the heir apparent. This was presumably in 605 as appointments to the Crown Prince's household were made on August 25 (a *chia tzŭ* day), 605 (*Sui shu* 3). As *Sui shu* 57 says he was then 70 (Chinese) years old, he must have been born in 536, a dragon year. Now, besides his regular *tzŭ*, Tzŭ-chün 子均, Ch'ang-hêng had also a nickname which was " son of a dragon," Lung-tzŭ 龍子.

3. A less definite instance of a chronogram may be seen in the name of LIU Ch'iu 柳虬 (*Chou shu* 38, *Pei shih* 64), who died in the winter of 534, aged 54 (Chinese). He was then born in 500-501. If his birth took place in the first twelvemonth, it is likely that his name Ch'iu is chronogrammatic, as it means " young, dragon with horns," and 500 A. D. was a dragon year.[197]

4. A " son of a tiger " was undoubtedly HSIEH Hu-tzŭ 薛虎子 (*Wei shu* 44, *Pei shih* 25, which writes 彪子 for Hu-tzŭ to avoid the T'ang taboo on Hu). He died in 491 at the age of 51 (Chinese) and was then born in 450-451, and his name Hu-tzŭ (" tiger's son ") would indicate that he came into the world in 450 which was a tiger year. It is also possible that his father HSIEH Yeh-chu 野腊 (" wild pig," " boar ") was likewise named according to the year of his birth.[198]

---

[197] The dates of another Ch'iu 虬 who lived in the same period, Yü-wên Ch'iu (*Chou shu* 29), are unfortunately unknown. In the case of LIU Ch'iu 劉虬 (*Nan Ch'i shu* 54, *Nan shih* 50: 438-495), the " dragon " in his name has no chronological significance. We have, however, a " son of the dragon " in HSIAO Tsê 蕭賾 (pht. Shih-tsu Wu ti, *Nan Ch'i shu* 3, *Nan shih* 4), second emperor of the Southern Ch'i. He was born on July 17, 440 (17th year of Yüan-chia, *Nan shih* 4 has incorrectly 27th year) and died in 493 at the age of 54 (Chinese). His biography tells us that his childhood name was " dragon boy " 龍兒, and 440 was a dragon year.

[198] His biography (*Wei shu* 44) mentions one appointment to a governor's post during the Ho-p'ing era (460-465), followed by another, and then states that he died at the age of 61 (Chinese) after having won a reputation as an administrator. If we presuppose that he lived until 471, the date of his birth would be 411, a year of the boar.

It is possible that 壞 *huai* < *$\gamma^\omega ai$ which often appears in " barbarian " names is an abbreviation of a transcription of either Mo. *noɣai*—" dog " or *ɣaqai*—" pig " (cf.

5. We find still another "son of a tiger" in Lɪ Ling 李靈 (*Wei shu* 49, *Pei shih* 33). His *tzŭ* was Hu-fu 虎符—"tiger tally" (*Pei shih* writes, of course, Wu 武 for Hu), undoubtedly an allusion to the year of his birth, as Ling appears to have been born in 390, a tiger year; he died in 452, aged 63 (Chinese).[199]

6. In Southern China, in addition to Ts'ᴀᴏ Hu, we have CHOU T'ieh-hu 周鐵虎 (*Ch'ên shu* 10, *Nan shih* 67). That brave general, whose name means "iron tiger" was made prisoner in the great defeat of the Ch'ên forces by WANG Lin 王琳 in the tenth month of 557. T'ieh-hu, alone of all the officers of the ill-fated army, refused to respond to the advances made by the victor and was put to death by WANG Lin. If, as is likely, he was not executed until 558, he must have been born in 510, as his biography gives his age at the time of his death as 49 (Chinese). 510 was a metal tiger year and his name was thus in all probability chronogrammatic.

It is noteworthy that among the twelve cyclical animals only the dragon and the tiger seem to have been consistently used as chronograms in proper names.[200] This is probably to be explained by the popularity of the animals and the qualities they symbolized as well as by their astrological significance. A further study of the subject may reveal a more subtle use of cyclical terms in the onomasticon of medieval China and may help occasionally to clear up some mooted question of chronology.

HJAS 3.246). It appears to be so used in the personal name of I Huai 乙瓌 (*Wei shu* 44, *Pei shih* 25). Huai died in the middle of the period 460-465 at the age of 29 (Chinese). If his death took place in 463, he was born in 435, a pig (γaqai) year; if in 462, he was born under the sign of the dog (noχai).

[199] In the case of HAN Hsiu 韓秀, *tzŭ* Pai-hu 白虎 ("white tiger"), *Wei shu* 42, the cognomen is apparently not chronogrammatic. Hsiu was entrusted with a confidential post before 466 and was certainly over sixteen at the time, while the nearest "white tiger" year is 450. He died about 480, and it is barely possible, if we suppose that he lived to be a nonagenarian, that he was born in the preceding "white tiger" year, 390 A.D. His father Ping 枛 joined the Wei in 396. *Pei shih* 27, avoiding T'ang taboos, writes Pai-wu 白武 for Pai-hu, and Ching 景 for Ping.

[200] We suspect that T'ang T'ai-tsung's love of horses was conditioned, apart from the natural attraction that the noble animal exercises over a born cavalryman, by the fact that he was born in a horse year. As observed by the Ch'ien-lung editors, T'ai-tsung's age at the time of his death in 649 was 52 (Chinese) as given by the *Chiu T'ang shu*, rather than 53, as we have it in *T'ang shu* 2. According to *Chiu T'ang shu* 2, he was born on the day *wu-wu* (55 of the cycle) in the 12th month of the 18th year of K'ai-huang (January 23, 599). Note that the day had the same cyclical designation as the year (K'ai-huang 18 was a *wu-wu* year) and also corresponded to the horse in the cycle of the twelve animals.

1. Emperors of the House of Tʻo-pa, 386-557 A. D.

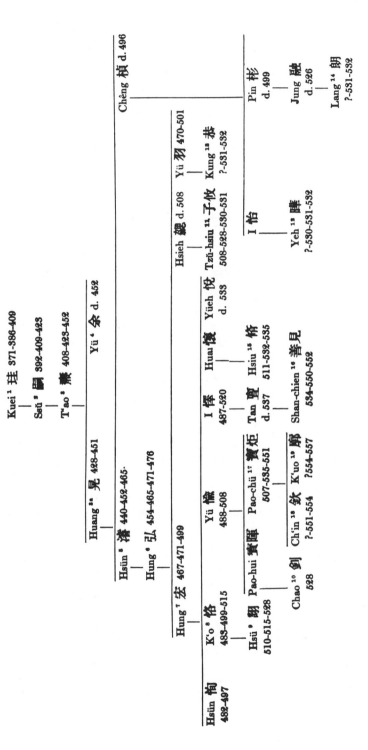

[1] Pht. T'ai-tsu Tao-wu 道武. Born August 4 (7th day of the 7th month) 371; king, Feb. 17, 386; emperor, 7 month, 396; murdered Nov. 6, 409. *Wei shu* 2, *Pei shih* 1.

[2] Pht. T'ai-tsung Ming-yüan 明元. Ascended throne Nov. 10, 409; died Dec. 24, 423. *Wei shu* 3, *Pei shih* 1.

[3] Pht. Shih-tsu T'ai-wu 太武. Ascended throne, Dec. 27, 423 (read 11th for 10th month in *Wei shu* 4a); died March 11, 452 (read 2nd for 3rd month in *Wei shu* 4b). *Wei shu* 4ab, *Pei shih* 2.

[3a] No pht. Kung-tsung Ching-mu 景穆. Died July 29, 451. He did not reign. *Wei shu* 4b, *Pei shih* 2.

[4] No pht. Placed on the throne by Tsung Ai 宗愛, the murderer of his father, he was killed by the same Tsung Ai on October 29, 452.

[5] Pht. Kao-tsung Wên-ch'êng 文成. Born August 4, 440; ascended throne, October 31, 452; died June 20, 465. *Wei shu* 5, *Pei shih* 2.

[6] Pht. Hsien-tsu Hsien-wên 顯祖獻文. Born, August 14, 454; asc. throne, June 21, 465; abdicated Sept. 20, 471; murdered, July 20, 476. *Wei shu* 6, *Pei shih* 2.

[7] Pht. Kao-tsu Hsiao-wên 孝文. Born, October 13, 467; asc. throne, Sept. 20, 471; died April 26, 499. *Wei shu* 7ab, *Pei shih* 3.

[8] Pht. Shih-tsung Hsüan-wu 宣武. Born, May 27, 483; asc. throne May 7, 499; died February 12, 515. *Wei shu* 8, *Pei shih* 4.

[9] Pht. Su-tsung Hsiao-ming 孝明. Born April 8, 510; asc. throne Feb. 12, 515; died March 31, 528. *Wei shu* 9, *Pei shih* 4.

[10] No pht. Asc. throne April 2, 528; murdered by Êrh-chu Jung on May 17, 528.

[11] Pht. Ching-tsung 敬 Hsiao-chuang 孝莊. Asc. throne May 15, 528; deposed Dec. 5, 530; died January 26, 531, murdered by Êrh-chu Chao. *Wei shu* 10, *Pei shih* 5.

[12] Pht. Tung-hai 東海 wang. Asc. throne Dec. 5, 530; deposed April 1, 531; died Dec. 26, 532.

[13] Pht. Chieh-min 節閔 ti, or Kuang-ling 廣陵 wang. Asc. throne April 1, 531; deposed June 6, 532; died June 21, 532. *Wei shu* 11, *Pei shih* 5.

[14] Pht. An-ting 安定 wang. Asc. throne Oct. 31, 531; deposed June 6, 532; died Dec. 26, 532. *Wei shu* 11, *Pei shih* 5.

[15] Pht. Hsiao-wu 孝武 ti (*Wei shu* 11 calls him 出帝 "the fugitive emperor"). Asc. throne June 13, 532; fled to Ch'ang-an, Aug. 21, 534. Murdered by Yü-wên T'ai, February 3, 535. *Wei shu* 11, *Pei shih* 5.

[16] Pht. Hsiao-ching 孝靜. Asc. throne, Nov. 8, 534; abdicated June 7, 550; died January 21, 552. *Wei shu* 12, *Pei shih* 5.

[17] Pht. Wên 文 ti. Asc. throne, Feb. 18, 535 (New Year's Day); died March 28, 551. *Pei shih* 5.

[18] No pht. Asc. throne, 3rd mo., 551; deposed, 1st mo., 554.

[19] Pht. Kung 恭 ti. Asc. throne 1st mo., 554; abdicated, Feb. 14, 557.

5

2.* The Family of YÜ-WÊN Hung

宇文肱 YÜ-WÊN Hung d. 526

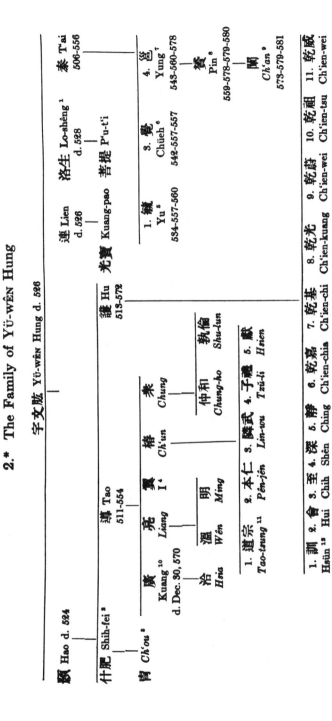

* The table is based on *Chou shu* 10-11. Names of YÜ-WÊN princes put to death by YANG Chien in 580-581 are italicized. Only the reigning sons of T'ai are given in this table.

1 Lo-shêng was put to death by ÊRH-CHU Jung. Posthumous titles were conferred upon the three elder brothers of YÜ-WÊN T'ai on August 1, 561 (*Chou shu* 5).

2 Shih-fei, Kuang-pao, and P'u-t'i were killed by KAO Huan, presumably in 534.

3 Ch'ou did not escape from Ch'i until early in 570 (*Chou shu* 5). Until his return Ch'ien-jên 乾仁 (= Hui 會, second son of Hu) was treated as Shih-fei's heir.

4 Died in his youth, leaving no posterity.

5 Pht. Shih-tsung 世宗 Ming 明 ti. Ascended throne November 5, 557 (*chia-tzŭ*, 9th month), died, poisoned by YÜ-WÊN Hu, on May 30, 560. *Chou shu* 4, *Pei shih* 9.

6 Pht. Hsiao-min 孝閔 ti. Ascended throne February 15, 557 (New Year's day, the Wei abdicated on the preceding day). Deposed by YÜ-WÊN Hu about November 1, 557. Died about a month later. *Chou shu* 3, *Pei shih* 9.

7 Pht. Kao-tsu Wu 武 Ti. Ascended throne June 1, 560; died June 21, 578. Until the third month of 572 reigned under the tutelage of YÜ-WÊN Hu. *Chou shu* 5-6, *Pei shih* 10.

8 Pht. Hsüan 宣 ti. Ascended throne June 22, 578. Nominally abdicated on April 1, 579. Died about June 8, 580. *Chou shu* 7, *Pei shih* 10.

9 Pht. Ching 靜 ti. Born August 1, 573. Became emperor April 1, 579. Forced to abdicate March 1, 581; died July 10, 581. *Chou shu* 8, *Pei shih* 10.

10 The inscription on his stele composed by the famous YÜ Hsin 庾信 has been preserved.

11 *Chou shu* 10 gives the list of Ch'un's sons without a clue as to how we should punctuate it.

12 All executed with their father in 572.

3.* The Family of Yü-wên T'ai

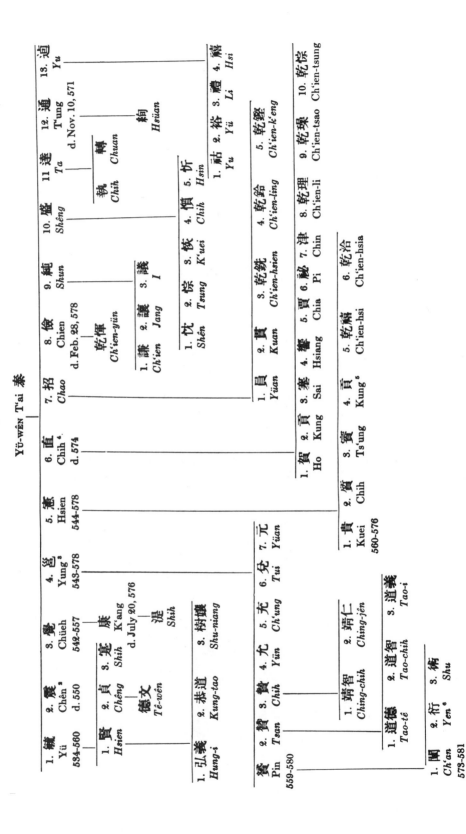

YÜ-WÊN T'ai 泰

NOTES TO TABLE 3

* The table is based chiefly on *Chou shu* 12-13, *Pei shih* 58. Names of the Yü-wên princes put to death by YANG Chien in 580-581 are italicized.

[1] YAO 姚 *fu-jên* bore Yü, "Empress" Wên-yüan 文元 (d. 541; she was a sister of T'o-PA Hsiu; her first husband CHANG Huan 張歡 was put to death on her complaint) bore Chüeh; "Empress" Wên-hsüan 宣 née CH'IH-NU 叱奴 (d. 573), Yung and Chih; the *fei* TA-PU-KAN 達步干 (a Juan-juan princess), Hsien; the *chi* WANG 王, Chao; the remaining sons were born of concubines of lesser rank.

[2] Married a daughter of T'o-PA Pao-chü.

[3] His dates are those given by *Chou shu* 12, confirmed by the inscription on his stele composed by YU Hsin. The *Pei shih* says he was 40 Chinese years old at the time of his death, July 18, 578. Both Yung and Hsien were raised in the home of LI Hsien 李賢 (*Chou shu* 25, Pei shih 59) and appear to have been of the same age. Hsien's sons (with the exception of the eldest who died before his father) were executed with him.

[4] Chih organized an uprising against Yung on Aug. 29, 574, was captured on Sept. 14, and was put to death, sometime later, together with all his sons. Chih's eldest son Pin 賓 was made heir to Yü-wêN Lo-shêng in the fifth month of 572 (*Chou shu* 5, 10). Is Pin identical with Ho?

[5] Kung is apparently identical with Fu 負, fourth son of Hsien (*Chou shu* 6) or Chên 真 (*Chou shu* 10) who was made heir to the same Lo-shêng in 576.

[6] Yen 衍 was the original name of Ch'an 闡. It is not impossible that after the name of Pin's eldest son was changed, Yen was bestowed as a name on the second son. On the other hand, 衍 Yen might be, as suspected by some, a corruption of K'an 衎.

Yü-wêN T'ai had several daughters: the P'ing-yüan kung-chu married Yü I (see note 155); the I-an kung-chu married a LI 李 (*Pei shih* 60); the fifth daughter, the Hsiang-yang kung-chu, became the wife of TOU I (*Pei shih* 61); SHIH Hsiung (*ibid.*) married another daughter, the Yung-fu kung-chu; the Hsi-ho kung-chu was the wife of LIU Ch'ung (*Pei shih* 65); the Hsiang-lo kung-chu, that of WEI Shih-k'ang (*Sui shu* 47).

Prince Yü-wêN Hsin, son of Yü-wêN Shêng, is to be distinguished from Yü-wêN Hsin of note 164.

4.* THE FAMILY OF YANG CHUNG

楊忠 Yang Chung 507-568 A.D.

堅 Chien 541-604 — 瓚 Tsan[1] 550-591 — 整 Ch'êng[2] d. 577 — 嵩 Sung[3] — 爽 Shuang[4] 568-587 — 集 Chi[6] 563-587

勇 Yung d. 604
廣 Kuang 569-618
俊 Chün 571-600
秀 Hsiu d. 618
諒 Liang d. 605

智積 Chih-chi[5] d. 616
智朋 Chih-ming
智才 Chih-ts'ai
訧 Shên[1] d. 618
靜 Ching d. 597

浩 Hao[7] d. 618
湛 Chan d. 618
瓜子 Kua-tzŭ[8] d. 618
顥 Hao d. 618
世澄 Shih-chêng
道玄 Tao-hsüan
綸 Lun
坦 Tan
猛 Mêng
溫 Wên

昭 Chao[9] 584-606
陳 Chien 585-618
杲 Kao 607-618
政道 Chêng-tao[12]

倓 T'an[10] 603-618
佑 Yu 605-619
侗 Tung[11] d. 619

儼 Yen[13]
裕 Yü
嶷 I
恪 K'o
詥 Kai
諶 Yun
昭 Shao
腹 Kung
孝實 Hsiao-shih
孝範 Hsiao-fan

* This genealogical table is based primarily on *Sui shu* 44, 45, 59 and *Pei shih* 71. Names of princes murdered by Yü-wên Hua-chi and his party in italics.

1 Ts'an was also called Hui 惠, probably identical with Hui 惠 mentioned in *Chou shu* 19 as one of the younger brothers of YANG Chien. Ts'an was married a daughter of Yü-wên Yung, the Shun-yang 順陽 kung-chu. YANG Chien and his wife hated them both and at the time of Ts'an's sudden death in 591, it was rumored that he had been poisoned when visiting his brother.

2 Chêng's wife was a daughter of WEI-CH'IH Kang 綱. In this case also a deep-seated enmity existed between the couple and YANG Chien and his wife. Chêng was killed in the campaign against Ch'i. Ts'an and Chêng were uterine brothers of Chien, born of the Lady Lü 呂.

3 Died in early youth. Ching, son of Ts'an, was made heir to him.

4 Shuang's *tzŭ* was Ming-ta 明達. Apparently identical with Ta 達 of *Chou shu* 19. Both he and Sung were sons of the Lady Li 李.

5 Chih-chi lived all his life in fear of his uncle Chien and his cousin Kuang, making every effort not to attract attention. He had five sons; only two are known by their names.

6 Exiled in 605 together with his cousin Lun and his brothers.

7 Established as emperor by Yü-wên Hua-chi. Murdered after the latter's defeat on November 23, 618.

8 Favorite son of Hsiu. The names of the others are not known.

9 *Pei shih* 71 says he was born on February 21, 584. YANG Chien is reported to have had (on April 29, 588) a dream presaging his conception. According to the same source, he was 23 (Chinese) years old at the time of his death in 606, which again would give us 584 as the year of his birth. Both *Sui shu* 59 and *Pei shih* 71 say, however, that he was 12 years of age at the time of his enfeoffment as Prince of Ho-nan 河南 which, according to *Sui shu* 2, took place on February 16, 590. This would mean that he was born in 579, when his father, Yang Kuang, was but ten years old.

On the same day, *Sui shu* 2 notes the enfeoffment of another grandson of YANG Chien as Prince of Hua-yang 華陽. I find no other record of that prince, named Ch'iai 楷, in the biographies of members of the imperial family. Was he a son of YANG Kuang? *Sui shu* 80 mentions him as the husband of Lady Yüan 元 and says he was killed by Yü-wên Hua-chi in 618.

10 Pht. Kung ti. Made emperor by Li Yüan, December 18, 617 (*Sui shu* 5) or December 19 (*T'ang shu* 1); deposed June 12, 618; murdered in the fifth month of 619.

11 Pht. Kung ti (not officially recognized). Made emperor at Lo-yang by WANG Shih-ch'ung 王世充 (*Sui shu* 85, *Pei shih* 79, *Chiu T'ang shu* 54, *T'ang shu* 85) on June 24, 618; deposed May 25, 619 and murdered in the sixth month of the same year.

12 The only member of YANG Chien's family to survive the fall of the dynasty. As a baby he was taken to the Tu-chüeh Turks where he remained until 630, when he returned to China. He died about 650.

13 All Yung's sons were first sent into exile and then put to death soon after YANG Kuang's accession to the throne. Yü-wên Shu and Yün Ting-hsing are said to have instigated the executions (*Sui shu* 61).

YANG Chien had at least five daughters: the eldest became the wife of Yü-wên Pin; another, the Hsiang-kuo 襄國 kung-chu, married Li Ch'ang-ya 李長雅 (*Sui shu* 54); the Kuang-p'ing 廣平 kung-chu married Yü-wên Ching-luan 靜亂 (*Sui shu* 50); the fifth daughter, A-wu 阿五, the Lan-ling 蘭陵 kung-chu, was married twice: first to WANG Fêng-hsiao 王奉孝, then to LIU Shu 柳述 (*Sui shu* 80).

Three Notes on the T'u-chüeh Turks

University of California Publications
in Semitic Philology,
vol. XI, Berkeley, 1951, pages 1-11.

I. The Chinese Name of the Turks

THIRTY YEARS and more have passed since the problem of the original form of T'u-chüeh (Ancient Chinese: $d'u\partial t$- / or $t'u\partial t$- / $-k\chi^w\upsilon t$),[1] the Chinese name for the confederation of the Turks in High Asia, was settled by Paul Pelliot[2] to the satisfaction of most orientalists.[3] Fortified by Karlgren's[4] solution of the difficulty presented by the alternation of the initials in the first Chinese syllable in favor of the voiceless initial,[5] Pelliot's equation $*T'u\partial t$-$k\chi^w\upsilon t$ = $*Türküt$, a "Mongolian" plural of the ethnonym Türk, is so convincing and has so well stood the test of time and repeated scrutiny that it is not without hesitation that I venture to reopen the question by suggesting the possibility of another reading for the Chinese compound.

While eminently satisfactory from a phonetic point of view and worthy of superseding other hypotheses in importance, Pelliot's solution is essentially a reflection of the scholarly spirit of our generation which seeks to solve the manifold of the history of Central Asia in the light of ethnographic and linguistic factors almost exclusively. Orientalists acquainted with the evolution of ideas on this subject in European historiography will not fail to notice, however, that the hybrid character of the form $*Türküt$, which is not attested in the old Turkish inscriptions, evokes indirectly an older, and often disregarded, approach to the problem of Central Asiatic ethnogenesis. That approach was typical for investigators of the late eighteenth and early nineteenth centuries, notably De Guignes and Father Hyacinth Bichurin, who were inclined to stress political economy as the dominant factor in the formation of the steppe confederacies and were not too much disturbed by linguistic incongruity. Their attitude was not only due to the inadequacy of the linguistic tools and methods of their day, but evidenced perhaps a surer insight into the political forces that shape human societies and even a certain instinctive prescience of the analytical failures of their successors, who were too prone to give primacy to ethnic and racial factors in the reconstruction of the history of High Asia in preference to the study of the interplay of political forces. For De Guignes and Bichurin, ethnic, and hence linguistic, hybridity was diathetic in the formation of large federations in the steppes, and all ethnogenetic and ethnonymic questions were viewed from that postulate. It is with these

---

[1] Karlgren, *Analytic Dictionary*, nos. 498, 503.

[2] *T'oung Pao* (1915), pp. 687–689. The same equation, possibly independently, but without critical discussion, was suggested by J. J. Hess in *Der Islam* (1918), pp. 99–100.

[3] Only E. Polivanov, in a note in *Izvestiia* of the Russian Academy (1927, p. 691), tried, not too convincingly, to reconstruct T'u-chüeh as *Türklär*, a pure Turkish plural of Türk, on the supposition of a *kl- initial cluster in the second Chinese syllable. So far as we know, *Türklär*, valid for later times, does not occur in Orkhon Turkish, which uses only the form *Türk* as a collective.

[4] In *Some Turkish Transcriptions in the Light of Irregular Aspirates in Mandarin* (Ts'ai Yüan P'ei Anniversary Volume; Peking, 1933), pp. 311–322.

[5] *Ibid.*, p. 322.

broad concepts in mind that I should like to discuss an admittedly tentative reading of the name of the T'u-chüeh.

First of all, it is to be observed that the present reconstruction of the name does not take into account all the information available in the Chinese sources. In the light of Karlgren's suggestion that the Chinese scribes had the tendency to select, for reasons of their own, unusual readings of characters for their transcriptions of foreign names, attention should be directed to the phonetic glosses appended to the *T'ang shu*.[6] Among these glosses there appears repeatedly the dimidiated (*fan-ch'ieh*) spelling $k(i\partial u) + (m)i\chi u\partial t$, that is, *$k_i u\partial t$, for the *chüeh* of T'u-chüeh. The reconstructed form for the whole compound must, therefore, be given as *$T'u\partial t$-$k_i u\partial t$*, rather than in the now traditional form *$T'u\partial t$-$k_i^w \partial t$*. This reading would indicate that the Chinese considered the compound as one of the so-called "rhyming" or "homoeoteleutic binoms," a class of two-term phonetic compounds the reconstruction of which presents peculiar problems. A study of these compounds in the light of evidence indicating the existence of an archaic consonantal cluster in the second syllable suggests that the Chinese favored the use of homoeoteleutic binoms for the conventional representation of vestigial consonantal clusters.[7] The final of the first syllable was then slurred in pronunciation in such a way as to bring the two initials as closely together as possible. The phonetic analysis of the group of words to which our *$k_i u\partial t$* belonged (most of them meaning 'short,' 'blunt,' 'curtailed,' 'stump') adumbrates indeed an archaic initial cluster *tk- in that semantic family.[8] In other words, while written *$t'u\partial t$-$k_i u\partial t$*, our homoeoteleutic compound may actually have been pronounced *$t'u$-$k_i u\partial t$*, if treated as a traditional rhyming binom. It is significant in this connection that the *T'ang shu* glosses consistently mark the pronunciation of the second syllable of T'u-chüeh, and ignore completely the first syllable, as if relying on their readers' foreknowledge of the treatment of such compounds.

Another important consideration to remember in trying to reconstruct the phonetic contour of the bisyllable is that our precise reconstructions of ancient Chinese words, particularly in Karlgren's system, are based on the study of rhyming dictionaries, that is, that of the phonetic values of syllables as they occur *in pause*. In the analysis of transcriptions of polysyllabic names, however, these "dictionary" reconstructions are not necessarily valid for every member of the complex and might even be misleading for unstressed syllables. Furthermore, it is not unlikely that some of the transcriptions of the sixth and seventh centuries reflect already a popular weak enunciation—or amissibility under certain conditions—of the final stops -*k*, -*p*, -*t* in the speech of Northern China.

Observe thus the transcription *$t'si\check{e}t$-nuo*[9] which without any doubt renders the Mongolian word *čino* ∼ *činoa*, 'wolf,' as is attested by the translation of the compound by Chinese *lang*, 'wolf.'[10] Similarly, *Pei Ch'i shu* 17 gives us as

---

[6] E.g., glosses to chaps. 1, 33B, 58, 215A, 217A, 218, 219.

[7] Cf. *Harvard Journal of Asiatic Studies* (*HJAS*), II, 353–360.

[8] I hope to be able to present the detailed evidence on the *tk- cluster in that group in the near future.

[9] Karlgren, *Analytic Dictionary*, nos. 1055, 674.

[10] Cf. *HJAS*, I, 177.

the barbarian name of Ho-lü Chin, a well-known warrior of the sixth century, the trisyllabic compound ʻA-lį̣uk-tuən,[11] which must be Turkish *altun*, 'gold,' his original appellation translated in Chinese by Chin, 'gold.' The second syllable obviously stands here for -*lŭ*-, rather than for *lį̣uk*, its registered "dictionary" value.

With respect to the syllable *t'uət* in the compound T'u-chüeh the foregoing argument would not appear, at first glance, convincing, since the character is well attested for the period as representing *t'uət* (for foreign *tür*) in a nonfinal position. It occurs in the firmly established equation T'u-ch'i-shih < *t'uət-gʻjię-śię*[12] = Turkish *Turgäš*. We can adduce, however, some occasions of the use of *t'uət* in transcriptions of foreign names, even in final position, where it seems to have, during the Northern Chou period, the value *tu* ~ *tü*. Most interesting is the occurrence of the character as the final element in the barbarian names of the Chou princes,[13] sons of Yü-wen T'ai (506–556). In all these names *t'u* appears to represent the Mongolian adjectival suffix -*tu* ~ -*tü*. Thus *Chou shu* 4 tells us that the baby name of Yü-wen Yu (534–560), the eldest son of Yü-wen T'ai, was T'ung-wan-t'u, in allusion to his having been born in the city of T'ung-wan. Another son's name was Mi-o-t'u[14] < *mjiă-ngâ-t'u(ət)*,[15] which may well represent Mongolian **miăngatu*,[16] written Mong. *mingɣatu*, 'chiliarch,' 'belonging to a chiliarchy.'

It is, therefore, within the realm of possibility that T'u-chüeh was pronounced **T'u-kį̣uət* even as early as the sixth century, when the transcription originated. Instead of **Türküt*,[17] then, it could have represented such forms as **Tuqut/r*, **Tüküt/r*, **Tuqud/z*, **Tüküd/z*, or corresponding forms with *o/ö*. Especially suggestive among these variants is the form **TUQUZ*, for it could well represent Turkish *Toquz* 'nine,' 'the nine,' a numerical designation for tribal federations which appears quite frequently in the eastern and northern parts of the Orkhon Turkish empire. The Chinese name of the union of the Turkish tribes may thus be based on the well-known appellation of a large part of the steppe league of Turkish tribes, the Toquz Oghuz, "the Nine Oghuz." The historical identity of the Toquz Oghuz has not been established with certainty for the early period of Turkish history,[18] but it is undeniable that it was sometimes applied to designate the parent body of the Orkhon Turks, whether united under one rule or divided into warring groups. Thus, while the Orkhon inscriptions mention fighting by men of the newly formed

---

[11] Karlgren, *op. cit.*, nos. 1, 563, 1143.

[12] *Ibid.*, nos. 498, 337, 223. Cf. also *Some Turkish Transcriptions* . . . p. 322.

[13] *Chou shu* 4, 12, 13.

[14] The complex occurs also as the name of a Kao-chü chieftain killed in 516 A.D., *Pei shih* 98.

[15] Karlgren, *op. cit.*, nos. 13, 679, 498.

[16] The form shows the phenomenon of *Brechnung* in the first syllable. Cf. Vladimirtsov, *Sravnitel'naia grammatika*, p. 177.

[17] Pelliot believed that the "Mongolian" plural of **Türküt* is to be explained by the supposition that the first information about the Turks was transmitted to the Chinese by the Juan-juan, whom he held to be Mongol-speaking. The name may, however, have originated with the Yü-wen of the Northern Chou dynasty, who, if the etymology of their name suggested in *HJAS*, III, 244, n. 67, is correct, were Mongol-speaking themselves.

[18] Cf. Grum-Grzhimailo, in *Zapadnaia Mongoliia*, pp. 285–289, who, after reviewing various scholars' statements respecting the identity of the Toquz Oghuz, exclaims in desperation: *"quot capita* . . ."

Turkish khanate of the East with some Toquz Oghuz under Baz qaghan,[19] the same inscriptions make Bilgä qaghan address his people as "people of Toquz Oghuz."[20]

This interpretation of the name in no way conflicts with the identification of Toquz Oghuz with the Uighurs, for the latter could have arrogated to themselves the proud title on their rise to power in 744 A.D.[21] In fact, setting up nine or ten tribal divisions is likely to have been considered the first step in announcing a group's pretensions to the hegemony of the steppes, with nine the traditional number for the eastern half of the potential empire and ten that for the west. It seems to me it is in this light that we should interpret the complex nomenclature found in the inscriptions, with Toquz Oghuz now synonymous with the Tölis, now designating the political organization ruled by the group calling itself Türk (in the narrow sense of the aristocratic clans stemming from A-shih-na, the progenitor of the T'u-chüeh, and from Bumyn and Istämi, the founders of the empire), while the dissident Turks of the west are called On-oq[22] or Tarduš. In contradistinction to their cousins in the east, the Western Turks maintain an organization based on a tenfold division, split into two groups of five each.[23] It is to this peculiar politico-geographical division of West-Ten and East-Nine that the tradition preserved by Rashid ed-Din and Abu-l-Ghazi refers, in the story of the On-uighur and Toquz-uighur.

Does the foregoing argument lead to the conclusion that we should favor the reading *Toquz over *Türküt for the Chinese transcription T'u-chüeh? Not necessarily so. In order to explain this rather paradoxical answer we must come back to the qualification "Mongolian" which Pelliot prefixed to his theoretical plural form of Türk, *Türküt. Evidence has been accumulating that this form of the plural, or collective plural, is really an archaic Turkish or "Turco-Mongol" formation and that the suffix -t interchanged dialectally with -r and -z, the latter two being perhaps more common in Turkish milieu than the former. L. Ligeti[24] established that it is this archaic plural suffix -z that explains best the name of the Qyrqyz, which is to be interpreted as a plural-collective of Turkish qyrq, 'forty.' The Chinese transcriptions of that name in the sixth century reproduce its second syllable by means of the character ku < kuət, with -t having the unmistakable value of -z, which is as normal as having -t render a foreign -t or -r. Nothing, then, prevents us from reading *Türküz for Pelliot's *Türküt and from considering this form an archaic but genuine Turkish, rather than Mongolian, plural of Türk. The two readings

---

[19] Kül tegin's monument, line 14.

[20] Bilgä qaghan's inscription, line 2.

[21] Or even some time before, when the "Uighur" faction of Bilgä qaghan's federation began to dispute his right to overlordship.

[22] On the compound *On-oq*, meaning 'ten arrows,' hence 'ten hordes,' see Thomsen, *Turcica*, in *MSFOu*, XXXVII, 4–26. The contrast of (*toquz*) *oghuz* (if *oghuz* is an archaic plural of *oq*) with (*on*)-*oq* may reflect dialectal differences between the speech of the eastern and the western parts of the Turkish empire.

[23] For an early reference to a division of the Turks into Ten Uighur and Nine Oghuz in an old Turkish inscription, see Ramstedt, *Zwei uigurische runeninschriften*, p. 12. For a general statement on the equivalence of the names Türk, Oghuz, Uighur, cf. S. Maksoudoff, *JA*, 1924, 141–148; also *HJAS*, IV, 230–239.

[24] *Die Herkunft des Volksnamens Kirgis*, Körösi Csoma Archivum, pp. 369–383.

for T'u-chüeh, **Türküz* and **Toquz*, are thus brought close enough together to be considered interchangeable in accordance with the conventions of Chinese transcription, the palatal reading being a precise "dictionary" enunciation of the two syllables, the velar, a binomial treatment of the compound.

To sum up, I believe that ethnic and politico-geographical designations were so interwoven in the nomenclatures of the steppe empires that the Chinese found it as difficult to keep separate the fast-shifting names and alignments in the territory of their nomadic neighbors as the scholars of our generation. The phonetic ambiguity in the Chinese rendering of the barbaric names sometimes permitted the Chinese to use their transcriptions with a flexibility which allowed, so to say, the telescoping of two similar-sounding names into a single transcription; for had they not shown themselves past masters in transcribing fairly accurately the sounds of a foreign name, at the same time semanticizing it by a proper selection of characters? Whether we have such a telescoping of *Türküz and *Toquz in the transcription T'u-chüeh only new data and further diligent investigation may tell.

II. The *Syr-Tardush Phantom and the T'ieh-lê

We have another homoeoteleutic compound in the Chinese transcription of the name of another large group of Central Asiatic tribes, the T'ieh-lê, illfamed in their heyday for their unruliness, and notorious in our generation for the grievous misinterpretation of their name. The early students of the Turkish Orkhon inscriptions, notably Hirth, tried to identify the T'ieh-lê ($<$ *t'iet-lək*)[25] with the Tölis repeatedly mentioned on the monuments as forming, together with the Tarduš, two main subdivisions of the Turkish confederation. This was done not only in the face of the insurmountable difficulty of the final -k in the second syllable, which could never transcribe Turkish -s or -š, but also in complete disregard of the evidence supplied by Chinese historians who equated the name T'ieh-lê with that of the Ti-li $<$ *d'iek-liek*,[26] the Ch'ih-lê $<$ *t''i̯ək-lək*[27] and the T'e-lê $<$ *d'ək-lək*,[28] and who mention them long before the rise of the Turks as a power.

The unfortunate equation T'ieh-lê = Tölis was accompanied by another, no less deplorable, lapsus on the part of Hirth, who implanted in the mind of other scholars the identification of the amalgamated name of two divisions of the T'ieh-le, the Hsieh Yen-t'o $<$ **Si̯ät (d)i̯än-d'â*,[29] with a supposed Turkish name of a division of Turks called *Syr-Tarduš. These inacceptable hypotheses received the imprimatur of such careful scholars as Radloff, Thomsen, and Chavannes,[30] and continue to affect the historical deductions of the

---

[25] Karlgren, *Analytic Dictionary*, nos. 991, 523.

[26] *Ibid.*, nos. 117, 536.

[27] *Ibid.*, nos. 909, 523.

[28] *Ibid.*, nos. 811, 523. On the initial of the first syllable, cf. further *Some Turkish Transcriptions*, p. 322.

[29] Karlgren, *op. cit.*, nos. 795, 235, 1011.

[30] A certain amount of responsibility for the ectoplasmic persistence of the nonexisting *Syr Tarduš is to be laid at the door of Chavannes, whose *Documents sur les Tou-kiue occidentaux* had undoubtedly a wider circulation than the less well known work of Hirth's. Chavannes, whose merits include the exposure of many of such ghostlike entities, philological and historical, was rather careless in constantly adding in parentheses the words Syr-Tarduš after every mention of the Hsieh Yen-t'o, as if giving the impression that he considered the equation as well established and justifiable as that of Ko-lo-lo = Qarluq.

majority of scholars interested in that period of Central Asiatic history to this day, with *Syr-Tarduš hordes roaming through the steppes of Asia "from Shantung to the Iron Gates." The only firmly dissenting voice on that subject was raised by the great Russian orientalist W. W. Bartold, and his doubts of the validity of both identifications[31] came to be shared by other Russian scholars of the prerevolutionary generation, particularly Melioranski, Aristov, and Grum-Grzhimailo. It appears clear from the Orkhon inscriptions that the terms Tölis and Tarduš were used primarily as designations of political and geographical divisions of the great Turkish confederation, and not as ethnic and tribal appellations. This fact was completely disregarded by European investigators, and the resulting confusion is well summarized in Bartold's conclusion of his criticism of Hirth's identification of the Hsieh Yen-t'o with the *Syr-Tarduš:[32]

". . . we are thus [that is, if we accept Hirth's thesis.—P.B.] forced to come to the following conclusion: originally the Syr-Tardush formed a part of the Tölis, who were distinguished by the Chinese from the Turks-T'u-chüeh; then they entered the T'u-chüeh confederacy under the name of Tardush and formed in it a western division to be distinguished from the Tölis, the eastern division. We leave the reader to judge for himself the probability of such a deduction."[33]

Bartold was also the only one who questioned the legitimacy of the combination *Syr-Tarduš itself. As pointed out by him, it is entirely a figment of Hirth's imagination, for the compound never occurs in the inscriptions. It was arrived at by the completely arbitrary combination of the genuine Turkish appellation Tarduš with the mysterious *Sir in the expression *türk-sir-budun*, 'Turk-*sir*-people,' which occurs several times on Tonyuquq's monument and seems to refer to the Eastern Turkish people brought back to vigorous life and political preëminence by Ilteres qaghan and his party, and was bolstered by the untenable reconstruction of Hsieh Yen-t'o as *Syr-Tarduš. The reading of the word *sir* is in itself uncertain. It is written with an *r* of the palatal series, hence *sir*, but, as the confusion between the velar and palatal *r* does occasionally occur in the inscriptions,[34] the reading *sïr* is not excluded. I wonder if we could not connect the trigrammaton, reading it *sïra* ~ *sirä*, with the well-known Turkish word *sïra*, 'sequence,' 'series.' The antiquity of that word in a political sense is evidenced by its occurrence in Proto-Bulgarian (registered by the Greeks as σειρά),[35] apparently in the meaning 'succession,' 'dynasty,' 'aristocratic elite.'[36] We could then interpret *türk-sirä-budun* (with palatal assimilation of *sïra* to *türk*) as "the (genuine) Türk dynasty and people," rather than see in it an evocation of the purely imaginary union of the Turks and the ghostly *Syr.[37]

[31] Bartold, *Die historische Bedeutung der Alttürkischen Inschriften*, p. 9; Grum-Grzhimailo, *op. cit.*, pp. 283–284.

[32] In his excellent review of Chavannes's *Documents*, in *Zapiski Vost. Otd. Imp. Arkheol. Obshch.* (*ZVOIRAO*), XV, 0162–0185.

[33] Translated from the Russian; Bartold, *op. cit.*, pp. 0172–0173.

[34] Melioranski in *ZVOIRAO*, XII, 36.

[35] Cf. J. Mikkola, "Die Chronologie der türkischen Donaubulgaren," *MSFOu*, XXX, 20.

[36] On the use of sira as a postposition cf. Deny, *Grammaire turque*, §906.

[37] The latest invocation of the *Sir as the name of a people (with a reference to Marquart, *Erānšahr*) is found in notes to a translation of Tonyuquq's epitaph (presumably by M. Sprengling), *AJSL*, LI, 370, n. 4.

Returning now to the question of the identity of the T'ieh-lê, it seems clear from our discussion in §I that the compound was likely to be read *Te-lek* or *Te-rek*, with the -*k* of the first syllable quiescent as suggested by the rhyming quality of the binom and the latter transcription *T'iet-lek*, where the final -*t* is undoubtedly to be assimilated to the *l*- or *r*- which begins the second syllable.[38] Now the T'ieh-lê were always said to be part of the Kao chü or "High Carts" confederation, and the latter are said to have derived their name from their use of carts with high, spoked wheels.[39] It is entirely appropriate, therefore, to seek an etymology for their name in some "Turco-Mongol" word meaning 'cart.' Such a word exists in Mongolian in the form *telegen, terge, tergen*.[40] The term "Carts" may then have been applied to a welter of tribes as a descriptive, functional, rather than ethnic designation, possibly in contradistinction to those tribes which mostly used pack animals.

The T'ieh-lê must thus be finally divorced from the Tölis. Where are we to find, then, the Chinese mention and transcriptions of the all-important names Tölis and Tarduš as designating the two main divisions of the Turkish confederation? As has been repeatedly suggested by Bartold and the older Russian scholars and finally expressly stated by I. A. Kliukin,[41] in the Chinese designations of the two halves of the Turkish empire, the Eastern (or Northern) and the Western Turks, and in the transcriptions of the names of qaghan Ta-t'ou (Tardou) and qaghan T'u-li (*t'uət-lji*). Chavannes's excellent book, which remains to this day one of our main guides to research on the subject of the early history of the Turks, would indeed have gained immeasurably in clarity if the great French sinologist had eschewed the fatal *Syr-Tarduš and T'ieh-lê = Tölis hypotheses and, instead, had parenthetically added the word Tarduš to the title of his work; for the Tarduš, the people of Tardou, are none other than "les Tou-kiue occidentaux."

III. Dilziboul and Istämi

Among the many philological problems facing the student of the fascinating story of "global" diplomacy and power politics in which the Byzantine, Persian, Turkish, and Chinese empires found themselves involved in the second half of the sixth century, is the problem of the name and identity of the Turkish representative in the "Big Four" alignment of that day.

Menander, our chief source of information on the diplomatic exchange between Byzantium and the Western Turks during Justinian's last years and through the reign of Justin II (565–578), calls the powerful leader of the Western Turkish confederacy Διλζίβουλος,[42] Διζάβουλος,[43] or Σιλζίβουλος.[44]

---

[38] On the relation of the T'ieh-lê to the Ting-ling see Otto Maenchen-Helfen's discussion of this mooted question in *HJAS*, IV, 77–86, esp. p. 83; also the latest contribution to the subject by Denis Sinor in *JA*, 1946–1947, esp. pp. 7–11. If the Ting-ling are to be identified with the T'ieh-lê, it is possible that their name is also to be read in "binomial" fashion, that is, as *Te-lieng*, rather than *tieng-lieng*.

[39] *Pei shih* 98, *T'ung Tien* 197.

[40] Already found in the *Yüan ch'ao pi shih*. See Haenisch's *Wörterbuch* to that work, pp. 147, 149.

[41] "New Data concerning the Tardushi" (in Russian), *Bulletin of the Far Eastern Branch of the Academy of Sciences*, 1932. Kliukin's argument is unfortunately weakened by his untenable hypotheses on the Chinese renderings of the Turkish terms *isbara* and *yamtar*.

[42] *Fragmenta hist. graec.* IV, 245, 247.   [43] *Ibid.*, p. 225.   [44] *Ibid.*, p. 205.

This name or appellation has mostly been thought the same as SinJibu[45] (Arabic: *snĵbw*), found in Tabari as the title or name of the Turkish khan who had conquered the Hephthalites.[46] In equating the two names it has become the fashion to give preference to the Arabic spelling on the ground that *ĵibu* represents the well-known title *jabɣu* borne by many of the Turkish chieftains in Western Turkestan. The *-los* ending of the Greek names is then entirely ignored and speculation is concentrated on the possible meaning of the first syllable Sil- or Dil-,[47] in which case priority is, usually and inconsistently, given to the Greek version, on the ground of the number of variants.[48] The procedure could easily be reversed and the lone Arabic example without difficulty brought into line with the Greek on the supposition that the reading *Snĵbw* is a corruption of **Silĵbl*, with *-n-* a graphic mistake for middle *-l-* and the final *w* a not unnatural misreading for final *l*.

According to Menander, Dilziboul died in 576, just as the embassy of Valentinus reached Turkish territory. The Romans first sojourned at the ordo of Dilziboul's son Tourxanth and then proceeded to the supreme headquarters of the Western Turks, now under the rule of Tourxanth's brother Tardou (Τάρδου). As early as De Guignes's day, this name was recognized as the first definite link between the evidence presented by Byzantine historians, on one hand, and that contained in the Chinese annals, on the other, for in Tardou one could easily identify the great Turkish chief Ta-t'ou whose career is sketched in the Chinese documents of the time, preserved mainly in the *Sui shu*, *Pei shih*, *T'ung Tien*, and the T'ang histories.[49] Tardou appears there as the son of Shih-tien-mi (*śi̯ĕt-tiem-mi̯ĕt*)[50] or Se-ti-mi (*s̞ɐt-tiei-miei*),[51] brother of the founder of the Turkish empire, the I-li khan T'u-men.[52] With the discovery of the Orkhon inscriptions, Shih-tien-mi was identified with one of the founders of the Turkish state mentioned in the runic inscriptions whose name is couched in the form *i/ä-s/š-t-m-i/ä*,[53] usually read *Äsitmi*[54] or *Istämi*[55] that is, as required by the runic spelling, as a word of the palatal class. Marquart further pointed out that *Istämi must be none other than the Στεμβισχάγαν mentioned in the famous letter of the Turkish khan (presumably Tardou) written in 598 to the Byzantine emperor Maurice, the substance of

---

[45] Nöldeke, *Geschichte der Perser und Araber*, p. 159.

[46] For a discussion and summary of the problem of Dilziboul's identity, see Chavannes, *Documents sur les Tou-kiue occidentaux*.

[47] Speculation goes here as far as substituting an *-r-* for the Greek *-l-* and the Arabic *-n-* and seeking in a form **Sir-jabɣu* the chieftain of the omnipresent *Sir.

[48] With the lone exception of E. Blochet in *Revue de l'Orient chrétien*, XXVII, 35–37, who defends the Greek forms, on the grounds both of consistency and of priority in time, but who emends the Arabic reading to conform with his mistaken idea that Sinjibu is the khan whom the Chinese knew under the name of Sha-po-lüeh.

[49] Summarized on pp. 48–50 of Chavannes's *Documents*.

[50] *Analytic Dictionary*, nos. 1214, 1162, 617. Cf. Pelliot's review of Chavannes's work in *BEFEO*, IV, 480 n.

[51] Karlgren, *op. cit.*, nos. 717, 986, 615.

[52] *T'ang shu* 215B.

[53] With (Kül tegin's inscription) or without (Bilgä qaghan's stela) the initial letter.

[54] Or *Äsitmä*: so Radloff, *Die Alttürkischen Inschriften der Mongolei*, N.F., p. 164; on p. 203 of the first volume of the *Inschriften*, Radloff abandoned his derivation of the name from *äšid*, 'hören.'

[55] Or *Estämi*, both according to V. Thomsen (*MSFOu*, V, 135; XXXVII, 17), whose reading is now widely adopted.

which is recorded by Theophylactus Simocatta,[56] and the Στεμεϊσχάγαν in Nicephorus Callistus'[57] recension of Simocatta's account.

No serious attempt has been made, so far as I know, to explain this curious appearance of one and the same individual under two different names. The suggestion naturally offers itself that Dilziboul was the chieftain's name or title during his lifetime, since all the references to him under that name are contemporary, while *Istämi is a posthumous appellation, for it appears in its Greek, Chinese, and Turkish forms in documents composed long after the khan's death, the earliest being Simocatta's, which purports to be dated some twenty-two years subsequent to his demise.

More exciting, however, is the possibility that the two names have some common semantic denominator and differ so signally because of dialectal variations in the speech of the Western Turks as contrasted with that of their Eastern brothers.[58] Indeed, Διλζι ∼ Σιλζι, the first part of what is undoubtedly a Turkish compound with the title *boila* as second element, should be of peculiar interest to Altaists, for it appears to be a Turkish word with a *δ-Anlaut, the alternation of which with *y-*, *d-*, *ǰ-*, and *s-*[59] serves so often as a basis for the classification of Turkish dialects and the reconstruction of their development.[60]

One of the roots with a common-Turkish *δ- initial that comes to mind in this connection is Turkish *yïlï* ∼ *yili* 'warm,' which yields forms with initial *d-* and *s-* for dialects in which the alternation is regular.[61] This root is further supposed to be reflected in Mongolian *doluγan* 'warm.'[62] Among its present derivatives in various Turkish dialects I fail to find a form *yïlči* < *δilči* that could serve as the original of Διλζι, but, surprisingly enough, one such form exists in Mongolian as *ilci* 'warmth,'[63] undoubtedly a Turkish loan word, as on Mongolian soil we should expect *ǰilči*. Dialectal Mongolian forms, such as *nilči*,[64] point, however, to the existence of a genuine Mongolian and common-Altaic form *δilči*, since Altaic *n-* belongs to the group of initials that give us Turkish *y-* but Chuvash *s-*,[65] while within the Mongol-Tungusic branch of the Altaic family *n-* interchanges with *ǰ-*.

Now the commonest and most widely distributed root for 'warm' in Turkish dialects, coexistent with *yïlï*, is *ïsï* ∼ *isi*,[66] already registered in both velar and palatal forms in Kashghari.[67] It has many derivatives, among which we note *ïsït* ∼ *isit-* 'to make warm,' 'to be feverish.' From this stem is regularly

---

[56] Theophylactus Simocatta, VII, 7–9. On the authenticity of the information contained in the letter as regards China, see *HJAS*, III, 223–243.

[57] *Ecclesiastica Historia*, 18, 30 (Migne, *Patr. Gr.*, CXLVII, col. 386).

[58] *T'ang shu* 215B.3a; *T'ung Tien* 197.

[59] The Turkish dialects of the Kirghiz steppe where Dilziboul's hordes roamed in the sixth century are still characterized by a predilection for these initials in preference to common Turkish *y-*.

[60] On some early examples of *δ-, see Marquart, "Kultur- und Sprachgeschichtliche Analekten," *UJ*, IX, 81–88.

[61] L. Gombocz, "Zur Lautgeschichte der altaischen Sprachen," *KSZ*, XIII, 26.

[62] *Ibid.*, and N. Poppe, "Altaisch und Urtürkisch," *UJ*, VI, 105.

[63] Kowalewski's Dictionary, p. 308.

[64] Mostaert, *Textes Ordos*; Vladimirtsov, *Grammatika*, p. 370.

[65] N. Poppe, *Die tschuwassische Sprache*, Körösi Csoma Archivum, II, 76.

[66] Without an archaic consonantal Anlaut, since the Chuvash form has no *ś-*.

[67] C. Brockelmann, *Mitteltürkischer Wortschatz*, pp. 68, 88.

obtained the nominal form *ïšïtma ∼ isitmä*,[68] 'warmth,' 'fever,' which is, in the palatal form, one of the possible readings for the complex of runic symbols to which is now commonly assigned the value **Istämi*. It is true that for the final *-ä* of the suffix *-mä* we should expect the runic sign 𐰀 instead of 𐰃, yet in the absence of examples of forms in *-mä* in the larger inscriptions, on one hand, and in view of the undeniable evidence that 𐰃 serves to transcribe *ä* as well as *i*,[69] on the other, the reading **Isitmä* for the name of the great khan seems to me quite probable and legitimate.

The Chinese transcriptions offer, however, some difficulties. The first one, **Śi̯ĕt-tiem-mi̯ĕt*, would favor some form such as **(I)sitimis*, which could represent **isitmiš*,[70] a verbal derivative in *-miš* (used as a substantive or an adjective) from the verbal stem *isit-*, except for the initial of the first Chinese syllable, which would indicate a *š-* rather than an *s-* in the Turkish original and the unexplainable *-i-* between *-t-* and *-m-*; the second Chinese transcription, **Svt-tiei-miei*, has the same puzzling vocalic element after the *-t-*. We must attribute it to a convention of Chinese transcription, namely, of unnecessarily expanding the syllabification of a foreign compound, such as we have in the well-attested equation Ku-tu-lu (< *ku̯ət-tu̯ət-luk*) = Turkish *Qutluq*.

We may have thus a possible and interesting coincidence in the meaning of the two names under which our hero is known in history. The Chinese sources remind us that the names and titles of Turkish khans, especially in the early period of their history, were more often bluntly descriptive, rather than high-sounding and flattering, and were more likely to have such meanings as 'Blackie,' 'Fatty,' 'Sit-at-home,'[71] than 'The Exalted,' 'The Majestic,' etc. The great leader of the Western Turks may thus have owed his title (in both versions of his name) to a sobriquet, referring perhaps to his having suffered from some febrile disease, or, even more probably, from the self-induced "fever" of alcoholics which distinguished so many famous leaders of the steppe.

In this connection it is interesting to recall that there occurs in the Orkhon inscriptions another term derived from the root *ïsïγ ∼ isig* (again in palatalized form), namely, *isigti*, which is included in the list of Chinese luxuries in line 5 of Bilgä qaghan's inscription and which Radloff and Melioranski were inclined to render as '(warming) alcoholic drinks.'[72] The latest form of our root leads us to a brief consideration of a problem in the Chinese accounts of the Turks in which our "febrile" hero may be directly involved.

In its brief story of the rise of the Turkish state in Central Asia the Chinese "History of the Northern Dynasties"[73] gives us two versions of the succession

---

[68] Often *sïtma ∼ sitmä*, with the loss of the first syllable because the stress falls on the suffix. Cf. J. Deny, *Grammaire de la langue turque*, p. 458.

[69] P. Melioranski, "Pamiatnik v chest' Kül'-tegin'a," *ZVOIRAO*, XII (1899), 21–24.

[70] The difficulty of explaining the form Istami, especially the final *-mi*, has early been recognized and has often led to the suggestion of an error in the inscriptions: 𐰃 for an original 𐰠 at the end of the word. Radloff, *op. cit.*, p. 203: Marquart, *UJ*, IX, 82, n. 5; W. Bang, *T'oung Pao*, VII, 327.

[71] *T'ung Tien* 197.

[72] Radloff, *op. cit.*, p. 151, cf. pp. 153–154; Melioranski, *op. cit.*, p. 87; V. Thomsen translates: Hirse (?), *ZDMG*, LXXVIII, 141.

[73] *Pei shih* 99.

of the first khans of the confederacy. According to the first, the great founder
T'u-men was succeeded upon his death in 552 A.D. by his younger brother,
A-i ($<$ '*A*-(*d*)*ït*)[74] khan, who in his turn passed the chieftainship to the next
brother, Mu-han khan (553–572), setting aside for the time being the rights of
his own son Shê-t'u (the future khan Sha-po-lüeh). According to the second
account, T'u-men was followed as khan by his son K'o-lo,[75] who then left the
throne to his brother Mu-han in preference to his son Shê-t'u, who thus becomes T'u-men's grandson rather than his nephew. It is obvious that the dis-
parity in the two traditions is owing to some confusion between a brother of
T'u-men's and the latter's son and successor. So far as the order of generations
is concerned, the second version is the correct one, but we are inclined to suspect that the neatness of its scheme of succession was obtained by the total
elimination of T'u-men's brother (the mysterious A-i khan of the first version),
possibly by the simple expedient of merging the two personages, brother and
son, into one. It is interesting to note that the title given to the son K'o-lo by
the Chinese sources is I-hsi-chi ($<$ '*ïĕt-si̯ək-kji*),[76] which gives us a Turkish
original **isiki* $\sim$ *isïqï* and possibly **isigi* $\sim$ *isïɣï*, another vocable seemingly
derived from our root *isig* 'warm.' In the light of the foregoing discussion, it
would not be too venturesome to suggest that in the I-hsi-chi of the early
Chinese sources (i.e., those prior to the T'ang histories) we have none other
than **Isitmä*, the "febrile" khan of the runic inscriptions or Dilziboul, the
"febrile" *boila* of the Byzantine histories, whose career, developing as it did in
the "Far West," was silently passed over in the first Chinese accounts, which
were primarily concerned with the successors of T'u-men in the eastern part of
the far-flung Turkish empire; and that the title under which he carried out his
great conquests was conferred by the Chinese historians upon his nephew
K'o-lo, with whom he undoubtedly shared during the latter's brief reign the
sovereignty[77] over the immense territory stretching from the limes of China
to the rim of Justinian's empire.

---

[74] Possibly, Turkish *ädiz* 'high.' *Sui shu* 84 has I k'o-han.

[75] Ancient Chinese: *k'uâ-lâ*. Possibly, Turkish *qara* 'black.' K'o-lo's reign was short and
probably did not last more than one year. In the third month of 553 he is said to have sent
to the Chou court 50,000 horses (*Chou shu* 50); he must have died soon afterward.

[76] *Chou shu* 50; *Pei shih* 99.

[77] According to Bartold (*ZVOIRAO*, XV, 0178–0179), Chavannes did not sufficiently
emphasize that the two halves of the Turkish empire had been from the very beginning
two independent and sovereign, albeit allied, states.

An Early Mongolian Toponym

Harvard Journal of Asiatic Studies, 19 (1956), 407-408.

The well-known early Sung gazetteer *T'ai-p'ing huan-yü chi* [*The Record of the Domed Precinct Space of the Era of Grand Complanation*], a work compiled in the period 976-983 A.D., contains, in its description of the northern marches of the Chinese empire, numerous local non-Chinese toponyms, several of which can be identified as transcriptions of Turco-Mongolian words.

Among them, we have *K'u-li* 庫利 (35.13a), the name of a river, also called in Chinese the " ' Slave ' River," thus permitting us to equate *k'u-li* with Turkish *qul*, " slave "; and the city of *Mo-le* 磨勒 (38.10a; Anc. Ch. *muâ-lək*) so named by the T'u-chüeh (according to the text) because of the excellent fish in the river nearby. The transcription undoubtedly represents Turk. *balïq*, " fish," with Ch. *m*- serving to render, as it frequently does, Turk. *b*-. *Chüan* 36.4b mentions also a *Ku-hu* 骨胡 (Anc. Ch. *kuəδ-ɣuo*) river, also called " ' Dry ' River." *Kuəδ-ɣuo* could well stand for **qurɣu*, a dialectal form of standard Turkish *kuruɣ*, " dry."

Of greater interest is the name of a river in I-ch'uan hsien 宜川縣 (modern Northern Shensi): *K'u-t'o* 庫碢 (Anc. Ch. *k'uo-d'â*). *K'uo-d'â* is a perfect transcription of Mongol *quda*, " affine," " relative by marriage," " go-between," " gossip," " trader," " monger," a term of great sociological import for the interpretation of early Mongolian tribal organization. According to the text (35.12a) which quotes an earlier atlas, this river derived its name from the fact that it formed a line of demarcation between the Chinese and the Barbarians and that the two peoples were in the habit of solemnizing contracts of marriage or alliance (with the burning of incense 香火) in the middle of the watercourse. The *t'u-ching* 圖經 (atlas) from which the *T'ai-p'ing huan-yü chi* derived its information cannot be identified with certainty, but is doubtlessly a T'ang or Sui work of the type mentioned in the bibliographies of the two dynasties. The I-ch'uan territory had never been under the control of the Sung, and their gazetteer must have utilized here sources a century or two older.

Quda is typical for the Mongolian branch of the Altaic family, since the root is practically unknown in Turkish environment. Mongolists will, I am sure, welcome this evidence of the important term attested possibly as early as the seventh century.

Some Proleptical Remarks
on the Evolution of Archaic Chinese

Harvard Journal of Asiatic Studies, 2 (1937), 329-372.

While studies of the graphic structure of Chinese characters have recently been greatly stimulated by the discovery of the " Bone Inscriptions," few attempts have yet been made to formulate the principles underlying the development of the Chinese script and to correlate them with those which determined the evolution of other forms of ' ideographic ' writing, particularly the cuneiform and hieroglyphic scripts of the Ancient Near East.

The investigation of the corner-stone problem of Chinese epigraphy, the relation of graph to vocable, has indeed been rather retarded than advanced by the new finds. Most students in the field have chosen to concentrate their efforts on the exotically fascinating questions of ' graphic semantics ' and the study of the living tissue of the *Word* has almost completely been neglected in favor of that of the graphic integument encasing it. As to the later (Chou) forms of the Chinese written language, they continue to be interpreted according to the principles laid down by native didactic and classificatory works, while less orthodox sources and evidence bearing chiefly on the ' phonetic ' aspects of the script are consistently disregarded.

It is, perhaps, inevitable that in the investigation of ancient ' ideographic ' scripts the ' phonetician ' and the ' epigraphist ' should often work at cross purposes. Even in Egyptology and Assyriology we frequently meet with such a situation, but in those sciences the outstanding philological achievements of both camps have considerably mitigated this wasteful division of labor. In the field of Chinese, however, where we are just beginning to formulate methods of philological approach, the division is greatly retarding the development of science.[1]

---

[1] The concentration of native scholars in China on epigraphical research to the neglect of ' phonetics ' is easily understandable. It is less excusable on the part of

While such ' phoneticians ' as Karlgren have successfully invaded the domain of the ' epigraphists,' the latter have shown some reluctance in availing themselves of the findings of the rival branch and exhibit a strange impotence whenever called to apply those findings to the study of graphic forms.

The fundamental problem of the relation of graph to word, or ' symbol ' to ' sound,' has not even been definitely formulated. The extremely valuable suggestions found in Karlgren's numerous works seem to have passed unnoticed by the ' epigraphists.' In the rare cases when these suggestions have attracted attention, their import has been misunderstood and the practical hints contained in them misapplied.[2]

It is in the hope of dispelling this fog of misunderstanding that the writer presents in the following pages for the consideration of Sinologists a few hypotheses on the evolution of ' sound and symbol ' in archaic Chinese, hypotheses that have in view the preparation of the ground for the discussion of this all-important problem. The complexity and the many ramifications of the question have in a large measure determined the choice of form of exposition and the grouping of the various problems under specific headings.

I. Graph, Semanteme, and Phoneme

The problem of the graphic representation of a vocable in archaic Chinese can best be approached by re-affirming some of the general principles which determined the evolution of prac-

---

western epigraphists. One would be inclined to commend to their attention the delightful " Pictographic Reconnaisances " that Dr. L. C. Hopkins has been conducting for the past twenty years in the *JRAS*, where, though phonology is scarcely touched upon, it is always invoked and important decisions are always with proper caution delayed pending phonological corroboration.

[2] Cf. particularly Dr. Herrlee Glessner Creel's essay " On the Nature of Chinese Ideography," *TP* 1936, 85-161, a well expressed, but most ineffectual attempt to demonstrate the unique ' ideographic ' characteristics of Chinese script and to combat ' phonological ' investigations of archaic graphs. Professor Pelliot's remarks appended to the article rightly condemn Dr. Creel's habit of divorcing writing from the living language. Apart from the author's impossible thesis, one must deplore the general

tically all known forms of writing. It would appear to the writer that they can be formulated as follows:

1. Any single symbol (or *Graph*) in so-called 'ideographic' writing should ideally have only one significance (represent only one *Semanteme*) expressed in the living speech by only one vocable (or *Phoneme*).[3]

As we know from the history of all writing, however, this theoretical desideratum is never definitely achieved, although in the late stages of development of graphic representation of speech it is sufficiently approximated to endow a written language with a high degree of efficiency as a medium of communication. Though fluctuating as it does even in 'phoneticized' scripts, the phonetic value of a graph in a written language standardized through continuous and wide-spread usage can be established with a sufficient degree of certainty, while the graph's semantic value is limited to a cluster of associations usually well defined historically and easily ascertained from the context.

2. Pictograms [graphic representations of natural objects] and symbolic signs do not constitute in themselves *Graphs*, i.e. elements of a written language. In order to become such, they must be conventionally and habitually associated with certain semantic-phonetic values. Thus the pictogram 馬, originally the picture of *a horse-like animal* was not necessarily the graphic equivalent of the Chinese word for *horse* [4] until it became definitely associated with this semanteme and was supplied with the appropriate phoneme (Chin. *ma*, not *hippos, equus, Pferd*, etc.). A symbolic sign such as Chinese 二 can be given its appropriate phono-semantic value *nyi—'two' only when forming a part of the conventionalized Chinese written language. As a symbol out of

---

tendency manifest throughout his article (and, alas, too prominently figuring in Sinological research on this continent) of insisting that the Chinese in the development of their writing, as in the evolution of many other of their cultural complexes, followed some mysterious esoteric principles that set them apart from the rest of the human race.

[3] When referring to Chinese, the term *phoneme* is used by the writer to designate a *syllabic phoneme*.

[4] Cf. W. Perceval YETTS, The Horse: a Factor in Early Chinese History, *Eurasia Septentrionalis Antiqua*, 9.236-240.

Selected Works of Peter A. Boodberg

its proper context, while it may represent the same semanteme
in any language, it may also convey such associations as ' parallel,'
' one thing on top of another,' ' division,' ' half,' [5] etc.

3. The habitual association of a graph (G) with the corresponding semanteme and phoneme (SP) which culminates in
the apprehension of the graph by the reader of the language of
which it forms an element as a single complex GSP can be
achieved only through a long usage of the language and the particular graph and only after conventions have been firmly established.

Once established, these conventional associations of symbol and
sound are, in a given linguistic medium, given up with extreme
difficulty, as everyone who has experienced the necessity of adjust-
ing his G-P associations from one system of spelling to another
can testify. These set conventions are also often in conflict with
factors of divergence and convergence (operating in all phases of
a language) which lead to a single phoneme being represented
by two or several graphs and one graph representing more than
one phoneme.

4. In a ' logographic ' script in its earliest stages of development a graph could and did indeed stand for more than one SP.
Every student of Sumerian and to a lesser degree of Egyptian [6]

---

[5] By ' associations ' we mean definite *words* such as the English terms given, not
' *ideas*.' The term ' ideograph ' which is so widely used by both layman and scholar
is, we believe, responsible for most of the misunderstanding of the evolution of
writing. The sooner it is abandoned, the better. We should suggest the revival of the
old term ' logograph.' Signs used in writing, however ambiguous, stylized, or symbolic,
represent *words*. If we associate with a graph several related words, unable to determine which of them it is supposed to represent exactly, this does not mean that the
graph *represents* the ' idea ' or ' concept ' behind those words. Whatever be the significance of these vague terms in psychology, in linguistics they mean absolutely nothing.
Linguistic science deals first and last with the word, its only reality. The ' disembodied
word ' which is what is generally meant by ' idea ' or ' concept ' does not exist for
the linguist. For him, " les idées ne viennent qu'en parlant."

[6] The fixation of SP values of graphs in Egyptian was facilitated through the
preservation of the realistic pictorial features of the script for a longer period than in
Sumerian or Chinese. Egyptian, on the other hand, ' alphabetized ' a considerable
number of its graphs which began early to be used as ' monophonemes.' We believe,
however, that the reconstruction of ancient Egyptian has been somewhat handicapped
by the belief that some of these specialized graphs had early completely lost their

is well aware of the many pitfalls bestrewn on his path by the
often seemingly capricious polysemy and polyphony of graphs.
The chief handicap faced by the investigator of archaic Chinese
writing consisted, and unfortunately still consists, in the fact that
the polyphony, if not the polysemy, of characters was not recognized as being as much an important feature of the Chinese
script as it is of those of the ancient Orient.

5. While early checked through necessity and by convention,
polysemy and polyphony, and reversely polygraphy, are inherent
in all 'logographic' writing, particularly in its first pictographic-
symbolic stage. Paradoxically enough, it was these confusing
characteristics of early graphic representation which made possible
its development towards greater and greater precision in conveying semantic and phonetic values and conditioned its evolution
into phonetic writing.

Let us take two simple cases of a graph G representing two
semantemes each with its phonetic value and one SP reflected in
two graphs:

$$G \left< \begin{array}{l} S^1P^1 \\ S^2P^2 \end{array} \right. \qquad\qquad SP \left< \begin{array}{l} G^1 \\ G^2 \end{array} \right.$$

Such a situation may cover several possibilities: [7]

In the first case, either the two S (S^1 and S^2) or the two P
(P^1 and P^2) or both pairs may be closely related, the second member of each pair being a cognate or derivative of the first. Thus
a graph with the fundamental meaning (S^1) $\sqrt{}$' two ' → P^1: ' two '
may also be used to represent the phonetic value ' twain ' or
' second ' (S^1P^2), a dialectical or morphological derivative of P^1,
still preserving its original S^1 value. Or it may, on the other hand,

---

' polyphonic' (bi- or tri-phonemic) value. Thus it would appear to me that the sign
for ʒ comprised originally a liquid (r or l) and, at least in some symbol combinations
as comparative semitic material tends to indicate, stood for ʒr or ʒl.

[7] To facilitate the discussion we shall in the few following paragraphs disassociate
for a time the S from P. It will become apparent that linguistically both form an
unbreakable unit SP, the phono-semanteme, which, as we have said, is the only
reality for the linguist. In the graphic representation of a phono-semanteme, the
semantic element can be gradually reduced to a minimum and eventually be eliminated,
but no power on earth can disembody the graph phonetically while it remains in
existence as a sign of communication.

be applied to represent a cognate word ' twin ' (*one* of a pair) or ' half ' (S^2P^2). Or, again, the original graph with its proper S^1P^1 may be found useful to represent ' too ' (S^2P^1), a homophonic semanteme supplanting through the association of sounds the original S.

Two entirely different SP may also become attached to the same G due to the graphic ambiguity of representation, as in the case of a pictogram of a *head* with long *hair* that may stand for either S^1P^1: ' head ' or S^2P^2: ' hair.'

In the second case of an SP reflected in two different graphs, with the standardization of scriptual forms one graph is bound to yield in precedence to the other and the ' weaker ' graph is likely either to attract another ' unattached ' SP or become a specialized or technical representation of the original SP (as a term in an esoteric vocabulary, as a proper name, *etc.*)

6. With increased usage for practical purposes and the consequent desire to limit, if not to eliminate, ambiguity in the written language and with the multiplication of signs created on the pattern of the few earliest graphs, the three great ' logographic ' languages of antiquity resorted to the device of adding another graph to the original ambiguous or ambivalent one with the purpose of fixing, determining, or specializing its S or P.

These appended graphs which are usually termed determinatives, may thus be *semantic* [8] and aphonic (but not necessarily so) or *phonetic* and asemantic (but again not necessarily so, as we shall see shortly).

Thus the graph exhibiting a fluctuation of $P^1 \sim P^2$ with a relative stability of the S would need a phonetic determinative (p^2d) to stabilize it in the second reading. In the case of a paronomastic displacement of S^1 by S^2 the graph would require the addition of a semantic determinative (s^2d) to fix the S^2 value of the graph, the original semanteme having been completely overshadowed by the phoneme. [9]

---

[8] Or ' signific ' in Karlgren's terminology.

[9] As in the case of a graphic ' pun,' the basic feature of the ' rebus ' stage in the development of writing.

7. At this stage of our discussion we must call attention to a very curious situation that arises in the use of determinatives, a situation in which lies the key to the understanding of many a problem connected with the evolution of the Chinese script.

A phonetic determinative (pd), originally an independent graph with its own SP, that is made to play a secondary role in the script by serving as an asemantic appendix to another graph the P of which it is intended to determine, must obviously belong to the class of graphs the P of which are well established by convention and, therefore, easily recognized. A graph of that sort has often a ' weak ' S that does not intrude much on the consciousness of the reader and helps him thus to concentrate on the P, or, though as an independent graph it carries its SP in an equally impressive manner, its contextual use as an auxiliary to another graph with which it has little semantic connection is so conventional that it is recognized as such (*i. e.* with its P value alone) very easily.

Now let us suppose that an original SP reflected in two different graphs has preserved its etymological unity although the second of the two graphs (G^2) has been attached to a special form of the etymon (as, *e. g.*, ' twain '$< \sqrt{}$' two '). The first graph (G^1SP $= \sqrt{}$' two ') now begins to acquire through usage the S^2P^2: ' twin,' thus exhibiting a divergence of both S and P from the original virgin SP and the necessity arises to fix it in that meaning and sound. Among the graphs that may serve as phonetic determinatives, G^2 would appear to be one made to order as it will not only determine G^1 phonetically but also semantically and will act as an s^2p^2d. Likewise an auxiliary graph called to serve as an s^2d may frequently be discovered to fulfill simultaneously the role of p^2d, acting therefore as p^2s^2d.

This important fact, dimly perceived by Karlgren, has been completely disregarded, so far as the writer is aware, by all other investigators. Homophones and homonyms in any given language are accidental only in the minority of cases, then chiefly through convergence caused either by phonetic attrition or semantic evolution. The greater number of homophones and homonyms especially in an early stage of linguistic development must be considered as etymologically related (after satisfactory demonstration, naturally) or all hope be given up for a rational analysis of linguistic facts.

Besides pd and sd pure and simple, unconnected with the graph determined, we thus have spd or psd which we should perhaps designate as *etymonic* determinatives (ed). In the first period that marks the appearance of determinatives in a written language it was inevitable, especially in the case of Chinese where the tendency towards monosyllabism is so marked, that a large number of the determinatives should belong to the third class and that determined and determinative should often form part of the same etymon.

8. The above theoretical consideration will have prepared the reader for the new method of attack on the problem of the structure of Chinese characters. Pedagogically sound and quite appropriate for purposes of static description, the terminology that we have been using for the analysis of the Chinese script, comprising such terms as radical signific, phonetic, ideographic, *etc.* appears entirely inadequate for the presentation of historical, evolutionary evidence on the vicissitudes of Chinese graphs and the development of Chinese vocables. Let us now proceed with this evidence and submit to the test the seemingly *a priori* principles outlined above.

II. POLYPHONY OF GRAPHS IN ARCHAIC CHINESE

As has been said, one of the blind-spots of Sinological epigraphy which gave rise to most disastrous misinterpretations of Chinese characters was caused by the evasion of the problem of polyphony in archaic Chinese. While the presence of polyphony in a limited way could not but be recognized by every student of Chinese, its import was always minimized and the average investigator proceeded lightly on his way on the premise that the fundamental principal underlying Chinese writing was 'one graph—one phoneme.' Little was even done to follow up the brilliant attempts of Conrady to explain by morphological factors the minor variations of initial and final observed in several Chinese vocables.[10]

The problem cannot, however, be longer ignored after the conclusive evidence gathered chiefly by Karlgren and Maspero on the existence of complex initial consonantal groups in over a score of ' phonetic series.' While revealing only relative polyphony in Anlaut, the material assembled on the subject yielded valuable clues for the further exploration of the phoneme hidden beneath the Chinese character.

Anticipating slightly the conclusions which we shall reach at the end of another section, we would begin our discussion by calling attention to the unmistakable fact that archaic Chinese possessed a variety of consonantal Anlaut complexes far exceeding in number the recognized *GL-, *BL-, *DL-, and problematical *BG-.[11] Among the ones that we shall postulate are **DN- and ***BD-.

The existence of these complexes explains away many of the puzzling statements that we find in such authoritative sources as the *Shuo Wên*,[12] which remains in spite of all recent discoveries our chief guide through the tortuous mazes of Chinese epigraphy.

[10] In the following discussion we shall concentrate chiefly on the archaic initial clusters as the problem of consonantal Auslaut has been already dwelled upon by Karlgren in *Word Families*. Moreover, the question of finals becomes of paramount importance only in the late archaic period where we have to deal with the very delicate problem of synalephe, *i. e.* with the reverse of the process of dimidiation of phonemes to which this article is substantially devoted. We shall give only one illustration of the phenomenon. Late archaic 弗 *$p\underset{\cdot}{i}u\partial t$—' not ' is undoubtedly a synalephe of 不 *$p\underset{\cdot}{i}\partial u$ and 之 *ti—' not it ' . . . (observe that ancient Chinese grammar required the pronoun object of a verb in negative sentences to follow immediately after the negative particle, cf. French *ne le* . . .). The fusion of the two elements 不 and 之 into one monosyllable represented by one graph could have happened only at the time when the archaic pronunciation of the two graphs had evolved into the comparatively simple phonemes indicated above.

[11] With capitals we represent the class of consonants. Thus G represents the velar stops g, k, γ, χ, and ng; B, the labials b, p, m; D, the dentals, palatals and affricates; N, the nasal; and L, the liquida. I consider *BG (*$m\chi$- as indicated in some phonetic series, such as 每, 黑, 微, etc.) as problematical for the archaic language, but possible at about the beginning of the ancient period. The evidence of the phonetic series would seem to indicate either a labio-velar G$^\omega$ initial in the phonetic series or the regular interchange of GL- with BL- within the semantic cluster.

[12] Hereafter quoted as SW.

In ch. 7 of his great work Hsü Shên analyzes the common character 年 *nien*—'year' < 'harvest' as consisting of 禾 *huo*— 'grain' ' as radical ' and 千 *ch'ien*—'thousand,' ' as phonetic' 从 禾千聲. The *Shih Ming* 釋名, a 3rd c. A. D. dictionary of popular or school etymology, paronomastically defines 年 *nien* by 進 *tsiĕn*, thus confirming Master Hsü's assertion.[13] Obviously the most satisfactory explanation of these two ancient glosses is that 千 *ch'ien* is derived from an archaic **tsnien*[14] and could thus well serve as a ' phonetic ' for the archaic term which eventually evolved into anc. *nien*. Now not all of the primitive graphs of 年 have 千 as the second element. Many substitute for it an element which seems sometimes to represent a man 人, and sometimes a cutting instrument or blade 刀. The polygraphy is easily explained as both graphs had the pronunciation *ńźiĕn < **źńiĕn*[15] and could thus serve for purposes of phonetic determination as well as 千. This is further indirectly confirmed by a common archaic form of 仁 *ńźiĕn*[16] (a derivative of 人) which is a compound of 千 and 心 where *ch'ien* appears as a ' phonetic.' In still other primitive forms of the graph that unmistakably stands for modern 年 *nien* we can discern nothing but the original form of 禾 without the addition of any other element (so on some of the Shang bones). The necessary conclusion that we are obliged to draw from these facts is that 禾 *ho*—' grain' was a polyphone (being also read **tsnien* in the sense of ' harvest ') and that the essential role played by the second element added to 禾 was that of a semantic-phonetic determinative to limit it in the sense of ' harvest.'

---

[13] The *Pai hu t'ung* phonetically equates 年 with 仍 *ńźiəng* indicating an instability of the final, further suggested by the common synonym of 年 in the sense of ' harvest,' 稔 *ńźiəm*.

[14] In the reconstruction of *ancient* phonemes we follow rather faithfully Karlgren's *Analytic Dictionary*. *Archaic* reconstructions are our own.

[15] All the evidence seems to point to an original *źń- (TSN: affricate + nasal) rather than *ńź- as reconstructed by Karlgren for the ancient language. The sequence of initials in alliterative binoms (see *infra*) indicates unequivocally *TSN.

[16] It is interesting to note that both 仁 and 人 have the not uncommon meaning ' kernel,' ' pit,' ' seed of grain.' Individual grains are often represented around 禾 in some ancient forms of 年.

Before we pass on to still more important cases of polyphony of a more absolute character, it would be well to sound a warning against offering this interpretation when we are in the presence of limited polyphony caused by the beginning of the break-up of the Anlaut consonantal complexes. Dr. Herrlee Glessner Creel (*op. cit.* p. 117-118) begins the exposition of his utterly phantastic theory of " the profoundly ideographic and non-phonetic genius of Chinese " by a discussion of the characters 自 *tzŭ* < **dz'i'* and 鼻 *pi* < **b'ji'*. Admitting the fact that the first character now chiefly meaning ' self,' ' from,' originally had the significance ' nose ' and was also pronounced **b'ji'*, that is in S and P was the equivalent of 鼻 *pi* < **b'ji'*—' nose,' he draws from it the amazing generalization that 自 must have had an ' ideographic ' value alone since it served as a symbol for " two differently pronounced words, ' nose ' and ' self.' " [17] The rational and obvious solution of Dr. Creel's puzzle lies naturally in the archaic initial of the phoneme that represented both semantemes (or rather the semanteme ' nose ' of which ' self ' is but a derivative) and constituted the archaic SP of the G: 自, namely ***BDZi*. This *archaic* phoneme with an initial consonantal complex was differentiated into two *ancient* readings of the graph, **dz'ji'* and **b'ji'*, and the latter was specially ' determined ' through the addition of the pd: 畀 **pji'*.

Now the commonest synonyms of *tzŭ*—' self,' ' from ' are in archaic Chinese 己 *chi* < **kji*—' self ' and 由 *yu* < **i̯əu* < ***DiuG* —' from.' [18] The latter graph, as is well known, early became interchangeable with another character 甾 **tsi* (SW 12B) a dialectical (Eastern Ch'u) term for ' earthenware.' [19] This in

---

[17] Professor F. Lessing reminds me that in the Far East the tendency of pointing to the nose rather than to the breast in indicating one's own person is almost universal.

[18] Also ' to follow.' Cf. 從 **dz'i̯ong—' id.'* **BDZ-* is well attested in this etymon. Compare the following synonyms all of which, as will be shown in occasional references to their respective ' phonetics,' exhibit a **BDZ-* initial: 跡 **tsiäk*, 緣 **di̯än*, 徒 **d'uo*, 徇 **zi̯uĕn*, 隨 **dz'ⁱa*, 循 **dzi̯uĕn*, 遵 **tsi̯uĕn*, 蹟 **tsiäk*, 踵 **tśi̯ʷong*, 俾 **pjʷie̯*, 踐 **ts'i̯en*.

[19] 缶 **pi̯ạu* < ***pi̯ôg* < ***BDoG*. 缶 was often graphically confused with 去 **ki̯ʷob*, witness 缶 used as a phonetic in combinations with det. 厂, 广, 辰, 口 + 厂, 言 + 厂, all pronounced **k'ŋp*. **BD-* is particularly indicated by 匋 ~ 陶 **d'âu-G*—' earthen-

4

turn was primitively a 'homograph' of 田 *si̯ĕn—'head' (the 'phonetic' in 思 *si and 細 *siei'; not to be confused with 田 t'ien—'field'). The curious interchange is explained by the fact that the proto-graph of these words was so pictorially ambiguous that it was variously apprehended as the picture of 1) a head with flowing hair, 2) a basket, and 3) a primitive earthen vessel with osier framework.[20] It is this 'head'—'basket' graph which serves also as the 'phonetic' in the characters 畀 *pji', 畁 *kji', 其 ̥*kji, and 異 **gjiG.[21] The P value **Di̯uG (as in 由) of this graph reflects one of its S: 'head' (i.e. 頭 **d'əuG, 首 *śi̯ou; cf. 道 *d'âu < **d'aŭG,[22] where the latter is 'phonetic,' vs. 迪 *d'iek, and 胄 **d'i̯əŭG—'helmet'),[23] a semanteme which, as we have seen, possessed another P: *Si ~ **SieR. The initial *S- appears to be derived from **BS- as indicated ·by 毘 *b'ji— 'navel' where 田 is 'etymonic' and 比 only a phonetic determinative (cf. the more common synonym 臍 *dz'iei—'navel,' often dimidiated 肶臍 *b'ji—*dz'iei[24]). 己 kji—'self' seems, on the other hand, to be derived from **KSi.[25]

The hypothetical archaic 'etymon' **BSi ~ **KSi (perhaps, more correctly **GSI)—'nose' ~ 'head' ~ 'self' ~ 'from,' would serve to explain many otherwise unexplainable graphic and phonetic forms. Thus it would not be unreasonable to suppose

ware,' 'kiln,' where 缶 is etymonic and 勹 *pauG < *BDauG is phonetic. On 甾, see Wang Kuo-wei's essay 釋由.

[20] The versatile graph represented also a bird's nest and as such was used to render the word *Sier—'West' (now 西) and *Sier < *BSeR—'to roost' (now 栖, 棲).

[21] Cf. L. C. HOPKINS, Pictographic Reconnaissances, IV, *JRAS* 1922, 54-57.

[22] < *BDOG < *GLoG. Cf. 路 *luo < *gloG—'road.' The archaic Anlaut of the last word explains how it came to serve in old texts as the equivalent of 車 *ki̯ʷo— 'chariot.'

[23] < *BDoG. Cf. 冒 *mauG—'cover,' 'hat'; also 兒 *mauG, the phonetic of 兜 *təuG—'helmet.'

[24] Cf. 脺腔 *b'ji-tsi̯ĕd, 脾肶 *b'ji̯e-tsi̯e, 脾析 *b'ji̯e-siek—'crop of a fowl,' 'psalterium of a ruminant,' in the latter meaning folk-etymologized as 百葉 *pŋk-di̯ä̆p (~ Engl. manyplies). There is a faint possibility that 鼻子 pi-tzŭ coll. 'nose' is a similar survival of an original *BDZ- in the word for 'nose.'

[25] Or **BSI. Cf. its appearance as 'phonetic' in 妃 pronounced *p'ji and *źi; also 紀, 記 *kji < **KSI—'to record,' fundamentally the same word as 史 *si < *BSI— 'record' > 'history.'

that 自 **BDZi~**BSI is etymonic in 息 *si̯ək—'to breathe.' [26]
The etymonic and graphic connection of 'head' with 'nose' explains the Lesser Seal convergence of the two graphs for these *words* (百 and 自),[27] while, in the light of the preceding, we can scarcely doubt that 自 (in its variant form 白, SW 4A) is 'phonetic' in 百 *pɒk—'hundred' > 皕 *pi̯ək—'two hundred,' which again appears as the 'phonetic'[28] in 奭 *śi̯äk (SW 4A: 从大从皕皕亦聲).

Space forbids a detailed discussion of each of the following cases of polyphony. It would suffice to say that it is time that, armed with the knowledge that we now possess concerning the phonetic structure of archaic Chinese, we should attack boldly the problem of so-called 'imperfect' 'phonetics' (the 亦聲 'also phonetic' of Hsü Shên), and subject to close scrutiny, etymologically and phonetically, all cases where the early Chinese sources indicate the slightest possibility of 'etymonic' rather than 'ideographic' analysis of characters. We shall now submit for discussion the following polyphones:

1. 豕 *śi̯a—'hog,' 'pig.' Synonym and homograph of 亥 *γâi < **G'aG. Undoubtedly 'phonetic' in 家 *ka—'house.' SW 7B states that 豭 *ka is the abbreviated 'phonetic' in the latter which is the equivalent of saying that 豕 was also read *ka.[29]

---

[26] In the light of most recent investigations it would appear that the majority of ancient syllabic phonemes with vocalic Auslaut are derived from archaic closed syllables. One of the commonest final consonants in the archaic language was the velar trill -R (= French or German uvular or pharyngal *r*) or -ʁ (Spanish *jota*, represented by an inverted R); both interchange easily with χ and γ, and in some phonetic series often give us final -*g*, -*ng* and -*k*. Thus 自 **BSIR ~ **BSIʁ through its derivative 息 **BSEK is cognate to 呬 **GSIʁ ~ **BSIʁ and 栖 **BSER. For the sake of simplicity we shall continue to designate this final consonant by -G.

[27] The graphic prominence given to 自 in the archaic form 面 *mi̯än—'face' is undoubtedly to be explained by *mi̯än being derived from *BDZän. Note that 面 (with det. 目, 見, 皮) is also pronounced *t'ien and is etymologically related to 前 *dz'ien < *BDZ—'fore-part.'

[28] More correctly, it is a phonetic determinative. Note the position of the two 百. It 大 indicates that the fundamental picture is not 大 *ta*, but 亦 *i* < *zi̯äk < *BZi̯äk originally the same graph as 大 but with two strokes to point to the sides or arm-pits (Chin. 腋 *zi̯äk).

[29] According to *Fang Yen* 8, 豭 *ka for 豬 *ti̯wo—'pig' was current in the northeastern dialects. SW 9B defines *ka by 'boar' and gives also a variant of the old graph for 'hog'

2. 三 *ṣam*—'hair.' Also read ***pi̯og*. 'Phonetic' and not 'co-signific' in 髟 ***pi̯og*—'long hair,' 彪 ***pi̯og*—'tiger's hair.' Etymologically related to 毛 **mog—'hair.'[30]

3. 名 **mi̯äng*—'name' is generally interpreted, on the authority of SW 2A, as being an 'ideographic' compound of 夕 **zi̯äk*—'evening,' 'dark,' and 口 **k'ɔu*—'mouth,' 'to utter' ('name' = 'what is *called out* 口 in the *dark* 夕'). The SW, however, specifically states that 夕 is the equivalent of 冥 *mieng—'dark' 夕者冥也. What Hsü Shên undoubtedly wanted to imply is that 夕 in the meaning of 'dark' should not be read **zi̯äk* but *mieng.[31] This character was possibly not more than a phonetic *determinative* for 口 **k'ɔu* which as we can infer from 鳴 **mi̯ʷng*—'sound' and 命 **mi̯ʷng*—'command' was also read ***Mi̯ʷng* in the meaning 'to utter.'

which was pronounced *χa. The original scription 豕 possessed also the phonetic value *TUN especially in the sense 'fat,' 'suckling pig' as indicated by 豚 **d'uən*—'young pig' and the graphic derivative of 豕 — 彖 **t'uân*—'hog.' Already on the bones **d'uən* is composed of 月 and 豕. 月 is here not to be taken as **ẑńi̯uk*—'meat' but as a pd representing the word 'fat,' archaic *BDUN ~ BDʒNG attested in 腯, 胖, 腤, 胖, 朦, 腔, 腥. The same etymon in the form *BSA we see in 肥, 髓, as *BSI in 脂, 胵, and probably in its oldest form *BLoG ~ *GLoG > *BDoG > DoG in 膏, 臚, 朧. 油, 澤, 灌, 膝.

豬 **ti̯ʷo* < *BDo is really only a variation of 豭 *ka as the latter was also pronounced *kuo. As attested by numerous archaic rhymes and proverbs *kuo was also one of the variant readings of 家 *ka—'family,' 'house.' The last etymon which was undoubtedly *GSO is reflected in 居 **ki̯o* 'to dwell,' 戶 **g'uo* ('phonetic' in 所 **si̯o*)—'door,' 'house.' For initial dental forms of the same cf. 都 *tuo—'capital,' 'to dwell,' 處 **tśi̯wo*—'to dwell,' 住 **d'i̯u*—'to reside'; with velar Auslaut 宋 *gsuong ~*bsuong—'to dwell,' and 宅 **d'ɒk*—'family,' 'house' (*BDak is indicated by its being phonetic in 亳 **b'ɒk*—'the name of the old capital of the Shang dynasty').

[30] The reading *ṣam* < *Gsam was probably acquired by the graph due to its similarity to 三 *sam* < *Gsam—'three.' Ancient ***pi̯og* is undoubtedly derived from archaic **BLog ~ **BSog : **GLog ~ **GSog as evidenced by graphic and phonetic derivatives from √'hair': 修 *si̯əuG*—'ornament,' 飾 **si̯əG*—'id.,' 老 *GLog—'old' (where 毛 is 'phonetic') vs. 壽 **ẑi̯əuG*—'old,' 須 **si̯uG*—'beard,' 首 **si̯əuG*—'head with hair,' 長 **ti̯ang*—'elder,' 'long' (the original graph represented 'long hair'; in later forms 亡 **mi̯ʷng* was added as a 'phonetic' indicating an archaic *BDang), 鬃 *muk (with *GLɒk as 'phonetic')—'fine lines,' 彫 *tieuG < *BDuG—'to engrave' 鬍 *tieuG—'abundant hair,' etc.

[31] The different readings can well be explained on the supposition of an original *BZek ~ *BZeng.

4. 目 *miuk—'eye'[32] had the variant reading **GEN as evidenced by 眼 *ngan (Ph. *kən) —'eye,' 看 **k'ân*—'to look' and its appearance in a slightly different graph in 臥 *kien.[33] It is also 'etymonic' in 見 *kien—'to see,' where 儿 *ńźiĕn is most probably a phonetic 'complement.'

5. Among the early partially recognized polyphones we must note 寸 **ts'uən*—'inch' < 'thumb' < 'hand,' which is graphically identical with 手 *śiəu—'hand' and in this last reading is 'phonetic' in 守 *śiəu, 討 **t'âu*, phonetic sub-determinative in 導 **d'âu*, 'etymonic' in 肘 **tiəu—'wrist,' and 'phonetic' in 紂 ***d'iəu*.[34]

6. 火 **χwâr—'fire' in the meaning of 'burn' was probably pronounced **TSÄK [35] ~ **TSUG and served as 'phonetic-etymonic' in 炙 **t'śiäk*—'to roast,' 焦 *tsiäu—'to burn,' 鱁 **TsuG—'to scorch' (ph. in 秋 **ts'iəu-G*—'autumn') and possibly 狄 **d'iək*.[36]

7. 木 *muk—'tree' had also the phonetic value **BSUG and was 'phonetic' in 宋 *suong,[37] 相 *siang,[38] 桑 *sâng—'mulberry-

---

[32] Archaic *BLuk ~ *BDuk. 目 is 'etymonic,' not 'signific' in 睦 *liuk, and phonetic' in 蜀 **d'iⁱᵒok*, probably 'etymonic' in 睪 *diäk—'to spy out,' where the phonetic is 幸, not in the reading *niäp, but as *piäk 辟 < *BDek, *BD- in this last phonetic series being well attested by binoms.

[33] 臣 in its oldest graphic forms is identical with 目. *kien is derived from *GLen which root had also a variant form *GLam which is reflected in 監 *klam; with the pd 品 **p'iəm*, also in 臨 *liəm < *BLəm.

[34] As we shall see presently, the original archaic form of 'hand' being *BDu ~ *BTSu, 寸 is also 'phonetic-etymonic' in 付 *piu—'to hand over.' As 寸 *tsuən, on the other hand, goes back to *btsun, the two readings of the graph are evidently variants of one and the same SP.

[35] That is as if equal to 赤 **t'śiäk*—'red' < 'fiery' where 火 is 'etymonic.' In 赤 reduplicated > 赫 *χᵥG we probably have the graph reverting to the phoneme *χwâr.

[36] Some ancient graphs seem to indicate, however, that the symbol on the right of the 'dog' was 亦 *źiäk* < *BSiäk which is a much more satisfactory phonetic. This appears to be confirmed by the paronomastic equation of 狄 with 辟 *piak < *BTSiäk, the initial cluster of which is substantiated by its being defined in turn by 積 *tsiek (see the *Kuang Shih Ming*, chs. 1 and 2).

[37] This graph representing the name of the state of Sung, the last remnant of the Shang 'Empire,' presents problems of peculiar interest. The tree 木 under the roof 宀 symbolized originally the sacred tree of a city-state altar above which, upon the conquest of the state, the victors erected a shed; the roof of the shed was supposed to

tree' (dimidiated into 扶桑 *b'i̯u-sâng) [39] and as 'signific-phonetic' in 樹 *zi̯u—'tree,' 'to plant' (cf. the pd of this character 尌 > 廚 *d'i̯u—'kitchen' *vs*. 庖 **b'auG—'kitchen').[40]

8. The archaic graph of 明 *mi̯ʷɒng—'bright,' as is well known, consisted not of 'sun' 日 and 'moon' 月, but of 囧 *ki̯ʷɒng—'bright' (originally the picture of a window)+月 as a sd. The interchange of the labial and velar initials in the etymon √'bright' indicates clearly that 囧 is 'phonetic-etymonic' in 明. On the other hand, the graph 日 which we find as the left

cut off the communication that existed between the altar and heaven. The state of Sung as well as the Shang Dynasty had two sacred trees: the mulberry 桑 *sâng and the pine 松 *zi̯ʷong < *GSung, the latter probably inherited from the Hsia. 松 is indeed supposed by many scholiasts to be (in abbreviated form) the 'phonetic' of 宋 *suong. It is not unusual, however, to find the state of Sung designated in Middle Chou texts by the characters 商 Shang < *si̯ang (i. e. by the name of the fallen dynasty which it represented) and 宗 tsung < *tsuong ('ancestor,' 'ancestral temple'). In other words, the name of the state undoubtedly goes back to a term the evolution of which can be roughly stated to be: ' √tree' > ' √ (ancestral) wooden tablet' > ' √shrine.' For synonyms, cf. 算 *tsuən < *BTSUN, 主, 尘 *ti̯u < **BSu, 祖 *tsuo < **BTSuo. The *Shih Ming* equates 宋 ... tically with 送 *sung—'to escort,' the pd of which represents graphically hands carrying a torch. The etymon of this graph is reflected in 廾 *ki̯ʷong, 共 *g'i̯ʷong, 奉 *b'i̯ʷong, all which go back to *GSong ~ *BSong; cf. also 烽 *pi̯ʷong—'beacon fire,' 襮 *b'uk < **BDZuk (举 *dz'âk is 'phonetic'!). For 廾 *GSong < *GLong cf. 弄 *lung. For the *GSi ~ *GSiG variation of the etymon ' √two hands,' cf. above 昇, 巽, 其, also 异, 奕. The same graph serves as the pd of 兵 *pi̯ʷɒng < **BDZang and of 具 *g'i̯u, etymonically identical with 舉 *ki̯ʷo < 與 *zi̯o.

In the light of the above it would appear that the original name of the 商 Shang dynasty was *BSang or *GSang. The 'phonetic' of 商 is 音 > 竟 *ki̯ɒng, 章 *ti̯ang, both etymologically connected with 明 *mi̯ʷɒng, 方 *pi̯ang, and 行 *g'ɒng. In some archaic scriptions of 章 *ti̯ang the 'phonetic' appears to be 東 *BDâng ~ *BSung. Cf. note 44 音—'sound' was a polyphone: the common pronunciation was ·i̯əm (曰 = 廿 *ɣam was then considered to be the 'phonetic'), but there was also a pronunciation *Gi̯ang which was reflected in 竟 *ki̯ɒng, 競 *g'i̯ɒng, 響 χi̯ang—'echo' (in which 鄉 is the pd). *Gi̯ang is derived from *GSang—'sound,' cf. 聲 *si̯äng—'sound,' where 殼 *k'ieng is 'phonetic.' 曰 as the abbreviated form of 音 *Gi̯ang < *GSang appears in 香 *χi̯ang—'fragrance,' < *GSang ~ *BSang, as indicated by 芳 *pi̯ʷang—'fragrant' and 馨 *χieng—'id.' Cf. also 芭苴 *pa-tsa—'fragrant herb.'

[38] The *Pai hu t'ung* equates phonetically 霜 *si̯ang with 亡 *mi̯ʷang.

[39] Or 榑桑 *b'i̯u-sâng. Another variant 空桑 *k'ung-sâng indicates also *GSang.

[40] For 包 *pauG—'placenta' < *BSoG, cf. *infra*. Compare also 鮑 *b'auG—'preserved fish' with 胥 *si̯ʷoG, 膮 *si̯uG—'id.'

part of some archaic forms was not necessarily phonetically equivalent to $*\acute{n}\underline{z}i\breve{e}t$, but as a polyphone could also represent the etymon √ ' bright ': $*mi^wang \sim *ki^wng \sim *tsi^wng$.

III. 'IDEOGRAPHIC' COMPOUNDS AND THE PHONETIZATION OF GRAPHS

We have already sufficiently indicated in our discussion and examples that the entire class of so-called *hui-i* 會意 or ' ideographic ' Chinese characters should be made the subject of a rigid investigation, and that it was often our ignorance of archaic phonetics that led us into classifying as such characters in which the Chinese lexicographers clearly perceived phonetic elements, and that even among the 740 pure *hui-i* listed in *T'ung Chih* 32 the majority have to be immediately re-classified as phonetic compounds.

It is indeed highly improbable, as has been already suggested in Section I, that the method of construing new characters through a combination of two old ones, neither of which retains its P value, could be used extensively in any script. Though often fluctuating due to the ambiguity of many graphs, the SP value or values of a graph must have been so early conventionalized and fixed that to suppose that G (SP) + G¹ (S¹P¹) creates a complex G + G¹ (S²P²) with a complete change of the SP associations of the component graphs is to underestimate the power and value of those early associations and to imply that the creators of Chinese writing were arbitrarily violating the fundamental laws of economy inherent in the development of any script and that the archaic script was used in an esoteric, cabalistic function rather than as the effective medium of graphic communication that it was.

We do not deny, of course, that in a limited way such characters made their appearance in Chinese writing. Mystagoguery and pedantocracy was as much a part of the life of the Chinese world of learning as elsewhere, but as elsewhere, East or West, people in China were writing to be understood and practical considerations must have outweighed whatever childish delight individuals, however influential in their day and generation, derived from the composition of puzzling graphic charades.

Apart from a few exceptional cases, then, ' ideographic ' characters as a class, we make bold to assert, simply do not exist.[41] Those characters which appear to be such in the later forms of the script

[41] In a little excursus we may be permitted to discuss here one of the most interesting polyphones of the archaic script which will serve to illustrate the persistence of the SP associations of a graph. This polyphone is the modern 卩 *tsiet* ' seal.' As correctly indicated by Dr. Creel (*op. cit.* 121-124) the protograph of this character was the picture of a kneeling man, and originally did not refer to a ' seal ' at all. Dr. Creel's aversion to phonetics, however, causes him to overlook the semantic implications of this statement. Now the word ' kneel,' was derived in Chinese (as it is in English) from ' knee ' which in the archaic language was *BTSiet ~ *BTSien, as reflected in 膝 *si̯ĕt and 臏 *b'i̯ĕn—' knee-cap ' < *BS- (cf. particularly 賓 with det. 香 and 禾 meaning ' fragrant '). The term ' knee ' also covered ' shin-bone ' which was designated by 脛 *g'ieng < GLeng ~ *BDeng (cf. note 44). Thus the graph for ' to kneel ' came to be associated with the two phonemes, which, however, go back undoubtedly to the same etymon. These two variant pronunciations are reflected in the use of the graph 卩 as a phonetic. In the reading *GLeng it serves as such in 令 *GLeng ~ *BLeng—' order ' and 鄉 *χiang < *GLang ~ *GSang—' to confront ' (possibly also in 客 *GLak, some early forms of which show a kneeling man under a roof). As to *BTSiet, with a -k Auslaut it is phonetic in 卽 *tsi̯ak (which is in turn phonetic in 節 *tsiet—' joint '), 色 *si̯ak, and 辟 *p'iek < *BTSiek—' to govern,' while as *BSien it appears in 印 *·i̯ĕn—' seal ' < *hi̯ĕn ~ *si̯en (the s- being preserved still in the cognates 信 *si̯ĕn and 璽 **si̯er, cf. also 瑑 *d'i̯wän < *BD-). In the same reading it enters also into several ancient graphs of 賓 *b'i̯ĕn < *BS—' guest,' a synonym of 客, and the phonetic of 臏—' knee-cap.' Now, as we shall have occasion to notice in the course of this article, *BS- ~ *BTS- constantly interchanges with *TSN- in a given phonetic series. It is not surprising, therefore, that 卩 —' kneeling man ' is confused in old graphs with 人, 儿—*ńi̯ĕn—' man '; the protograph of the second character can even be said to represent a *half-kneeling* human figure. As to the meaning ' seal ' acquired later by 卩 , it is derived from ' credential ' < ' tally ' < ' joint ' < ' knee.'

After a study of another fundamental graph, that of a hand holding a stick, we can dismiss one more of Dr. Creel's ' ideographs.' This GSP, derived from the primeval etymon ' hand,' had the following readings, all being the modification of one root: *BSi, *BSien, *Bsiet, *Bsuk, *Bsut; the BS- comes undoubtedly from an older *BL-. With the reading BSi we have: 尹 *gsi ~ *gsuən (in 君), 史 *Bsi < *BLi, some of the phonetic derivatives of 聿 (as with det. 歹, 镸), 隶 *BDi < *BLi; with *Bsuk 肀, in 肅 (besides the graphs discussed *infra* and in note 82); *BSut < *BLut is registered in 聿 (律, 筆) *BLut—' pencil,' while *BSien and *Bsiet appear chiefly in 肂 *tsi̯ĕn < *BTS—' a pencil writing strokes ' and 彗 *dzi̯wäd—' broom ' > ' to sweep ' ~ ' to clean ' (a variant of the graph that underlies 帚 *t́si̯əu—' broom,' phonetic in 婦 *b'i̯əu—' wife '). The ' simple pictograph of dish-washing with a brush or swab ' that Dr. Creel sees in 盡 represents thus the *word*—' to clean with a

are predominantly 'learned' creations of Chinese schoolmen, graphical modifications of either original pictograms and symbols or perverse rationalizations of 'organically' developed phonetic compounds.

Of the ten most often adduced examples of ideographic compounds we have already dismissed four 年, 名, 家, and 明, all of which had never been regarded as purely ideographic by the best Chinese authorities. Only two of the remainder cannot be interpreted on phonetic grounds, and it is precisely these two that form excellent illustrations of rare analogical creations on the pattern of an 'organic' graph.

This famous graph is the character 東 *tung*—'east' consisting of 木 *muk*—'tree' and 日 *ńźiĕt*—'sun,' interpreted usually as indicating the region of the sunrise by picturing "the sun rising behind a tree." It is rather disheartening to be obliged to re-assert again that the graph never represented the above, but, as has been known for the past two thousand years depicted (when treated as an 'ideographic' compound) *the sun climbing on the Tree of the East* and reflected the old myth of the *fu-sang* 'world-tree.' As recently correctly pointed out by L. C. Hopkins [42] the

brush' derived from the comprehensive etymon 'to do something with the hand armed with a stick, broom, brush, or any wooden instrument (cf. BSUK—'wood').'

Dr. Creel's 'ideographs' coming next are 降 *g'nng* < GLâng and 陟 *tiṇk* < *BDiǝk. The author's graphical analysis of these two characters (the first representing in its essential part footprints going down > 'to descend'; the second footprints going up > 'to ascend') is perfect, but he fails again to realize that the graphs must have represented definite words, and not 'ideas.' Dr. Creel is also unjust to the *Shuo Wên*: when the latter says that 夅, the phonetic of 降, equals in meaning *fu* 服, to give the latter the translation 'to submit' is not to render adequately what Hsü Shên wanted to convey. Indeed 服 = 'to submit,' but also 'to subdue' < 'to bring down' ~ 'to come down,' in other words it is a synonym of 下 *g'a and 降 *g'nng which are both derived from a proto-archaic root *GLa, 'down' > 'come down' > 'reach' (the last reflected in 各 ~ 格 *klnk, 來 *kləg, etc.). In other words, already one footprint (especially pointing downward) could stand for *GLa ~ *GLåG (as it does in 麥 *BLnK < *GLåK) while the addition of a second footprint below the first would strengthen not so much the 'idea,' but leave no doubt as to what *word* was represented. Similarly with 步, the essential part of 陟, the etymonic of which is the root *tiek—'step' ~ 'stop' which is reflected in 彳 *t'iäk, 辵 *t'iak, 止 **tiəg, 尺 *t'iäk etc. *Tiek goes back to an original *BDeG ~ BDoG meaning 'foot' ~ 'step' (cf. 足, 正, 步), a cognate of GLåG.

[42] *JRAS*, January 1937, 29-31.

primitive form of 東 was a pictogram representing a sack or bundle of faggots. What seems to have escaped the learned English commentator is the identity, long suspected by Chinese scholiasts, of 東 with 束 *ṣi̯ʷok*—'faggot,' 'to tie together' (which as a 'phonetic' is often read *si̯ʷong*). Now **SUK (> *śi̯ʷok*) ~ **SUNG is derived from an archaic **BSUG ~ **BSUNG as evidenced by a whole series of 'etymons' clustering around the root **BSUG—'tree' to which we have already drawn attention.[43] *tung*—'east' would appear, therefore, to be *etymologically* connected with **BSUNG—'the *fu-sang* tree,' the *graphic* presence of which in Lesser Seal forms was never questioned.[44] It is immaterial whether the mythological theme entered originally into the pictogram or was *read* into it at a latter period, the main point is that it could not have been attached to the graph unless there existed between the mythological term and the pictorial representation a common bond of semantic association through the *living word*.

[43] In 欶 *ṣâk*, *ṣiuk*—'to breathe' and 嗽 *ṣɒuG*—'to cough,' 束 *BSUG renders the etymon *BSEG—'to breathe.' See note 26.

[44] Observe that 東 *tung* is 'phonetic' in Lesser Seal graphs of 重 *d'i̯ʷong* which is in turn 'etymonic' in 量 *li̯ang* < *BLang and 'phonetic' in 童 *d'ung, and 動 *d'ung*. Semantic grouping and binomial forms (especially in the case of 童 where compounds of the type 蒙童 *mung-*d'ung are well attested) point to the fact that 重 and 童 go back to *BDung. The 'etymonic' of 重 is 壬 *t'ieng < *BDeng—'good.' originally the picture of a stalk of a plant. *BDeng goes back to *BLeng (cf. 令 *BLeng—'good') or *GLeng (cf. 莖 *kieng—'stalk,' where 壬 is 'phonetic'; 頸 *ki̯äng—'neck' vs. 領 *li̯äng—'neck'). Besides 'good' and 'stalk' the etymon had the meaning 'balance,' 'weigh' (cf. 程 vs. 秤, 兩, 量; also 聽 *t'ieng—'to hear a case' vs. 聆 *lieng—'to hear,' 平 *b'i̯ʷng—'to weigh,' 'to settle,' 定 *d'ieng—'to settle').

As *BSeng ~ *BSang it is phonetic in 聖 *śi̯äng—'perspicacious' (耳 is 'etymonic' in this character; besides *źṅi, 耳 had in the archaic language the readings: *GSeng, hence 耿 and 聲; *źṅung, hence 茸; *GLung ~ *GSung in the the meaning 'deaf,' hence 聾 and 聳) and 望 *mi̯ʷang—'to look from a distance,' 'to pay homage' (cf. 相, 朝 *BTSiau, also 廷 *d'ieng < *BDeng—'court,' 'hall,' 堂 *d'âng < *BDang—'hall'). In connection with 堂 *BDang, it is interesting to observe that *ming-t'ang* 明堂 *mi̯ʷng-d'ang*, the mysterious hall around which centered the ancient Chinese rituals, is probably nothing more than the dimidiated binomial form of *BDang > **Bang-Dang, rationalized into an adjective-noun formation. For the evolution of the term 'hall,' 'palace,' 'temple' cf. 郎 *lâng < *GLang ~ *BLang, 麗 *b'âng < *BLâng, 京 *ki̯ɒng < *GLɒng, 閣 *kak < *GLak, 宗 *tsung < *BSung, 廟 *mi̯äu < *BTSi̯auG, 寺 *dziG < *BDZiG, and 廳, 庭 *BDeng, 殿 *d'ien < *BDen.

It is only after the mythological significance became firmly
implanted in the character that it could begin to live an independent life severing its tie with the phonetic association. The
graphic elements could now be re-arranged to continue with the
mythological story, and it is at this point that the two 'ideographic' characters of which we spoke above made their appearance, namely 杲 *kâu representing the sun atop the fu-sang tree >
'sunrise,' 'bright,' 'high,' and 杳 *·ieu, the sun at the root of
the tree > 'dark' (observe that phonetically the two graphs are
only reproducing the two more common terms 高 *kâu—'high' ~
暠 *kâu—'bright' and 幽 *i̯ə̯u—'dark').

Another common character interpreted as an 'ideographic'
combination is 鮮 *si̯än ~ *si̯är—'fresh,' consisting of fish 魚 and
羊 mutton, to indicate, they say, the common desirable quality
of these two articles of diet! In spite of the final, 羊 **ziang is
here the 'phonetic' as indicated by 羨 *zi̯än, 善 zi̯än, and 羴
*śi̯än, the last serving, according to SW 11 B, as the original
'phonetic' of 鮮 *si̯än.[45]

---

[45] 鮮 is a very important character used in Chinese transcription of foreign words.
It appears in the term 鮮卑 *si̯er-pji̯ę which designated both the 'animal-style'
buckle and a nomadic people on China's northeastern frontier (cf. HJAS 1.306).
This last name may be identical with 鮮于 *si̯er-gi̯u, 鮮牟 *si̯er-mi̯u, the second
part of the binom rendering a syllable with a labio-velar initial. The same character
enters into the compound 鮮支 *si̯er-ti̯ă or *si̯er-g'i̯ă used as: 1) the name of an
aromatic and dye-producing plant, 2) a term designating plain silk, 3) the name of
district near the bend of the Yellow river above Lan chou. In the last function it is
also written 賜 (*si̯ĕg ~ *si̯ĕR) 支 and 析 (*si̯ĕk ~ *si̯ĕR) 支 (or 枝), the name
dating back to the Chou period (it is found in the Yü kung). The phonetic restoration
of the original of all these transcriptions would demand a special study. The
possibility that the second character of the compound was primitively pronounced
*g'i̯ă raises the interesting question whether we have not to deal here with an old
eastern Asiatic term which designated at the same time the great Kansu emporium of
Chinese-Western trade situated near Lan chou and the three chief articles of that
trade, silk, dyes, and 'animal-style' decorations (as well as the people trading in
them). In our belief, it is in an investigation of these linguistic complexes associated
with the paramount theme of transasiatic trade and its articles that lies the solution
of the great Serica question, the land of the Seres originally being not the entire region
of Northern China, but only its northwestern part, the Kansu-Shensi nexus of trade
routes and the approaches to Central Turkestan, the Chinese 'Western Regions,' Hsi
yü 西域; the archaic pronunciation of the last term, *si̯er-gi̯ʷək again leads us to
Serica.

As suggested in a previous paragraph the archaic etymon for 'self,' of which 己 *kji was but one of the graphs, had two forms **GSI and **BSI. This would explain away another of those quaint 'ideographic' characters, the graph 妃 *pʻjʷe̥i—'wife' ('a husband's own 己 woman 女!'). 己 *kji in its variant **BI < **BSI is again obviously 'phonetic' (cf. SW 12B that says so in so many words).

We come now to the last, and most curious, example of the selected ten 'ideographs,' the character 好 χâu < **χôg—'good,' 'to love,' consisting of 女 *ni̯ʷo—'woman' and 子 *tsi—'child.' Both of the components are polyphones. 女 *ni̯ʷo in its oldest form (so on bronzes and bones) is often interchanged with 母 **muG. 子 *tsi < **tsləg (it is 'phonetic' in 李 *lji < ** (ts) ljig) had also a common archaic reading **KOG, which is reflected in such graphs as: 孩 **gʻâG—'child,' 穀 *gʻuk—'suckling pig,' 觳 *kʻəu—'chick,' 穀 *kʻəu—'to suckle.'[46] In the form **kəu the same semanteme appears in 狗 *kəu—'dog,' originally 'whelp,' 駒 *ki̯u—'colt,' 犅, 牿 *ɣəu—'calf,' and is *phonetically* and graphically rendered in the early graph which evolved later into the characters 后 *gʻəu and 後 *gʻəu—'posterity' and which represented in its most primitive stage the act of parturition.[47]

---

[46] 子 *KOG < *KLOG is undoubtedly etymonic also in 孔 *kʻung < *KLung—'hole,' 'to penetrate' both meanings being derived, acc. to Chinese lexicographers, from the etymon 'parturition.' The significe 'swallow' 乙 *·at presents here a problem of considerable interest. The Chinese ritual of spring mating was associated with the arrival of the first swallows (other terms for which were 燕 *·ien, undoubtedly connected with 乙 *:at ~ *iaR, and 玄鳥 'black bird'). This association is reflected in the characters 堊 *·i̯ĕn—'swallow's nest' > 禋 *·i̯ĕn—'spring sacrifice of purification and prayer for children' and in the legend of the origin of the ancestor of the Shang dynasty whose mother conceived him by swallowing the egg of a swallow (玄鳥). The same motif re-appears in the story of the founder of the preceding dynasty. Yü's mother conceived him, says the legend, through swallowing the seed of the 薏苡 *·iek-źi plant. Now the same binom forms also another term for 'swallow' 意怠 *iek-źi or 鷾鴯 *iek-źńi which appears in *Chuang tzŭ*. Observe in this connection that the three supposed surnames of the great first dynasties, 姒, 子, and 姬 all go back to *GSiG ~ *BSiG, an etymon probably meaning essentially 'child,' 'progeny.'

[47] Cf. Herrlee Glessner Creel, *op. cit.*, pp. 99-101, where the author, while correctly following his Chinese predecessors in the interpretation of the graphic significance of the early forms, fails grievously in estimating their phonetic values. The 'inverted

In brief, an archaic Chinese phoneme **KOG~GOG covering the cluster of associations: ' mother '~' to give birth '~' child '~' to love '~' posterity ' was variously represented in the graphs 子 —' child,' 母~女—' mother ' and a combination of the two (as in 好 and the proto-graph of 后, 後). Again we see that, however pictographic in form was the original graph, to serve effectively as a real graph it could not be dissociated from the SP it conveyed.

We come now to the consideration of a most important phase in the development of Chinese writing. It appears that with the gradual conventionalization of early elaborately pictorial graphs the users of the Chinese script then had at their disposal a number of simple graphs the SP value of which had been relatively well fixed. These graphs consisting often of a few strokes could safely be *graphically woven* into the texture of more complex pictographs so as to serve, so to say, as *matres lectionis*, without necessarily distorting completely the original picture. Acting, therefore, as phonetic determinatives, these graphs should be distinguished from the usual pd in that they were *inner* modifications of a graph and not external accretions to it. In my belief two very early recorded instances of an inner phonetization of graphs are evident in the bones and bronze forms of the characters 馬 ' horse ' and 龍 ' dragon.'

Students of the primitive forms of Chinese writing must often have been puzzled by the fact that the pictogram for ' horse,' which at first depicted the noble animal faithfully, begins to be attested immediately after its appearance in forms where the original pic-

---

child' 𠫓 **t'uət* is, as has been recognized since Hsü Shên, equivalent in etymonic value to 突 **t'uət*—' to come out suddenly ' (in which 穴 **g'i^ωet* is probably ' phonetic '), a synonym of 出 **t'iuĕt* < *BDuət—' to come out,' on one hand, and of 忽 *χuət—' sudden ' and 猝 **ts'uət* < BTsuət—' sudden,' on the other. *BDut~ *BSut is also related to *BSoG < *GLoG which appears in 足 *BTSi^ωoK—' foot ' (the protograph is very similar, however, to 子), 疋 *Bsi^ωo—' *id.*' > 疏 *Bsi^ωo—' to come through (as a child at birth)' *BSiG in 巳 [KD 808] *dzi < *Bdzi—' foetus ' (胎), which on the oldest inscription is again represented by 子. *GLoG ~ *BLoG is shown by the reading **li̯ạu* < *GLəu for 㐬 (cf. note 83) > 流 —' to flow.' It is probably this phono-semanteme ' to flow ' > ' fluid ' which is represented by the alleged ' hair streaming down ' in the lower part of 㐬. As to 月 in 育 *iuk < **z̧iuk*, it is un-doubtedly phonetic.

ture becomes strangely distorted. While the horse's legs and tail continue to be clearly reproduced, the primitive picture of the head is supplanted by a graph which represents nothing but the *eye* of the animal, now with a flowing *mane*, now without, the resulting ensemble being grotesque to the utmost. Now, besides the common reading *ma, the graph for 'horse' possessed a by no means unusual phonetic value *muo[48] < **MOG (cf. its use as 'phonetic' in 媽 *muo—'mother,' = 母 **MuG, and 馬 *muo— 'horse running'; since the earliest time it was also considered to be a homonym and synonym of 武 *miuG—'martial'). Given this P value, the reasonable explanation of the grotesque distortion of the original pictogram for 'horse' is that through pictorial emphasis on the *eye*, Chin. 目 **miôg, or *mane* < 'hair,' Chin. 毛 **mog, the early graphologists of China were endeavoring to indicate the pronunciation of an early pictograph which although quite satisfactory as the representation of a 'horse' did not necessarily convey to the reader the *word* which it symbolized.

As to the 'dragon,' SW 11B distinguishes in the pictogram an abbreviated form of the character *d'ung 童 which acts as 'phonetic.' Indeed, even on the bones we see the head of the pictogram for dragon conventionalized into 孚 the 'etymonic' protograph of *d'ung. As we shall see shortly *d'ung could very well serve as a pd for **KLung,[49] the archaic term for 'dragon,'

---

[48] Besides the evidence from the rhymes of the *Shih ching*, we have numerous cases from Han poetry where 馬 *muo rhymes with 土, *t'uo, 虎 *χuo, 魯 *luo, 戶 *g'uo, 鼓 kuo, 古 *k'uo, and even with 主 *tiu, 武 *miu, and 宇 *g'iu. The surname 馬 Ma was in Han times undoubtedly pronounced *muo as we can see from *Han Shu* 6 (Hou-yüan 1, 88 B.C.) where 莽 *muo (< *muoG ~ *mang) is substituted for 馬 as the surname of the two officials, Ma Ho-lo 何羅 and Ma T'ung 通, who were executed in the 6th month of that year (under the year 90 B.C. Ma T'ung is referred to as 馬通 and not 莽通). According to the annotator MÊNG K'ang 孟康 (3rd c. A.D.) the substitution of Muo 莽 for 馬 was ordered by the Empress Ma of the Second Han Dynasty who did not wish her honored surname to appear as that of a rebel. As observed by SUNG Ch'i, however, the original surname could only be supplanted by a homophonous character: 馬 must, therefore, have been pronounced *muo.

[49] *GLung ~ BLung is indicated by 龐 *b'âng, 驡 *p'iung and 尨 *mâng, the pronunciation of 龍 in the meaning 'dapple'; also by the interchange of *lung with 降 *liung < *GLung (降 *g'âng is 'phonetic'!). The change from *GL- to *D- is shown in 竉 *t'iwong ~ *liwong and 龍 with det. 糸 and 長, also pronounced *t'iwong. In

and while it is only one of the possible explanations of the ambiguous graph, Hsü Shên was quite justified in advancing it for he must have been aware of the principle of graphic phonetization underlying the evolution of many pictorial forms analyzed by him.

IV. ARCHAIC "ANLAUT" AND DIMIDIATION OF GRAPH AND PHONEME

In the course of our discussion we have had occasion to call attention to the fact that archaic Chinese was strongly characterized by the presence of complex consonantal groups in the Anlaut of its monosyllabic phonemes and that these groups were the dominant feature of the early language rather than the exception as heretofore believed.[50] We have also suggested that certain of these Anlaut groups were interchangeable in some representative semantemes and that in the light of the evidence that has been slowly accumulating during the past decade, archaic Chinese emerges as a language which was almost unbelievably undifferentiated in its glottological structure.

---

the meanings 'to fly' or 'variegated,' 龍 had also the reading *DZap as evidenced by 襲 *dziəp, 龍 doubled and tripled, 龍+言, 龍+舟, all pronounced *dzap ~ *tap (cf. 昜 *tʻap, 習 *dziəp—'to fly,' and 雜 *dzʻáp—'variegated' < 集 *dzʻiəp—'to flock together'). *GLung—'dragon' is also connected with 翏 *liuG < *GLuG—'to fly high' (cf. the binom 蚴蟉 *gəu-liəu—'dragon-like').

[50] It is curious to note that the same lack of recognition of the existence of initial consonantal complexes that handicaps so much our investigation of archaic Chinese prevails also in Sumerology. The polyphony of Sumerian graphs would indicate that many of the Sumerian syllables that we believe to possess a simple consonantal Anlaut go back to forms with biconsonantal initials. Thus the Sumerian graph that we usually equate with the syllabic phoneme LU 'man' possessed also the readings: GU-LU, GUL, MU-LU, MUL, GALU, GAL. It would seem obvious that the original phono-semanteme for 'man' was in Sumerian *gʷlu, probably > glu in eme-ku, and > *mlu in eme-sal. We suggest that it was this Sumerian word that served as the original of Akkadian awêlu < agʷêlu—'man,' 'freeman.' Likewise, RA (DEIMEL. Sumerisches Lexicon, No. 206)—'to go,' which is also read A-RA, GI-E, GIR, RI, would appear to be derived from *GRA ~ *GRE, while No. 166: RAS, KAS comes undoubtedly from *KRAS ~ *GRAS. These examples can easily be multiplied. Sumerian apparently possessed in its early stage of development a variety of initial complexes the most stable of which was the velar + liquid combination. Often the first member of an Anlaut complex is vestigially represented by a prosthetic vowel.

Karlgren's work on *Word Families* has, in so far as the Auslaut of Chinese roots is concerned, prepared us somewhat for a sober consideration of this amazing situation, and we feel that in spite of being forced to abandon our established semasiological methods, we should not entirely give up hope of bringing some order into the semantic chaos that appears inevitable through the convergence of so many archaic stems into one semanteme.

That this convergence had not been observed before was due, as we have noticed, to the overemphasis placed on the study of the graph at the expense of the vocable or phoneme that the graph represented and to the lack of an understanding of the nature and evolution of graphic representation. At the same time, until Karlgren's latest work Chinese semantics could be said to have been non-existent.

Had we for a moment primarily considered the phoneme rather than the graph in our study of archaic Chinese, the solution of one of the great problems in the structure of the language would have immediately revealed itself to us. I refer to the nature of alliterative binoms of the type *KUNG-*LUNG that are so representative a part of the language at a certain stage of its development.[51]

An unfounded opinion is widely held among western students of Chinese that the dimidiation method of indicating the pronunciation of a given character by means of two others, the first of which supplies one with the Anlaut, the second, with the key vowel and Auslaut of the character determined, the *fan-ch'ieh* 反切 " spelling " of the rhyming dictionaries, originated in China under the influence of Buddhist missionaries who initiated the Chinese into the mystery of phonetic representation of vocables. It has been sufficiently indicated by old Chinese scholars, however, that the *fan-ch'ieh* method of " spelling " was of native origin and is but a universal application for lexicographical purposes of an essential feature of Chinese writing: the dimidiation of a graph into two related ones, the digraph being an attempt

---

[51] A convenient source of information on the binoms in the ancient literature is the *P'ien Ya* 骈雅.

to render phonetically (in cases of a rhyming binom) the complex structure of the consonantal Anlaut of the original phoneme.[52]

These rhyming binoms, the so-called *tieh-yün* 疊韻, originated, in my belief, in the majority of cases not as " jingles " of the " ding-dong " type, as heretofore believed, but precisely in the manner adumbrated by Chinese scholars. The process of reduction of a primitive biconsonantal (and sometimes even triconsonantal) complex to a single Anlaut consonant was in archaic Chinese obviously not uniform for all phono-semantemes or even for all the units of a phono-semantic complex or cluster. Let us take, for example, the well-attested consonantal complex **GL- in such a semanteme as **GLəu 婁—' to confine.' [53] As we know, this original syllabic phoneme developed on one hand into ancient *g'i̯u, on the other into *li̯u~ləu, and only in a few derivatives was the archaic complex retained in any measure. Now graphs representing the original phoneme would at the period when the majority of stems derived from **GLəu were pronounced *ləu or *g'əu become associated with these values rather than with the primitive reading **GLəu. The representation of the latter, then, in the cases where it had survived as a semanteme, would offer peculiar difficulties.[54] In what way, indeed, can one (in a system of writing the unit of which is a *syllabic phoneme*) represent a syllable **GLəu, when only *ləu and *gəu are available as phonetic values for semantically cognate graphs? The method

---

[52] SHÊN K'uo 沈括 of the Sung dynasty was, I believe, the first to call attention to binoms representing a single dimidiated phoneme.

[53] Originally *GLəuG ~ *BLəuG—' a woman in bonds.' The etymon is the same as in 母 —' mother,' 毋 *mi̯uG—' not ' < ' bound,' 陋 *ləuG—' narrow,' ' vulgar ' < *BLəuG, as shown by the binom 鄙陋 *pi-lou*.

[54] As phonetic ' erosion ' attacked the consonantal complexes in the North sooner that in the South while the written language was essentially the property of Northern cultural centers, we have in Chou texts many attempts to render Southern initial consonantal clusters by means of graphs prefixing ' complemental ' characters which, though having monophonemic initials in the regular northern pronunciation, still possessed a biconsonantal Anlaut in the South. Thus 夫 *b'i̯u in the proper name 夫差 Fu-ch'a (a king of Wu) restores undoubtedly the *B- of archaic *BTSa in 差 *ts'a. In the *Yüeh chüeh shu* ch. 1, ' reed ' is dimidiated as 前蘆 *pi̯u-luo < *BLu indicating that the labial form of the word prevailed in the South over the more common *'Lu < *GLu in the North. Note that the velar was commonly reconstructed in the North also in the binom 葫蘆 *g'uo-luo*.

5

by which the Chinese solved the problem is essentially the extension of the method of phonetic determination. The needed phonetic determinative could not, however, be incorporated into the graph to be determined, as most graphs had become firmly stabilized and conventionalized. The determinative now was used as an independent graph prefixed or affixed to the graph determined [55] and again, as in the case of older pd, the GSP selected for the role of a determinative inevitably would be one related in its GSP to the graph determined.

Thus a *$g'\partial u$ (descended from an original **$GL\partial u$) could be " reconstructed " into its primitive reading by affixing to it a graph read *$l\partial u$ while a *$l\partial u$ could serve as a basis for " reconstruction " with a prefixed graph read *$g\partial u$. In both cases we would have a binom consisting of two independent graphs *$g\partial u$-*$l\partial u$, the purpose of which would be not so much to represent *two* words *$g\partial u$ and *$l\partial u$ as to render an obsolescent *$gl\partial u$.

In this way our graph 婁 *$l\partial u$ was used as the foundation for several *$GL\partial u$ the commonest prefixed graph being 句 *$k\partial u$~ *$g'\partial u$. The binom 句婁 renders: 1) with Dt. 104: *$k\partial u$-$l\partial u$— ' hunchbacked,' 2) with Dt. 97: *$\gamma\partial u$-$l\partial u$—' cucumber,' 3) with Dt. 46: *$k\partial u$-$l\partial u$—' mountain top,' ' n. pr. of a mountain.' In other binoms with 婁 *$l\partial u$ as the basis, the lost initial velar is reconstructed by 區 *$k'iu$, 侯 *$g'\partial u$, 于 *giu and 禺 *giu.

The alliterative binoms would thus appear to offer us a new approach to the problem of the initial consonantal complexes in archaic Chinese and constitute an excellent auxiliary means in ascertaining the nature of the complex in a given phonetic series. One might object, however, to the above theory of the origin of binoms by pointing out the existence of binoms such as *$l\partial u$-$g\partial u$, where the order of the initial consonants is reversed. This would indicate either that the complex *lg- was a representative as *gl- in a given series, or that the binoms are in no way related to the consonantal complexes and are purely alliterative compounds so arbitrarily construed that the order of the members of the binoms was considered unimportant.

---

[55] This class of phonetic determination is thus fundamentally identical with the ' phonetic complements,' so extensively used in Babylonian and Egyptian writing.

In answer to this objection, one must admit that at a period when the significance of the process of phonetic determination had disappeared, it was indeed frequently the case that binoms were treated as copulative (dvandva) compounds of two independent terms and their position was often reversed.[56] With a view to ascertaining the normal sequence of binom initials, we have examined, therefore, over 600 binoms exhibiting alliterations corresponding to initial consonantal complexes the existence of which is indicated through other evidence. The statistical table below shows the frequency of an *a-b* (*e. g.* G-~L-) sequence of the members of the binom *vs.* a *b-a* (*i. e.* L-~G-) 'reversed' order of members in each group.[57]

---

[56] A 'reversed' binom such as **lǝu-gǝu* may, however, go back itself to **glǝu-glǝu*, a reduplicated form of the etymon. As such binoms later came to convey an adverbial or 'progressive' form to verbs it would appear that morphological distinctions began to play some role in the arrangement of the members. Binomization as the result of the intercrossing of dialectical forms is possible. I have heard German-Americans wishing one another "Glück and luck"! The whole question deserves serious and intensive investigation.

[57] A few examples for each group will suffice:

1. *G ~ *L: 康良 **k'âng-lâng* (with det. 山，宀，穴，身); 鬼鼬 **k'uai-luai* (with det. 人，山，石).
2. *B ~ *L: 麻羅 **mâ-lâ* (with det. 日，心); 蒙龍 **mung-lung* (with 日，月).
3. *G ~ *S: 夆雙 **γang-ṣang* (with det. 舟，足，豆，竹); 瞿叟 *kiu-sǝu* (with 毛，虫); 巩松 **kung-sung* (with 髟).
4. *B ~ *S: 夆松 **b'iung-sung* (with 髟); 旁喪 **piang-sang* (with 馬); 辟析 **piäk-siek* (with 歹).
5. *G ~ *DZ: 空恩 **k'ung-ts'ung* (with det. 人 and 心); 甲葉 **kap-tsap* (with 革 and 魚).
6. *B ~ *DZ: 孛卒 **puǝt-ts'uǝt* (with 鳥，毛. etc.); 蒙童 **mung-d'ung* (with 舟，山，毛，鳥).
7. *G ~ *N: 奇尼 **kja-nja* (with 肌，香，衣，犬); 匡襄 **kuang-nang* (with 足，力，髟).
8. *B ~ *N: 逢農 **b'iung-nung* (with 心，廾); 辟兒 **piäk-ngieR* (with 車，土，日).
9. *DZ ~ *NG: 且吾 **tsuo-nguo* (with 金，山，齒); 乍牙 **tsa-nga* (with 疒，厂，广，心).
10. *B ~ *G: 方皇 **piang-hʷang* (with 彳，衣); 分 or 賁盆 **puǝn-'uǝn* (with 車，香，廾，气，糸).
11. *S ~ *L: 良桑 **lang-sang* (with 衣), 祿速 (with 廾，衣).
12. *DZ ~ *L: 龍同 (or 童，重) **lung-d'ung* (with 身，人，彳，足，穴); 黨良 **dang-lang* (with 火).

Binom initials	Initial Complex	Total number of Binoms	a-b sequence	b-a sequence
1. *G-~*L-	*GL	97	66	31
2. *B-~*L-	*BL	49	37	12
3. *G-~*S-	*GS	40	37	3
4. *B-~*S-	*BS	36	30	6
5. *G-~*D (Z)	*GD (Z)	54	41	13
6. *B-~*D (Z)	*BD (Z)	76	62	14
7. *G-~*N	*GN	26	25	1
8. *B-~*N	*BN	14	14	..
9. *D (Z) ~*N (G)	*D (Z) N (G)	78	78	..
10. *B-~*G-	*BG	77	58	19
11. *S-~*L-	*SL	26	10	16
12. *D (Z) -~*L	*D (Z) L	87	37	50

It appears clear from the above that for the first ten classes of binoms in the predominant majority of cases the sequence of initials reflects the order of consonants in the Anlaut consonantal complex which the binoms served to reconstruct. In the last two classes the distribution is about 60% to 70% in favor of a reversed order of initials indicating apparently a real alliteration rather than a " phonetic reconstruction." [58]

In this connection it is to be noted that the *S-, *D-, and DZ- initials of the characters listed in the last two classes of binoms seem to be secondary developments from originally biconsonantal or triconsonantal complexes, chiefly *GL- and *BL- [59] (cf. the

[58] Metathesis of the members of the initial consonantal complex is also to be reckoned with. Only one case of such metathesis is known to me, however, for primary roots. This possibly occurred in a southern Chinese dialectical variant for the word ' tiger,' registered already in the *Fang Yen* in the form 李父 *lji-b'iu < *LBu. The common archaic for ' tiger ' was 虎 *GLuo~*BLuo. The phonetic evolution of this term is rather interesting. Dialectically the liquid was often registered as a dental as we see from the following forms: 伯都 *b'nk-duo or *b'iu-d'uo 榑都 (in the *Pai hu t'ung*, ch. 五行) and 於菟 *huo-d'uo (Ch'u dialect), which undoubtedly go back to *BDo~hDo.

[59] After careful investigation we have not been able to find a single semanteme where *S- or *D-, or *DZ- is primary. This forms the basis of our chief objection to the ' glottological ' theory of the primary D- (synchronous in origin with B- and G) in H. N. von Koerber's *Morphology of the Tibetan Language*, with the other theses of which we are in substantial agreement.

identical phenomenon in Tibetan where *kr-*, *tr-*, and *pr-* > ṭ-; *gr-*, *dr-*, and *br-* > d).[60] In the case of initial *S- the problem is more complex: we may be dealing there sometimes with a prefix of morphological value which came to serve as the initial owing to the disappearance of the true initial or initials between the prefix and the head vowel.[61]

A further investigation of the semantemes possessed by the first nine classes of the above consonantal complexes reveals, moreover, a consistent interchange within the same semantic cluster of the labial and velar initial consonant and that of the velar and the *DZ-. We thus can pair them as follows:

1. *GL-~*BL-
2. *GS-~*BS-
3. *GDZ-~*BDZ-
4. *GN-~*DZN-

The interchange of the first three pairs would seem to indicate that *G- and *B- are developed from a primitive labio-velar *Gᵂ- which probably also lies at the basis of the tenth class *BG-.

---

[60] Thus Tibetan *'brong* > *ḍong*—'wild yak' is, in my belief, to be compared with archaic Chinese 夆, 犎 *b'iung* < *BLung—'wild humped ox,' vs. 犝 *di̯wong*—'id.'; Tibetan *p'rug* > *ṭ'ug*—'calf,' with archaic Chinese 犢 *d'uk* < *BLuk—'calf' (note that 丵 *li̯uk* < *BLuk is 'phonetic' in 賣 *d'uk*; cf. *Shih Ming* 19, where 犢 *d'uk* is defined by 陸 *mi̯uk*).

It would seem that in archaic Chinese *BLuk developed both into *BDUK and *DLuk. Thus 薰陸 *hi̯uən-li̯uk* < *GUN-DLUK—'frank-incense' (attested since the 3rd c. B.C.) appears to be an early loan-word from Sanskrit *kunduruka*—'frank-incense.' Cf. also 六 *li̯uk* < *BLuk—'six' vs. Tib. *drug*—'six.' A propos of loan-words in Chinese, the *GL- complex in 虎 *χuo*—'tiger' would indicate that 琥珀 *hu-po*—'amber' is indeed a loan-word from western or southern Asiatic *χarupah—'amber.'

[61] There are indications that *B- also acquired in the archaic language a morphological significance as a prefix. Prefixation and infixation did not, however, arise until comparatively late in glottological development. Before individual phonemes such as *B- or *S- could be used functionally, their individual existence must have been realized. In our opinion, this individual existence could have been recognized only through the 'dialectical' contrast of the primary variations such as *GL- vs. *BL- vs. 'L, and through the conventionalization of 'tongue gestures' *within* the primary syllabic complexes (i. e. not as extraneous additions to a root, but as organic variations of the same, until through usage the organic 'prefix' or 'infix' could be 'abstracted' and begin to lead an independent life).

The problem now looms so laden with possibilities and so un-
prepared are we for a scientific analysis of such a primeval stage
of glottological development that nothing more can be done than
to indicate its momentous existence.[62] We can only mention the
fact that comparative linguistic studies have long made us realize
that the oldest Anlaut complexes in all languages appear to be
combinations of stops with liquids or nasals.[63]

V. Some Problems of Semantics and Morphology

Early archaic Chinese shows itself to be in such a primitive
stage of development that one would be inclined to despair of
any possibility of investigating it scientifically along orthodox
phonetical or morphological lines. The number of homophones
in the archaic period of the language, our study would indicate,
was probably greater and the number of individual syllabic
phonemes even more limited than in modern Mandarin.[64]

[62] Glottologically, proto-Chinese appears to have developed somewhat in the following fashion:

$$G\omega L \begin{cases} GL \begin{cases} GL > G\omega; \, > DL \\ G' \\ GN > G'N > DN \text{ (chiefly DZN)} \\ GD \text{ (chiefly GS)} > \text{'D} \\ \text{'L} \end{cases} \\ BL \begin{cases} BL > B\omega \\ B' \\ BN > \text{'N} \\ BD \text{ (chiefly BS, BDZ)} > \text{'D} \\ \omega L \end{cases} \end{cases}$$

Although this scheme of development has been found by us to apply to literally
hundreds of etymons, we shall not, for the present, insist on its universality.

[63] Cf. *e. g.*, Father W. Schmidt's *Die Sprachfamilien und Sprachkreise der Erde*,
Heidelberg 1926, 288-295.

[64] Whatever be the fate of the glottological theory outlined in these pages, one fact
remains firmly established in all recent investigations of archaic Chinese, namely.
that instead of further divergence of phonemes as their reconstruction is carried into
the past we must reckon with a catastrophic convergence of the relatively complicated phonemes of ancient Chinese into a very few archaic etymons. It would
seem that the Chinese language is finally justifying the hope entertained by its
students in the 17th and 18th century that it would be through the study of this
'language of philosophers' that linguistic science would tackle the great problem of
glottogony.

The graphological and glottological principles outlined above make it possible, however, to envisage the problem of the evolution of the Chinese language almost in its entirety and throw considerable light on some major questions of semantics and morphology of the archaic period. They also give a new construction to problems of textual criticism especially as regards the evolution of Chinese mythological themes and the development of the philosophical terminology of the Chou period. We shall endeavor to illustrate the application of these various principles to some specific cases.

1. The humble 'phonetic' of a composite graph was often, as we have seen and as has been previously suggested by Karlgren, the real 'radical' ('etymonic') of the word represented by the graph. An important task is, therefore, lying before us in reviewing our dictionary material in the light of this important principle. Let us take the archaic phoneme *ngâ 我—'I,' 'we' which, as has been long recognized, is 'phonetic' in 義 *ngiǎ a word designating the peculiar Chinese moral ideal which is usually inadequately rendered into English by 'justice,' 'righteousness.' Anyone well acquainted with early Chou texts will recognize that this term in the feudal period was more the equivalent of 'loyalty to one's feudal lord and to one's clan' rather than of 'justice.' [65] Now *ngâ as the 'etymonic' of *ngiǎ links this term closely with the set of connotations expressed by the etymon 'we,' 'I.' We should suggest, therefore, that the original meaning of *ngiǎ can best be rendered by 'we-ness' 'allegiance to the *we* group.'

Towards the end of the Ch'un-ch'iu period *ngiǎ begins to be encountered in the texts coupled with another term designating a social ideal of the time, namely *ńźiĕn 仁—'humanity,' benevolence' (more correctly **tsniĕn~źńiĕn, cf. *supra*, section III). It would appear that the intrusion of the new term on the consciousness of the philosophers of the time was caused by deep political

---

[65]* *Ngiǎ* was indeed the cornerstone of the 'bushidō' code of honor of the Chinese warrior of the Ch'un-ch'iu period. The original meaning of the term was preserved in Japan where it designates above all the feudal ideal of Loyalty.

and social upheavals of the epoch which was witnessing the amalgamation of the small social units of the time into larger groups. The narrow loyalty to the ' we ' group, an ideal sufficient to sustain the knights of a small city state of the preceding period, conflicted now with duties towards a larger whole, the extensive state of which the self-satisfied original unit was now a sub-ordinated part. ' Fellowship,' ' otherliness,' ' menness ' (taking **źńiĕn* 仁 as a derivative of **źńiĕn* 人—' man ') had now to be recognized as a moral factor necessary for the preservation of the smaller ' we '-group; ' neighborliness ' (**źńiĕn* is essentially the same word as 鄰 **liĕn* < ***źliĕn*—' neighbor ' and 親 **ts'iĕn* < ***ts'niĕn*—' kin ') had now to be cultivated lest the newly created socio-political groupings disintegrate. Viewed in this light, the twin terms so dear to Confucian philosophers become heavily pregnant with meaning and many a moralizing passage in their texts becomes throbbing with the live problems that faced the Chinese world about 500 B. C.[66]

2. One of the simplest of the early pictograms of the Chinese script is 山 **san*—' mountain,' originally ᴧᴧᴧ a graph representing a jagged lines of hills. This unpretentious graph has never been suspected of being a polyphone. Its significance is, however, not at all obvious. Should anyone unacquainted with archaic Chinese be asked what the picture represents he would undoubtedly answer: ' possibly pointed teeth, or the edge of a saw, or an uneven surface, perhaps a line of hills.' We shall see that it was precisely these associations that the graph conveyed also to the early Chinese.

There exist a dozen archaic binoms written with Dt. 46 山

---

[66] *Etymologically *ngiă* and **źńiĕn* correspond thus to ' egoism ' and ' altruism ' (人—' man,' in contrast to 我—' I,' often connotes ' others '). Cf. *Ch'un-ch'iu fan-lu*, ch. 8, section 29: 春秋之所治人與我也所以治人與我者仁與義也以仁安人以義正我故仁之爲言人也義之爲言我也. This can be literally translated: " That which is governed by the ' Spring and Autumn ' (Annals) is *men* and *we*. The wherewithal (the ' Spring and Autumn ') govern *men* and us is **źńiĕn* and **ngiă*. Through **źńiĕn* (one) appeases *men*, through **ngiă* (one) regulates *us*; thus **źńiĕn ipso verbo* equals *men*, *ngiă ipso verbo* equals *we*." **Ngiă* is thus essentially subjective consciousness (of the species, rather than the individual) contrasted with **źńiĕn*, expedient objectivity towards the genus.

(or Dt. 170 阝—'hillside') all going back to variant forms of a root *TSNGᵪ and all apparently registering the same semanteme: 'high,' 'uneven,' 'line of hills.' The commonest among them are 崔嵬 *tsʻuâi-nguâi, 岨峿 *tsʻuo-nguo, 嵯峨 *tsʻâ-ngâ, 崷崷 *tsʻəu-ngəu. Many of these binoms appear also with Dt. 211 齒— 'teeth' in the meaning 'uneven,' 'jagged teeth,' 'teeth of a saw.'[67]

All these words are derived from the root *TSNGᵪ the fundamental meaning of which seems to be 'teeth-like,' 'uneven.' This etymon was originally represented by graphs similar to the above ᴧᴧ and picturing teeth or teeth-like projections. One of these graphs lies at the basis of the character representing the very word 齒 *tʻi < **tʻʻiĕg—'tooth.' Now we possess a common synonym of the last, 牙 *nga—'tooth' which undoubtedly goes back to **tsnga as evidenced by the use of 牙 as the primary member of numerous binoms (chiefly of the type 乍牙 + various determinatives) also meaning 'uneven,' 'tooth-like.'[68] As the modern graph 齒 was originally written without the phonetic determinative 止 *tʻi and contained only a pictograph of 'teeth'

---

[67] Such are: 巉巖 *tsʻɐm-ngɐm, 盧牙 *tsʻa-nga, 皆牙 tsʻak-nga, 且吾 *tsʻuo-nguo, 取㝢 tsʻiu ngiu. Cf. 嶃巖 (with 山 and 石) *tsʻam-ngɐm—'mountainous'; 且吾 (with 金) *tsʻuo-nguo—'uneven.'

[68] Also 'notch,' cf. 柞鄂 *tsâk-ngâk—'spring of a trap.' The archaic term for 'musical instrument stand' was also derived from the same etymon as we can see from 崇牙 *tsʻung-nga, 業 *ngiɐp < *TSNGap, and 筍虡 *siuĕn-giʷo. If 作 *tsuo ~ *tsak—'to do' goes back to *TSNGaG, it would be reasonable to suppose that so does 爲 *giʷa ~ *nguâ—'to do.' Now 爲 in its protograph was the picture of an elephant 象 *ziang, 豫 *diʷo (for the last cf. note 70). It seems thus that the archaic Chinese term for 'elephant' was derived from 'tooth' (> 'tusk '~'ivory,' later etymologized as 象牙); it is, on the other hand, connected with *GLang—'bull' (Chinese 牨, 犅 *kâng < *klang, Tib. *glang*—'bull,' 'elephant'). A phonetic survival of *TSNGa in the word for 'elephant' is indicated in 藏牙 *tsâng-nga, a designation of the elephant that arose through the association of the original term with the current Asiatic legend that elephants bury their tusks in some secret place. The linking of the legendary 'emperor' Shun with elephants was caused by phonetic association (see *infra*) and through the name of his wicked brother Hsiang 象 ('elephant'!). Elephants plow for Shun when the latter occupies himself with farming and his grave at 槍吾 *tsʻang-nguo < *TSªNGO! is visited by herds of elephants. The later euhemerists rationalized the elephant motif in Shun's story by making out of the pachyderm a brother of their hero, who, as they claim in all seriousness, was enfeoffed by Shun (when the latter became emperor) as the lord of Yu-pi 有鼻, literally "possessor of the (elephant's) trunk."

it would be legitimate to raise the question whether the word *t'i* that we now associate with 齒 is not an 'abstraction' from an original binom *t'i-nga* < *TSnga. This last etymon was registered primitively in three graphs: 1) the ancestor of 牙, 2) that of 齒 *minus* the pd 止, 3) and that of modern 山—'mountain.' In the last case the phonetic value did not survive and was chiefly represented by binoms which undoubtedly reflected a colloquial survival of the old Chinese term *tsnga*—'mountain' < *'jagged elevations.' In the case of 齒 the graph, through being supplied with a phonetic 'complement,' came to be associated in phonetic value with the pd alone, while originally it must have been sounded like the modern binom 齒牙 *t'i-nga*.[69]

3. The fact that 我 *nga* and 吾 *nguo* serve as basic members of binoms read *TSNGᴕ suggests the possibility that both these words possessed in the archaic language a more complex consonantal Anlaut than we suspected. In fact SW 12B states that an old form of 垂 *d'ʷa ~ *t'ʷa* is 'phonetic' in 我. In the bronzes and bones this part of the graph resembles a rake or trident while the archaic form of 垂 contains the element ∧∧, one of the graphs for 'tooth.' There is, therefore, the likelihood that 我 *ngâ* is indeed derived from **tsngâ*. This primitive form of the phoneme designating the pronoun of the first person would serve to explain the rarer forms of the same pronoun, 予, 余 *diʷo* and *dia*.[70]

---

[69] From the etymon *TSNGᴕ—'tooth' were derived, besides 'elephant,' the archaic names of several other beasts, notably that of the 'lion' which appears in ancient texts in the forms 狻猊 *suan-ngiei*, 夋耳 *tsuən-nji*, and 騶虞 *tsi̯u-ngi̯u* (or *tsi̯u-nguo ~ nga*, with 吾 or 牙). In the case of the last binom 騶 serves only to restore the affricate of *TSNG- in 虞, 吾, and 牙, as 虞 alone stood in the archaic language for the name of the animal in question. 吳 *nguo* < *TSNGo, the phonetic of 虞, consists of 矢 *tsək—'to incline the head' with 口 *k'əu added as a pd. It is significant that 虞 'lion' < 'toothed monster' appears as the title of Shun to whose connection with *TSNGᴕ—'tooth' > 'elephant' we have already drawn attention. Another scription for the same term for 'lion' is found in 檮杌 *tâu-ngut* also used as the name of a primeval monster. The oldest form of the etymon was probably *GNGO—'monster of Chaos' > 'chaos,' 'mixed.' Cf. additionally 窮奇 *Gung-Gi̯a—'a winged tiger-monster,' 鶬鶊 *si̯uĕn-ngi̯a*, and 昆吾 *kuən-nguo*.

[70] 豫 'elephant' would indicate an original *DNGo in 予 *di̯ʷo*. The semanteme 'to give' attached to the latter form would indicate on the other hand that *di̯ʷo* goes back to *BDi̯o. It would then appear to be connected with the etymon for 'self,' *BSi.

If we follow the principles of phonetic reconstruction outlined above, it would appear that a similar anlaut complex underlies also the archaic forms of the pronoun of the second person 女 [~汝] *žńi̯wo < **TSNO,[71] 若 *žńi̯ak < **TSNak,[72] 而 *žńi̯əG < **TSNəG,[73] and 爾 *žńi̯ă < TSNa.[74] The pronouns of the first and second persons seem thus to belong to the same glottological formation distinct from the one which is based on the root **GSI ~ **BSI and served to build the reflexive and demonstrative pronouns 己 *kji < **ksi and 自 *dz'i < **BDZiG [75] and the following deictic particles:

**GS: 其 *g'ji < *gsi, 斯 *si̯e < *gsi̯e
    伊 *zi < *gsi
    兹 *tsi < *gtsi
    渠 *ki̯wo < *kso
    所 *si̯wo < *gso
    厥 *ki̯wɐt < *kswɐt

*BS: 此 *tsi̯a < *BTSi̯ă
    彼 *b'i̯ă < *BTSi̯ă [76]
    之 **ti̯əg [77] < **BDəg

---

[71] *TSN- is well indicated for 女—'woman' both in the phonetic series and by the binoms, especially in 妥, 如, and 奴.

[72] In 若 *žńi̯ak, *TSN- indicated by the binoms, is supported even in the ancient period, where with the loss of the final consonant it transcribes -jña in Sanskrit *prajñā* 般若.

[73] 而 *TSNəG in later texts is equivalent to 則 *tsək—'then.' Its derivative 需 *TSNəu—'beard' > 'soft' ~ 'weak' ~ 'meek' ~ 'dwarf' has the *TS- initial restored in 侏儒 ~ 株檽.

[74] It would appear in this connection that 子 *tsi < *TSləg that has always been considered an 'honorific' form of the pronoun of the second person is nothing but a *tsl- variation (probably older) of the common pronoun *tsnəg. In 爾 *TSNa, derivatives would indicate the presence of the older labio-velar + liquid substratum, the etymonic being *BLa—'net,' graphically 𝕏𝕏, the same that is reflected in 羅 *lâ < *BLâ, where a whole series of binoms reveals the lost labial, and 罔, 网, etc.

[75] Possibly related to Tibetan *bdag*—'self.' 自 *BDZiG ~ *BDZuG is also probably phonetic in 臭 *xi̯əuG, *tś'i̯əuG—'to smell.'

[76] 匕 *pji is 'etymonic' in 此 and 止 is the pd. That 彼 *b'i̯ă and 此 *tsi̯ă both go back to an undifferentiated deictic particle *BDa is indicated by the survival of the dental in a late synonym of 彼, 他 *t'â—'another,' coll. 'he,' 'she,' 'it.'

[77] This is the latest reconstruction by Karlgren. An interesting commentary on the continuity of the development of the Chinese language is found in the close

是 *žịa < *BZịa
者 *tịa < *BDịa [78]
也 *śịa < *BSịa [79]

It would seem, in fact, that all the Chinese particles without exception are deictic in origin. 是 and 也 representing the copula ' is ' in archaic Chinese can indeed best be interpreted as demonstrative particles which, as in many other languages, perform the role of the verb ' to be.'

4. One of the most interesting particles, graphically and phonectically, is the conjunction 且 *ts'ịa ~ *tsịʷo. The graph originally represented ' a stand for sacrificial meat ' and served to

similarity of the ancient pronunciations of 之 and its modern equivalent 的 *tị < *tiek,* in the archaic period *tiek < *BDek as evidenced especially by 豹 *pauG ~ *peuG < *BD—' leopard.'

[78] Note that 白 *BZi—' nose ' is ' etymonic ' in 者, which is phonetic in 書 *Bsịʷo—' to write.'

[79] The *Shuo Wên* (12 B) says that graphically this character represents the female *pudenda.* This has been disputed by almost all commentators since. The majority inclines to the opinion that 也 is identical with 它 ~ 蛇 *d''ịa, originally the picture of a hooded serpent. Now this last character was pronounced in proto-Chinese *BDa, as evidenced by binoms, phonetic glosses, and its synonym 巴 *pa < *BTSa—' python.' The initial *BD- is well indicated through this series for the words ' father ' and ' mother,' and through the last for ' earth ': thus SW 12B gives 姐 *BTSa an 社 *sịa as dialectical (Southern China) terms for ' mother ' while the *Fan Yen* 6 gives 父姼 *b'ịu-žịa and 母姼 *muo-žịa as the Southern Ch'u terms for ' father ' and ' mother.' Rhyming dictionaries give 爸 *pa and 爹 as the Wu dialect word for father.' Cf. also 爺 žịa and 爹 *da. It would seem that the affricate survived in the colloquial (in a semantized form) in 父親 and 母親. Now graphically the etymon ' mother ' is often represented (as in 后) by the graph 匕 *pji < *BSeR originally a human figure in a half-sitting posture. Both graphically and phonetically 匕 is identical with 尸 *si < *BSiR—' corpse.' The GP represents, in our opinion, the etymon ' hind parts,' ' buttocks ' > ' tail '; it is reflected in 展 *BDun—' buttocks,' 屔 *kịǎ < *GSa—' id.,' 尾 *mjʷei < *BSeR—' tail '; also in *BDZeK—' back ': 北 *pǝk *vs.* 脊 *dzịäk. The etymon had also a reading *GLo(G) ~ *GSo(G) as evidenced by 居 *kịʷo—*GSo—' to sit on haunches ' (cf. 蹲 *btsun), and 尻 *GLo(G). We can see now how the G representing a half-sitting female figure could serve as ' phonetic ' in 后 (cf. note 47). The interchange of *BSiR and *GLoG explains then how 后 reversed > 司 came to be pronounced *si < *BSi and mean (in 嗣) " posterity." Returning to 也, it is quite probable that the G represented the same etymon: ' rump ' ~ ' os sacrum ' ~ ' womb ' ~ ' the mound symbolizing mother earth,' 社 or 地 *d'iei < *BDei (cf. *Kuang Shih Ming* 1, where 地 is paronomastically equated with 媲 *b'ji and 麗 *liei, indicating *BLei > BDei).

render the following group of semantemes: √'past '~ √' old '~ √' ancestor '~ √' original '~ √' coarse '~ √' sour,' all of which go back to etymons with a *GS-~*BS- initial. In several meanings 且 interchanges with the phonetic series 古 *kuo < **GSO [80] (cf. especially the particle 姑 *kuo—' then ' which in old texts often forms with 且 the binom 姑且 *kuo-tsuo < **GTSO—' then '). Graphically 且 is connected with 豆 *d'ₒu < *BDₒuG—' sacrificial vessel,' also ' head,' ' principal,' while in the meaning ' ancestor ' (祖) [81] it becomes associated with 父 *b'iu < BSu—' father.'

This last etymon presents features of peculiar interest. The protograph represents a *hand* 又 **GiuG holding a torch (the original of the modern 主 *tiu, 燭 *t'i^ʷok, 炬 *ki^ʷo—' torch ') and is fundamentally the same picture as 叟 *sₒuG—' old man,' originally depicting a ' hand ' 又 with a torch 火 under a roof 宀. Both ' torch ' and ' hand ' are phonetic and etymonic in our graph: [82] ' torch ' undoubtedly being derived from **BSUG—' branch,' ' faggot ' while **BS- in the word for ' hand ' is easily established through the comparison of the following: 受 *źiₒu—' to hand,' [83] 付 *piu—' to hand over ' (寸 is etymonic!), 與 *zi^ʷo—

---

[80] 古 *GSo < *GLoG is connected with the etymon ' gourd '~' neck of a bottle '~ ' neck '>' throat '~' dewlap ' (胡) ~' opening '~' mouth ' (of a vessel). For *GS- in 古, cf. 居 *ki^ʷo < *GSo, 罟 *kuo—' net ' vs. 罝 *tsuo—' net.' *GL- is well attested in 葫 *g'uo—' bottle-gourd,' 鹽 *kuo (cf. 鹵) —' salt bed.' An interesting survival of *GS- in 沽 *kuo—' coarse ' (= 粗 *ts'uo, 鹵 *luo, 魯 *luo), ' stupid ' we see in colloquial 糊塗 hu-t'u—' stupid.'

[81] An interesting dimidiated form of 祖—' ancestor ' we find in 鼻祖 *b'ji-ts'uo— ' progenitor,' later etymologized into 始祖 shih-tsu—' first ancestor.'

[82] Cf. 支 *puk < *BSuk—' to strike ' where both ' hand ' 又 and 卜 (which represented as much a stick or branch of a tree as the alleged ' cracks in a tortoise shell ') are phonetic-etymonic. Also 肅 *siuk < *BSuK where ' the hand holding a stick ' is phonetic.

[83] Note that the middle part of the protograph of 受 represents a ' boat ' 舟, while the ' two hands ' form the primitive graph 爰 *b'iau which is etymonic. 舟 *tiₒu is, then, a phonetic determinative. Cf., in the light of the above discussion, the following terms for ' boat ': 俞 *diu (余 *di^ʷo seems to be the pd in ancient forms), 艘 *sau < *BS- (with 叟 as pd), the binom 帽艛 *miuk-siuk, 舫 *pi^ʷang < *BS-, 航 *g'âng < *GS-; also 'raft': 栿, 橃 *b'i^ʷɐt < *BS-, 泭 *biu, 查 *dz'a < *BDZ-; also 般 *b'uân < *BS- and 前 *dz'ien where 舟 (= 船 *dzi^ʷän is phonetic). 舟 tiₒu is connected with the etymon *BLₒu~*GLₒu—' to float ' which appears in 浮 *biₒu (cf. 桴 *b'iₒu-' raft '), 流 *liₒu, 游 iₒu, 漂 *p'iäu. Cf. also Tib. gru—' boat.' Observe that an original *BL- in 流 is confirmed by 琉璃 *liₒu-lia, an early

'to give,' 予 $di^{w}o$—'id.,' 齎 $*tsiei$—'to give,' 施 $*si\ddot{a}$ [84]—'to grant,' 貽 $*di$—'to bestow,' 畁 pji—'to present' and other numerous synonyms derived from the etymon 'hand' and all having a $*BS\text{-}\sim*GS\text{-}$ in their archaic Anlaut.[85]

5. Such investigations can be easily multiplied. It is curious to note that semantic classification of graphs reveals that the old designation of the signific determinative of a graph by the term 'radical' introduced by early western students of Chinese often tallies well with facts.[86] This is well illustrated by the following two 'radicals' which serve as 'significs' for a limited group of characters.

The fundamental graph 冫 $*pi\partial ng$ which conveys the meaning 'ice' 'cold' goes back to a phoneme with $*GL\text{-} *BL\text{-}$ initial as revealed by 涼 $li\underline{a}ng < *gl\text{-}$, 凌 $*li\partial ng$, 冷 $*lieng$, 汪 $*kieng$, 澗 $*ki^{w}eng$, 況 $*\chi i^{w}ang$, 溟 $*mieng$, 僵 $*g'i\underline{a}ng$, 凝 $*ngieng$, 亢 $*ki\ddot{a}ng$, 瀝 $*liek$, 逵 $li\underline{u}k$, 澆淶 $*li\partial uG\text{-}g'i\partial uG$ (cf. also 雹 $*b'\mathring{a}k$ and 露 $*gloG$). The same etymon appears also with Auslaut $-m$, $-n$ and $-t$ in: 㳘 $*li\ddot{a}m$ 凜 $*li\partial m$, 潜 $*g'i\partial m$, 涵 $*\gamma\hat{a}m$, 澰 $*g'i\partial m$, 瀲 $*ngi\partial m$; 匽 $*i\check{e}n$, 硜 $*ngi^{w}\partial n$, 寒 $*\gamma\hat{a}n$; 列 $*li\check{e}t$, 㵪 $*li\ddot{a}t$, 瀨 $*l\hat{a}d$, 渾淽 $*pi\check{e}t\text{-}pi\underline{u}\partial t$.

---

transcription of vaiḍurya ～ vilurya, 琉 $*li\partial u$ being derived from $*BL\partial u$ (as a phonetic 充 in two or three cases is pronounced $*muo$, $*p\partial u$).

[84] Dimidiated and etymologized in the binom 布施 $*puo\text{-}si\ddot{a}$.

[85] In connection with the etymon ∨ 'hand' > 'to hand over' > 1) 'to give' ～ 2) 'to take' one is tempted to discuss one of the most interesting problems of language revealed by this investigation as lying at the basis of the whole speech-complex of the archaic period of Chinese culture. This problem is that of the 'polarity' of etymons which is so characteristic of both the archaic language and early Chinese philosophy. It would appear indeed that the undifferentiated state of the language in which 'black' and 'white,' 'give' and 'take,' 'go' and 'stop,' 'hand' and 'head,' 'we' and 'you,' 'die' and 'live,' etc. were designated by the same term strongly conditioned the sense of balance and the firm belief in the *coincidentia oppositorum,* so pronounced a feature of Chinese mentality. While from a glottological point of view this is characteristic of all languages in a limited way, nowhere except in China did the 'plus' and 'minus' of a complex drift so little away from the etymonic core where they were originally merged one in the other.

[86] In general, it would seem that we owe an apology to our predecessors, the 'unscientific' pioneers of the type of Edkins. Their ingrained belief in linguistic monogenesis fostered by the biblical tradition often enabled them to perceive more quickly the truths of linguistic evolution at which we hope to arrive through the laborious inductive process. Thus, the 'absurd' transcription *hs*- appears now to be fully justified on the basis of the common archaic $*GS\text{-}$.

On the basis of the theory that the dental archaic initials developed in Chinese from original *GʷL-~*GʷS-~*GʷN- we can explain the following minority of words meaning 'cold' and having 冫 as their 'radical':

冰 *dʼieng, 瑭 *tʼâng, 清 tsʼiäng, 倉 *tsʼâng, 凍 *tsʼiang, 凌 *tsiɔm, 恫 *dʼung, 冬 *tuong, 汀 *tieng, 淒 *tsʼiei, 滲 *tsʼiɔm, etc.

All the words classified under 冫 are thus derived from one 'etymon' or root, and 冫 *piɔng is indeed the 'radical' of the entire group, the majority of graphs being explained as the product of the enlargement of the primitive graph by *phonetic determinatives*.

Again, the phonetic analysis of characters listed in the *Shuo Wên* under 示 would indicate that all the graphs reflect but various forms of only two etymons: **GʷLeR (with corresponding initial dental variations) and **GʷLuG.

Under the first we would classify: 示, 祇, 祠, 神, 禧, 禮, 齋, 禰, 祕, 禋, 禩, 祺, 禔, 禪, 祈, 祀, 禘, 祡, 社 (cf. also 天 [87] and 帝).

Under the second: 祿, 福, 褶, 禱, 祚, 祖, 祜, 祝, 宗, 祐, 禦。

Both primitive roots served essentially to convey the meaning 'sacred,' 'sacrifice,' 'blessing,' the first seeming associated with the semanteme 'sacrificial stand'~'altar,' the second more with that rendering 'sacrificial vessel.' [88]

---

[87] The all-important graph 天 *tʼien—'heaven'~'deity' was, acc. to *Shih Ming* ｜, also dialectically pronounced *χien (= 顯). This is further substantiated by its being phonetic in 祆 χien. The proto-archaic word was undoubtedly *GLen~*BLen as revealed by 旻 *miĕn < *BL- 'autumn sky' (*BL- is well attested in this group). The question arises whether the famous Hsiung-nu term 祁連 *gʼi-(or *żi)-lien—'heaven' is not Chinese after all, or at least reflects an etymon common to the Chinese and their neighbors. The dot or circle on top of 大 in the old graphs for 天 should cease to worry the epigraphists. It is, in our belief, 'phonetic-etymonic' and stands for the archaic word now represented by 顛 *tien—'forehead,' 'top,' the -ng variant of which is reflected in 頂 *tieng—'top of the head'< 丁 *tieng, which on the bronzes and bones is represented by a dot or black circle.

[88] Cf. 酋 in 酓, 酒 **dzʼiɔu < *BDZuG and 尊 *tsuɔn—'honorable' (Tib. btsun); also 良 *liang, which in the Lesser Seal form is a compound of 畐 *bʼiuk—'a vessel full to the brim' and 亡 *miʷang as phonetic acc. to SW 5B; hence liang < *BLang. The wine vessels represented among other graphs by 酉, 品, 壺 *gʼuo < *GLog were designated by the same etymon that we find in 鬲 *glɒk—'cauldron' and 角 *glɒk—'horn' > 'drinking horn.' The phono-semanteme of the first series above for 'sacred' is reflected in such characters as 卮, 觶, 觚, 也 > 匜 etc. representing the etymon

6. It would be impossible to consider even briefly some of the important problems that the above hypotheses raise. We shall limit ourselves to indicating a few interesting questions that arise in this connection in the investigation of the early Chinese onomasticon, mythology, and history.

1. In 唐堯 T'ang Yao, the first character *d'âng* rationalized into the name of the mythical emperor's fief represents probably the restoration of the initial dental of 堯 *ngieu* < **Dngeu [89]— 'mountain,' 'high place.' [90]

** (B) T̯i̯eR—'drinking vessel.' The existence of a proto-Chinese term *BDuG for 'wine' ~ 'wine vessel' obviates the necessity of looking further for the foreign origin of 葡萄 *b'uo-*d'au—'vine, grape, wine.' Cf. also the curious term 服匿 *b'i̯ək-ni̯ək—'wine vessel' < *BNek, possibly **BDNek. As the term appears in connection with the Hsiung-nu, we may have there, on the other hand, a form derived from tk. *bigni*—'wine,' the history of which has been studied by Pelliot.

[89] *Dngeu evolved into archaic *žñeu. In the meaning 'noisy' (嘵, 譊, 鐃 *njau < *žñiau) the old archaic complex has survived in the colloquial binom 熱鬧 *jo-nao* —'noisy,' 'crowded.' It is likely that the names of all the three legendary emperors, Yao, Shun, and Yü go back to *DNGʁ: Yao:*DNGeu; Shun, *i.e.* 虞 Yü, which is his title: *TSNGuo (one of the possible explanations of the origin of 舜 *si̯uĕn is that it was abstracted from **SUN-NGO), Yü:*SNGi̯u (cf. 肉 *TSNi̯ʒu which is phonetic in 禹.

[90] The "Flood Story" of the archaic texts is, as is well known, nothing but a euhemerized Creation Legend. It must have passed through a stage where it was interpreted as a myth of the primeval struggle between the powers on high (the 'high places,' abode of the gods) and the monster of Chaos. The latter was undoubtedly designated as *GLUNG ~ *GLUN, an etymon which is reflected in 龍 *GLung—'dragon,' 洪 *GLung—'flood' (as in 洪水 and 共工), 鯀 *GLun— the name of Yü's father, and most probably in 舜 *si̯uĕn < *GSun < *GLun, as Shun, the virtuous successor of Yao, was originally an avatar of Yü's father.

It would be comparatively easy to demonstrate how most of the names of the mythological characters in the Flood Story are but variations (dialectical or graphic) of only two or three original etymons which composed the primeval mythological theme of the Creation Legend, and how many motifs in it were developed through the semantization of graphs or specialization of complex semantemes.

We shall limit ourselves to one example: the mountain name Pu-chou 不周 *pʒu-tʒʒuG, the northwestern 'pillar of the sky' against which butted the monster Kung-kung doubtless is a semantic 'individualization' of an original 觸 *BTSi̯ʷok—'to knock against' in the phrase 觸山—'to butt against mountains.' The same phoneme appears in 燭 *BTSi̯ʷok—'torch,' 'torch-like,' the epithet of the dragon-monster of the Northwest. The etymon covered the meanings: 'horn' > 'to butt.' 'pillar,' > 'altar,' 'ancestor,' 'torch,' and with a velar initial is reflected in Hou Chi 后稷 *GʒuG-TSʒg < *GTSUG (~ 后土 *γʒu-tʒu < *GʒuG-TʒuG < *GTuG), the demiurge-ancestor of the Chou and its *chu* 主 ~ 柱 < *BTSuG.

2. In 麒麟 *g'ji-liĕn—'the kilin,' 'the mysterious animal of good omen,' we have undoubtedly a binom the first member of which serves but to restore the original velar of 麟 *GLen which primitively was used alone to render the animal's name.

A case of reversed 'enclitic' binomization is observed in the name of an ancient state in Shantung written 鄒 *tsɔu* and 邾 *tsiu* as a 'monograph,' but sometimes spelled out as 邾婁 *tsiu-liu*, showing clearly an original *TSLɔu.

3. One of the most vexing problems in Chinese epigraphy is the similarity, if not identity of the graphs for 月 *ngiʷɒt—'moon' and 月〈肉 *źńiuk—'meat.' We have already sufficiently indicated that a similarity of graphs reflects phonetic or semantic relationship between the words represented by the graphs. In this case on first examination we can not observe either. The application of methods of investigation outlined above, however, soon brings definite results. The protograph of 月 represented the crescent of the moon. Now we possess the term 朔 *sâk— 'new moon,' probably derived from *SNGâk as indicated by its phonetic 屰 *ngâk.[91] Can we be sure of a *SNG- sequence in the consonantal complex? The binoms 縮朒 *siuk-niuk and 仄匿 *tsɔk-nɔk—'first appearance of the moon in the East' confirm the supposition that the initial was *SN ~ *TSN and not *NGS-. It would seem, therefore, that the etymon for 'moon' was *TSN (G) u with two different finals, -t and -k. *DN- 〈 *GN- is also evidenced through binoms in the phonetic series 多 *dâ[92] which is a graphic derivative of the 夕 form of the moon crescent. This last character had apparently two readings:[93] the usual *dziäk and the rarer *siuk, both of which derive from *BS ~

---

[91] The older form of the etymon, *BLak ~ *GLak, is registered in 霸 ~ 魄 *p'ɒk— 'new moon.' Note that the phonetic of 霸 is 革 *kɒk—'hide,' 'to change' (p'ɒk with det. 雨、水, and 頁; *lɔk with 力) while the protograph of 屰 is identical with that of 牛 *ngləuG—'ox' and represents a pair of *horns* (Chin. 角 *klɒk).

[92] Several derivatives of 多 (notably with 髟, 黍, and 川) are read *na. 可 (or 奇) 多 is the usual binomial combination. An interesting survival of *GL- in the word for 'many' we have in the old dialectical (Ch'i) term 夥 *g'ua 〈 *GLa— 'many.' Cf. also 矮 *·wa—'id.' (a variant current in the state of Yen).

[93] Besides the unusual phonetic value *ming (冥) that we have discussed above.

6

*BDZ-.[94] A corresponding -*t* Auslaut form we see in 歲 *si̯wät < *BSut—'year,' originally 'unit of time'~'month.'[95] This interchange between *TSN- and *BS-, as we have observed is regular in almost all phonetic series. In one of its readings, then, 月 'moon' was a homophone of 月—'meat,' both being pronounced *TSNuK~*SNGuK, and the identity of the graphs is thus explained. Now if 月 *ngi̯wɐt is derived from DNGut,[96] one of the great problems in Chinese transcription of foreign names is seemingly nearing solution. The weary reader will, we hope, at least concede us the possibility that Yüeh-chih 月氏, the Chinese transcription of the name of the 'Indo-scythians,' the great tribe that played such an important role in the history of Asia, may have been pronounced in the archaic language * *tngut-ti̯a* or *sngut-ti̯a*. Whether this transcription is connected with Tangut, the medieval name of the Kansu-Shensi uplands and the people inhabiting them or, which appears less likely, represents an eastern Asiatic variant of Σκύθαι, Scyths is a problem that we hope to discuss at greater length in the future.

---

[94] Cf. 莫 *mɒk < *BSɒk—'dark' and 昔 *si̯äk—'formerly,' 'yesterday,' 'dried meat.' *BS- in the last is indicated by the synonyms: 脩 *si̯ɒuG, 脯 *pi̯u, 俎 *tsi̯wo—'sacrificial meat,' 鱐 *si̯ɒuG—'dried fish'; for 'dark,' cf. the binom 覭髳 *miek-tsiek—'obscure.'

[95] The etymonic in 歲 is 戌 *si̯uet < BS- as indicated by 威 *miet. The graph for 'halberd' 戈~戉 that is sometimes added as a phonetic to 月 in the bone inscriptions represented an etymon with a *TSNG- initial at least in one of its readings, possibly in the special meaning 'to wound,' 'to cut'~'cutting instrument' as we can see from 戔, 戋, 戕, 截. The same etymon with *BS- appears in 伐 *bi̯wɐt < *BSat—'to smite'~'kill.' *BS- is well attested in the root 'to kill' < 'to die.' Cf. 死 *sid *vs.* 斃 *b'iäd, 殺 -*sat, 喪 *sang (亡 *mang* is phonetic in this character, says SW 2a), 沒 *muət *vs.* 卒 *tsuət < *BTS- (observe that *piet is phonetic in this graph; cf. also numerous binoms of the type 孛卒 *buət-tsuət).

[96] Used as a phonetic 月 *ngi̯wɐt is interchanged with 兀~阢 *nguət—'highland,' 'plateau' which we know must go back to *tsngut as it is often equated with the binom 崔嵬 *ts'uâi-nguâi—'id.' < *TSNGai, discussed above.

'Ideography' or Iconolatry?

T'oung Pao, 35.4 (1940), 266-288.

With martial stalk, the ghost of 'Ideography' haunts again the platform of sinological Elsinore. In *TP* 34. 265—294, Professor Herrlee Glessner Creel, taking exception to some statements in the present writer's 'Proleptical Remarks' (*HJAS* 2. 329—372), directed against his efforts to revive 'ideography' as a method of interpreting Chinese characters, attempts to re-state his position in a curiously constructed article entitled 'On the Ideographic Element in Ancient Chinese'. Though written in a lively, controversial vein, the paper fails to produce a single new fact which would help us to clarify the important problem of the structure and genesis of Chinese writing, and enlightens us very little on the nature of 'ideographic' ectoplasm.

The article makes it painfully obvious, on the other hand, that the discussion of the cardinal points of the origin and development of the Chinese written language cannot be fruitfully continued, so long as the champions of 'ideography' refuse to define what they mean by an 'ideogram', and to explain coherently their reasons for disregarding in specific cases long-established evidence pointing

1) [Tout en publiant volontiers le présent article de M. Boodberg, nous considérons qu'il doit clore, en ce qui concerne le T'oung Pao, une controverse dont les éléments sumériens sortent du cadre et de la compétence de notre revue. — Note de la rédaction].

to the phonetic and logographic nature of what they term 'ideograms'. One of the chief purposes of my article was not, as Professor Creel imagines, to combat 'ideography' (for I am quite open-minded on the subject, especially as I do not know what on earth 'ideography' signifies concretely), but to protest against the loose use of the vague term 'ideogram' whenever 'logogram' is meant. It is true, at the same time, that, as a philologist and teacher of Chinese, I am naturally perturbed by—and cannot remain indifferent to— the rise of a methodology which produces, not in comparatively innocuous special articles, but in text-books through which a new generation of sinologists is expected to be trained, puerilities such as the following:

膚 fu[1].... "The skin, flesh. Superficial". [A 虍 tiger's 胃 stomach, *to feed which it rends the flesh of other animals*]. (H. C. CREEL, *Literary Chinese*, vol. 1, character No. 67).

朝 chao[1]. "The dawn. Early". Chao[2] "Court, dynasty. To have audience". [The 日 sun shining on 屮 grass *on* which 川 water *is standing*, i. e. wet with dew. This *typifies* the dawn, the hour at which court was commonly held by Chinese rulers]. *Ibid.* No. 296a.

夜 yeh[4].... "Night". [A man with 夕 the moon under one arm; *night as black as if the moon were concealed under a man's armpit*]. *Ibid.*, No. 304 [1]).

---

1) The italics are mine. Cf., in addition, *ibid.*, Nos. 6a, 13, 14, 22, 27, 29, 55, 65, 85, 136, 141, 154, 156, 178, 181, 195, 212, 213, 227, 229, 337, 379, 388, 419, 477, 495, 529, 650, 666, 767, 772, 776, 834, 842, 872, and many other less forced interpretations. Had Professor Creel not refrained altogether from analyzing a considerable percentage of graphs included in the notes, the number of monstrosities would have been over-whelming. All of those characters not only can, but have been, explained as phonetic logograms. To ignore those explanations and to substitute for them the charades that appear on almost every page of the book in order to build up a case for 'ideography', is unforgivable.

As to the three graphs above, in each the phonetic element is clearly discernible. 'Armpit' 亦 > 腋 *ẓjäk is phonetic in 夜 *ia < *ẓiag-* 'night' (with 夕 *ẓjäk* etymonic); this has been known for eighteen centuries and has never been seriously

To invite anyone to accept similar interpretations as the correct 'ideographic' analysis of Chinese writing is, to put it mildly, to incite him to disregard the laborious gains of scholarship of the past two thousand years and to make sinology a subject fit only for Kindergarten instruction.

This note is not written, however, to discuss the general thesis advocated by Professor Creel, nor as a rejoinder to the rather sophistic argumentations in his latest article but in appreciation of his sincere perplexities over certain minor points raised by my paper, and in answer to some specific questions he puts to me. I shall be as concise as possible in stating the particular difficulties and the solutions thereof:

1. P. 270—271. Professor Creel's discussion of the dvandva compound 門戶 *mên-hu*—'doors' is entirely irrelevant to the hypothesis I had advanced as to the origin of a certain class of binoms which seemingly arose as the result of the dimidiation of an initial consonantal cluster in an archaic syllabic phoneme. In each specific case, it is apparently necessary to remind Professor Creel, who refuses to recognize the numerous *sapienti sat* interspersed through my paper, the hypothetical dimidiation is arrived at by a 'triangulation' of:

disputed. In his analysis of 朝, Professor Creel is mistakenly dealing with *ch'ao*[2] 潮 ('morning') tide' consisting originally of 水 'water' and 卓, rising sun' as phonetic-etymonic, for which see note 1 on p. 274. In 膚 *pi̯u* 'skin', flesh' the 'tiger' element is phonetic, not as *χuo, but as *pi̯u (now written 彪) 'tiger's stripes'. The two archaic pronunciations of the 'tiger' element explain why 'two thousand years ago, the best etymologist of the time failed to see ..., etc.' (CREEL, *op. cit.*, 10). As a good paleographer and philologist, Hsü Shên knew that the 'tiger' graph stood both for the name of the animal and the designation of its skin, and registered this distinction in his work. Originally the two words formed, however, the same etymon, probably *GLOG ~ *BLOG — 'wild animal and the hide, skin thereof' and the differentiation of the two was slow. Note that our *pi̯u* was archaically interchanged with 臚 *li̯wo* < *GLʷO, in which graph the 'tiger' element is phonetic in its more usual reading *χuo* < *GL —.

a) data indicating the existence of a consonantal cluster in a given phonetic series, such as an alternation of initials in that series, supported by evidence of early lexicographical works as to the role of phonetic elements in a complex graph;

b) the study of synonymic interchange of words represented by substantially the same phoneme, but exhibiting a similar alternation of initials, and of word families;

c) comparison of paronomastic definitions, phonetic glosses, ancient dialectical variants, and, whenever possible, evidence supplied by related languages.

This material being available to any scholar, is perfectly testable, and the validity of the reconstruction demonstrable in each particular case [1]).

2. p. 273—274. Professor Creel's puzzlement over the V-shaped line which joins the abbreviations used on p. 333 of my article, *viz*:

$$G \left< \begin{array}{l} S^1\ p^1 \\ S^2\ p^2 \end{array} \right.$$

is most surprising. This V-shaped line stands for nothing more mysterious than the word 'represents' [2]), outside of the context or the paragraph in which it was used, it does not mean anything. Should one take this line in the conventional value of the sign $\langle$, = 'derived from' or 'converge into', it would not at all tally with

---

1) Here, pp. 272—273, follows, after a quotation of my note 5, some irrelevant *non sequitur* about behaviorism and my supposed attachment to Watsonian principles. I did not deny the existence of visual images, the genesis of pictograms as such, that is as pictures, nor the existence of ideas or concepts. The linguist and the epigraphist, however, can deal only with *words* and their representations. Whether thought is possible without language or not is a question which, whatever be our opinions on the subject, is in no way connected with our business at hand—Professor Creel's and mine—, the discussion of the Chinese *language*.

2) As very clearly stated by me in the paragraph beginning: 'Let us take two simple cases of a graph G *representing* two semantemes each with its phonetic value . . . .'

my statement, immediately preceding the use of the 'graph' [1]).

3. p. 276—277. Graphic 'determination' of homophonic graphs by 'significs' does in no way transform the graphs into 'ideograms'. Perhaps the issue could be clarified and all this tempest in a glass of water avoided, if Professor Creel should tell us whether pictographic elements put at, let us say, the right hand corner of a series of English homonyms would turn each of these English words into an 'ideogram' [2]).

4. p. 277—278. The character 明. A reference to pp. 344—345 of my article (last sentence of the paragraph) should quickly dispel Professor Creel's inability to understand why I 'ignored' the *ku-wên* form of 明 given by the *SW* as composed of 'sun' and 'moon'. I mentioned the form and explained it, but unfortunately too briefly (another case of *sapienti sat*). A fuller explanation is apparently in order.

'Ideographers', we suppose, imagine the composition of the character 明 *ming*—'bright', 'shining' somewhat as follows:

"The Chinese creators of the script said to themselves: 'How shall we write 'bright'? Now the sun is 'bright' and the moon is 'bright'. We shall put the pictures of the moon and the sun together, and that shall represent the 'idea' of 'bright'. Henceforth

1) In the second case of the use of the V-shaped line on the same page it stands for 'is reflected in'. Note that, strictly speaking, it was entirely unnecessary for me to resort to the use of these signs for the clarification of the preceding sentence: the graphic 'formula' was used primarily as a mnemonic notation.

2) As, *e. g.*, in the sentence: 'Washer, fix the washer in that washer', perfectly intelligible, in spite of the three homonyms, in the proper context and situation, such as involving a laundry 'boss' giving an order to his helper in a mechanized laundry. Should we meet this sentence out of its proper context, it would surely help us to understand it if the first *washer* had been supplied with a graphic picture of a man, indicating that the word should be taken as equivalent to 'washerman'; the second *washer*, with the picture of a ring, indicating that the term refers to the well-known plumber's gadget; and the third *washer* be decorated with a picture of a washing machine.

we should endeavour not to 'call' this 'ideogram' *sun*, or *moon*, or *sun-moon*, but 'bright'."

The obvious questions that immediately occur to anyone with linguistic sense hearing this story of the genesis of an 'ideogram' are: Did the Chinese have a *word* for 'bright', what were its semantic affiliations, was it in any way related to the vocables for 'sun' or 'moon', would not the 'ideogram' be confused with a picture of the conjunction of the sun and moon? For the 'ideographer' these questions are both unanswerable and irrelevant; lost in the contemplation of his little icon representing the 'idea' of 'brightness', he only shrugs his shoulders at the irreverent questioner.

The graphic and phonetic data at the disposal of any philologist who has studied Chinese free from the mania of 'ideography' almost automatically supply the following answers to the above questions.

The commonest Chinese *word* for bright was *GANG registered in numerous graphs, the simplest of which is 囧 *kiweng* [1]) which takes the place of the sun in some forms of our 明 *miăng*. Han lexicographers testify that this graph was also sounded with a labial initial and was a homophone of 明 *miăng*. 囧 forms with 皿 *miăng* 'vessel' a graph which appears already in the

---

1) It is the business of paleographers to discover what 囧 represented graphically in the oldest forms: a window, some other kind of opening, or an eye. Whatever be the final verdict, we know what phoneme it stood for and the general semantic group to which it belonged. It is undeniable that it was connected with one form of the etymon for 'eye', namely *GSANG ~ *GSOG; as indicated by its appearance in *ku-wĕi* scriptions of 省 *siăng-* 'look', 'examine' and its interchange with 'the double-eye' graph two 臣 back to back, and 朋, *Gʷang and *Gịʷăk. The last two roots, graphically represented by two eyes, in derivatives regularly serve to render the etymon 1 'fright' with the same pronunciation. This should solve Professor Creel's perplexity (pp. 267—268) over Karlgren's material indicating so many homophones for √ 'brigh VS √ fright'.

earliest inscriptions and is equivalent to 盟, both variations being pronounced *miăng. With the phonetic determinative 亡 mi'''ang (which itself exhibits an alternation of labial and guttural) 明 was pronounced ɤ''âng.

This word 'bright' *GANG was used to indicate the brightness of the sun in 景 kiăng—'sun-bright' and related words, 晃 g'wâng, 曠 kwâng, and 旺 giwang, all of which have the sun as a semantic determinative. Another primary word meaning 'sun-bright' was *DANG, registered in the elemental graphs 易‹昜, 陽 diang 'sun coming out of the clouds' ~ 'sun' ~ 'bright', and 昌 t'jang—'sunshine' [1]); in both the sun is prominent graphically. 陽 diang is, moreover, early attested as a common term for 'sun' [2]). There seems to have existed, therefore, three archaic Chinese words meaning 'sun-bright': *GANG, *DANG, *BANG.

Can these be traced back to a common root? Have we here an alternation of *G-~*D-~*B-, or the result of the break-up of a consonantal cluster? The latter seems to be the case, at least so far as the two *DANG are concerned. 昜 *DANG is usually interpreted as a graph rendering 'the sun breaking through the clouds' and occurs as the second part of a dozen binoms with the underlying meaning of V 'scatter' ~ 'dissipate', all of which have a *B-initial protom [3]), and it is significant that 昜 *DANG itself is glossed

1) Interchanging with 明 as in the quotation from the *Shih Ching* in the *SW* 7 A s. v.

2) Already in the *Shih Ching* and *Mencius*. This term for the sun is hardly due to the polarity of the cosmological ideas of *yang* and *yin*, as the moon begins to be designated as 太陰 (vs 太陽 'sun') much later. Observe also that SW 10 A, under 炅 *k'wong — 'to appear', 'bright', says (ap. Younger Hsü) that 日 'sun' is *phonetic* in that character. The statement is quite understandable on the supposition of 日 having had a reading *GDANG in addition to the more usual *ńjĕt.

3) Such as 波蕩 BA-d'âng — 'dissipated', 簸揚 or ｜颺 BA-(d)ang — to winnow', 播揚 BA-(d)ang — 'to winnow', 'to scatter abroad', 播蕩 BA-d'âng — 'to flee afar' 放蕩 BANG-d'âng — 'to roam', 'dissipate', *etc.*

SW 9 B by 飛楊 *BUI-DANG — 'to rise', 'to soar', while 陽 *DANG is explained in *SW* 1 by 發楊 *BAT-DANG — 'to expand', 'to manifest itself', and 颺 *DANG — 'tossed by the wind', by 飛楊 in *SW* 13 B. There are a few 易 binoms with a *G-protom, and several *B-initial binoms with 昌 *DANG as the second member. It is thus likely that both *DANG go back to an etymon of the form *BDANG (~ *GDANG) with the fundamental meaning *V* 'rise' ~ 'spread' ~ 'brighten' ~ 'sun coming out'. It is apparently this etymon that is registered in one of the earliest binoms 昧爽 *muâi—ṣiang*—'the first light of dawn' [1]).

It is clear, therefore, that in the Chinese language, 'bright' *BDANG was a syntagm of 'sun'—'light'—'spread', connoting *becoming* rather than *being*, 'bright' conceived more *in posse* than *in esse*, and it is thus not surprising to find the same phoneme in the meaning of 'twilight', > 'dim', > 'dark'. As to the character 明, the 'sun' 日 in the left part of the picture is, as I suggested, etymonic (that is phonetically equivalent to *BDANG—'bright) as clearly indicated by its interchanging with 囧 and the graphic and phonosemantic affiliations of *V* 'bright' with *V* 'sun' [2]).

In answer to the last question, we must say that treated as a *pictogram*, the character 明 represented indeed a *visible* conjunction of the sun and the moon, a perceptive, and not conceptive, union of the two luminaries [3]), the same union that appears in a 'Bone'

---

1) Observe that *siang* alone is the equivalent of *mi̯ăng—'bright', and interchanges also with 猛 *mʌng—'fierce'; sometimes with 亡 *mi̯wng.

2) 'Bright' is connected with 'moon' chiefly through the form *GLANG as in 亮 *liang* < *GL (as indicated by its phonetic 京 *ki̯ʌng*) and 朗 *lâng*—'moon-bright'. In binoms with these two characters as a base, we usually have a *G-protom. Cf. also 望 *mi̯wang 'full moon'—'bright'.

3) Although as a pictorial representation of actual astronomical facts it can hardly be described as faithful, the graphical combination of the 'sun' and 'moon' was undoubtedly often interpreted as representing the appearance of the crescent of the two-or-three day-old moon near the sun at the beginning of the lunar month. Some bronze graphs could even be interpreted as picturing 'the old moon in the arms of the new'.

graph believed to be a variant of 朝 *tįog, d'įog*—'dawn' < *BDOG, and consisting of the sun and moon surrounded by four 山 [1]).

5. This leads us to the consideration of another of Professor Creel's perplexities (pp. 278—281). Protesting against the suggestion that the 'tree' 木 is 'phonetic-etymonic' in 東 *tung*—'east', my critic waxes indignant at the old mythological interpretation of the graph and, insisting on an 'ideographic' analysis of 東 and the related graphs 杲 *kâu* < *kog and 杳 *°iəu* < *°iog, even ascribed to me the admission that the two last characters are 'ideograms'.

It is quite clear from the conclusion of my discussion of these two graphs on p. 349 that I considered them logograms based on the pictorial representation of a sun myth. In simple language, this meant:

When the Chinese created the graph 杲 *kâu*, representing the sun above a tree, did they look at it and say 日在木上 *ńźįet-dz'âi-muk-źiang* 'the sun is atop the tree'? No, that would have been quite meaningless for the purpose of using the character as a written sign. Anyone familiar with the graph would explain it to a tyro as 日高 *ńźįet kâu*, 'the sun is *high*' with emphasis on *kâu*—'high'. Similarly 日在木下 'the sun under the tree' is a graphic explanation, and not a definition of 杳 *°ieu*, unless the phonetic value be explained by *°ieu*—dark' [2]).

As to the mythological significance of the 木 'tree' in these graphs, it is quite obvious that our Columbuses of 'Ideography' would have never discovered that 東 represents 'the sun rising *behind* a tree' from the pictograph alone, had it not been for the entry

---

1) Observe that 朝 represents the same etymon *BDOG (a variant of *BDANG) which appears in 昭 *Bʻįog*—'shine', 'brilliant'. The *B in 'dawn' is indicated by its being phonetic in 廟 *mįäu*—'ancestral temple'. The 'grass' element is phonetic, as it is in some forms of 早 *tsâu* < *BDOG—'early'.

2) The mythological association of our °ieu [~ 幽] with Yu tu 幽都, 'the region of darkness', 'the winter abode of the sun', is very probable.

in *SW* 6A which explains the character graphically by 日 在 木 中 *lit.* 'the sun *in* tree' or, possibly, 'the sun *among* tree(s)'. That 'tree' meant here '*the* Tree' is clear from the fact that the related graphs 杲 and 杳 are entered in the *SW* immediately after 榑, 'the *fu-sang* tree of the sun'. This mythological interpretation is in no way invalidated by the existence of the character 莫 *muo*, *mâk*—'sunset', 'evening' representing, 'as the Shuo Wên tells us', the sun setting amid shrubbery, grass, or trees. Have ideographers never heard of 'the tree of the West', the 若 木 *jo-mu*, the mythological counterpart of the *fu-sang*, where the sun was supposed to alight in the evening? [1]).

But what is more important, is that the analysis of the character 莫 confirms what we had said on the archaic phonetic form of *tung* 東 which we reconstructed as *BD*V*NG. The Shuo Wên tells us, indeed, (in Younger Hsü's edition) that *mâng* (the 'double grass' graph) is 'also phonetic' in *mâk* 莫. This is supported by entries on the two remaining graphs classified under the 'double grass' radical, 茻 *mâng* and 葬 *tsâng*—'to bury', 'to hide' glossed in the *SW* by 藏 *dz'âng*—'to hide'. The last word suggests that the etymonic of all three characters was *btsang ⟨ *BDANG ~ *BDOG, which hypothesis is confirmed by the binom 莽蒼 *mâng-ts'âng*—'color of grass', 'dim' [2]) and Tib. *γsang*— 'to hide'. Thus, besides representing the same picture as 東, 莫

---

1) The *jo-mu* is, in all probability, but a variant form of *fu-sang*. Thus the *SW* 6 B (ap. Hsü the younger) says that 叒, the original form of 若 *jo*, is phonetic in 桑 *sang*; was *jo-mu* originally *sang-mu?

2) 黨茻 (with 日) *DANG-MANG—'the sun obscured' would indicate a reversed order of initials, but it is likely that the terms of the binom had been transposed for syntactic reasons in the *Ch'u tz'ǔ*, where the expression occurs. That the *B- came first in that etymon is seemingly confirmed by 麼羅 (with 日) *BA-LA — 'dim' (as the light of the sun) 蒙龍 (with 日) 'dim', (with 月) 'the moon clouded or about to set', both *BUNG-LUNG, *etc*. Cf., however, 童龍 (with 日) *DUNG-LUNG—'sun coming out'. *DB—in √ 'dim' is, therefore, not altogether excluded.

also rendered a phoneme closely related to *BDYNG. In both the 'vegetation element', whether depicting trees or grass, was etymonic-phonetic. It is the same phonetic-graphic element that appears in 朝 *BDOG—'dawn', now as two 屮, now as four 屮; its essential purpose is to render the phonosemanteme *BDANG ~ *BDOG V 'twilight' (dawn *or* sunset). That it also satisfied the pictographic sense of the users of the script by supplying their imagination with a picture of the sun rising or setting 'amid shrubbery' is undeniable, but the important point is that, however pretty the picture, it would not be a graph unless it were associated with a phonosemanteme.

Similarly, the other 'ideogram' that Professor Creel adduces to demonstrate the 'ideographic use' of 日 'sun', namely 旦 *tân* — 'dawn' which depicts 'the sun rising above the horizon' is best explained as a *pictographic* logogram. On bronzes the same character appears as a picture consisting of a circle 'left in white' connected with a round or elongated black mass and semantic analysis indicates clearly that as a logogram it represents the word 'black-and-white' ~ 'light-and-dark' ~ 'twilight' > 'dawn', archaic *tân ~ tât* which appears in its primary sense in 旦 enlarged by 黑 —'white mixed with black' 白而有黑 (*SW* 10), and, as binoms would indicate, is derived from *GDAN [1]).

---

1) Cf. particularly the various forms of writing the name of the 'Chinese nightingale': 曷旦 *GAT-*tán* (in *SW* 4 A with 水 and 鳥; often with 鳥 as determinative in both cases; 干旦 *GA(N)-*tán* (with Dt. 196; first character also written 旱); 侃旦 GA-*tán*; semantized as 求旦 *GIU-*tán* ('seeking the dawn') or 盍旦 *GA(P)-*tán* ('why no dawn?'). Another very important dimidiated form with 旦 *tán* < *GDAN as a basis is found in the name of the Shang ruler Ho-tan chia 河亶甲 *GA-*tân* kap, where ho 河 is used to restore the amissible *G- of *GDAN. On the bones the name of the same ruler is written ╳ 申, with only one character preceding the cyclical term. That character appears to be a form of 戔 *dz'ân* < *G/bDAN. Cf. WALEY *Book of Songs*, Suppl., 16. The *GAN form of 'dawn' appears in 斡人 *kán* 'dawn' said to contain 旦 *tán* as etymonic and 扚 °*ǵịvn* as phonetic.

6. Finally, on pp. 281 ff., Professor Creel, dishearteningly continuing to discover Americas, attempts to dismiss my arguments concerning the convergence of the graphs for 肉 'meat' and 月 'moon' and the endomorphically phonetic role of 目 in the graph 馬 'horse'. All the points advanced by him are perfectly known to 'anyone who can read' the Chinese works on the bone inscriptions. We are not interested in their constant reiteration; but we are still expectantly waiting for the 'ideographers' to stop playing with 'ideographic' charades and cease ascribing the different forms of Chinese characters to 'scribal conventionalization', a term that does not explain anything, and least of all the convergence of graphs[1]). For, we would like to know, how was it possible that

---

[1] The 'long and intricate task' of investigating scribal convergences on the basis of the hypothesis that these convergences were due to *semantic* and phonetic affinities, far from 'yielding results of very dubious validity' (p. 283) could prove to be one of the most fruitful studies for epigraphists, if they only would try not to close their eyes to the problem. Thus, the seemingly accidental convergences that Professor Creel mentions on pp. 282—283 are not so fortuitous as he claims them to be. The similarity of some forms of 'eye' and 'net', though comparatively late, is based on the semasiological connection of 'eye' 目 with 'mesh' < 'eye', 'loop of a rope'. That the topmost element of 若 is not a form of 'grass' 'vegetation', but represents 'hair standing on end from fright' (CREEL, *op. cit.*, No. 770) is one of the 'sur-realistic' phantasies of the 'ideographers'. May we ask them for the tiniest bit of substantiating evidence that the Chinese ever observed hair (some $2^1/_2$ ft. long judging from the proportions of the figure) 'standing on end from fright'? That the convergence of 玉 'jade' and 王 'king' is late no one has ever denied, but it is undoubtedly pre-Han. The *SW* graphic explanation of 王 which Professor Creel discusses on pp. 291—292 is perfectly understandable in the light of what the same work says on 玉 'jade' as representing three pieces of jade strung together, an interpretation generally, and almost universally accepted cf. CREEL, *op. cit.* No. 65*d*) Professor Creel should not blame Hsü Shên for his mistranslation of that worthy's text: thus, on p. 291, 叄 does not mean 'to assist', but 'thrice after other' or as a verb "to 'thrice'", and, in the quotation ascribed to Confucius 貫 means 'string together', and not 'penetrating'. In other words, however fanciful the cosmological interpretation of 王 by Tung Chung-shu may appear, it was based on a sincere and logical effort to explain the similarity of thetwo graphs, 'jade' and 'king' in their bronze forms. Again, in the oldest form of 王 'king' that 'represents man standing boldly erect, with outstretched arms on a line representing the earth,

the Chinese, so 'ideographically-minded' as they are described to us, permitted themselves to commit the blunder of progressively 'converging' a graph representing 'a piece of meat' and that of the 'crescent moon'. The obvious answer is, as suggested in my article and evident to anyone who would take the trouble of continuing the investigation, even along the lines laid out by Professor Creel, that the graphs became confused because from the very beginning they represented (*graphically*, though not always pictorially) [1]) the same etymon, probably 'sliced' 'ribbed' [2]).

i. e. a piece of territory, which he holds against all comers' (*op. cit.* No. 10; a rather naive conception of kingship, by the way), how does Professor Creel know that the human figure is not represented as *walking, going*, and could, therefore, be understood as equivalent to 往 *wang* — 'to go'?

As to the graphic convergence of 阜 and 邑, it is, of course, not absolute, the former being distinguished from the latter by position. Even there, though we are not at present able to prove the semantic connection, we should give the benefit of the doubt to the ancient Chinese who may have seen the link between 'bluff' and 'city' in 'acropolis'.

1) Professor Creel's inability to understand the important distinction between a graph and a picture lies at the bottom of our present imbroglio. In a picture, however stylized, ambiguity is to be avoided at all price; in a graph, it is an asset and, within certain limits, is highly desirable. The double-entendre whether based on two related, but already divergent senses of an etymon, or on a mere *idem sonans* of two terms, is the very soul of pictographic forms of writing.

2) Pictorially, the moon may be represented as a thin crescent, a 'full' crescent. in the first quarter, and even slightly gibbous, but as graphs all those pictograms represent the *word* 'moon'. What the graph for 'meat' represents pictorially is not easy to decide, a 'rib chop' is perhaps the best interpretation. Now in both the protographs of 'moon' and 'meat' the projecting ends of the 'rib' are quite characteristic. Highly significant is also the slant given to some forms of 夕 'the half-moon' which makes many of them undistinguishable from forms of 'meat' with a single cross-line. That the thin crescent and the piece of meat are easily differentiated nobody has ever denied, but that the 'slanting moon' *ZNUK and 'slice or chop of meat' *ZNUK were both graphically and phonetically closely connected is neither astonishing or particularly 'curious'. Before accusing Hsü Shen of making blunders and forcing his 'arbitrary' etymologies in preference to their own, Shang epigraphists should endeavor to give us better explanations than all-powerfull 'conventionalization' for convergences noticeable already on the bones. Professor Creel's omission from the discussion of 夕 and 多, and consequently of the 'double meat' in 俎 (and 宜) forces us to postpone further

As to the head being represented paleographically by the eye, the mere statement of the fact does not lead us anywhere, especially as it can and has been observed *nudis occulis* decades ago. Quite cognizant of the presence of an 'eye' 目 instead of the head in some forms of the character for 'deer' 鹿 *luk* [1]), I ascribed to it at the time of the writing of my article the same role of phonetic determinative as to the 'eye' of 馬 'horse'. Unfortunately, the demonstration of this point involved a lengthy discussion of the bone graphs, a review of many of the identifications so far made by Chinese scholars, the validity of which I made it a point not to question [2]), and that of the relationship between *BL- and *BD-initials in archaic Chinese. Two years ago, I was inclined to believe *BL- to be chronologically more primitive than *BD-, to-day I am in possession of data indicating a practically simultaneous development of the two phonemes. This does in no way invalidate the existence of a *BD- ~ *BL- complex in the word for 'eye' which determines phonetically the graph 鹿 *luk* ⟨ *Bluk, as it does 馬 and 蜀 *d'įʷok* ⟨ *BDUK [3]). In the 'eyebrowed eye' 首 we have,

elucidation of this point, pending his pronouncement on the subject (cf. my analysis of the connection of those characters with 'moon' at the close of my 'Proleptical Remarks'). $\sqrt{}$ 'Slanting' and $\sqrt{}$ 'defective' form another semantic connection between 'moon' and 'meat' ~ 'flesh'. The similarity of 夕 and 歹, another 'convergence' not entirely accidental, is also a pertinent point that could be discussed here with profit.

1) Derived from *BLUK, as indicated by 麤 *BOG. In the binom 麚鹿 'deer' (coll.) the protom *BI served in Han times to restore the *B of the original *BLUK (Cf. the similar use of *BI in ｜黎 and ｜壽). Binoms with *luk* as second member point also to *GLUK.

2) Thus the identification of the Shang graph, representing a doe(:) and a fawn or a single hornless deer-like animal, with 麀 seems to me highly problematical. The modern character is much more probably 麛 —'fawn'. 麑 *ngiei* in the meaning 'fawn' is a late derivative from 兒 'young', 'child'. In the case of 麋, the equation of the Shang form with the modern character is equally doubtful.

3) The 'eye' appears in that character already in Shang graphs. While a purely scribal conventionalization of the head of such animals as the horse and the deer into 目 is conceivable, to suppose that the same happened with the head of a silkworm is carrying paleographical phantasy too far.

just as in some forms of 馬, a 'digraphic' representation of 'eye' and 'hair'. The relationship of the two etymons to each other and to that for 'head' involves a long story to which we hope to return in the near future [1]).

The above dismisses the essential problems raised by Professor Creel's article, and, we hope, settles some of his perplexities. In attenuation of several harsh words that we have penned in reference to Professor Creel's methods of research and critism, we feel it our duty to say that inwardly we do not believe that his case is as bad as it appears. Given time to shake off iconodulic obsessions and opportunity to revise his terminology [2]), Professor Creel may yet find that the Tertullianian *certum est...*, whatever its potency in iconolatric pursuits, is not a safe devise in the work of scholarship.

There now remains to us the highly onerous task of considering the closing portion of the paper. On pp. 286—289 and 293—294 we find Professor Creel enlisting the collaboration of Prof. Arno Poebel who directs at my little note 50, dealing with the possibility of the existence of initial consonantal clusters in Sumerian, a heavy barrage of criticism.

I cheerfully concede Professor Poebel his privilege as an eminent sumerologist of the land [3]) to blast to pieces a theory of an obscure amateur, trespassing on the science which the author of the *Grund-züge* has so brilliantly served. Had he limited himself to a regal *vix credibile*, I would have no choice but to utter a humble *nil*

---

1) Some evidence points to the 'eyebrow' (Chin. 眉 *BI) as being a proclitic phonetic complement in *BSEU < *BSOG—'head'. On *GSOG—'eye' cf. note 1 on p. 271.

2) In the majority of cases, Professor Creel follows the interpretations of modern Chinese epigraphists and shares their natural predilection for 'ideography'. In his case however, this predilection, couched as it is in Western terminology and not in the more flexible Chinese nomenclature. becomes a definite bias.

3) Not 'as an authority on phonetic phenomena', however, as Professor Creel over-enthusiastically re-introduces him on p. 293. This highsounding and slightly absurd title Professor Poebel, I am sure, would be the first to disclaim.

ultra quaero plebeius. The superficial manner in which Professor Poebel disposes of my little suggestion forces me, however, out of respect to the same science of sumerology, to make the following reservations to the seemingly imposing evidence he has marshalled against me.

It is clear to an unprejudiced observer that the whole problem of the phonetic value of the sign Lú—'man' hinges on the question of the origin of the Emesal word mu-lu—'man'. As suggested, but not demonstrated by Professor Poebel in the work indicated by him [1]), mu-lu could be interpreted as a dvandva compound of mu (the Emesal form of g i š — 'man', 'male', of the main dialect) and the regular word for 'man', l ú.

There are several obvious objections to such an explanation of mu-lu:

1. It is based on a preconceived tendency to analyze dissyllabic words as compounds of two monosyllabic roots, a procedure that is justified only in cases when the semantic values of the component parts are clearly indicated in the script or when textual evidence supports it directly or indirectly. In both cases we must be careful to distinguish real semantic derivation from school- or folk-etymology [2]).

---

1) S i p a-(d) 'Hirte' im Sumerischen, *Studia Orientalia* I, 122. '... m u-l u 'Mensch' allem Anschein nach auch eine Zusammensetzung von *mu* 'Mensch' und *lu* (= *lù*) 'Mensch' 'Mann' ist...' is all that Professor Poebel says. He suggests the explanation as a parallel to a hypothetical *mu-sub reading for PA-sub — 'shepherd' (on the basis of a dialectical pronunciation of PA as mu). On the same page, however, he admits the possibility that PA might be a kind of phonetic complement as in the compound PA + SI which regularly stands for s i p a. A layman is naturally astonished at Professor Poebel's operating with mu-sub (~ munsub) with the view of forcing *mu into the meaning 'man' without even discussing its relationship to the synonym munsùb < *mu-n-sub?, in form an obvious deverbal substantive (cf. POEBEL, *GSG*, § 123) or with munsub- 'hair', 'wool', 'shearer' (*gallabu*).

2) Semantic metaplasis through the use of unrelated graphic forms for phonetic purposes seems to be as much characteristic of Sumerian as of Chinese.

2. The unmistakable predilection of Emesal texts for the phonetic rendering of logograms is not considered beyond the assertion that m u stands for GIŠ and l u for LÚ. Now, as m u-l u in Emesal supplants LÚ — 'man' alone, before offering his interpretation, Professor Poebel should have satisfied our curiosity as to the existence of a main dialect dvandva *GIŠ-LÚ — 'man', of which m u-l u would be the Emesal rendering. Such a form, so far as I am aware, is not attested [1]).

3. It is highly improbable that a dvandva compound of that type should be used as a pronoun. Yet m u-l u is the regular Emesal form of LÚ — 'one', 'some-one', 'whoever' ⟨ 'man' (POEBEL, *GSG*, § 253). M u-l u appears also as the Emesal form of LÚ in the sense of 'possessor of' (*bêlu*); it remains unexplained why Emesal should resort to the use of a compound to render the simple 'man' (LÚ) of the main dialect in this idiomatic usage.

4. In m u-l u-GÀL-l u — 'men', 'people', where m u-l u again takes the place of LÚ, a compound, apprehended as such by the users of the script, is again very unlikely to be employed.

It is, therefore, much more probable that m u-l u represents the Emesal pronunciation of the sign LÚ dimidiated or 'spelled out' in the fashion of texts written in that dialect.

As to the question of stress which is one of the points raised by Professor Poebel in his objections to a possible *GLU ⟩ LÚ, it should have been clear, in the light of my discussion of the development of Chinese, that I considered the hypothetical *gal and *gul readings of LÚ [2]) as *apotomized* forms of *GLU, arising

---

1) It is usual to ascribe the change of the vocalization in GI/FŠ ⟩ MU(š) to the labialization of an original *i* vowel in GIŠ under the influence of the initial M-. The question of the phonetic relation between the two initial sounds G and M is generally passed in silence. It is more likely, however, that both dialectical forms go back to an original *gʷüš ⟩ giš (main dialect); ⟩ *müš ⟩ m u (š) (Emesal).

2) ZIMMERN's note, in *Babylonische Busspsalmen* 14—16 (where the hypothetical readings were first suggested), though written 55 years ago, is still worth reading and some of its arguments still worthy of consideration.

from the ectasis of an *Einschubvokal* between *ɢ- and *ʟ-:
*ɢʟᴜ ⟩ *ɢᵊʟᴜ ⟩ ɢᴀ̆ʟᴜ́ ⟩ *ɢᴀʟ-ʟᴜ́, and not as having developed from
*gₐ-lù. In this connection, it is pertinent to observe that my
hypothetical form *ɢʟᴜ 'man' should be definitely rejected only
after a sufficiently valid demonstration that Sumerian lugal —
'king' (graphically both ʟᴜ́.ɢᴀʟ and ɢᴀʟ.ʟᴜ́) had never been read
by the originators of the script as *gal-lu[1]). The semantic development 'man' ⟩ 'king' is not all improbable, while the semantization
of lugal as 'great man' may well have been primarily graphic
and scholastic.

The uncertainty of the reading *ɢᴀʟ in lú-ɢᴀ̀ʟ-lu is a
point I readily grant Professor Poebel. It is, however, to be
remarked that if ɢᴀ̀ʟ-lu had originally been, as he suggests, a
geographical or ethnic term, it soon became a rather comprehensive
one, as, already in early texts, lú-ɢᴀ̀ʟ-lu (Emesal mu-lu-ɢᴀ̀ʟ-lu)
~nam lú-ɢᴀ̀ʟ-lu is used in the sense of 'people', and possibly
even in that of 'mankind'.

To complete this discussion of ʟᴜ́—'man', we should note
that Professor Poebel's derisive comparison of my *ɢʟᴜ ⟩ ʟᴜ́
with a phantastic derivation of *clamo* from *exclamo* does not only
reveal his failure to follow the trend of my argument [2]), but is

---

1) Cf. note 1 on p. 281. The reading of the component parts of a Sumerian compound
in reverse order is by no means unusual. Gal—'great' may have been pronounced gol~gul.
Cf. Poebel in *JAOS* 57, pp. 69, 71.

2) Another indication of the same failure is his pronouncement on pp. 288—289:
... since Sumerian is written in a system of syllabic writing, it would have been quite
impossible for the Sumerians to render two consonants at the beginning of a word;
even if words beginning with two consonants existed in the spoken language, in the
written language the first consonant would always appear with a vowel after it.' 'Critical'
observations of that sort show that Professor Poebel neglected to favor me with the
simple courtesy of reading my article carefully, or informing himself of the existence
of exactly the same situation in Chinese with its *syllabic* writing, where, due to painstaking phonetic investigation the existence of initial clusters has been clearly demonstrated inspite of the seeming impossibility of registering this cluster in syllabic writing
(I am not referring here, naturally, to my own reconstructions, but to those of better

manifestly unfair, as he never demonstrated that either the mu-
of mu-lu or GÀL in lú-GÀL—lu has ever had a morphological
value similar to that of the prefix *ex-* in Latin.

In the second part of the criticism, Professor Poebel's fundamental objection is that the synonymous Sumerian words for 'to
go' 'actually have in common *merely* their *ideogram*, which represents
the foot' (the italics are mine), and that comparison of the phonetic
values of the different terms is, therefore, entirely valueless. In
order to answer this objection, we must review the words mentioned.

The sign DU — 'to go' (a pictogram of the foot) had, Professor
Poebel admits, the readings:

rá, ge (possibly derived from gen).

Also ri and ir, both in the sense 'to go' (*alāku*) [1]) which he
chooses to ignore.

While it is true that no verb gir—'to go' is attested, in
Professor Poebel's argument it would appear that I produced it
out of thin air. He does not deny apparently that the sign DU
had the reading gir, although not in the meaning 'to go'. Now
if DU is the pictogram of a foot, it is very unlikely that the
'idea' of a foot existed in the Sumerian mind entirely apart of
the Sumerian word for 'foot'. In fact, that last word written
phonetically with sign DEIMEL 444 was gìr (Emesal merí). That the
'foot' in its gìr phonetic garb was not conceived as stationary, but
in its dynamic function of locomotion, is indicated by the Sumerian

and more conservative scholars, of whose dependable work Professor Creel should have
informed his collaborator). While the existence of the clusters cannot be demonstrated
directly, there are sufficient indications that justify the assumption of their occurence
in Sumerian even as seen in syllabic writing. Thus, whence the 'amissibility' of vowels
in compounds of the type kaprig < ka + pirig? Whether the disappearance of the first
i reflects the slurring of a short vowel of the word pirig (when part of the compound)
or whether it represents a return to an original *shewa* after the p (*i.e.* to the first
stage of the evolution *prig > *pᵊrig > pirig) is a legitimate question, the discussion of
which cannot be 'completely useless' even 'for practical purposes'.

1) ir₉ also written with DEIMEL 232.

word g i r—'road', written with the same sign and occasionally with
g í r (Emesal m e r i), Deimel 10. In addition, we have in Deimel 483,
the Sumerian words g u r, g i r, k i r, g i r i m—'to run' *garāru*)[1]).
Finally, the Chicago Syllabary gives the value 'to go' (*alāku*)
for GA (p i s á n).

Recapitulating, we have thus:

1. g i r — 'foot'
2. g á, g e, g e n, r á, r i, i r — 'to go'
3. g ì r, g u r, g i r i m — 'to run'
4. g ì r — 'road'

Apart of any theory as to the original form of a possible etymon
underlying all these words (V foot $> V$ 'to foot' could easily be considered the common denominator for all the groups), does comparing
them with a view of establishing a common origin resemble in
any way the wild combination of 'go' and 'run' into **grun* or 'go'
and 'walk' into **gwalk*, of which Professor Poebel accuses me?

Now to the KASKAL problem. Here again Professor Poebel
seems to make a strong case against the unrestrained speculations
of an amateur, but, as before, neglects to discuss fully the implications
of his own statements.

Anyone even superficially acquainted with cuneiform research
would naturally query Professor Poebel on his idea as to the
relationship of the two Akkadian words for 'leek', *karāš(u)* (pure
Akkadian) and *qa'iššu*[2]) (a Sumerian loan-word, $<$ g a ' e š). If he
believes them totally unrelated, well and good; if, however, he

---

1) Cf., however, Th. Bauer, *ZA* 7 (1933), pp. 216—218, on the meaning of
garāru in Akkadian.

2) The doubling of the š has no semantic or morphological significance. It indicates
that the preceding vowel was stressed. Basically short, stressed vowels in Sumerian are
often signified by the doubling of the following consonant; in Akkadian writing, this
v C[2] complex may be represented by $\bar{v}$ C, *i. e.* by a long vowel followed by a single
consonant. Hence -*āš(u)* in *karāšu* vs. *qa'iššu*. On this question, cf. Poebel in
JAOS 57, 47—49.

should concede the possibility of their having a common origin, his evidence is only supporting my seemingly absurd suggestion of a possible *GRAS reading for the KASKAL sign, a suggestion that I made in full knowledge of the facts adduced by Professor Poebel.

In fact, both examples 2 and 3 in my little note were advanced on the basis of perhaps amateurish, but honest and thorough search for the substantiation of Professor Poebel's own speculation on the *Schwund* of Sumerian intervocalic r (*GSG* § 56, cf. § 89, end). One example is adduced, that of the sign KUŠ (DEIMEL 110) for which the Chicago Syllabary gives also the phonetic value k u r u š (= Akk. *marū*). Professor Poebel favors the supposition that the r disappeared in that word by being assimilated to the final š, but does not preclude the possibility of a *Schwund*. It would seem, indeed, that some of the Sumerian r were typical uvular r, akin to the Semitic 'ayin, and easily amissible in pronunciation, when aperture was slightly increased. The hiatus in sumerian g a ' è s ⟩ Akk. *qa'iššu* is in all probability due to the disappearance of such a uvular r[1]. Ga'eš (also written EŠ-GA) could indeed be read *g a r-e š ~ *g a ꜥ-e š as the sign GA has a well attested reading *gar* which is probably the original phonetic value of the sign, GA being derived from *GA' ⟨ *GAꜥ ⟨ *GAR ~ *GAʁ. The phonetic value RAŠ of the KASKAL sign, instead of being 'a more or less accidental innovation of the late Akkadian scribes', could thus have organically developed from the reading of GA + KASKAL as *g a ꜥ-ꜥe š ⟨ *g a ʁ-ʁa š. We are also naturally curious to know if the

---

1) The disappearance of the r may also have taken place in g i š—'man', 'male' 'strongman'. Note that l ú-GIŠ is read l ú-g u r u š in the same meaning of *marū* that we have above for k u r u š. It would seem legitimate to raise the question whether GIŠ ~ g u r u š is not another graphic form of g u r u š (DEIMEL *ŠL* 322)—'strong', 'powerful' 'hero'. The reading may even explain the interchange and the graphic identity of GIŠ ~ g u r u š with the Sumerian word for slave u r u d (see POEBEL in *TP* 34, 288), possibly derived from *ʷu r u d̠.

reading g a r a š for GA + KASKAL in the meaning *purussû* [1]) is also due to an 'Akkadian innnovation'.

Believing thus that the e š value of KASKAL was derived from *ḫaš~ḫeš, I saw at the time no difficulty in accepting r a š as a reading for KASKAL. My study of the development of Chinese dimidiation suggested to me further that GA in GA-KASKAL, might be a phonetic complement (prefixed) to indicate a *GARAŠ reading of KASKAL, rather than an independent word or a mere syllabic sign. I confess that, in addition, I indulged in the following 'speculations':

Whereas: 1) the sign KASKAL with the value k a s takes in some texts the place of k a š—'alcoholic drink', and 2) in the meaning 'road' it is read ḫarran, supposedly an Akkadian word, but not demonstrably so and 3) in the compound GA.KASKAL it is read *eš* ⟨*ḪEŠ ⟨*RAŠ, giving us g a r a š⟩g a'e š as the reading for the combination, it is not improbable that the oldest value of KASKAL was *g a r a š ⟍ *g a r a n.

Now as k a s ⁓ k a š—'alcoholic liquor' has as its synonym k a r a n ⁓ k u r u n [2]) again supposedly an Akkadian loan-word, but not necessarily so, and the alternation N ⁓ Š is attested in Sumerian [3]), the possibility is not excluded that the various readings

---

1) Also written KA.AŠ and EŠ.BAR (read *bar-eš?)

2) On which cf. POEBEL, Zu den alkoholischen Getränken in Gudea, Zyl. B Kol. 6, 22 ff., *ZA* N.F. 5 (1929), pp. 146—164.

3) Mostly in Anlaut (cf. *GSG*, § 83). A very interesting case of such an interchange at the end of a root may be registered in DEIMEL 87 which, as the logogram for the name of the Euphrates is read *Buranuna* (interpreted as an abbreviation of id.UD.KIB.NUN.ki, but not necessarily so). As the sign is said to represent originally a cypress, it would be interesting to ascertain whether it is not connected with Akk. *burāšu*—'cypress' and whether *Purat, the original of Euphrates, is not to be linked with a term for cypress. As the name of the twin river Tigris < *Idiglat*, it has been suggested, may have been associated (folk-etymologically?) with Semitic (?) *daqal* دقل—'date-palm', the often recurring representations of the date palm and the cypress on ancient Mesopotamian monuments may indeed symbolize the two great life-giving rivers. The connection of the name of the cypress with terms for 'copper', also reflected in the name of the Euphrates, could be made the subject of a very fruitful study.

of the KASKAL sign are based on the interchange of the following phonetic values of the sign: *karaš (dial. variant of karan) — 'intoxicating drink'; *garan ⟨ harran — 'road'; *garaš ⟩ *ga'eš — 'leek'.

Finally, Professor Poebel's objection to my supposition that an initial velar could occasionally be dropped in Sumerian, on the basis of the assertion that no case of dropping *k* or *g* initially is known to him, is likewise unjustified. I never supposed a dropping of the *k* in my hypothetical reading *kras for KASKAL. As to initial *g*, a careful reading of my note should have made it clear that in the case of both the hypothetical *glu and *gra I had suggested the dropping not of a *g*, but of a labio-velar *gw-[1]). I do not consider it impossible, however, that in Sumerian an initial *g* might also become amissible through first being weakened into a *ḫ-*.

In short, it pains me to say, Professor Poebel, in order to disprove the existence of my alleged castle in the air, built himself a house of cards. I may have committed a grave mistake in broaching a big problem in a small note and in behaving like a foolhardy bull in the China shop of Sumerology, but I cannot, in the light of the above discussion of some of the ramifications of a very complex question, refrain from closing our argument with a respectful *non licet Jori* towards my critic. According to my understanding of the conventions of scholarship, angels—and 'cautious Sumerologists'—should undertake to correct the misdeeds of alleged fools in the light of reason and of *all* the facts of the case, or not at all.

---

1) Based obviously on the interchange of *g* of the main dialect with a *m*- in Emesal.

The Final -t of 弗 fu

The inversion of the regular order of verb and pronominal object in negative sentences in classical Chinese has been repeatedly observed and commented upon. Grammarians have, however, passed over the fact that this inversion, whenever the pronominal object was that of the third person, i.e., chih 之, affected the negative. In pre-Han Chinese the rule seems to require the use of the negative fu 弗 in such cases instead of the more common pu 不.

Von der Gabelentz's grammar is inaccessible to me, but it appears that even he and his disciples and followers have overlooked this rule, judging from v.d. Gabelentz's Die Sprache des Čuang Tsï and Haenisch's Lehrgang, L 110, where fu is defined as "nicht (auch prohibitiv)" without further comment, while in his text 國亡而弗知 is a clear example of the peculiar use of fu.

In more than 90 percent of cases of the use of fu in authentic Chou texts, fu followed by a verb contains an inherent chih 之 (him, her, it, them). In other words, fu 弗 regularly replaces 不之 pu chih in such examples as the following:

子知之曰弗知也
"Do you know it?" "I do not know it" [= 不之知]
弗為耳
Mencius VI, ii, 2, 3; Legge: "It is only that he will not do that thing." [= 不之為]
時至而弗失
"When the time comes they will not lose it." [= 不之失]

Indeed, the final -t of fu, KD 47 pi̯u̯ət can be well explained as the vestige of an original enclitic chih KD 1210 t́śi̯ < t́- attached to the regular negative pu KD 37 pi̯əu < -ui̯. Pu and fu (i.e., pu chih 不之) were clearly distinguished until the Late Chou period

---

* [Serial published by P.A.B. in the same manner as his HTHYFC (9). We have only numbers 1 through 4, all dated October 1934. -- Ed.]

when pu in the pronunciation puət (cf. Karlgren, loc. cit.) displaced fu entirely, the distinction between the two being preserved only in the style of the consciously archaizing writers.

Such an explanation of the final -t would be also justified in the case of the prohibitive wu 勿 KD 1278 mi̯uət (e.g., in 勿聽 "do not listen to him" [her, it, them]) and may also explain the final -t in such verbs as 曰 KD 1346 ji̯wɐt "to say it," which never is followed by chih 之 in contrast with 謂, 言, and 語.

NOTES ON CHINESE MORPHOLOGY AND SYNTAX, II.

Some Cases of Synaeresis in Archaic Chinese

In a preceding note the author has attempted to interpret the final -t of 弗 *pi̯uɐt and 勿 *mi̯uɐt as the vestige of an archaic 之 *ťi in the contraction of two original syllables *pi̯u-ťi ~ *mi̯u-ťi with the resulting apocope of -i. Heretofore only one case of such contraction had been recognized for archaic Chinese, namely that 諸 KD 1187 ₍ťsi̯wo is the result of the synaeresis of (1) 之 ťsi + 於 KD 1323 ₍ʔi̯wo, or (2) 之 ťsi + 乎 KD 85 ₍ɣuo [cf. KD p. 336]. Cases of synaeresis through syncope or apocope are, however, comparatively numerous in ancient and archaic Chinese, and a thorough study of such combinations and contractions of syllables will undoubtedly throw considerable light on some obscure morphological questions, especially those pertaining to the original significance, form, and evolution of grammatical particles.

In the following list of characters representing monosyllabic contractions of two original syllables the analysis of the component parts is well substantiated by the evidence of ancient texts.

1. 叵 KD 24 ᶜpᶜuâ 'impossible' [graph 可 KD 414 ᶜk'â reversed, so says the Shuo Wên] = 不可 *pi̯u-kᶜâ > *pᶜuâ 'im-possible.'

2. 盍 KD 75 ɣâp 'why not' = 何不 KD 414 *₍ɣâ-*pi̯u > *ɣâp(u) 'why not'.

3. 佣 *pəng 'unwilling' = 不肯 KD 314 ᶜk'əng 'be willing!, *pi̯u-k'əng > *pəng [cf. Kuang Ya IV]. 粃 *pj̯wi̯a [音彼 KD 721] dial. 'do not know' = 不知 KD 1218 *pi̯u-*ti̯a > *pj̯wi̯a (Kuang Ya ibid.).

4. 者· KD 1187 ᶜt'ṣia < t'- as a particle forming <u>nomina</u>
<u>actionis</u> can often be best interpreted as = 之也 KD 223 *t̂'i- *(d)ia
> t̂'ia.

5. 奚 KD 126 ꞔɣiei< gᶜ'why, how, what.' This particle is
used for 何 whenever a 以 KD 182 ᶜi< z- is implied before the
following verb (e.g. <u>Lun Yü</u> II.21: 子奚不為政 (為 = 以為)
and must be, therefore, equal to 何以 *ɣâ- *i > ɣiei.

6. 曷 KD 73 ɣât = 何之 *ɣâ-*t̂'i > ɣât. So also 害 KD 57
ɣât. The latter possibly = 何時 KD p. 399 ꞔzi< d̂ - 'what time,
when?'

7. 然 KD 929 ꞔńzïän < ń- must = 而 KD 10 ńźi< ń- plus
焉 KD 243 ꞔjïän.

NOTES ON CHINESE MORPHOLOGY AND SYNTAX, III.

The Morphology of Final −N and −T

When one attempts to trace the evolution of a Chinese etymon
through synonymy one is struck by the amount of evidence pointing
not only to the existence of prefixes in archaic Chinese, but also
to the predilection of particular aspects of the root for distinct
suffixes. Thus even a summary survey of Karlgren's <u>Dictionary</u>
yields considerable material indicating that final −N seemingly
served to designate the 'neuter' or 'intransitive' aspect of a
'verbal' root in archaic Chinese, while −T appears to have been the
mark of the 'active' or 'transitive' form.

These two aspects of the root appear sometimes in the same
character, e.g. KD 153 讞 ngïän° and ngïät 'to deliver a judicial
decision' or KD 767 散 ᶜsân° <u>vs.</u> 撒 sât 'to scatter', where <u>sât</u>
is strongly active (to disperse, let loose, distribute) and <u>sân</u>°
'neuter' (as indicated by ᶜsân 'broken, powder'). The distinction
between <u>−n</u> and <u>−t</u> is especially clear in the case of 'amphisbaenic'
roots such as **DZI̯U 'to lead' ~ 'to follow' and **LI̯A 'to meet' ~
'to separate' (cf. lat. <u>altus</u> 'high' ~ 'deep', <u>altum</u> 'heaven' ~
'ocean').

Thus, **DZIŲ appears in its <u>passive</u> aspect (i.e. 'to follow')
in 循 KD 1142 ˳ziuĕn <dz- and 導 KD 1112 tśiuĕn, and its active
sense in 率, 帥 KD 922, 1137 śiuĕt< -d and 述 KD 903 dźʿiuĕt <
dʿ- 'to follow' (but also 'transmit', 'state', 'expound'). **LIA
preserves both of its meanings in 離 KD 533-4 ˳ljie< -a (cf. the
controversial title of Ch'ü Yüan's famous poem, the "Li Sao", which
can mean either "Falling into Trouble" or "Tristesse de la séparation";
see <u>TP</u>, 1931, 93, P. Pelliot's remarks on H.A. Giles' preface to
Dr. Lim's translation). The same root appears, I believe, in KD 551
連 ˳liän 'connect in a row' (passive, neuter) and KD 548 列 liät
'to classify', '<u>dis</u>connect in a row'.

The final -N in these cases seems to supply the root with an
'introvertive' aspect with the action reluctantly moving away from
the subject to the object, while -T has a strong 'extravertive'
connotation, accelerating the movement toward its terminus, the
object. (Some of the final -T can doubtless be connected with an
original pronominal object ti 之.) Another good example of this
distinction is the radical ***PI-U, which combines such meanings
as 'to divide, together, part, mate'. It deposited itself in:
KD 29 piuᴀn 'to be divided', bʿiuᴀn 'part'; KD 689 半 puân
'half', <u>vs.</u> KD 682 /\ pʷat 'to divide', KD 728 別 bʿiät 'to
separate'.

In an earlier note the writer has suggested that the final
-t of 曰 KD 1346 jiʷɐt 'to say, speak' (always used in a strong,
'active' sense) represents an ancient pronominal object suffixed
to the 'verbal' root 'to speak'. This root must appear in its pure
form in 于 KD 1317 jiu< g- and undoubtedly underlies the following:

    謂 KD 1309 jʷeiˀ< g- 'to say'

    語 KD 1281 ngiʷoˀ 'to talk'

    言 KD 234 ˳ngiɐn 'word'

    云 KD 291 ˳jiuən< g- 'to say', 'is said'.

The last two words ending in -N are always used in ancient
texts in a 'passive' sense, and 云 jiuən is distinctly used as a
'neuter' form of 曰 jiʷɐt (e.g. 子曰 'the Master says:' 子云 ...
'it is said by the Master that...').

Karlgren suggests an archaic *ml- for KD 1315 文 $_c$mi̯uən 'lines, strokes, written character' on the basis of KD 553 吝 li̯ĕn ^{ɔ} where 文 is phonetic. In the light of the foregoing discussion one can, I believe, connect 文 $_c$mi̯uən < **bli̯uən with KD 1321 聿 i̯uĕt < **bli̯uĕt 'stylus'. We would have thus **bli̯uĕt 'that which <u>writes</u>', **bli̯uən 'that which <u>is written</u>.'

NOTES ON CHINESE MORPHOLOGY AND SYNTAX, IV

The <u>Xk</u> Form of Some Chinese Particles

Several particles appear in ancient texts under two forms: one ending in a vowel, the other in a <u>-k</u>. As the two forms were represented by entirely different characters (belonging mostly to the class of so-called 'borrowed' characters), the close relationship between the two has seldom been recognized, and whenever observed, the similarity of form was dismissed either by postulating 'dialectical variations' or as one word being 'cognate' to the other, without discussing the question which of the two is the original or radical form.

The following six pairs of particles are frequently met with in archaic texts and not a single one of the twelve characters can be explained as a dialectical variation from standard archaic Chinese as they all occur indiscriminately in authentic Chou texts, the two members of a pair being found often on the same page, or even together in one sentence.

1. 如 KD 944 $_c$ńźi̯^{w}o < ń- <u>vs.</u> 若 KD 938 ńźi̯ak < ń- 'like, as, if'

2. 誰 KD 1265A **$_c$zʷi̯e < d̑-a̱ (and 疇 KD 899 $_c$d̑^{c}i̯əu < d-) <u>vs.</u> 孰 KD 912 źi̯uk < d̑- 'who, what, which'

3. 苟 KD 484 kə̯u 'if' <u>vs.</u> 或 KD 118 ɣʷək 'if, someone'

4. 烏 KD 1288 ~ 胡 KD 91 $_c$ɣuo < g^c 'how, why' <u>vs.</u> 惡 KD 209 ˙uo ^{ɔ} < -g (˙âk) 'how'

5. 無 KD 1289 $_c$mi̯u 'not' <u>vs.</u> 莫 KD 683 mâk 'none'

6. 也 KD 223 ^{c}i̯a < d- 'emphatic particle' <u>vs.</u> 亦 KD 187

iäk < z- 'even, also'. (也 eventually came to mean 'also' in the
colloquial.)

     After careful analysis of the contexts in which the terms
with a final -k occur, one must come to the conclusion that the Xk
form was used in archaic Chinese whenever a <u>pronominal</u> or <u>optative</u>
其 ᴄgᶜji was implied before the following word. Thus 或 means in
most cases 'if one', i.e., it takes the place of 苟其 *kəu- *gi >
γʷək; 莫 equals 'no-<u>one</u>', 若 equals 如其 'if, as <u>one</u>' or 'if +
(<u>gi</u> + verb) equals optative or subjunctive form of the verb, and 惡,
differs from 胡 in that it always precedes a verb expressing subjective
opinion or option. 孰 in the majority of cases equals 'que<u>l</u>, which,
which <u>one</u>' as opposed to 誰 'who, qui'.

     These particles can, therefore, be considered as forms
produced by the synaeresis of corresponding vowel terms with a
following *<u>gi</u>.

The Etymology of 筆 pi 'stylus, brush'

Under No. 1321 Karlgren gives the old pronunciation of 聿 yü, lü, the phonetic of pi and itself an old term for 'stylus', as i̯uĕt < bl- ? (pi < pi̯ĕt < pl- ?). Ancient dictionaries, notably the Shuo wen, have preserved for us several dialectical terms for 'stylus' current in ancient China: pi 筆 in the state of Ch'in; yü 聿 in Ch'u; fu < KD 47 pi̯uət 弗 in Yen; and pu-lü 不聿 *puət-li̯uĕt in Wu and Shu. The modern reading lü for 聿 , its being phonetic in 律 lü < li̯uĕt, and the ancient Wu pronunciation fully justify Karlgren's reconstruction of an archaic *bl- in this group. (Attention to the archaic dialectical terms has been called by P. Pelliot in the TP; the exact reference escapes me for the moment.)

It is to be observed, however, that the fan-ch'ieh of i̯uĕt 聿 give for the initial term characters with archaic *d-, *z- 余 KD 1322, 允 KD 293, and that the Shih ming, a third century A.D. dictionary of popular etymology, equates pi 筆 with 述, KD 903 dz'i̯uĕt 'to transmit, expound, state'. (CF. also Yen Shih-ku's commentary to the Chi-chiu chang, ch. IV, where 律 li̯uĕt is explained by 率 KD 922 s^{w}i' > -d, ṣi̯uĕt and by 述 .) Note, moreover, 聿 i̯uĕt's etymological connections with 惟 KD 1265 *ᴅd^{w}i and 遂 KD 827 z^{w}i' < dz-, as well as with 自 KD 1091 dz'i'. (Cf. as an interesting parallel to our group 鼻 KD 716 b'ji', a cognate of dz'i'; for a possible archaic final in dz'i', Cf. 臬 KD 666 ngiet, ngi̯ät, where 自 dz'i' is phonetic according to the Shuo wen.) It is also probable that 聿 is phonetic, and not co-signific, in 肆 si', *si̯ĕt (a rare pronunciation), which is semantically connected with

---

*[Serial published by P.A.B. in the same manner as his HTHYFC (No. 9). There are only numbers 1 through 4, dated August 1934 to September 1935. "KD" denotes "Karlgren's Dictionary", i.e., Bernhard Karlgren, Analytic Dictionary of Chinese and Sino-Japanese, Paris, 1923. -- Ed.]

突 KD 498 t'uət, d'uət.

It seems, therefore, safe to reconstruct for ancient i̯uĕt 聿
an archaic initial *S-, Z-, D-, DZ-, and connect thus i̯uĕt with 書
KD 1187 ꜀si͡ʷo 'to write', 'book', as well as with 述 dź꜀i̯uĕt.
The *bl- (or *ml-?) prefix, in a term designating the instrument of
writing, I am tempted to interpret, in the light of the morphological
principles so brilliantly set forth in S. N. Wolfenden's Tibeto-
Burman Linguistic Morphology, b- as a subjective prefix, -l- as a
directive infix (cf. particularly pp. 25, 45, 50).

In all probability the original root which appears in the
archaic name of the stylus **B-L-S(D)i̯uĕt would be found in 鋭
KD 1138 i̯͡ʷâi < d-d, 劇 *si͡ʷ̈ad (cf. Kuang Ya II) 'sharp', 'to sharpen'.

KD NOTES 2   August 1934

The Archaic Initials of KD 529

Under No. 529 in his Analytic Dictionary Karlgren lists the
following characters in which 里 ꜀lji is 'phonetic': 娌 ꜀lji, 理
꜀lji, 裡 ꜀lji, 鯉 ꜀lji, 狸 ꜀lji; and one character 埋 ꜀mai in
which 里 is 'co-signific.'

The ꜀lji phonetic group presents, however, some interesting
peculiarities disregarded by Karlgren. While "lji" seems to be the
predominant 'phonetic' as shown by the obvious additions to the list
(瘦 , 鋰 , 運 , 緷 , 艃 , 魖 , 蜸 , etc., all pronounced 里
꜀lji or 釐 ꜀lji KD 535), six members of the group offer a curious
alternation of initials.

1. 悝 (also pronounced "li"). Fan-ch'ieh: 苦 (or 枯) 回
= *꜀k꜀uâi. That 里 is not 'co-signific' is shown by another
character.

2. 趣 (a) *꜀k uâi (枯 回); (b) *꜀ɣâi < g- (何 開).

3. 㾗 , a rare character, where 少 is signific. 謨 皆 =
*꜀mai.

4. 㘴 , another rare character. 莊 皆 = *꜀tsai < ts-.

5. 耟 , a variant of 耜 ^{c}zi < dz-, KD 180.

6. 裡 , for which the rhyming dictionaries give five different readings:

       a. $_{c}$lji

       b. *^{c}zi < dz- (象齒 ; 詳里); = 耜

       c. *$_{c}$tṣai < ts- (莊皆)

       d. *$_{c}$ɣai < g^{c}- (pr. 言皆)

       e. *^{c}k^{c}ji (口巳); = 杞 . Observe that in Karlgren's
series No. 319 巳 is possible 'phonetic' in 妃 $_{c}$p^{c}j^{w}ei and 配
p^{c}uâi^{ɔ}.

There is no doubt that in all these characters 里 lji is
'phonetic' and not 'co-signific', and 少里 $_{c}$mai indicates that in 埋
$_{c}$mai, the 'title-word' must also be considered as 'phonetic'. 霾
$_{c}$mai, with 貍 $_{c}$lji as 'phonetic', also shows that there must have
been somewhere in the KD 529 group a 'labial + l' initial consonant
complex. This is further substantiated by the various ancient names
of the fox: 貍 $_{c}$lji, 豾 *$_{c}$b^{c}ji, 狉 *$_{c}$p^{c}j^{w}i, 貊 *$_{c}$p^{c}j^{w}i, 豽
$_{c}$lâi (cf. the <u>Chi Chiu chang</u>, ch. IV). The two characters pronounced
$_{c}$k^{c}uâi and the *^{c}k^{c}ji of 裡 point furthermore to an archaic
'guttural + l'. The 里 series thus shows the same irregularity
which is observable in the initials of 翏 KD 546, K- ~ L- ~ M-, and
it should be possible, therefore, to postulate in some words of the
group an archaic **KLI: KLAI ~ **MLI: MLAI.

For the curious appearance of *zi, **tsai twice in the series
<u>cf.</u> Chang Ping-lin's interesting suggestion as to the possible
connection of 里 , 來 with 矣 *zi (新方言 ch. I).

KD NOTES, 3   October 1934

<u>Shih Ming</u> 'Etymologies'

One of the heretofore neglected sources for the reconstruction
of archaic Chinese is the <u>Shih Ming</u>, a dictionary of popular (or
school?) etymology of the 3rd century A.D. attributed to Liu Hsi of the

Han dynasty. The word material in this dictionary is classified
according to the <u>Erh Ya</u> categories and most of the definitions are
based on homophony with the usual curiosities of <u>lucus a non lucendo</u>
etymologies. The phonetic equivalences do not seem to be arbitrary
and far-fetched, however, and, with the great number of homophones
available in Chinese even at that early date, must have been quite
accurate. In most cases where the two members of the phonetic equation
do not seem to correspond perfectly according to the pronunciation
of the 6th century as reconstructed by Karlgren, the divergence seems
to confirm some of the hypotheses advanced in the reconstruction of
archaic Chinese, especially those concerning initial consonant
groups. The dictionary contains also several interesting observations
on dialectical variations in pronunciations which may serve to
supplement the material in the <u>Fang Yen</u>.

    The few following notes are based chiefly on phonetic
equations from the first of the eight <u>chüan</u> of the <u>Shih Ming</u>:

    1. 天 KD 996 ꞈtʻien 'heaven'. Pronounced 顯 KD 150 ꞈχien
in the provinces of Yü, Ssŭ, Yen, and Chi, and 坦 KD 966 ꞈtʻân
in Chʻing and Hsü. The first pronunciation indicates clearly that
天 ꞈtʻien is phonetic in 祅 ꞈχien, and not co-signific (according
to KD 996) and suggests an interesting dialectical shift of dental ~
guttural initials.

    2. 風 KD 18 ꞈpi̯ung < m (phonetic ꞈbʻi̯ᵂɐm). In the first of
the two regions indicated above, 泛 KD 60 pʻi̯ᵂɐm, in the second, 放
KD 25, 26 pi̯ᵂangꞋ. Karlgren's theory of pi̯um > pi̯ung through dis-
similation (cf. KD p. 30) must now take cognizance of a very ancient
dialectical divergence. (Incidentally 風 *pi̯ᵂɐm may be phonetic in
嵐 KD 36 ꞈlâm, which would pre-suppose an archaic *pl-, *bl- in
this group.)

    3. 年 KD 699 ꞈnien 'year, harvest'. Curiously enough, the
<u>Shih Ming</u> equates this character with 進 KD 1265 tsi̯ĕnꞋ, thus
supporting the <u>Shuo Wên</u>, which gives 千 KD 1076 ꞈtsʻien as the
<u>phonetic</u> (not-co-signific!) in <u>nien</u> 年 . In this case 幸 KD 664
ni̯ăp must also be 'phonetic' or 'cognate' in 妾 KD 1071 tsʻi̯ăp and
執 KD 1222 t́śi̯əp < t́-.

4. The equation 歲 KD 831 si$_\curvearrowright^{W..}$ăt = 越 KD 1348 ji$_\curvearrowright^{W}$ɐt< g- and similar ones may throw additional light on the nature of the lost initial guttural.

5. 霾 mai = 晦 χuâi$^{\circ}$ KD 607 seems to substantiate further the hypothetical mχ- in KD 529.

6. 坤 KD 868 ｃk'uən = 順 KD 1261 dź$^{\,c}$ｃiuĕn$^{\circ}$< d^c- seems to indicate that 申 ｃsi̯ĕn ~ 神 dź^{c}i̯ĕn< d^c is really <u>phonetic</u> in 坤 .

7. 鼻 KD 716 b'ji$^{\circ}$ = 嚊 *dzi$_\curvearrowright^{W..}$ai seems to support my contention that b'ji$^{\circ}$ is a real cognate of 自 dz^{c}i$^{\circ}$ (<u>KD Notes</u> 2).

8. 老 KD 515 ｃlâu = 朽 KD 358 ｃχi̯əu (ph. ｃk'âu) indicates clearly that the ancient lexicographers were right in believing that 考 ｃk'âu and 老 ｃlâu were originally one and the same character and that an archaic initial *kl- must be postulated for both phonetic groups.

KD NOTES 4   September 1935

The Archaic Initial *<u>lng-</u>

The double pronunciation of KD 568 樂 lak ~ ngâk has long aroused, in those interested in the reconstruction of archaic Chinese, the suspicion that words with initial *ng- could have been used as "phonetics" in characters with initial *l-.

Such is apparently the case with two common characters usually classified as "logical compounds" (會意), i.e., as consisting of two "co-signific" elements:

1. 魯 KD 580 ｃluo, explained as "fish 魚 (unable to) speak 曰 " = 'simple', 'stupid'.

2. 牢 KD 673 ｃlâu 'pen, fold', '<u>prison</u>' = "enclosure 宀 for 牛 oxen."
Should we suppose an archaic initial *lng- in 魚 KD 1332 ｃngi̯^{W}o and in 牛 KD 673 ｃngi̯əu, 魚 and 牛 could have very well served as "phonetics" in ｃ<u>luo</u> and ｃ<u>lâu</u>.

A little excursion into synonymy, a field heretofore neglected in the reconstruction of ancient Chinese pronunciation, will help us in making the supposed *lng- a historical reality and not a mere conjecture, at least in the case of the second word under consideration.

There exist, attested in ancient Chinese texts, several other words meaning 'prison' (which is one of the common meanings of 牢 ｃlâu), among which those most in use are the following:

1. 獄 KD 1336 ngi̯^{w}ok
2. 圉 KD 664 ｃngi̯^{w}o (also meaning 'enclosure', 'groom')
3. 圄 KD 1281 ｃngi̯^{w}o

*Ngi̯^{w}o seems to be the common root of these three; it is connected by the Chinese lexicographer with the root represented by 御, 禦 KD 1334 ngi̯^{w}o？ and 敔 *ｃngi̯^{w}o meaning 'to restrain', 'to hinder'. 牛 ｃngi̯əu cannot, therefore, be considered as a mere "phonetic accident" in 宀 + 牛 = 牢 ｃlâu 'prison'.

The "Yüeh ling" 月令 section of the Li Chi, as well as the Shuo Wen and Shih Ming V, supply us, however, with a fourth synonym for 'prison' (most probably a Ch'in word), the missing link bridging the gap between *ngi̯^{w}o ~ *nguo and *ｃlâu. This is the term:

4. 令圄 KD 558, 1281 ｃlieng-ｃngi̯^{w}o 'prison'.

We have undoubtedly in this binom an extremely rare case of a word "spelled out" by means of an archaic fan-ch'ieh method which unmistakably reveals the nature of the initial consonantal group in the archaic Chinese word for 'prison'. *Lieng-ngi̯^{w}o can, indeed, represent only *liengi̯^{w}o ~*lienguo > **lnguo, the parent word of both *ngi̯^{w}o and *lâu.

**Lnguo's connection with the KD 1280-1281 series 五 , 吾 opens interesting possibilities for the reconstruction of the archaic Chinese terms for 'five' and 'speak'. An archaic *lng- in KD 1280 五 ｃnguo 'five' would tighten the bonds that link it with Tibetan ᭴ lnga 'five', while in 1281 吾 ~ 語 ｃngi̯^{w}o？ 'speak', 'speech', an initial *lng- reunites the following word-family:

1. 語 *l-ｃngi̯^{w}o？
2. 言 234 ngi̯ɐn, in the light of the preceding, undoubtedly the "phonetic" in 戀 KD 590 ｃli̯^{w}an ~ luân. The *bl- consonantal complex of the latter makes the role of 言 less incomprehensible in 詈 ljie？< -a and 罰 b'i̯^{w}ɐt and connects 言 with 辯 734 ｃb'iän 'to argue'.
3. 論 KD 583 ｃluən？ 'to discourse', 'discourse' < *lnguən ?, Cf. 云 KD 291 ｃji̯uən < g 'to be said'.

Chinese Zoographic Names as Chronograms

Harvard Journal of Asiatic Studies, 5 (1940), 128-136.

The chronogrammatic use of some of the terms comprising the Chinese animal cycle in proper names, several examples of which have been discussed on the pages of this journal (*HJAS* 3. 243-53; 4. 273-5), appears, after further study of the subject, to be of much greater antiquity than heretofore supposed. It will be remembered that the majority of instances of such use of cyclical terms was culled from the onomasticon of the fifth and sixth centuries of our era, with the earliest example (in a nomadic milieu) dated in the last decade of the third century. Several corrections to be made to our list necessitate a brief review of the roll of the historical personalities with chronogrammatic names or nicknames enumerated in " Marginalia " 2 and 6. The surest cases appear to be the following:

Rat: KAO Huan, referred to as " rat " by YÜ-WÊN T'ai, born in 496 A. D., a rat year.[1]

Tiger: SHIH Hu, born 294;[2] Ts'AO Hu, b. 438; HSIAO Ying-ch'ou, spoken of as " tiger " in a prophetic ditty, b. 462; CHOU T'ieh-hu, b. 510, a " metal tiger " year; possibly LI Ling, *tzŭ* Hu-fu, b. 390.

The name of HSIEH Hu-tzŭ (*HJAS* 4. 274, paragraph 4) is to

---

[1] We may have a chronogram, rather than a derisive epithet, in " son of a rat " applied by SUN Ch'üan to KUNG-SUN Yüan, the ruler of Liao-tung, in 233 A. D. (*San kuo chih* 47 comment., quoting a *Chiang piao chuan*). We unfortunately do not know the year of his birth. He was a small boy at the time when his uncle KUNG-SUN Kung succeeded Yüan's father, K'ang, sometime between 208 and 220. In 228 he was old enough to dispossess his uncle of the governorship. It is not, therefore, impossible that he was born in 208, a rat year. The quotation presents, however, a minor chronological difficulty: SUN Ch'üan speaks of himself as having lived sixty years, yet in 233 he was but 51 years old. Either the speech was delivered on some other occasion and someone else is meant by " son of a rat " or " sixty years " is to be understood in the sense of " going on sixty."

[2] Read 294 A. D. for 296 A. D. in *HJAS* 3.252, line 6.

be deleted from the list. Dying in 491 at the age of 51 *sui*, Hu-tzŭ
was born in 440 or 441 A. D., in a " dragon " or " serpent " year,
and not in a year of the tiger as we had incorrectly stated.[3]

Dragon: LIU T'êng, *tzŭ* Ch'ing lung, b. 464; HSIAO Yen,
" dragon " in a prophetic verse, b. 464; HSIAO Tsê, baby name
Lung êrh, b. 440; LU Ch'ang-hêng, nicknamed Lung tzŭ, b. 536;
LIU Ch'iu if born in 500; [4] possibly SHIH Lê, *tzŭ* Chi lung, if born
in 272.

Dog: possibly YÜ-WÊN T'ai, if born in 506.

Pig: HSIAO Pao-chüan, spoken of as " wild pig," b. 483.[5]

Many other seemingly cyclical designations used as proper
names proved upon investigation to have no chronogrammatic significance, at least so far as the year of birth of the given individual
was concerned. Thus, for instance, TS'AO Piao [6] 曹彪, *tzŭ* Chu hu

---

[3] The unpardonable blunder that we committed in computing the date of his birth
was caused by an inadvertent transposition in our notes, where for his age at the
time of his death (51 *sui*) was substituted that of his son Shih-tsun 世遵 whose
biography immediately follows that of Hu-tzŭ and who died aged 42 *sui*. The mistake was subsequently corrected only partially and our humiliating error in making him
" a son of the tiger " resulted.

[4] In *HJAS* 4. 274, line 16, read 554 A. D. for 534 A. D. LIU Ch'iu died in the first
year of Kung ti of Western Wei. In line 18 on the same page delete the comma
after " young."

[5] We may have a case of a " son of the pig " in an allusion to YANG Yung, the
eldest son of YANG Chien. *Sui shu* 23 records the story of the apparition, sometime
about the end of the K'ai-huang era, of a big hog, followed by ten little pigs, to
some Buddhist monks. This was supposed to forecast Yung's downfall (he had at least
10 sons). It is not improbable that the unfortunate prince was born in 567 A. D., a
pig year, and was thus only two years older than YANG Kuang. The point cannot be
pressed, however, for in the next entry in the same text YANG Hsiu, another brother,
is also alluded to as a pig.

[6] *Piao* " striped like a tiger " is not used chronogrammatically here, but possibly so
in the name of WANG Piao-chih, *tzŭ* Shu-wu 叔武 (especially if *wu* is a T'ang substitution for *hu* " tiger "), *Chin shu* 76, who died in 377 A. D., at the age of 73 *sui*.
He was thus born in 305, possibly 306, which was a tiger year. *Pao* 豹 " leopard "
was used as a chronogram (probably for " tiger ") as early as the second century
A. D. Cf. the biography of KUNG-SUN Tu 公孫度, *San kuo chih* 8, whose baby
name it had been. Tu found protection in the home of a distant kinsman who became
attached to him because his own son whom he had lost was also born in a " leopard "
year and likewise named Pao. I am indebted for this reference to my colleague, Dr.
D. VON DEN STEINEN.

朱虎 " red tiger," seemed at first a promising " son of a tiger." His biography in *San kuo chih* 20 does not give the date of his birth, but according to *San kuo chih* 29 (biography of the diviner CHU Chien-p'ing), he was 57 *sui* at the time of his forced suicide in 251 A. D.: he was thus born about 195, while the nearest red tiger year is 186.

A true " son of the horse," however, was LIU Chün 劉駿 (pht. Shih-tsu Hsiao-wu huang-ti 430–453–464; *Sung shu* 6, *Nan shih* 2).[7] His name means " noble horse " and 430 was indeed a horse year.[8] That the chronogram is not accidental seems to be supported by the fact that his younger brother (by another of the wives of LIU I-lung[9]) LIU Shuo 鑠, prince of Nan-p'ing (pht. Mu, *Sung shu* 72, *Nan shih* 14) was known to members of the family as Wu yang 烏羊 (*Sung shu* 99, *Nan shih* 14). *Yang* " sheep " is undoubtedly chronogrammatic as the prince was born in 431, a sheep year; the date is attested by the *Nan shih*, which states that he was nine (Chinese) years old at the time of his enfeoffment in 439, and by *Sung shu* 72, which gives his age as 23 *sui* in 453 when he was poisoned by LIU Chün.[10]

SUN T'êng 孫騰, *Pei Ch'i shu* 18, *Pei shih* 54, 481-548 A. D., may have borne a chronogrammatic name. His *tzŭ* was Lung ch'iao 龍雀 " dragon-like birdling," the second character possibly referring to the date of his birth 481 A. D., which was a year of the cock.[11]

---

[7] Born Sept. 19, 430; asc. throne May 20, 453; died July 12, 464.

[8] In his *tzŭ* Hsiu-lung 休龍, *lung* " dragon " is probably to be taken as an epithet of " horse," " dragon-like (horse) " or " dragon among horses," and not as confusing in any way the chronogrammatic designation, while *Hsiu* is the common element in the names of all the sons of LIU I-lung.

[9] Pht. T'ai-tsu Wên huang-ti, 407-424-453. Asc. throne Sept. 17, 424; murdered by his eldest son, March 16, 453. *Sung shu* 5, *Nan shih* 2.

[10] On Sept 17, 453. *Nan shih* 2, *Sung shu* 6. He was the fourth son of LIU I-lung. The nickname of the second son Hsün 濬 which was Hu-t'ou 虎頭 (" tiger's head ") is not chronogrammatic; he was born in 429, a serpent year; *Sung shu* 99, *Nan shih* 14. Shuo's year of birth was a " white sheep," and not a " black sheep," year as his nickname Wu-yang might imply.

[11] *T'ang shu* 34 gives us an example of an interesting chronogrammatic association. Emperor Hsüan-tsung was fond of cock-fighting; this was later interpreted as portending the disastrous wars of the second half of his reign as the emperor was born under

For our next illustrations of onomatological chronograms we must go back a thousand years into China's dimmer past. In *Shih chi* 67, a chapter devoted to the disciples of Confucius, Ssŭ-ma Ch'ien gives in a score of cases the age of Confucius' best-known followers in relation to that of their master. Thus, Yen Hui is said to have been thirty years Confucius' junior,[12] Chung Yu (Tzŭ-lu), nine, Tsêng Ts'an, forty-six, etc. The thirty-fifth and last of that group is Kung-sun Lung,[13] *tzŭ* Tzŭ-shih 公孫龍 子石 who, according to Ssŭ-ma Ch'ien, was fifty-three years younger than Master K'ung. If we take the traditional date of Confucius' birth as the end of 551 or the beginning of 550 B.C., fifty-three years later would bring us to 498-497 B.C. In the cyclical chronological system 497 B.C. was a *chia-ch'ên* or a dragon year. Kung-sun Lung's name, "Dragon," is thus undoubtedly chronogrammatic. His *tzŭ*, however, presents some difficulty. The onomatological rule which prescribed a close semantic parallelism between the *ming* and the *tzŭ* was followed in ancient China very strictly,[14] yet no such connection in meaning

the sign of the cock. Indeed, according to *Chiu T'ang shu* 8, he was born on Sept. 8 (*mou-yin* of the 8th month), 685 A.D., a cock year. Both *Chiu T'ang shu* 9 and *T'ang shu* 5 say, however, that he was 78 *sui* at the time of his death in the 4th month of 760, which would place the year of his birth about 683 A.D.

[12] See, however, note 21.

[13] *Chia yü* 9 has Ch'ung 龍 instead of Lung. He is to be distinguished from the famous Kung-sun Lung, the logician.

[14] This rule is well exhibited in the names of many of the other disciples. Two of them (of the Ssŭ-ma and Jan clans) have as their *ming* 耕 *kêng* "to plough" and 牛 *niu* "ox" in their *tzŭ*, indicating that, at least in the state of Lu, ploughing in the sixth century B.C. was done with oxen. In Tsêng Ts'an's name, Ts'an 參 obviously stands for *ts'an* with Dt. 187 "third horse in a team," as indicated by his *tzŭ*, Tzŭ-yü 輿 "chariot" (on *ts'an*, cf. H. G. Creel, *Studies in Early Chinese Culture*, 186-7). Tzŭ-lu 子路 (with *lu* "road"), the cognomen of one of the famous of Confucius' followers, suggests that his *ming*, 由 *yu* < *D'uG must be taken as equivalent to 迪 *ti* < *D'iek "path," *yu* being anciently a cognate of 道 *tao* < *DâG "road," "way." Hui 回, the name of his favorite disciple Yen Hui, must be interpreted as if the character were written with Dt. 85 (*hui* "whirlpool") to match his adult name, Tzŭ-yüan 淵 "abyss," "whirlpool." The ancient meaning of 及 (with Dt. 9) *chi*, now used only as a proper name, must have been "solicitous," "anxious" (as if written with the near homonym 急 *chi*, which has the same phonetic), for in the *tzŭ* of both Confucius' grandson K'ung Chi and his disciple Yen Chi it is matched by 思 *ssŭ* "to think," "to reflect." 蜀 *shu* in the name of the disciple Shih-tso Shu must

of *lung* " dragon " and *shih* " stone " is immediately perceptible, especially if we take *lung* as a chronogram pure and simple.[15]

Another disciple's name, on the other hand, would indicate that our interpretation of " dragon " in KUNG-SUN Lung's name is not based on a mere chronological coincidence. Thirtieth in the *Shih chi* list stands the name of LIANG Chan 梁鱣, *tzŭ* Shu-yü 叔魚. The name of that worthy, when used as a common noun, designated in ancient China some cyprinoid fish and, according to P'EI Yin, LIANG Chan was also known as LIANG Li 鯉 " Carp." [16] It is well known that the early Chinese believed the carp to be a sort of embryo dragon capable of assuming the shape of the king of waters upon reaching a certain age or after passing a difficult test.[17] It is thus not unlikely that in the cycle of the Twelve Animals the carp may have occasionally taken the place of the dragon.[18] Now LIANG Chan or LIANG Li was twenty-nine years younger than Confucius [19] and must have been born in 522-521 B. C. And 521 was a *kêng-ch'ên* or dragon year.

If " Carp " LIANG's name is chronogrammatic, there immediately arises the question whether a more famous " Carp," Confucius' son K'UNG Li, *tzŭ* Po-yü, did not owe his name to the fact that he was born in a dragon year. According to tradition, Confucius married at 19 *sui* [20] and Li was born in the year following the marriage. The master's first-born received his name in grateful remembrance of a carp sent as a present by the Duke of Lu. This legend has always been suspect as there is no evidence of Con-

be an old form of 燭 *chu* " torch," " illuminate," as it is parallel to 明 *ming* " bright " in his *tzŭ*. 瞿 *chü* in the name of SHANG Chü must stand for the same character with Dt. 75 *chü* " rake," " twisted roots of a tree " to be parallel to his *tzŭ* Tzŭ mu 木 " tree." These examples can be easily multiplied.

[15] Should *lung*, then, be taken as equivalent to *lung* (with Dt. 170 or 32) " tumulus," " ridge " or *lung* (with Dt. 112) " to grind " ?

[16] In *Shuo wên* 11B, the two characters are used to define each other.

[17] Such as successfully negotiating the passage through the Lung-mên gorge of the Yellow River.

[18] Note that in the early Turkish cycle *balïq* " fish " takes the place of the dragon (*HJAS* 3.252).

[19] *Chia yü* 9 makes him 39 years younger than the Master.

[20] As a village youth, and not a tradition-bound member of an old house as he is painted in legend, he may have married a year or even two earlier.

fucius having enjoyed such high esteem at the court of his
sovereign so early in his career. As K'ung Li was born in 533 or
532 B. C. and 533 was a *mou-ch'ên* or dragon year, the likeliest
explanation of his cognomen is that he was named " carp," i. e.
" baby dragon," from the fact that he was conceived or came into
the world under the sign of that animal.[21]

We have been unable to find any other examples of the use of
Animal Cycle designations as names in that early period. While
many well-known individuals of the Ch'un-ch'iu period bore zoographic names, it is in most cases impossible to ascertain their
exact dates of birth.[22] It is also unlikely that the names of all the
animals of the cycle should have been used as chronograms, for
several of them, as one may infer from later usage, must have
already had unpleasant or uncomplimentary connotations,[23] and
it would seem that only " dragon," " tiger," and " horse " were
considered suitable or auspicious as proper names.

Confucius himself was probably born under the sign of the dog,
551 B. C. being a *kêng-hsü* year. There is no direct evidence that
the Master ever considered his fate as being in any way determined by this astrological fact, but it is interesting to note that

---

[21] K'ung Li died in his fiftieth year, in 484 or 483 B. C. According to *Lun yü* 11,
he pre-deceased Confucius' favorite Yen Hui. Yet if we accept the traditional chronological data on Hui (30 years younger than Confucius, died at 32 *sui*), Hui's death
must have taken place about 488 B. C. The only way out of the difficulty is to emend
30 to 39 in *Shih chi* 67 and have Yen Hui die in 481 B. C., the year of " the capture
of the unicorn." *Chia yü* 10 is well off the mark in making Duke Ting (509-495)
send his condolences to Confucius upon the passing of Yen Hui. We suspect that the
brazenness of Hui's father in requesting the Master's carriage to make an outer coffin
for his son can only be explained by the supposition that they were close relatives,
i. e. that Yen Yu was an uncle or cousin of Confucius, a brother or nephew of his
mother, *née* Yen. This would explain in a way the inordinate affection that Confucius
felt for Hui. We must remember that all through his childhood and early youth
Confucius was entirely ignorant of his being a scion, alleged or real, of the house of
K'ung, and knew, therefore, no other relatives but those on his mother's side, members
of the Yen family. Note that his closest friend, Tzǔ-lu, was also related to the Yen
through marriage.

[22] One of the earliest is " boar," the given name of Duke Kung of Ch'in (reigned
608-604 B. C.), *Shih chi* 5, *So-yin*.

[23] " Dog " became early a term of abuse, " hare " usually connotes lewdness, " pig,"
wildness and grossness of character.

3

he showed a rather pronounced concern for dogs. Among the few fragments of comments on the structure of Chinese characters attributed to Confucius and preserved chiefly in the *Shuo wên*,[24] two are on the term " dog ": one on the pictographic nature of the character *ch'üan* 犬, the other, a phonetic gloss on *kou* 狗, interpreted as equivalent to *k'ou* 叩 (*Shuo wên* 10A). *Chia yü* and *Li chi* 2B record the incident of the touching care Confucius took in burying his dog.[25] Finally, we may point to the famous description of his appearance given by a man of Chêng to Tzŭ-kung after the discomfiture suffered by the Master and his faithful in Sung. Confucius accepted as perfectly true the last part of it where he was said to resemble in his forlorn attitude " a dog of a house in mourning " 喪家之狗 (*Shih chi* 47).[26]

Evidence also seems to indicate that in popular belief cyclical animals were considered to be the real progenitors of individuals born in the year dedicated to them, capable of endowing their sons with at least some of their own physical characteristics. *Shih chi* 8 and *Han shu* 1B insist that Kao-tsu was conceived by his mother from a dragon, his divine origin being stamped on his " dragon forehead."[27] Kao-tsu's year of birth is a matter of conjecture. According to Fu Tsan, the commentator on the *Han shu*, Kao-tsu was 53 *sui* at the time of his death in 195 B. C. (*Han shu* 1B), but Hsü Kuang asserts that he was already forty-eight in 209 B. C.,[28] while Huang-fu Mi says that he was 63 *sui* at the time of

---

[24] The quotations from the *Shuo wên* are gathered together in *K'ung tzŭ chi yü* 5.

[25] While the *Chia yü* text is not necessarily the original one, the order of Confucius' words in it appears to be preferable to that of the *Li chi* version. The last seven characters in the latter form an obvious afterthought, derived from the opening of Confucius' speech in *Chia yü* and loosely added to the original paragraph.

[26] Cf. *Han shih wai chuan* 9 for the explanation of Confucius' considering the comparison a compliment.

[27] Cf. H. H. Dubs, *The History of the Former Han Dynasty*, 1. 28-9.

[28] Cf. Dubs, *op. cit.*, 37. As proved by Dr. Dubs, Kao-tsu was of such low origin that he originally had no given name. It is even doubtful, in our opinion, that he even had a surname, Liu 劉 being probably a nickname given to him or to his father, possibly meaning " dagger " or " *sicarius*," " spadassin " (the ancient meaning of *liu* was " to kill," " sword "). Cf. Dubs, 34-5, on the legend of the sword, Kao-tsu's proud possession, supposedly inherited from his father. It would be interesting in this connection to investigate certain alleged surnames of ancient Chinese who rose up from

his death and was born in 256 B. C. (*Shih chi* 8, 63 being corrected to 62 by HANG Shih-chün, one of the Ch'ien-lung editors of SSŬ-MA Ch'ien's work). The evidence, then, would seem to favor 257-256 B. C. as the year of Kao-tsu's birth and there is no doubt that the emphasis put on dragon omens in the legends of his early life was to a great degree determined by chronogrammatic associations, as 257 B. C., the year of his birth or conception, was a *chia-ch'ên* or dragon year. His elder contemporary Ch'in Shih huang-ti was born in the first month [29] of a tiger year, 259 B. C., dying in 210 B. C. at the age of 50 *sui* (Hsü Kuang in *Shih chi* 6).[29a] According to *T'ung chih* 4, he had "a tiger's mouth," a characteristic undoubtedly popularly believed to be inherited from his supernatural parent, rather than being descriptive of his political voracity.[30]

Taken singly, each of our examples of the chronogrammatic significance of zoographic names is not conclusive, but together they form a sufficient nucleus of evidence for postulating the popular use of the Animal Cycle in China as early as the sixth century before our era.

---

among the nameless masses. We believe, for example, that the name of P'ÊNG Yüeh 彭越, one of Kao-tsu's famous generals, is undoubtedly to be taken as one word, and not as consisting of the aristocratic surname P'ÊNG and the given name Yüeh. According to his biography in *Shih chi* 90 and *Han shu* 34, P'ÊNG Yüeh was a humble fisherman who later turned to banditry as a profession. His name represents the binom *Bang-Gut* or *Bang-Gi* "a kind of crab found on the lower Yangtse," usually written with the same characters (with or without Dt. 142) or with 骨 *Gut* or 其 *Gi* as the phonetic of the second and 旁 *Bang* as the phonetic of the first. "Crab" would indeed have been a very suitable nickname for a fisherman. CHUNG 仲, the surname of Tzǔ-lu, the disciple of Confucius, is also likely to be not a surname, but a mere nickname indicating that he was a second son, as all sources attest to his being of low rustic origin.

[29] Note that anciently the first month of the year was also dedicated to the tiger. The influence of the animal of the year was naturally taken to be greater should the birth of a person fall on a day or in a month of the same animal designation.

[29a] Aged 51 *sui*, according to *Shih chi* 5.

[30] *Hai* in the name of Hu-hai 胡亥, Shih huang-ti's son and successor, has no chronological significance. *Shih chi* 6 says he was 21 *sui* when he became emperor in 209 B. C. (in another place it is said he was but 13 *sui*). This is usually accepted as correct and would make 229 B. C. the year of his birth, while the nearest pig year is 226. Cf. CHAVANNES, *Mémoires historiques* 2.195, 241.

We should like, in addition, to take this opportunity for correcting a few minor, but aggravating errors in " Marginalia " 5 and 6:

On p. 263, note 155: read *yün-tou* for *wei-tou* [L. C. GOODRICH].

On p. 268: read 601 for 581 in line 9.

On p. 278: the names of Yü-wên Liang and his sons, Wên and Ming, should not be in italics, since they were put to death by Yü-wên Pin, and not by YANG Chien.

On p. 280: note 3 refers to Yü-wên Hsien, not to Yung as indicated.

On p. 281: the Hsiang-lo kung-chu, wife of WEI Shih-k'ang, was not the child of Yü-wên T'ai, but one of the seven known daughters of T'o-PA Pao-chü. The error in *Sui shu* 47 was caused by the fact that both Yü-wên T'ai and Pao-chü had the same posthumous title of Wên-ti. Cf. *Hsi Wei shu* 12.

[For pages 263, 268, 278, 280, and 281 above, read: 329, 334, 344, 347, 348. —Ed.]

Notes on Isocolometry in Early Chinese Accounts of Barbarians

Oriens, 10.1 (1957), 119-127.

In honor of Leonardo Olschki

The equidimensionalism of graphs, that unique feature of the Chinese system of writing, the syntactical structure of the Chinese language with its wondrous terseness always amenable to judicious dilation through the optional use of particles and expletives, and the traditional addiction of Chinese stylists to rhythmic parison, all these make colometry an important adjutory in the textual criticism of Chinese historical sources. A colometrical survey of texts extending over the millenium from Han to Sung, particularly that of shorter essays and of the introductory parts of longer historical accounts where the writers took special pains to array their material, reveals that Chinese historiographers had a tendency to calibrate their statements and align their data in cola of three typical lengths: the minimal, of 16 to 20 characters (henceforth referred to as "M"), the normal, of 21 to 25 graphic units (abbreviated "N"; columns of 22 and 24 characters were distinctly favored), and the oblong, of 26 to 33 characters (abbr. "O"). Closed syntactical units with a low count of characters (less than 16 in number, (abbr. "L") appear to be rare, serving chiefly as necessary complements to bring paragraphs to a desirable "standard" length, and should always be tested as to possible affiliation with dicolic or tricolic periods nearby, or else closely scrutinized as suspected interpolations or *membra disjecta*. Our survey which covered literally hundreds of passages of crucial historiographical importance convinces us that isocolometrical analysis is an almost absolute prerequisite to all formal interpretation and translation of a text.

Colometry and Paragraphing. An exemplary illustration of the value of colometry in attempting to ascertain an author's intention in marshaling his periods may be found in the opening section of Ssu-ma Ch'ien's famous chapter on the Hsiung-nu (*Shih Chi*, 110, to be compared with *Han Shu*, 94 which follows the text of the *Shih Chi* with minor variants). At first glance, the text might well be paragraphed as in De Groot's translation

(*Die Hunnen der vorchristlichen Zeit* [Berlin, 1921], pp. 1-4). We mark in parentheses the number of characters in the Chinese original: 1. The origin of the Hsiung-nu (15). 2. Under various names, they lived in the north since times immemorial, moving about with their flocks (21). 3. Enumeration of animals found in their territory (23). 4. They migrate in search of water and grass, have no walled cities or agricultural settlements, but apportion (grazing) lands. (20). 5. They have no script. Contracts are made verbally (9). 6. Their youth is early trained in riding and the use of the bow against animals (18). 7. A long paragraph describing their strong men as mounted archers, their "natural" mores as herders, huntsmen, and predatory warriors; their weapons, their headlong advances and retreats in raids, their bent on mere gain (62). 8. They know no "propriety". Food and clothing: the best going to the vigorous whom they honor, with remnants to the old and weak who are despised. They marry their fathers' and brothers' widows (51). 9. They have proper names, but no taboo on them; no clan names or cognomina (10). The above divisions are well justified syntactically and suggestions for minor revisions can easily be shrugged off on the ground that most sentence-units in the passage follow one another in loose paratactical order and precise periodization (if at all intended by the author) cannot be objectively determined in view of the paucity of commatic particles and conjunctions. From a colometric point of view, however, the paragraphing, with its haphazard sequence of "L", "M", "N", and "O" cola, becomes immediately suspect. Two or three syntactical units appear to be of the "O" type and our first attempt at re-alignment should be made on the hypothesis that the whole section is composed on that pattern. The hypothesis is substantiated forthwith, as the following table shows (see Plate A for text):

| *Shih Chi*: | 30 | 29 | 29 | 27 | 27 | 30 | 32 | 25 | Total: 229 |
| *Han Shu*: | 28 | 30 | 29 | 26 | 26 | 30 | 33 | 24 | Total: 226 |

Observe further that the first three cola of the *Han Shu* and the last three in both texts yield the same total of characters, 87 in each case, as if an effort had been made of fitting the periods into three columns of 29 characters each; and that the first three periods of the *Shih Chi* have but one supernumerary character above the same total. The two middle periods in both texts are somewhat short, although well within our limits for the "O" pattern of colometric length. Such "catalexis" is normal, but it is interesting to note that paragraph No. 4 contains the only solecistic locution in the entire text: in the *Han Shu* version, following the words ". . . (youngsters) shoot foxes and hares", instead of "to use as

food" (*yung wei shih*) of the *Shih Chi*, there appear the rather myste-
riously elliptical characters *jou shih*, "meat food" or "meat-eating", the
Chinese construction being in this case as awkward as the English
rendering would suggest. The anacoluthon was noticed by the commentator Yen Shih-ku, who lamely explained: "meaning: 'they have no
grains (*mi-su*) and only eat meat (*shih jou*)'". The *Han Shu* text may
well be defective with at least one character missing. A rough paraphrase
of the text in the light of its colometric structure follows with sentence-
units misplaced by De Groot's punctuation underlined in their proper
position:

1. Origin and names under which they lived in the north (30, 28).
2. *They move about with their flocks*; their animals, common or bizarre,
are enumerated (29, 30). 3. As nomads, they have no cities and agricultural settlements, but apportion grazing lands; *this, having no writing,
they effect by verbal contract* (29, 29). 4. Their boys early start practising
riding and the use of the bow, *so that when they reach manhood and are
able to draw the bow to the full they all become armed horsemen* (27, 26).
5. Their "natural" mores, in peace or under stress (27, 26). 6. Their
weapons; they advance or retreat, bent only on gain, *for they are ignorant
of propriety and ethical principles*. (30, 30). 7. Food and clothing, with
preference shown to the vigorous, and the aged and the weak held in low
esteem (32, 33). 8. Marriage customs; *in their undeveloped onomasticon
they use no ritual taboo on names* (one of the Chinese preventives against
the abomination of incest (25, 24). This division of the text not only
eliminates the jerkiness of "L" sentences that appear interspersed in
the former paragraphing, but ties every period together in one cogent
and well-articulated statement. Ssu-ma Ch'ien is undoubtedly utilizing
here archival material, much of it possibly verbatim, yet manages to
weld it into a rhetorically effective and logically developed whole.

Pattern and Patchwork. Some seven centuries after Ssu-ma Ch'ien, we
find the historiographers of the T'ang dynasty describing, somewhat in
the same manner, the customs of the T'u-chüeh Turks, another great
nomadic confederacy threatening China from the North, in chapters or
sections of chapters specially devoted to them (*Chou Shu*, 50, *Sui Shu*,
84, *Pei Shih*, 99). The precise date of the compilation of each of these
important sources and their filiation constitute one of the most mooted
problems in Chinese historiography. It is almost impossible to establish
with certainty which of them quotes which, except in the case of fairly
obvious interpolations by later editors of passages from the *Pei Shih*
to fill in lacunae in the *Chou Shu*. Colometric evidence leads us to be-

lieve, on the other hand, that some of the repetitions, redundancies, inconsistencies, and contradictions in the three accounts (henceforth to be referred to as C, S, and P) might be explained on the supposition that all their compilers had access to archival material of diverse character and provenience, supplied perhaps from different governmental bureaus and on stationery of different dimensions, and that the historians honestly attempted to incorporate the most significant data contained in the documents, only occasionally attempting to adjust the wording stylistically to their own chosen colometric pattern. It may well have been that they trusted their readers, who were well versed in these bureaucratic details, to identify easily the provenience of some contradictory or repetitious passage by the indelible stamp of its standard stationery length. Thus P and C show evidence of being partial to one source of information on T'u-chüeh customs written in the "O" tradition. Observe, for instance:

1. Paragraph comparing the titles of the Turkish royal pair, qaghan and qaghatun, to those of rulers of the ancient Hsiung-nu. P and C: 29. Not in S. 2. List of titles of dignitaries. C 31, P 29 (so also S). 3. Description of the rite of the mock-strangling of a newly elevated ruler. C: 25, 32, 26, total 83; P: 24 + 32 + 26 = 82; not in S. 4. Reckoning by tallies and use of arrows for credentials. C and P : 27. The P version of this paragraph will be discussed later. 5. Criminal code: P. 79 *vs.* C 53, presumably 3 *vs* 2 columns of 26 characters each. The single supernumerary may well have been the initial *"ch'i"*, *"their"*, made necessary in the larger context of the historical work. The S version has 44 (dicolic 22 ?). 6. Description of the royal holy places. C: 29 + 24 + 28 = 83; P : 28 + 24 + 27 = 79. Not in S. On that text, see Peliot, *T'oung Pao* (1928-29), 26, 212-216.

By contrast, we have:

1. A paragraph comparing the mores of the Turks with those of the Hsiung-nu in terms reminiscent of the *Shih Chi* introduction (nomadism, food, clothing, despising the aged and honoring the vigorous, shameless ignorance of "propriety"). P 46 (two perfect cola of "N" 23). C 38 (imperfect dicolic "M" 19) following the P sequence, but omitting in it 9 characters, 8 of them on food and clothing, and adding at the end a stylistically required commatic *yeh* which P must have dropped to insure the perfection of its dicolon. S reshuffles the elements of the paragraph, omits a dozen characters, including a reference to the Hsiung-nu and comes up with a period of 34, arranged in a somewhat assymetrical dicolon of 18 + 16. (See Plate B). No colometric justification for the different length of the three versions can be found in their contexts *infra* or *supra*.

2. Significantly tagged at the very end of its description of Turkish customs, C has an "M" colon of 16 characters stating that the written characters of the Turks (*shu tzǔ*) resemble those of the Hu, but that they have no knowledge of calendrical reckoning (see Plate C). The treatment of this piece of information from an "M" source is exceedingly interesting in P: there it is coupled with an "M" dicolon of 36 characters (forming 52 in all, presumably an "O" dicolon) dealing with Turkish men's and women's games, their drinking, worship of spirits and belief in shamans, "much in the same manner as that of the Hsiung-nu". Instead of the sentence on writing, S has an "L" 10 on the sacrifice of sheep and horses to Heaven in the fifth month and 38 characters corresponding to the 36 of P, but with a better parisonic reading. Its total is 48, a dicolon of "N" 24. It is obvious that S quotes correctly the original "N" source. P attempted, rather clumsily, to telescope the unwonted 16 into the original "N" 48 by substituting the 16 for S's initial "L" 10 which it could justifiably discard for it had already mentioned a fifth month sacrifice in its "O" section on "royal sacred places" (see above). The clues are unmistakable: the cautious reserve of C in leaving the 16 isolated and thus identifying it as originating in "M" environment, the perfect isocolometry of S stamping the "games and spirits" passage as being of "N" type, and the telltale parisonic slip in P. (Circled characters on Plate C illustrate the lack of balance in P.).

3. The statement "their written characters resemble (those of) the Hu" is contradicted in P and S by a phrase of three characters (*wu wên tzǔ*) as a last element in an "L" 9: "They excel in horse-riding and archery and are innately ruthless and cruel; they have no script". In P this precedes the "O" 27 passage on "reckoning by tallies and the use of arrows for credentials" (also found in C), while in S the "L" 9 forms the first half of an "N" 21 reading ". . . (they have no script) (9) but make notches on wood for credentials (4); they wait for the moon to be about full and forthwith carry out their predatory raids" (8). These last 8 characters are put by P at the end of the "O" 27 item, the entire sequence being thus 9.27.8, or a total of 44 (dicolic "N" 22). Plate D attempts to show how P broke up the "N" 21 sequence, blending the "N" information with that of the "O" source.

The three chapters on the T'u-chüeh contain at least fourteen similar cases involving the juxtaposition of "M", "N", and "O" cola. The most fascinating one is that of the colometry of the three versions of the legend of the lupine origin of the Turks. The patchwork of sources there being most intricate and the colometric solution of the filiation of the texts extremely complicated—this major problem in the prehistory of the Turks can only be alluded to within the scope of these brief notes.

PLATE A   *Shih Chi* text (significant *Han Shu* variants below)

1. 匈	1. 隨	1. 逐	1. 兒	1. 其	1. 其	1. 自	1. 父
2. 奴	2. 畜	2. 水	2. 能	2. 俗	2. 長	2. 君	2. 死
3. 其	3. 牧	3. 草	3. 騎	3. 寬	3. 兵	3. 王	3. 妻
4. 先	4. 而	4. 遷	4. 羊	4. 則	4. 則	4. 以	4. 其
5. 祖	5. 轉	5. 徙	5. 引	5. 隨	5. 弓	5. 下	5. 後
6. 夏	6. 移	6. 毋	6. 弓	6. 畜	6. 矢	6. 咸	6. 母
7. 后	7. 其	7. 城	7. 射	7. 因	7. 短	7. 食	7. 兄
8. 氏	8. 畜	8. 郭	8. 鳥	8. 射	8. 兵	8. 畜	8. 弟
9. 之	9. 之	9. 常	9. 鼠	9. 獵	9. 則	9. 肉	9. 死
10. 苗	10. 所	10. 處	10. 少	10. 禽	10. 刀	10. 衣	10. 皆
11. 裔	11. 多	11. 耕	11. 長	11. 獸	11. 鋋	11. 其	11. 取
12. 也	12. 則	12. 田	12. 則	12. 爲	12. 利	12. 皮	12. 其
13. 曰	13. 馬	13. 之	13. 射	13. 生	13. 則	13. 革	13. 妻
14. 淳	14. 牛	14. 業	14. 狐	14. 業	14. 進	14. 被	14. 妻
15. 維	15. 羊	15. 然	15. 兔	15. 急	15. 不	15. 旃	15. 之
16. 唐	16. 其	16. 亦	16. 用	16. 則	16. 利	16. 裘	16. 其
17. 虞	17. 奇	17. 各	17. 爲	17. 人	17. 則	17. 壯	17. 俗
18. 以	18. 畜	18. 有	18. 食	18. 習	18. 退	18. 者	18. 有
19. 上	19. 則	19. 分	19. 士	19. 戰	19. 不	19. 食	19. 名
20. 有	20. 橐	20. 地	20. 力	20. 攻	20. 羞	20. 肥	20. 不
21. 山	21. 駝	21. 毋	21. 能	21. 以	21. 遁	21. 美	21. 諱
22. 戎	22. 驢	22. 文	22. 彎	22. 侵	22. 走	22. 老	22. 而
23. 獫	23. 驘	23. 書	23. 弓	23. 伐	23. 苟	23. 者	23. 無
24. 狁	24. 駃	24. 以	24. 盡	24. 其	24. 利	24. 食	24. 姓
25. 葷	25. 騠	25. 言	25. 爲	25. 天	25. 所	25. 其	25. 字
26. 粥	26. 騊	26. 語	26. 甲	26. 性	26. 在	26. 餘	
27. 居	27. 駼	27. 爲	27. 騎	27. 也	27. 不	27. 貴	
28. 於	28. 驒	28. 約			28. 知	28. 壯	
29. 北	29. 騱	29. 束			29. 禮	29. 健	
30. 蠻					30. 義	30. 賤	
						31. 老	
						32. 弱	

5, 12. ○ 30. 邊	I+: 車	Ditto	16-18: 肉食	7. ○ 8. 田	Ditto	23+: 飲	24. ○

PLATE B

P

1. 其
2. 俗
3. 被
4. 髮
5. 左
6. 衽、
7. 穹
8. 廬
9. 氊
10. 帳、
11. 隨
12. 逐
13. 水
14. 艸
15. 遷
16. 徙
17. 以
18. 畜
19. 牧
20. 射
21. 獵
22. 爲
23. 事
24. 食
25. 肉
26. 飲
27. 酪
28. 身
29. 衣
30. 裳
31. 褐
32. 賤
33. 老
34. 貴
35. 壯
36. 寡
37. 廉
38. 恥
39. 無
40. 禮
41. 義
42. 猶
43. 古
44. 之
45. 匈
46. 奴

S

1. 其
2. 俗
3. 畜
4. 牧
5. 爲
6. 事
7. 隨
8. 逐
9. 水
10. 草、
11. 不
12. 恒
13. 厥
14. 處、
15. 穹
16. 廬
17. 氊
18. 帳

19. 被
20. 髮
21. 左
22. 衽
23. 食
24. 肉
25. 飲
26. 酪
27. 身
28. 衣
29. 裳
30. 褐
31. 賤
32. 老
33. 貴
34. 壯

C

1. 其
2. 俗
3. 被
4. 髮
5. 左
6. 衽
7. 穹
8. 廬
9. 氊
10. 帳
11. 隨
○
12. 水
13. 草
14. 遷
15. 徙
16. 以
17. 畜
18. 牧
19. 射
20. 獵
21. 爲
22. 務

○
○
○
○
○
○

23. 賤
24. 老
25. 貴
26. 壯
27. 寡
28. 廉
29. 恥
30. 無
31. 禮
32. 義
33. 猶
34. 古
35. 之
36. 匈
37. 奴
38. 也

PLATE C

S　　　　　　　　　　　(C) P

1. 五	25. 歌	1. 其	31. 歌
2. 月	26. 呼	2. 書	32. 呼
3. 中	27. 相	3. 字	33. 相
4. 多	28. 對	4. 類	34. 對
5. 殺	29. 敬	5. 胡	35. 敬
6. 羊	(30) 鬼	6. 而	(36) 鬼
7. 馬	(31) 神	7. 不	(37) 神
8. 以	32. 信	8. 知	38. 信
9. 祭	(33) 巫	9. 年	(39) 巫
10. 天	(34) 覡	10. 曆	○
11. 男	35. 重	11. 唯	16. 男　40. 重
12. 子	36. 兵	12. 以	17. 子　41. 兵
13. 好	37. 死	13. 艸	20. 好　42. 死
14. 樗	38. 而	14. 青	21. 樗　○
15. 蒲	39. 恥	15. 爲	22. 蒲　43. 恥
16. 女	40. 病	16. 記	23. 女　44. 病
17. 子	41. 終		24. 子　45. 終
18. 踏	42. 大		24. 踏　46. 大
19. 鞠	43. 抵		25. 鞠　47. 抵
20. 飲	44. 與		26. 飲　48. 與
21. 馬	45. 匈		27. 馬　49. 匈
22. 酪	46. 奴		28. 酪　50. 奴
23. 取	47. 同		29. 取　51. 同
24. 醉	48. 俗		30. 醉　52. 俗

PLATE D

S	P	P = C	P
		(10) 1. 其	(24) 15. 并
1. 善	1. 善	(11) 2. 徵	(25) 16. 一
2. 騎	2. 騎	(12) 3. 發	(26) 17. 金
3. 射	3. 射	(13) 4. 兵	(27) 18. 鏃
4. 性	4. 性	(14) 5. 馬	(28) 19. 箭
5. 殘	5. 殘	(15) 6. 及	(29) 20. 蠟
6. 忍	6. 忍	(16) 7. 諸	(30) 21. 封
7. 無	7. 無	(17) 8. 稅	(31) 22. 印
8. 文	8. 文	(18) 9. 雜	(32) 23. 之
9. 字	9. 字	(19) 10. 畜	(33) 24. 以
10. 刻		(20) 11. 刻	(34) 25. 爲
11. 木		(21) 12. 木	(35) 26. 信
12. 爲		(22) 13. 爲	(36) 27. 契 ↑
13. 契		(23) 14. 數	
14. 侯°			
15. 月			(37) 10. 侯
16. 將			(38) 11. 月
17. 滿			(39) 12. 將
18. 軏			(40) 13. 滿
19. 爲			(41) 14. 轉
20. 寇			(42) 15. 爲
21. 抄			(43) 16. 寇
			(44) 17. 抄

Philological Notes on
Chapter One of the *Lao Tzu*

Harvard Journal of Asiatic Studies, 20 (1957), 598-618.

The opening sequence of the most celebrated text of Chinese literature is usually divided into ten stichoi:

	0	1	2	3	4	5	6	7	8
S 1		道	可	道	非	常	道		
S 2		名	可	名	非	常	名		
S 3		無	名	天	地	之	始		
S 4		有	名	萬	物	之	母		
S 5	故	常	無	欲	以	觀	其	妙	
S 6		常	有	欲	以	觀	其	徼	
S 7		此	兩	者	同	出	而	異	名
S 8		同	謂	之	玄				
S 9		玄	之	又	玄				
S 10		衆	妙	之	門				

S 1.1. The etymological background of *Tao* 道 is usually dismissed by scholars fascinated by its exalted metaphysical status with a brief twofold statement: that the primary and concrete meaning of the word *tao* < *d'ôg* is "way," "path" ("la voie," "der Weg," "via") and that its graph is a compound of two graphic elements, "head," *shou* < *śjôg*, used as a phonetic, and the semantic "to proceed," "walk." Though essentially correct, the statement is in need of amplification and closer philological scrutiny. In ancient scriptions of the graph, "proceed" (classifier 162) interchanges with 行 "march in order," "act" (classifier 144) and occasionally the two classifiers are telescoped together. *Shuo Wen* 2B offers as a *ku wen* form of *tao* a digram of "head" and 寸, modern classifier 041 *ts'un*, "inch," but anciently an allogram of 手 *shou* < *śjôg*, "hand." Some Bronze scriptions have

this fork-like " hand " element added to *tao* with C144, while in
a few of them the " hand " appears to emerge as a graphic modification of the lower " footstep " element (modern 止, C077) in
the telescoped C162 + C144. This " *tao* with the hand element "
is usually identified with the modern character 導 *tao* < *d'ôg*, " to
lead," " guide," " conduct," and considered to be a *derivative* or
verbal cognate of the noun *tao*, " way," " path." The evidence
just summarized would indicate rather that " *tao* with the hand "
is but a *variant* of the basic *tao* and that the word itself combined
both nominal and verbal aspects of the etymon. This is supported by textual examples of the use of the primary *tao* in the
verbal sense " to lead " (e. g., *Analects* 1.5; 2.3) and seriously
undermines the unspoken assumption implied in the common
translation of *Tao* as " way " that the concept is essentially a
nominal one. *Tao* would seem, then, to be etymologically a more
dynamic concept than we have made it translation-wise. It would
be more appropriately rendered by " leadway " and " lode "
(" way," " course," " journey," " leading," " guidance "); cf. " lodestone " and " lodestar "), the somewhat obsolescent deverbal
noun from " to lead."

Another etymological problem concerns the element " head "
in *tao*. *Shou* < *sjôg* is undoubtedly phonetic in *tao* < *d'ôg* (the
alternation of spirant and stop being common in a given phonetic
series), but is it merely phonetic or etymonic? Semasiological
analogy (English: " to head " meaning " to lead " and " to tend
in a certain direction," " ahead," " headway ") would suggest
that the latter is the case; Chinese synonymy seems to confirm it.
Of the three common aspects of HEAD, topmost protuberance
(*caput*), uppermost turning point (*vertex*), and tip (*apex*), *shou*
favors the first two, the last being expressed by 顛 *tien* and 頂
ting. *Shou* as " vertex " is well attested in verbal function (it is
then read in the fourth tone) as " to turn to," " to obvert."
Besides " leadway " and " lode," *tao* would then also connote
" headway," and perhaps " headlead," " headlode," and " lodehead." With *shou* commonly meaning " foremost," " chief,"
" arch-," we are perilously near seeing in it an equivalent of Gr.
archēgos, archēgon, " first cause," " archegetic (leading, primary)
principle."

To avoid soaring into the rarefied atmosphere of first causes, the Archeus, and the *anima mundi*, let us turn to the recorded pedestrian connotations of *tao*. Paronomastically, *tao* is equated with its homonym 蹈 *tao* < *d'ôg*, " to trample," " tread," and from that point of view it is nothing more than a " treadway," " headtread," or " foretread "; it is also occasionally associated with a near synonym (and possible cognate) 迪 *ti* < *d'iôk*, " follow a road," " go along," " lead," " direct "; " pursue the right path "; a term with definite ethical overtones and a graph with an exceedingly interesting phonetic, 由 *yu* < *djôg*," " to proceed from." The reappearance of C162 " walk " in *ti* with the support of C157 " foot " in *tao*, " to trample," " tread," should perhaps serve us as a warning not to overemphasize the headworking functions implied in *tao* in preference to those of the lower extremities. The " *tao* with the hand " scription further complicates the picture by introducing into it a third, " hand-leading," cheiragogic element to counterbalance the archegetic and podegetic factors. The displacement of the fork-like " footstep " grapheme by the fork-like " hand " element noted above is significant not only semantically but phonetically. 寸 as *shou* < *sjôg* " hand " shows as a phonetic the same fluctuation between spirant and stop that we postulate for " head ": 守 *sjôg*, 肘 *tjôg*, 討 *t'og*, 壽 *shou* < *djôg*, " longevity," 疇 *ch'ou* < *d'jôg*, " ploughed field." The phonetic series of the last two (Karlgren, *Grammata Serica* 1090) gives us in addition *d'ôg* and *tôg* in other compounds; the primary phonetic of that series is a protograph of " ploughed field " supposed to represent the S-like pattern of three furrows running boustrophedon through an agricultural strip; according to the *Shuo Wen* 2 A, the " hand " element that appears in the lower right corner of the expanded protograph is phonetic in KGS 1090 f, *ch'ou* < *d'jôg*, " who." Semasiologically, " ploughed field " is not necessarily remote from the immediate problem of *tao*, " leadway " or " vertex-way." Cf. Gr. *ogmos*, " furrow " < *agō*, " to lead," and L. *versus*, " furrow," *versura*, " turning at the end of the furrow," " boustrophedon ploughing." Having established the phonetic importance of the " hand " we must ask ourselves what etymonic contributions, if any, it would bring in. What aspect of "hand" activities does the graph suggest? Leading (*manu-duco*), drawing-dragging (*traho*), or catching-heaving (*capio*)? Offhand, one would favor the first two, *tao* being primarily a *ductus* (a "leading") or *tractus* ("line" of "course"), but the third should not be entirely overlooked, even though we cannot give it full consideration at present. It will suffice to say for the present that the pursuit of this particular etymological path would lead us to a wonderland of semantics where Chinese "head" *śjôg* and Chinese "hand" *śjôg* would merge in the same way as "head-Haupt-caput" mingle their etymological strands with "capio-catch-have-haft" in the Indo-European linguistic subconscious.

The great semantic complexity of *tao* may have predetermined the rich system of associations surrounding *Tao* in its metaphysical and literary career. In the light of its semasiological ancestry, it is not surprising that the *Tao* can be both "headlong" and "beforehand," "precipitate" (from *caput*) and "preceptive" (from *capio*), "proverse" (and thus "progressive") and "obverse" (and "regressive," as boustrophedon ploughing: 反者道之動 "antistrophe is the movement of the *Tao*," says *Lao Tzu* 40); that it may connote at the same time the Archductor of the universe and a mere "viaduct," "the Lodehead," "Weird-head" ("weird," destiny, < "worth," "to turn," "become," G. *werden*), and all-comprehensive Becoming (*das Werden*) of all life, on one hand, and a "lode-shire" (*tao* as a political subdivision), a lowly "foot-track," or a practical "method" of procedure on the other.

Possibly as early as the end of the Chou period *tao* formed with the word 路 *lu* < *luo* < *glâg*, "road-way," the binom *tao-lu* usually interpreted as a *dvandva* compound, but in the light of the preceding probably meaning "leading road." It may have been originally a colloquial term, but is attested in polite literature since the beginning of the Han. One is strongly tempted, in view of the etymological connections of *Tao* with "head," to invoke *tao-lu* < *d'ôgluo* < *d'ôgglâg*, as a colloquial designation of the *Tao*, as a possible foundation for the popularity of early Taoist stories describing a philosopher or poet discoursing upon the cosmological

Tao with a skull, the Chinese term for " skull " being a disyllabic homoeonym 髑髏 *tu-lou* ‹ *dʻukglu* (also written: 毛盧 , with C181 頁 , *tu-lu* ‹ *dʻuklo*) .

To sum up, we feel that the traditional translation of *Tao* as " the Way " does little justice to the wealth of the Chinese term's semantic connotations. What word should be substituted for " way " is a matter of choice and taste. Personally, I am partial to " lodehead " in clearly metaphysical contexts, and to " head-lead " (nominal and verbal) in mixed or commonplace discourse.

S 1.2-3 and S 2.2-3, *kʻo-tao* and *kʻo-ming*, are rendered by all translators as " may be *tao*'ed " and " may be named "—in various circumlocutions. This is fully justified in the light of our knowledge of Chinese grammar: in 97% of cases verbs following *kʻo*, " may," " can," must be construed in the Indo-European passive, for never (*sc.* hardly ever) does a verb in binomial union with *kʻo* take or tolerate an object. The active, transitive force of such a verb is restored by the insertion of the particle *yi* 以 after *kʻo* (*mutatis mutandis*, the same rule is valid for *so* 所 + verb) . Thus: *kʻo chien* 可見 " (X) may be seen," *kʻo-i chien* 可以見 " (X) may see." The question arises, however, how was that construction understood in Chinese, a language in which the category of the passive was not primary? How can it be parsed in our linguistic terms without having recourse to the passive? The answer is not easy and can be formulated at present only in the form of an etymological hypothesis as to the primary meaning of the auxiliary verb *kʻo* ‹ *kʻâ*, " may," " can." In spite of the difficulty presented by the initial consonant, archaic *kʻâ*, " may " may well have been a cognate of the homoeographic concrete verb *ho* ‹ *gʻâ* 荷 (archaically 何) , " to bear, to carry, to sustain "; and, more remotely, an affine of its near synonym 許 *hsü* ‹ *χjo*, " to permit," " to allow," " to admit." In that case, *kʻo* + verb might be interpreted as " bear " (" brook," " allow," " admit," etc., as a finite verb) + verbal noun (as the object of *kʻo*) . Then, *kʻo chien*, " (X) may be seen " would equal " (X) bears seeing "; *kʻo-i chien*, " (X) bears to see (something) ," the particle *i* performing its familiar function of marking the infinitive of purpose, or " in order to," " so as to," " for to," between two verbals.

S 1.4 and S 2.4. In the present state of our knowledge of Archaic Chinese we face a troublesome dilemma in the analysis of 非 *fei* < *pjwər*, the Chinese pre-substantival negative, usually equated with " to be not." If the word be a fusion of the negative element *p-* with a verb equivalent to the Indo-European verb " to be," why is it that we never encounter that verb in its positive form? *Pjwər* could well be a fusion of *p-* and *(d)jwər* (modern *wei*, graphs: 唯, 惟 or 維), a copula-like particle common in the language of the *Shih* and *Shu*. If this be the lost Chinese verb " to be," one would have to postulate a serious break in the continuity of the Chinese language between the eighth and the sixth centuries before our era, a break or shift in the dominant dialect resulting in the total disappearance of the " ontological " verb except in the negative form. One could, on the other hand, interpret 唯 *wei* < *(d)jwər* as a " verbal " of affirmation, i. e., " to yea," " to say aye," and *pjwər*, as " to n'aye " (i. e., " to negate ") functioning in many constructions as a pre-substantival equivalent of our " no," " non." The close juncture of *fei* with the following word often results in a certain syntactic ambiguity. There is, for instance, no grammatical criterion which would enable us to decide whether 非常人也 *fei ch'ang jen yeh* means " (X) is-not (*fei*) a common (*ch'ang*) man," or: " (X) (is an) uncommon (*fei-ch'ang*) man." Idiom-conscious readers will incline towards the second choice, *fei-ch'ang*, " uncommon," " extraordinary " being a common idiom (as an adjective), readers well-grounded in the syntactical pattern *fei . . . yeh* might insist on the essential correctness of the first. This dilemma must have affected the thinking of many a translator of the first couplet of the *Lao Tzu* with its two *fei-ch'ang*.

S 1.5 and S 2.5 常 *ch'ang*, " constant," " regular," " common," " ordinary," " persistent," " conventional," " enduring," never meant " eternal " or " absolute " in our sense, as wrongly used by so many translators of the first couplet of the *Lao Tzu*. As an epithet, it is used to characterize " long-customed," " long-vested " things and habits, both in the positive sense of " time-honored " (" regular," " customary," and " enduring ") and in the negative sense of " time-worn " (" commonplace," " ordinary," and " routine "). It is difficult to find a single English word to do etymological justice to the connotations of *ch'ang*. Its phonetic, and possibly etymonic, 尚 *shang* < *djang*, "high," "put high," "exalt," *adv.*, "still," "as before," a close cognate of 上 *shang* < *djang*, "up," "above," "top," "rise," "raise," appears to convey in the compound graphs in which it plays a " phonetic " role an overtone that may be expressed by the English prepositional formant "fore- " and by Latin " *prae-*." Thus: 嘗 *ch'ang*, "to taste," "to try" < " to foretaste," "pregustate "; 當 *tang*, "to appose," "apposite," < " to foreset," "foregainst "; 掌 *chang*, "palm of the hand," perhaps < " forehand "; 掌 *chang*, "to manage," "be in charge of " (尚 *shang* itself has that meaning in archaic terminology), < " to forehandle," "forehold," "forekeep," "to be preposited to "; 賞 *shang*, "reward " < " premium." In the light of this suggestion, our *ch'ang*, "constant," etc., could be rendered "forewonted " ("forecustomed," "forefound," "foreheld," "prestituted," etc.). Syntactically, *ch'ang* functions chiefly as an adjective or adverb. As we shall find in the discussion of S 5 and S 6, on a rare occasion one can encounter a case of amphibology where *ch'ang* could be parsed as either. Since English is one of those versatile languages in which many adjectives do not differ in form from corresponding adverbs (e. g., "fast," "forward," "lengthwise "), one should, as a matter of philological discipline, make some effort to reproduce this amphibology of *ch'ang* in English. I am inclined to coin the word "wontwise " ("wont," "custom," usage + the adverbial-adjectival " -wise ") to serve this particular problem.

S 2.1. The graph 名 *ming* < *mjĕng*, "name," "to name," presents some interesting graphophonetic problems. It is unmistakably a compound of 口 *k'ou* < *k'u*, "mouth " and 夕 *hsi* < *dzjäk*, "evening " (graphically, "moon crescent "). *Shuo Wen* 2 A (*Shuo-wen chieh-tzu ku-lin*.578-579) suggests a phonetic rationalization of the graph by equating the ' moon crescent ' element with 冥 *ming* < *mieng*, "dark," quaintly explaining: "when it is dark (*ming*) and one cannot see one another, one names (*ming*) oneself by word of mouth." Paronomastically, *ming*, "name," is equated with 明 *ming* < *mjäng*, "bright," "made clear or distinct," with 命 *ming* < *mjăng*, " fate," " decree " (graphically: " mouth " + " command "), and with 鳴 *ming* < *mjĕng*, " to call, as a bird or other creature " (graphically: " mouth " + " bird "). The first equation suggests that some ancient Chinese graphosemanticists thought of the ' crescent ' element in the graph for " name " as reminiscent of the " *ming*-crescent " of the dextral part of the graph 明 *ming*, " bright," rather than being equivalent to the " *hsi*-crescent." The " mouth " element in " decree " and " to call " points to the possibility that there existed in the oldest form of Chinese writing a " mouth " graph which was not phonosemantically equal to *k'u* ' mouth,' ' opening,' but was read *ming* and meant perhaps " call," " to call," and that that " *ming*-mouth " graph served as etymonic in the three graphs: 名 *ming*, " name," i. e., " name-call "; 鳴 *ming*, " bird-call "; and 命 *ming*, " hight-call," " fate-call," " call of destiny."

S 1 and S 2. We may now proceed to the consideration of the first couplet as a whole, with particular attention to syntactical structure.

A philologist with the naïve belief in the rigidity of Chinese syntactical patterns must find peculiarly disconcerting the prevailing tendency among otherwise competent sinologists of translating *tao k'o tao* and *ming k'o ming* by " the *tao* that can be *tao*'ed " (irrespective of the value assigned to second *tao*) and " the name that can be named," as if *k'o tao* and *k'o ming* were relative clauses modifying the first *tao* and *ming*. The supposed requirements of idiomatic usage in the translating languages probably serves as the unspoken excuse for this unjudicious violation of the fundamental axiom of Chinese grammar: modifier precedes principal. Indo-European relative clauses are expressed in Chinese by adjectival ones. ' The name that can be named ' would have been an appropriate translation for *k'o-ming chih ming* 可名之 名; it is a bad distortion of the original for *ming k'o ming* which is either a finite sentence (" the name may be named," or: " the name be named," as a precative or imperative subjunctive) or a conditional clause (" if the name were namable," " . . . is namable," " . . . be namable "). It seems sometimes that we are actually regressing in grammatical acumen: compare, for instance, Rudolf

BACKOFEN's 1949 rendering typical of so many recent versions, " Der Begriff, durch den man begreifen kann . . . ," with the venerable (but substantially correct) 1870 wording by Victor VON STRAUSS: " Der Name, kann er genannt werden, (ist nicht) . . . ."

As indicated previously, all students of the *Lao Tzu* are somewhat obsessed with the supposedly fundamental nominal character of the term *tao*. This makes them overlook entirely a perfectly legitimate and cogent way of construing the famous opening couplet of our text, namely the syntactical construction in which the first *tao* and *ming* are interpreted as transitive verbs: *tao* as " to lead," " to head," " to treat or consider as the (or: a) way "; *ming* as " to name," " to treat as a name." This syntactical pattern appears in the *Lao Tzu*, ch. 3: 不見可欲 *pu chien* (= *hsien*) *k'o yü*, " do not make manifest what might be desired "). In addition, it is quite possible grammatically, though not quite as satisfactory contextually, to take *fei*, " is not," as a transitive verb: " to negate," " deny," " gainsay," " disparage."

If we dismiss as outrageously solecistic all the interpretations of the couplet based on parsing *k'o tao* and *k'o ming* as relative clauses, we are reduced to four possible syntactical versions of the couplet:

I. *tao/ming* (noun-subject) *k'o-tao/ming* (verbal predicate), *fei* (is not) *ch'ang* (adj) +*tao/ming* (n.) (complement)

II. *tao/ming* (v. t., with subject understood) *k'o-tao/ming* (substantivized verbal phrase as object of *v. t.*), *fei* (is not) *ch'ang* (adj.) +*tao/ming* (n.) (complement).

III and IV. The same as I and II, but with *fei* (*v. t.*) *ch'ang* (adj.) +*tao/ming* (n.) (object of *v. t.*)

I. (If/when/though) the way is way-able (i. e., brooks/admits treatment as a way), it is no common way.
    (If/when/though) the name is namable (i. e., brooks/admits treatment as a name), it is no common name.

II. (When we) way (i. e., treat-as-the-way) the wayable (i. e., what brooks/admits treatment as a way), it is no common way.
    (When we) name (treat as a name/its name) the namable, it is no common name.

III. If the way is wayable, (we) gainsay the common ways; if its name be namable, (we) gainsay the common names.

IV. Waying the wayable, (we) gainsay the common ways; naming the namable, (we) gainsay the common names.

The polysyntactical ambiguity and seeming confusion and contradiction of the above renderings will prove, after a moment's reflection, more apparent then real. It is not impossible more-over to construct a crude English replica of the original text reproducing all of its ambiguities. With the use of English *-ing* forms demarcation lines between verbs and nouns will be properly blurred; with the suppression of 'the' and 'is,' a procedure not entirely illegitimate in what purports to reproduce an epigramatic —and somewhat doggerel—verse, and the secondary reading of 'no' as an imperative (i. e., "say no to . . ."), we may achieve the desired degree of ambiguity in syntactical construction; finally, the discreet use of a colon as a noncommittal punctuation mark will serve to suggest both the rhythm and syntactical juncture of the Chinese original:

> Waying wayable : no common waying
> Naming namable : no common naming

In conclusion, with some help from semi-juridical Anglo-Latin, one could reproduce not only the tautology of the Chinese forms, but suggest also the 'imperative subjunctive' construction in the first hemistichs:

> Waying *licet* waying : no common waying
> Naming *licet* naming : no common naming.

S 3.1 and S 4.1. The philologist should protest with the utmost vigor the common translation of Chinese 有 *yu* ‹ *gjŭg* and 無 *wu* ‹ *mjwo* as "Being" and "Non-being" respectively, or even as "Existence" and "Non-existence." There is no doubt that prior to the invasion of China by Buddhism with its Indo-European glosso-philosophical paraphernalia which made ontological specu-lation possible, these two Chinese terms, even in Taoist environ-ment, remained securely within the semantic and philosophical category of habit or possession, being both essentially transitive verbs: "to have (something)" and "not to have (something)," with objects following them in the normal course of grammatical and philosophical events. These essential facts of the Chinese language are best kept in mind by endeavoring to maintain some consistency in translation and keeping *yu* and *wu* within the range of "have-aught" and "have-naught," or "habit-aught" and "habit-naught" (verbally or nominally) without yielding too readily to the temptation of substituting for them the idiosyncratically occidental concepts of "being" and "non-being." The legerdemain substitution of the latter pair for the former must be tremendously baffling to an uninitiated student of *Lao Tzu* confronted with the following disparate versions of stichoi 3 and 4:

Without a name, it is the Beginning of Heaven and Earth; with a name, it is the Mother of all things (*Wisdom of the East*, 1905, Lionel GILES).

The term Non-being indicates the beginning of heaven and earth; the term Being indicates the mother of the ten thousand things (*Wisdom of the East*, 1954, J. J. L. DUYVENDAK).

Professor DUYVENDAK's note on p. 19 of his edition while cogent enough for the specialist is not very enlightening to the general reader who would hardly be able to figure out how the shift of a non-existing (in Chinese texts) punctuation mark from S 3.1 to S 3.2 would produce the above startling difference in meaning.

The mystery is immediately dissipated if the couplet be translated, however clumsily, following strict philological principles (the colon marks the rhythmical and syntactical pause in the stichos):

Having-naught namecalling : Heaven-&-Earth's beginning;
Having-aught namecalling : myriad creatures' mother.

It is obvious from the above that L. GILES reads with one school of Chinese commentators: "Having naught anaming . . ."; J. J. L. DUYVENDAK, following another school: "The Having-Naught anaming . . . ," "Having-naught" simply becoming an abstract noun. Now, although the latter interpretation is philosophically very attractive and tempting, its champions should inform the reader that the construction, when thus parsed, does read as awkwardly in the original Chinese as in the English rendering above. Being myself a partisan of this reading, I would give a great deal to be able to tone down that statement, but philological experience would not permit it.

S 3.6 始 *shih* < *śjəg*, usually unimaginatively translated here "beginning," is one of several Chinese words with that significance. Both hemigrams composing its graph (the semantic 女.

" woman," and the phonetic 台 *t'ai* < *t'əg*, also phonetic in 胎 *t'ai* < *t'əg*, " foetus," " embryo," " beginning "; cf. *Erh Ya*, I) indicate that we have to deal with a word connoting " organic beginning " (" fetation," " gestation," " pregnation," " parturition," " incience " < L. *inciens*, " cyesis," " feture ' < L. *fetura*), as contrasted with other forms of " beginning," e. g., 初 *ch'u*, " insective beginning," 元 *yüan*, " principiate beginning," 首 *shou*, " capitate beginning," 基 *chi*, " foundation beginning," 開 *k'ai*, " beginning as opening," etc. There is no need to go so far as to suspect in this stichos a hint of a theory of a cosmological virgin-birth (as does, I believe, John C. H. WU), but one could defend the view that the emphatic use of a graphic element connoting natural sex characteristics could suggest to the Chinese reader something approaching our concept of gender, that is: " fetation," with a slight semantic grace note " a fetating she ", or " pregnancy " of a " pregnant she."

S 4.4. The etymological background of 物 *wu* < *mjuət*, " thing," " creature," " wight " is not without importance for the understanding of the genesis and evolution of the Chinese philosophy of nature. Without attempting to marshal the large evidence on the subject, one must remind the reader that ancient texts beginning with the Oracle Bones commonly use *wu* in the meaning " color of the coat of an animal, particularly cattle," " variegated thing." Indeed, *wu* < *mjuət* appears to be a cognate of another all-important Chinese term, 文 *wen* < *mjuən* " striae," " streaks," " pattern of lines "; " tattoo "; " variegated," " brindled," " dappled "; " design," " ornament," " ornamental markings," " written character," " pattern of writing," " composition," " essay," " literature," " arts of peace," " culture," etc. (as regards the difference of the finals, observe that final -*n* is often found in the 勿 phonetic series). The natural " maculation " of things must have deeply impressed the Chinese and " variate " or " mottling " became their designation for all things. The broad diapason of the root MUEN is not without analogy in Indo-European: cf. L. *macula*, G. " Mal," " Muttermal," believed to be cognate to Gothic *mela*, " writing."

S 5.0. The character is frequently omitted in quotations of that stichos. It is generally agreed that *ku* 故, as an adverbial con-

junction, lacks the conclusive force of our " therefore " and " consequently," albeit as a noun it seems to connote " reason," " cause,"
and that it should be conservatively rendered (until the Chinese
concepts of causation are adequately explored, philosophically
and semantically) by " truly," " indeed," " assuredly." In the
vast semasiological area covered by the phonetic group represented by the graph *ku* 古, one can block out the etymon OLD –
DURE – FAST – FIRM – DRY (cf. *ku* with classifiers 31, 85 + 31,
75, 104, 140, 188), so to say: ELDFAST, " made fast-and-dry
by age." Semantically, then, our *ku* 故 may equal " affirmably,"
" affirmedly," " made fast."

S 5.5 and S 6.5: *kuan* 觀, in most translations of this passage
weakly rendered by " see," connotes " to behold," " to view (an
important, impressive, distant or supernal, or extraordinary
sight)," " to contemplate," " to surview (rather than " survey "),"
" to be a spectator of," " to observe," in one word: " to spectate."
Kuan frequently appears, however, in a causative sense, " to cause
to view," " put in view." In our text, a causative interpretation
is not entirely excluded. Perhaps " to descry the view," " descry
in view (prospect, perspective) " would be sufficiently indicative
of the possibility. *Kuan* undoubtedly belongs to the etymon
KAN KUAN, " to look," but some connection with the root
HUAN, " outcry," " clamor," is not ruled out grapho-phonetically;
cf. 讙 *huan*, " clamor."

S 5.7 妙 *miao* < *mjog*. It is not certain whether the original text
contained this particular graph or a homophonous one, such as
眇 *miao* < *mjog*, " make one eye small," " squint," " squinting,"
" blind on one eye "; " to squint," " to sight peering into the distance "; " to the utmost," " endmost," " minute," " mite," " minim," " infinitesimal," " subliminal." The technical (metaphysical)
meaning of 妙 *miao* (with the " woman " classifier) is not at all
clear and the various suggested renderings for it are mainly based
on its inferential interpretation in this particular context and in a
similarly obscure passage in the *Book of Changes*. Otherwise, it
connotes " petite," " slender," " youthful." *Miao* can hardly be
as unspecific as the over-conservative translation " wonder,"
"wondrous" would make it, nor as packed with peculiarly western

notions as the over-exuberant renderings " secret of life," " spiritual essence," " quintessence," " the logically unknowable," etc.,
would suggest. In all probability 妙 *miao* is but a graphically
specialized form of 眇 *miao* which, as may be surmised from the
rough sketch of its etymological development given above, can
be defined as " too small to be seen," " minuend to the vanishing
point," in one word: " subliminal." One could continue the line
of speculation adumbrated under S 3.6 and suggest that the substitution of " woman " for the classifier " eye " in 眇 *miao* was
effected to emphasize the Taoist preoccupation with the " Eternal
Feminine," thus transforming a sexless " micromorph " into a
" microgyne," or a " minim " into a dainty " minikin." Further
exploration of the problem of " graphic gender " in Chinese writing will show how valid is this line of argument. At this point,
we shall limit ourselves by giving a slight feminine accent to *miao*
in addition to the " syntactical plural " form in which we have to
cast it in view of the unmistakable plurality of the *miao* indicated
in S 10. " The subliminaria " would, I believe, endow the *miao*
with a sufficiently discreet degree of femininity and plurality to
perform properly their philological and metaphysical duties.

S 6.7. In contrast to the dearth of specific information on *miao*,
the interpretation of its matching rhyme word 徼 *chiao < kiog*
suffers from too many conflicting glosses. Composed of the
" marching " classifier C060 as a semantic element and the
phonetic hemigram *chiao*, " make bright," *chiao* is attested in
various texts in the following meanings: " patrol," " to make
rounds," " to patrol," " follow a course," " path or sideroad,"
" (patrolled?) border or stockade defense line on the frontier with
southern barbarians." The core meaning seems to be, then, " am-
bitus," " going round," " circuit." " Going round " is registered in
other graphs derived from the same phonetic. Thus, 繳 *chiao*
(with C120, " silk "), " to wind around "; 幑 chiao (with C050,
" cloth "), " leggings." The basic meaning of the phonetic, " make
bright," survives not only in compound graphs with classifiers
associated with luminosity (" moon," " sun," " white," " eye ")
but also, in the opinion of glossographers, in such as 檄 (with
C075, " wood ") *hsi < g'iek*, " writing tablet sent around with

summons (as for mobilization)," " proclamation "; gloss (paraphrased in English): i. e., a " declaration " " made CLEAR." All
this is important in connection with the fact that so many of our
uncertainties as regards the *Lao Tzu* stem from our inability to
identify for sure which particular determinatives of relatively rare
complex graphs stood in the original text and which were added
or substituted later. If " luminosity " was indeed a semantic
factor in the phonetic group *chiao*, then the contrast between
miao and *chiao* in couplet 3 (S 5 and S 6) is not only that of the
subliminal with the extensional, but also that between the indistinct and the clearly delineated. Among the possible substi-
tutes for our *chiao* is the character 窔 *ch'iao* < *k'iog*, " hole,"
" opening." This alternate reading that has been defended by
able commentators does not make too much sense until we realize
that " hole " connotes in the usage of this particular character
" aperture," " vent-hole," L. *lumen*. To convey all these overtones
we may have to use the compound " lumen-ambital," with " am-
bitus " suggesting quite effectively " periphery," " extension "
(both physical and logical), and " circuital motion " (and return
to the starting point, cf. WANG Pi's comm.), and " lumen " im-
plying both " lighted " and " passageway."

These rather cumbersome translations for *miao* and *chiao*
possess some etymological merit, but do not shed sufficient light
on the philosophical problem of the couplet to challenge seriously
previously suggested renderings. Personally, I wish I had a little
more confidence in all the comments that have been written on
this passage for the past sixteen centuries and that some authority
would allay my uneasy suspicions that—while *miao* and *chiao*
have some connection with a theory of cosmogonical particles or
atoms—the terms themselves originated as part of the obscure
vocabulary pertaining to ancient Chinese string instruments (cf.
the rather baffling entries in *Shuo Wen* 12 B under the now obsolete classifier 弦 *hsien*, " chord," where there is also found the
supposedly ancient form of *miao*). As a reminder of this dis-
turbing possibility, we should like to retain the word " minikin,"
in association with " subliminal," as a translation for *miao* (English " minikin ": 1. " diminutive," " dainty "; 2. " thin treble

string on the lute," " treble pitched "). It is difficult to decide
whether the close matching of *chiao* with *miao* extends to a
conception of the *chiao* (in whatever sense) as plural. I am inclined to think it does, and—while in this mood—would translate
chiao as " circuit-luminaria."

S 5 and S 6. As is well known, the third couplet of our text
presents a problem similar to that in the preceding couplet: shall
yu and *wu* be taken as simple verbs with the following *yü* as
their object, i. e., as " (to) have-aught " / " have-naught desired "
/ " desirable," or as abstract nouns with the *yü* as predicate, i. e.,
" the Have-aught " / " Have-naught desires " / " desired." The
ch'ang preceding *yu* and *wu* would correspondingly function either
as an adverb or a verb. In our analysis of the opening distich we
have adumbrated a third possibility, that of *ch'ang* being a transitive verb; in that case *yu* and *wu*, as nouns, would be its objects,
with the following *yü* starting a new verbal sequence; or, as is
more likely, *yu yü* / *wu yü*, " having-aught " / " naught desired,"
serving as compound substantival objects of the verbal *ch'ang*.
Using " forewont " simultaneously as an adjective (i. e., ' forewonted "), as a transitive verb (" to accustom "), and less
successfully as an adverb (" wontwise ") and aligning the translation of the verse so as to keep the nominal (and metaphysical)
capitalization of " Have " as inconspicuous as possible, we offer
the following approximation of the threefold ambiguity of the
original:

> Forewont
> Have-naught/aught
> Desired for to contemplate . . . .

S 5.6 and S 6.6. As frequently in involved sentences or contexts,
the antecedents of the two *ch'i* 其 " demonstrative adjective or
pronominal adjective of the third person (singular or plural) "
are difficult to ascertain. They could be reflexive with nominal
yu and *wu* as immediate antecedents (a very tempting reading),
or could refer to any single substantival term or combination of
terms in the previous lines, or indeed to the main subject of discourse, the *Tao*. To avoid irrevocable commitment as to antecedent (in the gender or number of the English pronoun) the

cautious translator has no choice but to render *ch'i* by " of the same," or by an emphatic " *the*," italicized to distinguish it from the numerous " the " injected into the translation due to the requirements of the English idiom.

S 7. The key word in this stichos is 同 *t'ung*, " alike," " same," " together." As in Latin (*simul~similis*) , " sameness " and " togetherness " may be expressed in Chinese by the same root, and it is difficult to decide between the two semantic poles when it comes to commit oneself in another language. In addition, the problem of translating *t'ung* is complicated by the fact that the stichos can be construed in three different ways, each syntactically justifiable (' S ' = subject; ' P ' = predicate; ' O ' = object) :

1. *tz'u liang-che* (S) *t'ung* (P^1); *ch'u* (P^2) *erh* (junctive) *i* (adv.) *ming* (P^8). The eight characters form in this case two stichoi, a reading preferred by several judicious editors.
2. *tz'u liang-che* (S) *t'ung* (adv.) *ch'u* (P^1) *erh* (j) *i* (adv.) *ming* (P^2).
3. *tz'u liang-che* (S) *t'ung* (P^1) *ch'u* (O^1) *erh* (j) *i* (P^2) *ming* (O^2).
1. These coupled ones are the same;
   Coming out, they are differently named.
2. These coupled ones come out alikened (or ' simultaneously ') , but are differently named.
3. These coupled ones aliken (as a transitive verb : ' make one ') (their) coming out, but differentiate (their) names.

There are two possible solutions of the philological problem in English. Vestigially, English " same " retains some faint connotation of " together " (AS. *samen*) ; it remains to force " same " into the verbal category, postulating a form " to same " (lit., " be the same "; 2. " make the same ") . A better solution would be to revive the obsolete etymological sense of " to atone " (< " at one "; *tr.* " to join in one "; *intr.* " to come into unity ") . Then, using " diverse," as the dictionary seems to permit it, either as an adverb (= " diversely ") , or as a verb (" to be or to make different ") , and " name-call " as either a noun or a verb, we obtain:

1 A. These coupled ones same (*v.i.*) ;
       Egressing, diverse namecall.
1 B. These coupled ones at-one (*v.i.*) ;
       Egressing, diverse namecall.
2. These coupled ones at one (adv.; or : ' same ') egressing, diverse namecall.
3. These coupled ones at-one (*v.t.*; or : ' same ') egressing, diverse (*v.t.*) namecall.

As in the original Chinese, version 1 AB would differ from versions 2 and 3 only in the punctuation, or—omitting the latter —only in alignment.

S 8.2 謂 *wei* ⟨ *gjwɔd*, " to say," " tell," " call," " address (some-one) ," appears to be a cognate of 曰 *yüeh* ⟨ *gjwăt*, " to say," " quoth " (introducing direct quotations) , and of 云 *yün* ⟨ *gjwən*, " said," " to be said " (of indirect quotations) . Morphologically, it seems to equal *GJWE- (the etymon " to say," " speak ") plus an element of unknown function (Karlgren's -*d*, perhaps -*s* or -*z*) , to be contrasted with the final -*t* of *gjwăt* (possibly the vestige of a pronominal object such as 之 *chih* ⟨ *tjəg*) and the final -*n* of *gjwən* (a final consonant seemingly associated with the intransi-tive or static aspects of verbs) . Should one desire to have a single translation for *wei* applicable to most of its usages one would have to revive the obsolescent transitive functions of English ' to speak ' or ' to bespeak ' in the senses: " to speak to," " to address " (" we spoke a ship ") and " to speak about," " to term designate," " call."

S 8.3 之 *chih* ⟨ *tjəg*, " pronominal object of the third person: him, her, it, them." The gender and number distinctions in pro-nouns force the Indo-European translators to commit themselves, often *à contre-coeur*, as to the antecedent of *chih*. Since *chih* appears to be originally a demonstrative (in adjectival function obsolete even in archaic Chinese, except in a few expressions) , it would be better to keep it on that level in pedantically precise translations, rendering it as " this," " that " or " such." We would particularly favor the last as noncommittal in number as well as gender.

S 8.4 *hsüan* ⟨ *g'iwen* 玄, " somber-colored," " brownish," " dark-ling (as the color of depth, such as that of water or of the darken-ing sky)," " fuscous," " fusco-hyaline (dusky, but semitrans-parent)," " dim," " dun." Probably a cognate of 熏 *hsün* ⟨ *χiwən*, " smoky," and 纁 *hsün* ⟨ *χjwən*, " purple," " brown." By exten-sion, particularly in the Taoist vocabulary, " darkling into the distance ": " profound," " mysterious," " abstruse," " mystical," *n.* " mystery." All these traditional translations seem to be too precise and may not be quite justified after scrutiny. However supercharged the word may have become in esoteric literature, its specific semantic contour may not have extended beyond " darkling," " darkful," " fuscating," " the fuscated."

S 9. The persistent rendering of this stichos as "mystery of mysteries," " mystère des mystères," " das Geheimniss der Geheimnisse," " *gen no mata gen*," etc. by highly competent translators presents a puzzle of puzzles to the pedantic philologist. For him, the sentence *hsüan chih yu hsüan* is a clearly verbal one that must be construed: verb (transitive) + pronominal object + adverb + verb. Every tyro student of Chinese knows that *yu* (S 9.3) " once more," " moreover," " again," is above all an adverb, its non-adverbial usage being limited to functioning as an archaic junctive between two numerals, as in 二十又三 " twenty *yu* three " (analogous to English " and " in " three-and-twenty "), and that even in that function it may be interpreted as operating as a verbal (equivalent to 有 *yu*, " have," the locution being: " twenty having three "). The adverb *yu* makes it impossible, then, to read the following *hsüan* as a noun, nor the *chih* preceding it as the possessive *chih* in the construction: " noun *chih* noun = noun's noun," i. e., " mystery's (or mysteries') mystery." How shall we explain this flagrant disregard of the principles of grammatical analysis by responsible translators? Lawyers for the defense will plead attenuating circumstances. First, Chinese commentators, ancient and modern, are curiously evasive, if not silent, on the structure and meaning of this stichos. Second, *hsüan* appeared to the defendants to be a noun and was not found to be attested as a transitive verb lexicographically. Third, a considerable part of the *Lao Tzu* (our chapter included) being in verse, poetic license coupled with the daring and originality of the author's thought and verbalization might be considered sufficient to outweigh a petty point of grammar. A philological court would, however, easily dismiss these excuses as irrelevant, immaterial,— and irreverent towards Lao Tzu. First, there is not a single passage in the entire *Lao Tzu* text where a similar departure from the grammatical norm of the language of the period is indicated or suspected. Second, an identical construction with an adverbial *yu* appears in *Lao Tzu* 48: 損之又損 *sun chih yu sun*. Our mis-

translators of *hsüan chih yu hsüan* as " mystery of mysteries,"
etc. show here no hesitation in parsing the sentence as verbal and
translate correctly: " decrease it and again decrease," " décroître
encore décroître," " nimmt ab und wiederum nimmt ab," " *kore
wo sonjite mata sonzu,*" etc. Of course, *sun* is registered in all
dictionaries as a verb, consistency is a pedestrian virtue out of
place in mystic environment, and naïve occidental mystai looking
for " the decrease of decreases " (and corresponding " Abnahme,"
" décroissance," and " *son no mata son* ") to match " the mystery
of mysteries " should not expect to find philosophical translations
cluttered with pedantic notes. Third, while it is true that *hsüan*
is not registered in lexicons as a verb, neither are countless other
nouns which a philologist would identify as functioning verbally
in the proper grammatical context. *Hsüan* is, incidentally, an
adjective-verb, and only secondarily a noun. To illustrate the
problem with a primary noun, would a knowledgeable student of
Chinese literature think offhand of 弦 or 絃 *hsien*, " bowstring,"
" chord," " string of a musical instrument," as a verb? Yet he
would have no difficulty in translating it as " to string " in 弦
之 *hsien chih* " to string it (musically) " (Mao's comm. to *Shih* 91;
Shen Chien 申鑑, opening paragraph), i. e., " give it (or ' them ')
expression on stringed instruments," parallel to the following 舞之
wu chih, " express it (them) in dancing." We conclude, therefore,
that while translating *hsüan chih yu hsüan* as " mystery of mysteries " may have some justification in the translator's mind in
the context of his interpretation of the chapter, his conception of
the philosophy of the *Lao Tzu*, and his understanding of the
duties, rights, privileges, and liberties of a translator, the universal evasion of the problem of the grammatical structure of the
stichos by the translators and the mysterious silence on that
problem which they observe in their footnotes constitute a philological misdemeanor of the first order. As a verb, *hsüan* must
have meant " to darken (transitive or intransitive) ," " to darkle,"
" to deepen," " to be (become, or make) fuscous," " to be (become, or make) mysterious," etc. Structurally, then, the supposed " mystery of mysteries " should read: " to mysterize it, the
more (it) mysterizes," or " mysterizing it, and once more mys-

terizing. . . ." We use " mysterize " in the sense: *v. t.* " to make mysterious "; " interpret mystically "; *v. i.* " to cultivate mystery or a mysterious air " (WEBSTER's *Unabridged*). The only rendering of the stichos approaching this verbal construction is, to the best of my knowledge, that of LIN Yutang (in *The Wisdom of Laotse*, p. 42) : " Reaching from the Mystery into the Deeper Mystery."

S 10 presents no difficulties. Its first word *chung*, " multitude," " host," " crowd," " throng," " to be many," " all," is usually translated by " all " which renders its narrowest, adjectival meaning. The full flavor of the verb-noun complex would better be expressed by " thronging " or " thronged." The whole line may be construed as being in apposition to S 9, as the predicate of S 9 (if erroneously interpreted as nominal: " the mystery of mysteries "), or as the object or complement of the verbal in S 9.

The following translation of the entire text has little literary merit. It reflects, however, to the best of my ability, every significant etymological and grammatical feature, including every double entendre, that I have been able to discover in the original in an endeavor to establish a solider philological foundation upon which a firmer interpretation of the *incipit* of Taoist philosophy might be built.

>   Lodehead lodehead-brooking : no forewonted lodehead;
>   Namecall namecall-brooking :no forewonted namecall.
>   Having-naught namecalling : Heaven-Earth's fetation,
>   Having-aught namecalling : Myriad Mottlings' mother.
>   Affirmably,
>   Forewont
>   Have-naught
>   Desired—for to descry in view *the* minikin-subliminaria,
>   Forewont
>   Have-aught
>   Desired—for to descry in view *the* circuit-luminaria;
>   These pairing ones at-one
>   Egressing,
>   Diverse namecall :
>   At-one—bespeak such : Darkling,
>   Adarkling such, again adarkling
>   The thronging subliminaria's gate.

Tolstoy and China
—A Critical Analysis*

Philosophy East and West,
1.3 (1951), 64-76.

This neat and compendious study of Tolstoy's interest in China's ethical heritage and of its possible influence on the illustrious Russian writer in the years of his sageship is intelligently planned, painstakingly compiled, and sincerely, though perhaps a little too expeditiously, written. The specialist may find it professionally competent, though by no means definitive or exhaustive; the layman, factually dependable, yet hardly conclusive. It is a pity that the author and his collaboratrice succumbed to whatever temptation offered itself for launching their candid and stimulating, yet somewhat unfledged, essay in the form of a book, rather than allowing it to incubate first, as an *ébauche* of a monograph, in a review of "comparative" literature or culture. Its many admirable architectonic qualities would have stood out as prominently, while the uncompleted gestation of the whole, partly attributable to imperfect nutrition from defective sources, would not have received libriform emphasis.

Following a brief but cogent introduction on China, the West, and Tolstoy (pp. 3–10), the Boddes ably analyze Tolstoy's readings on the Middle Kingdom (pp. 11–29), basing their statements on a list of Western works on Chinese civilization ascertained to have been accessible to Tolstoy (with some forty literary items tidily enumerated in Appendix B, pp. 95–102). They proceed then to a consideration of Tolstoy's writings and publications on China, most of which are unavailable outside Russia, with particular attention devoted to the three fragments entitled collectively *Chinese Wisdom* (pp. 30–46). A recapitulation of the story of Tolstoy's contact with Chinese intellectuals in the last years of his life follows (pp. 47–58). The authors conclude with an attempt at evaluating the meaning of China to Tolstoy (pp. 59–74) and with the formulation of a threefold hypothesis of China's imprint on some of Tolstoy's fundamental ideas, namely, his censorious views on music, his nihilistic doctrine of the state and of non-

* Mr. Boodberg's review of *Tolstoy and China* by Derk Bodde, with the collaboration of Galia Speshneff Bodde ("History of Ideas Series," No. 4; Princeton: Princeton University Press, 1950), is printed in this section of the journal because of its extensive analysis of the subject.—*Editor's Note.*

resistance, and his nullifidian notions on immortality (pp. 75–89). Appendix A (pp. 91–94) recounts for Occidental readers a Chinese piece of self-reportage on a visit made in 1945 by Kuo Mo-jo, one of contemporary China's most distinguished pseudo-Marxists and Stalinodules, to the Tolstoy Museum at Yasnaya Polyana.

Though still incomplete (as only half of the projected ninety-five volumes of the Soviet Centennial Edition of Tolstoy's works begun in 1928 have been published), the evidence of Tolstoy's concern with the Chinese ethos in both its Confucian and Taoist aspects is extensive. It has been marshaled by Bodde with the skill and precision of Hesperian scholarship which contrast sharply with the inept treatment of the same material by the Sinologically illiterate Soviet editors whom Bodde rightly takes to task for their unscholarly nonchalance (see, e.g., p. 43, note; p. 60, note). So much more deplorable is Bodde's own uncritical acceptance of hints and tentative conclusions by the same uninspiring annotators or by other informants on points crucial to his argument and the development of his theme. This grievously affects both his acumen as a Sinologue and his understanding of the genesis of Tolstoy's Sinophilia. Thus in his perconctatory assay of Tolstoy's earliest piece of writing on China, *Chinese Wisdom* (presumably composed in 1884, pp. 36–44), Bodde goes off on an utterly false track, with his philological moiety strangely unable to subject the fabric of Tolstoy's essay to elementary linguistic tests and his otherwise sound bibliographical instinct remaining unaccountably dormant. The case is rather illustrative of the pell-mellish technique of modern corporate scholarship and as such deserves admonitory analysis.

First, Bodde and adjuvant experts labor here under the entirely unwarranted assumption that Tolstoy decocted his little tract chiefly from English publications on China. They seem to be oblivious of the fact that, however competent Tolstoy may have been in utilizing English and German writings on the Orient, French remained for him, as for most Russian intellectuals of his day, the main fountainhead of both general and specific cultural information. The volume of quotidian consumption of French printed goods, trademarked or contraband, was so large in Tolstoy's milieu that citatory reference was precluded in all but the highly exceptional cases. The modern bibliographical *douanier* must be, therefore, constantly on the *qui vive* lest he pass by a mass of Gallic goods while his attention is distracted by a few bales of a consignment stamped London or Leipzig. Had Bodde followed this monition, comparison of pertinent texts would have immediately revealed to him that the translation of the introductory chapter of *The Great Learning* (*Ta Hsüeh*) included in *Chinese Wisdom* was not made by Tolstoy from the English version of J. Legge's *Chinese Classics,* as claimed by Bodde and the sciolists of the Soviet "Jubilee Edition" (henceforth quoted, Bodde-fashion, as JE), but is an almost verbatim rendering of G. Pauthier's French interpretation (taken from either *Le Ta hio ou La Grande Étude,* 1837, or *Confucius et Mencius: Les Quatre Livres,* 1868; these are not included in Bodde's list of Tolstoy's readings). Second, the paragraphs of *Chinese Wisdom* dissected by Bodde on pages 41–43 do not contain "a curious parody of the picture of ancient Chinese education"; nor are they based "upon some secondary European account written by someone who had none too good a knowledge of the original texts," but represent from beginning to end a faithful transposition into Russian of portions of Chu Hsi's famous preface to *The Great Learning.* This, Bodde should have easily recognized from the opening sentence, had he not been blinded by his crotchet in favor of Legge (whose edition of *The Great Learning* does not carry the Sung master's preface). In his paraphrase, Tolstoy indulges in but one serious *ad libitum,* that probably induced by his misunderstanding of French *"arroser"* as "to water plants," instead of "to sprinkle the ground (as a measure of dust-abatement in the school-yard)." Third, Tolstoy hardly needed to obtain his information on Chinese immigration into the United States from such unlikely quarters as "American visitors or American newspapers," as suggested by E. J. Simmons in a "personal communication" quoted by Bodde. The French and Russian periodicals of the time would have yielded abundant material on that question. For example, the well-known Russian monthly *Russkaya Mysl'* in its first issue for 1883 contained (pp. 138–161) a thoughtful firsthand report on the anti-Chinese agitation on the Pacific Coast and the first Exclusion Act. Five years previously, the *Revue des deux mondes* carried an article entitled "L'invasion chinoise et le socialisme aux États Unis" (1878, pp. 589–613), and the review *Le correspondant* (*livraison* of July, 1878, pp. 92–113), another, "Les chinois hors de chez eux," both with considerable attention paid to the question of the status of the Chinese in California. The reading routine of every educated Russian comprised the perusal of half a dozen leading French and Russian reviews, and Tolstoy must have seen one or all of these articles. Fourth, the idealistic picture of China that Tolstoy had conjured in his mind when he wrote his sketch must have been to a large extent evoked by another French work discussed in detail and correctly appraised by Bodde (pp. 17–19), but mistakenly believed by him to be unknown to Tolstoy before 1887, namely, Simon's *La cité chinoise.* Bodde and the Soviet editors on whom he apparently bases himself entirely overlooked the fact that most of Simon's ecstatic disquisition had been serialized, prior to publication in book form, in the popular French bimonthly *La nouvelle revue* in four of its issues between April, 1883, and April, 1884 (Vols. XXI, XXII, XXV, and XXVII). Tolstoy not only knew the periodical but had some of his own work published in it the same year (Vol. XXIII, July–August, 1883; cf. letters to the Countess, June 8 and November 14, 1883, JE 83, 385, 411) and must doubtless have seen E. de Cyon's study on himself entitled *Un pessimiste russe* (Vol. XXII, pp. 619–657), which is found almost next to the second chapter of Simon's work in the same volume (pp. 528–567). It is on page 541 and page 549 of that installment that Tolstoy must have found mention of the ritual of spring plowing by the Chinese emperor, to which he refers at the beginning of *Chinese Wisdom.* Another laudatory account of Chinese civilization by a Chinese colonel, Tcheng-Ki-Tong, military attaché at the Paris embassy, ran in the *Revue des deux mondes* in the May and June issues of 1884, but probably too late to have affected Tolstoy's composition, as no traces of it can be recognized in *Chinese Wisdom.* The colonel's essay was also later published under separate cover and stirred sufficient interest in Russia to be synopticized in the popular magazine *Niva* (1887, pp. 1123–1124). It is, incidentally, in the next (1884) volume of the celebrated French *Revue* that appeared the penetrating critical article on Tolstoy by E. M. de Vogüé, which provoked a rejoinder in December of the same year by N. N. Strakhov, one of Tolstoy's best friends and greatest admirers, reprinted in Strakhov's *Kriticheskiya stat'i* (Vol. I, pp. 366–387, Kiev, 1908).

To sum up, one must come to the conclusion, with reservations discussed below, that the main inspiration of Tolstoy's *Chinese Wisdom* stemmed primarily from three French works: Pauthier's translation of *The Great Learning,* Simon's *La cité chinoise,* and Julien's version of the *Tao Tê Ching.* Only the last one is recognized as a source by Bodde. I believe that it can be demonstrated further that the impact of these three works on Tolstoy was such that to the end of his days they—or rather the notes he had taken on them—remained in his mind as constituting the very epitome of Chinese civilization. They were digested and assimilated by him to such an extent that most of his subsequent reading on China never displaced that first impression and only feebly registered itself on his consciousness; it is even doubtful that any other work on China, known or unknown to us, with the exception of other versions of *The Great Learning, The Doctrine of the Mean,* and the *Tao Tê Ching,* was ever read through by Tolstoy.

The main source of Angloform information on China for Tolstoy in 1884 remains, then, as demonstrated in workmanlike fashion by Bodde (pp. 14–16), the excellent book by Meadows, *The Chinese and Their Rebellions.* There is no doubt, however, that Tolstoy limited himself to reading only the second, more philosophical and least informative, part of the tome (from p. 326 on, and particularly beginning with p. 493). Besides the quotation discussed by Bodde on page 16, Tolstoy noted with warm approval (*Complete Works,* translated by Leo Wiener, Vol. XIX, p. 109) Meadows' philosophizing on the fourfold character of civilization in his *Essay on Civilization and Its Present State in the East and West* incorporated in the volume (the passage commented upon by Tolstoy is found on pp. 501–503). This entry was missed by Bodde; his slip was unquestionably due to his misunderstanding and unjustified censure of Wiener's editorial craft, as shown in the note on pages 16–17, where he attributes to Wiener the misspelling of Meadows' name as "Medov," unaware that the conscientious American scholar had merely faithfully reproduced the Russian original. Now, the work translated by Wiener under the title *Thoughts and Aphorisms* is based on a "pirated" publication by D. R. Kudryavtsev of farraginous excerpts from Tolstoy's correspondence under the title *Spelye Kolos'ya* (*Ripe Ears of Grain,* Geneva, four installments from 1894 to 1896), where the two citations from Meadows appear on pages 175 and 56. In the latter case Meadows' name is again distorted, this time as "Medor" (and so again accurately copied by Wiener in the English edition). Not all the epistolary fragments are dated in the original; the two in question are not, and the date given by Bodde refers to another cutting close by. This inaccuracy Bodde also ascribes to Wiener without any justification whatsoever. The origin of Kudryavtsev's compilation is obscure and has been little discussed in the Jubilee Edition and other available Russian sources. The provenance of the letters is not clear, although a message from Tolstoy to the compiler is prefaced to the publication, giving, seemingly *à contre coeur,* postfact permission for its circulation. I would hazard the explanation, subject to correction by Tolstoy specialists, that the material was surreptitiously supplied to Kudryavtsev by Chertkov, since the only identifiable fragments in the first half of the book come from Tolstoy's letters to the latter. It would seem that Chertkov, as Tolstoy's literary executor and the chief editor of the Jubilee Edition, refrained from mentioning this bit of indiscretion toward his teacher and friend, while other Tolstoyists remained silent on the subject as long as the man called Tolstoy's evil genius was alive.

It is also likely that the shorter work of Meadows, *Desultory Notes* (mentioned above), was accessible to Tolstoy at the time, for it appears to be the only book of the period which gives prominence (p. 202) to the quotation from Mencius which lies at the basis of Tolstoy's statement on the anti-war sentiments of the Chinese in the second paragraph of *Chinese Wisdom.* It is an almost verbatim rendering of *Mencius* VII.2.4, not a paraphrase of IV.1.14, as stated by Bodde (p. 40).

Returning now to our theory that Confucian thought assumed in Tolstoy's mind a pre-eminently Francicized form, I believe that it can be further substantiated by an analysis of the quotations from the first three of the Confucian Four Books that are scattered through Tolstoy's later works. The most fruitful source is of course *For Every Day* (1906–10) and its earlier versions, *Thoughts of Wise Men* and *Circle of Reading,* the composition of which was inspired by Tolstoy's Chinese reading of 1884 (Bodde, p. 34). My own comparison of the various renderings of the twenty-two identifiable quotations or paraphrases from *The Great Learning* and *The Doctrine of the Mean* found in Tolstoy's works shows the following: only one or two can be derived from Legge; two or three parallel the Russian version made by the Japanese D. Konishi; the remainder are without any doubt translated verbatim from Pauthier or inspired by his interpretation. This is unmistakably shown by the phraseology, by the tautological rendering of a single Chinese term by two synonyms, a favorite device of Pauthier's, and, in the quotations from *The Great Learning,* by references to "the luminous principle of reason received by us from Heaven," the somewhat Johannine translation given by Pauthier to the Chinese *ming tê,* soberly rendered by Legge as "illustrious virtue." This idiosyncrasy of Pauthier's, Bodde erroneously ascribes to Tolstoy (p. 65) and consequently fails to see that it must have been that wording that prompted Tolstoy to write in a letter to Strakhov in June, 1882, thanking him for sending what had apparently been Tolstoy's first special book on China: "The thought of [Jesus'] talk with Nicod [emus] is clearly stated there by Confucius" (JE 63.98; cf. Bodde, p. 7). Only Pauthier's exposition of "the light of reason received by us from Heaven" could have made Tolstoy think of Confucius in connection with St. John 3.19–21. That passage of the Gospels preyed at the time on Tolstoy's mind as evidenced by reference to it in the famous letter to Engelgardt penned soon thereafter, about Christmas, 1882 (JE 63.113). In June, 1885, Chertkov in a letter to Tolstoy from England reminds him of one of his preferred bits of Chinese wisdom, the well-known legendary inscription on Ch'êng T'ang's bathtub enjoining daily "renovation" (*The Great Learning* II.1). It is quoted in Pauthier's unmistakable emphatically redundant version (JE 85.236; M. V. Muratov, *L. N. Tolstoi i V. G. Chertkov,* Moscow, 1934, p. 125). It must also have been Pauthier's enthusiasm for *The Great Learning* that had inculcated in

Tolstoy the belief that that work together with *The Doctrine of the Mean* represented the most authentic and direct sayings of the Chinese sage, and not Konishi's translations of 1892 and 1895, as suggested by Bodde (p. 60). One must concede, however, that the ingenuous Konishi must have confirmed Tolstoy in his illusion by going as far as identifying Ch'êng Tzŭ, Chu Hsi's master, as a direct disciple of Confucius (*Voprosy filosofii i psikhologii*, Vol. XVI, p. 30). In his transcription of Chinese names Konishi followed an incongruous practice of mixing together Chinese and Sino-Japanese transliteration, through which phonological maze Tolstoy somehow managed to steer a relatively true course. It is only the Orientalogically hapless editors of the Jubilee Edition who still seem to believe that Konishi's impossible hybrid "Laosi" is one of the recorded names of Lao-tzŭ (JE 25.884). A sad contrast indeed with the seeming competence prevailing in the Russia of 1893 in matters pertaining to Chinese literature, as shown by the interchange of letters between Tolstoy and Stasov (see Bodde, pp. 24–25). Incidentally, Bodde's wonderings on page 92 concerning Konishi's sojourn in Russia can be set at rest for it is well known that Konishi had repeated conferences with Tolstoy in September, 1909 (in Moscow), and in June, 1910 (at Yasnaya Polyana). See, for instance, A. B. Goldenweiser, *Vblizi Tolstogo* (2 vols., Moscow, 1922 and 1923). I cannot resist the temptation of pointing out from that work two pertinent bits of Tolstoyana, the first not without piquancy in this year of grace 1951. It seems, according to the pianist Goldenweiser (Vol. II, p. 53), that Konishi told Tolstoy, probably with a grain of Nipponese malice, that the Chinese on Formosa were not averse to practicing cannibalism at the expense of the natives and that Tolstoy roguishly recounted later some of the gruesome details. On page 56 of the same volume, the sage and the pianist are recorded as having indulged in some cruel remarks apropos of samples of Japanese folk-music which Konishi had hopefully left with the master, who, together with the musician, failed dismally to appreciate its quality, either as to words or melody. Bodde's doubts as to the availability of Konishi's 1893 translation of *The Great Learning* (p. 102) must be due to his not being privy to the fact that Tolstoy was a member of the Moscow Psychological Society (he was made an honorary member on January 24, 1894, *Voprosy filosofii*, Vol. XXIII, p. 457) and as such could not have overlooked its journal and the translations of his fellow member, Konishi, published in it. As to quotations from *The Analects* of Confucius, of which there are also over a score in the *Circle of Reading* and *For Every Day*, we find again that the predominant majority of them are translated from Pauthier, with only two or three traceable back to Legge. Even the lone paraphrase from *Mencius* V.2.8 (*Circle of Reading* 2.497) is recognizable as coming from Pauthier (*Les Quatre Livres*, p. 403) on the basis of the preposterous Chinese name "Nikonshau," which could only be a transmogrification of the French "Nieouchan," but by no stretch of the imagination that of Legge's English *"New* mountain." It all points to the conclusion that Tolstoy never read much of Legge's *Chinese Classics* beyond the *Prolegomena* to Volume I and to Volume II (on Mencius), whence he extracted the information on Mo-tzŭ (Bodde, pp. 26–29). Bodde's belief (p. 59) that Tolstoy had used Legge's *Classics* as "his primary source for Confucianism" is therefore erroneous; he used the work so occasionally and so listlessly that it is no wonder at all that he could not even remember Legge's name in 1890 (pp. 28, 59). Tolstoy's predilection for translating from the French is further indicated by his use of a singular source of Confucian quotations, Louis Rochet's *Sentences, maximes et proverbes mantchoux et mongols* (Paris, 1875), a collection of aphorisms culled chiefly from Manchu and Mongolian translations of the Chinese classics. After much searching, I have been able to identify this work as the source of "Manchu proverbs" appearing in the *Circle of Reading* (1.154 and 2.358). I have not been successful, however, in attempts to trace the ten "Chinese proverbs" quoted in the *Circle*. They must be ascribed to one of the unknown Tolstoyan sources on China, postulated so often by Bodde. Tolstoy's reading on Chinese Buddhism was limited, as pointed out by Bodde, and was probably confined, to the two works of S. Beal, *A Catena of Buddhist Scriptures* and *The Romantic Legend*, perused in the late eighties (p. 101). In the first work, it must have been the *Sūtra of Forty-two Sections* (pp. 188–204) that attracted Tolstoy's attention because of its purely ethical character. Twenty years later, we find in the *Circle* (1.35) a quotation without the shadow of a doubt gleaned from page 196 of the *Catena. Circle* 2.257 has a short quotation from the *Fo pen hsing chi ching* which cannot be identified with surety, but may have been extracted from *The Romantic Legend.*

In his studies of the *Tao Tê Ching* Tolstoy used a variety of translations of that text, French, German, English, and Russian (pp. 99–100), but again it could be demonstrated that in this case also he remained in a large measure true to his first love of 1884, Julien's French rendering. In at least two cases of purported quotations from Lao-tzŭ included in *For Every Day* (JE 43.224; 44.306) Tolstoy incorporates Julien's commentary into the text. Contrary to expectation, Victor von Strauss's "theosophist" translation had made little impression upon Tolstoy, so far as I can judge after a quick analysis of the fifty-odd quotations from the *Tao Tê Ching* scattered through Tolstoy's writings. In the last years of Tolstoy's life Paul Carus' widely known edition of 1898 (Bodde, p. 100) seems to have superseded Julien's as Tolstoy's favorite, and he exchanged several letters with the translator at the turn of the century (P. Carus, "A Tribute to Tolstoy" [in Russian] in *O Tolstom*, Moscow, 1911, Vol. II, pp. 50–52; *Tao Teh King*, Chicago, 1898, p. 25). At least once (JE 44.168), Tolstoy used Carus' version without checking his translation with other renderings as can be seen by his misconstruing English "arms" *sc.* "weapons" as "hands" (Russian *"ruki"*) in a passage from the seventy-sixth chapter of the *Tao Tê Ching* (Carus, p. 135), a mistake which would have been impossible had Tolstoy consulted French and German versions. Two interesting echoes of Pauthier and Simon are to be noted for that late period of Tolstoy's life. In his *Memoirs* (2d ed.; Moscow, 1938, p. 404; see also *Zhivaya Zhizn*, Moscow, 1922, p. 169), the well-known Russian writer Veresayev (Smidovich) recounts his visit to Yasnaya Polyana in August, 1903, and reports, with some puzzlement as to the sources of Tolstoy's Sinological information, the following. It seems that, during a conversation with Veresayev, Tolstoy waxed indignant toward Metchnikoff's *Essai de la philosophie optimiste* and invoked in the discussion the Chinese concept *shu,* generally translated "reciprocity" (so by Legge, *Analects* XV.23), but misinterpreted by Tolstoy to mean "respect," "respect towards all life," toward every manifestation of nature, every blade of grass, every cloud in the sky, or even a pool of dirty water on a country road. The erudite Veresayev, who seems to be cognizant of the *locus classicus,* wonders whether Tolstoy obtained this unusual interpretation of the Chinese term from Chinese visitors to Tolstoy's estate who initiated him into an esoteric tradition relating to the passage. There is no doubt that here again Tolstoy's inspiration comes from Pauthier, who was fond of referring to the concept, using the Chinese word untranslated (*Les Quatre Livres*, p. 192, with a footnote reference to his 1837 edition of *The Great Learning*, which is inaccessible to me). The plain Chinese word must have been iridized in Tolstoy's mind by passing through the prism of Simon's paean to the Chinese philosophy of labor and agriculture ("Le travail" in *La cité*). There the Chinese attitude toward nature is characterized by the use of such extravagant terms as gentle solicitation of nature's co-operation, caressing understanding, and spiritualization of the earth, in contrast to Western agriculturists' gross pretensions, violent impositions, scientific maltreatment, and mechanical ruses. Tolstoy's curious misconception of Chinese *shu* may also have been slightly colored by Tcheng-Ki-Tong's discussion of "le respect" in *Revue des deux mondes* (1884, pp. 288–290).

Another echo of Simon's reverberates in *For Every Day*. Among the entries for February 2, we find a passage beginning "Confucius says . . ." (JE 43.64), a unique way, for Tolstoy, of citing Confucian wisdom. The quotation appears in fuller form in *Circle of Reading* under November 10 and was entered in *Thoughts of Wise Men* as a thought for November 29 by Tolstoy in his diary, rereading the passage on November 29, 1905 (JE 55.281). One is inclined to be indulgent toward the Soviet editors for failure to recognize under this specific reference a quotation which Simon extracted, in the mysterious way peculiar to him, a man confessedly ignorant of the Chinese written language, from the little-known Taoist work, *Kuan Yin Tzŭ* (see *Ssu-pu pei-yao* ed., 5a), and cited in the second chapter of *La cité chinoise* (6th ed., p. 98). In an equally unexplainable manner, Tolstoy had transformed the name Kouang yun tse (so spelled in the French text) into "Confucius." This editorial innocence as to the sources of Tolstoy's information is matched, however, by a pontifical mis-interpretation on the part of the same editors in the index of the second volume of *For Every Day* (JE 44.491). Under December 5 (p. 332; under July 18 in *Circle of Reading* 2.59), Tolstoy entered a quotation which he attributed to "Kvan-Khin." It is not difficult to recognize in the quotation the celebrated vow of Kuan-yin (or Ti-tsang), the Bodhisattva of Mercy, possibly (though not probably) found by Tolstoy on page 406 of Beal's *Catena*. Our fatuous editors enigmatically identify the quotation as coming from the pen of Ch'ang Kien (English transcription in the original), described as a poet of the T'ang dynasty.

We adduce these two bits of Muscovite Orientalistic perspicacity as an illustration of the type of pitfalls encountered or felicitously bypassed by Bodde in his peregrinations through the Jubilee Edition and as evidence of the amount of philological detective work which is still to be done before the full story of "Tolstoy and China" can adequately be told. There remains now to estimate the validity of Bodde's hypothesis of the influence of Chinese thought on Tolstoy's ideas on music, non-resistance, and immor-tality. I am afraid that most thoughtful students of Tolstoy who will un-doubtedly be grateful to Bodde for his earnest and orderly exposition of Tolstoy's preoccupation with Chinese civilization would, at this juncture, be obliged to part company with him.

In spite of the seemingly imposing evidence of a radical change of in-terests that Tolstoy experienced during his great moral crisis of the late seventies and early eighties, most competent Russian students of his life agree that the virile creator of *War and Peace, Anna Karenina,* and other great bellettristic works and the doctrinaire writer of jejune tracts, however paradoxical it may seem, co-inhabited, Janus-like, the depths of Tolstoy's being from the very beginning of his conscious life; that the dichotomy of his literary activity is more apparent than real; that the "new ideas" he began to expound in the post-1880 period emanated from the quintessence of his cloven soul; and that the Tolstoy of the "Nekhlyudov and Sage of Yasnaya Polyana" era was but the inspissated soul-substance of the Tolstoy of the "Olenin-Prince Andrew-Pierre-Levin" cycle. This organic unity of Tolstoy has been, *en dernier lieu,* authoritatively reiterated by that master craftsman of Slavonic literary criticism, Professor Waclaw Lednicki, in his review of E. J. Simmons' *Leo Tolstoy.* Andrei Byelyi's essay "Lev Tolstoi i kul'tura" (*O religii L'va Tolstogo,* Moscow, 1912, pp. 142–171) also comes to my mind as well worth rereading in this connection. If one leaves aside the few powerful personality-shaping influences of Tolstoy's adolescence and youth, such as that of Rousseau, the term "influence," with its inescapable connotation of an inflow of extraneous power and authority, must be applied with extreme caution to that colossus of bathmic energy that was Leo Tolstoy. The elements of the great exothermic chain reaction that constituted his creative life were inwrought in the endothermic substance of his adolescent being, and most surmised "influences" seem at best to be but catalytic agents. Thus, Tolstoy's moralistic attitude toward music was only a facet of the "categorical imperative" he applied to all art and the only prophylactic this man endowed with the sensuousness of a titan had found to be effective, from his youth on, against the soul-shaking potency of organized tone. Music, as he well knew from intimate personal experience, could not be treated as an adiaphoron. This attitude antedates any possible acquaintance with Chinese doctrines on the subject. True, as pointed out by Bodde (pp. 78–79), the famous indictment of music in *The Kreutzer Sonata* (1889) contains a specific mention of China in the words "in China music is a state matter," but this does not in any way presuppose that Tolstoy had read any detailed Chinese disquisition on music, such as the *Li Chi* treatise. I am inclined to believe that we have here again an echo of Tolstoy's 1884 studies. It is significant that among the apparently deliberate omissions made by Tolstoy in his translation of Pauthier's version of Chu Hsi's preface to *The Great Learning* are two references to music as forming part of the Chinese state-sponsored educational curriculum. It may well be that Tolstoy had been at the time intrigued by Chu Hsi's emphasis on "music being a state matter in China" and had filed the notion away in his mind for future application to a purpose such as presented itself five years later.

As to the possible influence of Lao-tzŭ on Tolstoy's concepts of non-resistance, though it is undeniable that the legendary Chinese sage was one of Tolstoy's favorites among the wise men of the world, we must insist that we have here another instance of Tolstoy's phenomenal protopathy, rather than a response to a stimulus from the shadows of the ancient Far East. One could as well attempt to trace Tolstoy's ideas on the subject of non-resistance to the New World and to William Lloyd Garrison, with whose works Tolstoy became acquainted in 1886 (JE 63.343). It must be conceded that Tolstoy may have heard of some of Lao-tzŭ's doctrines as early as 1869, the date of the first *popular* Russian reference to Lao-tzŭ known to me (in S. M. Solov'yev, *Nablyudeniya nad istoricheskoi zhizn'yu narodov, Vyestnik Evropy,* December, 1869, pp. 693–694). Yet even at this early date Tolstoy's "native Taoism" had already found unmistakable expression in *War and Peace* (1864–69). Indeed, what better exposition of the workings of the Tao, as the historical process unaffected by the spastic efforts of a man of destiny, could we have than in that epic of life's majestic continuity? What truer exponents of clear-cut Taoist "non-action," of "doing nothing so that nothing would remain unaccomplished" than in the figures of Kutuzov and Karatayev? Neither is it necessary to look to China for discovering the sources of Tolstoy's concept of immortality. A recusant all through his life, never able to find solace from his preter-natural horror of death in any orthodoxy, Tolstoy had no need of seeking inspiration in the pantheistic doctrines of Asia to develop his non-Christian conception of deathlessness in Nature and in God. He had already evolved the notion in his twenties and expressed it in one of the most powerful of his early stories, *Three Deaths* (1858), as well as in his letters of the period to his confidante, Countess Alexandra Tolstoy. In short, Bodde's threefold hypothesis of Chinese influence would appear to be untenable, be it only on the ground of anachronism.

All in all, *Tolstoy and China* is a well-meant and relatively successful attempt to add to our understanding of Tolstoy and of the process of the seepage of Chinese ideas into the Western world, but it definitely lacks the spark of philological imagination and the breadth of literary culture that could have made it a genuine contribution to the "History of Ideas." Chapter V ("The Meaning of China to Tolstoy") is especially disappoint-ing in this respect. Written in the prim and complacent tone of an aca-demic thesis, it is full of stereotyped observations on Tolstoy's "theism," "puritanism," "anti-imperialism," and "eclecticism," and on the "natural-ism," "hedonism," and "feudalistic roots" of Chinese philosophy. It reveals Bodde's innocence of the vast interpretative literature on Tolstoy's complex personality and betrays the black-and-white naiveté of the skin-deep sociological approach to an interpretation of the Russian and Chinese scenes, both old and modern. Curiously enough, for the necessary tools are all at hand, Bodde completely misses here the matchless opportunity of boldly delineating the striking diachronic congeniality of the strongly polarized patriarchalistic-anarchistic, aristocratic-plebeian, elitarian-egalitarian (Professor Lednicki's happy phrase), egotistic-humanitarian, aesthetic-ethical mentality of Tolstoy, so astonishingly free from any middle-class propensity, with the similarly polarized Confucian-Taoist psyche. The few pedestrian remarks he makes on the subject do justice to neither Tolstoy nor the great molders of Chinese thought.

Finally, a few bagatelles. To readers conversant with Russian, Simmons' transcription adopted by Bodde is somewhat annoying in its inaccuracy and capriciousness. On page 33, note 11, Bodde guilelessly observes that *A Surat Café*, published in 1910 together with a short tract on Lao-tzŭ, "has nothing to do with China." He seems unaware of the fact that this beautiful story by Bernardin de St. Pierre, translated by Tolstoy in January, 1887 (JE 86.18), and a favorite of his for many years (it appears in *Circle of Reading* 1.212–219), has as its protagonist *"un lettré de la Chine, disciple de Confucius."* To note 3, page 31, is to be added the information that Tolstoy had denied the authorship of *Le mensonge chinois* in two letters to Chertkov, dated October 14 and November 8, 1900, and that the disavowals were made public by Chertkov in *Listki Svobodnago Slova* (No. 18, pp. 17–18).

Tolstoy and China is handsomely printed. We have noticed but one aggravating misprint, that on the jacket, where the year of Tolstoy's death is given as 1919, instead of 1910.

CHRONOLOGY OF PETER A. BOODBERG

1903	Born April 8, Vladivostok, Russia, the second son of Baron Alexis Paul and Valentine (Nazaroff) Boodberg.
-1915	Student, Military Academy, St. Petersburg.
1916	Graduated from high school, Harbin, Manchuria.
1919	Student, Far Eastern University, Vladivostok.
1916-20	Lived in Manchuria and China.
1920	Immigrated to the United States.
1924	A.B. in Oriental Languages, University of California, Berkeley.
1928	Married Helen S. Petroff.
1929	Birth of daughter Xenia (Mrs. Richard Henry Lee, III).
1930	Ph.D. in Oriental Languages, University of California, Berkeley.
1932	Instructor in Oriental Languages, University of California, Berkeley.
1935	Assistant Professor of Oriental Languages, University of California, Berkeley.
1937	Associate Professor of Oriental Languages, University of California, Berkeley.
1939	Guggenheim Fellow.
1940	On staff of Harvard Chinese Dictionary Project, Harvard-Yenching Institute.
1942-44	Director of the Army Specialized Training Program, Chinese Language School, University of California, Berkeley.
1948	Professor of Oriental Languages, University of California, Berkeley.
1955	Taught summer school classes at Harvard University.
1956	Guggenheim Fellow.
1960	Agassiz Professor of Oriental Languages and Literature, University of California, Berkeley.
1963	Guggenheim Fellow.
1964	President of the American Oriental Society.
1967	Trip to Europe: first time out of the U.S. since immigrating.
1970	Agassiz Professor of Oriental Languages and Literature, Emeritus, University of California, Berkeley.
1972	Died of a heart attack, June 29, Berkeley.

Bibliography of
Peter Alexis Boodberg*

Journal of the American Oriental Society, 94.1 (1974), 8-13.

By Alvin P. Cohen

MONOGRAPHS AND TEXTBOOKS

1. "THE ART OF WAR IN ANCIENT CHINA: A STUDY BASED UPON THE *DIALOGUES OF LI, DUKE OF WEI,*" unpublished Ph.D. dissertation in Oriental Languages,. University of California, Berkeley, June 1930
2. HIEROGLYPHICA POLYSYLLABICA: A SUGGESTION AS TO THE SIMPLIFICATION OF THE CHINESE SCRIPT, published by P.A.B., Berkeley, 1932 (9 pp.).
3. EXERCISES ON THE 214 DETERMINATIVES: I. DETERMINATIVES #1 - #60, published by P.A.B., Berkeley, February 1933 (14 pp.).
4. EXERCISES IN CHINESE PARALLELISM, University of California Press, Berkeley, 1943.
5. UCI: AN INTERIM SYSTEM OF TRANSCRIPTION FOR CHINESE, University of California Publications in East Asiatic Philology, Vol. 1, No. 1, University of California Press, Berkeley, 1947.
6. UCJ: AN ORTHOGRAPHIC SYSTEM OF NOTATION AND TRANSCRIPTION FOR SINO-JAPANESE, University of California Publications in East Asiatic Philology, Vol. 1, No. 2, University of California Press, Berkeley, 1947.
7. with Shih-Hsiang Chen, TWENTY-FIVE CHINESE QUATRAINS, WITH VOCABULARY EXERCISES, University of California Press, Berkeley, 1948.
8. INTRODUCTION TO CLASSICAL CHINESE, University of California Press, Berkeley, 1947, revised edition 1951.

---

* The compilation of this bibliography has required extensive searching, especially because most of P.A.B.'s personally published writings are very rare and are not listed in any bibliographical sources. Therefore, I wish to express my gratitude to the many people all over the world who so kindly responded to my inquiries and provided information and copies of the rare publications. As far as can be determined this bibliography is complete except for items 9c, 9 g, and 15. The compiler would be grateful to receive copies of these missing items.

ARTICLES AND SERIALS

9. HU T'IEN HAN YÜEH FANG CHU[a], serial published by P.A.B., numbers 1-13, dated from March 1932 to March 1936.
The title page to HTHYFC has two pairs of parallel phrases in Chinese: "If you write it, then write it (completely); it you erase it, then erase it (completely)." "For major concerns, write them on tablets; for minor concerns, strips and slips are enough."
The introductory page to number 1, March 1932, reads:

> The title of this publication, HU T'IEN HAN YÜEH FANG CHU, which can roughly be translated "The Mirrorings of the Chinese Moon in a Barbarian Sky" has been suggested by the often recurring passages in Chinese poems describing 'the watch on the Wall', where the moon appears as the symbol of civilization and home, and the cold winter sky is pictured as unhospitable as the wastes of the North.
>
> The HU T'IEN HAN YÜEH FANG CHU will be devoted to the study of Chinese documents relating to the cultural and political history of Central and Eastern Asia. Half of the publication will be reserved for annotated translations of selected biographies from the Dynastic histories.
>
> The present number begins the series of biographies of famous Chin dynasty barbarians. Glossaries will be appended to the last issue of the series.
>
> It is hoped that this "journal" will be made a trimestrial one.
> > Peter A. Von Budberg
> > Baron Peter Budberg (in Cyrillic type)

This seems to be the last time he used the spelling 'Budberg'.

9a. 1 (March 1932)

Biographies:	pages
T'ieh-fu Liu Hu[b]	1-3
Liu Wu-huan[c]	4
Liu O-lou-t'ou[d]	5
Liu Hsi-wu-ch'i[e]	5
Liu Wei-ch'ên[f]	6-11

10. SINO-ALTAICA. This is actually a sub-
series within HTHYFC, numbers 5, 7, 8, 9,
10, 11, and 13 (see items 9e through 9m above),
although P.A.B. also circulated copies of the
individual articles as separates.
With the exceptions of S-A IV.4 and IV.6,
the separates are identical with the corresponding articles in HTHYFC. The two exceptions were revised when reprinted in
HTHYFC, number 13, March 1936 (see item
9m above). The originals (i.e., the separates)
are:
   IV.4 (September 1935): "La lengnée de celz
   Argon" (3 pages)
   IV. 6 (September 1935): Hsiung-nu Titles
   (2 pages)
11. SINO-TIBETAN NOTES. This is actually
a sub-series within HTHYFC, numbers 11
and 13 (see items 9k and 9m above), although
P.A.B. also circulated copies of the individual articles as separates.
12. with Esson M. Gale and T. C. Lin, "Discourses
on Salt and Iron (YEN T'IEH LUN, Chapters
XX-XXVIII)," JNCBRAS, 65 (1934), 73-110.
P.A.B. also did extensive work on the initial

part of this work: Esson M. Gale, DISCOUR-
SES ON SALT AND IRON: A DEBATE ON
STATE CONTROL OF COMMERCE AND
INDUSTRY IN ANCIENT CHINA, Chapters
I-XIX, Sinica Leidensia, Vol. II, E. J. Brill,
Leyden, 1931.
13. NOTES ON CHINESE MORPHOLOGY AND
SYNTAX, serial published by P.A.B., numbers 1-4, all dated October 1934.
   1. The final -t of *fu*^{m} (2 pages).
   2. Some cases of Synaeresis in Archaic Chinese
   (2 pages).
   3. The Morphology of Final -N and -T (3 pages).
   4. The *Xk* Form of Some Chinese Particles
   (2 pages).

14. KD NOTES, serial published by P.A.B., numbers 1-4, August 1934-September 1935. ("KD"
denotes "Karlgren's Dictionary," i.e., Bernhard Karlgren, ANALYTIC DICTIONARY
OF CHINESE AND SINO-JAPANESE,
Paul Geuthner, Paris, 1923)
   1 (August 1934): The Etymology of *pi*^{n} 'stylus,
   brush' (2 pages)
   2 (August 1934): The Archaic Initials of KD
   529 (2 pages)
   3 (October 1934): *Shih Ming* 'Etymologies'
   (3 pages)
   4 (September 1935): The Archaic Initial *lng-
   (3 pages)

15. HSI HSIA NOTES, n.d. but probably mid-
1930's, (2 pages, incomplete).
16. "The language of the T'o-pa Wei," HJAS,
1 (1936), 167-185.
17. "Two notes on the history of the Chinese
frontier"
   1. Hu^o colonies in northwestern China under the
   Han
   2. The Bulgars of Mongolia
   HJAS, 1 (1936), 283-307.
18. "Some proleptical remarks on the evolution
of archaic Chinese," HJAS 2 (1937), 329-372.
   (This article was provoked by H. G. Creel, "On the
   nature of Chinese ideography," TP, 32 (1936),
   85-1·1).
19. "Marginalia to the Histories of the Northern
Dynasties"
   1. Theophylactus Simocatta on China
   2. On the use of the animal cycle among "Turco-
   Mongols"
   HJAS, 3 (1938), 223-253.

3. The Altaic word for "horn" in the political nomenclature of the Steppe
4. The coronation of T'o-pa Hsiu
5. The rise and fall of the House of Yang
6. Addenda and corrigenda to Marginalia 1-2 and genealogical tables
6a. The chronogrammatic use of animal cycle terms in proper names

HJAS, 4 (1939), 230-283.

20. "'Ideography' or iconolatry?," TP, 35.4 (1940), 266-288.

(This article is a rebuttal to H. G. Creel, "On the ideographic element in ancient Chinese," TP, 34 (1938), 265-294).

The editor of T'OUNG PAO, Paul Pelliot, added an editorial footnote on the first page:

Tout en publiant volontiers le présent article de M. Boodberg, nous considérons qu'il doit clore, en ce qui concerne le T'oung Pao, une controverse dont les éléments sumériens sortent du cadre et de la compétence de notre revue. — Note de la rédaction.

21. "Chinese zoographic names as chronograms," HJAS, 5 (1940), 128-136.
22. "Three notes on the T'u-chüeh Turks"

1. The Chinese name of the Turks
2. The *Syr-Tardush phantom and the T'ieh-lê
3. Dilziboul and Istämi

SEMITIC AND ORIENTAL STUDIES, PRESENTED TO WILLIAM POPPER, University of California Publications in Semitic Philology, vol. XI, Berkeley, 1951, pages 1-11.

23. "The semasiology of some primary Confucian concepts," PHILOSOPHY EAST AND WEST, 2.4 (1953), 317-332.
24. CEDULES FROM A BERKELEY WORKSHOP IN ASIATIC PHILOLOGY, published by P.A.B.; 54 numbered "Cedules" dated from July 1, 1954 through December 20, 1955. (26 of these were reprinted in 1969; see item 31 below). (Dates are noted in the form "540701", i.e., July 1, 1954).

001-540701: On Crypto-Parallelism in Chinese Poetry
002-540710: Proto-Bulgarian **ičirgü* ∼ *ičürgü*
003-540720: A Triplex Fusion in Ancient Chinese
004-540801: Chinese *Hsiāng*[p], 'country-wick', and *Ch'ing*[q], 'grandee'
005-540810: Philology in Translation-Land
006-540820: On the Translation of Chinese Binoms
007-540901: *Shih Ching* 1, a Re-Translation
008-540910: On Chinese *ts'ing*[r], 'blue-green'
009-540920: On Latent Predicates in Chinese Poetry
010-541001: Chinese TZU[s], 'child'
011-541010: On Ancient Chinese Titles
012-541020: On Allotonic Overtones in Chinese Poetry
013-541101: On Fishing Snow
014-541110: Imperial Aurigation in China
015-541120: Some Basic Grammatonomic Characteristics of the Chinese Script
016-541201: Chinese 'State' and 'Nation'
017-541210: Syntactical Metaplasia in Stereoscopic Parallelism
018-541220: On 'H'/'T'/'M' Progression in Quatrains
019-550101: Translations, Hyperbatic and Hyperbathetic
020-550110: Prolegomenon to *Lao Tzu* 1.1: TAO[t]
021-550120: The Necessary Nuisance of Grammar
022-550201: On Chromatographic Effects in Chinese Poetry
023-550210: On the Verbal Use of Topochronological Univocals
024-550220: On Colloquialisms in Tu Fu's Poetry
025-550301: Semantics, Chromatics, and Grammar
026-550310: A Neglected Aspect of Chinese 'Epistemology'
027-550320: Diction and Poetic Unity
028-550401: Self-Criticism in Eighth Century China
029-550410: On the Virtue of the Infinitive
030-550420: 'T'/'M' Parallelism Once More
031-550501: On Indo-European Prosopocentricity
032-550510: On the Semasiology of Chinese 'Poetry' and 'Thought'
033-550520: On Tu Fu's Humour
034-550601: Two of Tu Fu's 'Last Poems'
035-550610: Elements of Chinese Grammatonomy
036-550620: Hemigrams, Their Juxtaposition and Composition
037-550701: Towards a Philological System of Notation for Chinese Characters
038-550710: On Uniliteral Classifiers: Minuscules
039-550720: Uniliteral Classifiers: Italicized Majuscules
040-550801: Some Special but Simple Notations
041-550810: The 214 Classifiers: Classifiers 001-020
042-550820: Classifiers 021-040
043-550901: Classifiers 041-060

044-550910: Classifiers 061-080
045-550920: Classifiers 081-100
046-551001: Classifiers 101-120
047-551010: Classifiers 121-140
048-551020: Classifiers 141-160
049-551101: Classifiers 161-180
050-551110: Classifiers 181-200
051-551120: Classifiers 201-214
052-551201: The 214 Classifiers in Alphabetical Order
053-551210: On Coding Phonetic Hemigrams
054-551220: On Semantic Notation for Phonetic Hemigrams

25. "An early Mongolian toponym," HJAS, 19 (1956), 407-408.

26. "The Chinese script: An essay on nomenclature (The first hecaton)," BIHP, 29 (1957), 113-120.

27. "Notes on isocolometry in early Chinese accounts of barbarians," ORIENS, 10.1 (1957), 119-127.

28. "Philological notes on chapter one of the LAO TZU," HJAS, 20 (1957), 598-618.

29. "Comments on 'Some great books of the Oriental traditions'," in APPROACHES TO THE ORIENTAL CLASSICS: ASIAN LITERATURE AND THOUGHT IN GENERAL EDUCATION, ed. W. T. de Bary, Columbia University Press, New York, 1959, pages 166-170. (This is the proceedings of a conference held at Columbia University, September 12 and 13, 1958).

30. "Ancient and archaic Chinese in the grammatonomic perspective," in STUDIA SERICA BERNHARD KARLGREN DEDICATA, ed. Søren Egerod, Copenhagen, 1959, pages 212-222.

31. "Cedules from a Berkeley workshop in Asiatic philology," TSING HUA JOURNAL OF CHINESE STUDIES, 7.2 (1969), 1-39. Chinese postscript by Chen Shih-Hsiang. This is a selection of 26 "Cedules" from the complete group of 54 (see item 24 above). The original serial numbers of the 26 reprinted here are: 001, 005-009, 012-013, 017-034.

BOOK REVIEWS

32. "Tolstoy and China—A critical analysis," PHILOSOPHY EAST AND WEST, 1.3 (1951), 64-76. This is a review of Derk Bodde, TOLSTOY AND CHINA, Princeton University Press, 1950.

33. review of Erwin von Zach, HAN YÜ'S POETISCHE WERKE, Harvard University Press, Cambridge, 1952, in JAOS, 73.1 (1953), 35-36.

34. review of Fung Yu-lan (trans. by Derk Bodde), HISTORY OF CHINESE PHILOSOPHY, Princeton University Press, Princeton, 1952-53,

(review of vol. I) in FEQ, 12.4 (1953), 419-422;

(review of vol. II) in FEQ, 13.3 (1954), 334-337.

UNPUBLISHED MANUSCRIPTS**

35. STUDIES IN CHINESE LEXICOLOGY

(Introduction) Binoms and their Semantization
Chapter 1. "Snag", "Crag", and "Music"
Chapter 2. "The Human Crotch"
Chapter 3. "Circle", "Eye", and Man Recumbent
Chapter 4. Bramble, Sprout, and Pike
308 handwritten pages of text, plus 97 pages of footnotes for the text through chapter 2; n.d. This appears to be the MS of a two volume book that was to be published by the Harvard University Press about 1940. According to footnote 1, the basis of this study was the product of research performed during 1938-39 under a grant from the John Simon Guggenheim Memorial Foundation.

36. *Untitled.*

88 handwritten pages; n.d. This is a lecture and appears to be the text of P.A.B.'s unpublished lecture "Turk, Aryan and Chinese in Ancient Asia," presented in 1942 at the University of California, Berkeley, under the auspices of the Graduate Division.

37. "A Philologist's Creed"

Two typewritten pages; n.d.

OTHERS

38. Extensive bibliographical research for: Robert J. Kerner, NORTHEASTERN ASIA: A SELECTED BIBLIOGRAPHY: CONTRIBUTIONS TO THE BIBLIOGRAPHY OF THE

** These few items are the only surviving MSS. It appears that P.A.B. destroyed several other MSS of books and articles relating to his interests in philology and the history of the Chinese frontier.

RELATIONS OF CHINA, RUSSIA, AND JAPAN, WITH SPECIAL REFERENCE TO KOREA, MANCHURIA, MONGOLIA, AND EASTERN SIBERIA, 2 vols., Bert Franklin, New York, 1939.

39. Research and preparation of the Chinese materials used in: Frederick J. Teggart, ROME AND CHINA: A STUDY OF CORRELATIONS IN HISTORICAL EVENTS, University of California Press, Berkeley, 1939.

a. 胡 天 漢 月 方 諸
b. 鐵 弗 劉 虎
c. 劉 務 桓 陋 頭
d. 劉 關 陋 祈
e. 劉 悉 勿
f. 劉 衛 辰
g. 劉 庫 仁
h. 劉 眷
i. 劉 顯
j. 赫 連 勃 勃

k. 字
l. 孫 子
m. 弗 筆
n. 胡
o. 胡
p. 鄉
q. 鄉
r. 青
s. 子
t. 道
u. 劉 羅 辰